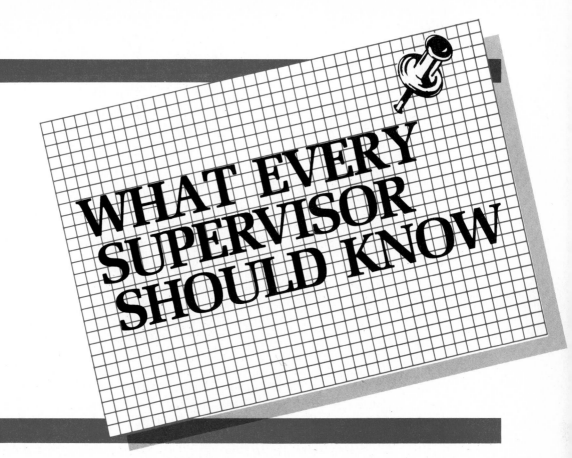

About the Author

Lester R. Bittel is currently professor of management and director of the Center for Supervisory Research at the School of Business of James Madison University in Harrisonburg, Virginia. Before accepting his academic post, he was employed as industrial management editor, editor in chief, and publisher of *Factory* magazine, and copublisher of *American Machinist, Product Engineering, Industrial Distribution,* and *Purchasing Week.* He also held the position of director of information systems for McGraw-Hill Publications Company. Prior to joining McGraw-Hill, he was field engineer for the Leeds & Northrup Company, industrial engineer for Western Electric Company, Inc., and plant manager and training director of the Koppers Company. He is a past chairperson of the Gantt Medal Board and the Silver Bay Conference on Human Issues in Management and a fellow of the American Society of Mechanical Engineers.

Mr. Bittel is the editor in chief of the *Encyclopedia of Professional Management* and coeditor of the original *Training and Development Handbook,* sponsored by the American Society for Training and Development. He is the author of *Business in Action, Improving Supervisory Performance, Management by Exception,* and *The Nine Master Keys of Management.* He also coauthored *Practical Automation.* He is the designer of the *Shenandoah Management Games for Supervisors* and has contributed to the *Industrial Engineering Handbook, Handbook of Business Administration,* and *Maintenance Engineering Handbook.*

Mr. Bittel was a principal consultant and contributor to the massive *Modular Programme for Supervisory Development* published by the International Labour Office in 1981. He is also the designer of the Professional Development Certificate Program used as a standard by the Commonwealth of Virginia for training its public service supervisors. Along with David Engler, he was a principal consultant to CRM/McGraw-Hill Films in the conception and preparation of its extensive *Supervision* series of multimedia behavioral model programs. Most recently, Mr. Bittel, along with Dr. Jackson E. Ramsey of the Center for Supervisory Research, completed the largest, indepth study of supervisory attitudes and practices ever made. Data gathered in this nationwide survey of more than 8,500 supervisors, reported widely in such publications as the *Harvard Business Review* and the *Training and Development Journal,* has become the basis for the design of supervisory training and development programs in hundreds of companies throughout the United States.

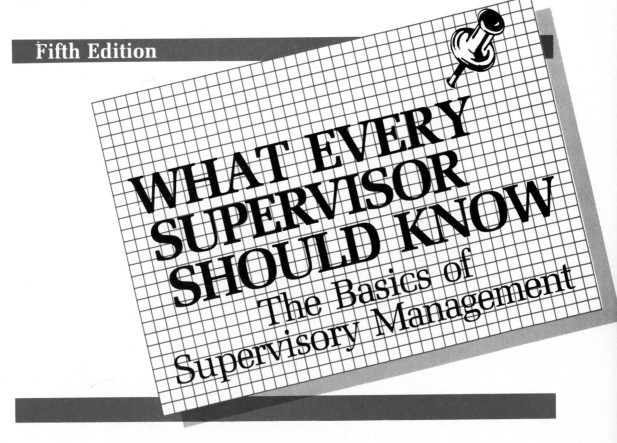

Fifth Edition

WHAT EVERY SUPERVISOR SHOULD KNOW

The Basics of Supervisory Management

Lester R. Bittel

Professor of Management and
Director, Center for Supervisory Research
School of Business
James Madison University

Gregg Division/McGraw-Hill Book Company

New York   Atlanta   Dallas   St. Louis   San Francisco   Auckland
Bogotá   Guatemala   Hamburg   Johannesburg   Lisbon   London   Madrid
Mexico   Montreal   New Delhi   Panama   Paris   San Juan   São Paulo
Singapore   Sydney   Tokyo   Toronto

Sponsoring Editor: Edward E. Byers
Editing Supervisor: Mitsy Kovacs
Design and Art Supervisors: Caryl Valerie Spinka and Nancy Axelrod
Production Supervisor: Laurence Charnow

Text Designer: Michaelis/Carpelis Design Associates, Inc.
Cover Designer: Ed Butler
Illustrator: Wallop Technical Arts. Steve Burnett, Inc.

Library of Congress Cataloging in Publication Data

Bittel, Lester R.
  What every supervisor should know.

  Bibliography: p.
  Includes index.
  1. Personnel management.   2. Supervision of employees.
Title.
HF5549.B52 1985   658.3′02   84-12579
ISBN 0-07-005574-2

What Every Supervisor Should Know, Fifth Edition

2 3 4 5 6 7 8 9 0   DOCDOC   8 9 1 0 9 8 7 6 5

ISBN 0-07-005574-2

PREFACE

Several years ago, when the first edition of this book appeared, its aim was to tell the truth about supervision. There is some evidence that it has succeeded. This book has been consulted by over a half million supervisors and potential supervisors. It has been translated into Dutch, Danish, Portuguese, and Spanish and reprinted in paperback by the Tata Press in Bombay, India. It is the basic text for supervisory management in over 100 two-year colleges. It has been adopted for in-house supervisory training programs by hundreds of industrial companies, commercial firms, and nonprofit institutions. And it has stood the toughest test of all—the test for validity and practicality. Thousands of practicing supervisors have bought, read, and kept in ready reach this handbook, which tells them everything they ought to know about their jobs. So, in this fifth edition, let us once again examine the basic premises of *What Every Supervisor Should Know*.

The Truth About Supervision

This phrase defines the focus of the book, which I view as an antidote for too much preaching and too little understanding of the problems that face first-line supervisors. Ever since I plunged into my first supervisory job many years ago, I've had the urge to put into writing what I believe are the realities of supervision. I wanted to examine both the techniques that really work and the ones that are liable to backfire, to show supervisors' proper functions in the organization, and to indicate the extent to which supervisors can exercise their judgment and authority.

Integrated Objectives

The overall approach of this book is based on six interrelated objectives:

1. To offer reliable assistance with real-life situations.
2. To take into account the everchanging social and organizational environments.
3. To provide insights based on experience.
4. To cover all the vital aspects of supervision.
5. To reflect the most up-to-date views of supervision.
6. To maintain a good-humored perspective on one of the world's toughest jobs.

With objectives like these, *What Every Supervisor Should Know* should prove to be a useful aid to a wide and diverse readership, which includes:

● *Instructors,* who would use it as a basic text for preparing their students for the complex world of supervisory management.
● *Students* of human affairs in commerce, government, and industry, who would turn to it as a centralized source of information about the job of supervision.

- *Supervisors,* who would find it a handy reference manual of methods for handling people, managing their jobs, and planning their advancement.
- *Their bosses,* who would gain an insight into the problems—human, technical, and personal—that supervisors must face daily.
- *Training directors* and other human resources specialists, who would use it as a text or guide for training supervisors in interpersonal relations and in technical job skills.

Comprehensive Update

This latest edition reflects an extensive re-examination of every aspect of coverage. Revisions benefit, too, from (1) my work with the International Labour Office in identifying 32 key skills areas of supervision (published in 1981 as *Modular Programme for Supervisory Development*), (2) consultations in supervisory job competency analysis with the Office of Management Development and Training of the Commonwealth of Virginia in 1982, which led to its Professional Development Certificate Program for supervisors and middle managers, (3) the extensive research into supervisory problems, practices, and attitudes conducted by Dr. Jackson E. Ramsey and myself at the Center for Supervisory Research (which is described in detail below), and (4) my consultation in 1983 with CRM/McGraw-Hill regarding the design and application of behavioral modification techniques to supervision. As a consequence, there are hundreds of modifications and amendments in this edition to provide readers with the very latest information and the most current points of view from authoritative sources.

New or greatly revised materials range from such topical subjects as Quality Circles and robotics to perennial problems that are receiving renewed attention, subjects such as productivity improvement and job design. There is a new chapter on time and stress management and chapters offering contemporary guidance on career-path planning and maximizing personal effectiveness in the organization.

Of special importance to supervisors is the new or extended coverage of topics like quality of work life, ergonomics, conflict management, cost-benefit analysis, organization development, legal aspects of and record-keeping for performance appraisals and employee discipline, comparative worth concepts in job evaluation, active listening and body language, work distribution charting, assertiveness training, avoidance of sexual harrassment, employee rights to privacy, right-to-work laws, office automation, and the impact of personal computers and management information systems.

Of the thirty class-tested case studies in this text, twelve are brand new or revised. They have been chosen to provide a broad range of organizational settings—in industry, government, and service organizations.

Unique Learning Components

This edition retains the two unique learning methods that differentiate it from most other texts in the field. It continues to rely heavily on:

1. *A question-and-answer approach with immediate feedback.* This helps to reinforce understanding and to develop application proficiency in a manner similar to that of programmed learning. Additionally, the format en-

ables readers to relate concepts to the problems they face daily at work. It also makes the text a convenient desk or workbench reference source.

2. *Dozens of practical do's and don'ts.* Especially when offering advice in interpersonal relations, this didactic approach borrows heavily from examples set by various behavioral models throughout the text. Readers are given suggestions for conducting effective dialogues with employees and are also given examples of exchanges that are likely to fail.

Readers will also benefit from two substantive new features of this edition:

3. *Survey data showing how other supervisors think and act.* Survey data appears at the introduction to each major part of the text. This data helps to orient supervisors to the larger scope of their chosen field. Most important, it helps to provide perspective on common problems that supervisors often feel are unique to their own situations. When the data shows that other supervisors find certain situations difficult to handle, this provides an incentive for readers to master skills that others find to be effective in these situations.

The survey data reported here is drawn from the National Survey of Supervisory Management Practices (NSSMP) which was based on a sample of approximately 8,500 supervisors, the largest ever collected. Data were gathered by written questionnaire from 116 participating businesses, nonprofit institutions, and public agencies and from 43 chapters of the International Management Council representing 448 companies for a total of 564 organizations in 37 states.

4. *Nine comprehensive behavioral models, illustrating effective supervision.* These detailed models of effective dialogue appear in an appropriate context at the end of each of the first five parts. Each model illustrates a carefully prescribed, step-by-step behavioral procedure for dealing with a specific interpersonal problem. Students are directed to identify each of the steps and then to imitate the model, first in group sessions and later in similar situations on the job. The instructor may also choose to broaden the use of the models into a full-scale behavioral modification program, which is described in the *Course Management Guide.*

All of the models that appear in the text were prepared by David Engler, a noted authority on the application of technology to instruction, training, and communications. Mr. Engler is the president of General Educational Media, Inc., of Wilmington, Delaware, which designs and produces training programs.

All of the behavioral models in this text are part of a series of three-hour multimedia modules entitled *Supervision.* The behavioral model dialogues appear here through the courtesy of, and with the permission of, the copyright holder, CRM/McGraw-Hill Films, P.O. Box 641, Del Mar, California 92014. These dialogues may not be reproduced in any form without the express consent of the copyright holder.

Acknowledgments

I accept the responsibility for everything written in this text. I would, however, be doing a great disservice to many others associated with supervisory management who assisted or advised me if I did not acknowledge their contributions. In particular, I am indebted to Joseph T. Allmon of Riegel Textile Corp., Albert Benglen of the International Management Council, Ernest Balkany of Steelcraft Company, Paul Deysher of AMP, Inc., Frank Diehl of Sheller-Globe Corp., Hubert E. Dobson of FMC Corporation, Edwin B. Feldman, author of the *Housekeeping Handbook,* Robert Johnson of Blaw-Knox Division, Dr. Donald L. Kirkpatrick, professor of management development at the University of Wisconsin at Milwaukee, Ronald Leigh, executive director of the National Management Association, Marie Leonard of Morton-Norwich Products, Inc., Dr. Richard Mignery, executive director of the Institute for Certified Professional Managers, Patricia Moran of Veterans Administration Hospital in Downey, Illinois, Dr. Joseph Prokopenko of the International Labour Office, Carson Tucker of Philip-Morris Corp., Richard Reardon of Virginia Distributive Education Adult Inservice Training, Ray Vogt of Pullman Standard Company, Wallace Richardson, professor of industrial engineering at Lehigh University, and Lisa P. Watts of Management Performance International, Inc.

Finally, I am deeply indebted to other talented individuals who made significant and direct contributions to this text and its associated instructional program: Ronald S. Burke, president of Management Planning Services, who prepared the test banks and much of the material that appears in the *Skills Development Portfolio* and also in the *Course Management Guide*; David Engler, who created and wrote the behavioral model dialogues that appear at the end of the first five parts of the text; Edmund Zazzera, vice president and executive producer of McGraw-Hill productions, and Brian Sellstrom of CRM/McGraw-Hill Films, who extended permissions to use the behavioral model dialogues; Dr. Jackson E. Ramsey, director of the Center for Supervisory Research at James Madison University, who worked so effectively with me to gather and analyze the data in the National Survey of Supervisory Management Practices; Helen Royall, my ever-expert typist; and my wife, Muriel Albers Bittel, who so ably managed our editing schedules and hundreds of other details associated with manuscript preparation.

Lester R. Bittel

CONTENTS

Case Studies in Human Relations

*The Case of the Snarled Parking Lot is also available in either 16-mm color film or videotape from CRM/McGraw-Hill Films, Del Mar, California.

Behavioral Models

PART

1

SUPERVISORY MANAGEMENT AND HUMAN RELATIONS

Management at any level accomplishes its tasks and goals through the actions of other people. At the supervisory level the interpersonal relations are most frequent and most intense. Accordingly, this part emphasizes five key objectives.

- To grasp the full extent of the supervisory job so as to be able to integrate technical know-how, administrative skills, and sensitivity in employee relations.
- To understand how people view their work so as to be able to sustain conditions that provide the most satisfaction and the least dissatisfaction.
- To be aware of the individuality and basic needs of your employees so as to be able to motivate them in a variety of ways.
- To recognize the extent and the power of group influence so as to be able to direct its energy toward productive ends.
- To accept the presence of conflict in organizations but to be able to minimize it and build an atmosphere that encourages cooperation.

What supervisors say about the job of managing people

The great majority of supervisors (82 percent) say they are generally satisfied with their jobs. They then single out their relationship with their employees as one of the most important sources of that satisfaction. Listen to these typical comments about the most rewarding aspect of supervisory work:

"I enjoy developing people and seeing them grow."
"Seeing the pleasure my employees get out of a job well done."
"Having all employees work together toward a common goal."
"Working with people."
"Helping a marginal employee to become an outstanding one."
"Resolving conflicts and providing fair treatment."
"Seeing our employees make the department look good."
"Being able to say that we did it as a team."

Survey figures show that most supervisors speak well of their employees' desire to do a good job, as indicated by these figures:

Statement	Percentage expressing a high degree of agreement
Most employees appreciate praise from their supervisor.	98
Most employees want to do a good job.	93
Employees in my department generally like working there.	88
Most employees willingly accept responsibility for their work.	83

On the other hand, some supervisors still have their doubts about employee motivation, as indicated by these figures:

Statement	Percentage expressing a high degree of agreement
Most employees have to be pushed to produce.	41
Most employees require close supervision.	28
Most employees do not work harder after receiving a pay raise.	20

Information in the next five chapters should help to clear up the reasons for these differing viewpoints.

1

THE SUPERVISORY MANAGEMENT JOB

Why does first-line supervision get so much attention?

First-line supervisors in industry and commerce represent just about the most important force in the American economy. Over two million strong, they carry out a management tradition that dates back to the building of the pyramids. And yet time has not simplified their work. First the industrial revolution with its division of labor and now high technology with its accelerated mechanization and computerized office have changed the supervisor's role to one of bewildering and often frustrating complexity.

Today's supervisor (whether a first-line supervisor, a front-line supervisor, or a section or department manager) must be a vigorous leader, a shrewd and effective planner, a source of technical know-how, and a deft mediator between policy-setting management on the one hand and rank-and-file workers on the other. Small wonder that the cry goes up again and again: "We need better supervisors."

Recognition—and acceptance—of supervisors by top management has helped them to emerge finally as essential and integrated members of the management group and to assume all the responsibilities of full-fledged managers. The way hasn't been easy. Too often it has been painfully slow. Even today there are companies where the supervisor's status is shaky. But on the whole, no single group of men and women has achieved and deserved such stature and attention in so short a time after so long a wait as has supervisory management.

Who is a supervisor?

Anyone at the first level of management who has the responsibility for getting the "hands-on-the-work" employees to carry out the plans and policies of higher-level management is a supervisor.

Where did the term come from?

In earlier days the supervisor was the person in charge of a group of towrope pullers or ditch diggers. That person was literally the "fore man," since he was up forward of the gang. His authority consisted mainly of chanting the "one, two, three, up," which set the pace for the rest of the workers. In Germany the supervisor is still called a *Vorarbeiter* ("fore worker"); in England the term *charge hand* is used. Both terms suggest the lead-person origin.

The term *supervisor* has its roots in Latin, where it means "looks over." It was originally applied to the master of a group of artisans. One hundred years ago it was not uncommon for the master in a New England shop to have almost complete power over the work force. The master could bid on jobs, hire his own crew, work them as hard as he pleased, and make his living out of the difference between his bid price and the labor costs.

Today the supervisor's job combines some of the talents of the "fore man" (or leader) and of the "master" (skilled administrative artisan).

Legally, what makes a supervisor a supervisor?

The federal laws of the United States provide two definitions of a supervisor.

1. The Taft-Hartley Act of 1947 says that a supervisor is:

> ... any individual having authority, in the interest of the employer, to hire, transfer, suspend, lay off, recall, promote, discharge, assign, reward, or discipline other employees, or responsibility to direct them, or to adjust their grievances, or effectively to recommend such action, if in connection with the foregoing the exercise of such authority is not of a merely routine or clerical nature, but requires the use of independent judgment.

The act specifically prohibits supervisors from joining a union of production and clerical employees, although they may form a union composed exclusively of supervisors.

2. The Fair Labor Standards Act of 1938 (or Minimum Wage Law) specifies that supervisors can spend no more than 20 percent of their time doing the same kind of work as the people they direct. It also stipulates that supervisors be paid a salary (regardless of how many hours they work). This latter provision makes some supervisors unhappy, since it makes them exempt from the provision of the law that calls for overtime pay after a certain number of hours have been worked. Many employers voluntarily compensate supervisors for overtime in one way or another.

The thrust of these two laws is to make supervisors, once and for all, a part of management.

Are supervisors permitted to do the same work as the people they supervise?

There is no law stopping it. Most companies with labor unions often have a contract clause that prohibits the supervisor from performing any work that a union member would ordinarily do (except in clearly defined emergencies, in which the supervisor would do as she or he sees fit).

This is a point on which most managements agree with unions. Few companies want supervisors to do the work their employees are hired to do. Supervisors are most valuable to their employers when they spend 100 percent of their time supervising. It makes little sense for a $350-a-week supervisor, for instance, to do the work of a $200-a-week laborer.

Where do most supervisors come from?

Three out of four supervisors rise from the ranks of the organization in which they serve. Typically, they are long-service employees. They have greater experience, have held more different jobs in the organization, and have significantly more education than the men and women they supervise. Usually it is apparent that supervisors are chosen from among the best and the most experienced employees in the organization.[1]

What personal characteristics does higher management find most desirable in supervisors?

The job of supervision is so demanding that higher management tends to look for *super*people to fill the role. Most firms establish criteria against which supervisory candidates are judged. Here are some of the qualities most commonly sought.[2]

- Energy and good health
- Leadership potential
- Ability to get along with people
- Job know-how and technical competence
- Initiative
- Self-control under pressure
- Dedication and dependability
- Positive attitude toward management

Obviously, these are fine attributes in any person. Obviously, too, people who measure up are hard to find. Fortunately, however, many of these attributes can be acquired or improved through supervisory training and development programs.

How can a newly appointed supervisor make the job of crossing over to the managerial ranks a less turbulent one?

A person who is made a supervisor crosses over from one style of thought to another. As an employee, an individual's concerns are with self-satisfaction in terms of pay and the work itself. As a manager, this same person is expected to place the organization's goals above all other job-related concerns. This means that a supervisor worries first about meeting quotas, quality, and cost standards; second about the employees who do the work; and last about himself or herself.

To make the task more difficult, the newly appointed supervisor usually has already made the long climb to the top of the employee ranks. Now the person must cross over to a new field of achievement—management, as shown in Figure 1-1. It will take a while to get a toehold at the supervisory level. For many, however, it will be the beginning of another long climb—this time to the top of the management heap.[3]

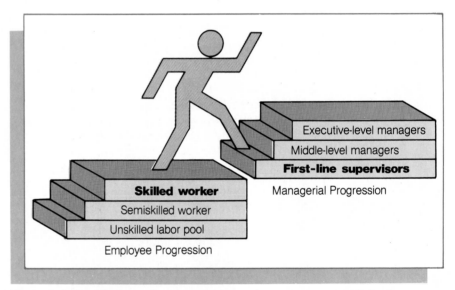

Figure 1-1. Crossing over from employee ranks to managerial ranks, from "top of the heap" to "bottom of the heap."

The pressure from above and below makes some new supervisors uncomfortable. One supervisor in the *1981 National Survey of Supervisory Management Practices* (NSSMP) survey said that the most frustrating part of his new job was "not being allowed to work with my hands anymore."[4] Another supervisor on a Ford Motor Company assembly line once put it this way: "The foreman is a punching bag. You get your ears beat off from both sides of the fence."

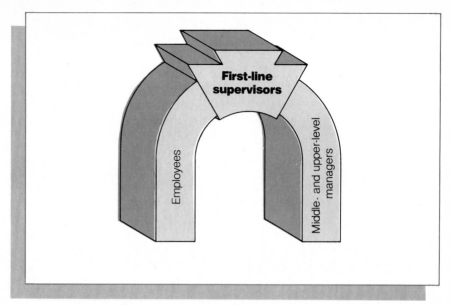

Figure 1-2. Supervision as the keystone in the organizational arch.

This need not be so, says Professor Keith Davis, one of the most astute observers of organizational relationships. Davis agrees that the supervisor takes pressure from both sides, but he likens the role to a keystone in the organizational arch (Figure 1-2). Says Davis:

> The keystone takes the pressure from both sides and uses this pressure to build a stronger arch. The sides can be held together only by the keystone, which strengthens, not weakens, the arch. The keystone position is the important role of supervisors in organizations.[5]

Experienced supervisors add this advice to the new person:

> Don't throw your weight around. Admit your need for help and seek it from other supervisors and your boss. Make a practice of coming in on time and sticking to your job for the full day; employees despise supervisors who push for productivity but who goof off themselves. Keep yourself physically prepared and mentally alert; the job will be more demanding than you expect. And don't indulge in petty pilfering of supplies or use of shop equipment and time to do personal work; employees may try this themselves but they sure don't respect management people who do.[6]

When it comes to job responsibilities, what is expected of supervisors?

Responsibilities encompass four—and occasionally five—broad areas.

Responsibility to Management. Supervisors must, above all, dedicate themselves to the goals, plans, and policies of the organization. These are typically laid down by higher management. It is the primary task of supervisors to serve as a "linking pin" for management to make sure that these are carried out by the employees they supervise. (See Figure 1-3.)

Responsibility to Employees. Employees expect their supervisors to provide direction and training; to protect them from unfair treatment; and to see that the workplace is clean, safe, uncluttered, properly equipped, well lit, and adequately ventilated.

Responsibility to Staff Specialists. The relationship between supervision and staff departments is one of mutual support. Staff

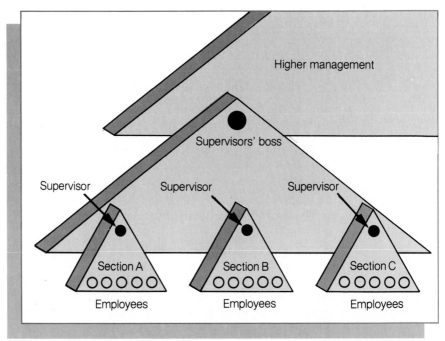

Figure 1-3. Supervisors as link pins. Rensis Likert envisioned supervisors as the linking pins of an organization, serving to connect employee work groups to the goals of the organization. Adapted from Rensis Likert, *New Patterns of Management,* McGraw-Hill Book Company, New York, 1961.

people are charged with providing supervisors with guidance and help as well as prescribing procedures to be followed and forms to be completed. Supervisors, in turn, aid the work of the staff departments by making good use of their advice and service and by conforming to their requests.

Responsibility to Other Supervisors. Teamwork is essential in the supervisory ranks. There is a great deal of departmental interdependence. The goals and activities of one department must harmonize with those of others. This often requires the sacrifice of an immediate target for the greater good of the organization.

Relationships with the Union. Labor union and management views are often in conflict, and the supervisor and shop steward are often at loggerheads. It is the supervisor's responsibility, however, to keep these relationships objective, to neither "give away the shop" nor yield responsibility for the welfare of the organization and its employees.

How will supervisory performance be judged by higher management?

It will be judged by two general measures: (1) how well you manage the various resources made available to you to accomplish your assignments and (2) how good the results are that you get from them. (See Figure 1-4.)

Management of Resources. These are the things that, in effect, set you up in business as a supervisor. They include:

● **Facilities and Equipment** such as a certain amount of floor space, desks, benches, tools, production machinery, computer terminals, and microfiche readers. Your job is to keep these operating productively and to prevent their abuse.

● **Energy, Power, and Utilities** such as heat, light, air conditioning, electricity, steam, water, and compressed air. Conservation is the principal measure of effectiveness here.

● **Materials and Supplies** such as *raw materials,* parts, and assemblies used to make a product and *operating supplies* such as lubricants, stationery, cassette holders, paper clips, and masking tape. Getting the most from every scrap of material and holding waste to the minimum are prime measures here.

● **Human Resources** such as the work force in general and your employees in particular. Since you do little or nothing with your hands, your biggest job is to see that these people are productively engaged at all times.

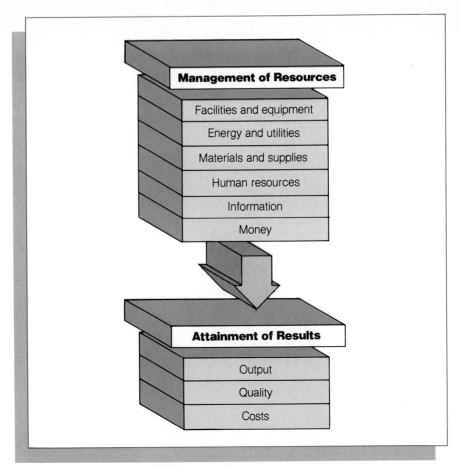

Figure 1-4. Measurement of supervisory performance.

● **Information** such as that made available by staff departments or found in operating manuals, specifications sheets, and blueprints. Your success often depends on how well you can utilize the data and know-how made available to you through these sources.

● **Money**—all the above can be measured by how much they cost, although the actual cash will rarely flow through your hands. Nevertheless, supervisors are expected to be prudent in decisions that affect expenditures and may have to justify these in terms of savings or other benefits.

Attainment of Results. It follows that if you manage each of your resources well, you should get the desired results.[7] Whatever your particular area of responsibility and whatever your organization, you can be sure that you will be judged in the long run by how well you meet these three objectives:

- **Output, or Production.** Specifically, your department will be expected to turn out a certain amount of work per day, per week, and per month. It will be expected that this will be done on time and that you will meet delivery schedules and project deadlines.
- **Quality and Workmanship.** Output volume alone is not enough. You will also be judged by the quality of the work your employees perform, whether it be measured in terms of the number of product defects, service errors, or customer complaints.
- **Costs and Budget Control.** Your output and quality efforts will always be restricted by the amount of money you can spend to carry them out. Universally, supervisors attest to the difficulty in living up to cost and budget restraints.

Of all that is expected of supervisors, which tasks loom largest?

Three types of problems seem to persist:

1. Meeting tight production or operating schedules. Take all the fancy talk away, and the supervisor's basic job is still one of "getting out the production." You must see that the goods are finished on schedule, deadlines are met, and projects are completed when promised.

2. Keeping operating costs in line. In simple words, supervisors must do more than getting out the production. They must also attain their operating goals efficiently. More to the point, they must keep their expenses within the allowed or budgeted limits.

3. Maintaining cooperative attitudes with employees. Automation and computers or not, it's the employees who turn the crank. Getting the employees to turn the crank when they should, how they should, and as fast as they should is the ultimate problem for supervisors.

What does it really take to succeed as a supervisor?

No one knows for sure, but there are a number of qualities, or dimensions, of the supervisory job that experts look for. For example, General Electric Company, at its Columbia, Maryland, facility, singles out seven important dimensions of the supervisory job: technical know-how, administrative skill, ability to develop a plan to meet department goals, ability to deal with the manager to whom you report, communications skills, ability to deal with people inside and outside the operating unit, and ability to deal effectively with people who report to you.[8] Other researchers also identify such success-related qualities as creativity, stress tolerance, initiative, independence, problem analysis, decisiveness, tenacity, flexibility, risk taking, and use of delegation.[9]

The American Telephone and Telegraph Company (AT&T) promotes about 12,000 men and women from the ranks into supervisory positions each year (throughout its system and its now-independent constituent companies). To make the choice of these candidates more reliable and to better prepare them for their new jobs, AT&T spent several years studying the "job content" of its master supervisors (those whose performance is the very best). On the basis of this study, AT&T developed a list of skills that supervisors must acquire if they are to be effective at their work. This list is reproduced in Table 1-1. It is generally regarded as applicable to almost any

TABLE 1-1 PRINCIPAL DUTIES OF FIRST-LEVEL SUPERVISORS
(Ranked According to Time Required and Frequency of Occurrence)

Rank Order	Duties	Percent of Time Spent*	Frequency of Occurrence
1	Controlling the work	17	Every day
2	Problem solving and decision making	13	Every day
3	Planning the work	12	Every day
4	Informal oral communications	12	Every day
5	Communications, general	12	Every day
6	Providing performance feedback to employees	10	Every day
7	Training, coaching, developing subordinates	10	Every day
8	Providing written communications and documentation	7	Every day
9	Creating and maintaining a motivating atmosphere	6	Every day
10	Personal time management	4	Every day
11	Meetings and conferences	4	Twice monthly
12	Self-development activities	2	Weekly
13	Career counseling of subordinates	2	Bimonthly
14	Representing the company to the community	1	Monthly

Adapted from Charles R. MacDonald: *Performance Based Supervisory Development: Adapted from a Major AT&T Study*, Human Resources Development Press, Amherst, Mass., 1982, p. 20.
*Percentages add up to more than 100 because of overlap of duties—i.e. *planning* of the work at a *meeting* called for that purpose.

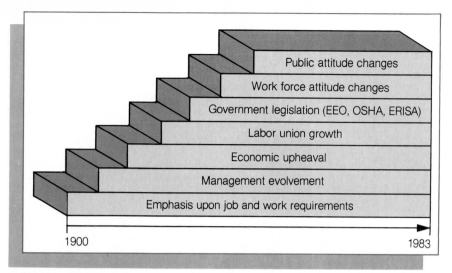

Public attitude changes	
Work force attitude changes	
Government legislation (EEO, OSHA, ERISA)	
Labor union growth	
Economic upheaval	
Management evolvement	
Emphasis upon job and work requirements	

1900   1983

Figure 1-5. Evolving sources of pressure on first-line supervisors. Based on a concept in Herbert R. Northrup, Ronald M. Cowin, Lawrence G. Vandon Plas, and William E. Fulmer, *The Objective Selection of Supervisors,* Manpower and Human Resources Studies No. 8, The Wharton School, University of Pennsylvania, 1978, p. 6.

supervisor. The list may seem formidable, but most of the talents it requires can be acquired by supervisors who learn from their experience and take advantage of training and developmental opportunities offered by their employers.

How are the pressures on supervisors changing?

What started out as mainly a technical job at the turn of the century has gradually shifted. Pressure is now being put on supervisors to accommodate an increasingly demanding work force, as shown in Figure 1-5. This trend will continue. In the 1980s and 1990s the general public will ask employers to accept greater responsibility for employment whether or not this employment contributes to profits or effectiveness. This means that supervisors will be expected to make work for their employees in slack times and to motivate them to be more productive in active times.

Where do supervisors fit into the management process?

They are an essential part of it. Supervisors perform exactly the same managerial functions as all other managers in their organiza-

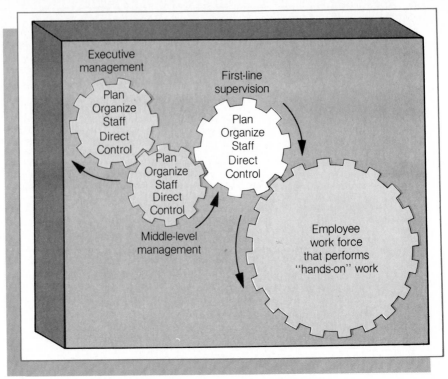

Figure 1-6. All managers take part in the managerial process: planning, organizing, staffing, directing, and controlling.

tion—up to and including the chief executive. Each specific task, every responsibility, all the various roles that supervisors are called on to perform are carried out by the managerial process (Figure 1-6). This process, which is repeated over and over, daily, weekly, and yearly, consists of five broad functions:

● **Planning.**   Setting goals and establishing plans and procedures to attain them.
● **Organizing.**   Arranging jobs to be done in such a way as to make them more effective.
● **Staffing.**   Selecting and placing just the right number of people in the most appropriate jobs.
● **Directing.**   Motivating, communicating, and leading.
● **Controlling.**   Regulating the process, its costs, and the people who carry it out.

The managerial process is explained in detail in Parts 2 and 3 of the text.

How do supervisory job roles differ from those of other levels of management?

They differ only in degree. Higher-level managers spend more time planning and less time directing, for example. Two people who studied this matter came up with three useful guidelines.[10] They first divided all the tasks and responsibilities we have listed so far in this text into three kinds of roles. Roles are the parts played by actors on a stage; they are also the real-life parts played by managers and supervisors in an organization. These three roles can be classified as those requiring:

● **Technical Skills.**   Job know-how; knowledge of the industry and its particular processes, machinery, and problems.
● **Administrative Skills.**   Knowledge of the entire organization and how it is coordinated, knowledge of its information and records system, and an ability to plan and control work.
● **Human Relations Skills.**   Knowledge of human behavior and an ability to work effectively with individuals and groups—peers and superiors as well as subordinates.

The observers then concluded that the role of the supervisor emphasizes technical and human relations skills most and administrative skills least. This emphasis tends to reverse itself with higher-level managers, as illustrated in Figure 1-7.

Supervisory balance: What does it mean?

It is a simplification of a very valuable dictum: Pay as much attention to human relations matters as to technical and administrative ones.

In other words, be as *employee-centered* as you are *job-* or *task-centered* in your interests.

Or, said still another way, spend as much time maintaining group cohesiveness, direction, and morale as you do pushing for productivity or task accomplishment.

This view has been borne out by a number of studies. The basis, however, is research carried on by Rensis Likert, the man who saw supervisors as linkpins. In a survey of clerical, sales, and manufacturing employees, he found that, on the average, employees who worked for supervisors who were job- or production-centered produced less than employees who worked for employee-centered supervisors.[11]

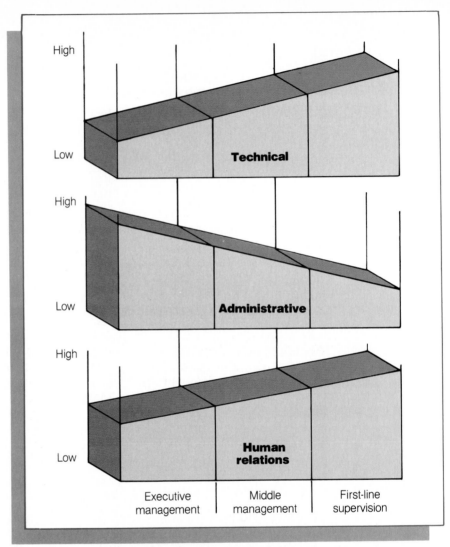

Figure 1-7. Skills needed according to managerial level.

It would be dangerous to draw the conclusion from Likert's studies that being a nice guy is the answer to employee productivity. It isn't. As in sports, nice guys often finish last. The important conclusion from these studies is that supervisors who focus on job demands to the exclusion of their interest in the welfare and the development of their people don't get the results they are looking for. Conversely, supervisors who bend over backward to make work easy for their employees don't get good results either. It takes a balance between the two approaches, as shown in Figure 1-8.

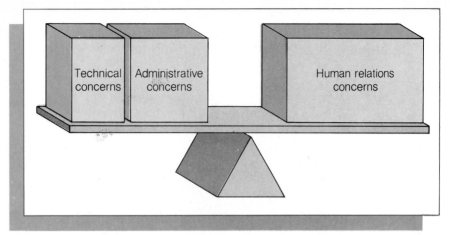

Figure 1-8. The balance of supervisory concerns.

For example, "Red" Goss, a section supervisor in a West Virginia coal mine, speaks of his major headaches. These are directing traffic in the mine's darkness, rearranging power cables, safety, and equipment breakdowns, because—as his boss says—"If there's no production, we're down his throat." Yet Red is relaxed and friendly with his workers. His aim, he says, is to treat the miners "like people, like trained men." As a result, Red's crew routinely turns in the mine's highest production. His boss says, "The men respect Red. He knows how to talk to them." Red "gives" a little in accommodating individual wishes among his men, but his men often go out of their way to be helpful. Red points to an instance where the cutting crew used their own initiative to open a new vein without waiting for him to first mark out the next cut, as is traditional.[12]

B eing a supervisor can't be all good news. What are some of the drawbacks? What can a supervisor do to minimize them?

Generalizations about the negative side of supervision can be misleading because every job is different, companies and industries vary, and each individual is unique. It is usually true, however, that the advancements are limited: The managerial pyramid gets narrower at the top, and college-educated people usually have an inside track. Often the pay isn't much better than that of the people you have to supervise; efforts to widen the gap often fail. The hours are long, and the human relations part of the job can be torturous. The supervisor is typically torn between loyalties to management and to the work group. In some companies a supervisor's ideas for improving methods may be taken for granted instead of being rewarded via the suggestion box. In most instances a supervisor's security depends not on seniority or union membership but on his or her ability to produce results. Frequently, the supervisor does not have all the resources needed to attain them.

Why do so many supervisors keep on plugging? Because of the reward *not* found in the paycheck.[13] Supervisors keep supervising because of the challenge inherent in the work itself and the sense of accomplishment gained from doing a difficult job better than anyone else can. A few supervisors quit or step down, but most of them hang in. They may grouse and complain, but they keep on trying—and getting results.

How professional is the work of supervision?

It is getting more professional every day. Two leading management organizations, made up primarily of first-line supervisors, are working hard to make it that way. The International Management Council (IMC), affiliated with the Young Men's Christian Association (YMCA), and the National Management Association (NMA) have pooled their resources to form the Institute of Certified Professional Managers (ICPM). The institute, working with the American College Testing Program (ACT), has devised and is administering professional certification tests. Certification is based on a combination of experience and examinations in three areas: (1) personal skills, such as skills in communications, government regulation, and time management; (2) administrative skills, such as planning, decision making, staffing, and controlling; and (3) human relations skills.

Addresses of participating organizations are:

International Management Council
2250 East Devon Avenue
Des Plaines, Illinois 60018

National Management Association
Dayton, Ohio 45439

Institute of Certified Professional Managers
P.O. Box 386
Dayton, Ohio 45409

What's ahead in supervision for women and minorities?

The road ahead is smoother than it once was, but it is still steep. In 1960, only 2 percent of blue-collar supervisors were black. By 1972, 6 of every 100 were black, and by 1980 7 percent were black. The growth seems to have leveled out since then. The gains among white-collar supervisors appears somewhat the same. For example, in 1972, 10.1 percent were black; today the figure is just under 12 percent.

Women have always been a dominant force among white-collar supervisors. In 1972, 57.8 percent were female; over 70 percent are female today. Women have also made steady inroads into blue-collar supervision, although they are in a distinct minority there. In 1972, 6.9 percent of all blue-collar supervisors were women; today, the figure is closer to 12 percent.

At the higher levels of management, both blacks and women remain in the minority. One out of every four managers and administrators is a woman; only about one out of every twenty is black or a member of another racial minority.

Obviously, there is still considerable room for improvement. Nevertheless, pressures from equal employment opportunity legislation and demonstrated competence in minority and women incumbents should ensure their continuing gains in the supervisory and managerial ranks.

Why do some supervisors fail?

The NSSMP survey turned up the dismaying fact that 20 percent of all supervisors feel themselves unsuited for the jobs they hold. The reasons vary, of course, according to individual situations. Sometimes the fault lies in the supervisor's boss or in the job conditions. But often as not, the trouble lies in the supervisor himself or herself. So, if you'd like to avoid being a misfit, check yourself against the six supervisory pitfalls pointed out by the NMA after a study of 86 companies:

● Poor personal relations with workers or with other management people.
● Individual shortcomings, such as lack of initiative and emotional instability.
● Lack of understanding of the management point of view.
● Unwillingness to spend the necessary time and effort to improve.

- Lack of skill in planning and organizing work.
- Inability to adjust to new and changing conditions.

Note how many of the items on this list have to do with the human relations side of the job. Skill in handling the technical and administrative aspects is always important. But these skills will mean very little if you do not master your relationships with other people in the organization and especially with the people who work for you.

Key Concepts

1. Supervisors play a vital role in every management group; they add strength to an organization by serving as the linking pin between middle and executive levels of management and the employees who "put their hands on the work."

2. Supervisors must bring to their work a unique combination of technical competence, individual energy, and the ability to get along with—and motivate—others.

3. The performance of supervisors will be judged by how well they manage the *resources* assigned to them (facilities and equipment, power and utilities, material and supplies, information, money, and human resources) and the *results* they get from them in the way of output, quality, and cost control.

4. The supervisory management job generally requires three skills: technical skill, administrative skill, and human relations skill. The human relations skill is often the most demanding.

5. It is essential for successful supervisors to balance their skills and efforts rather equally between that part of the work that is production- (or task-) oriented and that which is employee- (or group-) centered. Too much of an emphasis in a single direction is likely to be self-defeating.

Supervisory Word Power

Employee.   A person who works for a company or an organization for wages or salary and who (for purposes of this text) does not hold supervisory or management status and responsibility. Employees are also called workers, laborers, artisans, technicians, clerks, engineers, and the like. Employees are people who "put their hands on the work."

Supervisor.   A person in charge of, and coordinator of, the activities of a group of employees engaged in one type of operation. In the ranks of management the supervisor's position is at, or just above, the entry level. Supervisors determine work procedures, issue written and oral orders and instructions, assign duties to workers, examine work for quality and neatness, maintain harmony among workers, and adjust errors and complaints. Supervisors are also called foremen, group leaders, section chiefs, section heads, and department managers.

Manager. A person who directs supervisory personnel to attain the operational goals of a company or an organization. In the ranks of management a manager's position may range from the entry level to the uppermost echelon, but it usually is in the middle level. Managers plan, initiate, and execute programs; interpret and apply policies; establish goals and standards of operational activities; and motivate, direct, and control supervisors. Managers are also called general supervisors, superintendents, directors, and general managers.

Executive. A person in charge of, and responsible for, the performance of a group of managers. In the ranks of management the executive is in the upper echelons. Executives establish broad plans, objectives, and general policies; they motivate, direct, and control the managers subordinate to them.

Job- or Task-Centered Supervision. Emphasis on the job or task that employees are expected to perform; a major concern for production or operating results.

Employee- or Group-Centered Supervision. Emphasis on a genuine concern and respect for employees as human beings and on maintaining effective relationships within the work group.

Reading Comprehension

1. What is the essential point of the legal definitions of *supervisor?*

2. Why would a company be likely to object if the supervisor of the molding department spent most of his or her time setting up and operating the molding machines?

3. Name four groups within the organization for which a supervisor has responsibilities, and briefly describe the nature of the responsibilities to each.

4. Which two broad categories of performance are typically used to judge the effectiveness of supervisors at their work?

5. Contrast the likely priorities of a production worker in a glass factory with those of the department's supervisor.

6. AT&T's master supervisors have ranked fourteen important tasks that supervisors must perform (Table 1-1.) Sort these out according to three categories of supervisory roles: (1) technical, (2) administrative, and (3) human relations.

7. How is supervisory management similar to higher-level management? How is it different?

8. When a supervisor is told to achieve supervisory balance, what is it that should be balanced? Why is it important?

9. Describe four drawbacks to a supervisory position.

10. If you had to point to one key area that is most likely to produce failure for a supervisor, what would it be?

Supervision in Action

A. The Case of the Divided Loyalties. A Case Study in Human Relations Involving a Supervisor's New Job, with Questions for You to Answer.

Rick López looked neither to the right nor to the left as he headed back from the shop floor to his desk. Friday had been a long day. In fact, it had been a long week. It seemed like five years, rather than five days, since he had walked into the shop last Monday on his first day as a supervisor in J Shop. Much longer, he thought, than his eight years as an employee in several other departments of the company. Rick had started as a bench hand with only a high school diploma and a three-year hitch of military service under his belt. He had moved ahead quickly through a series of six jobs. The last three years he had been a head assembler in M Shop and then setup person for all the machines in P Shop. On the basis of his quickness, his all-around knowledge of shop processes, and his general popularity, Rick had been appointed supervisor of J Shop to replace a veteran supervisor who had retired.

Today, as with every other day this week, Rick had encountered situations for which his shop expertise and previous experience had not prepared him. He had expected that, but not what had just happened. Rick was walking the shop—supervising. He stopped for a minute or two to watch each operation and to chat with each employee about his or her work. One particular operation caught his prolonged attention. The point at which a subassembly was joined to a final assembly was going very slowly. The assembler, Jennie Barnes, was a relatively new employee. She was very slow in fitting the two parts together. To pick up her speed she often "forced" the process. In so doing, she damaged an occasional final part. Rick saw that Jennie not only was damaging the final product but also was holding up the rest of the assembly line. "Look, Jennie," he said, "why don't you take a rest for a few minutes. I'll take over here for a while and see that you get caught up with the rest of the lines."

Jennie went off to the lounge while Rick sat in for her. With his quick, deft hands he was able to accomplish two or three times as much as Jennie. When Jennie remained away longer than Rick had anticipated, he began to fix some of the damaged final assemblies. At that moment Rick's new boss, Mr. Tower, came along. "I have been looking all over for you," said Mr. Tower. "We have a rush order I want you to track down for me. But what are you doing here?"

"I'm straightening out a bottleneck in the line," said Rick. "The operator is new at this job and hasn't learned how to do it right—or fast enough, either."

"Where is the operator?" asked Mr. Tower.

"She went to the lounge a few minutes ago," said Rick.

"I've been looking for you for a half hour," said Mr. Tower. "She must have been gone longer than that."

At that moment Jennie returned to her bench. "It's about time you came back," said Mr. Tower. "It's bad enough that you can't do the job right without your taking half the afternoon off." Jennie looked at Rick, who said nothing. Mr. Tower then called Rick aside. "If Jennie can't do her job, get rid of her. We've got better things for you to do here than covering up for an incompetent employee."

1. What do you think Rick was doing wrong in this situation?
2. Was Mr. Tower fair in his judgment of Jennie? What should Rick have done about this, if anything?
3. What advice would you give to Rick the next time a problem like this comes up?

B. The Case of the Complaining Keypunch Operator. A Case Study in Human Relations Involving a Supervisor's New Job, with Questions for You to Answer.

Ruth Smyth was the best all-around clerk that Gibraltar Finance Company's data processing section ever had. She was a natural for being promoted to supervisor when the time came. During Ruth's first few weeks as section supervisor, everything went well. She obviously knew the work flow from A to Z. Given this chance, she quickly cleared up long-standing bottlenecks and eliminated a number of duplications. Her experience and good judgment easily won the respect of the people who worked for her. On the other hand, Ruth was a stern and serious taskmaster. She was fair and courteous with her employees, but she showed little interest in them beyond their ability to get the work done.

As Ruth settled into the job, however, she had an uneasy feeling that something wasn't quite right in her section. Her employees came to depend on her decisions in the slightest matters. If a problem arose, they were likely to sit at their machines waiting for orders from Ruth. At first Ruth felt flattered by this dependence. But this caused her work load to gradually build. Increasingly she found herself giving curt instructions and short answers to people in her work group.

One employee in particular, Woodie Beck, a keypunch operator, really irritated her. Regardless of what the assignment was, he found some fault with it. In addition, Woodie regularly complained about his machine, his chair, the lighting, the temperature, or his co-workers. Ruth responded to each of Woodie's complaints and requests with some attempt to accommodate him or to set the problem straight.

To make matters worse, the quality of Woodie's work, which had been unspectacular but acceptable, began to fall off. He made errors. Frequently his tapes had to be checked and repunched. When this continued, Ruth called Woodie into her office. "I've been very patient with your unending complaints and requests," Ruth said, "but lately your work has been far below what is considered satisfactory. It it continues, I'm going to recommend that you be suspended or discharged."

"I'm sorry about my work," said Woodie. "I've had all kinds of problems at home. My oldest son was expelled from high school for drug dealing a couple of months ago. Neither my wife nor I can seem to keep him out of trouble anymore. It's driving us both crazy."

"Family troubles are a bother, I know," said Ruth, "but you can't let them interfere with your work. What's important right now to you is the fact that the quality of your work is no longer acceptable here. If it continues, you will lose your job. My advice to you is to find some way to keep your concerns about your son from affecting your work. Otherwise, your problems will be even worse. I've been very fair with you, but you owe your first attention now to improving your work. Unless it improves, I'll have to put you on notice."

1. What are Ruth's strengths and weaknesses as a supervisor?
2. How well do you think Ruth handled the problem with Woodie's work? What was good and what was bad about her approach? What do you expect will be the results of Ruth's conference with Woodie?
3. If you were Ruth, how would you have handled Woodie's problems?
4. What suggestions can you make to Ruth in order for her to improve the quality of her supervision?

References

1. Herbert R. Northrup, Ronald M. Cowin, Lawrence G. Vanden Plas, and William E. Fulmer, *The Objective Selection of Supervisors,* Manpower and Human Resources Studies No. 8, The Wharton School, University of Pennsylvania, 1978, pp. 58–69.
2. Ibid., p. 77.
3. Carl A. Benson, "New Supervisors: From the Top of the Heap to the Bottom of the Heap," *Personnel Journal,* April 1978, p. 176.
4. Lester R. Bittel and Jackson E. Ramsey, *Summary Report: 1981 National Survey of Supervisory Management Practices,* Center for Supervisory Research, James Madison University, Harrisonburg, Va., 1982, pp. 65–85.
5. Keith Davis, "The Supervisory Role," in M. Gene Newport (ed.), *Supervisory Management: Tools and Techniques,* West Publishing Company, St. Paul, Minn., 1976, p. 5.
6. *Foreman in Indiana Industries,* Manpower Report 70-2, Office of Manpower Studies, Purdue University, Lafayette, Ind., November 10, 1970, pp. 8–10.
7. Saul W. Gellerman, "Supervision: Substance and Style," *Harvard Business Review,* March-April 1976, pp. 89–99.
8. *What's Ahead in Personnel,* No. 181, Chicago, March 1978, p. 3.
9. William C. Byham, "Assessment Centers," in Lester R. Bittel (ed.), *Encyclopedia of Professional Management,* McGraw-Hill Book Company, New York, 1979, pp. 55–58.
10. Basil S. Georgopolous and Floyd C. Mann, *The Community General Hospital,* The Macmillan Company, New York, 1962, "Supervisory and Administrative Behavior," p. 431.
11. Rensis Likert, *New Patterns of Management,* McGraw-Hill Book Company, New York, 1960.
12. Bob Arnold, "The Coal Boss: Foreman's Job Grows Harder as the Miners, Technology Change," *The Wall Street Journal,* November 6, 1975, p. 1.
13. Michael J. Abboud and Homer L. Richardson, "What Do Supervisors Want From Their Jobs?" *Personnel Journal,* June 1978, pp. 308–312.

2

PEOPLE AT WORK

What is meant by work?

Webster helps here. The dictionary is on target with five related definitions:

- Activity in which one exerts strength or faculties to do or perform.
- Sustained physical or mental effort valued to the extent that it overcomes obstacles and achieves an objective or result.
- Labor, task, or duty that affords one the accustomed means of livelihood.
- Strenuous activity marked by the presence of difficulty and exertion and the absence of pleasure.
- Specific task, duty, function, or assignment, often a part or phase of some larger activity.

Note the key words: *physical, mental, effort, exertion, obstacles, difficulty, result,* and *means of livelihood.* Note, too, the implication of work as a part of a larger activity and its age-old association with the absence of pleasure. Modern-day supervisors try to combine work with pleasure for their employees as measured by the degree of personal satisfaction derived from it.

Why do most people work?

For two reasons: first, for the money it brings and for what necessities and pleasures that money will buy; second, for the satisfaction work can bring—either from being with other people or from a sense of personal accomplishment.

Which reward is more important to most workers, money or job satisfaction?

That depends. Most of us want both, of course. But until each of us has a paycheck that is big enough for our own highly personal situation, job satisfaction may take a back seat.

In what ways is work different from many other things people do?

Four factors make work unique.

1. Rules, regulations, and procedures are necessarily designed to demand a degree of conformity in each employee's action and thus to limit free choice. Many people find it hard to channel their efforts into paths that are set by others. Modern supervision tries to keep rules to a minimum and to stress the opportunity for self-control.

2. A chain of authority makes each person more or less beholden to the boss, and the boss in turn to another boss, and so on. In practice this means that most companies are run by relatively few top-level managers. Lower-level managers and employees at the bottom of the organizational pyramid often feel that they have little say in what happens. Employees typically think the only right they have is to complain, not to make constructive suggestions about how to run the business. Supervisors who invite help from employees tend to make the work more appealing to them.

3. Those who hold managerial responsibility are expected to place their own personal interests behind those of the organization. It is no secret that a great many managers do not do so. Instead, they take care of themselves first and the company's resources, especially employees, later. Employees who work for this kind of manager may find their job satisfactions very small. And they may expend their effort in complaints.

4. Much of what happens or is expected to happen is put into written records. Outside of work, most of our activities are loosely defined and rarely put into writing. Written documents—those that record the past and those that set goals for the future—are threatening to many people. There is the fear that no mistake will be forgotten and that every promise will be remembered. Because of so much formal communication, employees often feel more comfortable with supervisors who pass on the word in easy, give-and-take conversation.

These four factors were first identified in the 1890s by a German sociologist named Max Weber, who prescribed them for an "organized system of work directed by hired managers." He called this system *bureaucracy.*

How many people are truly happy at their work?

According to a number of authoritative studies, more than 85 percent of all employees are satisfied with their jobs. This doesn't necessarily mean that they are ecstatic about them. The figures also show that blacks (as well as other minorities) and women are not as satisfied as whites and men. (See Figure 2-1.) Furthermore, factory workers tend to be less satisfied than white-collar workers. And one of the clearest conclusions is that job satisfaction tends to improve with age. Younger people are by far the most dissatisfied with their work.

The trend toward job satisfaction seems to have peaked during the 1970s. Nevertheless, it is still surprisingly high. High enough, it seems, to give supervisors an even break in attempting to move employees toward organizational and departmental goals.

What is it that today's workers expect from their jobs that is often lacking?

Something that challenges their skills and offers fair pay in return for this extra effort. According to Daniel Yankelovich, a noted surveyor of public opinion and director of the nonprofit Public Agenda Foundation, most people can choose to work hard—or to just get by. Only one person in five, reports Yankelovich, says he or she does his or her very best. For one thing, workers assume that an increase in out-

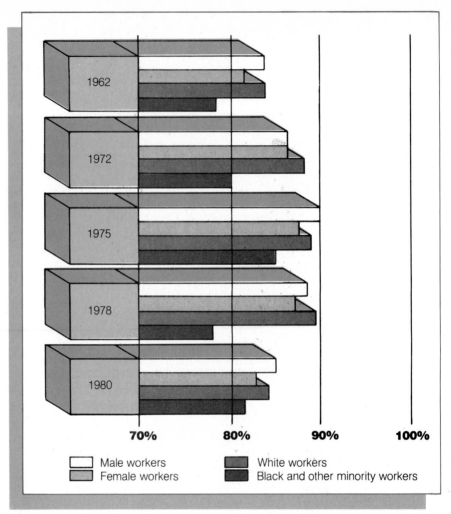

Figure 2-1. Percent of all workers in a particular classification who are "satisfied." Percent satisfied includes the following responses: "very satisfied," "somewhat satisfied," and "fairly satisfied." Adapted from "Satisfied Workers as a Percent of Total Workers: 1962 to 1980," Table No. 676, p. 405, *Statistical Abstract of the United States: 1980*, U.S. Department of Commerce, 1981.

put may not benefit them—only the consumer, stockholders, or management. Down deep, however, most employees will work harder and better, says Yankelovich and other observers, if the work they do makes sense to them and is truly appreciated by their bosses. In fact, eight out of ten Americans say that their jobs are too easy, that they'd prefer a difficult job to an easy one where they merely "put in their time."

Supervisor can minimize both kinds of employee complaints. First, they can make sure that employees have enough to do, especially of the kind of work that capitalizes on their initiative. Second, supervisors can live up to their promises about promotions or relief from boring assignments for those who do go all out to do a good job.

Why do so many people approach their work with a "show-me" or "please-me" attitude?

Times are no longer simply "a-changing." For many people, the future has arrived. The Woodstock generation has grown up and reported for employment, if not work. They are better educated than any work force in history, and this induces higher expectations. Applicants and subordinates are aware of their civil rights, too. There's a widespread feeling that "I'm entitled." Many people feel that society owes them a living, and a pleasant one at that. Relatively few believe that hard work, dedication, and perseverance make the best road to success. It's no wonder, then, that so many employees place the burden of their need for job satisfaction on the supervisor. In turn, the supervisor need all the skills and patience that he or she can muster to motivate today's workers to perform at the levels that society—to say nothing of their employers—expects of them.

Is there any cure for boring work?

Yes. Listen to Barbara Garson, author of *All the Livelong Day: The Meaning and Demeaning of Routine Work* (Doubleday & Co., New York, 1975). She observed: "People need passionately to do real and serious work: to set a problem for themselves, devise a means whereby the problem can be solved, and then see their realized efforts in a completed task...the need to use judgment, individual skill, or work-educated insight." Garson, a harsh critic of business, points to the solution. Hard and challenging work is real and serious. "Mickey Mouse" jobs are soft and nondemanding. A supervisor can help employees to see the job as a problem to be solved, since that's what a job really is. Supervisors can also show employees what the final results are, even on a short-cycle job such as mounting a relay to an electronic breadboard for a TV set. Employees should know that supervisors do want the use of their judgment, not indifference or carelessness; personal skill, not automatic machine-dependency; and know-how based on work experience.

What can be done to improve the quality of working life?

There are two views. The first is that improved productivity—greater output from the inputs of labor, materials, money, and machines—continues to be the foundation for a better work life. Higher productivity buys the tools that make work easier and the time for each employee to find the best way of adapting to the task. The second is the conviction on the part of many qualified observers that a greater involvement in decision making at the job level is essential. The early managers believed just the opposite. They divided jobs into the smallest and easiest pieces. Their goal was to create foolproof jobs for "dumb" human beings. The trouble with this view is that the majority of human beings are not dumb at all. They *want* to "work smarter," although not necessarily harder. As a consequence, they will respond to job conditions that make fullest use of their manual and mental skills. They like working in situations that enable each woman and man to make a demonstrably valued contribution to the finished product or service.

To most people, an improved quality of work life simply means that their hours spent at work will not be wasteful ones. They want to feel that, somehow, their lives will be more worthwhile as a result of their working than if they had no job at all.

One good example of how employees respond to an opportunity to improve the quality of their work life is the popular acceptance of *quality circles.* These are small groups (see pp. 456–458) in which employees are invited to participate on an equal footing with management to solve operational problems and to develop employee potential. They may focus their attention on quality, but their efforts are often effective in attacking every aspect of poor productivity. Regardless of what form an improved quality of work life takes, certain characteristics of both supervisors and employees are present:

- An open rather than a rigid reaction to change.
- Cooperation rather than reliance on authority and conflict.
- A problem-solving rather than a blame-placing approach.
- A win-win rather than a win-lose attitude toward solutions.
- Mutual respect for what each person can contribute.

What are the chances of developing a 100 percent enthusiastic work force?

Very slim. If the statistics presented in Figure 2-1 can be taken as representative, one out of ten employees is likely to be truly dissatisfied. To be one the safe side, you can judge your supervisory performance as "good" if you have only two out of ten employees who regularly sing the work-force blues.

Is there any sure way to make work more enjoyable?

Given the differences in expectations, the answer must be no. Some basic approaches, however, will make for greater satisfaction among employees in general.

Offer Employees an Opportunity for "Bottom-Upward" Feedback. This is one good way to find out what each person expects from work, even if it cannot always be provided.

View Many Supervisory Functions as Facilitating Rather Than Directing. Few people want to be told how and when to do every little thing. Not every worker who is given an inch will take a mile. So try to provide the kinds of information and tools an employee needs to get the job done—the right blueprint or specification, a key bit of know-how. A physical or mental assist, when needed or asked for, encourages employees to enforce their own discipline.

Stay Flexible When and Where You Can. The supervisor whose department rules can't be bent to accommodate a worker's individuality on occasion makes employees feel hopelessly locked in. Keep to a minimum all directives that begin with the words *always* or *never*. Think in terms of *most of the time*, or *on the average*, when you will not permit this or insist on that.

Try to Be a Part of the Total Organization. Know your boss as well as you can. Find out the company's basic objectives about costs, production, and quality. Understand the real intent of company policy toward employees. If you have this information, you will be in a better position to intercede for your employees. The boss who goes to bat for the gang is often the boss an employee can face on a rainy Monday morning when there is a temptation to remain in bed.

Key Concepts

1. Work is a unique activity that requires conformity from employees, the exercise of authority by managers who are able to subordinate their own interests to company goals, and the presence of written records.

2. The great majority of employees are reasonably satisfied at work, although each individual may seek satisfaction in a different way.

3. Many jobs are inherently boring, but a creative supervisor can find ways to provide variety and challenge and thus to stimulate and sustain employee interest.

4. Workers are capable of improving the methods with which they perform their jobs and, when offered this opportunity, are more likely to find satisfaction in their work and to strive to meet company goals.

5. Supervisors help to improve the quality of work life when they maintain a flexible approach while discharging their managerial responsibilities, facilitate rather than direct their employees' work, and encourage feedback from them.

Supervisory Word Power

Bureaucracy. An organized system of work directed by professional managers and not, by definition, necessarily enmeshed in red tape.

Facilitating. An approach to management in which a supervisor assists and guides employees in their efforts to perform their jobs rather than emphasizing orders and instructions.

Quality of Work Life. The idea that work must—in addition to being productive in a material way—be rewarding in a psychological or spiritual way to the person who performs it.

Work. That task, job, or employment in which a person applies mental or physical skills in order to earn a livelihood.

Reading Comprehension

1. Contrast the work or job you have done for pay with a task that you may have done on a voluntary basis. Into which did you put more physical or mental effort?

2. List five tasks that you would perform only for money and five that you would perform for personal satisfaction alone. How might you combine a "money" job with a "pleasure" job?

3. Provide an example of an acquaintance who values money as the most important satisfaction from a job. What do you know about the person that would contribute to that viewpoint?

4. Think of persons you know who are happy in their work. Describe one such person, the work performed, and the kind of supervision provided.

5. Describe a job that you consider boring. Can you think of some other person who doesn't feel that way about it?

6. Ron is a file clerk in an insurance company. His task is to take hundreds of documents each day—policies, completed forms, and correspondence—and file them alphabetically in the appropriate folders in file cabinets. What might he do to make his work less boring? Make at least five suggestions.

7. Think of your most recent job. Of the five or ten people you worked with regularly, how many would you judge to be satisfied with their work and how many dissatisfied with it? What did they say or do that led you to these judgments?

8. Describe the conditions that would make a job ideal for you. Try to be serious and realistic about this.

9. Have you ever had a job that was easy but dull? What could you have done to make it more interesting?

Supervision in Action
The Case of Mildred and the "Mickey Mouse" Job. A Case Study in Human Relations Involving a Bored Employee, with Questions for You to Answer.

Two employees of the Zebra Hosiery Mills were waiting outside the plant for transportation home on a cold, wet afternoon. Mildred lit a cigarette and said, "One more day like this and it's bye-bye Zebra for me."

"What's the problem?" asked Leon, her co-worker.

"This job is boring me to death," said Mildred. "It's a Mickey Mouse all day long. I work my fingers raw racking up those yarn spools. Two hours straight before the break. Then lunch. Then the afternoon break. That's the same routine four times a day. I handle over 800 spools. Toward the end of each period I can hardly wait until I count the two hundredth spool."

"Wow," said Leon. "I never thought of it that way. It just strikes me that it's an easy way to make $60 a day."

"Easy, nothing," said Mildred. "I could show them how to make it easier. All we'd need is some gizmo to let me rack up two spools at a time. But that pumpkin head I work for hasn't listened to a new idea in 30 years."

"That could be," said Leon. "But I'm satisfied just so long as the supervisor stays off my back. I just don't like to be hassled."

"If she were to hassle you, you'd know you were something besides a machine," said Mildred. "If there were some place closer to home, I'd walk out on Zebra tomorrow."

"I could get a job nearer to my home," said Leon, "but I'd only make $50 a day. The extra $10 is worth 15 minutes longer on the bus."

"Not for me," said Mildred. "I've got kids to feed when I get home. I don't want them out on the streets longer than they have to be. I'd take a cut if my job was next door to where I lived."

At this point Leon's bus arrived. "See you tomorrow—if you don't decide to quit," he said as he climbed aboard.

"Fat chance," said Mildred to herself. "What other choices do I really have?"

1. Contrast the difference in satisfaction Mildred and Leon get from their work. Which person seems more satisfied? Why?

2. If Mildred doesn't like her job, why wouldn't she simply get a more satisfying job elsewhere?

3. How far should Zebra Mills go to make its jobs satisfying to all employees? Why?

4. If you were Mildred's supervisor, what might you do to make the work less boring for her?

3

INDIVIDUAL MOTIVATION

Why isn't good human relations just plain horse sense?

Because this is a dangerous oversimplification. Life and business experiences are full of paradoxes and inconsistencies showing that good intentions and straight-line reasoning are not enough.

Take this example. Joe Smith supervises two men who work side by side on an assembly line in an auto plant. Their job is to attach the garnish (or trim) to the painted body. For some time Ed and Al, the men involved, had been complaining of nicks and cuts received from handling the sharp pieces of metal. Finally Joe decides the best way to cure the problem is to insist that both men wear gloves on the job. On Monday he approaches Ed and Al together, "Guys," says Joe, "the safety department has approved the issuance of work gloves for this job. This should prevent the rash of cuts you've been getting. Here's a pair of gloves for each of you. From now on I'll expect to see you wearing them all the time."

Next day Joe had to ask Ed on three separate occasions to put his gloves on. But Al wore his all the time. At the week's end Al was sold on the value of the gloves. But Ed just stuck his in his pants pocket. "They slow me down so I can't keep up with the line," he told Joe. But to Al he said, "This work-glove idea is just an excuse to justify speeding up the line. If you give in on this issue, they'll sock it to you even harder the next time."

Why do two men, handled the same way in the same situation, have such differing reactions? After all, weren't Joe's intentions good? Didn't he try to settle Ed's and Al's complaints about the cuts? Wasn't his solution a logical one?

Isn't human relations just applied psychology?

No. Human relations in industry is not psychology, sociology, or anthropology. Most of all, it is not psychiatry. Whereas these four sciences aid in our understanding of what happens to people when they come to work, labels such as these are more misleading than enlightening.

When a job applicant fills out an interview form, the science of psychology is being applied. When a manager asks a supervisor what the employees think about the new rates, the manager is acknowledging the presence of sociological forces. When a plant in Michigan shuts down on the first day of the hunting season because it knows from past experience that most of the workers will take off anyway, anthropologists may identify this action as a concession to group cultures. And when an office manager listens to a near-hysterical clerk without interrupting, the manager may be borrowing a technique from the psychiatrist.

All the above actions involve the behavior of people at work. It has become common—and convenient—practice to call this behavior *human relations.* The operative words are *people, behavior,* and *work.*

Where do you find the important action in human relations?

Human relations is something that takes place between people. It takes place between an employee and the boss, between one worker and another, between a staff specialist and a line supervisor, between a manager and a superior. It takes place between individuals and between an individual and a group. The human interactions may be between executives and their departments, between managers and their associates, or, inversely, between workers and management in general. It also takes place between two or more groups. It may occur between the sales department and the accounting office, between the production department and the maintenance department, or between two factions in the same group. One noted authority concluded that the number of potential interactions for a person supervising 14 employees is 114,872.

Why do people act the way they do?

If you mean, "Why don't employees act the way you wish they would?" the answer will take a long time. But if you are really asking, "Why do people act in such unpredictable ways?" the answer is simple: People do as they must. Their actions, which may look irrational to someone who doesn't understand them, are in reality very logical. If you could peer into their backgrounds and into their emotional makeup, you'd be able to predict with startling accuracy how this person would react to criticism or how that person would act when told to change over to the second shift.

The dog who's been scratched by a cat steers clear of all cats. Workers who have learned from one boss that the only time they are treated as human beings is when the work load is going to be increased will go on the defensive when a new boss tries to be friendly. To the new boss such employee actions look absurd. But to the workers it's the only logical thing to do.

So it goes—each person is the product of parents, home, education, social life, and work experience. Consequently, when supervisors deal with employees, they are dealing with persons who have brought all their previous experiences to the job.

Then are all people different?

Each person *is* a distinct individual. In detail his or her reactions will be different from anyone else's. But to understand human relations, you must first know *why* people do things before you can predict *what* they will do. If you know that Bill dislikes his job because it requires concentration, you can make a good guess that Bill will make it hard for you to change the job by increasing its complexity. If

Mary works at your company because of the conversation she has with her associates, you can predict that Mary will be hard to get along with if she's assigned to a spot in an isolated area.

The important tool in dealing with people is the recognition that although what they do is likely to differ, the underlying reasons for their doing anything are very similar. These reasons, incidentally, are called motives, or needs.

What determines an individual's personality?

Just about everything. An individual's personality cannot be neatly pigeonholed (as we so often try to do) as pleasant or outgoing or friendly or ill-tempered or unpleasant or suspicious or defensive. An individual's personality is the sum total of what the person is today: the clothing worn, the food preferred, the conversation enjoyed or avoided, the manners and gestures used, the methods of thought practiced, the way situations are handled. Each person's personality is uniquely different from anyone else's. It results from heredity and upbringing, schooling or lack of it, neighborhoods, work and play experiences, parents' influence, religion—all of the social forces around us. From all these influences people learn to shape their individuality in a way that enables them to cope with life's encounters, with work, with living together, with age, with success and failure. As a result, personality is the total expression of the unique way in which each individual deals with life.

What do employees want from life—and their work?

Most of us, including employees, seek satisfaction from life in relation to what a very famous psychologist, A. H. Maslow, called the "five basic needs." (See Figure 3-1.) And we seek a good part of these satisfactions at our work. Dr. Maslow outlined the basic needs this way and conceived of them as a sort of hierarchy, with the most compelling ones coming first and the more sophisticated ones last. **We Need to Be Alive and to Stay Alive.** We need to breathe, eat, sleep, reproduce, see, hear, and feel. But in today's world these needs rarely dominate us. Real hunger, for example, is rare. All in all, our first-level needs are satisfied. Only an occasional experience —a couple of days without sleep, a day on a diet without food, a frantic 30 seconds under water—reminds us that these basic needs are still with us.

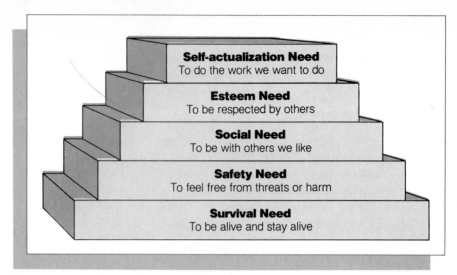

Figure 3-1. Maslow's hierarchy of needs.

We Need to Feel Safe.   We like to feel that we are safe from accident or pain, from competitors or criminals, from an uncertain future or a changing today. Not one of us ever feels completely safe. Yet most of us feel reasonably safe. After all, we have laws, police, insurance, social security, union contracts, and the like to protect us.

We Need to Be Social.   From the beginning of time we have lived together in tribes and family groups. Today these group ties are stronger than ever. We marry, join lodges, and even do our praying in groups. Social need varies widely from person to person—just as other needs do. Few of us want to be hermits. Not everyone, of course, is capable of frank and deep relationships—even with a wife or husband and close friends. But, to a greater or lesser degree, this social need operates in all of us.

We Need to Feel Worthy and Respected.   When we talk about our self-respect or our dignity, this is the need we are expressing. When a person isn't completely adjusted to life, this need may show itself as undue pride in achievements, self-importance, boastfulness—a bloated ego.

But so many of our other needs are so easily satisfied in the modern world that this need often becomes one of the most demanding. Look what we go through to satisfy the need to think well of ourselves—and have others do likewise. When a wife insists her husband wear a jacket to a party, she's expressing this need. When we buy a new car even though the old one is in good shape, we're giving way to our desire to show ourselves off.

We even modify our personalities to get the esteem of others. No doubt you've put on your company manners when out visiting. It's natural, we say, to act more refined in public than at home—or to cover up our less acceptable traits.

We Need to Do the Work We Like.   This is why many people who don't like their jobs turn to hobbies for expression, and why so many people get wrapped up in their work. We all know men and women who enjoy the hard burden of laboring work, or machinists who hurry home from work to run their own lathes, or bored terminal operators who stay up late in their own homes playing with their own microcomputers. This need rarely is the be-all and end-all of our lives. But there are very few of us who aren't influenced by it.

In the 1960s and early 1970s many young people dropped out of society or set out to "do their own thing." This was largely an expression of the desire to fulfill oneself—what Maslow called "self-actualization."

Which of these needs is the most powerful?

The one or ones that have not yet been satisfied. Maslow's greatest insight was that once a need is satisfied, it will no longer motivate a person to greater effort. If a person has what is required in the way of job security, for example, offering more of it—such as guaranteeing employment for the next five years—will normally not cause a person to work any harder. The supervisor who wishes to see greater effort generated will have to move to an unsatisfied need, such as the desire to be with other people on the job, if this employee is to be expected to work harder as a result.

In what way can a job satisfy a person's needs?

It's a fact: Many people are happier at work than at home! Why? Because a satisfying job with a good supervisor goes such a long way toward making life worth living. Whereas all of us may complain about our job (or our boss) from time to time, most of us respond favorably to the stability of the work situation. At home Jane may have a nagging husband, sick children, and a stack of bills to greet her at the end of the month. At work Jane can have an appreciative supervisor, a neat job with a quota she can meet each day, and assurance of a paycheck (and other benefits) at the week's end. No wonder Jane enjoys herself more at work than at home.

Or look at it this way. A rewarding job with a decent company and a straight-shooting boss easily provides the first two basic needs: (1) a livelihood that keeps the wolf away from the door and (2) a sense of safety from the fears of layoff, old age, or accidents. Satisfaction from the other three basic needs—to be social, to be respected, and to do the work we like—is often more a function of a person's supervisor than of the job itself.

A good supervisor can see that a person's job satisfies the *social need* by demonstrating to the rest of the work group the desirability of taking in a new worker. For instance, "Fellows, this is Pete Brown, our new punch press operator. We're glad to have him with the company. And I've told him what a great bunch of guys you all are. How about taking him along to the cafeteria at lunchtime and showing him how to get a cup of java?"

To satisfy the *esteem need,* a good supervisor will make sure workers know that their work is appreciated. For example, "Pete, here's you locker. I think you'll agree that this is a pretty clean washroom. We feel that if we hire a good man, we've got to give him good conditions to work in so that he can do the best possible work."

To satisfy the *desire to do worthwhile work,* a good supervisor gives a lot of thought to putting workers on the job for which they have the most aptitude and training. Like saying, "Since you've worked this type of machine before, Pete, suppose you start on this one. When you've gotten the hang of things around here, we'll see about giving you a chance to learn some of the better-paying jobs."

I f people all have the same fundamental needs, how far can a supervisor go in "push-button" human relations?

Not very far at all. There is a great danger in oversimplifying the analysis of human needs, especially at work.

One explanation of human behavior, for example, is that it depends on each employee's expectancy (or estimate) of what his or her actions may or may not bring. In effect, the employee makes three estimates: (1) Can I do what management is asking me to do? (2) If I can do it, will management be satisfied and reward me? (3) Will the reward given me be worth the effort? As you can see, a person's effort will be greatly influenced by the answers to these questions. According to Maslow, the supervisor may go through the right motions and still find that the employee doesn't perform as anticipated.

In what important ways does dissatisfaction differ from satisfaction?

One noted behavioral scientist, Frederick Herzberg, made these distinctions between them:

Satisfaction for an employee comes from truly motivating factors such as interesting and challenging work, utilization of one's capabilities, opportunity to do something meaningful, recognition of achievement, and responsibility for one's own work.

Dissatisfaction occurs when the following factors are not present on the job: good pay, adequate holidays, long-enough vacations, paid insurance and pensions, good working conditions, and congenial people to work with.

Herzberg bases these definitions on his two-factor theory. He says that every human being has two motivational tracks: (1) a lower-level one, animal in nature and bent only on surviving, and (2) a higher-level one, uniquely human and directed toward adjusting to oneself. Herzberg labels the first set of motivations "hygiene," or "maintenance," factors. We need to satisfy them, he reasons, to keep alive. People try to avoid pain and unpleasantness in life: they do the same on the job. Satisfaction of these needs provides only hygiene for the person. They physically maintain, but they do not motivate. If they are not present in the workplace, an employee will be dissatisfied and may look for a job elsewhere that provides these factors. But the employee will not work harder just because these factors are given to him or her. Said another way, a general pay increase may keep employees from quitting, but it will rarely motivate an employee to work harder. (See Figure 3-2.)

How can supervisors provide the kind of satisfaction that motivates employees?

Herzberg feels that those job factors that provide genuine and positive motivations should be called *satisfiers*. (See the upper portion of Figure 3-2 for some typical satisfiers.)

Without splitting hairs, we can see that generally the company must provide the factors that prevent dissatisfaction. The supervisor tends to provide the factors that satisfy. Few supervisors can establish the basic pay rates for the organization. Almost all supervisors can motivate. For example, the supervisor can provide an employee with a specific, challenging goal: "Not many people can

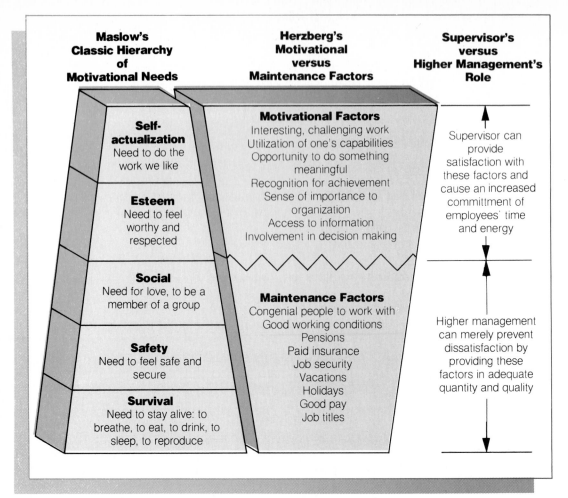

Figure 3-2. Employee needs that supervisors can satisfy.

stack more than 200 cartons an hour. If you can stack 220 today, you'll be a great asset to this department."

Similarly, a supervisor can let an employee know that the work is appreciated: "The boss asked me today who it was that typed these especially neat reports. I was pleased to be able to say it was you."

The supervisor can also help to make work more interesting by suggesting: "Why don't we take 15 minutes today to see whether together we can find a way to break the monotony in your job?"

And the supervisor can always extend responsibility by saying to an employee: "Beginning today, will you make the decision as to whether off-grade products should be reworked or thrown away? If you make an occasional mistake, don't worry about it. Your judgment is as good as mine, and I've learned that we can't be 100 percent perfect in these decisions."

How important is achievement to today's employee?

It is probably more important to supervisors than to employees. One noted observer, David McClelland, believes that the need for achievement is especially strong among most people who enter the management ranks. Nevertheless, a great many people feel its strong pull.

You can recognize the achiever, according to McClelland, if the person:

1. Likes to be able to control the situations in which he or she is involved;
2. Takes moderate risks but not long chances;
3. Likes to get immediate feedback as to how well he or she has done; and
4. Has a tendency to be preoccupied with the job to be done.

This last quality is one that supervisors must guard against lest it distract them from the need to relate well to their subordinates.

McClelland believes that most people learn their motivation patterns from life's experiences rather than by feeling them instinctively, as Maslow suggests. In fact, McClelland believes that in addition to achievement, the needs for power and affiliation are the most common motivators.

Individuals who are *power*-motivated may see every situation in your department as one in which they must seize control or otherwise submit to your domination. The power seekers tend to be abrasive, insisting on doing the job their own way rather than going along with your instructions.

Employees who are motivated by *affiliation* are usually friendly and like to socialize. The affiliation seekers are often hard to motivate toward production for production's sake but may respond to the appeal for cooperation.

Achievement seekers will rise to challenges and seek freedom of choice in deciding how to do the job. But they may be inclined to take off in an independent direction and balk at working with other employees.

Is the object of good human relations to have one big happy family?

Have you ever known a family in which there wasn't some discontent? Where one child didn't feel that another one was favored by a parent? Or where there wasn't an occasional spat between husband and wife? Or where there wasn't a disreputable relative hidden somewhere? I can't believe you haven't. It's the same way in business. As a responsible supervisor you strive for harmonious relationships with your employees and with the others with whom you associate. But it would be foolish to expect that everything is going to be as smooth as cream all the time—or even most of the time. It's only natural for people to have differences of opinion and arguments.

What you should aim for in your area is to have the arguments settled in a peaceful and reasonable manner. Keep emotions and epithets out of it. Sure, you can expect occasional name calling —and loud voices and red necks. But the *general* level of human relations in your area should be friendly, with an attitude of: "Okay, let's pull this issue apart. Tell me exactly what's eating you about this assignment. When I've seen your point, I won't promise you I'll agree with you. But I'll be a lot better able to give you a straight answer then." And after your decision: "Don't apologize for making an issue about it, Bill. That's your prerogative. And I'm glad you exercised it to get this matter cleared up. But how about in the future coming to me first before you get so hot and bothered about it?

What happens when workers don't get satisfaction from their jobs?

Morale will be down, attitudes will not be "right." But most important to you, unsatisfied workers don't produce as much or as well as those who find work rewarding.

Isn't job satisfaction primarily the company's responsibility—not the supervisor's?

The company's stake in good human relations is just as big as the supervisor's. And when a company helps the supervisor to establish the right climate for good human relations, the supervisor's job with people is much easier. But your relationship with your employees is a very personal one. And no amount of policies and procedures, fancy cafeterias, generous fringe benefits, or sparkling toilets can take the place of supervisors who are interested in their people and treat them wisely and well. From your point of view, responsibility for employees' job satisfaction is one you share jointly with the company.

Does good human relations really pay off?

Early in your career as a supervisor you'll find this recurrent criticism of the practice of human relations in industry: It makes good talk, but it doesn't pay the bills; whenever the squeeze is on to cut costs, all the frills will go out the window. That's the trouble with human relations. It's been hard for many companies to prove that its practice saves money. And whenever you come across supervisors who don't believe in good human relations (or who mistake softness for the real thing), they will be able to quote you examples of the well-meaning supervisors who got trampled on by employees they'd tried to do right by.

On the other hand, the casebooks document that supervisors who are intelligent in their dealings with people are able to show more production, lower costs, and greater quality. Good human relations doesn't mean being soft or weak or negligent. But neither does it mean treating people as if they weren't people. Good human relations is an art and a science. It is firm, yet flexible; and it's the most difficult ambition in the world to achieve. But be assured that the results are rewarding—in dollars and cents as well as in personal satisfaction for you and the people you supervise.

Key Concepts

1. There is no one best way to handle interpersonal relationships. They are dependent on what the particular situation is (its urgencies and its technical, social, or economic pressures) and who is involved in it. All human relationships are complex, with many influencing elements often hidden deep beneath the surface evidence

2. Individual behavior is dependent on a vast heritage of geneological characteristics and is shaped by the forces of home environment, educa-

tion, and work experience. This individuality causes people to behave the way they do, even though such behavior often appears illogical to others

3. Although it may appear that most people work mainly to satisfy their needs for food, shelter, and clothing, it is a fact that in this industrial age most people expect much more from their work in the way of social relationships, self-esteem, and meaningful work.

4. A contented work force and above-normal productivity do not necessarily go hand in hand. Permissiveness and indulgence, for example, induce careless and indifferent work habits. By setting high work standards and motivating employees to attain them, a supervisor must expect occasionally to cause tensions and outspoken disagreements. These exchanges, when resolved without delay, are healthy and tend to hold morale high.

5. Good human relations at work rarely occur accidentally. They are instilled and nurtured by the supervisor in charge. A supervisor can go a long way in establishing good human relations merely by treating his or her staff with respect and granting each person the consideration that persons deserves as a unique individual, regardless of his or her relative status within the organization.

Supervisory Word Power

Achievement Need. A desire for accomplishment, which motivates many people at work. Employees who are motivated by this need usually like to control their own work, like to know immediately whether their work is satisfactory, take moderate risks, and concentrate closely on tasks and goals.

Affiliation Need. A desire to interact with other people and to enjoy social contact. Meeting this need is an important source of job satisfaction for some people.

Behavior. The actions people take, or the things they say, while coping with other people, with problems, with opportunities, and with situations. Because behavior depends on so many influences, it may or may not accurately reflect a person's true feelings.

Dissatisfaction. The state that takes place when "maintenance" or "hygiene," factors such as good pay, fringe benefits, and desirable working conditions are lacking. Merely avoiding dissatisfaction is not adequate to motivate most workers.

Expectancy. An individual's judgment about the attractiveness of an assignment, based on (1) whether or not he or she can actually do what is requested, (2) whether there will be a reward for this performance, and (3) how highly the person values the promised benefit in view of the effort required.

Individuality. The character that heredity, environment, education, and experience combine to develop in each person—a unique hierarchy of motives and a unique way of behaving.

Motivation.   The process that impels a person to behave in a certain manner in order to satisfy highly individual needs for survival, security, respect, achievement, power, and sense of personal worth.

Personality.   The individual's unique way of behaving and of seeing and interpreting the actions of other people and things. Personality is shaped by heredity, parents' beliefs, upbringing, work experiences, and many other factors.

Power Need.   A desire to control the actions of others and to manipulate events. The control and manipulation may often be seen as ends in themselves rather than as ways to accomplish other important things.

Satisfaction.   The state that occurs when truly motivating factors—such as interesting and challenging work, full use of one's capabilities, and recognition for achievement—are provided.

Reading Comprehension

1. Provide an example from your own experience that shows how two or three people reacted differently to almost the same set of circumstances. Give an explanation of the reasons for these differences.

2. Find the dictionary definitions for *psychology* and *sociology*. Give an illustration of each science taken from everyday life.

3. Think of a possible confrontation between an employee and a supervisor. Show how their viewpoints and objectives might vary.

4. Do you think that a person's order of priorities for Maslow's five basic needs changes as he or she matures? Why?

5. Comment on the relationship between an individual's need for esteem and his or her need to do meaningful work.

6. Describe the three estimates an employee makes about a work assignment in deciding whether or not he or she will try harder.

7. When worker motivation in a department is still low despite good pay, fringe benefits, and desirable working conditions, what can a supervisor do to increase motivation?

8. Give some examples of behavior that might be expected from three individuals: one has a strong need for power, another has a strong need for affiliation, and the third has a strong need for achievement.

9. How would you draw the line between *(a)* a supervisor who is well liked and whose department is productive and *(b)* a supervisor who is well liked but whose department is not particularly effective?

10. Contrast a supervisor who tries to manipulate employees and one who tries to motivate them.

Supervision in Action
The Case of the Three Disappointing Employees. A Case Study in Human Relations Involving Three Potentially Good Employees Who Don't Quite Hit the Mark.

Pete is perplexed. Six months ago, the personnel manager turned up three promising candidates to fill vacancies for general labor jobs in his department. Pete was impressed by all three. After a brief trial period, he asked that all three be permanently assigned to the department. Since then, however, Pete has begun to mistrust his judgment.

The three employees—Mary, Mike, and Manuel—all came from a similar section of town. Their education was about the same: they had finished high school and nothing more. They were the daughter and sons of first- and second-generation Americans. These were families of modest circumstances. Everything about these three employees had led Pete to believe that what was good for one should be good for the other. Accordingly, in his approach to supervising them, Pete made it almost a point to treat each person equally. "I don't play favorites," he declared with pride.

Nevertheless, each of the three seemed to have developed his or her own peculiar set of characteristics. Take Mary, for instance. She was completely dependable so far as attendance was concerned, but she was no world-class performer when it came to output. Furthermore, when Pete tried to get her transferred to a department where she might have a better chance of getting promoted, she refused the opportunity. "I'd rather stay here where I know the job," she said.

Mike, on the other hand, was a quick study. He caught on to each new job very quickly. But as soon as he had learned it, he wanted to try something different. He routinely complained about being bored with the work in the department. And his attendance seemed to reflect it. When questioned by his less than outstanding attendance record, Mike replied: "You can't miss me that much when I'm absent. There's nothing I'm asked to do that someone else in the department can't fill in on with only a moment's notice."

Manual presented still another problem. His performance was all right, but he was continually complaining about something. If it wasn't about the pay scale being too low, it was because there were no hot meals in the cafeteria. Or the company down the road had ten paid holidays, whereas this one had only nine. Pete moved Manuel around the department trying to find the kind of assignment that would keep him satisfied.

Finally, Pete spoke to the personnel manager: "You sure let me pick three odd-balls this time. All three work for the same company and under the same circumstances, but only Mary seems reasonably satisfied. And, while she's steady, she sure is slow and afraid to take on anything new. Mike could be a top-notch employee, but he's undependable and doesn't want to stick with anything. Manuel isn't a star performer, but he's better than average. Yet his continual complaining is driving me up the wall."

"Well," said the personnel manager, "I never told you that supervising would be easy—or that everybody was going to be happy in their work."

1. What was wrong with Pete's belief that by treating every employee the same, he would get the same results from each?
2. On the basis of the information presented, which motivational need seems to be the most dominant for each of these employees? How does this affect each employee's performance?
3. What might Pete do, if anything, to improve the level of satisfaction —and performance—for each of these three employees?

4

WORK GROUP
BEHAVIOR

What is meant by group dynamics?

This term is applied to the forces brought to bear by individuals, singly or collectively, in a group activity. The choice of the word *dynamics* is especially important. It implies change. For example, you set out to explain to Paul why he should operate a slightly more complex machine without receiving an increase in his pay rate. He enters the situation with the conviction that you are trying to take advantage of him. You begin with the view that he's got to accept your word, willynilly. After five minutes of talking, you see that Paul isn't going to take this decision lying down; furthermore, you feel he has a legitimate argument you hadn't anticipated. Paul, on the other hand, feels that you aren't going to go to bat in his behalf, and although he's still apparently listening, he's made up his mind to see his shop steward as soon as he can. Since the conversation began, your attitude has changed and so has Paul's. That's dynamic.

Any two people can make up a group. Their interaction is group dynamics. As more and more people get into the group, the situation gets more dynamic. As time elapses, the situation gets more dynamic. And as new factors enter the situation (a change in workplace lighting, an announcement of a pay increase at the plant next door, etc.), the situation gets even more dynamic.

Two or more persons interacting—plus change—add up to group dynamics.

Why are group relations more important today than they were in years past?

Business, industrial, service, and government enterprises are larger and more complex. As a result they depend more on the effectiveness of group effort. At the turn of the nineteenth into the twentieth century, employees worked more by themselves, and their productivity often depended on their efforts alone. Then, too, many of the jobs were unskilled. People were hired to do routine work or to perform a specific task that a machine performs today. Automation, computers, and modern technology made those jobs scarce. Instead, modern jobs involve great interdependence among individuals and among departments and demand close cooperation among all parties.

What does this have to do with the supervisor?

Just about everything. You must first recognize that all situations are dynamic. Then you've got to develop a way of following the direction of, and coping with, the evolving situation. All too often in group dynamics the supervisor is a couple of laps behind the field. He or she is trying to solve the situation as it was five minutes ago—or five days ago—not as it is right now.

Which groups take priority: the formal or the informal ones?

Formal groups do, such as your own department or assigned work teams within your department. They have been set up routinely to carry out the work in the best fashion. But informal groups require your attention and consideration, too. A supervisor must be realistic about formation of informal groups within the department:

1. Informal groups are inevitable. They'll form at the water fountain and in the locker room. They will be made up of car poolers and those with common interests in sports or politics. You will find them everywhere. There is no way to blot them out.

2. Informal groups can be very powerful. They influence your employees strongly. They command their loyalty and often demand conformity. Most important, such groups can work on your behalf or they can work against you.

What causes employees to create their own informal groups?

There are a number of reasons. Most powerful is a common specialty or skill. For example, the keyboard operators in a data processing office are naturally going to find things in common to talk about. Other common experiences, backgrounds, or interests will also serve to pull parts of a formal grouping of employees into "cliques." Proximity plays a role, too. Workers who are physically close together tend to form close relationships to the exclusion of others in the department who are in more remote locations.

Membership in informal groups is developed gradually. Over a period of time, an individual begins to feel that he or she is accepted by the others. In return, the individual begins to accept—and carry out—the interests and behavior of the group. The bonds are tighter when the attraction is fostered by a desire for protection or support (often with regard to the company or management). Groups are less cohesive when the common bond is more casual, as with hobbies and sports. Since these groups are purely informal, membership depends on a feeling of being an "insider," "fringe-sider," or "outsider," as shown in Figure 4-1. All ten members report formally to the same supervisor, but only five consider themselves insiders. They work closely together and regularly eat lunch together. Three other employees under the same supervision associate, sometimes closely, with one or two of the "in" group, but not all of them. Two other employees are considered outsiders by the group. Few of the in group talk to them. The outsiders tend to eat lunch with people in other work groups.

A supervisor must be careful in his or her relationship with these informal groups. They can't be ignored; more often they can be help-

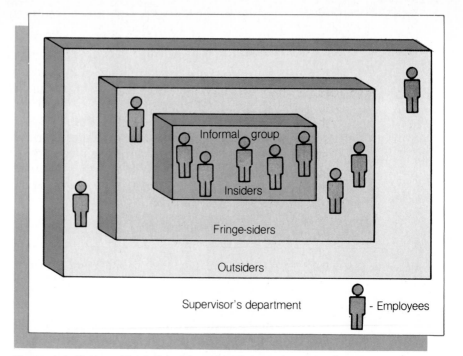

Figure 4-1. Pattern of relationships of an informal group of employees within a formal group of employees under the same supervisor.

ful. On the other hand, giving them too much attention, especially to the exclusion of the outsiders, will surely bring about dissension and lack of cooperation.

To whom does the individual employee owe loyalty: the group or the supervisor?

There is no reason why an employee cannot be loyal to both. An employee warms up to various informal groups for friendship and companionship. A rank-and-file worker is more likely to identify with a buddy than with the boss. And in a time of layoffs or other threats, an employee may reasonably look to the group for protection.

On the other hand, an employee looks to the good supervisor for knowledge about the job, personal training and development, direction and instruction, encouragement, respect, and understanding. The wise supervisor doesn't force an employee to choose between the group and the boss.

Which goals come first: the individual's, the group's, or the organization's?

If anything is to be accomplished, groups as well as individuals must place their goals second to those of the organization. The trick to good supervision, however, is to find a way to keep the goals of all three in harmony. Mary, for example, wants to get the job done as soon as she can so that she can take a break. The group wants to stretch it out so that there will be overtime. The supervisor, who must represent the organization, wants to get the job done on schedule so that a shipment can be made on time and at specified labor cost. Mary and the supervisor are pulling in the same direction. The group is not. The supervisor has to find a way to persuade or insist that the group go along with the company goals, such as "We'll all lose this order if we don't get it out by 4 p.m." Or "Our deadline is 4 p. m. We've been able to make it dozens of times in the past. And regardless, there will be no overtime approved for this shipment."

How does a group of employees differ from any single employee in the group?

Take a group of ten employees who work in a small can-filling line in a food-packing plant. This group is respected and feared by its supervisor as one of the most productive, most-likely-to-strike groups in the plant. Yet in the group are three people who, polled separately, are strongly against a walkout. And there are another three who, when working with other groups, are low producers. This is typical. Each person in a group may be a fairly strong individualist when working alone. But when people work in a group, the personality of the group becomes stronger than that of any single individual in the group. The group's personality will reflect the outlook and work habits of the various individuals, but it will bring out the best (or worst) in some and will submerge many individual tendencies the group does not approve of.

Furthermore, each group sets the standards of conduct—or *norms*—for its members. Norms are accepted ways of doing things, an accepted way of life within the group. The group's ways may not be the best ways. Often, group norms stand in the way of doing things the way the company and the supervisor want them done. But the group will support the group standards. Individuals who don't confirm will be cut off from the group's gossip sessions and social activities. It's not uncommon for the group to ridicule those who don't "play ball" or to purposely make it difficult for outsiders to get their own work done.

What are work groups likely to do best?

Solve work problems. Groups, formal or informal, seem to have an uncanny knack for unsnarling complex work situations. In a few minutes they can straighten out crossover procedures between employees. They often know causes of difficulty hidden from the supervisor. Typically, they are acutely aware of personality conflicts between their members. Thus, a group's ability to put together jointly held know-how in a constructive manner is one that experienced supervisors like to tap. The technique of securing group aid this way in solving departmental problems is called *participation*.

In what ways are groups most likely to cause problems?

By ganging up to present mass resistance (spoken or silent) and by pressuring individual members to conform to the group's standards. Strong work groups stick together. They will protect one of their loyal members, and they will force a nonconformist to go along with the majority. The pressure can be so strong that even an eager beaver or a loner can be made to fall in line—or to quit. Groups are powerful. Their support is to be cherished. Their enmity can be awesome. For these reasons prudent supervisors seek the group's help in establishing attainable work goals.

How changeable are group attitudes?

They can be very changeable. Take a group's attitude, for example, on a proposed change in its work procedure. Initially all members may resist it. Then one or two try it out and find that it is not so bad as they thought. They persuade a few of their friends to try it out. Soon, like passengers who rush from one side of a boat to another, they can dramatically change the weight of the group's position. Even the reluctant members are swept along with the crowd. Obviously, this effort can be helpful or troublesome. It is a considerable force to be dealt with.

Why are some groups influential, others weak?

Strong groups, contrary to what you might suspect, are ones in which there are lots of conflict and frequent arguments. But where arguments are welcomed, agreements are stronger, too. And the pressure to conform is great.

Weak groups are those in which the objectives are not very important to most members or in which a few strong leaders make all the decisions.

In the work groups you supervise, try to find out what the workers want as a group. Then help them to set these goals themselves. Try to show that your interest is in seeing that group goals are achieved, that you aren't the roadblock to job security, better pay, more rewarding work. That way the work groups you supervise will be strong groups. And properly inspired, their goals will be very similar to yours.

It's when supervisors set themselves against work groups that the group becomes either strongly against the supervisor and the company or weak and easily seized by a strong leader who may be against the supervisor or the objectives which best satisfy both company and worker.

How can a supervisor set goals with the work group without sacrificing authority?

Unless the group of people you supervise believes that what you want them to do is to their advantage as well as to yours, you'll have little success as a supervisor. The solution lies in permitting the group to set their goals along with you and in showing them that these goals are attained through group action—teamwork.

It may be only natural for you to feel that to permit the group to get into the decision-making act will be hazardous to your authority. It needn't be. First of all, make it clear that you'll always retain a veto power over a group decision (but don't exercise it unless absolutely necessary). Second, establish ground rules for their participation beforehand. Explain what's negotiable and what's not. Make these limitations clear. Finally, provide enough information for the group so that they can see situations as you do. It's when people don't have enough facts that they rebel against authority.

In dealing with work groups, try to make your role that of a coach. Help employees to see why cost cutting, for instance, is desirable and necessary to prevent layoffs. Encourage them to discuss ways to

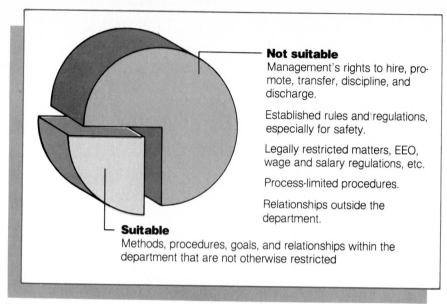

Not suitable
Management's rights to hire, promote, transfer, discipline, and discharge.

Established rules and regulations, especially for safety.

Legally restricted matters, EEO, wage and salary regulations, etc.

Process-limited procedures.

Relationships outside the department.

Suitable
Methods, procedures, goals, and relationships within the department that are not otherwise restricted

Figure 4-2. Areas suitable for—and negotiable by—participatory management methods.

cut costs. Welcome their suggestions. Try to find ways of putting even relatively insignificant ideas to work. And report the team's achievements frequently. Emphasize that good records are the result of the team's united effort, not your own bright ideas.

Of course, it goes without saying that certain decisions—such as those concerning work standards or quality specifications—may be beyond the group's control or even yours. (See Figure 4-2.) Consequently, you should make it clear at the start what work conditions are off limits as far as group participation is concerned.

What makes group participation so effective?

You'll hear a lot about the wonders of participation in one form or another, such as "consensus management," or "quality circles." Most of what you'll hear is true. In today's employer-employee relations, few techniques have been as successful in developing harmony and the attainment of common goals as has the development of participation by management and supervision.

Participation is an amazingly simple way to inspire people. And its simplicity lies in the definition of that word: "to share in common with others."

Sharing, then, is the secret. You must share knowledge and information with others in order to gain their cooperation. You must share your own experience so that employees will benefit from it. You must share the decision-making process itself so that employees can do some things the way they'd like to. And you must share credit for achievement.

How often can group participation be expected to work in your behalf?

Only as often as the group's perception of a situation leads them logically or emotionally, or both ways, to the conclusion that what you wish is good for them. Keep in mind that merely permitting participation will not manipulate the group to your point of view. And the larger the group, the more forces are at work in it with which your ideas must cope.

If the majority can be expected to agree with your inclinations when given the same view of the facts you have, then the majority may sway group attitudes in your direction. But even this won't always be the case. If, for example, Carlos is cantankerous, but because of seniority or outspokenness has the respect or fear of the rest of the people in the word processing pool, the group may never buy an idea of yours that discredits him. Conversely, the group may (for reasons that are hard to determine) rebel against Carlos and accept your new idea.

There are two rules of thumb to guide you: (1) Without group support your chance of achievement is slim, and (2) your best chance for winning group support is to let the forces within the group itself struggle toward a decision with minimum interference from you. This isn't to say you must stand by helplessly while the group strikes off in the wrong direction. You can supply sound direction by proving facts that might be overlooked and by asking the group to weigh pros and cons of various alternatives.

Which comes first, the individual or the group?

It's almost impossible to say. We do know that the group is not just the sum of the individuals in it. Individually each of your employees may be loyal and honest. But as a group each person may be more loyal to the group's interest than to you. As a result, the individual may cheat a little on output or quality, if that's the standard the group respects.

It seems unavoidable that you must place your bets on the group's being collectively stronger than any of its individuals. Hardly any one person can stand up to group pressures for long. The person who does so may keep on working in your area but is no longer a member of that group. Such persons become oddballs, difficult for you to deal with fairly and intelligently because you're never sure what standards of performance to impose on them—theirs or the department's. For that reason don't press individuals to support you in favor of the work group. Accept the fact that they will be loyal to you when this loyalty doesn't put them at odds with their peers.

By and large the supervisor's charge is to treat each person as individually as possible without challenging the prerogatives of the group the individual works in. The work group is an organization for which you are expected to provide direction and inspiration, not moral judgments.

Key Concepts

1. Because supervision is involved with organized human effort, group relations are present in every situation and the characteristics of a group's behavior must be weighed just as carefully as the characteristics of an individual. Work groups may be either formal, established by management, or informal, spontaneously created by members because of mutual interests.

2. With groups especially, the principle of participation presents an effective approach. By recognizing a group's efforts to attain (or block) goals, a supervisor who invites participation encourages the group to direct its influence in a productive manner.

3. Employees can be loyal both to the group and to the supervisor. Little is to be gained by forcing an individual to choose between the two, since both provide certain satisfactions.

4. Because groups exert such tremendous influence in the work situation, supervisors must tune their senses to the feelings of groups as well as of individuals. Before supervisors can successfully cope with or redirect nonproductive behavior, they must know how people in the work force feel about themselves, their work group, the group itself, and their supervisors.

5. Supervisors must respect the power and legitimate interests of work groups without abandoning the responsibility of management to the group

or relinquishing essential authority. Adequate care will usually allow organization goals to be met without ignoring the rights and expectations of individuals or groups.

Supervisory Word Power

Group Dynamics.   The interaction among members of a work group and concurrent changes in their attitudes, behavior, and relationships; similarly, the interaction—and changing attitudes, behavior, and relationships—between a work group and others outside the group, in particular, the supervisor.

Group Norms.   Beliefs held by the group about what is right and what is wrong as far as performance at work is concerned.

Formal Work Groups.   Those groups or teams of employees who are assigned by management to similar activities or locations with the intent that they work together toward goals established by management.

Informal Work Groups.   Those groups that form spontaneously among employees who work near one another, or who have common personal interests, or who work toward common job goals, whether or not these goals are the ones set down by management.

Participation.   A supervisor's or manager's sharing with work groups of work-related information and of responsibilities, decisions, or both. Participation may be used to determine the way a job should be performed, how a group should divide up the work, and what the work goals might be.

Reading Comprehension

1. Why are the forces that operate within groups called group dynamics?

2. Describe a situation you have been in, in which you were part of both a formal group and an informal group within the same organization.

3. Should a supervisor force an employee to choose between loyalty to the group and loyalty to the supervisor? Why or why not?

4. Why would an experienced supervisor encourage group participation in solving a work problem?

5. Give an example of how a group's norms might differ from the standards of performance set by the company or by the group's supervisor.

6. What kind of problems can work groups cause that a supervisor should be especially conscious of?

7. Think of a supervisor or a teacher you have had who never revealed personal feelings and reactions to the work group. Was this a good idea? Why or why not?

8. Think of a group that has changed some of its attitudes or beliefs over a period of time. What caused the change? Was it rapid or gradual? How did it take place?

9. What are some forces likely to create a strong group? A weak group?

10. As a supervisor, what would be your overall goals in establishing relations with your work group?

Supervision in Action

The Case of the Unsuccessful Procedures Change. A Case Study in Human Relations Involving Group Dynamics, with Questions for You To Answer.

When Barbara was promoted to supervisor and moved to the claims department of an insurance company, she was viewed with suspicion by the men and women in the new department. Because Barbara was soundly grounded in the clerical procedures used there, she believed there were many improvements that could be made. Not wanting to give the impression of being too eager, however, Barbara spent the first week or two just getting to know the people in her department. On the whole, the staff was pretty standoffish. This was especially true of Jack, one of the older claims analysts. On the bright side, Barbara was able to make friends with Tony, one of the sharp, young new clerks.

One of the costly practices Barbara noticed was that the claims form was initially posted to a logbook by a clerk, then given a preliminary classification by an analyst before being returned to the clerk for detailed verification of the data on the form. After this, the form went back to an analyst for completion. Barbara reasoned that the clerk who entered the form in the logbook could be trained to make the preliminary classification. This same clerk could also verify the detailed data on the form. This way, unnecessary doubling back of the form would be eliminated, and the analysts could spend more of their time on the complex aspects of claims processing.

Barbara waited until Friday and then proposed to the clerks and analysts that on Monday, the new procedure should be followed. She demonstrated to all the clerks how the classifications could be made with the same master list used by the analysts. Since there were no objections and only a few questions, Barbara presumed that the work group understood the new procedure.

On Monday Barbara made a point of working along with Tony because he was the newest clerk in the office. He easily caught on to the new way. Tony seemed sold on the improvement, and by noon he had finished as much work as he normally would have before the additional step was added to his job. That afternoon, however, Tony reported to Barbara that he had run into all sorts of difficulty in following the new procedure. The next morning Barbara discovered that Tony was doing the job in the old way. Barbara checked the rest of the staff and found that no one other than Tony had even given the new method a try. In fact, when she queried Jack about it, Jack said this was an old idea that had been tried before and found to be full of problems. Barbara then went back to Tony and suggested he try a variation in which his problems with the new method might be worked out. Tony shook his head and said: "This is not as good an idea as it looked at first. If it were, other people in the department besides me would be trying it. Anyway, I would rather follow the old procedure. It's much simpler."

1. Why do you suppose Tony gave up on the new procedure so soon?
2. How might Jack's reaction have influenced the other employees?
3. Should Barbara persist in trying to install the new procedure? Why?
4. How might she have gotten her idea accepted in the first place?

5

CONFLICT AND COOPERATION

Is the presence of bickering and disputes a sign
of poor supervision?

Not necessarily. It is human to quarrel and complain. When many
people must work together, conflict is inevitable. Accordingly, a
small amount of conflict can be a good thing. It is when there is no
end of quarreling and confrontation that supervisors should begin to
worry about how good a job they are doing.

What are the main sources of conflict in an organization?

They are many. People with different ideas about what should be
done and how to do it are a common source. Departments that are

sometimes at cross-purposes—such as production and maintenance, production control and sales, sales and credit, accounting
and retailing, purchasing and engineering—cause intergroup difficulties. But most of the causes of conflict in a supervisor's department are closely related to the work itself: how it is laid out and the
way in which the supervisor manages the employees. In particular, a
supervisor should be on guard against:

1. An appearance of an unfair allocation of tools, materials,
supplies, and other resources. There are few shops where there is always enough of everything to go around equally. The supervisor
must often make the hard decisions about who will have what, how
much, and when. When these decisions are made openly and fairly,
employees are more likely to accept them without quarreling with
one another. If allocations are made slyly or on the basis of favoritism, trouble will brew.

2. Expressed disagreements about what's important and what is
not. If these are the result of lack of information or misinformation,
they should be cleared up right away. If the disagreements arise
because individuals see things differently, the supervisor must try to
get to the root of the problem. For example, a press operator may
constantly push his benchmate for work to be processed, whereas
the benchmate may insist that her work can't be released because its
quality isn't good enough. The first individual sets priority on output,
the other on quality. The supervisor must find an answer to this question: Are these priorities (or goals) merely a reflection of each individual's values—or are they related to the department's established
goals and standards?

3. Changes in work flow or conditions that imply a change in status.
If in the past, Anita handled incoming orders first before passing
them on to Jack for posting, Anita may regard her work as more
valued than Jack's. A change in the order of flow so that Jack
handles the orders first may disturb Anita's sense of status. And she
may begin finding fault with everything that Jack does.

4. A growing sense of mistrust among employees. This is liable to
occur when things in the department are generally going wrong. If
business is bad, or if the department has been criticized for mistakes or low productivity, employees may look around for others on
whom to place the blame. The production department, for example,
will blame off-grade products on the maintenance people—the
equipment was faulty. The floor salesperson may blame the cashier
for a lost sale. The nurse may blame the nurse's aide for upset patients.

5. Lack of stability in departmental operations. Change is so threatening to many people that they will naturally take out their fears and

anxieties in quibbling and complaints. Many times, change is something beyond the supervisor's control. But the supervisor can pour oil on troubled waters simply by maintaining an air of calm. He or she can, for example, talk with employees about the reasons for the change, how long it will last, and how it will affect—or not affect—normal operating conditions.

How does competition differ from conflict?

The former is usually productive; the latter is often counterproductive. The right kind of competition can stimulate a healthy, controlled battle between two individuals. Informal contests allow employees to try to excel at meeting departmental goals that are mutually beneficial. Carried too far, however, the contestants may lose sight of the common good and become antagonistic.

Conflict tends to pit individuals and groups against one another in trying to control the department's resources in pursuit of their own goals. A lathe operator, for example, may insist on taking the only available tool in order to finish his or her *own* quota on time. He or she may not worry about whether or not this slows up another operator or the department in meeting its goals. Or a salesperson may demand the major portion of the section's travel expenses because his or her *own* customers are most important. (See Figure 5-1.)

What's a good way to handle conflict in your department?

First, be alert to its presence. Next, seek out its causes. Then meet it head-on. A basic approach involves five steps:

1. Decide What It Is That You Wish to Be Accomplished. Do you want peace and quiet at any price? Or do you want better quality? Greater productivity? A project finished on time? Fewer mistakes in transcribing? An end to delays caused by quarrels between the maintenance person and your production operator? Nothing will be resolved unless you first make up your mind what the desired outcome should be.

2. Call Together the People Who Can Best Settle the Issue. If the conflict is strictly between you and an individual, limit the confrontation to the two of you. If others are involved, invite them into the discussion. If a disinterested party, such as the quality-control department, can shed light on the subject, ask for its participation. If a referee or someone who can speak authoritatively about the company's viewpoint is needed, then get your boss into the act.

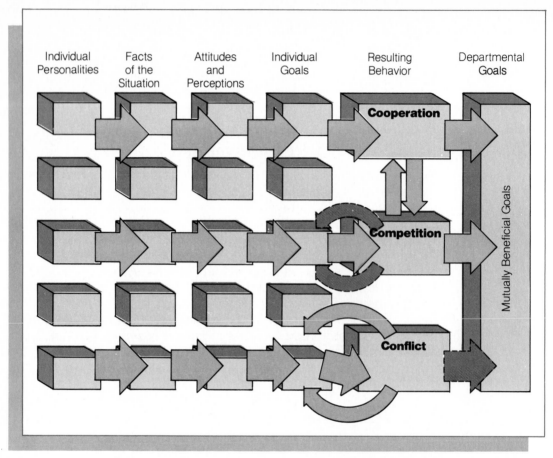

Figure 5-1. Factors in the processes of conflict, competition, and cooperation. Conflict takes precedence over competition and cooperation when individuals strive to meet their own goals with little or no regard for group goals.

3. Be Ready to Bargain, Not Hand Out Edicts. Conflicts are truly settled by negotiation. A short answer tends only to put off the problem, and it will keep recurring. If you keep your eye on the objective you have set, there are usually many ways to attain it. Remember that each individual has an objective, too. If the maintenance department, for example, can provide the necessary repairs while still keeping their costs in line—and dependable repairs are your objective—then let the maintenance people do it their way.

4. Don't Be Distracted by the Red Herring of Personalities. Whereas many people do rub one another the wrong way, most conflicts have a much more tangible basis. That's the value of keeping the eyes of all concerned on the main objective. It tends to push personality conflicts into the background. Finally, try not to get emotionally involved yourself. Above all, don't choose sides.

5. Focus Attention on Mutually Beneficial Outcomes. Above all, don't make performance comparisons between individuals. This will only heighten competition and stress. Instead, hold up total organizational results as the criterion for success. If Kevin insists that Sharon takes up more than her share of the keyboard time, for example, try to reach a solution that makes the most effective use of the keyboard. That way, both Sharon and Kevin can contribute to departmental effectiveness, even though both may have to give in a little while doing so.

How can you avoid prolonging a touchy situation?

As we said earlier, the best thing is to face up to conflict as soon as you are sure it has substance. In other words, don't heat up a minor dispute by jumping the gun. But do try to resolve it clearly once you've seen more than smoke. Because conflict is unpleasant to most of us and because it is not easy to settle, you should guard against certain practices that tend to prolong it. For example, check to see that you are not making any of the following mistakes:

● Avoiding conversations or contact with those who are involved. You're angry at Sue, for example, and you're not going to speak to her. Or you purposely cut out the bowling night with the purchasing supervisor who is undercutting you.
● Emphasizing orders and instructions while shutting off an employee's opportunities to talk to you. Or relying on a flurry of written memos and bulletin board notices. This encourages employees to inflate the issues and make them harder to resolve.
● Switching from compliments to complaints. You feel you were nice to Sam, for example, and he didn't cooperate. Okay, now you'll show him what it's like by throwing a few zingers to him.
● Allowing the injured parties to gang up. One unhappy person can "infect" several others. If it is your department against the sales-order department, for example, continued silent combat will build up their solidarity. And when you finally do try to settle the issue, it will be stickier than ever.

People speak of the value of gaining sensitivity. Why?

In dealing with other people who are members of your work force, many authorities believe that you can establish better long-term relations with them if you are sensitive to the way they feel—both about you and about your behavior toward them. The rationale goes something like this: If you're in tune with employee's feelings, your timing of instructions, changes, requests, and criticisms—and your way of going about all this—will be more effective.

The sensitivity point of view assumes that few of us really know how we affect other people. It also assumes that if we had a chance to see ourselves as others see us, we'd change our ways and adopt a more acceptable manner. Unfortunately, these sensitivity authorities generally assume that under normal conditions others disguise their true feelings so well that the chances of our finding out about ourselves are very slim. Accordingly, the prescribed way to acquire this learning is to take part in a sensitivity-training laboratory, often called laboratory, or controlled, training.

What's the significance of a hidden agenda?

One point of view of the sensitivity-training people is that so many ordinary business meetings (where, for instance, supervisors sit down to resolve production or cost problems) get nowhere because each member nurses a "hidden agenda." This hidden agenda prevents the group from making real progress in solving their mutual problems. For example, Teresa, the production-control supervisor, may feel the meeting has been called to make her the scapegoat of a delayed shipment. Consequently, she comes to the meeting with the intention of placing the blame on the purchasing agent for not having stocked the right quantity of subassemblies. This is Teresa's hidden agenda. Until the group gets Teresa to put this agenda on the table, the group meeting will accomplish very little. Proponents of sensitivity argue that it would be far better for the purposes of the meeting if Teresa were to say what is on her mind—that she thinks she's going to be made the goat, that others are to blame. That way, other participants would know how Teresa feels and could clear the air of recriminations before settling down to solutions that usually require teamwork.

Must you be superhuman to get along with everybody?

You would be if you did. That's why psychologists stress the value of accepting yourself pretty much as you are—not smugly, of course, but recognizing that you have many faults, faults that keep you from doing a perfect job and sometimes make you difficult to live with.

If you expect perfection from yourself, for example, chances are that you are almost impossible for others to get along with because you tend to expect perfection from them, too. Worse still, you expect perfection from them in a lot of matters they couldn't care less about. On the other hand, it's just as dangerous to shield yourself from your own personality deficiencies and to make excuses for them. Admitting your weaknesses is far better. Try to make concessions where they cause others trouble. But don't blame others for your shortcomings.

Whether you strive for perfection or cover up your weaknesses, it often adds up to misery for others. Sensitivity experts believe that (1) just knowing more about yourself may make you more acceptable to others and (2) permitting others to comment to you about your shortcomings can work magic for you. People will then accept you for what you are and will make allowances for you. And they will also more readily accept—and act on—your criticism of them.

Does sensitivity imply that a responsive manager doesn't demote, discipline, or fire anybody?

Not at all. If the demands of a particular job are such that a subordinate cannot perform it properly, the supervisor must take action. Sensitivity does not interfere with this action. Its purpose is to help people who are working to do a better, more effective job. Sensitivity flourishes in an atmosphere of success (not failure), and vice versa.

How can you invite candid, open discussion with others without recriminations?

First, get the talk candid. That takes guts on your part. Later, the recriminations won't be bad, if they don't disappear altogether. The trick in getting others to level with you is to try to separate feelings from facts.

Take an employee who has an irritating way of making remarks to other employees while you're explaining the lineup for the day's work. Get this employee aside and say something like this: "I have no idea what it is you're saying when I'm talking. But it irritates me beyond reason. It makes me want to give you the heaviest kind of work I can find. It's crazy for two grown people to get a hang-up like this. Maybe my impression of your attitude is all wrong. Is it?" Given this chance, the person may say, "You bug me, too, the way you lecture us each morning as if we were kids. What's more, you always seem to find a way to make me look like a fool." At that point the employee is beginning to bring a hidden agenda into view—because you've been willing to expose yours. Surprisingly, once feelings have been discussed—not necessarily resolved—the chances are infinitely better that the two of you will be able to agree better on factual matters.

What is an attitude?

An attitude is a person's point of view. It's a way of looking at something. But even more important, an attitude is a person's readiness to react—and to react in a predetermined way.

Baseball batters ready to swing at a pitch, for instance, set their feet, cock their bats, keep their eyes on the pitcher. They've learned from experiences that this attitude gives the best chance of getting a hit. In the same way, you—and your employees—learn from your experience to assume a readiness to react when faced with a situation. Employee attitudes toward lateness determine how conscientiously they try to get to work on time. Your attitude toward lateness will determine how much emphasis you place on tardiness as a measure of employee performance.

When are attitudes positive or negative?

Attitudes that reflect optimism and enthusiasm—what professional athletes call desire—are positive. People who are positive in their thinking look for good things in other people and in their own work. They seek to change and improve those conditions that they don't like rather than merely to complain about them. People who have negative attitudes tend to see only the bad side. They dwell on their own misfortunes and those of others. Unfortunately, negative attitudes, like positive ones, are contagious. An employee who begins a working career cheerfully may have that positive outlook eroded by the constant carping of sour-dispositioned associates.

What causes poor attitudes?

When an employee faces a situation the way you'd like—such as accepting your corrections in good grace—you're likely to say that the worker has a good attitude. But if the same worker irks you by habitually failing to keep the area neat, you may find yourself saying that the employee's attitude is poor. How do you explain this contradiction? How can the same person's attitude be good one time, bad the next?

It could be that the employee's attitudes (from the employee's point of view) are fine. In the first instance you seem considerate and helpful when it comes to explaining how to do a job. Your favorable action has developed in the worker a good attitude toward criticism. In the second instance this same worker may have learned that you are pretty soft about discipline for sloppy housekeeping. The worker's observation is that you complain a lot about poor housekeeping, but your bark is worse than your bite. So this worker's attitude toward housekeeping is the one you've taught, even though it's bad.

Is the supervisor always responsible for a worker's attitudes?

No. An employee, just like yourself, has many teachers. Parents, childhood pals, schoolteachers, the man or woman at the next desk, and union representatives have all been teaching him how to react to things for a long time. These other people may have shown him hundreds of times that he could get away with anything just by giving lip service to what the boss says. So he keeps on doing what he pleases. If that's the case, as it often is, you'll have to try hard to build up new, different experiences with this worker. You'll have to show him that his old attitude won't be a good one in his relationships with you.

You can recognize when others have done a better job of teaching attitudes than you have if you find yourself saying, "I've told her and told her. But she just keeps on doing it the way she wants to." Do you really blame an employee if she continues to find out that she can get away with a bad attitude? For her the attitude is a good one to assume with you.

What can you do to change attitudes?

Quite a lot. Understanding attitudes often points the way to changing them. Employees *learn* the attitudes they have. You can teach them new ones. Don't try this by preaching. Do it by setting favorable examples, by providing employees with favorable experiences.

Suppose Mark is a troublemaker in your department. He complains about his own assignment, continually charges discrimination, stirs up the other employees to make grievances. In your eyes his actions show his attitude to be bad.

Now you want Mark to change his attitude. But why is Mark a troublemaker? That's hard to say. And it takes experience and understanding to find out. But think for a moment about what Mark's experience shows him about his troublemaking attitude: It provides him with plenty of attention, it makes him a hero, it wins grudging admiration from his associates.

Now suppose that you could find a way of providing Mark with experiences where his troublemaking didn't get him attention or admiration. And you found other, more favorable ways of providing experiences that give him the attention and admiration he desires.

For instance, you might find good reason to compliment Mark openly and frequently about his work. You might ask his opinion about new methods that are under consideration. You might enlist his aid in telling other employees about job changes. All these actions on your part are healthy. And they provide Mark with the type of job satisfaction he looks for. And suppose, for instance, that each time Mark made trouble, you handled his actions discreetly and impersonally. And you avoided any show of emotion or upset. Chances are that the effect would be to change his attitude for the better.

You should be cautioned, of course, that attitudes and behaviors aren't often easy to pin down to actual cause and effect. But if you approach each human relations problem without a preconceived notion and with real humility and warmth, attitudes can be changed. The point in Mark's case is that you want to help him, not outsmart him.

Can you always change someone's attitude?

Theoretically the answer is yes, but in practice, no. Some people are just too fixed in their ways to yield very much. Sometimes you, as a supervisor, can do little to change the organizational situations that create unfavorable attitudes. And some combinations of circumstances may be too complex to do much about without help from the personnel office, or from a psychologist or a psychiatrist.

What's the supervisor's responsibility for the general condition of employee attitudes?

A supervisor is logically in the best position to influence attitudes among rank-and-file employees. Since your contact as supervisor is personal and frequent, you can do much toward understanding attitude changes and taking action to improve attitudes or to keep them from getting worse.

It would be misleading, however, not to recognize that middle management and top management have a significant effect on attitudes. Supervisors are human beings; they're also employees. It's only natural that supervisors should reflect in their attitudes the consideration they get, or do not get, from higher management. And the supervisor's attitude—good or bad—is often reflected among first-line employees. But, by and large, the supervisor holds the key to employee attitudes.

What is an attitude survey?

An attitude survey is a systematic way of finding out how employees feel about their company, their pay, their supervisors, their working conditions, their jobs, and so forth.

The most common attitude survey is based on a multiple-choice questionnaire. This way, a company can take a kind of vote among its employees to find out their attitudes. Questions are phrased something like this:

> Check the one answer that most nearly describes how you feel about the following statement: There's too much pressure on my job. Do you agree, are you undecided, or do you disagree?

Another typical question:

> My boss really tries to get my ideas about things. Do you agree, are you undecided, or do you disagree?

As many as 100 questions may be asked, with room left for written comments. To make the survey more meaningful, it is kept confidential: No employee signs his or her name, and the tabulation is done by a university or a consulting firm so that company officials never see even the handwriting of the employees surveyed.

Questionnaire answers are tabulated and analyzed. Most companies report survey findings either generally or in specific terms to their employees. It's especially important that, once management finds out what employee attitudes are, it take immediate action to improve conditions where attitudes are unfavorable. For instance, a survey may show that most employees don't feel free to discuss job matters with their supervisors. Most people who have studied the relationship of attitudes to effort feel that such a condition is unhealthy and prevents a supervisor from getting the type of cooperation needed. Consequently, the company—and the supervisor—should take steps to improve the condition. For you, it may mean changing your own attitude and conduct to show that you will set aside time to listen to employee questions, complaints, or suggestions; and that you will do this listening with interest and welcome the ideas that are presented.

Just how good is good morale?

You'll never be able to please all your employees all the time. It would be a mistake to try. The supervisor's job requires that you enforce rules, mete out discipline, and encourage people to do many things they may not be eager to do. The supervisor who strives too hard for popularity may sacrifice some of these important requirements of leadership.

How's your own morale?

Want to measure you own attitudes against those of the average supervisor? Then ask yourself these questions: Are you management-oriented? Do you feel rather secure in your work? Do you feel that the company gives you enough recognition and opportunity? To be normal, you should answer *yes* to all of these.

But do you think there's a lot more that can be done to improve efficiency? That the company's come a long way, but that it has lots more to do before it operates as efficiently as you'd like it to? If you feel this way, chances are you're a pretty good supervisor.

It's normal, too, for you to be a little sensitive on pay matters—to feel that the men and women you supervise get almost too much in relation to your own salary. But if you feel that staff departments are out to get you, or that other supervisors don't cooperate, you're off target. Your attitude is unhealthy and is probably standing in the way of your success.

Why don't some people cooperate?

For a very natural reason: They see no personal advantage in doing so. A terrible attitude? Not at all.

Not one of us does anything for nothing. We do some things for money, others for lots of other reasons. Joe works well because he likes the feeling of being with a gang of people. Jane works hard because she gets a sense of accomplishment from what she is doing. Louise puts in top effort because her job makes her feel important.

Hardly anyone works for money alone. We all expect different satisfactions in different proportions from our work. So don't be annoyed when a worker's attitude seems to say, "What's in it for me?" That's your signal to get busy and to find some way of providing satisfaction for that person on the job.

Why isn't high pay the key to cooperation?

Good pay rates are important, but many companies that have taken the high-wage route to workers' affections have been sadly disappointed. Pay means much to most employees; yet experience shows that it isn't enough.

One big trouble with pay as an incentive is that employees don't enjoy it while they work. It is after work that the pay brings tangible rewards and good feelings. Consider vacations and pensions. Employees can take advantage of neither while actually on the job. As Herzberg pointed out, your solution to winning employee cooperation is to appeal to employees' needs for respect, for challenge, for interesting work. We agree that each employee has a different set of these needs. Still, the supervisor's skill lies in trying to adjust the employee's work and working relationships to satisfy these "motivating" needs as much as is reasonable. The belief is that employees will cooperate to get this kind of treatment.

What's the best formula for winning cooperation?

The best formula is not to seek one. Despite the simplicity of the basic reasons people work, there is no easy road to securing cooperation. Don't be misled into believing there are gimmicks or pat things to say. There are no standard ways to react that, once memorized, will have employees eating out of your hand. If you attempt to outsmart employees, they will spot your lack of sincerity. And resistance will go up in proportion.

The best way to achieve cooperation is to change your own way of looking at people until you see in them some of the good and bad qualities you see in yourself. Make a point of being sensitive to people. Pause again and again to imagine how employees think about what you tell them or what you ask them to do. Stop talking, too, and listen to what they say about themselves, about other workers, and about you. For not until you begin to *know* people will you be able to put into practice some of the simple ideas expressed here for getting along with people.

How do you go about getting cooperation from your associates?

The secret of getting along well with other supervisors is much the same as that of winning cooperation from your employees: Find out what they want most from their work, then satisfy these desires. With your associates, though, it's not so much a problem of providing satisfaction as it is of not blocking their goals and ambitions.

Face up to the fact that, to a degree, you and your associates are competing—for raises, promotions, praise, popularity, and a host of other things. If you compete too hard, or compete unfairly, you won't win much cooperation from the other supervisors. And your chances of getting ahead depend on your ability to run your department in smooth harmony with those departments that interlock with yours.

Winning friends among other supervisors means intelligent sacrifice. Occasionally you'll have to put aside your wish to make your department look good just so that you don't put the supervisor of the next department behind the eight ball. Willingness to lend a hand when another supervisor falls behind and avoiding hairsplitting when allocating interdepartmental charges and responsibilities will help.

Above all, let other supervisors run their own shows. Don't try to give orders in their departments or encourage disputes between your workers and theirs.

Just as when an individual employee doesn't play ball with the others, if you don't conform to a reasonable degree, you'll have the supervisory group down on you—and cooperation will be long in coming. To turn this group solidarity to your advantage, aim at giving the supervisory organization the advantage of your own positive leadership. Help other supervisors set worthwhile goals, and the chances of all of you working together will be improved.

How can you get along best with staff people?

Generally speaking, staff people in your organization are almost entirely dependent on the cooperation of you and other supervisors. And in this case cooperation will breed cooperation. When you cooperate with staff people, their jobs are made infinitely easier. Their superiors judge them by their success in getting your assistance and on the degree to which you accept and act on their advice. So when you cooperate with staff people, you're actually helping them to get more satisfaction from their work. And you can be pretty sure that they'll go a long way toward helping you make a good showing on *your* job.

Wouldn't you like to have a data processing specialist report to your boss: "It's a pleasure to work with a supervisor like Jill. She never seems to hide things or get her back up when I offer suggestions. She is quick to see how what we're doing will improve operations in the long run. Not that Jill buys everything I say. She doesn't. She has her ideas, too. But together, I think Jill and I are really accomplishing things out there."

How can "I'm okay, you're okay" help to resolve personality conflicts?

This kind of analysis, often called *transactional analysis* (TA), helps to provide insights because it simplifies some of the apparently complex interactions that take place between people. This analysis maintains that there are four possible views of a relationship that can be held by the employee, the supervisor, or both:

1. I'm not okay. You're not okay. This is a negative view that implies an employee's dissatisfaction with her or his own behavior, but also, in effect, says that the supervisor's actions are just as bad. It is somewhat like the attitude of a rebellious child quarreling with a parent. At work it might arise when an employee accused of pilfering materials says that the boss does the same thing.

2. I'm not okay. You're okay. This is often the mark of the person who has lost self-respect, or of a person who places all the responsibility on the boss's shoulders. This person often feels unable to do the job without continual assistance from the supervisor. Supervisors should strive to get out from under this kind of dependence.

3. I'm okay. You're not okay. This is the parental kind of role supervisors often assume. Essentially it means treating the employee like a child. Such an attitude invites rebellion or loss of any hope the employee may have that the job can be done to the supervisor's satisfaction.

4. I'm okay. You're okay. This is the mature, or adult, way to handle conflicts. It assumes that each individual respects the other. Starting from a point of mutual respect, each person tries to understand—although not necessarily agree with—the other's point of view. The supervisor says to the employee, "I understand why you may think I'm taking advantage of your good nature, but listen to me long enough so that you understand my point of view. Once we're sure we understand one another, maybe we can come to some sort of agreement that gives you some satisfaction while making sure that the job gets done."

When transactional analysis is used, any of the first three approaches tends to keep the conflict going, even to heat it up. The fourth approach, sometimes called *stroking,* can be very effective if carried on honestly. It helps to provide a solid basis for cooperation and compromise.

Individual or group of individuals — what's the best way to avoid misunderstanding and to gain willing cooperation?

The starting place is respect for others' points of view, no matter how much they vary from your own. For the manager this implies an appreciation of subordinates for what they really are. It's wishful thinking—and downright harmful—to measure someone against a mythical ideal such as the perfect person for the job.

Try to remind yourself that by definition you, as a supervisor, deal in other people's lives. An order to take any action in the company is interpreted all down the line in terms of personal effects on people. And the effectiveness of the implementation of any order is a matter of approval or disapproval on the part of your subordinates and your associates.

Many managers never learn that their subordinates are constantly evaluating the manager's actions and varying their efforts accordingly. It's certainly the rare subordinate who will risk telling the boss when he or she is making mistakes, particularly if the boss isn't one who takes criticism willingly. Thus many supervisors never get any critical feedback about themselves. Fortunately, if you can make the first step, you'll find yourself a new and better kind of supervisor. You'll gain a new awareness that there are more consequences to any action involving people than those on the surface. And the consequences often interfere with productivity, because people who are working on their own frustrations have less energy to devote to the job.

Of course, it isn't always possible to solve the human problems that can result from a necessary and unpleasant management action. But sensitive supervisors enjoy two distinct advantages over their less sensitive counterparts:

1. An awareness of others' needs aids in avoiding unnecessary human problems that ordinarily seem to be cropping up each day.
2. A pattern of awareness of others' needs in itself tends to blunt the edge of problems and conflicts that cannot be avoided, because subordinates and associates know that the supervisor has tried.

I s it smart to show you appreciate employee cooperation, or should you act as if it's something you've got coming to you?

You can overdo your show of appreciation. But neither should employees think you take their efforts for granted. It would be ridiculous, for example, to stand by the time clock congratulating each employee for coming in on time. But it makes sense to look over the attendance record every six months and take a minute to say to each person with a perfect record, "I just reviewed the department's attendance records for the last six months, and I see that you went through these six months without missing a day or being late once. We appreciate that around here. It helps make the department an easier place to work in. Hope you can keep it up."

Yes, it's better to err on the generous side than to get the reputation as a supervisor who takes a pound of flesh each day but never so much as says thank-you.

Key Concepts

1. Conflicts are natural in any organization. The supervisor's responsibilities are to try to understand the causes of conflicts and resolve them in a way that will contribute to meeting the objectives of the work group. Establishing open communications among the people really involved is the key to accomplishing this.
2. Conflict is best resolved by focusing on mutually beneficial goals, by seeking areas of compromise, by examining facts, and by keeping personality differences out of the discussion.
3. Being sensitive to others is a technique for building mutual understanding, not for shucking off supervisory responsibility to individuals in the

group. The supervisor still maintains discipline and makes decisions as needed.

4. Attitudes and the degree to which they influence behavior of both individuals and groups are highly individualistic. Furthermore, attitudes are the result of long-term conditioning; consequently, they cannot be ordered into existence by management. It is likely, however, that when a supervisor's attitudes are positive, his or her subordinates' attitudes will also be positive.

5. Understanding the reasons for an employee's point of view—especially when the understanding is indicated to the employee by attentive listening—is one of the most effective ways for a supervisor to induce cooperative attitudes. Transactional analysis can provide insight that may help in avoiding certain blocks to the needed communication.

Supervisory Word Power

Attitude. The way in which an individual or group looks at, and consequently reacts to, a work situation. Attitudes are formed toward associates and superiors, the various conditions of employment, and the job itself.

Competition. A relatively healthy struggle among individuals or groups to excel in striving to meet mutually beneficial, rather than individual, goals.

Conflict. From a managerial point of view, a disruptive clash of interests, objectives, or personalities between individuals, between individuals and groups, or between groups.

Cooperation. Individuals or groups of people working together in reasonable harmony toward mutual objectives.

Morale. A measure of the extent (or level—either high or low) of voluntary cooperation demonstrated by an individual or a work group and of the intensity of the desire to attain common goals.

Sensitivity. The development of an acute awareness of other people's feelings, attitudes, and motivations, especially as they have an influence on, or are influenced by, your own behavior and work situations.

Transactional Analysis (TA). A way of improving relationships between people that emphasizes communications and is based on an understanding of parental, childish, or adult (mature) attitudes toward one another.

Reading Comprehension

1. Why do conflicts arise in an organization?

2. Distinguish between competition and conflict.

3. If two employees were quarreling over who should have the use of a lift truck first while loading cartons for shipment, what steps would you take to settle this dispute?

4. Give an example of a hidden agenda in some sort of group meeting or discussion.

5. Would it be wise for a supervisor to insist that an employee's attitude be changed? Why or why not?

6. In what ways might an employee give evidence of a poor attitude toward work?

7. Describe some steps that a supervisor might take to change employee attitudes.

8. Contrast the attitude of employees toward their pay with their attitude toward status and recognition.

9. What kind of action should supervisors take as a result of information gathered during an attitude survey?

10. How can transactional analysis (TA) be of practical value in handling conflicts?

Supervision in Action

The Case of the Shaky Foundation. A Case Study in Human Relations Involving Conflict and Cooperation, with Questions for You to Answer.

Crews at a construction site for a new supermarket were preparing the foundation. The excavation had been completed. Now the forms crew was busy installing the wood and metal framework into which the cement crew would pour the fresh concrete from the mixer. Duncan, the pouring supervisor, was watching the placement of the forms. "Be sure that inside form is properly secured," he told one of the crew. "That outside form isn't level yet," he advised Wendy, another member of the forms crew. "Last time, your sloppy forms made us look bad." The crew and Wendy just kept on about their work without paying too much attention to the instructions handed down by Duncan. After a while, Duncan left the site to round up his own crew for pouring which would begin that afternoon.

Nick, the forms supervisor, who had been at the site office verifying the blueprints, returned to his crew shortly after Duncan had left. He jumped into the foundation pit to show the crew how to make the final alignment of the forms. Wendy, however, told him that the forms had already been leveled and locked up. "They aren't in the right position," said Nick. "Why didn't you wait until I got back before bolting them into place?"

"Duncan was here and showed us what to do," replied Wendy.

"Well, he was wrong. And it is none of his business, anyway," said Nick. "I take charge of the forms. All he and his crew do is to dump the concrete into them after we've done the precision work."

At that point the concrete truck rolled up to the excavation. "Get out of the pit!" shouted Duncan, who was now on the site with his crew. "We're ready to pour."

"You'll have to wait," said Nick. "Your meddling has held up the job. We are going to have to realign the forms according to these prints."

"That was what I was trying to tell your crew," said Duncan. "If they had listened to what I told them, we could go ahead."

"Talk to me the next time," said Nick. "But meanwhile, take you and your crew of apes and get out of here."

"You get out," said Duncan. "Or you'll all get a cement overcoat." With that, he opened the chute door on the mixer just enough to let a couple of buckets of wet cement splash into the pit and on Wendy and Nick.

Wendy jumped out of the pit and pushed Duncan against the mixing truck. Duncan shoved back and in a minute there was a free-for-all as the two crews—forms and pouring—pushed and shoved and swung fists.

Finally someone called the site boss to the scene. The fighting stopped. "What's this all about?" he asked.

"Duncan and his pouring crew put their noses into our job once too often," said Nick. "And he dumped a load of cement on us."

"That's a laugh," said Duncan. "If I wasn't here to check up on what they were doing, we would have one more shaky foundation. And we'd get the blame. I was just making sure that the forms were right before we poured."

1. If you were the site boss, what approach would you use to resolve this dispute? Which supervisor would you sympathize with?
2. What did Duncan do to bring on this conflict?
3. What might Nick have done to avoid the conflict?
4. How might the site boss make sure that similar disputes do not arise in the future?

Introduction to Behavioral Models

If you have learned to drive a car, you know how difficult a seemingly simple skill can be to learn. Someone could tell you exactly how it is done, including all the key points, but it's unlikely that you would know how to drive well enough on the basis of that discussion alone to pass a driving test. It's much more effective to first sit in a car and watch an expert driver demonstrate the skills that he or she has told you about. Then, after having watched the model driver, you would begin to learn by practicing driving. Typically, you would begin by trying the most uncomplicated maneuvers first. And you'd be wise to try them on uncrowded streets where traffic was at a minimum. Later, you would proceed step-by-step to the more difficult aspects of driving under increasingly more difficult traffic conditions. At each step you would try to imitate the expert (or model) driver until you became proficient yourself. Ultimately, you would have learned to drive by observing and practicing the skills of a proven model.

So it is with the skills of supervision. The words and exercises in this textbook may help you to understand the skills of supervision. But they do not provide you with practice in developing the skills yourself. That's the purpose of the human relations skills models that are presented below and later on in this book. Each model will consist of a tried and tested, step-by-step procedure to be followed in handling a certain kind of situation. Use of the model, or procedure, will then be demonstrated by a transcript of the dialogue between a model supervisor and an employee.

Your assignment will be to listen to the dialogue in the model as if you were watching a play. It will be a very real play with realistic people, but it will be stripped down to its essentials so that you can see how the model procedure works. Try not to be distracted by the fact that the people or the situations aren't exactly the same as those in your work area. Instead, focus on what is happening in the play. It's similar to learning to play the piano. You begin by learning the notes (the skill points) and their location (where and how the skill points are applied). Later on you can practice these simple exercises (like scales on a piano) in a real work situation that involves you. Just as your musical scales won't be as perfect as a Mozart sonata (realistic), you will have to practice your basic skills before you can attempt more difficult pieces (real situations).

Model 1*

Dealing with Employee Conflicts

Experience shows that supervisors who follow this sequence of steps are likely to get better results when handling conflicts between employees than are supervisors who don't.

Step 1. Ask each employee to state the problem as he or she sees it.

*These scripts are reproduced with permission from the CRM/McGraw-Hill *Supervision* Series.

Step 2. Ask each employee to state the other person's view of the problem.

Step 3. Ask each employee to confirm the accuracy of the other's repetition.

Step 4. Focus on objective facts and areas of mutual need or mutual goals.

Step 5. Ask each employee to suggest solutions to the conflict.

Step 6. Bring both to an agreement on specific steps or actions that they would take to resolve the conflict; then set up a date for a review of the outcome.

The Situation

Jim, the supervisor, is troubled by the continual bickering between two employees in his department. Betty and Judy have been quarreling for some time now. Jim has spoken to each of them separately, but with no success. Now he has decided that this condition must be corrected, since the conflict between the two employees is beginning to affect others in the department.

Dialogue

1. Jim: I've asked you both to come in this morning because I'm aware that you have been having a lot of arguments with each other. I'm concerned about that because it's beginning to affect other people in the department and because it may affect your performance. Now, I've talked to each of you separately about this problem in the past two weeks, but it's still with us. So I thought the three of us should sit down and talk about it together. What I'd like for us to do is try to get a clear fix on what the problem is and figure out a way to solve it. So I want each of you, one at a time, to tell me what you think the problem is, and I want each of you to get a clear understanding of how the other sees the problem. Okay?

2. Betty: Okay.

3. Judy: That's fine with me.

4. Jim: Okay. Betty, let's start with you.

5. Betty: All right. The problem is that Judy goes out of her way to take all day to make copies of my work. Now this creates serious problems for me because I can't get copies out to the engineers on time and they blame me. I've tried talking to Judy about this, but she is always hostile and we end up arguing.

6. Jim: All right. Now, Judy, you tell us what the problem is.

7. Judy: Well, the problem is that I do copying for the whole department, not just for her. When she has copying for me to do, she expects me to put everyone else's work aside to do hers. I can't do that. Other people are in a hurry for their copies, too, but she thinks she's special and she's very rude to me when she complains about how long it takes for her copies. I don't see why I should let her get away with being rude.

8. Jim: All right. Now, Judy. I want you to tell us what Betty said the problem was.

9. Judy: What do you mean?

10. Jim: I want you to tell us in your words what you heard Betty say the problem was.

11. Judy: She said the problem was that I go out of my way to take all day with her work. That's just not true.

12. Jim: Judy, please. Just tell us what Betty said, not what you think of what she said.

13. Judy: Okay. She said that waiting all day for her copies gave her problems because she can't get the copies back to the engineers on time and they blame her.

14. Jim: I think that there's one other point she made.

15. Judy: Oh, yes. That she's tried talking to me about it but that I'm hostile and we end up arguing.

16. Jim: Betty, is that what you said?

17. Betty: Yes.

18. Jim: All right. Betty, now you tell us what Judy said the problem is.

19. Betty: Well, let's see. She said that she works for the whole department and that when I have work for her to do, I expect her to do my work first. She said she can't do that because other people are also in a hurry for their work. She said I'm rude when I complain about how long my copies take. She doesn't think she should let me get away with being rude.

20. Jim: Judy, is that what you said?

21. Judy: That's what I said.

22. Jim: All right. Now each of us has a clear understanding of how the other sees the problem. What I want to do now is try to focus on the objective facts in the problem. I don't want to deal with what you two think of each other or what you think the reason is for the other's behavior. It's not my job to make you like each other, but it is my job to make sure that the work gets done effectively. So, let's get at the objective facts here. Betty, what are the objective facts as you see them?

23. Betty: It's simple. It takes almost all day to get my copies made and I need them sooner.

24. Jim: Good. Judy, what are the facts as you see them?

25. Judy: The facts are that I work for a lot of other people and I can't do her work faster than I do anybody else's. I do my work on a first-come, first-served basis.

26. Jim: All right. Now let's look at these facts a little more closely. Betty, what do you mean when you say it takes "all day" to get your copies?

27. Betty: It means all day. If I give her my work in the morning, say at 10 o'clock, I usually get it back after 4, when it's too late to get it out to the engineers.

28. Jim: So it takes six hours.

29. Betty: Okay. It takes six hours.

30. Jim: And is that true every day?

31. Judy: No, it's not.

32. Jim: Just a minute, Judy. Betty?

33. Betty: Not every day, but most days.

34. Jim: Four days a week, three days a week, on the average?

35. Betty: Not less than three.

36. Jim: And tell me more specifically what it means when you say you need them sooner.

37. Betty: I need them in about three hours at the latest.

38. Jim: Good. Judy, what do you mean when you say other people are in a hurry for their copies?

39. Judy: I mean that other people ask me to rush their jobs, too.

40. Jim: How many others every day on the average?

41. Judy: I don't know. I don't keep track of that.

42. Jim: Well, is it ten people a day?

43. Judy: No. But at least one or two people every day.

44. Jim: Then there may be some people who wouldn't mind waiting a little longer for their copies?

45. Judy: I don't know. I have no way of telling. That's why I do everything in the order I get them in.

46. Jim: But you do take work out of order when you get a rush, don't you?

47. Judy: Yes, but only when you tell me to specifically.

48. Jim: Would it take less than six hours if Betty got her work to you earlier in the morning?

49. Judy: Yes, on most days. If I had her work at 8:30, I could probably get it back to her by 1:30 or 2 o'clock.

50. Jim: Would that help, Betty?

51. Betty: Well, 1:30 would probably work for me, but in most cases 2 would be too late.

52. Jim: I think we have a partial solution. What do you think?

53. Betty: Well, I think I could probably get my work to Judy by 8:30 on three days out of four, but there are days when it's just not possible.

54. Jim: And on how many of those three days could you get Betty's work back to her by 1:30?

55. Judy: I'd say two out of three.

56. Jim: That's half the problem solved. I'll tell you what I think we should do about the other half. Judy, on those days when you think you can't get Betty's work back to her by 1:30 or on those days when Betty can't get her work to you before 10 o'clock, come in and show me your schedule, and I'll tell you whether or not we can move her work up on your schedule; and if we can't, then you'll let her know. How does that sound to both of you?

57. Betty: That's fine with me.

58. Judy: It's fine with me, too.

59. Jim: Good. Let's go over this again. Just to make sure it's all clear. Betty?

60. Betty: On most days I will get my work to Judy by 8:30. On other days by 10 o'clock.

61. Jim: Okay. Judy?

62. Judy: On the days I can get Betty's work back to her by 1:30, I will do so. If I can't do that without changing the schedule, I'll bring the schedule to you and you will decide. If we can't get it done by 1:30, I'll let Betty know.

---

63. Jim: Great. Well, that should eliminate the objective reasons for this conflict between you. This should work, but just to make sure, let's plan to get together again at 8:30 on the 14th and review how it's working out. Okay?

64. Betty: I'm satisfied. I'll do whatever I can to make it work.

65. Judy: I have no problems with it. It's fine with me.

66. Jim: I'm glad to hear that. I appreciate your both coming in and helping me out on this. Thanks. See you on the 14th.

Model Analysis

A. Identify where in the dialogue Jim applied Step 1 by asking Betty and Judy to state the problem (use line numbers).

B. Identify where Jim applied Step 2 by asking each employee to state the other's problem.

C. Identify where Jim applied Step 3 by asking each employee to confirm the accuracy of the other's restatement.

D. Identify where Jim applied Step 4 in forcing Betty and Judy to focus on objective facts and areas of mutual need or mutual goals.

E. Identify where Jim applied Step 5 by asking Betty and Judy to suggest solutions.

F. Identify where Jim applied Step 6, first by bringing Betty and Judy to agreement on the specific steps to be taken in resolving the conflict and then by setting up a review date.

G. Recall, and describe briefly, a situation involving employee conflict. Try role playing the supervisor, with others in your group taking the parts of the subordinates. Get feedback from the group and from the instructor to sharpen your sense of when to apply each of the model's steps and to improve the skill with which you handle each of these steps.

Over the past century, trial, error, observation, and research have laid the foundation for the practice of management. Managers and supervisors in all kinds of organizations perform several universal functions. Accordingly, this section stresses the need for supervisors to understand the workings of the management process itself:

● To observe the management process as a whole in which supervisors perform key managerial functions and follow time-tested principles.
● To understand the vital importance of planning so as to set departmental goals and establish effective procedures.
● To acquire an understanding of problem-solving and decision-making concepts and practices so as to be able to plan and manage more effectively.
● To link the concepts of planning with control so as to be able to keep your processes and employees aligned with prescribed policies and standards of performance.

How supervisors view their planning and control responsibilities

Supervisors speak of the value gained from sound planning and control and also about some of the problems that arise when planning and control aren't implemented properly. Supervisors also remark about the good feeling that comes when goals are met and problems are solved. Here are some representative comments:

Supervisors say they are frustrated when there is:
"...lack of planning."
"...an unexpected schedule change."
"...panic-style planning."

Supervisors say they get real pleasure from the following:
"...putting a plan into action and seeing it develop successfully."
"...meeting our deadlines."
"...completing orders on time."
"...bringing a project in on time and within budget."
"...achieving monthly goals."
"...solving production problems."
"...being in control and operating as planned."

Survey figures show that planning and control take a good part of their time; yet some problems persist. For example:

Activity	Ranking*	Percentage who say they spend "above-average" time on this activity
Planning production schedules	4	20
Solving cost- or expense-related problems	8	16
Solving production-schedule problems	9	15
Solving quality-control problems	13	13

*Sixteen activities were rated: Number 1, with 26%, was "dealing with supervisors and staff people from other departments"; number 16, with 9%, was "employee grievance and/or disciplinary matters."

Other figures show that supervisors feel considerable pressure from their bosses to control departmental output, quality, and costs. For example: Ranking of results or conditions that get "more than moderate attention from your boss or other superiors."

Condition	Ranking	Percentage who say that attention is more than "moderate"
Quality or accuracy of work	1	57
Keeping operating expenses in line	2	53
Maintaining output or volume of work	3	53

6

SUPERVISION AND THE MANAGEMENT PROCESS

How does managerial work differ from other kinds of work?

Managerial work is concerned with the work that others do. Supervisors and managers plan, direct, and coordinate the work that their subordinates do rather than do the work themselves. As a consequence, supervisors often have to restrain themselves when they'd rather jump into a sticky situation and do the work with their own hands. Instead, they must stand back and direct the people who are paid to work with their hands or with a particular skill. Unlike rank-and-file employees, supervisors are paid to manage, not to do the work themselves.

What is the so-called management process?

It is the name given to functions or activities ordinarily performed by managers and not performed by rank-and-file blue-collar workers or clerical employees. These managerial functions are pursued in an orderly sequence. They are carried out, to a greater or lesser degree, by supervisors at every level, by middle managers, and by top executives. Regardless of where these functions are performed by managers—in factories, on construction sites, in banks and retail shops, in hospitals, or at government agencies—they include the following:

Planning. This is the function of setting goals or objectives. Often this specifically means production schedules, quality specifications, cost budgets, deadlines, and timetables. The results of planning include policies or guidelines, operating plans and procedures, and regulations and rules. Chapter 7 tells you more about this most important of all managerial functions.

Organizing. In performing this function a supervisor lines up all available resources. These resources include departmental tools and equipment, materials, and methods, but especially the work force. It is at this stage that the work is divided up in a department and jobs are assigned to various employees. Chapter 10 describes this activity in detail.

Staffing. This is the function whereby the supervisor figuratively puts flesh on the organizational structure. The supervisor first figures out exactly how many employees the department will need to carry out its work and then interviews and selects those people who appear to be most suitable for filling the open jobs. Chapter 11 provides the basic groundwork for effective staffing.

Activating. It is at this point that the supervisor directs all the department's resources into action by issuing orders and instructions, by communicating, and by providing motivation and leadership. Part 3 offers suggestions for carrying out this pivotal function.

Controlling. Once departmental plans are in motion, supervisors must periodically keep score on how well they are working out. Supervisors must measure results, compare them with what was expected, make a judgment of how important any difference may be, and then take whatever action is needed to bring the results into line. In formal language, such activities are called evaluating and controlling. Chapter 8 outlines the essentials of the control function.

In theory, supervisors perform the five basic functions of the managerial process in the order listed above. In practice, supervisors perform all of the management functions in one way or another each time a corrective action is in order. They may find themselves shortcutting the management process sequence or turning back on it, inasmuch as each problem situation is unique and calls for its own solution.

Why is it called a process?

Because it moves from one stage to another progressively in a fairly consistent order (Figure 6-1). In a production shop, for example, a supervisor first plans the daily schedule, then organizes the resources by assigning people to their work stations, then activates the process by giving orders and instructions, and finally, controls, or checks up on, results. In a typical office a similar management process takes place as supervisors plan the workday, organize the work and the clerical force, activate by communicating and motivating, and control by seeing that paperwork procedures are followed properly.

This process is carried on over and over again, day by day, month by month, and year by year. For this reason many people refer to it as the *management cycle.*

This process must have an objective, mustn't it?

Yes, of course. The purpose of the management process is to convert the resources available to a supervisor's department into a useful end result. Said another way, a supervisor is in charge of seeing that inputs are transformed into outputs in his or her department, as illustrated in Figure 6-2. This end result, or output, is either a product or a service.

A *product* might be a pair of shoes, a loaf of bread, a bicycle, or steel strings for a guitar. Your product may be partially complete, so that it becomes the material resource for the next department in your factory. Or it may become the raw material for use in another manufacturing plant. Or it may be ready, like a pair of shoes, to be sold directly to a consumer without further work performed on it.

A *service* may be in the form of accounting information provided for a production department, inspecting a product as it is being made, or drawing up a schedule for others to follow. A service may be provided directly for a consumer, as with an insurance policy or handling of cash and checks for a bank customer. It may be maintaining machinery in a plant or washing windows in a shopping center.

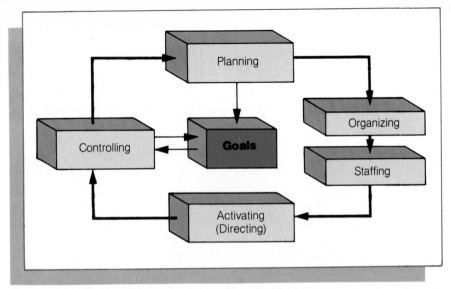

Figure 6-1. Functions in the management process.

Whether the end point is a product or a service, the management process is expected to make sure that the result is at least as valuable as the combined cost of the initial resources and the expense of operating the process. In a business enterprise a *profit* is made when the end result can be sold at a price that is higher than the cost of providing it. If the reverse is true, the business assumes a *loss.*

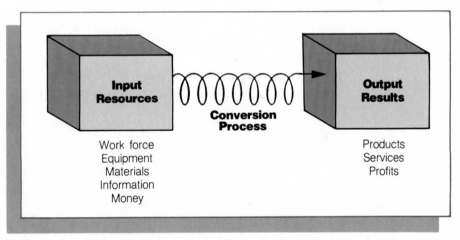

Figure 6-2. Managers are responsible for converting an organization's resources into useful results.

What are the resources managed by the management process?

The six important resources (or inputs) that supervisors must manage during the management process are:

1. **Men and Women, the People Who Make Up the Labor Force.** For a supervisor these are the employees, skilled and unskilled, assigned to the department.

2. **Machinery, Buildings, and Tools and Equipment Needed to Make the Goods or to Render the Services.** In a manufacturing company these facilities range from blast furnaces to baking ovens; in construction, from bulldozers to wheelbarrows. In a department store the facilities range from display counters to cash registers. In a bank the equipment includes tellers' cages and coin-counting machines. In an insurance company the equipment may include file cabinets, typewriters, calculators, and computers. In a hospital the facilities include beds, bedpans, x-ray machines, and thermometers.

3. **Materials That Go Into the Final Product or Service or Are Consumed While Making Them.** Raw materials in manufacturing and construction run the gamut from iron ore for steel, flour for bakeries, and tires for automobiles to transistor chips for TV sets. Other materials are operating supplies, such as grease for machinery and protective clothing for employees. Materials consumed in service industries such as banking or insurance include tons of paper, gallons of ink, and millions of paper clips. In retail trades the "raw" materials are the merchandise manufactured by others and placed on display for sale.

4. **Money, the Capital Needed to Purchase the Machinery and the Materials and to Meet Work Force Payrolls.** Supervisors may see little cash pass through their hands, but every action they take depends on the availability of funds to pay for these actions and the results of them.

5. **Information, Methods, and Technology That Make Up the Know-How of a Particular Company and Its Industry.** Sometimes this information is written in manuals and procedures. Often it exists only in the minds of talented employees and staff specialists. Regardless of its source, it is invaluable to the efficiency of the conversion process.

6. **Markets, the Consumers Who Buy and Use the Products and Services That Result From the Management Process.** Except in sales, supervisors rarely have direct contact with the market served by their company. Nevertheless, it is the market that makes the process meaningful, because consumers buy the end results (products or services) and thus provide the money needed to pay for the input

resources. In this sense the market is an input, or resource, of the management process.

What do all the phases of the management process have in common?

Each requires that a supervisor solve problems and make decisions. Some people believe that these two talented activities are what management is all about. If operations ran smoothly, a company could depend on a computer rather than a supervisor to make decisions. But the organizational workday is crowded with unexpected events. Each represents a problem to be solved, a decision to be made. For supervisors, most of these problems require an immediate solution. Otherwise, employees would be standing around waiting for instruction. Machines would be idle. Materials would be damaged. Shipments would be delayed. Chapter 9 gives you dozens of tips on how to improve your problem solving and decision making.

How much of the management process can be handled routinely?

Once your planning has been completed, much of your work can be done routinely—within certain limits. That is, you can apply the same solution you used to handle a problem in absenteeism last month to a similar problem this month. Or you may find that your decision about a particular shipping problem will apply to many others like it. On the other hand, there are any number of other problems that are entirely different. These will need fresh inputs. You may have to create a new way to make assignments on the assembly line. Or you may have to initiate a new method of scheduling your keypunch operators. These new situations require that a supervisor be an innovator.

What makes the management process work?

Management and managers: executives, managers, supervisors. Each helps to turn the wheel. Supervisors are out on the cutting edge; higher-level managers are closer to the hub (Figure 1-6).

TABLE 6-1   DIFFERENT APPROACHES TO MANAGEMENT

Approach	Emphasizes productivity as a result of the following	Impact on supervision
Systematic Management Also known as scientific, classic, traditional, rational, process, or functional management	Systematic process, management principles, measurement and standards, and firm direction and control	Greater reliance on established company policies and procedures and on prescribed relationships in formal work groups
Human Relations Management Also known as behavioral or organizational behavior management	Individual or group motivation stimulated by management's concern for people and their relationships	Greater reliance on participatory techniques and upon individuals and groups to solve operational problems
Quantitative Management Also known as management sciences or systems theory management	Use of advanced mathematical and statistical methods as well as theories about how information and other resources interact in an organization system	Greater reliance on staff-directed and/or automatic programs to prescribe operating procedures and to signal for control actions
Contingency Management Also known as situational management	Belief that supervisors and other managers must choose one or more of the three basic approaches to fit the conditions that prevail in a particular situation	Greater need for sensitivity to the demands of different situations along with the skills and flexibility to apply different management approaches selectively

To what extent can supervisors follow their own inclinations in carrying out the management process?

There is a great deal of leeway. In fact, there are three distinct approaches for management to draw from. Or you can use a combination of all three. (See Table 6-1.) The three approaches are sometimes called schools or theories.

1. Systematic Management Approach. This is known by other names, too, such as scientific, classical, traditional, process, functional, or rational. All names imply a systematic approach that relies on measurement and analysis of the various tasks and activities that take place at work.

2. **Human Relations Approach.** This is also known as the behavioral school, because it is based on the thought that a manager who understands human behavior well enough is able to get employees to willingly cooperate with, and produce toward, company goals.

3. **Quantitative Approach.** This approach emphasizes the use of numbers and relies on the sciences of mathematics and statistics. It is also known as the management sciences or systems theory of management.

Many latter-day students of management are skeptical about the value of depending too much on any one of these three approaches. They insist that each management situation be studied carefully and approached as a uniquely different problem. Sometimes, they say, the scientific approach will be best. Other times the human relations approach will get the best results. Still other times the quantitative approach should be chosen. Because of this iffy kind of advice, this approach has been labeled situational, or contingency, in that what a manager should do depends (is contingent) on the particular situation at hand.

When does the systematic management approach work best?

A systematic approach is almost always a good way to attack any problem.

It requires that you gather facts first. What has really happened to the agitator tank? When did it happen? Who was operating it? Were reasonable production rates set for its operation? How close has actual output been to what was expected?

It emphasizes the value of accurate measurements. How much? How big? How long? How many?

It presumes that most activities are best performed according to a set path. Are the procedures carefully spelled out? Were they followed?

The problem with the systematic approach is that it too often expects perfection from organizations or that people will function like machines. Its founder, Frederick W. Taylor, was an engineer who hoped that human beings could be motivated by wage incentives to imitate machines. Later advocates of scientific management were also engineers—Henry L. Gantt, who conceived the production control chart, and Frank B. Gilbreth, who perfected the art of motion study of workers. Other proponents were mainly business people. Harrington Emerson, one notable contributor, believed that efficiency would result from better organizational arrangements and elimination of waste—human as well as material. Henri Fayol, a French factory owner, laid down a number of guiding principles that are still useful today. You will read about these in the pages that follow.

At what times should human relations management be used?

There is rarely a time when it shouldn't be considered. The stickiest problems in business or elsewhere involve human beings. Supervisors need to know all they can about why people act the way they do. Exaggerated human conflict can be very wasteful. Use of what we know about the psychology and the sociology of human behavior can minimize this conflict. A large platoon of authorities, beginning with Elton Mayo and extending to Burleigh Gardner, has demonstrated the controlling influence that human relations can have in any organization. Mayo, in his famous experiment at the Hawthorne Works of the Western Electric Company in the 1930s, indisputably demonstrated that the performance of workers is more nearly related to psychological and social factors than to the physical makeup of the workplace. In 1945 Gardner wrote a basic text summarizing many research studies. Optimism for this approach was highest in the 1950s, when it was thought that a cookbook of methods could be given to supervisors. The idea was that if you follow the right directions and prescriptions, people will act the way you want them to. Alas, the real world never came up to this promise.

Recent investigations by such authorities as Herbert Simon and Chris Argyris strongly suggest that supervisors should use great caution in applying human relations theory. Their watchwords would appear to be: Go slowly. Clear up technical problems first. Let people try to solve their own problems. Don't oversimplify management tasks. They are all complex because so many factors—materials, machinery, instructions, time pressures, conflicting objectives, hidden relationships—can influence the outcome of a supervisor's actions.

Where will the quantitative approach be most reliable?

Where people problems are fewest and process factors are greatest. The quantitative method is a numbers approach. It helps in setting up production and maintenance schedules, in balancing assembly lines, in controlling quality, in mapping out shipping routes, in setting work loads for bank tellers and airline ticket clerks. Quantitative methods (Part 6, "Managing Work Productively," shows supervisors how to apply a number of statistical and quantitative techniques, as does Chapter 9, "Problem Solving and Decision Making") can be and have been applied successfully to just about any management problem where an employee's interests and motivation aren't controlling factors. Without any doubt the management sciences approach should be in every supervisor's tool kit. More often than not, of course, supervisors will need the help of industrial engineers, statisticians, or systems people to put the techniques to work. But these specialists will, in turn, need the supervisor to spot potential applications.

Exactly what are the principles of management?

Just about any good rule of thumb qualifies as a principle. And you will find dozens presented to you in this book. But the basic, or original, principles of management were set down by the French businessman Henri Fayol in 1916. They still make a lot of sense today, as you may agree after examining this list of his more important principles.

1. Work should be divided so that each person will perform a specialized portion. In making a sailboat, for instance, one person will lay up the hull, another caulk, and another make sails. In running an office, one person will enter orders, another type letters, and another file correspondence. Fayol called these ideas *division of work* and specialization.

2. Managers must have the right (authority) to give orders and instructions, but they must also accept responsibility for whether or not the work is done right. A supervisor needs the right to ask a work crew to load a freight car, for example, but if the car is loaded improperly, the supervisor must accept the blame.

3. Managers are responsible for extracting discipline and building morale among members of their work force, but they must also be true to their word in return. Said another way, if you want loyalty and cooperation from employees, you must be loyal and cooperative in return.

4. An individual should have only one boss. Fayol called this *unity of command.* Experience bears this out: If an employee reports to more than one superior, confusion and conflict result.

5. Every organization should have only one master plan, one set of overriding goals. Such *unity of direction* is lost if the purchasing department, for example, slows down the production department's output by buying materials from a less costly but undependable supplier when the company's overall commitment is to ship orders on time.

6. Similar to the principle of unity of direction is Fayol's insistence that all individuals, especially managers, must place their interests second to those of the total organization. If persons in authority went their own way, Fayol reasoned, all others in the organization would suffer as a result.

7. Pay and rewards (remuneration) should reflect each person's efforts and, more important, each person's contribution to the organization's goal. It was a novel idea in Fayol's time that each employee should be paid according to individual worth rather than at the whim of a manager who might be inclined to play favorites.

8. Orders and instructions should flow down a *chain of command* from the higher manager to the lower one. Fayol also said that formal communications and complaints should move upward in the same channel. In practice, however, it has proved to be a good idea to permit and encourage the exchange of work information sideways between departments (or commands) as well. The real trouble seems to occur when a manager bypasses a supervisor with instructions to an employee or when an employee goes over a supervisor's head to register a complaint.

9. Materials should be in their proper place. Fayol extolled the virtue of all kinds of order; he believed that routine procedures minimized effort and waste.

10. Employees should be treated equally and fairly. Fayol called this equity. It invites dissatisfaction and conflict among employees, for example, when a supervisor gives one employee a break while picking on another.

11. Managers should encourage initiative among employees. Fayol advised: "It is essential to encourage this capacity to the full.... The manager must be able to sacrifice some personal vanity in order to grant this sort of satisfaction to subordinates. Other things being equal, a manager able to permit the exercise of initiative on the part of subordinates is infinitely superior to one who cannot do so."

A contingency approach was mentioned earlier. What is its significance for supervision?

It adds realism—and safety—to the supervisor's job. The contingency approach (sometimes called the situational or operational approach) implies that a supervisor must be ready to employ one or all three of the management approaches. What is used depends on—is contingent on—the particulars in the operation or situation. If you are starting a new project or revising an old one, the scientific, or systematic, approach makes sense. If you are enmeshed in a situation (such as a radical change in procedures) where people's reactions are unusually sensitive, a concern for human relations should prevail. If your employees are looking for a solution to a difficult or recurring operational or process problem, the quantitative approach might get first call. Rarely, however, can you rely entirely on a single approach. Just as there is a continuum of leadership styles, there should be a balance in the application of management approaches. In general, choose the first approach that fits your personality and talents best, but do not rely on it exclusively. Always, or almost always, double-check your results to see if you should apply a second or a third approach to the problem. Above all, try to keep Fayol's management principles in mind.

Key Concepts

1. Managerial work is different from nonmanagerial work in that managers devote most of their time and energy to planning, organizing, staffing, activating, controlling, problem solving and decision making and innovating rather than doing the work themselves.

2. The main task of managers is to oversee the efficient conversion of a company's input resources into useful outputs. When the value of the outputs exceeds the cost of its inputs, a business firm makes a profit. When the reverse is true, it sustains a loss.

3. Effective managers are able to apply all three managerial approaches —systematic, human relations, and quantitative—to business and organizational problems.

4. Most problems that face management are complex and are influenced by many factors; thus, the approach selected or emphasized should depend on an analysis of the particular situation.

5. Professional managers base many of their decisions and actions on established management principles.

Supervisory Word Power

Chain of Command. The formal channels in an organization that distribute authority from top to bottom.

Contingency Management. The selection and use of the managerial approach (or combination of approaches) that is most appropriate for a particular problem or situation.

Division of Work. The principle that performance is more efficient when a large job is broken down into smaller, specialized jobs.

Human Relations Management. A management approach that seeks to stimulate cooperation on the basis of an understanding of and genuine concern for employees as individuals and as members of a work group.

Management Process. The major managerial functions of planning, organizing, staffing, activating, and controlling carried on by all managers in a repetitive sequence or cycle.

Outputs. (of the management process). The products or services produced by converting resources into results.

Quantitative Management. A management sciences approach to management that emphasizes the use of advanced mathematics and statistics and the application of information and systems theory.

Systematic Management. The traditional approach to management that emphasizes the functions performed in the management process as well as the systematic measurement and analysis of the various tasks and activities of the workplace.

Unity of Command. The principle that there should be a single set of goals and objectives that unifies the activities of everyone in an organization.

Unity of Direction. The principle that each individual should report to only one boss.

Reading Comprehension

1. Give a specific example of an activity that would be included in each of the five functions of the management process.

2. What makes the management process a "process?"

3. How can managers tell whether the process of converting resources to end products is successful?

4. Name six resources on which the management process depends.

5. If supervisors and other managers have plans, why do they have to make decisions and solve problems on a day-to-day basis?

6. Why can't a supervisor rely all the time on the systematic management approach?

7. Name some applications for which the quantitative management approach has been found successful. What do the applications have in common?

8. Why did Henri Fayol say that an organization should have unity of command?

9. In light of modern experience, should communication be rigidly confined to an up-and-down direction in the chain of command?

10. What is the basic message of the contingency view of management?

Supervision in Action

The Case of "Who's in Charge Here?" A Case Study in Human Relations Involving the Management Process, with Questions for You to Answer.

While working as a machinist for a large corporation, Joe Schreck saved his money so that he could start his own business. In 1980 he opened a small custom machine shop with a lathe, a grinder, a milling machine, and an all-purpose tool. At first Joe operated all the machines himself with the aid of a helper. Business grew, and within a few years Joe had six mechanics and four helpers working along with him. It wasn't long thereafter that Joe hired Ruby Burns to take care of his recordkeeping and to handle purchases.

More and more, Joe found himself letting Ruby make decisions about purchases and accounts. He still spent most of his time in the shop working at one or another of the machines. If a difficult job came up, Joe would move the regular operator aside and do the special work himself.

Whenever Joe was busy working on one of the machines, Ruby found herself arranging the job assignments for the employees. If there was a question from a customer, she would handle it directly. In addition Ruby found there were fewer tie-ups if she laid out the work schedules each week.

One day Ruby approached Joe with a suggestion that a new scheduling ticket be used to keep track of jobs as they progressed through the shop. Joe listened to the idea and commented: "That's a good idea, but you should spend your time purchasing and keeping our books. I'm the manager here, and keeping track of jobs is really my job."

Ruby replied: "I don't care what you call yourself, Joe, but I'm doing more to make sure that this shop turns a profit than you are. You act more like one of the hired hands. A skillful one, but really a machinist, not a manager."

"You must be joking," said Joe. "I own this shop, and I am its manager. It is you who are just one of the workers."

"I'm sorry you feel that way," said Ruby. "I've been taking on more and more of the managerial responsibility here, and I've been hoping that you'd give me the title of general manager."

"If anyone should carry that title," said Joe, "I should. The workers in the shop accept your schedules and the way you lay out their work, but if I weren't there, nothing would happen. They get the job done because they know I am boss and that I am the real leader on the floor."

"Let's not argue about it, Joe," said Ruby. "If you want me to be just another worker in the shop, I'll stop managing and stick to calling in purchases and doing the books. But if I do that, you will have to stop most of the 'hands-on' work. And you'll have to spend most of your time managing."

1. What managerial functions was Ruby performing? What about Joe?
2. What was Joe doing that was not managerial work? Why did he do it? Who would do it if Joe didn't do it?
3. What work did Ruby do that was nonmanagerial?
4. Do you think Ruby should be appointed general manager, or would it be better for Joe to assume that responsibility? Why?
5. Is the owner of the shop necessarily the manager? Why?

7

MAKING PLANS AND CARRYING OUT POLICY

W̲hy is so much emphasis placed on planning?

Because the resources that management applies must deal with the future, and the future is rarely the same as today. Planning is a tested way of coping with this change. It helps to make certain that you have enough employees on hand to do the job, the right amount and kind of materials, and tuned-up machinery when you need it. Most important, planning prepares a road map that enables a supervisor to move resources effectively.

Plans, planning, policies, goals: What is the difference?

If ever there was an area of management where the terms were mixed up, this is it. *Plans* are what come out of the *planning* process. Plans or programs are what you intend to do in the future. Before you can develop plans, however, you must set targets. These targets are called *goals, standards,* or *objectives.* After you have set these goals (that is the simplest term to use), you establish general guidelines for reaching them. These guidelines are called *policies.* Only after policies have been set should plans be formulated. As a final step, you may choose to lay down some *rules* and *regulations.* These will establish the limits (controls) within which employees are free to do the job their own way.

Take this example. You are thinking ahead—planning—about what your department will do during the annual spring cleaning. You make a list of things that you want to accomplish: filing cabinets cleared of all obsolete material, shelving cleaned and rearranged, tools repaired and in tip-top shape. These are your goals. Next you establish some sort of policy. For example, cleaning will be done during normal working hours without overtime; discarding obsolete papers will conform to legal requirements; repairing tools may be done by your own maintenance department or by an outside machine shop. Then you lay out a master plan of how the housekeeping will be done, when, and by whom. If this plan is detailed as to its exact sequence, it is called a *procedure.* Finally you set down some firm rules or regulations for your work crew: Only file clerks will make judgments about what paperwork will be discarded; before tools are sent outside for repair, employees must check with you; employees who clean shelving must wear protective gloves. Figure 7-1 illustrates common relationships among these terms.

What is the best way to begin the planning process?

By deciding where it is you want to go and what it is you want your department to accomplish. These are, of course, your goals or objectives. And you should set them carefully and systematically. This can be done by following the next seven steps.

1. Consider the goals of the entire organization, not just those of your department. Think about the needs and wishes of customers—those the company serves as well as those "customers" your department serves internally.

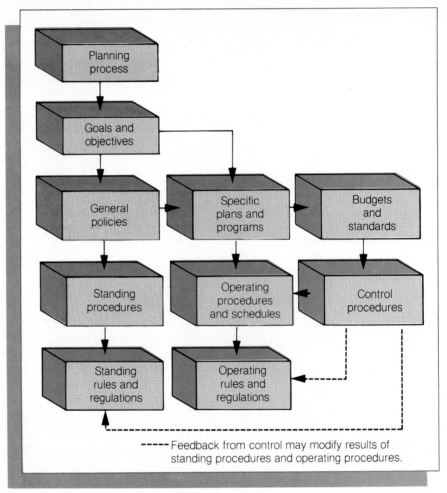

Figure 7-1. Relationship between the various outputs of the planning process.

2. Estimate the strengths and weaknesses of your department. Ask how they will help or hinder you in trying to meet company goals and in trying to serve external and internal customers.

3. Don't jump to conclusions at this early stage. Instead, keep your mind alert to new opportunities—such as ways to improve quality or reduce costs. Don't restrict your thinking to what your goals were last year or how you met them. If you can forecast what may happen to change conditions next year, this will help focus your attention on goals that will be more meaningful in the months to come.

4. Consult with those who will have to help you carry out your plans and with those who can offer you their support along the way. Employees who are involved in setting goals are more likely to be committed to success in reaching the goals. Staff departments that are consulted in advance may direct your attention to potential pitfalls or to goals that will get the full measure of their support.

5. Pick a reasonable set of goals. These should meet two standards. They should (a) contribute to the organization's goals and (b) be attainable by your department, given its strengths and its weaknesses.

6. Arrange your department's goals in a hierarchy of objectives. That is, place the most important ones at the top of your list and the least important at the bottom.

7. Watch out for limitations. Think about restrictions that may be imposed on you by your company or by the need to coordinate with or serve other departments. Your department cannot operate in a vacuum. It must base its plans on such realistic planning premises.

What kinds of goals are supervisors usually concerned with?

Typically, the goals you set for yourself—or that are set for you, at least partially, as part of a company's overall objectives—are targets to be aimed at in the near future. They pin down your department's output, quality of workmanship, and allowable expenditures. Often, they also include goals in such employee-related areas as departmental attendance, labor turnover, and safety, as shown in Table 7-1. These goals may be stated in terms of tomorrow, next week or next month, or as far ahead as a year. More often than not, the goals are quantitative (expressed as numbers or dollars) rather than merely qualitative (described with such words as "improve," "maintain," "good," or "better").

In many companies and organizations, the manner in which you and your department attain your goals becomes the determining factor in what kind of raise you'll get or how good a job you can be groomed for. This is one big reason why it is so important to lay out a detailed set of plans for meeting your goals.

Once goals have been decided on, what happens next in the planning process?

Effective plans flow from clearly stated goals, as shown in Figure 7-1. These plans, however, depend on following a systematic planning process, just as you did when setting goals. Here are six steps that ought to lead to success.

TABLE 7-1 TYPICAL PERFORMANCE GOALS FOR A FIRST-LINE SUPERVISOR

Area of Measurement	Last Year's Record	Next Year's Goals
1. Ratio of jobs completed on schedule to total jobs worked	85% average, 92% highest, 65% lowest in June	90% average, minimum acceptable 75%
2. Percentage of job costs held within 3% of standard costs	91% average, 95% highest, 75% lowest in June	90% average, bring up low figure to 87% or better
3. Rejects and rework	Less than 1% rejects; rework averages 7%	Keep rejects to less than 1%, but cut rework to 3%
4. Labor stability	Two quits, one discharge	No quits of employees with over three years service
5. Absences, latenesses	5% absences, 7% latenesses	5% absences, 2% latenesses
6. Overtime	Only on jobs okayed by sales department	Only on jobs okayed by sales department
7. Accidents	No lost-time accidents; 37 calls to dispensary for minor ailments	No lost-time accidents; reduce number of dispensary visits

1. Develop a master plan. This should focus on your main objective. If, for example, the company's goal is for higher-quality products or services, the master plan for your department should give this top priority.

2. Draw up supporting plans. This requires that you think about how each activity in your department can contribute to your master plan. Machinists may need more explicit blueprints. Assemblers may need brighter workplace lighting. Clerks may need a different order-entry procedure.

3. Put numbers and dates on everything you can. Plans work best when employees know how much or how many are required of them. Since plans are for the future—tomorrow, next week, or next month—times and dates are essential.

4. Pin down assignments. Plans are for people. Responsibility for carrying out each part of a plan or procedure should be assigned to a particular individual.

5. Explain the plan to all concerned. Plans should be shared. Their rationales should be explained and their goals justified. Employees who know *why* are more likely to cooperate.

6. Review your plans regularly. Circumstances and restrictions change. Your plans should be examined periodically to see whether they should be changed, too.

How strictly must the planning process be followed?

Experts say that nothing should be attempted without prior planning. There should be few exceptions to this rule of primacy. There is flexibility, however, as to how a supervisor goes about planning. Nevertheless, thought should be given to each of the steps outlined above.

In what way are plans or programs usually classified?

They are usually classified according to their duration and purpose.

Long-range plans are typically set by higher management and are expected to be in operation from two to five years.

Short-range plans are those that supervisors are most concerned with. These are usually based on operations of one year or less. At the department level, short-range plans may be in effect for a day, a week, a month, or a quarter.

Standing plans include just about any activity that goes on without much change from year to year. Standing plans cover general employment practices, health and safety matters, purchasing procedures, routine discipline, and the like.

Single-use plans are used only once before they must be revised. Departmental budgets and operating schedules are examples. They will be good only for a week or a month until new ones are issued.

Generally speaking, then, supervisors will follow short-range, single-use plans for day-to-day operations. But supervisors will also be guided by many standing plans that implement routine, relatively unchanging goals and policies.

When should supervisors plan and how often?

Before starting anything new or different. Planning should take place before a new day, a new week, a new product or service, or introduction of different materials or machinery. As a matter of routine, a supervisor should make up new plans each night for the next day, each Friday for the next week, and the last week in the month for the next month.

Which areas should be targets for a supervisor's planning process?

Just about anything qualifies. Any kind of change should trigger new plans. Every area within the supervisor's responsibility is a candidate for planning. For starters, here is a list of a dozen prime candidates:

- Use of facilities and equipment: departmental layout and working conditions, equipment utilization and maintenance.
- Use and care of materials and supplies: purchases, inventory levels, storage.
- Conservation of energy and power: electricity, steam, water, and compressed air usage; waste disposal; fire protection.
- Cash and credit management: petty cash, billing, collections.
- Work force management: forecasting requirements, safety and health care, sanitation, communications, absences and turnover, employee training and development.
- Information collection and processing: tallies and logbooks, recordkeeping, order processing.
- Time conservation: start-ups, shutdowns, personal time.
- Schedules: routing, delivery performance, shortages.
- Quality management: inspection and control techniques, rework methods, scrap reduction, employee training and motivation.
- Cost reduction and control: cost estimating, work simplification and methods improvement, correction of variances.
- Productivity: work simplification and methods improvement.
- Self-improvement: planning, organizing, communicating, public speaking, writing for business, leading conferences.

How do controls relate to plans?

Controls are like limit switches that keep plans in line. When a plan is moving directly toward its goal, the track is kept clear. The supervisor need apply no control. But when a plan strays from its target, the supervisor must take corrective action to bring it back in line. When planning a department's goals, a supervisor must also plan its control limits.

What is a good way to double-check your plans and projects?

Try using the five-point planning chart illustrated in Figure 7-2:

● **What** spells out objectives in terms of specifications for output, quality, and costs.

● **Where** sets the location for the assignment (its workplace) and the place where the product or service must be delivered: the adjoining department, the shipping dock, the home office.

● **When** records your time estimates for the work to be performed and, most important, pins down starting and finishing times and dates.

● **How** verifies short- and long-range methods, procedures, and job sequences.

● **Who** designates the individual responsible for the assignment and specifies that person's authority and extent of control over the resources needed: tools, machinery, additional labor, materials.

What is meant by company policy?

Company policies are broad rules or guides for action. At their best these rules are a statement of the company's objectives and its basic principles for doing business. They are intended as a guide for supervisors and managers in getting their jobs done. Many

FIVE-POINT PLANNING CHECK CHART		
What	Objectives	Specifications
		Cost/price limits
Where	Locale	Delivery point
When	Time elapsed	Starting date
		Completion date
How	Tactics	Methods Procedure Sequence
	Strategy	
Who	Responsibility	Authority Control Assignment

Figure 7-2.

policies give supervisors the opportunity to use their own best judgment in carrying them out. Others are supported by firm rules that supervisors must observe if they are to run their departments in harmony with the rest of the organization.

Does policy apply only at high levels?

Policy is generally set by managers high up in the company organization. But policy can be no more than a collection of high-sounding words unless the supervisor translates them into action on the firing line.

Take an example of a disciplinary policy. Here's how it might sound as it works its way down from the front office to first-line action by the supervisor:

Company President: "Our policy is to exercise fair and reasonable controls to regulate the conduct of our employees."

Manufacturing Vice President: "The policy on attendance in this plant is that habitual absenteeism will be penalized."

Plant Superintendent: "Here are the rules governing absences. It's up to you supervisors to keep an eye on unexcused absences and to suspend any employee absent or late more than three times in three months."

Supervisor: "Sorry, I'm going to have to lay you off for three days. You know the rules. You put me in a bad spot when you take time off on your own without warning or getting approval."

Note that no real action takes place until the supervisor puts the words of the policy into effect.

What sort of matters does policy cover?

A company may have a policy to cover almost every important phase of its business—from regulating its method of purchasing materials to stipulating how employees may submit suggestions. As a supervisor you will probably be most concerned with policies that affect (1) employees and (2) the practices of your department.

Employee policies most commonly formalized are those affecting wages and salaries, holidays and vacations, leaves of absence, termination of employment, safety, medical and health insurance and hospitalization, service awards, and retirement and pensions.

Department practices most often reduced to policy are requisitioning of supplies, preparation of records, access to data processing terminals, timekeeping, safeguarding classified materials, cost-control measures, quality standards, maintenance and repair, and acquisition of new machinery and equipment.

These listings are not all-inclusive. Some companies have more, others fewer policies.

Is policy always in writing?

Far from it. Many rigid policies have never been put down in black and white. And many firm policies have never been heard from an executive's lips. But employees and supervisors alike recognize that matters affected by such policies must be handled in a certain manner and usually do so.

The existence of so much unwritten policy has led many authorities to the conclusion that all policy is better put into writing so that it may be explained, discussed, and understood. Nevertheless, there are many companies that don't subscribe to this way of thinking, and their policies remain implied rather than spelled out.

How does policy apply to rules and regulations?

One of the great misunderstandings about policy is the belief that it's always something negative, such as "Don't do that" or "Do it this way or you'll get in trouble."

Policy can also be positive, encouraging, and uplifting. Just examine the written policy of a nationally respected company as expressed in a booklet published by its board of directors:

Importance of the individual. We believe the actions of business should recognize human feelings and the importance of the individual and should ensure each person's treatment as an individual.

Common interest. We believe that employees, their unions, and management are bound together by a common interest—the ability of their unit to operate successfully—and that opportunity and security for the individual depend on this success.

Open communications. We believe that the sharing of ideas, information, and feeling is essential as a means of expression and as the route to better understanding and sounder decisions.

Local decisions. We believe that people closest to the problems affecting themselves develop the most satisfactory solutions when given the authority to solve such matters at the point where they arise.

High moral standards. We believe that the soundest basis for judging the "rightness" of an action involving people is the test of its morality and its effect on basic human rights.

Words? Yes. Policy? Definitely. And as an official guide to action committed to print by the top officers of the organization, these statements are an excellent example of the positive side of policy.

Should a supervisor change policy?

No. That's a very dangerous thing to do. Policies are set to guide action. It's a supervisor's responsibility to act within policy limits.

Supervisors can influence a policy change, however, by making their thoughts and observations known to the boss, the personnel department, and the top management. After all, supervisors are in the best position to feel out employees' reactions to policy—favorable or otherwise. You do your boss and your company a service when you accurately report employees' reactions. And that's the time to offer your suggestions for improving or modifying the policy.

Do supervisors ever set policy?

In a way, supervisors always set policy at the departmental level. Supervisory application of policy is their interpretation of how the broader company policy should be carried out for employees. It's important for you to recognize that company policy usually allows you discretion at your level—even though this discretion may be limited.

Suppose your company has a policy that forbids taking or placing bets on company property. Anyone caught will be fired. You can carry out that policy in many ways. You can bait a trap, hide behind a post, and fire the first person you catch. Or you can quietly size up and warn the most likely violator that if caught, there won't be a second chance. You can put a notice on the bulletin board calling employees' attention, generally, to the policy. Or you can hold a group meeting and announce how you will deal with those who gamble on company property. You can choose to regard only the taking of horseracing bets as gambling, or to include professionally run baseball, basketball, and football pools. Or you can rule out any kind of gambling. Whatever you decide, so long as you carry out the intentions (and the letter, where it's spelled out) of the company policy, you are setting your own policy.

How responsible will employees hold you for company policy?

If you have done a good job of convincing employees that you fully represent the management of their company, your actions and company policy will be one and the same thing in their eyes. Naturally, you will sometimes have to carry out policy that you don't fully agree with—policy that may be unpopular with you or with your employees. Resist the temptation to apologize for your actions or to criticize the policy to employees. When you do, you weaken your position.

If you have to reprimand an employee, don't say, "I'd like to give you a break, but that's company policy." Or when sparking a cleanup campaign, don't say, "The manager wants you to get your area in order." Handle such matters positively. Give the policy your own personal touch, but don't sell the company down the river or you're likely to be caught in the current yourself.

How can you prevent your policy interpretations from backfiring?

Try to protect your actions in policy matters by asking yourself questions before making these decisions:

- Is policy involved here? What is the procedure? What is the rule?
- Am I sure of the facts? Do I know all the circumstances?
- How did I handle a similar matter in the past?
- Who can give me advice on this problem? Should I ask for it?
- Would my boss want to talk this over with me first?
- Does this problem involve the union? If so, should I see the union steward or should I check with our labor relations people first?

Must you consider more than one policy at the same time?

Yes. Frequently you will be called on to handle a situation that involves several policy matters simultaneously. For instance, suppose you are informed that the company is dropping a product from its line. It will mean reducing labor costs in your department by 25 percent, since the work volume will fall off the same amount. One of your employees, hearing of the cutback, asks whether instead of laying off people, the work can be shared—whether you will retain all the employees but have them all work fewer hours per week. You check with your boss, who says, "The company's policy (and it's written into our agreement with the labor union) is that we will not 'share work.' The employees we retain must work a full week. But anything else you can do to reassign work is all right with me—as long as it's in line with company policy."

What can you do? Company policy knocks out a work-sharing plan. How about keeping the most skilled workers and laying off the less skilled? No. Can't do that. Company policy is that in "permanent" layoffs, employees with least seniority will go first. How about reducing the number of material handlers? That's okay. Nothing to prevent you from doing that. How about having the setup person double as an inspector? Oops, policy says, "Quality will be considered before every other operating policy except safety."

"Well," you say to yourself, "what I propose to do needn't sacrifice quality, so I'll make the double-up move.

"Now what can I do with my direct labor? I can drop ten from the gang if I can work four operators to an assembly instead of our usual six. Let's see, the union contract specifies that the number of operators needed to staff an assembly job operation cannot be changed except when changes in work load warrant a reduction. That seems like pretty clear policy to me. But I better check with the shop steward to see if there's some angle I've overlooked."

Before you have made your final plans, you've had to check them—and adjust them—against five company policies. Yet you make your own decisions and run the department as you see fit—except that you are guided by the rules set down for integrating your action with that of all the other departments of the company.

What is a supervisor's policy manual?

Many companies have actually taken their general company policies and written down interpretations as a specific guide to supervisory action. Those written guides for supervisors are usually placed in a loose-leaf folder and called a supervisor's manual. Supervisors use these manuals as references whenever a policy question comes up that they aren't certain about handling. If your company has such a manual, it's a useful aid in handling your job.

What do employees want to know about policy?

Employees are rarely concerned with nice phrases. General statements of policy mean little to them. But they do have a keen—and critical—interest in the specific and concrete aspects of policy whenever it hits home.

If your company's policy is to "treat employees equitably in disciplinary affairs," this will probably be unclear to them. You can help a lot if you rephrase the broad statements of policy (which may be generalized out of necessity) into language that every employee understands. In this case: "We intend to give everyone a fair and square deal if a rule is broken. Everyone will receive exactly the same treatment."

But even such a clear summary of a regulation still doesn't answer for an employee the question, "What does this mean to me?" You'll have to be still more specific: "If more than three out of every hundred pieces you turn out don't measure up to standards, I'll give you a warning the first time. The second time, you'll be given time off without pay. If it continues, you may be discharged." You wouldn't get far with policy, for instance, if you say to the employee, "If the quality of your production is substandard, we may have to take disciplinary action." The employee may very well ask, "What's quality? What's my production? What's substandard? What's disciplinary action?"

██
██

Key Concepts

1. Planning is the process of systematically working out what you and your work group will do in the future. Plans establish a hierarchy of goals—based on the needs of the organization and on the strengths and weaknesses of the work group—and specific procedures, regulations, and policies designed to achieve the goals.

2. Objectives or goals for a work group should (a) support the goals of the overall organization and (b) be attainable, given the limitations and resources of the group. Objectives should be clearly and concretely stated. Supervisors usually deal with short-term objectives spanning a few days, weeks, or months.

3. Decisions and actions in every enterprise are guided by a body of operating principles that either have been set down in writing or have evolved informally (like common law) as a result of decisions and actions that management has taken under similar circumstances in the past.

4. Company policies are dynamic, too, in that they are influenced by the decisions and actions of supervisors and managers as they cope daily with ever-changing situations and circumstances.

5. In the eyes of employees, the supervisors are inseparably identified with the policy of the employing organization, since it is at their level that philosophies and principles are translated into specific actions.

Supervisory Word Power

Objectives. Goals, targets, and purposes—both short-term and long-range—toward which an organization strives; the long-range objectives in particular must be supported by guidelines for management action and decisions.

Policies. Broad guidelines, philosophy, or principles that management establishes in support of its organizational goals and which it must follow in seeking them.

Procedures. Methods prescribed by management as the proper and consistent forms, sequences, and channels to be followed by individuals and units of an organization.

Regulations. Specific rules, orders, and controls set forth by management restricting the conduct of individuals and units within an organization.

Standards. Specifications, criteria, and prescribed measurements that define the limits within which, or the level at which, an organization's performance is presumed to have met its goals.

Reading Comprehension

1. Give an example from your work or personal life of a time when prior planning would have made things work out better than they did.
2. How can you judge whether particular objectives are reasonable for your department or work group?
3. Name some specific areas in organizations to which planning should be applied.
4. How are plans and controls related?
5. Contrast the ways in which policy affects top management decisions and the supervisor's actions.
6. What are some of the things typically covered by company policies?
7. When would it be wise for a supervisor to check with the boss before carrying out a particular policy?
8. Give an example of how a supervisor's decision in a particular instance might be influenced by more than one policy.
9. One company's policy manual stated: "It is our intention to listen with an open mind to employees' complaints." What supplementary information might a supervisor add to that statement when explaining it to employees?
10. Which do you think is more important to a company in the long run: the policies it sets or the actions its supervisors take? Why?

Supervision in Action
The Case of the Excused Absence. A Case Study in Human Relations Involving Company Policy, with Questions for You to Answer.

"The company's policy regarding time off from work is a reasonable one, Dick," said the plant superintendent to Dick Deeds, the new supervisor in the stamping room. "If employees have personal emergencies to take care of during working hours, we're only too glad to let them punch out and take care of them. However, we frown on the practice of granting time off to fish or hunt or to take care of any other personal matters that can be attended to after working time."

Three weeks later Tad Wade, a machine operator, asked Dick if he could report in late the next morning. He needed to do so, he said, because he had just bought a new car and wanted to register it at the motor vehicle agency. There was always a long line of applicants at the lunch hour or in the afternoon. "Sure you can," said Dick. "But come to work as soon as you have tended to your business."

The following morning, while Dick was lining up the day's schedule, Laura Featherstone, supervisor of the mixing department, stopped by Dick's desk. "You certainly put me in a tough spot with a couple of my people today. The boys got wind of the fact that you let Tad off today to register his new car. I've never accepted an excuse like that. I tell my people that so long as it's urgent, I'll let them go. But nix on rearranging work schedules just to suit one man's convenience."

1. Do you think Dick was right in letting Tad have the time off? Why?
2. What do you think of Laura's interpretation of company policy? Of Dick's?
3. Would it be better if Dick's boss had been more explicit in explaining the policy to Dick? Why?
4. What can Dick do to avoid having this situation arise again?

8

EXERCISING CONTROL OF PEOPLE AND PROCESSES

What is the basic purpose of a supervisor's control function?

To keep things in line and to make sure your plans hit their targets. In the restrictive sense, you use controls to make sure that employees are at work on time, that materials aren't wasted or stolen, that some persons don't exceed their authority. These controls tend to be the don'ts of an organization, the rules and regulations that set limits of acceptable behavior. In the more constructive sense, controls help to guide you and your department to production goals and quality standards.

What can controls be used for?

For just about anything that needs regulation and guidance. Controls, for example, can be used to regulate:

- **Employee Performance** of all kinds, such as attendance, rest periods, productivity, and workmanship.
- **Machine Operation and Maintenance,** such as its expected daily output, power consumption, and extent of time for out-of-service repairs.
- **Materials Usages,** such as the percentage of expected yield and anticipated waste during handling and processing.
- **Product or Service Quality,** such as the number of rejects that will be accepted or the number of complaints about service that will be tolerated.
- **Personal Authority,** such as the extent of independent action employees can take while carrying out the duties outlined in their job descriptions.

What are the supervisor's roles in the control process?

Supervisors fulfill two functions, as illustrated in Figure 8-1. In the first role, a supervisor acts somewhat like a judge, watching what happens in the department to see whether or not activities, conditions, and results are occurring as they are supposed to. In the second role, supervisors act as problem solvers and decision makers. They do so in order to find out why something is going (or has gone) wrong and then deciding what to do about it.

In their *judgmental role,* supervisors observe what is happening (or has happened) throughout the conversion process and then compare these observations (or measurements) with the standards of what was supposed to happen. These standards are derived from, or may be exactly the same as, the goals that were set during the planning process. Here are two examples of how the judgmental role is handled: In the first example, a supervisor in a word processing unit of a bank expects that all ten operators will be at their stations within 5 minutes after the lunch break (a standard he has set for the operators). Now he observes that only eight operators are regularly at their stations when they should be. The supervisor knows that a standard condition is not being met; it is temporarily out of control. In the second example, an assembly supervisor in a video game factory has set a goal of completing 300 assemblies a day. At the end of one day, the production report tells her that only 255 games were as-

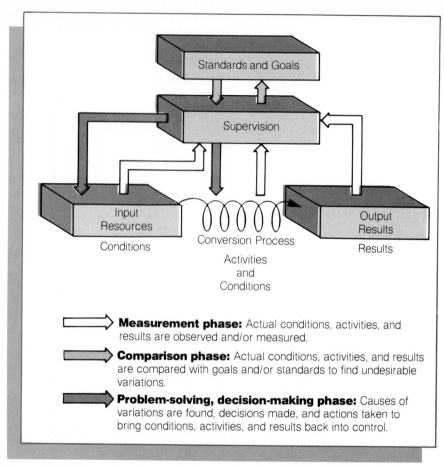

Figure 8-1. How goals and standards are used during the supervisor's control process.

sembled. The supervisor knows that her department is 45 assemblies below standard; production is temporarily out of control.

In their *problem-solving/decision-making role,* supervisors must not only find out why conditions or results are below standard, they must also correct conditions and bring results up to expectations. Here's how the supervisors might handle the two control problems spotted in the last paragraph: In the first case, the supervisor makes certain that the word processing equipment is in good operating order and that there is plenty of work available for all ten operators. Then he speaks to the latecomers to find out if there are any extenuating circumstances that prevent them from being at their stations immediately following the lunch break. He then outlines the need for promptness to ensure full usage of the equipment and the penalties for being late. Finally, he continues to watch for late arrivals so as to keep this condition in line with his standard. In the second case, the assembly line supervisor conducts a similar problem-solving search to find the cause of the missed standard. She might find that the cause arises from a number of conditions: faulty assembly tools, shortages of parts, changed specifications, employee absences, lack of training—or failure of one or more employees to apply themselves to their work. Once the true cause has been identified, the supervisor decides what to do and takes the steps needed to correct the problem and bring the conditions and/or results back under control.

In what way are plans and controls linked?

Controls are directly related to the goals that have been set during the planning process. In fact, controls are often identical with these goals. Suppose, for example, that as supervisor of a commercial office of a telephone company, you have planned that your department will handle 100 service calls per day during the next month. The quota of 100 calls per day is your goal. It also becomes your control standard. If your department handles 100 calls per day, you have met your target and need exert no corrective controls. If, however, your department handles fewer than 100 calls and begins to fall behind, it is below its control standard. You must take some sort of action to correct this performance.

Take another example. Suppose that you are the supervisor of a machining department in a brass foundry. Your superintendent has advised you that the company has set a goal of only 3 percent rejects of products scheduled to leave your area. In this case you may have to study each separate operation in your department to determine what you can consider its acceptable quality (or workmanship). You must keep in mind that the net effect must be only 3 rejects out of every 100 castings machined.

The lathe operators may be told that they cannot damage any castings at all, since their work is easiest to control. The boring machine operators may be given a standard that allows them to bore center holes no more than 0.1 inch off center. And the grinding machine operators may not be given a standard in terms of rejects at all. They may be told that the surface finish of casting they work on must meet the specified dimensions within ±0.005 inches. In your estimate, if everything went as wrong as it could for each operator, with operators still meeting the standards you set, the department would still meet its targeted goal of 3 rejects per 100, regardless of which operation used up all its tolerances.

If the department found that it was rejecting 5 of 100 castings, your job as supervisor would be to find which machine operator had exceeded the limits of control that you had set. And then you would have to decide what caused this to happen. It might be that the machine needs maintenance because it wobbles too much to bore a perfect center. Or the fixture that holds the casting in place while it is being machined might have slipped. Or the tools might need sharpening. Or the employee might need additional training to learn how to operate the machine more accurately. Or there is always the possibility that the operator was careless or willfully damaged a casting. Each of these causes would require a different kind of control action on your part.

Exactly what is a control standard?

A control standard, usually called simply a *standard,* is a specific performance goal that a product, a service, a machine, an individual, or an organization is expected to meet. It is usually expressed numerically: a weight (14.00 ounces), a rate (200 units per hour), or a flat target (4 rejects). The numbers may be expressed in any units, such as inches, gallons, dollars, or percentages.

Many companies also allow a little leeway from standard, called a *tolerance.* This implies that the performance will be considered to be in control if it falls within specified boundaries. A product, for instance, may be said to meet its 14.00-ounce standard weight if it weighs no less than 13.75 ounces or no more than 14.25 ounces. The control standard would be stated as 14 ounces, ±0.25 ounces. The tolerance is the ±0.25 ounces.

Where do the control standards come from? Who sets them?

A great many standards are set by the organization itself. They may be set by the accounting department for costs or by the industrial engineering or methods department for wage incentive (or time) standards. They may be issued by the production-control department for schedule quantities or by the quality-control people for inspection specifications. It is typical for control standards in large organizations to be set by staff specialists. In smaller companies supervisors may set standards themselves. But even in large companies the supervisor may have to take an overall, or department, standard and translate it into standards for each employee or operation.

On what information are control standards based?

Standards are based on one, or all three, of these sources.

Past Performance. Historical records often provide the basis for controls. If your department has been able to process 150 orders with three clerks in the past, this may be accepted as the standard. The weakness of this historical method is that it presumes that processing 150 orders represents good performance. Perhaps 200 would be a better target. This might be especially true if improvements have recently been made in the processing machinery and workplace layouts.

High Hopes. In the absence of any other basis, some supervisors ask for the moon. They set unreasonably high standards for their employees to shoot at. Whereas it is a sound practice to set challenging goals, standards should always be attainable by employees who put forth a reasonable effort. Otherwise, workers will become discouraged, or will rebel, and won't try to meet them.

Systematic Analysis. The best standards are set by systematically analyzing what a job entails. This way the standard is based on careful observation and measurement, as with time studies. At the very least, standards should be based on a consideration of all the factors that affect attainment of the standard—such as tooling, equipment, training of the operator, absence of distractions, and clear-cut instructions and specifications.

How accurate are standards and control measurements likely to be?

They won't be perfect. It is the supervisor's responsibility, however, to check regularly to see that measurements are being made as honestly and as accurately as possible.

Unintentional errors creep in as a result of carelessness when original figures are recorded, of mistakes when data is transferred from one record to another in keypunching, or of the halo effect when an observer is impressed by unusually high or low performance.

Deliberate falsification can take place when an operator or a salesperson whose wages depend on performance distorts the figures, when an employee covers up for a friend, when someone wants to give the impression of progress by holding up Friday's production count so that it appears in next week's record, or when someone works to lull the supervisor into thinking that everything is going all right.

Inaccuracies aside, it is also very important to check regularly to see that (1) the standards have not changed because of an improvement in machines or methods and (2) the measurements really do help you to make control decisions.

How is the control process carried out?

The control process follows four distinct steps, the last three of which are illustrated in Figure 8-1:

1. Set Performance Standards. Standards of quantity, quality, and time spell out (a) what is expected and (b) how much of a deviation can be tolerated if the person or process fails to come up to the mark. For example, the standard for an airline ticket counter might be that no customer should have to wait in line more than five minutes. The standard could then be modified to say that if only one out of ten customers had to wait more than five minutes, no corrective action need be taken. The standard would be stated as "waiting time of less than five minutes per customer with a tolerance of one out of ten who might have to wait longer." The guideline is that the more specific the standard, the better, especially when it can be stated with numbers as opposed to vague terms such as "good performance" and "minimum waiting time."

2. Collect Data to Measure Performance. Accumulation of control data is so routine in most organizations that it is taken for granted. Every time a supervisor or an employee fills out a time card, prepares a production tally, or files a receiving or inspection report, control data is being collected. Whenever a sales ticket is filled out, a sale rung up on a cash register, or a shipping ticket prepared, control data is being recorded—often with a computer-related terminal. Of course, not all information is collected in written form. Much of what a good supervisor uses for control purposes is gathered by observation—simply watching how well employees are carrying out their work.

3. Compare Results with Standards. From top manager to first-line supervisor, the control system flashes a warning if there is a gap between what was expected (the standard) and what is taking place or has taken place (the result). If the results are within the tolerance limits, the supervisor's attention can be turned elsewhere. But if the process exceeds the tolerance limits—the gap is too big—then action is called for.

4. Take Corrective Action. You must first find the cause of the gap (variance or deviation from standard). Then you must take action to remove or minimize this cause. If travelers are waiting too long in the airline's ticket line, for example, the supervisor may see that there is an unusually high degree of travel because of a holiday. The corrective action is to add another ticket clerk. If, however, the supervisor observes that the clerks are taking extra-long coffee breaks, this practice will have to be stopped as soon as possible.

To what extent can a supervisor depend on automatic controls?

More and more, operating processes rely on mechanical or automatic control. They try to minimize the human element. We all expect the thermostat to tell the furnace to keep the room warm. In many automobiles we expect a buzzer to tell us whether the seat belt is fastened or whether we are exceeding a preselected speed limit. In some cars we even let a mechanism take over the accelerator so that the speed of the auto is automatically maintained for us. Many processes in business and industry are controlled by the same principles. A worker feeds a sheet of metal into a press, and the machine takes over. A clerk slips a piece of paper into a copying machine, and the machine automatically reproduces the number of copies the clerk has dialed onto the control mechanism. The trend toward such automatic controls is very strong.

Human activities, however, still require supervisory control. Supervisors have to continually find ways to make sure that employees meet their job standards. Especially important are those of (1) attendance, (2) speed and care in feeding or servicing automatically controlled machines, and (3) even greater care needed by employees in joining their efforts with those of people in their own organizations and others they interface with in their company or client organizations.

What specific kinds of organizational controls are most likely to aid or restrict supervisory actions?

These depend largely on the nature of the organization in which the supervisor works. The following controls, however, are most common:

Quantity Controls.   These relate to the demand of almost every organization for some standard of output or production. The quantity of production required is often the basis for all other aspects of control. In other words, a supervisor must first make sure that output quantities measure up. Then the supervisor's attention can turn to controls that specify a certain quality or time, for example.

Quality Controls. If, in meeting the production standard, a department skimps on the quality of its work, there can be trouble. Quantity and quality go hand in hand. The inspection function is intended to make sure the final product or service lives up to its quality standards (specifications). As a supplement to routine inspections, many companies practice statistical quality control, a way of predicting quality deviations in advance so that a supervisor can take corrective action before a product is spoiled. (See Chapter 24 for details.)

Time Controls. Almost every organization must also meet certain deadlines or live within time restraints. A product must be shipped on a certain date. A service must be performed on an agreed-on day. A project must be completed as scheduled. Such time standards point up the fact that it is not enough just to get the job done if it isn't finished on time.

Material Controls. This is related to both quality and quantity standards. A company may wish to limit the amount of raw or finished materials it keeps on hand; thus it may exercise inventory controls. Or an apparel firm, for instance, may wish to make sure that the maximum number of skirts is cut out of a bolt of cloth so that a minimum amount of cloth is wasted—a material yield standard.

Cost Controls. The final crunch in exercising controls involves costs. A supervisor may meet the quantity and quality standards, but if in so doing the department has been overstaffed or has been working overtime, it probably won't meet its cost standard.

How do budgets fit into this picture?

Budgetary controls are very similar to cost controls and standards. Typically, the accounting or financial department provides a supervisor with a list of allowable expenses for the month. These are based on the expectation of a certain output, say, 4,000 units of production. These allowable expenses become its cost standards to be met for the month. At the end of the month the accounting department may issue the supervisor a cost variance report (Figure 8-2). This tells whether the department has met its standards, exceeded them, or fallen below them. Note that in Figure 8-2 the department has exceeded its overall budget by $800. It has, however, met a number of its standards while spending more for material handling,

COST VARIANCE REPORT

Department <u>Assembly</u>   Dept. no. <u>707</u>   Month <u>July</u>
No. of units scheduled for production <u>4,000</u>
No. of units actually produced <u>4,020</u>
Production variance +20 units

Account Title	Actual	Budget	Variance (+over −under)
Direct labor	$ 8,000	$ 8,000	0
Indirect labor			
Material handling	900	600	+300
Shop clerical	500	500	0
Supervision	1,200	1,200	0
Overtime	100	0	+100
Shift premium	0	0	0
Operating supplies	500	400	+100
Maintenance and repairs	1,900	1,400	+500
Gas, water, steam, air	1,600	1,800	−200
Electrical power	800	800	0
Total controllable budget	$15,500	$14,700	+$800

Figure 8-2.

overtime, operating supplies, and maintenance. The supervisor will be expected to do something to bring these cost overruns back into line next month. On the other hand, the department used less than was budgeted for gas, water, and steam. If this keeps up, the accounting department may develop a new standard for those expenses and allow the supervisor less money for them in the future.

Some authorities speak of systems control. What is meant by that?

In simplest terms, systems control means that you can't control one activity or performance factor without affecting the control of another. All activities carried on in a department or a process are interrelated. Quantity, quality, time, materials, and costs cannot really be separated if you look at the big picture. They are part of a system.

Take an example. If the sales department wants the shop supervisor to push an order in a hurry, the supervisor may have to sacrifice quality (by working too quickly) or costs (by working overtime). Something in the system has to give. In practice, someone must always decide whether the cost of getting out an order ahead of schedule can be justified by the benefits involved. One customer may be pleased (a benefit), whereas several others may be displeased because their orders were bumped back (a cost). Even the customer who is pleased to get an order sooner than expected may be displeased if the quality of the shipment doesn't measure up to expectations.

Supervisors are often at the receiving end of systems-control decisions. Just as frequently they may have to make systems-control decisions in their own departments.

Must supervisors spend all their time controlling?

It would appear that way. But by using a simple principle called management by exception, time taken for control activities can be held to a minimum. *Management by exception* is a form of delegation in which the supervisor lets things run as they are so long as they fall within prescribed (control) limits of performance. When they get out of line (as on the cost variance report in Figure 8-2), the supervisor steps in and takes corrective action.

Figure 8-3 shows how a supervisor can use the management-by-exception principle as a guideline for delegating much of the control work to subordinates.

Take, for example, a broiler chef in a fast-food restaurant. The boss says that the chef should expect to broil between 180 and 200 hamburgers per hour. This is control zone 1. So long as results fall within the prescribed limits, the chef is completely in charge.

If the requests for hamburgers, however, fall below 180 but above 150, the chef keeps the grill hot but puts fewer hamburgers into the ready position; or, if requests build up to 225, the chef moves more hamburgers to the completed stage. This is zone 2. The chef takes this action without first checking with the boss but tells the boss what has been done.

If business falls below 150 but is more than 100 hamburgers an hour, the chef may ask the boss whether the grill can be turned off for a while; or, if the requests build up to 250 per hour the chef may ask if one of the counter clerks can help. This is zone 3.

If conditions now move to either extreme—hamburger requests drop below 100 or exceed 250, the chef calls this to the supervisor's attention. This is zone 4. The supervisor may in the first instance (below 100) decide to shut down the grill, or in the second instance (above 250) decide to start up an auxiliary grill.

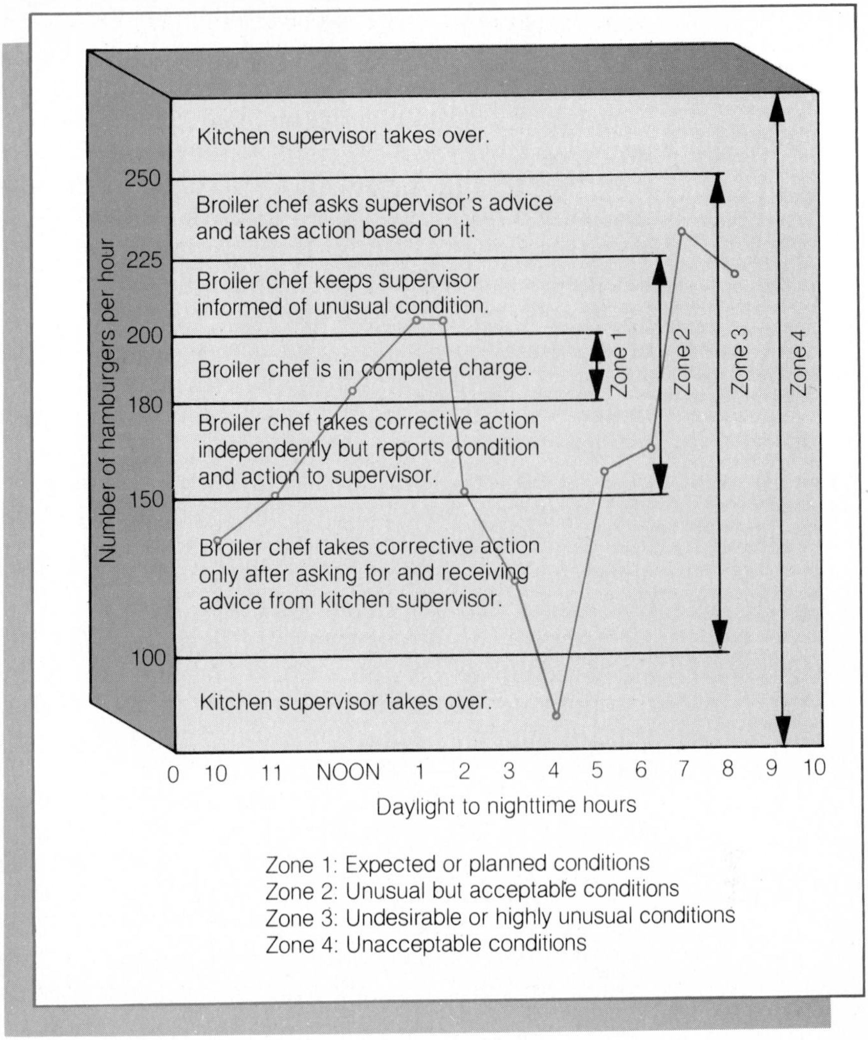
Kitchen supervisor takes over.
250
Broiler chef asks supervisor's advice and takes action based on it.
225
Broiler chef keeps supervisor informed of unusual condition.
200
Broiler chef is in complete charge.
180
Broiler chef takes corrective action independently but reports condition and action to supervisor.
150
Broiler chef takes corrective action only after asking for and receiving advice from kitchen supervisor.
100
Kitchen supervisor takes over.
Number of hamburgers per hour
Zone 1
Zone 2
Zone 3
Zone 4
0 10 11 NOON 1 2 3 4 5 6 7 8 9 10
Daylight to nighttime hours
Zone 1: Expected or planned conditions
Zone 2: Unusual but acceptable conditions
Zone 3: Undesirable or highly unusual conditions
Zone 4: Unacceptable conditions

Figure 8-3. Use of management-by-exception chart for controlling operation of hamburger grill.

How can you soften employee resistance to controls?

Many people do not like to be "controlled." They don't like to be told what to do, and they feel boxed in when faced with specific standards. Few persons like to be criticized or corrected. Yet criticism or correction is what control often comes down to. When correction means discipline or termination, controls can seem very harsh indeed. For this reason a supervisor should be realistic about controls. Thus controls can have a very negative effect on employees, to say nothing of what they may do to the supervisor.

The negative aspects of controls, however, can be minimized. Supervisors should consider any of the following more positive approaches:

Emphasize the Value of Controls to Employees. Standards provide employees with feedback that tells them whether they are doing well or not. Standards minimize the need for the supervisor to interfere and often allow the employee to choose a way of doing the job so long as standards are met. "You do the job, and I will stay out of your hair."

Avoid Arbitrary or Punitive Standards. Employees respond better to standards that can be justified by past records that support the standards. "Our records show that 150 per day is a standard that other operators have consistently met." Standards based on analysis, especially time studies, are even more acceptable. "Let's time this job for an hour or two so that we can be sure the standard is reasonable." Compare this with: "We'll just have to step up our production rate to 175 units each day."

Be Specific: Use Numbers If Possible. Avoid such expressions as "improve quality" and "show us better attendance." Instead, use numbers that set specific targets, such as "fewer than two days' absence in the next six months" or "decrease your scrap percentage from 7 out of 100 to 3 out of 100."

Aim for Improvement Rather Than Punishment. Capitalize on instances of missed standards to try to help employees learn how to improve their work. "Your output was below standard again last month. Perhaps you and I ought to start all over again to see what it is that is preventing you from meeting standards. There may be something I haven't shown you about this particular operation."

Make the Penalty for Nonconformance Absolutely Clear. A supervisor must balance rewards with punishment. Most employees respond to positive motivation. Many do not. All employees, however, good and poor alike, want to know what the "or else" is about their jobs. The guiding rule is to hold off punishment if you can, but to make it clear to everyone that standards must be met. Specify in advance what the penalty will be for those who don't meet them.

Avoid Threats That You Can't or Won't Back Up. If an employee is to be disciplined for failing to meet a quota or a standard of workmanship, be specific about the nature and timing of the discipline. "If you don't get your production up to 150 per day by the first of April, I will recommend that you be laid off for good." Don't say, "If you don't shape up soon, your head will be in a noose." If you do make the specific threat, it is good to make certain in advance that the company will help you make it stick. (See Chapter 20.)

Be Consistent in the Application of Controls. If you have set standards that apply to the work of several employees, it should go without saying that you will be expected to make everyone measure up to them. If you do feel that exceptions can be made, be prepared to defend that position. In the main, however, standards should be the same for everyone doing the same work. Similarly, rewards and punishment should be the same for all those who meet or fail to meet these standards.

What about encouraging self-control?

Self-control is beautiful for those who can exert it. Douglas McGregor insisted that many people need only to be given the targets for their work—the standards. After that, he said, they wish to be left alone and to be judged on the basis of their results in meeting or not meeting these targets. Employees will, Douglas McGregor said, provide their own control and do not need a supervisor to threaten them or cajole them into meeting standards.

My advice is to give an employee the benefit of the doubt. Give a free hand to those who take charge of themselves. Keep the rein on those who soon show that they need, or expect, the control to come from the supervisor.

When do management goals become control standards?

Very often, as shown when the linkage between planning and controlling was explained. More specifically, however, many companies convert their organizational goals into control programs by using a system of management by objectives. *Management by objectives* (MBO) is a planning and control process that provides managers at each organizational control point with a set of goals, or standards, to be attained. The process is usually repeated every 12 months. These MBO goals are similar to the supervisory performance goals listed in Table 7-1. It is presumed that if all supervisors reach their goals, the organization will also reach its goals. In companies where MBO is practiced to its full extent, the supervisors' goals literally become the standards of performance that must be met. The assumption is that the supervisors are capable of, and will exert, their own controls in striving to meet these objectives. The MBO system also presumes that the supervisors have been given enough freedom of action so that they can meet these goals with the allocated resources. In essence, MBO is simply a formalization at managerial levels of the principle of self-control.

Key Concepts

1. The control function is inseparably linked to planning. It requires that a supervisor keep continual track of progress toward departmental goals so that corrective action can be taken as soon as possible.

2. Good controls are based on reliable, attainable standards of performance. The best standards are those that are based on systematic analysis.

3. Budgetary controls place financial restrictions on the actions a supervisor can take in attempting to meet quantity, quality, time, and other interdependent or system-related goals.

4. Since controlling is only one of several functions supervisors must perform, they must take maximum advantage of the exception principle to delegate corrective action to qualified employees.

5. Resistance to controls is a natural human reaction. For this reason, controls should be fair, be specific and numerical where possible, motivate rather than coerce, be consistently applied, and encourage the greatest degree of self-control possible.

Supervisory Word Power

Budget. A financial or cost standard that establishes the amount of allowable expenses for operating a supervisor's department over a limited period of time.

Feedback. Relaying of the measurement of actual performance back to the individual or unit causing the performance so that action can be taken to correct, or narrow, the variance.

Management by Exception. A principle of control that enables a supervisor to delegate corrective action to a subordinate so long as the variances in performance are within specified ranges.

Management by Objectives (MBO). A planning and control technique wherein supervisors and their superiors agree on goals to be attained and standards to be maintained.

Specification. A collection of standardized dimensions and characteristics pertaining to a product, process, or service.

Standard. The measure, criterion, or basis for judging performance of a product or service, machine, individual, or organization.

Tolerance. The permissible deviation from standard.

Variance. The gap or deviation between *actual* performance or results and the *standard* or expected performance or results.

Reading Comprehension

1. How are control standards related to the goals established in plans?
2. Explain the difference between a supervisor's judgmental role in controlling and his or her problem-solving and decision-making role.
3. Of the three chief ways of setting standards, which is the best? Why? What's wrong with the other two?
4. What kind of errors should supervisors look for in control information or in the measurements on which standards are based?
5. What is the ultimate purpose of the control process?
6. Give some examples of automatic controls in everyday life.
7. Briefly describe five specific controls a supervisor is likely to be concerned with.
8. How are management by exception and control standard tolerances related?
9. Is there anything positive in controls for the *people* who work in an organization? If so, what?
10. How should a supervisor approach the issue of self-control among employees?

Supervision in Action
The Case of the Missed Bogey. A Case Study in Human Relations Involving Budgetary Controls, with Questions for You to Answer.

Ross J., supervisor of the assembly department of the Traverse City Transmissions Plant, had just received his budget for the month of May. Among other things, the production control department had increased his monthly output standard, or bogey, from 2,000 units to 2,500. The budgeting department had taken this into account when setting the various allowable expenses for the month. The department's total allowable costs were usually $100,000. For May this figure had been raised to $125,000. This was a one-quarter increase to balance the one-quarter increase in the output bogey. The budgeting department called this approach "flexible budgeting," since it increased or decreased Ross's allowable expenses in proportion to the monthly output bogey. If the bogey had been lowered to 1,500 units, for example, the allowable expense total would have been lowered also, probably to $75,000.

Ross studied his bogey and expense budget carefully. He saw that he would have to add another person to the assembly line. He also decided that the department would have to work overtime for an hour or two each day to meet the bogey. When Ross called this to the attention of his superior, his boss said, "I can't approve your adding another person in your department, but I will approve overtime—so long as you don't exceed the total allowable expense for the month."

"That won't be too easy," said Ross. "You are asking for an increase in output of 25 percent. I may have to work the department as much as 25 percent overtime to meet that bogey."

"The expense budget won't handle it," said Ross's boss. "It allows for only a 15 percent increase in overtime. You'll have to make up the difference by getting increased productivity from your regular workers."

Ross wasn't too happy about that decision. He did go back to his desk, however, to see what improvements he could think of. Then he went out to the shop floor to study the operations there. After considerable observation, Ross did discover a couple of places on the line where improvements could be made. At one point, where the gears were placed in the housing, there was a bottleneck. This slowed the line while employees downstream waited for housings to finish. On the basis of this observation, Ross decided to transfer one worker from the finishing operation to the gear-insertion stage. That way, the line would be better balanced. Production ought to rise the needed 10 percent.

Ross made the necessary changes in assignments the second day of May. There was some resistance to this. The employees in the finishing stage complained about being overloaded. Work at the gear-insertion station was somewhat crowded, as the additional employee tended to get in the way. Nevertheless, Ross stuck with his plan and by the end of the second week in May, the line was running pretty smoothly. Ross checked his output and found to his chagrin that the department had completed only 1,000 assemblies. The month was half over, and even with the increased production rate the department would probably fall short of its 2,500-unit bogey by 250 units. Accordingly, Ross took it upon himself to work his crew overtime every day for the last two weeks of the month. At the end of May, Ross was pleased that his department had, in fact, met the bogey of 2,500 units.

A few days after the end of the month Ross received a call from his boss. "What happened to your budget last month? the boss asked. "You went over it by $5,000."

"It must have been the overtime we worked during the last couple of weeks," said Ross.

"I thought I told you that you had to keep your overtime in line," his boss replied.

"I did, during the first two weeks," said Ross. "But when I saw that we wouldn't meet our bogey, I added overtime every day."

"You shouldn't have done that," said his boss. "Ordinarily it costs your department $50 to put together each unit. At the rate you were going, it cost more than that. In fact, it cost $130,000 to put together the 2,500 units, or $52 per unit. That's an increase of 4 percent. We hardly make that kind of percentage of profit on the transmissions in the first place."

"I am sorry about that," said Ross. "But I thought that the main thing you wanted from me was the 2,500 units. Besides, the changes I've made in setting up the assembly line will enable me to keep costs in line next month."

"It's too late now," said Ross's boss. "The scheduling department is cutting us back to 1,500 transmissions next month. You'll have to be thinking about cutting at least one person from your line. Meanwhile, I want you to write out a complete explanation as to why you failed to come inside your expense bogey during May. I have to meet with the general manager this afternoon, and she will want a full explanation."

1. How reasonable was Ross's boss in this situation? What might he have done to make the situation clearer to Ross?
2. What do you think of Ross's plan? What was good about it and what was bad about it? How does it reflect the need for a cost-benefit decision?
3. In what way might Ross have avoided this situation? How can he avoid a recurrence in June?

9

PROBLEM SOLVING AND DECISION MAKING

What, specifically, is a problem?

A problem is a puzzle, a mystery, an unsettled matter, a situation requiring a solution, a plan or an issue involving uncertainty. Your work is full of them. Problems can be classified three ways:

Problems That Have Already Happened.   Some examples are merchandise that spoiled, costs that got out of line, employees who quit, shipments that were missed. These may need immediate solutions to correct what has taken place.

Problems That Lie Ahead. Examples are how to finish the Ajax project on time, when to put on a second shift, where to place the new press, whether or not to tell employees of an impending change in their work. These, too, require immediate solutions to set effective plans and procedures.

Problems That You Want to Forestall. These lurk in the future. You'd like to take preventive action now so that they will never arise and thus never require solutions.

Problems, and their solutions, are, of course, inseparably related to the management process. Problems arise all along the way. Supervisors must solve them when they plan, organize, staff, direct, and control. Otherwise, problems will stand in the way of the attainment of the department's goals.

What causes a problem?

Change. If everything remained exactly as it should be, problems would not occur. Unfortunately, change, especially unwanted change, is always with us. Changes occur in materials, tools and equipment, employee attitudes, specifications received from customers, the work space itself, and just about anything else you can imagine. The trick to problem solving is often the ability to spot the unwanted and unexpected change that slipped into an otherwise normal situation.

About how many problems – or decisions – does a supervisor handle each day?

Counting minor as well as major ones, the total comes to about eighty, or about one every 5 or 6 minutes. Some of these are so routine that they are hardly noticed. For example: Employee Pat wants to know which batch to work on next. Or Mary wants to know whether she can check out a different tool from the stock room. Or Pete asks for permission to leave the shift a few minutes early. Supervisors handle these problems and make the necessary decisions without a second thought.

Other problems require considerable time and reflection. For example: What can be done to reduce the number of rejects on the finishing line? Is now the time to begin training Ramon to replace Janice during her vacation? How can the Ajax project be speeded up so that it is completed by the scheduled deadline? These

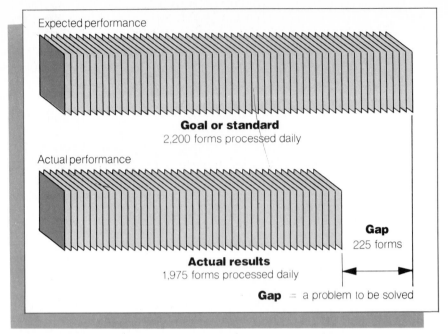

Figure 9-1. How gaps between actual performance and goals or standards help to identify or "find" problems.

problems will require a systematic approach if a good solution is to be found.

Problems and decisions fly so fast in the supervisor's world that some authorities believe that problem solving and decision making are what the job is all about.

How can you recognize a problem or a potential problem?

A problem exists when there is a gap between what you expect to happen and what actually happens. (See Figure 9-1.) Your budget, for example, calls for 2,200 insurance policies to be processed this week; the count at 5 p.m. on Friday shows that you completed only 1,975, a gap of 225 policies. Or you expected to hold the total number of employee absences in your department to 300 days this year; the total is 410, a gap of 110 days.

It is almost the same with potential problems. You know what you would like to have occur in the future: a project completed, a perfect safety record, fewer than ten customer complaints. These are your plans. But when you look ahead at your procedures and the potential for mishaps, you feel that your department will fall short of its targets—that there will be a gap. In a nutshell, you find problems by spotting a gap between actual and expected performance.

How are problems solved?

By removing whatever it is that has caused, or will cause, a gap between the expected (or desired) condition and the actual condition. That's the main idea, at least. Suppose, for example, that your hoped-for safety record of zero accidents is spoiled by three accidents on the punch press machine. You will want to (1) find their cause (bypassing of the safety guard by the operators) and (2) remove it (by designing a foolproof guard).

Finding and removing the cause or causes, however, is usually difficult and requires considerable examination and thought. There will be more discussion about the problem-solving process later.

What is the connection between problem solving and decision making?

The two processes are closely related. (See Figure 9-2.) A decision is always needed in the choice of the problem's solution. In many ways, problem solving *is* decision making. As you will see in a moment, any step along the way of planning, organizing, directing, controlling—and problem solving—that presents a choice of more

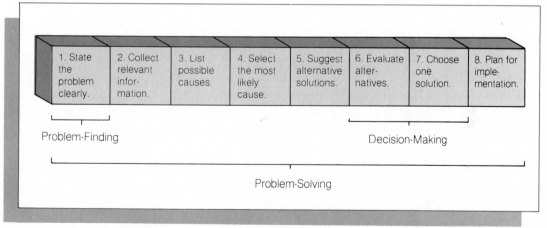

Figure 9-2. How problem-solving and decision-making overlap.

than one course of action requires also that a decision be made. Take the safety record on the punch press again. A truly complete analysis of the problem might have suggested that the cause could be removed in three different ways: (1) use of an automatic feeding device that would remove the need for a guard, (2) institution of an educational and disciplinary program to instruct operators about the proper operation of the present guard, or (3) design of a foolproof guarding system. The supervisor, as decision maker, would have to choose among the three alternatives. The first might be judged too costly, the second not completely effective, and the third the best choice because it is relatively inexpensive and foolproof.

How can you recognize the need for a decision?

Whenever there is more than one way of doing things, a decision is needed. Any kind of choice, alternative, or option calls for a decision. You might ask, "If this is so, why are so many decision opportunities overlooked?" The answer is that managers and supervisors alike get preoccupied with the status quo. In effect they say, "The way we are doing this is the only way." Such supervisors miss the point that there are always alternatives. There is always the choice to do something or not to do it, to speak or to remain silent, to correct or to let well enough alone. All too often a supervisor's decision is made by default. The supervisor does nothing. The tide of events carries the department until a crisis occurs. In reality, however, doing nothing represented a choice. It was a decision not to change, not to plan for improvement, not to anticipate a potential problem.

Must the approach to problem solving be systematic?

Yes. There are few exceptions to the rule that the best results come from a systematic approach. Here, as illustrated in Figure 9-2, is a fundamental approach to problem solving and decision making.
Step 1. State the Problem Clearly and Specifically. Stay away from a general statement, such as "We have a problem with quality." Instead, narrow it down and put figures on it if you can, as in "Between the first of the month and today, the number of rejects found at final inspection have totaled 32, compared with our standard of 15."
Step 2. Collect All Information Relevant to the Problem. Don't go too far afield, but do find data that may shed some light on

process changes, materials used, equipment function, design specifications, employee performance, and assignments. Much of the data will not tell you anything except where the source of the problem is not. If your information shows, for example, that there has been no change in the way materials have arrived or machinery has been used, good! You can look elsewhere.

Step 3. List as Many Possible Causes for the Problem as You Can Think of. Remember that a problem is a gap between expected and actual conditions. Something must have occurred to cause that gap. Most particularly, something must have been changed. Is the present operator different from the old one? Was a power source less regular than before? Has there been a change, however slight, in the specifications?

Step 4. Select the Cause or Causes That Seem Most Likely. Do this through a process of elimination. To test a cause to see if it is a probable one, try seeing (or thinking through) what difference it would make if that factor were returned to its original state. For example, suppose a possible cause of rejects is that compressed air power is now only 75 psi instead of 90 psi. Try making the product with the pressure restored to 90 psi. If it makes no difference, then power irregularity is not a likely cause. Or perhaps you think that the new operator has misunderstood your instructions. Check this out with the operator. See if your instructions are, in fact, being followed exactly. If not, what happens when your instructions are followed? If the rejects stop, then this is a likely cause. If the rejects persist, this is not a likely cause.

Step 5. Suggest as Many Solutions for Removing Causes as You Can. This is a good time for brainstorming. There is rarely only one way to solve a problem. If the cause of an employee's excessive absenteeism, for instance, is difficulty getting up in the morning, this cause might be removed in a number of ways. You might change the shift, insist that the employee buy an alarm clock, make a wake-up telephone call yourself, or show how failure to get to work is job-threatening. The point is to make your list of alternative solutions as long as possible.

Step 6. Evaluate the Pros and Cons of Each Proposed Solution. Some solutions will be better than others. But what does better mean? Cheaper? Faster? Surer? More participative? More in line with company policy? To judge which solution is best, you'll have to have a set of criteria like the ones just listed. Evaluation requires you to make judgments based on facts. Consult the information gathered in Step 2. Also consult anyone who can offer specialized opinions about the criteria you have chosen.

Step 7. Choose the Solution You Think Is Best. Yes, this—like what you did in Step 6—is the decision phase of problem solving. In effect, you will have weighed all the chances of success against the risks of failure. The strengths of your solution should exceed its weaknesses.

Step 8. Spell Out a Plan of Action to Carry Out Your Solution. Decisions require action and follow-up. Pin down exactly what will be done and how, who will do it, where, and when. How much money can be spent? What resources can be used? What is the deadline?

W̲hat approach is used for problems that involve the future rather than the past?

You must think forward rather than backward. What could change so as to cause a problem? An employee is retiring; you'd better have a trained replacement. The company has signed a contract with a new supplier; you'd better make sure the purchasing department relays the exact materials specifications to the vendor. Your plans call for ten new employees by the year's end; you'd better check with personnel to make sure these employees will, in fact, be available and fully trained when the new equipment is ready.

Potential problem analysis is essentially the same as basic, systematic problem solving. Its focus, however, is on Step 3, listing possible causes. The fundamental difference is that you must transfer what your experience has told you about past causes to estimates of what may possibly recur in the future. You must, of course, also use your imagination to anticipate new sources of problems—causes that have not occurred previously but which might in the future.

Opportunity finding is the happy—or positive—side of potential problem analysis. In this case, however, a possible cause or even a gap is a signal that something can be changed for the better. Suppose, for example, that you've been taking for granted that absences in your department are going to average about 5 percent. But you notice that the rate is either rising or falling. There's the gap. Then you examine the possible causes and find that they are related to rumors about changes in job assignments. Employees are reacting two ways. Some are sticking close to the work so that they can control the changes that might affect them. Others are looking around outside the company for jobs elsewhere. Either way, this is your opportunity to improve communications and develop a stronger sense of togetherness in your work group. The period may be rocky, but at its conclusion, you may not only build a more unified work group, you may also permanently reduce the department's absence rate.

How systematic must the decision-making process be?

Unlike problem solving, there are good reasons to believe that decision making need not always be systematic—nor even logical. System helps up to a point. But when you are dealing with the future, hunches and intuition often pay off.

The systematic, or rational, approach to decision making takes place during Steps 6 and 7 of problem solving: evaluating alternative solutions and selecting the best one on the basis of the facts available. This approach can be made even more rational and more reliable by first setting goals that the decision must enable you to reach. For example, a problem-solving decision about cost cutting must be effective for at least six months and not involve employee separations. Or, if you are developing future plans, the decision may be required to fulfill the requirement of assuring that production schedules be met without overtime.

This rational step of first setting a goal tends to make the quality of the decision better, even when it is ultimately made by hunch, because you know what your target is or what limitations will be placed on your choice or plans for implementation.

What is meant by mathematical decision making?

Mathematical decision making refers to the use of certain mathematical, statistical, or quantitative techniques to aid the decision maker. These are aids, very valuable ones in many instances, but they are only aids. The techniques do not make decisions. They arrange numerical information in such a way that it can be analyzed mathematically, but the executive, manager, or supervisor must make the final decision on the basis of an interpretation of the results.

How can supervisors make use of decision trees?

A decision tree is essentially a graphic portrait of Steps 5 and 6 in the problem-solving process. It shows how each alternative solution forks into various possibilities. Suppose, for example, that a supervisor is faced with a decision about how to treat Edgar, an employee whose attendance has been very poor. One alternative (A-1) is to enforce strict discipline by laying Edgar off for three days. A second alternative (A-2) is to provide constructive encouragement. A third alternative (A-3) is to try a little of both. Figure 9-3 shows how these alternatives work on a decision tree.

The supervisor can presume that there are only three ways Edgar can react. He may respond only to strict discipline, he may respond only to encouragement, or he may respond favorably to both. The probable changes in performance from each kind of response are diagramed, with a range of outcomes from very little improvement to

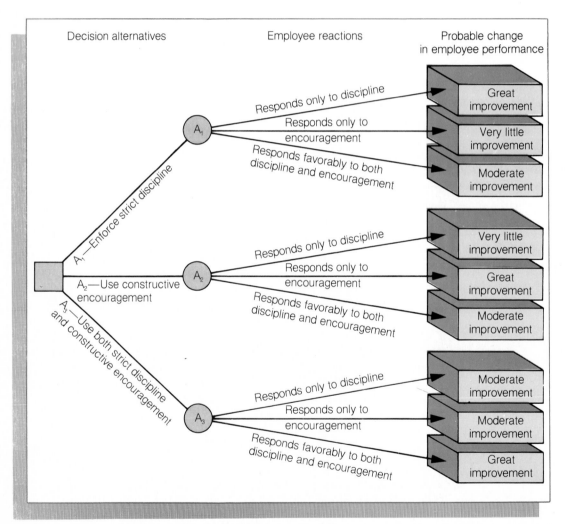

Figure 9-3. Basic decision tree: discipline versus constructive encouragement to improve an employee's performance.

great improvement. Thus, the improvement in Edgar's performance differs according to each decision strategy and to each possibility of how Edgar might respond to it.

Edgar may react three different ways to the A-1 alternative. If he responds to discipline there may be great improvement; if he responds only to encouragement, then there will be very little improvement. Or, if he responds favorably to both discipline and encouragement, there may be moderate improvement. Similarly, Edgar may react three different ways to alternative A-2 and to alternative A-3. The decision tree helps the supervisor to visualize the various outcomes or possible changes in Edgar's performance. On the basis of this analysis, you may be better able to choose the alternative that has the best chance of being effective.

Where do payoff tables fit in?

Payoff tables enable you to convert the various decision alternatives of a decision tree to numerical values. For example, in Figure 9-3, the probable change in employee performance shows three possible outcomes for decision alternatives A-1, A-2, and A-3. If "great improvement" were worth 5 points, "very little improvement" only 1 point, and "moderate improvement" 3 points, then you could compare the numerical value of each of the alternatives. A-1 would score a total of 9 points (5 for "great," 1 for "very little," and 3 for "moderate"). A-2 would score a total of 9 points, too. A-3, however, would score a total of 11 points. On the basis of these values, the supervisor might choose A-3 as the alternative with the best potential for succeeding.

Payoff tables have an obvious weakness in that they are dependent on your judgment of the possible outcomes for each alternative and also the values you assign to each. On the other hand, the great value of this method is that it forces you to make a firm judgment about what you think may happen and the worth to you of these outcomes. The payoff table won't make a decision for you, but it will force you to be more realistic about possible outcomes.

What is meant by cost-benefit analysis?

It is not unlike the closing steps in problem solving and decision making. This is the phase when you examine the pros and cons of each proposed solution. Cost-benefit analysis has become a popular technique for evaluating proposals in the public sector. Take a proposal for a local government to offer a child-care service to its residents. Cost-benefit analysis adds all the costs of implementation and equates them with the value of the services to the community. Typically, the benefits of such nonprofit services are hard to quantify; that is, it is hard to place a dollar value on them. Accordingly, many cost-benefit analyses include quality judgments of benefits as well as dollar estimates.

Cost-benefit analysis is similar to *input-output* analysis, which is an attempt to make sure that the cost and effort expended in carrying out a decision will at least be balanced by its outputs or results. In business, when outputs exceed inputs, the result is a profit. If there is an excess of benefits over costs in nonprofit organizations, the excess is called a surplus.

Some say that most decisions involve a trade-off. What is meant by that?

This is a way of saying that to attain your objective in one area, you must be prepared to give up something in another area. The department store maintenance supervisor who has only so much money to spend on new equipment may buy a powered floor sweeper and may have to forego the purchase of a powered platform to facilitate ceiling maintenance. Housekeeping will improve on the floors; meanwhile, it may get worse on the ceilings. This is a trade-off in which someone must decide which goal is more important at the moment.

Are decisions based on intuition as good as those based on logic?

If a decision works out well, it won't make any difference how it was reached. Many decisions based on hunch have proved to be correct. They are harder to defend, however, when they go wrong. More important, any decision is likely to be better if its goals are clearly understood. The logical approach helps to strip away distractions and irrelevancies. Intuition often adds a valuable dimension by calling on some inner sense we don't clearly understand. Many authorities believe the best decisions come from the dual approach—a combination of logic and hunch.

In seeking facts to solve a problem or make a decision, what should be the cutoff point?

Stop looking when the trouble and the cost of obtaining the extra information exceeds its value. The rule is: The more critical and lasting the effect of a decision, the more you can afford to look for the last scrap of vital information. Don't spend two days hunting for background data on a purchasing decision, for example, if the item plays only an insignificant part in your process and will only be used once or twice. On the other hand, it might pay to defer a decision to hire a full-time employee until you have made a reference check.

Do guard against using the absence of information as an excuse for procrastination. Some decisions are especially hard to arrive at and unpleasant to carry out. When you are faced with these situations, there is a temptation to put off an answer (yes, answers are decisions—or should be) by asking for more information. Rarely is the questioner fooled by this tactic, and rarely does the additional information add much to the quality of the decision.

One final comment on this question: don't be too eager to rush into decisions—especially those involving people. Employees will often press hard for a quick answer. They catch you with your guard down. They may imply, for example, that unless you arrange for a transfer next week, something drastic will happen to them. If you feel that the urgency is forced, it makes good sense to wait a while. The situation may relax; the individual may find that the request for a transfer was only a passing inclination.

What is a "programmed" decision?

Decisions that are spelled out in advance by a standard procedure or policy are said to be "programmed." That is, a supervisor has only to identify the problem correctly as one that has arisen before. There's no point in solving it a second time. As a consequence, the supervisor simply applies the previous solution or the decision that is dictated by standard procedures and policies. By avoiding the necessity of having to "reinvent the wheel" each time the same problem comes up, a supervisor saves time and energy.

Some problems occur so frequently that you can set up a routine decision for them. You must remember, however, that what worked before may not work again. It can be risky to follow past experience blindly without considering other possible solutions.

Do people approach decision situations differently?

Very much so. There are typically four kinds of decision makers.

- **Risk Seekers** actively look for opportunities to make changes, to improve, to force action. Within limits these people make the best supervisors—especially in dynamic business enterprises where technology and the outside environment are very fluid.
- **Risk Averters** tend to stand pat, to presume that what is working now should not be changed without very sound reasons. These people make good supervisors, too, especially in stable governmental organizations where it is important to have someone who can hold to a set and proved course.
- **Wishful Thinkers** try to control the impossible or hope that good intentions will override harsh facts. These people don't make very good supervisors under any circumstances.
- **Biased Thinkers** have limited vision. They often act from prejudice or misinformation. These people should not be supervisors.

Of course, all of us have a little of each kind of decision maker in us, depending on the situation. For this reason many experts advise that the best, and the most professional, approach to decision making is a contingency one. In effect, they say, use the technique and be the kind of person that best fits the problem at hand. Said another way, in times of great uncertainty, a stand-pat approach may be best. In times of great opportunity—when growth, for example, is taking place in your organization—look for chances to make changes.

What can be done to make your decisions more effective?

Besides starting with a specific goal in mind and laying a foundation of facts and systematic analysis, there are a couple of other kinds of insurance you can turn to.

Pick Your Spots.   First, avoid decision making, if you can, where risks are high. Second, try to make decisions only where the potential for payoff is great. You can identify the second kind of opportunity by using ABC analysis. (See Figure 9-4.) The ABC concept is based on an established economic fact: A vital few problems or opportunities for action account for the greatest loss or greatest gain. Most problems and opportunities are basically of little consequence. Economists call this the 20/80 syndrome. It means that 20 percent of your problems will account for 80 percent of your losses or profits. Then, to turn the idea around, 80 percent of your problems will account for only 20 percent of your losses or profits. ABC analy-

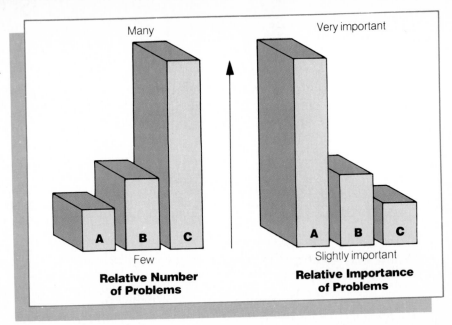

Figure 9-4. ABC analysis.

sis calls the vital few, "A" items; the inconsequential many, "C" items; and those that fall somewhere in between, "B" items. If you were to take an inventory of items in your stockroom, for example, it is a sure bet that only a relatively few items would account for most of its value. A great many items, however, such as paper clips and erasers, would account for only a small portion of the inventory's total worth. Astute purchasing managers concentrate on the vital few items, not the trivial many. You should apply the same principle to your problems and decisions selection.

Maintain Your Perspective.   Statistically, problems fall in what is called a normal distribution, and so do the results of most decisions. We say, "You win some and you lose some." That's really what a normal distribution tells us. If you make ten decisions, one or two will work out fine. One or two are likely to be "bombs." The rest will fall somewhere in between. Knowing this, you should keep the following guidelines in mind when you make decisions:

1. Don't reach too high. Don't set your objectives at the very top; allow some room for mistakes.
2. Don't overcommit or overextend your resources on one problem; you may need them later for an unanticipated problem.
3. Always prepare a fallback position, a way to alter plans and attain at least part of the objective.

When should you make decisions on your own and when should you go to others for help?

It depends on a number of factors. Table 9-1 shows how to look at the whole picture before deciding to handle a problem on your own or to ask another person or a group of employees for their assistance.

How good are group decisions?

They have their good points and their bad points. Where a decision can be aided by shared views and mutual responsibilities (such as

TABLE 9-1 GUIDE FOR SEEKING HELP IN PROBLEM SOLVING

Factors	1. You decide alone	2. You consult with one of your employees	3. You consult with a group of your employees
Whose problem is it?	Yours alone	His or hers	The group's (ours)
Amount of time	Not available	Have some time available	Plenty of time available
Expertise	Fully expert	Expert advice is needed to fill gaps in your own knowledge	Yes, as for No. 2
Technical know-how	Full know-how	Need to fill in gaps in your technical know-how	Yes, as for No. 2
Can others add anything to the decision?	No	Yes	Yes
Will you accept suggestions?	No, not likely	Yes, from someone you respect	Yes, from an effective unit
Will it help others to carry out the project if they are involved in the decision?	No significance; you will carry out the project yourself	Yes, helpful and essential	Yes, necessary and essential
Coordination of effort	Not needed; you will handle it all	Vertical; necessary with your superior or your employees	Horizontal; needed and necessary among your employees
Learning value	No value to anyone else	Value to one employee, potentially	Value to your whole group

those affecting safety), committees have proved to be effective. Where action must focus on benefitting a single area, group decisions may be weak and ineffective. The hidden objective of such group decisions often is, for its participants, to share the blame if anything goes wrong or to spread a scarce resource so that there are fewer complaints.

Generally speaking, decisions should be made by those charged with the responsibility to solve a particular problem. These decision makers may gain much, however, by seeking ideas and suggestions from others. But, in the main, they must make the final decisions themselves.

Just how good should you expect a decision to be?

The test of a good decision is: Did it meet the objectives set for it? Suppose, for example, the decision's goal was to prevent a recurrence of excessive turnover. At some point in the future, such as the end of the year, excessive turnover should have stopped.

How many of your decisions should be good ones? You probably make between 60 and 100 decisions a day. If two out of three of them can be judged to be good, you've attained an excellent batting average.

Key Concepts

1. An important mark of effective supervision is the ability (a) to recognize the existence of a problem or the need for a decision and (b) to identify opportunities for improvement and anticipate potential trouble spots.

2. Problems are characterized by a gap between what is expected to happen and what actually occurs. Gaps are usually caused by a change in procedures or conditions. Problems are solved by removing or correcting the cause of the change, which, in turn, closes the gap.

3. Decision making is an inseparable part of the problem-solving process. It is the phase in which solutions, ideas, and new courses of action are examined critically and then chosen on the basis of their chances for success or failure in meeting related objectives.

4. Problem solving should always be approached systematically. Decision making utilizes intuition and creativity as well as logic, but it is always more effective when based on firm objectives and adequate information.

5. Problem solving and decision making are often improved by seeking help from those individuals or groups of employees who are best informed about and/or most closely involved in the problem and in implementing its solution.

Supervisory Word Power

Cost-Benefit Analysis. A technique for weighing the pros and cons of alternative courses of action, especially in nonprofit organizations, in which both the intangible benefits of the action and its costs are assigned dollar values.

Decision Making. That part of the problem-solving process that entails evaluation of the alternative solutions and a choice among them of an effective remedial action.

Decision Tree. A graphic method of portraying, for comparative purposes, the possible outcomes of each of a number of alternative solutions or remedial actions.

Problem Solving. The process wherein the gap that occurs between expected and actual conditions or results is analyzed systematically in order to find and remedy its causes.

Programmed Decision. A decision that is indicated by the solution to a similar, recurring problem or by a procedure or policy that has been established for dealing with such a problem.

Reading Comprehension

1. Differentiate between problem solving and decision making.

2. How would you recognize the existence of a problem?

3. What is the essential ingredient in solving a problem?

4. What is the primary cause of most problems? What causes a gap to occur?

5. If one branch (or set of alternatives) of a decision tree showed a cumulative value of 25 points, a second branch a total of 17, and a third branch a total value of 22, which branch would have the greatest probability of succeeding if it were followed?

6. What special decision-making technique might be used for deciding which one of five projects should be chosen for a public health program? Why?

7. Given a decision concerning whether or not to institute a change in operating methods in a mail room, which approach would you choose—a logical or intuitive one? Why?

8. Give some examples of how a company's policies, rules, or standard procedures help to "program" a decision for a supervisor.

9. How might ABC analysis improve your problem solving and decision making?

10. Under what circumstances might it be better for a supervisor to seek help in solving a problem rather than handling it all himself or herself?

Supervision in Action

The Case of the Unreliable Inventory Figures. A Case Study in Human Relations Involving a Perpetual Inventory System About to be Replaced by a Computer, With Questions for You to Answer.

Connie T., warehouse supervisor for Office Suppliers Company, was puzzled by the performance of Buddy M., an inventory clerk. Buddy's main job was to maintain the perpetual inventory records. He was in charge of posting incoming and outgoing shipments to the record card for each particular item stored in the warehouse. Although not an outstanding performer, Buddy's work had always been acceptable. Lately, however, with the introduction of a computerized system in the accounting department that doubled-checked his work at the close of each month, it was apparent that Buddy's figures were no longer reliable. Connie hesitated to get too heavily on Buddy's case, since he was a long-time employee whose diligence had never been questioned. Finally, Connie could put the matter off no longer. She called Buddy into her office and told him of her decision.

"Buddy," she said, "you're going to have to get your act together or you and Office Suppliers will be parting ways."

"What do you mean?" asked Buddy.

"It should be clear to you," said Connie. "You've been letting your work slide downhill in the past few months. The figures you produce on your inventory record cards are no longer dependable. Every month, the computer report turns up an armful of errors in them."

"I'm surprised at that," said Buddy. "While I don't double check everything the way I used to do, I still thought my figures would be close to what the computer shows."

"Well," said Connie, "they aren't. You've gotten very careless. If you don't get back on track, I'll be recommending you for discharge."

"I suppose I shouldn't be surprised by that," said Buddy. "Once the company put the computer in the accounting department, I knew it wouldn't be long before it would be on line over here in the warehouse. I guess I'll be just one more person whose job is taken over by the computer."

"That isn't the idea at all," said Connie. "Regardless of where the computer is used, we will always need someone in the warehouse to feed data into the computer terminals. But if you can't keep up with the job as it is now, what's the point of trying to train you for the computer operation?"

"Ever since the computer came into the company, I've been wondering what it would do to me," said Buddy. "My wife tells me that it's got me talking in my sleep. The big thing going for me has always been my skill with figures. If the computer can do it all faster and better than I can, where will that leave me?"

"It will leave you with a better job than before, if you show that you can handle the changes that may come," said Connie.

"To tell the truth," said Buddy, "one reason my figures may not be as good as they used to be is that I can't see what use they are if the computer is going to do the same work anyway."

"That may come later," said Connie. "For the time being, we need the day-by-day figures that your running totals provide us. The computer system is set up now only to produce monthly totals from the data the accounting department gives it. For the time being, at least, we need your perpetuals as much as ever."

"That puts a different light on my performance," said Buddy. "I can get back on the track without your talking about firing me."

"Let's forget about that," said Connie. "I guess I was a little off-base."

"Okay," said Buddy, "but what makes you think my job might be even better because of the computer?"

"The computer will take a lot of the drudgery out of your record posting and tabulations. It will leave you free to spend more time verifying the counts of materials recorded on the incoming bills of lading and on the outgoing shipping tickets. This will make you more than a bean counter, valuable as that may be. You'll be helping the company to make sure that it gets what it's paying for and shipping to customers only as much as has been purchased."

1. How well did Connie identify the real cause of Buddy's deteriorating performance? What do you think was the main cause?

2. What do you think about Connie's decision to put Buddy on notice?

3. Where in the problem-solving process did Connie fail to give sufficient attention?

Model 2

Getting Employee Commitment to a Plan

Experience shows that supervisors who follow this sequence of steps are likely to get better results when seeking to get an employee's agreement and commitment to a plan of action and/or of planned goals than those supervisors who don't.

Step 1.   State the broad goal or plan.

Step 2.   Ask the employee's view of what his or her objectives should be in relation to the broad goal or plan.

Step 3.   Negotiate unrealistically high or low objectives.

Step 4.   Agree on objectives that are clear, specific, and measurable.

Step 5.   Confirm the details of the employee's commitment and set up a review date.

The Situation

Sara is an accounts receivable supervisor in the credit and collections department of a consumer finance company. She is outlining her department's goals for the next year. She needs the commitment of Jose, one of the telephone collectors, to the part he will play in carrying out the plan. Sara has called Jose into her office to talk about it.

Dialogue

1. Sara: The plan for our department for the next year includes a goal of reducing our average days outstanding for our accounts receivable from 45 days to 40 days. That's about an 11 percent reduction. We think that if everyone makes a real strong effort on this, we should be able to improve at least that much.

2. Jose: That doesn't mean that everyone has to be at 40 days, does it?

3. Sara: No. That's the department average. Some people will average 40, some will average below 40, and some above 40. The goal is for everyone to improve so that the overall average is 40 or less.

4. Jose: I see. Okay.

5. Sara: Now, you've done a good job this year with your accounts. You've got some difficult slow payers in your group. This year your average was 49 days. If we don't add any new accounts to your group next year, what do you think you could get that average down to?

6. Jose: No new accounts? Oh, I'd say maybe 47 days.

7. Sara: Well, that would be about a 4 percent reduction. That's not bad. But think about this: If you're not given any new accounts next year, you'll end up with fewer accounts at the end of the year. You know, we always lose some accounts each year and we also pick up new ones, but none of the new accounts will be assigned to you. So, you should have more time to spend on fewer accounts.

8. Jose: Yeah, I guess that would make a difference. Maybe I could get down to 45 days.

Actually, our annual turnover of accounts runs about 10 percent. So with 10 percent fewer accounts, you should be able to get your average down to 45 days.

10. Jose: That makes sense. I can do that.

11. Sara: Good. I'm glad you agree. We know from experience that the more often you call your overdue accounts, the sooner they're likely to pay their outstanding bills. If you use this extra time to call those accounts more often, your average will go down. But if you concentrate most of that extra time on your slowest payers, you'll get your best improvement.

12. Jose: And I've got some real slow payers.

13. Sara: If you use that extra time on—let's see—your ten slowest payers (they average about 55 days) you might get enough improvement just from them to bring your average below 45 days.

14. Jose: That's a good idea. I think it might work.

15. Sara: Okay. So your goal for the coming fiscal year is to get the average days outstanding for your accounts down to 45 days. No new accounts will be added to your group during the year. And you'll use the extra time you pick up from lost accounts to concentrate on calling your ten slowest accounts more often. Is that a fair statement of what we've agreed on?

16. Jose: That's right on the mark.

17. Sara: Great. Now, I want to check with you from time to time to see how things are going. For example, if your turnover of accounts turns out to be less than we expect, we may have to make some adjustments. Let's get together again on August 15. We'll have the July figures by then and we'll take a look at how the first month went.

18. Jose: Okay, Sara. I'll do my best.

19. Sara: I know you will. And I appreciate your cooperation, Jose.

Model Analysis

A. Identify by the numbers of the lines in the dialogue where Sara applied Step 1, stating the broad plan or goal.

B. Identify by line numbers in the dialogue where Sara applied Step 2, asking Jose his views about his objectives in relation to her plan.

C. Identify by line numbers in the dialogue where Sara applied Step 3 by negotiating with Jose to make sure that his goals were neither too high nor too low.

D. Identify by line numbers in the dialogue where Sara applied Step 4 by getting agreement on objectives for Jose that are clear, specific, and measurable.

E. Identify by line numbers in the dialogue where Sara applied Step 5 by (1) confirming the details of Jose's agreement and (2) by setting up a review date.

F. Recall, and describe briefly, a situation involving a problem with getting an employee's agreement with a plan or commitment to a goal. Try role playing the supervisor, with someone else in the group taking the part of the subordinate. Get feedback from the group and the instructor to (1) sharpen your sense of when to apply each of the model's steps and (2) improve the skill with which you handle each of the steps.

Model 3

Dealing with Employee Response to Controls

Experience shows that supervisors who follow this sequence of steps are likely to get better results when dealing with employee problems associated with their response and possible resistance to controls than supervisors who don't.

Step 1. State the problem caused by the employee's response to controls and confirm the purpose of the controls.

Step 2. Get the employee's view of the problem.

Step 3. Ask the employee for his or her solution.

Step 4. Agree on a solution that takes into account the employee's response as well as the purpose of the controls.

Step 5. Confirm the employee's commitment to the solution and set up a date for review.

The Situation

George, the supervisor of a shipping department, has set up a simple use, or tally, form at the strapping machine that automatically wraps steel banding around heavy cartons. He wants to maintain some sort of control over jobs for which the machine is needed. Bob, one of the shipping department employees, consistently fails to make the required entries on the form. George has called Bob into his office to discuss the problem that this causes.

Dialogue

1. Bob: Did you want to see me, George?
2. George: Yes, Bob. Come on in. Have a seat. Thanks for stopping by. I see your wrist isn't strapped. Is the sprain all healed?
3. Bob: Yes, it works okay now.
4. George: Good. Bob, I asked you to come in because I want to talk to you about the problems I have when you don't fill out the usage forms at the case-strapping machine, which happens often. You see, I use the information on that form to keep track of whether our materials use plan is on target. That means I don't have reliable information if someone doesn't fill out that form when he or she does a run on the strapping machine. Now, tell me, why don't you fill that form out every time you do a run?
5. Bob: I don't know.
6. George: You don't know.
7. Bob: No.
8. George: Do you object to filling it out?
9. Bob: No.
10. George: Do you understand why it's important to me?
11. Bob: Yeah, I guess so.
12. George: Bob, are you saying there is no reason why you don't fill out the form?
13. Bob: I guess I am.
14. George: Don't you think there must be some reason?
15. Bob: I guess so.
16. George: Try to think about what it might be.
17. Bob: I guess the reason is that I forget sometimes.

18. George: You sometimes forget to fill out the form. What do you think we could do that would always help you remember to do it?

19. Bob: I don't know.

20. George: Well, think about it.

21. Bob: Maybe someone in the shop could remind me.

22. George: That's a possibility. Who do you think might do that?

23. Bob: Well, maybe Joe.

24. George: Is Joe always around when you make a run?

25. Bob: No.

26. George: Then that wouldn't always work.

27. Bob: No, I guess not. Maybe we could put up a sign.

28. George: That's a good idea. Where could we put it to make sure you would look at it when you did a run?

29. Bob: Maybe on the strapping machine?

30. George: Okay. Where on the machine would you put it?

31. Bob: Well, I guess right next to the run button.

32. George: So, when you push the run button you'll see the sign and fill out the form while the job is running.

33. Bob: Yeah.

34. George: Will you make the sign and put it on the machine today?

35. Bob: Okay. I'll do it as soon as I get back to the shop.

36. George: I think you've come up with the solution. I don't see any reason why this shouldn't work. Do you?

37. Bob: No. It should work.

38. George: All right, let's go over what we've agreed on. You're going to make a small sign today—a label, I guess—and you'll stick it on the strapping machine right next to the run button. Then, whenever you do a run, that label will remind you to fill out the form while the job is running. So, it will no longer be possible for you to run a job and forget to fill out the form.

39. Bob: Right.

40. George: And you're confident this will solve the problem.

41. Bob: Yeah. I'm sure it will.

42. George: I'm sure it will, too. And I appreciate your helping me out with this problem. From now on I can be sure of my figures. That's one less headache for me. Bob, let's get together again first thing on Monday the 20th and see how this is going. Okay?

43. Bob: Okay. Monday the 20th, first thing in the morning.

44. George: And thanks again.

Model Analysis

A. Identify by the numbers of the lines in the dialogue where George applied Step 1 by stating the problem caused by Bob's failure to fill out the usage form.

B. Identify by line numbers in the dialogue where George applied Step 2 by getting Bob's views of the problem.

C. Identify by line numbers in the dialogue where George applied Step 3 by getting Bob's thoughts about a solution to the problem.

D. Identify by line numbers in the dialogue where George applied Step 4 by reaching an agreement with Bob about a solution.

E. Identify by line numbers in the dialogue where George applied Step 5 by (1) confirming Bob's commitment to the solution and (2) setting up a review date.

F. Recall, and describe briefly, a situation involving a problem with an employee's negative response to controls. Try role playing the supervisor, with someone in the group taking the part of the subordinate. Get feedback from the group and the instructor to (1) sharpen your sense of when to apply each of the model's steps and (2) improve the skill with which you handle each of the steps.

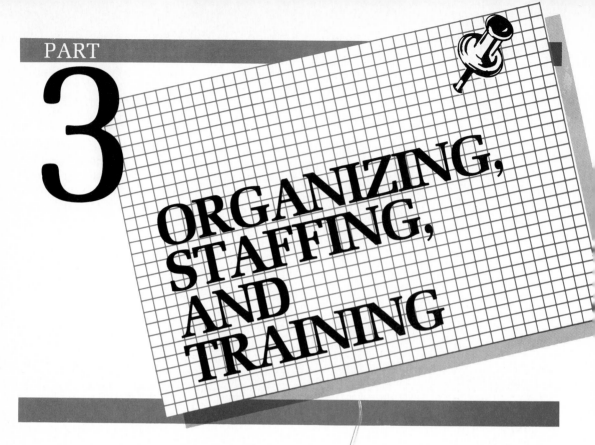

PART 3

ORGANIZING, STAFFING, AND TRAINING

Success in supervision turns on the ability to gather together the best available human resources in the most effective organizational arrangement. To do so, jobs and positions should be carefully specified. Employees must be selected and placed in these jobs with care. Employee performance should be appraised periodically. Training and development of employees is necessary to make and keep them fit for their jobs. In all, five aspects of human resources management will be stressed here:

● The need for organizational structures and for being able to design structures that suit a department's goals and resources.
● Use of your knowledge of human needs and behavior to provide the most effective staff for your organization.
● Further pursuit of an understanding of organization design so as to facilitate job analysis, job evaluation, and compensation processes.
● Relating job specifications to the performance requirements of those who perform these jobs and conducting appraisals that provide proper correction and motivation.
● Applying knowledge of job requirements and human resources to the training and development of employees.

Supervisors recognize the importance of the organizing and staffing function in that they appreciate the need to have authority commensurate with responsibilities. Survey figures demonstrate the following (figures indicate percentages):

1. Supervisors Usually Have Authority to Carry Out Their Responsibilities.

Overall, would you say that you are given enough authority to carry out your responsibilities?

82   Yes
18   No

2. Most Supervisors Say That They Have a Large Enough Work Force and an Adequate Say in Selecting New Employees.

Would you say that you are usually given enough people to get the work of your department completed properly and on time?

72   Yes
28   No

When new employees are hired or placed in your department, in most instances, do you have final say on acceptance or rejection?

63   Yes
37   No

3. Supervisors Believe That Performance Appraisals Are Worth the Effort.

If your company has a formal employee performance appraisal or merit rating program [80 percent say they do], what is your opinion of the program's effectiveness in achieving each of the following objectives?

	Very effective	Somewhat effective	Not effective
Motivating employees to improve performance	23	62	15
Providing a basis for division or discharge	32	53	15
Providing a basis for training and development	28	54	18

4. Supervisors Are Deeply Involved in Employee Training Programs.

How do employees in your department usually receive job training?

93   They work along with experienced employees.
44   They receive special training from the company training department.
28   They receive special training from outside the company.
58   I personally provide the training.
6   They receive no special training.

10

ORGANIZING AN EFFECTIVE DEPARTMENT

What is an organization?

An organization is a grouping together of people so that they can work effectively toward a goal that members of the group want to achieve.

The goal of a business organization is primarily profits for stockholders and salaries and wages for managers, supervisors, and employees. There are other important goals, too, such as supplying goods and services to the general population or producing military materials for our defense in time of war. And members of the organization all aim for other satisfactions, too, such as fellowship, accomplishment, and prestige.

Why organize in the first place?

We'd have nothing but havoc without organization. We take organization for granted because we have lived so long with it at home, in places of worship, and at school. Little we do together would be effective if we didn't agree among ourselves as to who should do what. And since business organizations are under tremendous pressures to be effective, their organization tends to be more formal and rigid.

After the Dallas Cowboys won the professional football Super Bowl in 1978, one sportswriter made the comment that the victory wasn't the real accomplishment. "The thing that sets the Cowboys apart from other strong National Football League teams," said Phil Elderkin of the *Christian Science Monitor,* "is their ability as an organization. From the front office to the playing field, everything is done with calculated precision."

The overriding value of an organization, then, is its ability to make a more effective use of human resources. Employees working alone and often at cross-purposes require the coordination and direction that an organization can provide. People working together within a sensible organizational structure have a greater sense of purpose and accomplish more than people whose efforts are allowed to run off in any direction they choose.

Are all organizations formal?

No. In a good many of our activities, even in complex manufacturing plants, some people just naturally take over responsibilities and exercise authority without anyone's ever spelling them out. Chances are that in a group of 15 employees who you might imagine are all at the same level, you'll discover some sort of informal organization. It may be that the person who sweeps the floors actually swings weight in that group. Acting as staff assistant may be the lift-truck driver, who is the informant. The rest of the group may either work hard or stage a slowdown at a nod from a third member of the group, who has authority as surely as if the company president had given it.

So be alert to informal organization—among the employees you supervise, in the supervisory group itself, and in the entire management structure.

What is meant by the division of labor?

Sometimes called the "division of work," this is the process whereby the total amount of work that must be done by an organization is divided up among its members. This process is called "organizing." Typically, it follows these steps:

1. Making a list of all the tasks that must be performed by the organization to accomplish its objectives.
2. Dividing up these tasks into activities that can be performed by one person. Each person will then have a group of activities to perform, called a job. This in turn allows each person to become more proficient at his or her special job.
3. Grouping together related jobs (such as production jobs or accounting jobs) in a logical and efficient manner. This creates specialized departments or sections of the organization.
4. Establishing relationships between the various jobs and groupings of jobs so that all members of an organization will have a clear idea of their responsibilities and, either their dependence on, or their control over people in other jobs or groups of jobs.

Which comes first, the organization or the work to be done?

If there were no job to do, there would be no reason for having an organization. So don't make the mistake of being organization-happy and trying to set up an elaborate organization just for the sake of having one. The best organization is a simple one that puts people together so that the job at hand gets done better, more quickly, and more cheaply than any other way.

What is the purpose of organization charts?

To help you understand organizational relationships. Such charts are really pictures of how one job or department fits in with others. Each box, or rectangle, encloses an activity or department. Those boxes on the same horizontal level on the chart tend to have the same degree of authority or power and to have their work closely related. Departments in boxes on the next higher level have greater authority; those at lower levels have less authority. Clusters of boxes that enclose departments performing closely related functions (such as shaping, fabricating, assembly, and finishing in a manufacturing plant) are typically connected in a vertical chain to the head manager of that particular function (such as the production manager).

Boxes containing line departments tend to descend from the top of the chart to the bottom (where supervisors' departments typically are) in vertical chains. Boxes that enclose staff departments tend to branch out to either side of the main flow of authority.

Organization charts can be drawn any way that shows relationships best, even in circles; but for practical purposes most charting is done in the manner just described and illustrated in Figure 10-1. One note of caution: Organization structures and staffing change constantly. Accordingly, organization charts go out of date very quickly.

What's the difference between line and staff?

An organization works best when it gets many related jobs done effectively with the minimum of friction. This requires coordination and determination of what to do and how to do it. Those managers and supervisors whose main job it is to see that things get done are usually considered members of the *line* organization. Other management people who help them to decide what to do and how to do it, assist in coordinating the efforts of all, or provide service are usually called *staff* people. (See Figure 10-1.)

In manufacturing plants, line activities are most commonly performed by production departments, sales departments, and, occasionally, purchasing departments. The production supervisor or first-line supervisor is likely to be a member of the line organization.

Departments that help the line departments control quality and maintain adequate records are typically staff departments. Industrial engineering, maintenance, research, accounting, and personnel relations are some other examples of typical staff activities.

In service organizations such as banks and insurance firms, the line organization may represent the primary "action" operations (such as deposits and withdrawals and recordkeeping, or premium collections and claim settlements) and the staff organization such support groups as computer departments and actuarial.

In hotels and motels the line may be everything connected with the operation of a geographic unit, and the staff such activities as advertising, accounting, and legal.

In transport companies the line department may be fleet operations; the staff department, equipment repair and maintenance.

In a hospital, medical and nursing may be the line groups, with laboratory, culinary, and housekeeping the staff groups.

It may help you to think of line people as the doers, staff people as the advisors. Each function—line or staff—is important in its own way, even though there has often been rivalry between line and staff people for credit and recognition.

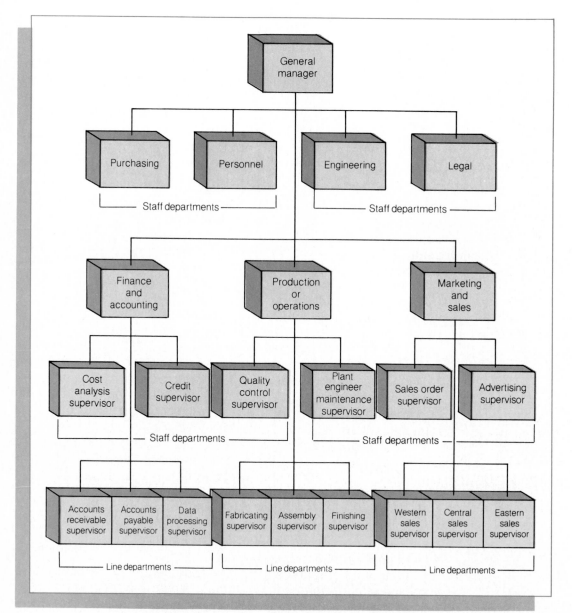

Figure 10-1. Line-and staff organization in a manufacturing company.

PART 3 • ORGANIZING, STAFFING, AND TRAINING

Is the line-and-staff structure the only way to organize?

No, although it is the most common and is found in most organizations. There are other commonly used ways to put together an organization:

Functional.   Each group of related activities is collected under one functional head, as shown in Figure 10-2. Most line-and-staff organizations tend to be somewhat functional in concept, however, and it may often be hard to make the distinction.

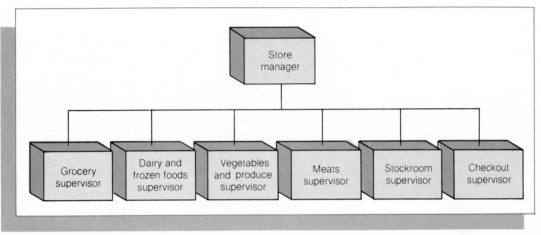

Figure 10-2. Example of functional organization design for a supermarket.

Divisional or Product.   All functions needed to make a particular product, for example, are gathered under one highly placed manager. If a firm manufactures tractors for farmers, road graders for construction contractors, and lawn mowers for home use, it might "divisionalize" in order to make and sell each major product in its product line, as shown in Figure 10-3. Note that under each division head this organization is essentially a functional one; as a consequence, labels such as "functional" and "divisional" can be misleading.

Geographic.   A firm may divide some of its activities, such as sales, or all of its activities according to the geographic region where these take place (Figure 10-4).

Customer.   A company may also choose to organize some or all of its activities according to the customers it serves, such as farmers,

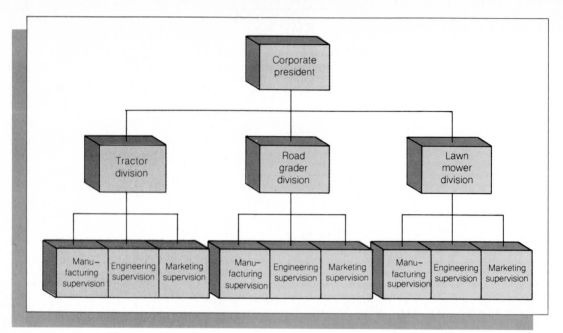

Figure 10-3. Example of product or divisional organization design for a manufacturing company.

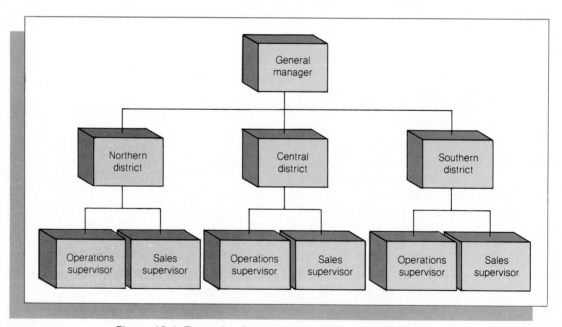

Figure 10-4. Example of geographic organization design for an insurance company.

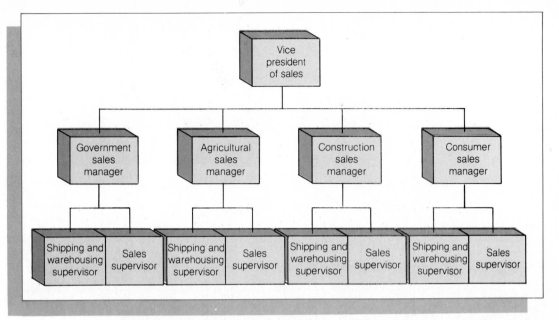

Figure 10-5. Example of customer-(or market-)oriented organization design. This is a line type of organization, with the main line of authority running from the vice president of sales through the sales managers down to the shipping, warehousing, and sales supervisors.

contractors, and home owners. This kind of organization (Figure 10-5) is closely related to the product organization.

Project, Matrix, or Task Force. This form is commonly used in research and development organizations and engineering firms for one-of-a-kind projects or contracts. It allows a project manager to call on the time and skills of personnel—for a limited period of time—with various functional specialties. When the project is completed, the specialized personnel return to their home units to await assignment to another project. Because project managers can exercise their authority horizontally across the basic organization while the specialists receive permanent authority from their functional bosses above them vertically on the chart (Figure 10-6), this form is called a matrix organization.

Regardless of organization type, always remember that the purpose of the organizational structure is to make your department's work more nearly fit together with the work of other departments.

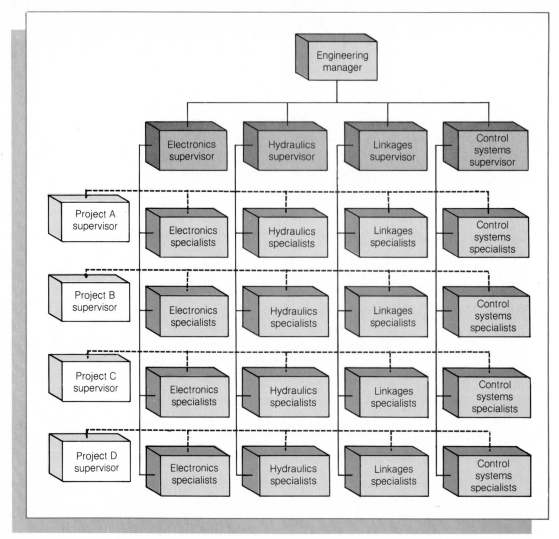

Figure 10-6. Example of project or task force (matrix) organizational design.

What is the distinction between a centralized and a decentralized organization?

A *centralized* organization tends to have many levels of management; to concentrate its facilities in one location; to perform certain functions (such as engineering, labor negotiations, computer operations, and purchasing) from a single source; and to gather together its power and authority at headquarters. A *decentralized* organization tends to have the opposite characteristics, especially when a company is divided into distinctly separate units with varying degrees of independence. These units may be set up along product lines, according to geography, or according to methods of marketing and distribution.

Centralized organizations tend to have more levels of management, to exert tighter controls, and to allow employees less freedom to make their own decisions. Decentralized organizations have fewer levels of management, have looser controls, and allow employees greater freedom in their actions.

What is the Table of Organization (TO)?

This expression (derived from military staffing practices) implies that, for each department or unit, (1) staffing is limited to certain specified positions and (2) a specified number of people are prescribed for each position. When a department is "not up to its TO," this means that either vacancies exist as positions with no incumbents, or the number of incumbents in one or more position classes is less than that prescribed, or some combination of the two. The TO principle can beneficially be applied to business if the specific TO capacity (or productivity) is carefully related to the organization's responsibilities and goals.

How wide can a supervisor's span of control be?

Authorities disagree on this point, but it is a good rule of thumb that no manager or supervisor should have the responsibility for more than six separate activities. The more specialized and complex the activities, the shorter the span of control. The more uniform and less complicated the activities (as with many supervisory responsibilities), the greater the span can be. Sometimes the span of control (or of management) is defined by the number of people rather than by the number of activities. When such is the case, it is not unusual for a supervisor to have a span of 30 or more employees, provided they are engaged in only a few simple, related activities. On the other hand, a middle-level manager might be responsible for the activities managed by the supervisors of six different departments.

Are authority and responsibility the same thing?

No. Authority should go hand in hand with responsibility, but the two are no more alike than are the two sides of a coin. Your *responsibilities* are those things you are held accountable for—such as costs, on-time deliveries, and good housekeeping. Responsibilities are also spoken of as your duties—such as checking time cards, investigating accidents, scheduling employees, and keeping production records. *Authority* is the power you need to carry out your responsibilities. A supervisor's authority includes the right to make decisions, to take action to control costs and quality, and to exercise necessary discipline over the employees assigned to help carry out these responsibilities.

It's an axiom that you shouldn't be given a responsibility without enough authority to carry it out. If a supervisor is given responsibility for seeing that quality is up to specifications, that supervisor must also be given authority to stop the production line when the quality falls off or to take any steps necessary to correct the condition.

Where does your organizational authority come from?

Authority, like responsibility, is usually handed down to supervisors from their immediate bosses. The bosses in turn receive their authority and responsibilities from their immediate superiors. And so it goes, on up to the company president, who receives assignments from the board of directors. This process of handing down responsibility and authority is known as delegation.

The biggest chunk of authority and responsibility rests with the company president, who may split this chunk in as few as 3 pieces (to the vice presidents of production, sales and financing) or as many as 20 (to vice presidents in charge of 20 different products). As the responsibilities and authorities come down the line to you, the pieces get smaller. But they also get much more specific.

Your plant superintendent may have the responsibility for producing goods in sufficient quantities to meet sales requirements, whereas your responsibility may be to see that ten milling machines are operated at optimum capacity so that 200,000 product units are produced each month. Similarly, the plant superintendent's authority may permit the exercise of broad disciplinary measures, whereas yours may be limited to recommending disciplinary action for employees who break rules or whose output is not up to production and quality standards.

Most companies try to make the responsibilities and authorities at each level of management fairly consistent. For instance, a supervisor in Department A should have the same general responsibilities as a supervisor in Department Z. And their authorities would be generally the same even though the specific duties of each might differ widely.

Figure 10-7 is a checklist that might help you and your boss to decide duties, policies, and actions for which you are held responsible.

What other sources can you draw on for your authority?

In addition to your organizational "right" to get things done, you may often need to draw from other, more personal sources. Your employer tries to establish your organizational rights by granting you a title or a rank, by depicting your position on an organization chart, and through some visible demonstration of status, such as a desk or an office or some special privilege. Ordinarily you must reinforce this authority—or power—with one of the following:

- Your job knowledge or craftsmanship
- Your personal influence in the organization (whom you know and can get to help you or your team)
- Your personal charm (if you have it)
- You ability to see that things get done (performance)
- Your persuasive ability (a communication skill)
- Occasionally your muscle or physical strength

All these sources are important because employees tend to restrict their acknowledgment of organizational rights over them. They expect their supervisors to show a little more real power than that. When employees come to accept your authority as deserved or earned (*acceptance* theory of authority rather than *institutional*), you will find that your people relationships will improve.

Should a distinction be drawn among authority, responsibility, and accountability?

Yes, although it may appear to you to be only a technical one. As your boss, for example, I might be held accountable to higher management for the way in which operating supplies are conserved in my department. But I have the prerogative to delegate this responsi-

SUPERVISORY RESPONSIBILITY SURVEY

Do you feel it is your responsibility to . . .		Yes	No	Don't Know
. . . select and train your employees?	1. Request that additional employees be hired as needed?	___	___	___
	2. Approve new employees assigned to you?	___	___	___
	3. Explain benefit plans to employees?	___	___	___
	4. Tell employees about upgrading and pay ranges?	___	___	___
	5. Make sure employees know rules of conduct and safety regulations?	___	___	___
	6. Train an understudy?	___	___	___
	7. Hold regular safety meetings?	___	___	___
. . . make work assignments and maintain discipline?	8. Prepare employee work schedules?	___	___	___
	9. Assign specific duties to workers?	___	___	___
	10. Assign responsibilities to assistants or group leaders?	___	___	___
	11. Delegate authority?	___	___	___
	12. Discipline employees?	___	___	___
	13. Discharge employees?	___	___	___
	14. Specify the kind and number of employees to do a job?	___	___	___
	15. Determine the amount of work to be done by each employee in your group?	___	___	___
	16. Authorize overtime?	___	___	___
	17. Enforce safety rules?	___	___	___
	18. Transfer employees within your department?	___	___	___
. . . handle employee problems with the union?	19. Interpret the union contract?	___	___	___
	20. Process grievances with shop stewards?	___	___	___
	21. Prepare vacation schedules?	___	___	___
	22. Recommend changes in the contract?	___	___	___
	23. Lay off employees for lack of work?	___	___	___
	24. Grant leaves of absence?	___	___	___
. . . know how pay and incentive systems work?	25. Explain to employees how their pay is calculated?	___	___	___
	26. Determine allowances for faulty material or interruptions?	___	___	___
	27. Approve piece rates or standards before they become effective?	___	___	___
	28. Answer employees' questions regarding time studies or allowances?	___	___	___

Figure 10-7.

SUPERVISORY RESPONSIBILITY SURVEY

Do you feel it is your responsibility to . . .		Yes	No	Don't Know

. . . make these operating decisions?

	Yes	No	Don't Know
29. Start jobs in process?	___	___	___
30. Stop jobs in process?	___	___	___
31. Authorize setup changes?	___	___	___
32. Approve material substitutions?	___	___	___
33. Requisition supplies to keep your department running?	___	___	___
34. Determine whether material should be scrapped or reworked?	___	___	___
35. Replan schedules upset by breakdowns?	___	___	___
36. Take unsafe tools out of service?	___	___	___
37. Correct unsafe working conditions?	___	___	___

. . . tie in with other departments?

	Yes	No	Don't Know
38. Know how an order flows through the company from start to finish?	___	___	___
39. Understand what the staff departments do? Your relationship to them?	___	___	___
40. Authorize maintenance and repair jobs?	___	___	___
41. Requisition tools?	___	___	___
42. Investigate accidents?	___	___	___

. . . be concerned with the way the job gets done?

	Yes	No	Don't Know
43. Make suggestions for improvements in operating procedures in your department?	___	___	___
44. Recommend changes in department layout?	___	___	___
45. Suggest material handling methods to be used in your department?	___	___	___
46. Discuss with staff members the operating problems caused by proposed design changes?	___	___	___

. . . think about how much things cost?

	Yes	No	Don't Know
47. Cut down on waste of materials and supplies?	___	___	___
48. Keep adequate production records for checking output per machine and per worker-hour?	___	___	___
49. Participate in setting up your department budget?	___	___	___
50. Investigate charges against your budget?	___	___	___

Figure 10-7 (continued).

bility to you—if I also grant you the authority to take any steps needed to protect these supplies. If you were to misuse these supplies or to lose track of them, I might discipline you for failing to discharge your responsibility in this matter. But I'd still be held accountable to my boss (and would be subject to discipline) for what happened—no matter which one of us was at fault. Similarly, when you delegate a minor responsibility to one of your employees (together with the necessary authority to carry it out), you will still be held accountable to your boss for the way in which this responsibility is fulfilled by your subordinate. In other words, you can delegate responsibility, but you cannot delegate accountability.

How much leeway do supervisors have in taking authoritative action?

You can't draw a hard-and-fast rule to follow. Generally speaking, a company may establish three rough classifications of authority within which supervisors can make decisions:

- **Class 1.** Complete authority. Supervisors can take action without consulting their superiors.
- **Class 2.** Limited authority. Supervisors can take action they deem fit so long as the superior is told about it afterward.
- **Class 3.** No authority. Supervisors can take no action until they check with the superior.

If many decisions fall into class 3, supervisors will become little more than messengers. To improve this situation, first learn more about your company's policy and then spend time finding out how your bosses would act. If you can convince them that you would handle matters as they might, your bosses are more likely to transfer class 3 decisions into class 2, and as you prove yourself, from class 2 to class 1.

Note that the existing company policy would still prevail. The big change would be in permitting supervisory discretion. And this would be because you have demonstrated that you are qualified to translate front-office policy into front-line action.

What is the chain of command?

The term *chain of command* is a military phrase used to imply that delegation of responsibility and authority and of orders and information in an organization should originate at the top, then proceed toward the bottom from each one-higher management level to the next-lower level without skipping any levels or crossing over to another chain of command. The same procedure would be followed by information and requests going up the line. Your boss needs up-to-date information about your work and its progress.

Is it a bad practice to go out of channels?

It's best to conform to the practice in your company. Channel is just a word to indicate the normal path that information, orders, or requests should travel when following the chain of command. The channel for customer orders to travel from the sales manager to the production supervisor might be from the sales manager to the production manager, from the production manager to the department superintendent, and from the department superintendent to the supervisor. It would be going out of channels if the sales manager gave the order directly to the supervisor.

The channel used by a supervisor to ask for a raise might be from the supervisor to the department head, from the department head to the production manager, and from the production manager to the manufacturing vice president. The supervisor would be going out of channels if the vice president were asked for a raise before each one of the other managers had been seen in progression.

Since authority and responsibility are delegated through the channels of a chain of command, for the most part it's better to handle your affairs (especially decisions) through them, too. It avoids your making changes without letting your boss know what's going on. And it prevents others from feeling that another manager is going over the boss's head.

On the other hand, there are occasions when chain-of-command channels should be circumvented. In emergencies, or when time is essential, it makes sense to get a decision or advice from a higher authority other than your boss if your boss is not readily available.

For purposes of keeping people informed and for exchanging information, channels sometimes get in the way. There's really nothing wrong with your discussing matters with people in other departments or on other levels of the company—so long as you don't betray confidences. If you do cross channels, it's a good practice to tell your boss you are doing so, and why. That way, you won't seem to be doing something behind your boss's back. And that is something you should never do.

How do staff people exert influence?

Staff departments exert influence, rather than real authority, because their responsibility is to advise and guide, not to take action themselves.

It's a mistake (in most cases) to assume that a staff department tells you how to do something. More often than not the staff department suggests that you do something differently, or advises that your department is off target (on quality, for instance), or provides information for your guidance. This isn't evasion. It's an honest recognition that the line people must retain the authority to run the department, but that to stand up to today's competition, you need the counsel of a specialist in some side areas.

If supervisors are smart, they will make every use they can of the staff department's knowledge. If you were building a house yourself for the first time and someone offered to furnish you free the advice of a first-rate carpenter, a top-notch mason, a heating specialist, and a journeyman painter, you'd jump at the chance. The same holds true in accepting the advice and guidance available from the staff departments and other specialists when you are tackling a management problem.

Who can delegate authority and responsibility?

Any member of management, including the supervisor, can usually delegate some responsibility—and authority. Remember, the two must go together.

A supervisor, for instance, who has responsibility for seeing that proper records are kept in the department may delegate that responsibility to a records clerk. But the clerk must also be given the authority to collect time sheets from the operators and to interview them if the data seems inaccurate. The supervisor wouldn't, however, delegate to the records clerk the authority to discipline an employee. Likewise, a supervisor can't delegate the accountability for seeing that accurate records are kept.

When should you delegate some of your work?

Delegate when you find you can't personally keep up with everything you feel you should do. Just giving minor time-consuming tasks to others will save your time for bigger things. Let one employee double-check the production report for example and send another employee down the line to see who wants to work overtime.

Arrange to have certain jobs taken over when you're absent from your department in an emergency or during vacation. Keep it to routine matters, if you will, and to those requiring a minimum of authority. But do try to get rid of the task of filling out routine requisitions and reports, making calculations and entries, checking supplies, and running errands.

How can you do a better job of delegating?

Start by thinking of yourself as primarily a manager. Recognize that no matter how good a person you might be, you'll always have more responsibilities than you can carry out yourself.

The trick of delegating is to concentrate on the most important matters yourself. Keep a close eye, for instance, on the trend of production costs: That's a big item. But let someone else check the temperature of the quenching oil in the heat treater. That's less important.

Trouble begins when you can't distinguish between the big and the little matters. You may feel you can put off checking the production record: It can wait until the day of reckoning at the end of the month. You may think that unless the quenching oil temperature is just right, the heat treater will spoil a $500 die today. But in the long run you'll lose your sanity if you don't see that the small jobs must get done by someone else.

Be ready, too, to give up certain work that you enjoy. A supervisor must learn to let go of those tasks that rightfully belong to a subordinate. Otherwise, larger and more demanding assignments may not get done. And don't worry too much about getting blamed by your boss for delegating to an employee work the boss has given to you. Generally speaking, supervisors should be interested only in seeing that the job is done the right way, not in who carries it out. See Figure 10-8 for an idea on how to decide what jobs to target for delegation.

Should you delegate everything?

Don't go too far. Some things are yours only. When a duty involves technical knowledge that only you possess, it would be wrong to let someone less able take over. And it's wrong to trust confidential information to others.

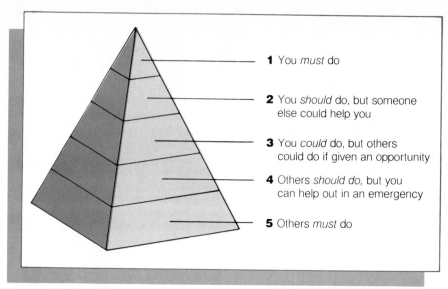

1 You *must* do

2 You *should* do, but someone else could help you

3 You *could* do, but others could do if given an opportunity

4 Others *should do*, but you can help out in an emergency

5 Others *must* do

Figure 10-8. Supervisor's task and delegation chart.

What should you tell employees about jobs delegated to them?

Give them a clear statement of what they are to do, how far they can go, and how much checking you intend to do. Let employees know the relative importance of the job so that they can judge how much attention it should receive. There's no point in letting an employee think that making a tally will lead to a promotion if you consider it just a routine task.

Tell employees why you delegated the job. If it shows you have confidence in them, they will try that much harder. But if they think you're pushing off all the dirty jobs on them, they may deliberately make mistakes.

Don't mislead employees about authority. You don't want them trying to crack your whip. But do define the scope of the task and see that others in your department know that this new task isn't something an employee assumed without authorization. Let it be known that you gave the assignment and that you'll expect cooperation from the other workers.

Why should employees accept a delegated job?

Employees who accept a delegated job outside of their own job responsibilities are really taking the job on speculation. They have a right to know what's in it for them:

- Employees who take on an extra duty get a chance to learn. If they have never seen how the individual records in the department are tabulated, here's a chance for them to get a better perception of what's going on.
- Delegated jobs provide more job satisfaction. Employees thrive on varied assignments. This is a chance to build interest by letting employees do something out of the ordinary.
- Delegation is sometimes a reward for other work well done. If you can truthfully say that you wouldn't trust anyone else with a certain delegated task, this will help build employee pride and a feeling of status.

Are there any organizational don'ts?

Yes, but not very many. Once an organization is set up, pragmatism and practicality ought to prevail. In fact, some odd—and informal—arrangements occasionally work out very well. For example, a highly successful Canton, Ohio, firm operated for years without a visual organization chart. Its president thought the staff would develop the most effective relationships without one, and apparently it did. Nevertheless, in the design stages, at least, there are a few hazards of organization that ought to be guarded against.

1. Don't let the chain of command get too long. Keep the number of responsibility levels at a minimum; otherwise, some information will never trickle all the way to the bottom.
2. Don't ask one person to report to two bosses. Anyone caught in this nutcracker knows the dilemma: Which boss's work comes first?
3. Don't make fuzzy job assignments. When there is a gray area between two positions, overlap, conflict, and duplication of effort are invited.
4. Don't be too rigid. Try to retain flexibility for contingent situations—those problems that inevitably crop up and need nonstandard assignments.

What can be done to help your department's organization adjust to changing conditions?

You can apply some of the techniques of organization development (OD). OD is a participative, rather than a purely management-directed, approach to organizing. It assumes that members of an organization (your employees, for instance) are more aware of conflicts and deficiencies caused by organizational constraints than the boss may be. To institute an informal OD program, a supervisor invites employees, singly at first and later when they are all together, to discuss their job roles and relationships. Specifically, employees are asked to comment on the appropriateness of their duties and responsibilities, the extent of their authority, and the way in which their jobs mesh with or abrade other jobs. Inevitably, this brings into the open problems that can be attributed to the division of labor and the organizational structure. At that point, the supervisor and employees try to solve these problems constructively, rather than to criticize and place blame on one another. For example:

1. OD strives to achieve clarity of each person's role in the organization. Group discussions consider such questions as: "What is Bill's role and what is my role?" "What is the extent of authority that Mary has when working on urgent, red-rush projects?" "What can we expect from the records department and how much must we do ourselves?"

2. OD helps to set priorities. It answers such questions as: "When we have six requests from sales for special handling of orders, which gets our attention first? Who decides this?" "In the event of a conflict between a quality standard and a shipping deadline, who makes this decision?" "When it comes to working on my job or helping out with Pete's job, which comes first?"

3. OD seeks to settle staffing problems. It encourages employees to find answers to questions such as these: "Which one of us will get the services of temporary help when it arrives?" "If my job gets to be too much for me during the Christmas rush, what kind of assistance can I expect?" "If there is a slowdown this summer, will Adam continue to work with me, or will he be transferred to another operation?"

Key Concepts

1. Organizations provide the structure within which different individuals with different skills can combine their efforts effectively in the pursuit and attainment of common goals. The first-line supervisor represents the cutting edge of most organizational structures, causing them to succeed or fail.

2. Charts and descriptions of organizational structures, although valuable as starting points, never fully define or stabilize the complexities of informal relationships at all levels, which may take precedence over the formally prescribed ones.

3. Whereas formal channels for discharging responsibility and authority must be respected in most instances, it is usually wise for supervisors to modify their decisions and actions in accordance with the organizational relationships observed by their peers and superiors.

4. Better-than-average supervisors are the ones who know how to appeal for and put to use the specialized advice and guidance available from staff departments.

5. The ability of a supervisor to divide up his or her work effectively among subordinates—to delegate—is probably the single most important factor in success or failure as a manager.

Supervisory Word Power

Accountability. A supervisor or manager's liability for the way in which organizational obligations are discharged, either personally or by those subordinates to whom he or she has delegated responsibility and authority to perform them.

Delegation. The assignment, or entrustment, to subordinates of organizational responsibilities and obligations along with appropriate organizational authority, power, and rights.

Line and Staff. The most common kind of organizational structure, in which line managers hold accountability for results that most directly affect profits, or other corporate goals, and staff managers hold accountability for results that most directly affect the processes by which line managers accomplish their goals.

Organization. The structure derived from systematic grouping of the tasks to be performed and from establishing formal relationships that strengthen the ability of people to work more effectively together in pursuing common objectives.

Responsibility and Authority. An obligation on the part of a manager or supervisor to see that certain organizational tasks are performed, coupled inseparably with the power necessary to carry out these tasks.

Reading Comprehension

1. What is the real purpose for creating an organization?

2. What is the purpose of an organizational chart? Is it possible to do without one?

3. Compare the formal organization with the informal organization.

4. In a manufacturing organization, which departments are likely to be line and which ones staff?

---

5. In a service organization such as a bank, which departments are likely to be considered line and which staff?

6. Managers and supervisors choose the kind of organization structure that will best fulfill its basic purpose in their work group or department. What is this purpose?

7. On the basis of what you know of human relations, should managers who have the choice stress authority derived from the institution or authority stemming from employee acceptance? Why?

8. Why must authority and responsibility be passed together to subordinates?

9. Give examples of companies, departments, or other groups that might be likely to use matrix organization. What do these groups have in common?

10. Would it be a good thing to have an especially versatile employee report to the maintenance supervisor as well as to the production supervisor? Why?

Supervision in Action
The Case of the Fast-Food Cleanup. A Case Study in Human Relations Involving Organizational Practices, with Questions for You to Answer.

"Which is it going to be?" asked Charlie J., a porter at the Bronze Burger, a fast-food franchise restaurant in Cincinnati. "Am I going to sweep the parking lot, or am I going to mop up the kitchen?"

Charlie's question was directed at Karen W., manager of the Bronze Burger.

"It should be obvious to you that the kitchen takes precedence over the parking lot," said Karen. "Food is our business. We must keep the kitchen clean at all times. And if the cook tells you to clean the kitchen, you better hop to it."

"That's what you tell me now," said Charlie. "But you should have heard the blistering I got from the out-front service chief a couple of minutes ago. He said that if I didn't get the parking lot swept before noon, I could look for a new job."

"The out-front chief is right," said Karen. "You've got to keep after the outside of the shop or we will be losing business from customers who drive in and see containers and slopped food all over the lot. But, for the moment, the kitchen job comes first. Grab your mop and get going."

"You better tell that to the out-front chief. He'll have my hide otherwise," said Charlie.

"Don't worry about him," said Karen. "Just get the kitchen mopped now. When you finish that, get your broom and go outside to the parking lot."

Charlie returned to the kitchen, got his mop, and within a few minutes was swabbing its quarry-tile floor. When he was half through, Jerry, the out-front chief, rushed into the kitchen. "What's going on here?" Jerry demanded. "I told you to get the parking lot swept before noon. It's a mess out there."

"I'm only doing what I've been told," said Charlie.

"No, you're not. I told you to sweep the parking lot."

"Tell that to the cook," said Charlie. "And tell it to Karen, too. She's the boss, and she said to do what the cook told me to."

With that, Jerry stomped out front to where Karen was watching the work of the serving clerks.

Jerry grabbed her by the arm. "Karen," he said, "you'll have to do something about Charlie. And about the cook, too. Charlie is paying no attention to me. And the cook keeps insisting that Charlie do the kitchen work first."

"In this instance," said Karen, "Charlie and the cook are right. The kitchen needs mopping before any more food comes out of it today."

"The parking lot needs sweeping," said Jerry, "if you are going to have any customers. The place is a mess. You told me that the outside areas must be kept spotless. You also told me that Charlie was assigned to me for that duty."

"He is," said Karen, "but sometimes the kitchen work will have to come first."

Jerry threw down his apron and walked away.

Two days later Jerry told Charlie that the restaurant tables needed cleaning and that he should get to them when he could. Charlie shrugged and said, "I'll get to them when I've finished in the kitchen."

Karen, coming on shift, took one look at the state of the uncleaned tables in the restaurant, found Jerry, and said "What's happening out front? The tables are in terrible condition. Your responsibility is to see that they are kept spotless. We'll lose customers if this keeps up."

Jerry replied, "I am doing all I can. I spoke to Charlie about getting them cleaned up. As you told me the other day, his first responsibility is to the cook. After he finishes in the kitchen, he will get to the tables."

"That won't do," said Karen. "You and the cook will have to work out a better way of sharing Charlie's time."

1. What do you suggest Jerry do now?
2. What do you think of Karen's organizational setup?
3. If you were Charlie, what would your reaction be?
4. If you were Karen, how would you organize Charlie's work and his reporting relationships?

11

STAFFING WITH HUMAN RESOURCES

What are the symptoms of poor human resources staffing?

Costs so high that they don't allow your department to operate at a profit are the most obvious symptom. And your first corrective step should be to see that you have only the right number of employees on the job.

Signs of inefficient work force management also include a high turnover rate, excessive absences and lateness, lots of grievances, poor quality of work, and lowered output. Each one tells you that there's a big chance you don't have the right person working for you, or if you do, that that person isn't working on the right job at the right time.

What does it cost to put a new employee on the payroll?

It is not unusual for a manufacturing company to find that it costs over $4,000 for one net addition to its labor force at the assembly-worker level. This is not unusual when you consider the costs of running want ads, operating an employment office, handling paperwork, and breaking in the new person. For a technician, engineer, or programmer the figure could be $10,000 or more.

How much does it cost to keep an employee on the payroll for a year?

A conservative estimate of the cost of keeping a semiskilled factory or office worker on the payroll for one year is $16,000. Figure it this way. Salary for a good employee runs more than $10,000 a year. It costs an average of $1,500 to train and bring a new employee up to normal production. Another $500 is included to offset the cost of the one in three employees who doesn't work out. Add $2,500 in fringe benefits that don't show up in salary. And cap this off with another $1,500—cost of the depreciation on the capital investment that makes the job possible.

Consequently, each employee who works for you must return about $16,000 in productive efforts before the company can break even. If you supervise ten employees, you can figure you're managing a payroll of more than $160,000 per year. That's why human resources management is so important.

What phases of work force staffing concern supervisors most?

The supervisor's chief responsibilities for a department's work force management could be summed up by saying the supervisor should have the right worker on the right job at the right time. How can this be done? By making accurate forecasts of the number of workers needed to staff the department, by taking an active interest in the kind of employees the company hires, and by maintaining working conditions that can attract and hold the best employees.

People are an organization's most vital resource. They will make or break your department's performance. People are very costly resources, however. You should select them the way you would a new car and take equally good care of them once they have been hired.

How do you forecast work force requirements?

It's really a matter of looking ahead—and applying simple arithmetic. Time studies and labor standards all make a forecast more accurate, but you can do very well without them.

Step 1. Find out what your department is scheduled to produce for the next week, month, quarter, or as far ahead as you can determine. If you don't know that, the chances are slight that you'll make efficient use of the people who work for you.

Step 2. Calculate how much the work schedule means in terms of total worker-hours. You can do this by getting an estimate from the methods, industrial engineering, accounting, or planning and scheduling department—if one exists in your company. Their schedules are certainly based on machine-time and work-force estimates.

If worker-hour requirements aren't available elsewhere, you'll have to make your own estimate. Do this either by checking times for previous or similar jobs or by making careful estimates of the time required for each job. Keep your figures in terms of worker-hours or worker-days. But be specific and allow time for setups and teardowns. Try to recall delays associated with each job and allow time for these.

Where jobs are machine-controlled (that is, the job can't be done any faster than the speed at which the machine runs), base your estimates on (1) how long the machine will take to do each job—allowing for breakdowns and idle time—and (2) how many operator-hours are needed to run the machine.

Step 3. Convert your totals to worker-hours and divide by 8 to see how many worker-days it will take you to complete your schedule for the period you've selected.

Step 4. Divide the total worker-days by the number of working days during the period to find the number of employees you'll need. But don't stop here.

Step 5. Check how many indirect persons—housekeepers, material handlers, setup persons—you'll need to service the required number of employees during this period (unless you included these in Step 2).

Step 6. Add the number of employees (direct labor) to the number of indirect persons to get the total needed.

Step 7. Make allowances for absences. How many days absent per month do employees in your department average? How many worker-days a month do all your employees combined lose? Suppose, for example, it's 5 worker-days a month. That's just the same as saying that you can expect to be short-handed 5 days a month, which may interfere with meeting your schedule. If you add an extra employee to cover absences, you can expect to be overstaffed 15 days a month—which is costly.

Can you give an example of forecasting work force requirements?

1. Suppose your schedule shows that during July your department must produce 1,000 widgets, 250 gadgets, and 60 umphlets.
2. Widgets and gadgets are hand-assembly jobs. Umphlets are produced on a machine. Previous production records, or time studies, or standards show the following:

Widgets: Average 50 per day with 10 employees

$$\frac{1,000}{50} = 20 \text{ days}$$

20 days × 10 employees × 8 hours = 1,600 worker-hours

Gadgets: Average 10 per day with 2 employees

$$\frac{250}{10} = 25 \text{ days}$$

25 days × 2 employees × 8 hours = 400 worker-hours

Umphlets: Average 3 per day, allowing for down time, require 1 operator

$$\frac{60}{3} = 20 \text{ days}$$

20 days × 1 operator × 8 hours = 160 worker-hours

Total worker-hours for all three units:

1,600 worker-hours (widgets) + 400 worker-hours (gadgets) + 160 worker-hours (umphlets) = 2,160 worker-hours

3. Convert to worker-days:

$$\frac{2,160 \text{ worker-hours}}{8 \text{ hours per day}} = 270 \text{ worker-days per month}$$

4. Average number of employees needed for the month:

$$\frac{270 \text{ worker-days}}{20 \text{ days/month}} = 13\tfrac{1}{2} \text{ employees for the month}$$

5. Add number of indirect employees. Three materials handlers take care of the gadget and umphlet operation. A combination setup per-

---

son and packer handles the widget line. That's four employees each day all month.

6. Average number of employees needed in July:

$$
\begin{array}{rl}
13\frac{1}{2} & \text{direct} \\
\underline{4} & \text{indirect} \\
17\frac{1}{2} & \text{employees}
\end{array}
$$

7. Allowance for absences. Record for department shows your employees lose on the average a half-day per month:

$$17\frac{1}{2} \text{ employees} \times 4 \text{ hours per month absent} = 70 \text{ hours absent per month}$$

70 hours is about one-half of one employee for a month. So

$$
\begin{array}{rl}
17\frac{1}{2} & \text{employees needed} \\
\underline{\frac{1}{2}} & \text{employee for absences} \\
18 & \text{employees needed for the month of July}
\end{array}
$$

You should be cautioned that this is a simplified example. In some cases the numbers of employees needed cannot be averaged by estimating gross worker-hours. Transfers of employees between operations can become impractical or can even be prohibited. The supervisor in the example, for instance, might not be able to use the umphlet operator on the widget line, or the widget operator on the umphlet line. In addition, you cannot presume that in practice you will have unlimited machines for assignment. Accordingly, you will encounter scheduling bottlenecks because of machine or space limitations and may have to plan second or third shifts.

Should you overstaff or understaff?

That depends. If you plan for too many employees, department costs will go up unless your schedule and machine availability will permit you to assign them to productive jobs. It's bad, too, to have idle people in the shop or to use them on make-work jobs. Overstaffing, however, does allow you to set up production in emergencies and ensures your meeting delivery dates.

Understaffing can be just as bad. It can get you behind in schedule and in trouble on deliveries. It can also give employees the feeling of being overworked. And it doesn't give you much flexibility.

Your company can minimize both overstaffing and understaffing by pooling the work force estimates of each supervisor and maintaining an optimum-size labor pool as a cushion against unpredictables—such as unusual absences or a sharp upward adjustment in schedules.

How far ahead should you plan?

As far as you can—even a year ahead, if possible. Demands by employees for a guaranteed weekly or annual wage have mainly been for a guarantee of a more stable job.

Job stability is just as desirable to management as it is to labor. Layoffs and rehiring are costly. One very good way to minimize both is to make your forecast of work-force requirements accurate and to make them as far ahead as possible. That way you can smooth the hills and valleys of your labor requirements. There's little point in laying off five workers this month if you're going to need ten more workers a month from now. It's much better if you can level out the scheduling in your department so that you can keep, say, seven or eight of these employees working continuously all the time.

It's recognized that such optimum forecasting cannot always be done—that interruptions in supply, restrictions in storage capacity, and unpredictable demands by customers interfere with even the best plans.

What is meant by balancing the work force?

Making sure that the number of employees on hand just matches the work load. Most departments have peaks and valleys that last an hour or a day. Mismatches that extend over a week, however, are costly and should be avoided. One way to balance your employee work load more consistently is to prepare a look-ahead work-force trial balance, using a work sheet like the one illustrated in Figure 11-1. This example looks 12 months ahead. If your work load is changeable, you could make such a sheet month by month.

How do you measure employee turnover?

Turnover is the name given to the measure of how many people come to work for you and don't stay for one reason or another. Turnover includes employees who are hired or rehired and employees who are laid off, who quit, or who are discharged. It also includes those who either retire or die.

WORK FORCE TRIAL BALANCE PLANNING SHEET*

Dept: _____ Period: from _____ to _____.

1. Number of workers needed to meet present work load:
   Direct   _____
   Indirect   _____
      Subtotal   _____

2. Number of additional workers to allow for:
   A. Scheduled workday losses
      Holidays   _____
      Vacations   _____
      Subtotal   _____
   B. Unscheduled workday losses
      Sickness and other excused absences   _____
      Unexcused absences   _____
      Subtotal   _____

3. Total number of workers needed to staff department at beginning of
period: (Subtotal line 1 + Subtotal 2A + Subtotal 2B)   _____

4. Number of workers to be added during the period to:
   A. Replace anticipated work force losses
      Retirements   _____
      Promotions and transfers   _____
      Discharges   _____
      Leaves of absence   _____
      Subtotal   _____
   B. Replace unanticipated work force losses†
      Resignations and quits   _____
      Disabilities   _____
      Deaths   _____
         Subtotal   _____

5. Total number of employees needed to replace losses during the
period
         Subtotal 4A + Subtotal 4B   _____

6. Number of employees needed to meet anticipated change in
department work load during the period
   A. Additions to meet increase in work load   _____
   B. Less removals to allow for decrease in work load   (−)_____

7. Total number of workers needed at end of period:
         Number on line 3   _____
         Number on line 5   _____
         Number on line 6A or B (+ or −)   _____
            Total   _____

*All entries are in number of workers.
†If no past records are available, use 5% of the total on line 1.

Figure 11-1.

For consistency's sake the U.S. Department of Labor suggests that the rate of turnover compare only the total number of separations (quits, fires, deaths, etc.) with the average number of employees on your payroll during a particular period. The *rate of turnover* is calculated as follows:

$$\frac{\text{Number of separations} \times 100}{\text{Average size of work force}} = \text{Turnover percentage}$$

For instance, if you had an average of 50 employees during the month, but you laid off 3, the turnover would be 3. Your turnover rate would be $\frac{3 \times 100}{50} = 6$ percent per month. If that rate persisted, your turnover rate for the year would be 72 percent (6 × 12).

Turnover rates vary from department to department, from company to company, and from industry to industry. The national average for all business in the United States is about 7 percent per month, or 82 percent per year!

Decisions as to what kind of separations and hires to include in turnover computations vary from organization to organization. Obviously, if certain kinds of separations or hires are excluded, the turnover rates will be lower. So it's good to know exactly what the specifications are when comparing turnover rates.

What causes turnover?

Turnover is generally considered to be the single best measure of morale. Poor morale can result from many things. Two of the most important of these are poor supervision and having the wrong person on the wrong job. The wrong person on the wrong job can mean poor hiring procedures—or poor placement procedures after a good person is put on the payroll. This chapter will discuss the latter causes.

What's so bad about absenteeism?

Absences (like turnover) are costly—to the company as well as to the employee. If it costs about $16,000 per year to keep a person on the payroll, then each day that person is absent could cost your department something like $65, based on 240 working days per year. Don't be misled, either, by the hourly worker who says, "I don't get paid when I'm not here, so what do you lose?" Absences frequently create a need for overtime through delays in getting an operation started or a machine running. And every supervisor can testify to the aggravation absence and lateness cause. It's the biggest obstacle you have in your work-force planning—from day to day or from month to month.

There are two popular ways to compute absenteeism rates:

$$\text{Absenteeism rate} = \frac{\text{Total days absent}}{\text{Average size of work force}} \tag{1}$$

$$= \text{Average days absent per employee}$$

$$\text{Absenteeism rate} = \frac{\text{Total days absent} \times 100}{\text{Worker-days worked and worker-days lost}} \tag{2}$$

$$= \text{Percentage of scheduled worker-days lost}$$

For example, suppose at the end of 6 months a supervisor found that the schedule showed a crew of 25 employees working for 120 days. Examining the record, the supervisor found that 10 employees had worked every day (10 × 120) for 1,200 worker-days; 10 employees worked 116 days (10 × 116) for 1,160 worker-days; 3 employees worked only 110 days (3 × 110) for 330 worker-days; and 2 employees worked only 100 days (2 × 100) for 200 worker-days. The total of worker-days worked is 2,890. If all 25 employees had worked every day for 120 days, the total worker-days would have amounted to 3,000. Therefore, 110 worker-days were lost (3,000 − 2,890). The department's absenteeism rate would be:

$$\frac{110 \text{ days absent}}{25 \text{ employees}} = 4.4 \text{ days lost per employee} \atop \text{in 6 months or 8.8 days per year} \tag{1}$$

The percentage of scheduled worker-days lost each year would be calculated as follows:

$$\frac{110 \text{ days absent} \times 100}{2{,}890 + 110} = \frac{110 \times 100}{3{,}000} = 3.7 \text{ percent of} \atop \text{scheduled} \atop \text{worker-days lost} \tag{2}$$

National averages for days lost per employee range from 9 days per year to as high as 3 days per month (36 days per year). Absence and lateness, like turnover, can be controlled by good supervision. But it's better to avoid this demand on your supervisory time and skill if you can. And you can, by screening out applicants who have displayed these undesirable characteristics in the past or are likely to develop them on the job in your company—simply because they are unsuited for the work they were hired to do.

How can better hiring reduce turnover and absences?

Selecting the proper person to fit first the company and then the available job opening hits the turnover and absenteeism problem at its source. There are hundreds of thousands of people looking for work who would be misfits almost anywhere. But there are millions who would probably be out of place in your company. Sue doesn't like close work. Pete can't stand heavy work. Joe wants a job with lots of room for initiative. Alma wants a job where she doesn't have to think. And so on. Turnover and absences show that Sue, Pete, Joe, and Alma didn't find work to suit them in your company.

To complicate the matter further, Joe may want a job that allows for initiative, but maybe he doesn't have the native ability to produce without close supervision. Alma wants a job where she doesn't have to think, but maybe all those jobs call for someone who can work rapidly and Alma is slow as can be.

A third complication, and perhaps the most serious, is that the ability to handle the human side of the job varies widely with different people. And, of course, the human relations requirements of jobs vary, too. If you put employees who like to be one of the gang back in the corner working alone, they won't be happy no matter how much they like the work or how skillfully they can perform it. Similarly, a person who has never been able to get along well with superiors won't be much of a help on a job where there has to be a lot of close supervision.

In what ways can you improve your hiring results?

Just formalizing the employment procedure and making it systematic help rule out the big mistakes that often occur during haphazard hiring. For instance, every applicant should fill out some sort of form before being given consideration. On such a form the applicant should furnish critical information about work experience and education. A glance at the form will rule out people who don't meet educational or job-experience requirements.

The application form can tell you something more. A work record will show up the job hopper who has held a dozen jobs in three or four years. This kind of person is usually an employment risk. Periods of prolonged employment are good indicators of stability, even if the indicator doesn't always prove reliable.

Chances are that your responsibility in your company will be limited to cooperating with the employment or personnel department. If you understand what they are trying to do for you, they'll be able to do a better job for you. A prominent personnel executive put it this way: "The personnel department gives the candidate the first interview, checks references, and may conduct mechanical or clerical aptitude tests. The medical department makes certain the applicant is physically fit. But there is no substitute for the supervisory interview. The supervisor has to live and work with the employee. The supervisor should be satisfied the new person fills the bill."

Will tests help to select better employees?

Over 50,000 firms think so. Properly selected, administered, and evaluated, so-called psychological tests can be a big help in picking better workers. Tests may be simple and direct, such as those that show whether an applicant can read and write or perform the simple arithmetic that recordkeeping on the job may demand. Other, highly specific tests may enable an applicant to demonstrate the ability to perform the special skills your job demands. For instance, any person looking for a job can claim competence in operating a multiple-spindle automatic or a calculator. A ten-minute tryout will prove whether the claim is valid. These "can do?" tests, called *performance tests,* are widely used.

Which tests are most sensitive to restrictions of the equal employment opportunity laws?

Psychological tests that attempt to find out whether a person has the ability to learn a particular kind of job (aptitude tests) can also be fairly reliable, but under present United States laws these are often open to challenge by the applicant. For that reason your company may or may not choose to use them.

Personality, intelligence, and job or career *interest* tests are widely used for applicants seeking higher-level management positions. But these, too, must be fully validated and their reliability proved before they can pass the civil rights hurdle. *Validity* simply means that the test really measures what it is supposed to measure. *Reliability* means that if an applicant were to take a test several times, the score would always be the same.

Underlying the challenges of validity and reliability is the requirement that any test given to applicants (1) should be directly related to the job's content and (2) should not discriminate unfairly against the person taking them. In other words, it would not be right to require that an applicant for a typist's job pass a test designed for an administrative secretary. Nor should the test be worded in such a way that it favors a person with a particular background over another who does not have it—unless it can be shown that the job requires that background.

What good are physical examinations?

As a supervisor, you'll want to know whether a person assigned to your department has any physical limitations. There's no way of actually finding out about poor eyesight, a hernia, or a heart condition, for instance, without a complete physical examination. A physical defect doesn't necessarily rule out an applicant, but knowledge of it does ensure that person's being put on a job where the best work can be done and where the disability is not aggravated.

What can a supervisor do to improve the selection process?

Whenever a supervisor is given a chance to interview a prospective job candidate, that's a golden opportunity to help make sure the department gets a first-rate employee. Interviewing points that apply most directly to selecting employees are reviewed here.

Know What Kind of Employee You Want. Don't describe the person vaguely as a good worker who will stay on the job. That doesn't tell you much about the qualities you are looking for to suit the job that is open. Try making a checklist of necessary or desirable qualifications, such as:

- Experience. The applicant should have worked a couple of years on multiple-spindle drill presses, for example, even though they weren't exactly like yours.
- Blueprint reading. The person has to be able to work directly from prints.
- Speed. This job doesn't require a quick worker as much as it requires a steady, consistent worker.
- Initiative. Does the applicant's previous experience show work without close supervision?
- Attendance. Has the applicant a good record of attendance (because this job needs someone who's going to be here every day)?

See Enough Candidates. Your personnel department will probably screen out the obvious misfits before an applicant is sent to you for approval. But if you do the hiring directly, make a point of interviewing at least three candidates before making up your mind. That way you get a chance to make comparisons and to get the feel of the prevailing labor market. For some hard-to-fill jobs requiring special skills, you may have to see as many as 20 or 30 persons.

What should you talk about to job candidates?

Preview the job for the applicant. It's a great time-saver to tell the applicant what the fixed requirements of the job are. Mention such things as job title and relationships to other jobs, and the main activities involved in the job, such as walking, standing, sitting, and performing heavy work. Tell the applicant what kind of materials and machines are used and describe the working conditions.

It's especially wise to forewarn an applicant about any undesirable conditions, such as fumes, dampness, and night work. Don't scare the applicant, but be sure the facts are known ahead of time. Better that the applicant turn down the job than walk off it after three days.

You can also describe the good parts about the job—what kind of advancement there is, the company's benefit programs, and so forth. This is the time to do some sound, factual selling, but don't make promises about raises or promotions. These can come back to haunt you later on.

What kind of questions should you ask the applicant?

Don't turn the interview into a "third degree" by asking too many point-blank questions—especially those that can be answered by a simple yes or no. The job seeker is likely to be on guard during the interview, anyway. For example, the answer will ordinarily be "yes" to a question like, "Did you get along well with your boss in the last place you worked?"

Ask "open-ended" questions that begin with what, where, why, when, or who. This gives the applicant a chance to talk and, while talking, to show you the kind of person he or she really is. If the applicant does most of the talking and you do most of the listening, you'll have lots of time to form an opinion. And that's the purpose of the interview.

Ask open-ended questions such as:

● What about your education? How do you feel that it would help you do the kind of work we do here?

- Where did you get your most valuable experience? Suppose you tell me about your working experience, starting with your first job.
- Whom did you report to in your last job? Can you describe that supervisor?
- When did you first decide you liked to do this sort of work? What have you found most difficult about it? Most pleasant?
- How would you describe your health? What kind of attendance record have you maintained during the last year?
- Why did you leave the job at the XYZ Company?

What kind of questions are you forbidden to ask a job applicant?

Be careful. Listen to whatever your personnel department advises. Otherwise, you as well as your company may get into trouble over some unintended equal employment opportunity infringement. The following is just a partial list of prohibitions:

- **Race or Color.** Don't ask. Don't comment.
- **Religion.** Don't ask. Don't say, "This is a (Catholic, Protestant, Jewish, or other) organization."
- **National Origin.** Don't ask. Don't comment.
- **Sex.** Don't ask. Don't comment. Don't indicate prejudgment about physical capabilities.
- **Age.** Don't ask, "How old are you?" Don't ask for a birth date. You *may* ask if the applicant is between the ages of 18 and 65.
- **Marital Status.** Don't ask for this, or for ages of children, or where a spouse works.
- **Disability.** You may ask if the person has a present disability that will interfere with the job to be performed, but not about past disabilities or illnesses.
- **Address.** You may ask for this and how long the person has lived there. You may ask if the applicant is an American citizen and, if not, whether the person has the legal right to remain permanently in the United States. It is generally unlawful to press for answers beyond this point.
- **Criminal Record.** You may ask if the person has ever been convicted of a crime and when and where it took place. You may *not* ask if a person has ever been arrested, nor can you deny employment on this basis unless it can be proved it would damage the employer's business.
- **Physical Capabilities.** Don't ask how tall or how strong an applicant is. This may indicate a sexist prejudice. You may explain

physical aspects of the job, such as lifting, pulling, and so forth, and show how it must be performed. And you may require a physical examination. The hope is that if the applicant has a clear chance to estimate the job's physical requirements, the application will be withdrawn if the job appears too demanding or beyond the person's capabilities. Legally, however, you may not make that decision during an interview.

Questions about *education* and *experience* are pretty much unrestricted. The main point to be sure about in any interviewing area is that the question's relevance to the job for which the individual is applying can undeniably be shown. This legal requirement is called a bona fide occupational qualification, or BFOQ.

What do you look for while interviewing an applicant?

Besides the factual things you obviously need to know about an applicant's skills and know-how, you'll want to be alert to what the interview tells you about:

Suitable Background.   Do the applicant's education and experience, and even residence and off-the-job associates, indicate that the person will be happy working with the people in your company? If education isn't a strong point and hobbies are bowling and baseball, the applicant won't find many friends among employees who take their education seriously and spend their spare time discussing opera and stamp collecting.

Desirable Characteristics.   Are the applicant's achievements outstanding? Did the person work five years at the XYZ Company without missing a day?

How about personal interests? If the jobs liked best in the past have been outdoor ones, such as truck driving, why is the applicant looking now for a confining job on an assembly line?

Try to spot attitude. Does the person act mature or sound as if given to childish boasting? Does the person listen to what you say? An example of an attitude you'll want to steer clear of is one where an individual goes out of the way to criticize the last company worked for, the people worked with, or the quality of the product. You'll probably be making no mistake to conclude this individual is the kind of person who'd find everything wrong at your company, too.

You can tell a lot about physical condition, too, from the interview. The person applying for a job who appears slow-moving and lethargic may put no energy into the job, either. Remember, most people looking for work are trying to put their best foot forward. If an interviewee can't show you a very good side during the interview, there's a chance that you won't see anything better on the job.

What should you avoid in conducting a job interview?

James Menzies Black, an old friend of mine who used to be a director of personnel for a major railroad, cautions:

1. Don't be overly formal. The more you do to help the applicant relax, the more effective the interview will be.

2. Don't take notes. A busy pencil writes off a productive interview. Train your memory so you can make your notes after the interview is completed.

3. Don't high-pressure applicants. If you paint a glowing picture to job seekers that quickly fades after they are on the payroll, you will have disappointed employees on your hands. Worst of all, you will have employees who don't trust your word.

4. Don't hire a chief when you really need a worker. If an applicant is too intelligent or experienced to be happy in the job and there is little opportunity for quick promotion, say so. You want employee and job to match. That's why you conduct an interview.

5. Don't tell applicants you are rejecting them for personality reasons. If you think the experience or the knowledge to hold a job is lacking, be frank and say so. If you are refusing to hire for intangible reasons such as a poor personality, uncertainty about reliability, or a dislike of general attitude, keep your reasons to yourself. Frankness may offend applicants and will certainly discourage them for no good reason.

6. Don't make moral judgments or give advice. The applicant's personal life is no concern of yours.

7. Don't ask trick questions that may embarrass. If you see that there is conflict in the applicant's statements, you should certainly explore the matter, but do so discreetly. Your job is not to "catch" the prospect. It is to find out what you can about the individual.

8. Don't let your facial expression, tone of voice, or gestures reveal your feelings. You give applicants confidence by showing interest and sympathy. If they think you disapprove of what they are telling you, they will become silent or try to shift ideas around to where they will please you.

9. Don't be impatient. Try not to let the applicant know you're in a hurry, even if you are. A look at a watch has killed many an interview.

10. Don't be misled by your prejudices. Keep an open mind. Good interviewers never allow their biases to cloud their judgment.

Whom should you hire?

Deciding which applicant to hire isn't easy. But you can make a better decision if you separate facts from hunches—not that you should ignore your intuition or inferences. It's a good idea to take five minutes after you've interviewed an applicant to jot down what you think are the significant facts, and list your hunches, too.

Facts may show that the job seeker has had ten years of experience on a milling machine, has good health, and can read blueprints. But your conversation may have brought out the feeling that the individual is stubborn and boastful and might be hard to supervise. Only you can tell which items you'll give most weight to. Some supervisors don't mind having a prima donna on their staff so long as that individual can produce. Others fear that a prima donna is likely to upset teamwork. And, of course, your hunches can be wrong.

You can be sure, however, that your choice will be better than flipping a coin if you've gone about your interview in a systematic way; and if you've kept personal prejudices pertaining to a race, religion, age, sex, or nationality out of your figuring.

How do you pick the best from the list of qualified applicants?

First, be sure that you have dropped no one from the list of possibilities because of discrimination or prejudice; in other words, be sure that all things are equal according to the law. Then, pick the applicant who fits your sense of what kind of person will do the job best. This is where your experience and intuition can help. For example, Bobby Knight, the highly successful Indiana University basketball coach, lists three things he looks for when recruiting basketball players:

(1) *Strength.* Wiry strength to hold onto the ball, to maintain a position on the boards or a defensive stance. (2) *Quickness.* The slow, plodding team will have trouble over the long season. (3) *Concentration.* There isn't a right way to play the game, but there are a lot of poor ways. You have to play in a way that utilizes the abilities of your team. Concentrate, and you will be successful.

Your department won't be playing basketball. But you can look for such things as (1) *perseverance,* as demonstrated by a work record that shows the applicant can stay with a difficult situation; (2)

alertness, as indicated by the applicant's ability to follow your description of the work to be done—since many jobs require a person who can sense when a deviation from rigid procedures is desirable; (3) *cooperation,* as illustrated by the applicant's willingness to go through the red tape of employment interviewing and processing without quibbling about it. Other jobs, of course, may need another set of personal qualities. Initiative in a salesclerk, for example, may be more important than cooperation. Single-mindedness may be more valuable than alertness in a chemical processing plant that requires rigid conformance to prescribed sequence.

Should you check employee references?

Absolutely yes! It's foolhardy to hire anyone without checking with the last employer to find out the actual job the applicant held and to verify dates of employment. Most former employers will not tell you much more for fear of legally prejudicing the applicant's chances. For this reason, it's wise also to tell the job candidate that you will be checking his or her education and employment statements. One good way to obtain the applicant's own views about his or her employment record is to ask, "What do you think your last employer would say about your performance, work habits, and attendance?"

Personal references, on the other hand, are usually not of much value. Few people will supply you with names of others who will say something bad about them.

Key Concepts

1. Conservation of human resources and labor costs through proper employee selection, placement, and utilization forms the foundation for a supervisor's effectiveness, and it is a responsibility over which he or she can and must exert maximum control.

2. No one can or should know better than the supervisor what kind of individuals the work in the department demands—their skills, aptitudes, and interests—and the number of such individuals needed to get the work done economically, on time, and well.

3. The supervisor should be prepared to exert a major influence in the selection of the right kind of people for his or her department by participating fully in describing jobs, setting criteria for applicants, and conducting employment and placement interviews.

4. A supervisor must maintain constant surveillance over work force assignments to make certain that there are neither too many nor too few employees and that they are neither overqualified nor underqualified for the work load in the department.

5. Control of absences and turnover is of considerable value in an organization's economic use of human resources, and it, too, is a control over which a supervisor has a major influence.

Supervisory Word Power

Application Blank.   A form used by a company to systematically gather and record information about a job applicant's qualifications, education, and work experience.

Attrition.   The gradual reduction of a work force by means of natural events and causes, such as retirements, deaths, and resignations, as opposed to reductions planned by management, such as discharges, layoffs, and early retirements.

Employment Interview.   A face-to-face exchange of information between a job applicant and an employer's representative in order to develop qualitative information about the applicant's suitability for employment.

Psychological Tests.   Written examinations, conducted by trained professionals, of a person's qualifications, interests, and aptitudes in order to judge objectively the individual's suitability for a particular job or kind of work.

Work Load.   The amount of work an individual, or a group of individuals, can be expected to perform during a given period of time under normal conditions.

Reading Comprehension

1. What is meant by balancing the work force? Why should a supervisor try to do it?

2. What are some of the hidden costs of adding an employee to, and separating an employee from, the payroll?

3. State a basic rule supervisors can follow to make their selection and hiring practices comply with the various equal employment opportunity laws.

4. What is the fundamental purpose of tests, application forms, and interviews that are used in hiring new employees?

5. What are some of the factors that contribute to turnover?

6. Would it be wise to hire a college graduate for a job that requires only a high school education, so long as the applicant were willing to take it at prevailing wage rates? Why?

7. Would a supervisor be likely to use more than one method of calculating absence rates? Why?

8. What's the difference between an aptitude test and a performance test?

9. What are some of the things you might want to know about an applicant that can be elicited in a job interview?

10. In conducting an employment or a placement interview, what are some of the techniques a supervisor can use to make the interview more effective?

Supervision in Action
The Case of Too Much Overtime. A Case Study in Human Relations Involving Work-Force Management, with Questions for You to Answer.

"This overtime has got to stop," stormed the plant superintendent to Jake Barnes, supervisor of the finishing department in a toy factory. "You've had to schedule overtime three times already, and the month has only just begun. What's the trouble out there?"

"Well, boss, it's this way," said Jake. "When the pressure was on to pare costs to the bone, I laid off three of our finishers. According to the schedule we got from sales, we would have been able to produce all they required without putting on any overtime. But the sales manager has been out here every day moving up orders. And increasing some, too. We'll still be in good shape by the end of the month. But right now I don't have as much help as I need to get the stuff out as fast as sales is calling for it."

"Jake, I've told you time and again not to accept delivery changes from sales without first making sure you can handle them. It's easy for sales to make promises. But the way you're running up overtime, we're the ones who will have to pay for those promises."

"To tell the truth," said Jake, "I thought we'd be able to move up those orders—and we would have, except that we had four employees out this week. Seems as if the flu is knocking out more people every day. I can't predict things like this. You tell me to keep my labor force down to the minimum. I don't want to recall anyone for just a few days. I think that if the company wants delivery, we'll have to schedule the overtime."

"Jake, I still don't think you've handled this problem well at all. There's going to be the devil to pay if you don't bring your labor costs into line."

Two days later, the finishing department was still in trouble. At 3 p.m. the phone rang. It was the sales manager. "Jake, the shipping department tells me you're holding up the McWorth order. It's got to go out tomorrow for sure. Can I call McWorth and promise the order will be shipped?"

1. What do you think of the instructions Jake got from his boss?
2. What do you think of the sales manager's request?
3. What do you think Jake should have said to his boss when the overtime problem arose?
4. If you were Jake now, how would you handle this situation?
5. What would you do to avoid the problem in the future?

12

JOB ANALYSIS, EVALUATION, AND COMPENSATION

What is the purpose of job analysis?

It serves two major functions. First, it provides the information needed to convert the principles of organizing and staffing (as discussed in Chapters 10 and 11) into clearly defined, specific jobs for employees to perform. Second, job analysis provides the foundation upon which a job evaluation plan can be built. Job evaluation, in turn, becomes the cornerstone of an effective and equitable wage and salary program.

How is a job analysis made?

Information is gathered for a job analysis by any of three methods:

● Sending a questionnaire to supervisors and employees, who fill the survey form out in detail. Accuracy and comprehensiveness of this method depend almost entirely on the supervisor and the employee.
● Interviewing supervisors and employees and recording significant facts on a survey form. This method depends on good cooperation from the people interviewed.
● Actually observing the job as it is performed. This is the most dependable way, although there can be a loophole if the operator performs a variety of jobs and the observer doesn't see a representative sample of all of them.

Who can make a job analysis?

Anyone, properly instructed, can make a job analysis. But most companies either employ a professional specialist to do this job or train someone to do it on a full-time basis.

What's included in a job (or position) description?

The job description is not a step-by-step account of the way a job is done. It summarizes in more general terms what the job entails.

A typical job description for a light assembly job might read:

Work performed. Assembles small electronic components such as capacitors, resistors, tubes, rheostats, shunts, etc., to radio chassis. Works with hand tools such as socket wrenches, screwdrivers, and pliers and with overhead power-driven wrench. Refers to instructions sheets and diagrams. Keeps tally sheet of the units worked on. Keeps workplace clean and performs miscellaneous related duties. Is under close supervision of supervisor.

How clearly are job requirements spelled out in a job description?

Through interviews with the employee and the supervisor and through comparisons with other jobs, the analyst determines specifically what the performance requirements are. For instance, in the light assembly job described in the last question, the analyst might enter on the job description:

Responsibilities. Is responsible for assembling parts according to specifications. Is responsible for care of tools and housekeeping.

Job knowledge. Must know how to read from job instructions and diagrams. Must know how custom changes are handled.

Mental application. Requires moderate concentration. Must recognize poor fit or parts that are faulty mechanically.

Dexterity and accuracy. Requires high degree of dexterity.

Machines or tools used. Hand tools and power-driven screwdriver.

The analyst will also specify other requirements, such as:

Experience required. None.

Training data. One week of vestibule training.

Education requirement. Equivalent of two years of high school.

Relation to other jobs. Transfer from other assembly work. Transfer to other assembly work such as soldering and wiring. Promotion to lead assembler.

Supervision. Under supervision of department supervisor.

The analyst may then run through a checklist of over 100 items that describe *physical activities* (such as walking, stooping, carrying, hearing, color vision); *working conditions* (such as hot, cold, dusty, noisy, or toxic conditions, electrical hazards); and *occupational characteristics* (such as strength of hands, ability to work rapidly for short periods, memory for written instructions, arithmetic computation, tact in dealing with people).

It is of utmost importance that the job requirements be truly justified and not in any way represent prejudices or habitual preferences toward white males, for example. All job-evaluation plans are subject to review by the Equal Employment Opportunity Commission (EEOC) for this reason.

What's the underlying purpose of job evaluation?

The purpose of job evaluation is to determine systematically the relative worth of jobs within plants and offices.

Have you ever wondered how the job of a washroom porter can be compared in terms of wages with that of a machine operator? Or the duties of a keypunch operator with those of a computer programmer? Do the unpleasant tasks of the porter's job make it worth as much as that of the machinist, who has better working conditions but who needs more skill? What's the worth of the continuous attention demanded by the keypunching job compared with the requirements of the programming job?

How would you compare the value to a company in dollars of a supervisor who supervises an assembly crew of 75 people with that of a quality-control engineer who supervises only 10 people but who needs much more technical education than the supervisor? Would you pay a steeplejack more than a toolmaker in order to reward the steeplejack for the risks taken? Job evaluation is designed to form a systematic basis for answering such difficult questions, and it leads to fairer pay systems.

What is the basic tool of job evaluation?

Job analysis. The information gathered by a job analysis not only defines the jobs and positions in an organization, it also provides the basis for determining how much each job is worth.

Job titles, in and of themselves, mean very little. In one plant a machinist is a lathe operator, in another a grinding machine operator. Even in the same plant, a grinding machine operator in Department B will work to 0.002 inch on routine work. In Department C, the operator will work to 0.001 inch on custom jobs. In Department G, a horizontal grinder may be operated; in Department H, a centerless grinder.

Only by studying the duties, requirements, and skills of a job can you find what the job really entails.

Which is rated, the individual or the job?

The first principle of job evaluation is that only the job is rated—not the individual who performs it. Here's why: Suppose two employees have identical jobs and turn out about the same quality and quantity of work. But one has a better education than the other. So far as the jobs are concerned, both should still be rated the same. In job evaluation, what is important is only what the job demands, not what extra personal qualities the employee may or may not bring to it. After all, if the job requires only an elementary school education or its equivalent, what purpose would be served in paying an employee extra for a college education when this extra education can't be applied to that job?

How foolproof is job evaluation?

It is pretty reliable, although it is not altogether without injustices. Job evaluation is a systematic art, but it is not a science yet. In job evaluation you still have to exercise judgment to appraise the worth of jobs. But job evaluation is the most reliable and the fairest way we know to compare the value of one job with that of another. Its checks and balances help rule out personal prejudices and see that each job is measured by the same set of yardsticks.

What are some of the values that come from job evaluation?

When jobs are rated fairly and employees are paid accordingly, there are usually fewer grievances about wages and pay rates. It's said that employees are not so much interested in "how much I get" as in "how much the person next to me gets." Job evaluation makes sure that people doing the same work under the same conditions get the same pay.

In addition, job evaluation provides a structure so that an employee may progress within defined lines to a higher wage grade. The same structure can be used to rate a new job quickly when it is added. And it can be used to compare the pay for jobs within the company with those in nearby or similar organizations.

How is a job analysis converted to a job evaluation?

Data collected during the analysis becomes the raw material for job evaluation. But without the analysis, job evaluation on a large scale is practically impossible. The more accurate the data, the better the evaluation.

Four principal methods are used to convert the job analysis data into a job-evaluation system. The first three are described just briefly here because only about one-fifth of all companies having job-evaluation plans use any of them.

Ranking is the simplest and earliest form of job evaluation. Simple title and descriptions of each job are written on separate cards. Then a committee sorts the cards, ranking them from highest to lowest worth. The trouble here is that it's almost impossible for everyone on the committee to know each job or to agree on the importance of the various factors—working conditions, supervision required, and so forth.

Classification is a refinement of the ranking methods. The committee begins by classifying all possible work at the location into grades of work: for example, A—messenger work, B—simple clerical work requiring no training, C—work requiring recognized clerical ability or considerable experience on certain machines. Next the committee slots the existing jobs into the various grades. Here again, the committee must guard against thinking of the individual rather than the job. Nevertheless, this system is simple and is used effectively in most government jobs.

Factor comparison is a reliable, but complicated, method of evaluating very different types of jobs—as in comparing manual jobs with jobs requiring creative thinking. Essentially, the method consists of ranking about 20 key jobs according to several different factors common to all jobs. A proportionate amount of the present wage for a key job will represent each of the factors. The sum of the amounts paid for each of the factors is the money rate for the job. This is the only job-evaluation method that brings money into the calculations before the job classifications are determined.

What is the most popular method for evaluating jobs?

The Point Method. Point plans have been installed in several thousand companies—small and large.

Under the point method, jobs are defined in terms of factors that are common to all—such as responsibility, skill, education, and effort required. The amount of each factor will vary according to the job. So the first step is to take the job analysis or job description and transfer the data to a point-system job-rating sheet (see Figure 12-1).

For each of the "compensable" factors (11 are in the illustration), there is a range of points (see Table 12-1). According to the demands of the particular job on each of the factors, the job will get a certain amount of points. To determine just how many points, it is common to rate each factor for each job according to the degree of demand for that factor (see Table 12-2).

For example, in the case of the engine lathe operator's job, look at the description of Responsibility for Material or Product. The basis for rating (obtained from the original job analysis) says that the prob-

JOB RATING—SUBSTANTIATING DATA

Job Name LATHE OPERATOR–ENGINE (Up to 30″)   **Class** A

Factors	De-gree	Basis of Rating
Education	3 (42)	Use shop mathematics, charts, tables, handbook formulas. Work from complicated drawings. Use micrometers, depth gauges, indicator gauges, protractors. Knowledge of machining methods, tools, cutting qualities of different kinds of metals. Equivalent of 4 years high school plus 2 to 3 years trade training.
Experience	4 (88)	3 to 5 years on wide variety of engine lathe work, including diversified setups.
Initiative and ingenuity	4 (56)	Wide variety of castings and forgings of complicated form. Close tolerances. Difficult setups of irregularly shaped parts. Considerable judgment and ingenuity to plan and lay out unusual lathe operations, select proper feeds and speeds, and devise tooling for varying materials and conditions.
Physical demand	2 (20)	Light physical effort. Setups may require handling of heavy material mounting on faceplate. Machine time greatest part of cycle. Most of time spent watching work checking, making adjustments.
Mental or visual demand	4 (20)	Must concentrate mental and visual attention closely, planning and laying out work, checking, making adjustments. Close tolerances may require unusual attention.
Responsibility for equipment or process	3 (15)	Careless setup or operation, jamming of tools, dropping work on ways, jamming carriage, may seldom cause damage over $500.
Responsibility for material or product	3 (15)	Careless setup or operation may result in spoilage and possible scrapping of expensive castings, forgings, shafts, etc., e.g., machining below size, inaccurate boring of diameter and depth. Probable losses seldom over $500.
Responsibility for safety of others	3 (15)	Flying chips may cause burns, cuts, or eye injuries. Improperly fastened work may fly from faceplate or chuck. May injure another employee when setting work in machine.
Responsibility for work of others	1 (5)	None
Working conditions	2 (20)	Good working conditions. May be slightly dirty, especially in setups. Some dust from castings. Usual machine shop noise.
Unavoidable hazards	3 (15)	May crush fingers or toes handling material or from dropped tools or clamps. Possible burns, cuts, or eye injury from flying chips and particles. Finger or hand injury from rotating work.
Total	311	Grade 4

Figure 12-1.

TABLE 12-1 POINTS ASSIGNED TO FACTORS

	First Degree	Second Degree	Third Degree	Fourth Degree	Fifth Degree
Skill:					
1. Education	14	28	42	56	70
2. Experience	22	44	66	88	110
3. Initiative and ingenuity	14	28	42	56	70
Effort:					
4. Physical demand	10	20	30	40	50
5. Mental or visual demand	5	10	15	20	25
Responsibility:					
6. Equipment or process	5	10	15	20	25
7. Material or product	5	10	15	20	25
8. Safety of others	5	10	15	20	25
9. Work of others	5	—	15	—	25
Job conditions:					
10. Working conditions	10	20	30	40	50
11. Unavoidable hazards	5	10	15	20	25

able losses are seldom over $500. On Table 12-2 this is considered a third-degree demand for that factor. Table 12-1 allocates 15 points for third-degree demand for this factor.

Points on the job-rating sheet are totaled, and the total for the job plus each of the point scores for each factor is posted to a master

TABLE 12-2 RESPONSIBILITY FOR FACTOR 7 (MATERIAL OR PRODUCT)

Degree	Requirements
First:	Value of material that may be wasted, damaged, or lost is small (maximum $50), or possibility of loss or damage is slight.
Second:	Probable loss due to damage or waste of materials or product is low (maximum $200).
Third:	Probable loss due to damage or waste of material or product is limited (maximum $500), or if amount of possible loss is high, probability of occurrence is exceedingly low.
Fourth:	Probable loss due to waste or damage of material or product is high (maximum $1,000).
Fifth:	Value of material that may be wasted, damaged, or lost by the employee is very high, up to several thousand dollars.

summary sheet. The analyst, together with the supervisor, can then compare the factor rating of each job with others that are similar, and next, the total points for each job with the total points for other jobs.

How are job points converted into job grades?

A typical point system sets up a range of cutoff scores. Minimum and maximum scores are established for each labor rating or grade. For example: 100 to 150 points is a grade 10 job (lowest on the scale); 151 to 180 is a grade 9; 181 to 205 is a grade 8; and so on up to the maximum number of points, which would rate as the number 1 job in the system.

It is not uncommon to find two very different kinds of jobs, such as a specialty machine operator and a roving inspector, with similar point totals and thus in the same labor grade. One job may build up points for experience and physical demand, the other for initiative, visual demand, and responsibility for product. It is the total of all factors, not just a high score on one, that counts.

Are all point systems the same?

No. There are many "standard" plans, such as the old National Metal Trades Association (NMTA), the National Electrical Manufacturers' Association (NEMA), and—for white-collar jobs—the Life Office Management Association (LOMA) plans. But even if your company uses such a plan, there's a good chance that it has been adjusted slightly to better fit the jobs that are peculiar to your organization.

Are job-evaluation plans different for white-collar than for blue-collar jobs?

Most of the time a different scale of points is used for white-collar jobs than is used for factory workers. Office plans may give special weight to "contacts with other departments." Service-type jobs may emphasize "client" or "customer" contacts.

Special plans are used (1) for highly creative work, such as research and development or editing, and (2) for management positions, where credits for number of people supervised, extent of initiative required, and responsibility for profits are heavily weighted.

Where do supervisors fit into this picture?

Supervisors can be of great help to the job-evaluation specialist. First, they can aid the job analyst in getting the true picture of the job. After all, supervisors probably know better than anyone else how a job might vary from time to time. And since they look at many jobs, their opinions as to the degree of the various demands are likely to be more objective than those of employees.

Supervisors are especially helpful in determining the degree to be assigned the various factors for each job. For instance, a supervisor may have felt originally that the experience factor for a heat treater was fourth-degree. But when comparing this job with other jobs, the supervisor might see that a layout person's job is rated fourth-degree also. The supervisor might then say, "No, the heat treater's experience isn't quite so necessary as that of the layout person, so let's drop the heat treater's rating back to third-degree."

When are the money values assigned to the various jobs classifications?

Only after the labor grades have been assigned. That way, the ratings are apt to be fairer, because the raters up until that point have been talking only in terms of the job itself—not the individual currently performing it or the wages that person should receive.

How are actual wages determined?

Job-evaluation ratings are usually converted to wage rates in three steps:

1. Plot a chart of money paid employees *now* against the evaluation job grade. This shows up the current inequities in job payment. It's not uncommon to find two persons working in the same job classification—one getting $5.00 per hour, another $6.25. This is a situation that job evaluation corrects.

2. Make a survey of wages paid by comparable companies in the community. In making this survey, the job-evaluation specialist is careful to compare job descriptions—not just job titles, since titles are misleading.

3. Combine the study of actual wages paid with wages other companies in the area pay to develop a pattern for paying wages in the particular organization.

What is the relationship between how much is paid for a certain job and how it is rated under

Under a job-evaluation plan, the job's rating should be the major factor in determining its pay, but there are other influences. The total wage can be affected by the prosperity of the company, the industry involved, or its geographic location. For instance, in 1984, a word processor in a Los Angeles electronics plant might receive anywhere from $1 to $3 more per hour than a word processor with the same classification in a steel company in Pittsburgh.

Another factor that influences wages is the power of the individual or of the group to bargain for higher wages. And where wage-incentive plans exist, two workers with identically rated jobs may draw the same base rate but have different earnings because of differences in their effort and output.

What are rate ranges?

Rate range is the term typically applied to the spread between the minimum and the maximum wage rate for each job grade. Many companies, however, pay only a single rate to wage-roll employees in each grade and prescribe rate ranges for salaried, white-collar, and supervisory jobs only.

What happens to employees' pay when they move from one job to another job in the same grade?

A transfer from one job to another in the same job grade is not considered a promotion, even though an employee may feel it is and consider one job more desirable. The employee will continue to get the same rate as on the old job. The only way for the employee to get more money (if there are no rate ranges) is to be promoted to a higher job grade.

How does job evaluation tie in with the concept of equal pay for equal work?

The law of the land (the Fair Labor Standards Act as amended by the Equal Pay Act of 1963 and again by Public Law 92-318 in 1972) stipulates that all employees, regardless of sex or other discriminatory identification, should receive the same pay for the same kind and amount of work. Job evaluation is the basic means for making sure that this occurs. The "equal pay for equal work" standard, like job evaluation, requires scrutiny of the job as a whole. Its intention is that job titles be ignored and attention focussed on actual job requirements and performance. The law examines four factors in particular: equal skill, equal effort, equal responsibility, and similarity of working conditions. Whereas the law does acknowledge some exceptions, it will not permit the concepts of "women's jobs," "men's jobs," "job lists for nonwhites," and the like. On the other hand, the law does permit the use of merit pay plans that recognize a difference, within a job pay range, of different levels of performance among individuals.

What is meant by "comparable worth"?

This refers to a concept used for evaluating widely dissimilar jobs. The Equal Pay Act charges discrimination if women aren't given pay equal to men's pay for equal work. In a great many instances, however, women perform work that is radically different from the work performed by men in the same organization. Nevertheless, these women often feel, with justification, that their pay is still not equal, all things considered. The concept of comparable worth is an effort to rectify this kind of situation. It makes it possible for the work—and the pay—of a toll collector, for example, to be compared with that of a nurse. Typically, this approach involves examination and comparison of four factors: level of know-how required, problem-solving entailed, accountability, and working conditions. The applicability of the comparable worth concept is challenged by some labor unions and women's organizations on the grounds that it emphasizes subjective judgments (often with a sexist bias) to a greater degree than do most traditional job evaluation systems. Some employers also contend that it is the supply and demand of labor that really determines pay. Many people also say that they have little faith in an evaluation system that compares apples with oranges, as in equating a clerk's worth with that of a craftsperson.

Merit pay: What is its connection with job evaluation?

Merit-rating systems (by any name) focus on the individual who performs the job, not the job itself. A job-evaluation program serves to define, classify, and establish the worth of jobs. In programs where rate ranges are also created, the range provides flexibility for rewarding above-average and exceptional performance. The rate range for a posting clerk in an insurance company may be from $170 to $215 per week. A clerk who just qualifies for the job may be paid the minimum: $170. A clerk whose performance is judged above-average may receive a $15 merit increase to boost his pay to $185. Later on, when his performance is judged to be exceptional, he may get another merit increase of, say, $20 to make his salary $205 per month. But no matter how good his performance becomes, no amount of merit increases will be able to lift his pay above the range limit of $215. Only a promotion to a job with a higher classification will do that for him.

Has a cost-of-living raise anything to do with job evaluation?

Not directly, although cost-of-living raises can affect differentials between grades. Cost-of-living, or escalator, raises usually are introduced to gear wages to rises and falls in the consumer price index of the U.S. Bureau of Labor Statistics, commonly referred to as the cost-of-living index. In some companies, if the index rises one full point, all wages go up 1 percent—or some agreed-on fraction of a percent.

Another factor that sometimes affects a company's pay system is when it adopts a raise in the federal minimum wage. If pay for higher-grade jobs is not raised proportionately, the lowest-grade job squeezes the pay scale from the bottom. The law's intention is not to require an across-the-board raise, but employees in the higher labor grades often feel that it is an inequity if their wage rates remain where they were.

How much should employees know about job evaluation?

Job evaluation takes the mystery out of why some jobs pay more than others. Nothing can destroy morale more than the thought that someone else is getting more for doing the same job that you are doing. So, within the limits of your company's policy, job-evaluation methods should be an open book to employees. Supervisors ought to make it their business to know more about how their company's plan works than any other employees know. That way supervisors remain the employees' main source of information. And supervisors can do much to explain what may appear to be discrepancies and thus keep grievances from growing.

In discussing job evaluation with employees, emphasize these points:

- Job evaluation rates the job, not the person performing it.
- Many factors are compared and evaluated—not just the one that seems most important to the particular individual.
- The same set of yardsticks is used to measure every job.
- Job evaluation is based on the gathering of factual evidence, not just a casual description of the job.
- Job titles are misleading and can mean different things in different parts of the company. Descriptions are what count.
- Whereas judgment still plays a role in determining a job's worth, it has been held to a minimum because the method is systematic and involves enough people so that discrimination and favoritism are practically ruled out.

When it comes to pay, how many companies rely on a job-evaluation plan for a foundation?

Relatively few small companies, but three-quarters of larger companies and almost all state and federal agencies use some form of job evaluation. For example, the classification system is prescribed by the Classification Act of 1949 for all jobs regulated by the United States Civil Service Commission.

Regardless of job evaluation, what are the basic ways in which employees get paid for their work?

There are essentially three different forms of direct compensation or pay.

1. Hourly Wages.   Pay is based solely on how many hours the individual works. If the job of a welder calls for $6.00 per hour and the welder works only 28 hours during a particular week, the pay will be $6.00 × 28, or $168. Hourly wage systems prevail for blue-collar workers.

2. Straight Salary.   Pay is based on a flat weekly or monthly sum and is often paid in full regardless of the hours worked, provided the hours not worked are excused. For example, the salary of a receiving clerk may be $210 per week. If the clerk has to miss six hours' work during the week for a legitimate reason, the full $210 is still received. The straight salary system prevails for office and clerical workers, white-collar employees generally, and managerial personnel.

3. Incentive Systems. There are dozens of variations in incentive-pay systems, but the principle is that pay is based in full or in part on the results attained by the individual. In an apparel factory, for example, sewing machine operators may be guaranteed a base wage rate of, say, $4.00 per hour. They will be given an additional percentage of that wage rate, however, in proportion to how much more they produce above a certain standard of output. Suppose the standard is 20 shirts stitched per hour, and the operator puts together 24 in an hour. The incentive (sometimes called a bonus) will be 20 percent (4/20) multiplied by the hourly rate ($4.00), or 80 cents. The total pay for that hour then would be $4.80. Many salespeople also work on similar incentive arrangements, based on how much they sell.

An organization may use any one or all three of these methods. The combination of payment methods and the resulting pay pattern within an organization is called its compensation plan.

What about profit sharing?

Like wage incentives, there are almost as many profit-sharing plans as there are companies that offer them to employees. Most plans are based on a system that shares the company's year-end profit with employees. Some plans attempt to relate the employees' share to the overall productivity of the company, based on some agreed-on standard of performance. There are arguments pro and con regarding profit sharing. Many workers would rather have their pay completely unrelated to how well their employers fare in business. Many others feel that a share in the profit is their due. Companies that offer profit sharing do so because they believe it improves internal cooperation and workmanship, and often productivity.

Are fringe benefits the same as pay?

Technically no. But the companies that provide employee benefits —and all companies do to a greater or lesser degree—it might as well be pay. Surveys regularly conducted by the United States Chamber of Commerce peg the cost of employee benefits at over 30 percent of base wages or salaries. Many of the fringe benefits most employees take for granted are included in this figure. These include vacations, holidays, sick leave, health care and insurance, life insurance, education assistance, and pensions. A person has only to be self-employed to find out quickly the staggering cost of social security payments and medical, hospitalization, and life insurance and to find out how costly it is to be sick or to take a vacation without an employer to share these payments.

Of special note is the law's view that supervisors, as agents of the employer, must be able to explain a company's benefit plan, especially its pension provisions, to employees.

Key Concepts

1. Job analysis is the process of gathering information about job or position duties, activities, skill and knowledge requirements, and responsibilities and arranging this information systematically in a written job or position description.

2. Job evaluation is the process of classifying jobs and positions according to their relative worth to an organization.

3. Employees tend to be just as concerned with the equitability of their pay as compared with that of other employees as with its absolute dollar value. Furthermore, it is desirable to provide an orderly visible pay structure so that employees can know and understand the normal progression to higher wages.

4. It is the job itself—its responsibilities, conditions, and demands—that is evaluated, not the aptitudes or performance of the person who fills it.

5. Compensation for work may be in the form of wages, salary, incentive pay, profit sharing, fringe benefits, and other monetary rewards, depending on the organization and the type of work. Job evaluation can contribute to setting fair compensation levels by establishing a progression of job difficulty and responsibility that corresponds to a progression of pay rates, with a specific rate (or range from minimum to maximum) for each job classification.

Supervisory Word Power

Compensation Plan. The total pay system set up by an organization to provide the direct financial return to employees in the form of wages, salaries, incentives, and other cash payments for the work they perform.

Job Analysis. The process of gathering information about, and determining the component elements of, a particular job by means of observation, interview, and study, for purposes of wage and salary administration.

Job Description. A combination of simply written, short statements that describe both the work to be performed and the essential requirements of a particular job or position.

Job Evaluation. The process by which the overall value of a particular job, as specified in its description and requirements, is measured.

Job Requirements. A listing of the specific knowledge and skills, education, and experience needed by an employee to perform the work described.

Reading Comprehension

1. Differentiate between job analysis and job evaluation.

2. List at least five factors typically itemized in a job or position description.

3. Compare the benefits derived by management from a job-evaluation program with those derived by employees.

4. Explain why it is so important in job evaluation to rate the job rather than the person who holds it.

5. Name the four principal methods used for job evaluation.

6. Give an example of the kind of inequity in pay that might irritate an employee.

7. What are some of the things that a supervisor should tell employees about the company's job-evaluation plan?

8. What is the difference between hourly wages and a straight salary? For what kinds of jobs are the two pay methods traditionally used? Give examples of jobs for which each might be used.

9. What is the basic principle according to which pay is determined in a wage-incentive system? Give an example of such a system.

10. In the point plan illustrated in the text, 11 factors are provided. Some factors are more heavily weighted than others. Which are they? Why do you suppose they are assigned the most points?

Supervision in Action

The Case of Who Is the Most Valued Employee. A Case Study in Human Relations Involving Job Evaluation and Compensation, with Questions for You to Answer.

"Hey, Jerry, I'm running out of stock. Will you get me a new load right away?" asked Arva, a press machine operator in a paper box factory.

"You'll have to wait a few minutes," called Jerry, as he trundled by with his walking lift truck. "There're six other operators shouting for stock right now."

"If you don't refill the paper stacker for this machine within five minutes, you'll put me out of business," said Arva. "I'm on a roll today and can make 50 percent bonus. But I won't if you don't get moving."

"Keep your shoes on," said Jerry. "I'll be there as soon as I take care of the rest of the prima donnas and crown princes in this shop. They all want service at the same time."

Jerry did get the stock to Arva in time for her to make her bonus. But at the lunch break, Jerry began hassling Arva on a favorite theme of his. "I work twice as hard as you press operators, but you get more money than I do. All of you sit around on a stool half the time, while I'm on my wheels, lifting, straining, hustling so that you can get rich."

"Any potato head can move stock," said Arva. "It takes skill to do what we press operators do. It takes at least a month to learn this job. And, if something goes wrong, we can ruin a thousand boxes before it gets straightened out, to say nothing of damaging a $1,000 loading mechanism."

"It may not take a college education to move this stock around," said Jerry, "but it sure takes a lot of muscle. And I have to keep nearly a dozen operators happy. All you have to do is to watch out so that a machine doesn't jam and shut down. You ought to give me half of your bonus, because without me you'd never make it."

"I make the bonus in spite of you," said Arva. "If you didn't spend so much time talking, your job would be a snap."

Rudolph, the department clerk, who had been listening to this conversation while he finished his sandwich, couldn't resist getting into the argument. "You two make me laugh. Neither of you could do *my* job in a thousand years. I had to take special courses in bookkeeping and statistics before I could get this job. And my pay at the end of the week is just about the same as Arva's."

"Yeah," said Arva, "but you're on salary. When you miss a day, you get paid anyway. If Jerry or I miss a day, we lose a day's pay."

"Furthermore," said Jerry, "both Arva and I and the rest of the press operators are lifting, pulling, racing around all day. In your job, you hardly ever break a sweat."

"I work with my brains, not my back," said Rudolph. "If I didn't keep on top of the department schedules, your work would be twice as hectic. Without me, neither of you would have any work to do."

"That's a lot of horsefeathers," said Arva. "Here comes Paula, our very own supervisor. Let's ask her who she thinks has the hardest job."

If you were Paula—Arva, Jerry, and Rudolph's supervisor—how would you resolve this argument?

1. Which of the three employees do you think has the hardest job?

2. Why might Rudolph, the department clerk, and Arva, a press operator, end up the week with the same pay?

3. Why might Arva and Rudolph have a higher pay rate than Jerry, the stock handler?

4. What job evaluation factors probably rank highest for Jerry's job? For Arva's job? For Rudolph's job?

5. Arva, Jerry, and Rudolph are each paid according to a different compensation plan. What is the plan used for each? Why would their employer choose to use a different wage plan for each of them?

CHAPTER

13

APPRAISAL OF EMPLOYEE PERFORMANCE

What is the difference between job evaluation and an employee performance appraisal?

In job evaluation, only the job is considered. In an employee performance appraisal (sometimes called a merit rating), you measure how well an employee is doing on that job. Essentially, one technique evaluates a job; the other evaluates an individual.

At its root, what is the true purpose of an appraisal?

There are three basic reasons for making an appraisal of employee performance:

1. To encourage good behavior or to correct and discourage below-standard performance. Good performers expect a reward, even if it is only praise. Poor performers should recognize that continued sub-standard behavior will at the very least stand in the way of advancement. At the most drastic, it may lead to termination.

2. To satisfy our curiosity about how well we are doing. It is a fundamental drive in human nature for each of us to want to know how well we fit into the organization for which we work. An employee may dislike being judged, but the urge to know is very strong.

3. To provide a firm foundation for later judgments that concern an employee's career—pay raises, promotions, transfers, or separation. It is a cardinal mistake, however, to stress the relationship of pay raises during the appraisal period. It is only human for persons who have been told their work is good to expect an increase in pay to follow. If your company's compensation plan doesn't work that way, you may suffer a very red face when an employee tells you later on that "you told me my good work would bring a raise or a promotion."

How formal will the performance rating procedure be?

It varies. Some companies prescribe and carefully follow through on their appraisal programs. Others leave it pretty much up to the individual supervisor. Many formal programs use a "forced choice" form (Figure 13-1) to record the supervisor's rating. Its purpose is to force the supervisor to make a decision on each of the rating factors considered. These ratings can often be converted to achievement scores, which are provided in the illustrated form.

Is it proper to ask an employee to help you make an appraisal of another employee's performance?

Evaluation of an individual's performance and ability is a definite management responsibility. You cannot properly share it or delegate it to someone else outside the managerial ranks. It's perfectly all right, however, and often helpful, to discuss your opinions with your boss or occasionally with your associates (such as an assistant

Employee Performance Rating Form

Dept. _____ Clock No. _____

Rating For _____

Factor	Range	
QUALITY OF WORK 1 Performance in meeting quality standards	Careless	Just gets by
	4	**8**
JOB KNOWLEDGE 2 Understanding in all phases of the work	Expert in own job and several others	Expert but limited to own job
	25	**20**
QUANTITY OF WORK 3 Output of satisfactory work	Turns out required amount but seldom more	Frequently turns out more than required amount
	8	**12**
DEPENDABILITY 4 Works conscientiously according to instructions	Dependable, no checking necessary	Very little checking
	20	**16**
INITIATIVE 5 Thinks constructively and originates action	Good decisions and actions but requires some supervision	Minimum of supervision
	9	**12**
ADAPTABILITY 6 Ability to learn and meet changed conditions	Prefers old methods, does not remember instructions	Learns slowly; reluctant to change
	3	**6**
ATTITUDE 7 Willingness to cooperate and carry out demands	Good team worker	Cooperative
	10	**8**
ATTENDANCE 8 Amount of excessive absenteeism	2 to 3 days normal or 2 days own accord	1 to 2 days normal or 1 day own accord
	6	**8**
SAFETY AND HOUSEKEEPING 9 Compliance with safety and housekeeping rules	Safe and orderly worker: equipment well cared for	Workplace clean and safe
	10	**8**
POTENTIAL 10 Potential ability to lead and teach others	Has no more growth	Future growth doubtful
	2	**4**
PERSONALITY 11 Ability to get along with associates	Disagreeable	Difficult to get along with
	2	**4**
SUPERVISORY ABILITY 12 Additional rating for supervisors only	Poor organization and planning	Inadequate supervision
	7	**14**

Date rated _____ Signed _____

Figure 13-1. Typical employee performance rating sheet to be completed by the supervisor. Note that to minimize halo effect, rating scales for some factors are

INSTRUCTIONS
1. Disregard your personal feelings. Judge this employee on the qualities listed below.
2. Study the definitions of each factor and the various phases of each before rating.
3. Call to mind instances that are typical of employee's work and actions.
4. Using your own careful judgment—check the phrase in each factor that is typical.
5. If employee performs no supervision—do not rate additional factor for supervisory ability.
6. Explain on reverse side any unusual characteristic not covered in regular factors.

Range			Rating
Does a good job **12**	Rejects and errors rare **16**	Exceptionally high quality **20**	
Knows job fairly well **15**	Improvement necessary —just gets by **10**	Inadequate knowledge **5**	
Slow—output is seldom required amount **4**	Exceptionally fast, output high **20**	Usually does more than expected **16**	
Follows instructions **12**	Frequent checking **8**	Continuous checking and follow-up **4**	
Thinks and acts constructively, no supervision required **15**	Requires constant supervision **3**	Fair decisions— routine worker **6**	
Normal ability: routine worker **9**	Short period for mental adjustment, willing to change **12**	Learns rapidly— adjusts and grasps changes quickly **15**	
Limited cooperation **6**	Passive resistance **4**	Poor cooperation, argumentative **2**	
No days lost **10**	3 to 4 days normal or 3 days own accord **4**	More than 4 days absence **2**	
Occasional warning about safety and orderliness **6**	Warned repeatedly about safety and cleanliness **4**	Area dirty, safety rules ignored **2**	
Slow development ahead **6**	Bright future growth **8**	Exceptional possibilities **10**	
Average or reasonable **6**	Well liked and respected **8**	Winning personality **10**	
Nothing outstanding **21**	Good planning and effective organization **28**	Outstanding leadership **35**	

TOTAL _____

reversed, such as for job knowledge, dependability, attitude, and safety and housekeeping. Other scales are mixed in order, such as for quantity.

supervisor). But management alone can determine the relative value of individual employees and their place in the organization.

It should be added that a few organizations use peer ratings successfully. But unless this is an established part of the appraisal program in your company, it should be avoided. Without proper preparation, it will cause far more problems than it will solve.

Doesn't an employee's rating represent only the supervisor's opinion?

A good performance rating includes more than just a supervisor's opinion. It should be based on facts, too. In the consideration of quality of performance, what is the employee's error record? As to quantity, what do the production records show? And as for dependability, what's the absence and lateness record? Can you cite actual incidents where you may have had to discipline the employee or speak about the quality or quantity of output? Answering these questions makes your rating less opinionated, consequently more valid and worthwhile.

Such documented incidents become critical examples (often called *critical incidents*) of an employee's performance. These incidents should undeniably represent the quality—good or bad—of an employee's work. It is a good practice to make notes of such occurrences and place them in the employee's file. At appraisal time they serve to illustrate what you consider good or subpar performance and to support the ratings you make.

What factors should you consider when appraising an employee?

These can vary from plan to plan. What you are trying to answer about an employee's performance, however, are these three questions:

● What has the individual done since last appraised? How well has it been done? How much better could it be?
● In what ways have strengths and weaknesses in the individual's job approach affected this performance? Are these factors ones that could be improved?
● What is the individual's potential? How well could the employee do if really given a chance?

Factors that are judged in appraisal also tend to fall into two categories: objective judgments and subjective judgments. *Objective factors* focus on hard facts and measurable results—quantities, quality, attendance. *Subjective factors* tend to represent opinions, such as those about attitude, personality, and adaptability. Distinguish between the two. Be firmer about appraisal of objective factors than about those involving opinion only. But even subjective factors can be rated with confidence if they are supported by documented incidents. The sample performance rating form shown in Figure 13-1 includes both objective and subjective factors, together with verbal definitions of the various kinds of performance.

How often should you rate an employee?

Twice a year is a happy medium. If you rate too often, you're likely to be too much impressed by day-to-day occurrences. If you wait too long, you're likely to forget many of the incidents that ought to influence your appraisal. Even if your company has a plan that calls for rating only once a year, it's good practice on your part to make an informal appraisal more often.

How can you make sure your ratings are consistent from employee to employee?

One good way to make sure you rate each employee fairly is to make out a checklist with the name of each of your employees down one side of a sheet of paper and the factor to be rated across the top. Look at only one factor at a time. Take quality, for instance. If you have previously rated Tom only "fair" and Pete and Vera "good," decide whether Pete and Vera should still be rated "good" when compared with Tom's rating. Perhaps you'll want to drop Pete's rating to "fair" because Pete and Tom produce about the same quality of work, whereas Vera's quality is consistently better than that of either of the other two.

Another way to check your ratings for consistency is to see whether there is a variation among your appraisals, or whether you have rated all your employees the same. In any group there should be a variety of performances. Roughly speaking, three-quarters of your employees should be in the middle ratings—"fair" to "good." About one-eighth will stand out at the top with "very good" to "exceptional." And another eighth will be at the bottom, rated from "fair" to "unsatisfactory."

How do you convert employee performance ratings to money?

This is strictly a matter of your company's policy. About the only generality that can be drawn is that employees whose ratings are less than satisfactory should not be recommended for pay increases. Where a company has a rate range (maximum and minimum wage rates) for each job, many people believe that only workers who are rated "very good" or "exceptional" should advance to the maximum rate for the job.

If you can't give an employee a raise, why rate the employee at all?

Performance rating is so often associated with money that supervisors and employees alike lose sight of the other important benefits. Periodic performance reviews help a supervisor to:

● Point out strengths and weaknesses to employees so that they can cultivate the former and correct the latter.
● Provide a fair and unbiased method for determining qualifications for promotions, transfers, and special assignments.
● Recognize those employees who have exceptional ability and deserve training for higher positions and responsibilities.
● Weed out those who aren't qualified for the work they are now doing and help assign them to more suitable work. Or, if they are wholly unqualified, to separate them from the company's payroll.

Why should you bother to tell employees where they stand?

People like to know how they shape up, as long as your evaluation is fair and constructive. Informal discussions of ratings with an employee will:

● Give the employee a clear understanding of how well the boss thinks the job is being done.
● Provide the employee with a chance to ask questions about your opinion and give views on his or her own efforts.
● Clear up any misunderstandings about what you expect from the employee on the job.

- Set a course for the employee to improve attitudes and job skills.
- Build a strong relationship based on mutual confidence between supervisor and employee.

Don't employees resent being told?

The biggest fear in most supervisors' minds is that an employee will dislike being criticized. Surprisingly, this fear is unfounded—if the appraisal is based on facts rather than opinion only and you display a willingness to change ratings if an employee can show you you're wrong. People want to know where they stand—even if it isn't good. But don't interpret this to mean that appraisal interviews are free from stress, or that employees will make it easy for you. Chances are they won't.

Furthermore, do not let your discussion with the employee being rated take on the nature of an end-of-term school report. Mature adults resist this. Subordinates can easily regard the performance appraisal as just another way for the company to increase its control over them if this attitude prevails.

How do you handle charges of bias or favoritism?

Unfavorable criticism stings an occasional employee so hard that it's not unusual for the person to react by charging bias or favoritism. Don't try to argue the employee out of it. Your direct denial probably won't be accepted anyway. Instead, try acknowledging that possibly you have erred in making your rating.

For instance, say, "Tony, why do you think I might be favoring Sam? If I've given you that impression, perhaps you can help me see where I've been wrong." So Tony says, "Well, you give Sam all the easy jobs, and I get all the junk that no one else wants."

Your reply ought to be along these lines: "I don't agree that I give Sam the easy jobs, but I do find that I ask him to do lots of jobs that need first-rate attention. He seems easier to get along with when I need something done in a hurry. On the other hand, I've been hesitating to ask you to do anything out of the ordinary. That's because you act as if I'm taking unfair advantage of you. Don't you agree that it's just human nature on my part to lean on people who show they want to cooperate? Maybe it's been my fault that you feel I've favored Sam. I'll watch that in the future. But how about your pitching in and taking your share of the load? Will you try it that way with me, Tony?"

How can you tell employees their work is way below par?

Don't be too harsh on poor performers. Be especially sure that your treatment has encouraged the best kind of performance. Otherwise they may feel that their poor showing is more your fault than their own.

Your guides should be these: Be firm. Nothing is to be gained by being soft. If work has been bad, say so.

Be specific. For example: "We've been over this before. During the last six months I've made a point of showing you exactly where you have fallen down on the job. Remember the rejects we had on the X-56 job? And the complaints on the motor shafts? Only last week you put the whole shop in a bad light by the way you mishandled the shaft job again. It looks to me as if you just aren't cut out for machine shop work. So I'm recommending that you be transferred out of this department. If there's no other suitable work available, I guess you'll have to look for work elsewhere."

Don't rub it in, though. Leave the employee's self-respect. End the discussion by summarizing what you have found satisfactory as well as the things that are unsatisfactory.

Isn't it true that no matter how well some employees do their job, there's little chance of their getting a better job?

Yes. It's especially hard on a good worker who is bucking a seniority sequence and who knows that until the person ahead gets promoted or drops dead, there is little chance to move up. Suppose a number 2 laboratory analyst said to you, "Each time I get reviewed, you tell me I'm doing a good job. But this hasn't done me any good. I'm getting top dollar for the job I'm on, and until the number 1 analyst changes jobs, I'm stuck. All the performance review does to me is to rub salt in the wound!"

A good way for you to handle this gripe is to admit the situation exists, but don't oversympathize. Try saying something like this: "Sure, I agree that it's hard waiting for your chance. But some workers make the mistake of depending entirely on seniority for their advancement. I don't want you to fall into that trap. When the next better job opens, I hope both of us can say that you're fully qualified. That's one of the good things about performance ratings. You can find out where your weak spots may be and correct them. For a person who has your ability and does as well on the job as you do, there's no reason why you have to limit your ambitions to the number

1 analyst's job, either. Maybe you'll be able to jump from a number 2 job here to a choice job in another department."

Should you discuss one employee's rating with another employee?

Not if you can possibly help it. Avoid comparisons when you can. And be sure that each employee knows that you treat each rating as confidential. Try to establish the entire procedure on the basis of confidentiality.

What is the best way to handle the appraisal interview itself?

Whereas there are any number of approaches you might use, there are seven steps that form a pretty good path toward understanding and acceptance of the appraisal.

Step 1. Prepare the employee, as well as yourself, to come to the meeting expecting to compare notes. That way, you have your facts at hand and the employee has the same opportunity to recollect about performance during the previous period.

Step 2. Compare accomplishments with specific targets. Don't be vague or resort to generalizations. Be specific about what was expected and how close the employee has come to meeting these expectations.

Step 3. Be sure to give adequate credit for what *has* been accomplished. It is a temptation to take for granted those things that have been done well and to concentrate on the deficiencies.

Step 4. Review those things that have *not* been accomplished. Emphasize where improvement is needed. And explore together with the employee how this can be done and why it is necessary for the employee to improve.

Step 5. Avoid the impression of your sitting in judgment. If there is blame to be shared, acknowledge it. Don't talk in terms of mistakes, faults, or weaknesses. Never compare the employee with a third person. Stick to a mutual explanation of the facts and what they imply to both of you.

Step 6. Agree on targets to be met during the period ahead. Be specific about them. Relate them to what has not been accomplished during the current period. This sets the stage for a more objective appraisal discussion next time around.

Step 7. Review what *you* can do to be of greater help. Improvement is almost always a mutually dependent activity. An employee who knows that you share responsibility for it will approach the task with greater confidence and enthusiasm.

Where should you carry on performance rating or appraisal interviews?

Do it privately, in your own office or in a private room. You'll want to be able to give the interview your undivided attention. And you won't want to be in earshot of other employees, either. Allow yourself enough time—at the very least a half hour. Otherwise the whole procedure will be too abrupt.

What's the "sandwich" technique for telling employees about unfavorable aspects of their work?

The sandwich technique means simply to sandwich unfavorable comments between favorable comments, as shown in Figure 13-2. For example, say: "I've been pleased with the way you've stepped up your output. You've made real improvement there. I am a little disappointed, however, by the quality of what you produce. The records show that you're always near the bottom of the group on errors. So I hope you'll work as well to improve quality as you did quantity. I feel sure you will, since your attitude toward your work has been just fine."

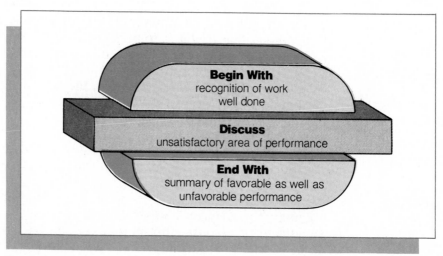

Begin With
recognition of work
well done

Discuss
unsatisfactory area of performance

End With
summary of favorable as well as
unfavorable performance

Figure 13-2. The "sandwich" technique.

The same technique is a helpful guide to the entire appraisal/review discussion. Use it by starting the talk off with a compliment. Then discuss the work that must be improved. Finish by finding something else good to say about the employee's work.

Should you leave room for employees to save face?

Call it what you want, but give employees every chance to tell you what obstacles stand in the way of their making good. Don't interrupt or say, "That's just an excuse." Instead, take your time. Let the person talk. Often the first reason given isn't the real one. Only if you listen carefully will you discover underlying causes for poor attitude or effort.

Confidence in you as a supervisor and in the performance rating system is important. So don't be too anxious to prove that the employee is wrong. Above all, don't show anger, regardless of what kind of remark the employee makes. That advice goes even if the employee becomes angry.

Isn't it dangerous to give employees a high rating? Won't they expect to get an immediate raise or a promotion out of it?

Knowledge of where an individual stands with the boss is every bit as important to a top-notch performer as it is to a mediocre employee—maybe even more so. If you fail to show your recognition of a good job, an employee is likely to feel, "What's the use of doing a good job? No one appreciates it."

Good workers are hard to come by. They should know how you feel, even when you can't show them an immediate reward. Remember, people work for lots more than what they get in the pay envelope.

What's the halo effect? How can you avoid it?

Nearly all of us have a tendency to let one favorable or unfavorable trait influence our judgment of an individual as a whole. This is called the *halo effect*. The range of halo biases is shown in Figure 13-3. You may feel that Carl is a hard person to socialize with, that

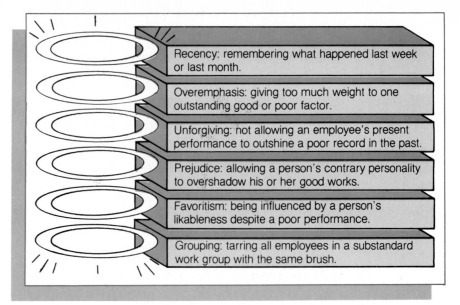

Figure 13-3. The range of halo biases.

his attitude is wrong. This becomes a halo effect if you let this one trait color your whole judgment of Carl so that you forget that Carl's workmanship is outstanding or his attendance is good. In the other direction, you may be so impressed with a worker's loyalty that you may tend to overlook shortcomings. Either kind of halo effect is bad.

To avoid the halo effect, it's helpful to rate all employees on one of the rating factors before going on to the next factor.

What are some common errors a supervisor may make when appraising employee performance?

Plain old bias or prejudice is something that will ruin an otherwise good appraisal unless you make a definite effort to keep it out. Ask yourself, "Am I measuring this person's performance only against the job? Or am I dragging in dress, accent, color or nationality, physical appearance?"

Overemphasizing a single incident will also distort your rating. Guard yourself against saying, "Mary is one of the best people we have. I remember three years ago when she saved our skin by turning out the Thompson job in six hours." Or, "Mack will never be any good. He proved that to me last year when he botched the Smith job."

What sort of follow-up should a supervisor make after the performance rating interview?

Appraisal isn't something that's done today and finished until next year. For it to be of lasting value to you and your employees, you should follow up the appraisal interview this way:

Stick to Your Side of the Bargain. If you have promised to examine an employee's work more carefully to see if you've given a fair rating, do so. Check the past record and show the employee any of the data that's been questioned. If you must change your rating, do it promptly and let the employee know that his or her point of view has been supported.

Provide Avenues for the Employee's Development. An employee will need your help to improve—especially in skills. Give the worker the kind of instruction that your review indicated would help. If the employee needs more versatility, broaden the assignments by giving him or her different and challenging jobs to do. If workmanship is inferior, study what the worker is doing wrong and show how it can be done right.

Continue to Show Interest in the Individual's Work. Drop by the workplace occasionally with a view toward letting employees know they have improved—or gone downhill—since the interview. If they're making progress, give them credit. If they are slipping, point out where you're dissatisfied.

What are the legal implications of a performance appraisal?

There are several. Most of them are related to the following legal doctrines:

● Equal pay for equal work.
● Absence of discrimination on the basis of age, sex, religion, color, or national origin.
● Accommodation of the physical and mental needs of the handicapped and of veterans of the Vietnam era.

To minimize accusations of noncompliance with these legal requirements, try to do the following:

1. Make certain that your appraisals are based on what the job actually requires employees to do, not on what you'd like them to be able to do. That's the value of job analysis and a detailed job description.
2. Be especially cautious in making subjective judgments. Ask yourself, "Could I back them up if challenged?"

3. Stick to facts that can be documented. When in doubt, keep a record of an occurrence that might be disputed.

4. Never say anything, even in the spirit of "leveling" with an employee, that could possibly be interpreted as meaning that your appraisal was based on a favorable or unfavorable reaction to the individual's race, color, religion, age, sex, national origin, or veteran's status. It is difficult, of course, to be so neutral in your judgments, but you must do everything possible to avoid even the appearance of prejudice or discrimination. To do otherwise might bring you and your employer into court.

Should a supervisor keep a written record of what transpires during an appraisal interview?

First ask your employer or personnel department for advice on this one. Then listen to my answers. I'll give you two:

No. If you have developed a rapport during the interview that promises that the two of you will go forward with mutual confidence, you may destroy this valued atmosphere by putting a summary of your interview in writing.

Yes. If your appraisal has been negative and you expect that improvement may not be forthcoming, it's wise to make a written record that summarizes the interview, especially what you expect from the employee in terms of improved performance in the future. If you do make such a record and place it in the employee's official file, you will be expected by law to give a copy to the employee. That's the problem. You'll have documentation if you need it later on, but you may make an enemy of the employee (or at least make him or her wary).

It is also a good idea to collect in an employee's official files some sort of documentation of critical incidents. These might include: regularly kept reports that show the level of and/or quality of output, written complaints or compliments from customers or internal staff members, and examples of very good or very poor work, such as a report filled with arithmetic or typing errors.

Will the management by objectives approach work with your employees?

Yes, if you don't carry it too far. At Step 6 of the appraisal interview, described above, you can be very specific about performance goals for the next period. If you and the employee agree on them, they become objectives of the employee, who can provide self-control (or self-management) in order to attain them. The MBO approach (see pages 131 and 132) appeals to well-motivated, self-starting, responsible individuals. It is less attractive to, and less effective for, those employees who rely heavily on the supervisor for planning and control of their work.

Some employees try very hard, but their performance remains below par. What is the reason for this? What can be done about it?

If there is a weakness in performance appraisal programs, it is that management assumes employees have only to try harder in order to measure up to standards. This is often not the case. Many factors can contribute to employee performance.

1. Individuals may be assigned to work that does not match their capabilities. It may be too easy or too difficult. One solution is a transfer to a more suitable job. Or the job might be redesigned to give the employee a better fit. An employee may not be able to handle the paperwork required. Perhaps it can be done by someone else. Or the job may require too little judgment for a highly intelligent person. Perhaps it can be rearranged to provide options that use this person's analytic ability.

2. Employees may not have received proper training. In any case of continued poor performance, the supervisor should first reexamine the training program and find a way to review the job procedure with the employee from start to finish. A key operating point may have been missed.

3. Individuals may be victims of pressures from the work group. An employee may be trying to conform to your job standards, but co-workers may be giving him or her a hard time. To correct this situation, you may need to approach it from the group's point of view to change or modify their position.

4. Workers may not be up to the job requirements, physically or emotionally. A checkup by the company nurse or doctor may be in order. If there are persistent family problems—divorce, death, severe illness—you may try gentle counseling. Your objective should be to show that you are sympathetic, but that there is a limit as to how long the related poor performance can be accepted.

5. Your own supervision may be at fault. It takes two to tango, and poor performance may be related to a supervisor's failure to provide clear-cut standards, to train employees effectively, or to help with problems and changes as they arise.

6. There is always the possibility, too, that there is some hitch in the operating process—improper tools, materials, or equipment—or a conflict in prescribed paperwork procedures. You may want to review these problems with your own boss or with the appropriate staff departments.

Key Concepts

1. The objective of performance rating is to help the employee improve the caliber of his or her job performance. When made aware of those areas in which he or she is already doing a good job and of those in which there is room for improvement, an employee can be encouraged to develop strengths and to overcome weaknesses.

2. Just as employees consider themselves to be individuals who are valuable to the organization, they want to know how valuable the organization considers them. Because of this desire to be appreciated, employees welcome the chance to talk candidly with their supervisors about how well they are handling their jobs now and how they can improve their performance in the future.

3. The careful and fair application of both objective and subjective factors in appraisals will help assure employees that their ratings are based on facts and not opinions. This assurance helps the people being rated to recognize criticism for what it is: advice that will help them along the way to complete mastery of their jobs.

4. An appraisal interview should first accentuate the positive by giving credit where credit is due. It may then shift to areas where performance can be improved by underlining goals called for by the job but not yet attained by the employee.

5. When supervisor and employee meet in an appraisal interview, it should be on a two-way street highlighted by a mutual examination of job requirements, a mutual review of how adequately they are being fulfilled, a mutual agreement on new targets, and a mutual responsibility for improvement.

6. Carelessness or lack of effort are not the only causes of inadequate performance. Supervisors must be alert to other causes and remedy them when possible. Mismatches between jobs and workers, ineffective training, pressures from other employees, physical or emotional stress, poor supervision, and inadequate procedures may all bring about poor performance in spite of employees' best efforts.

Supervisory Word Power

Appraisal Interview.   A meeting held between an employee and the supervisor to review the performance rating and, using that rating as a basis, to discuss the overall quality of the employee's work.

Critical Incident.   An actual and specific occurrence—either favorable or unfavorable—that serves to illustrate the general nature of an employee's performance.

Halo Effect.   A generalization whereby one aspect of performance, or a single quality of the individual's nature, is allowed to overshadow everything else about that person.

Objective Factors.   Those signs in an employee's job record that can actually be measured: quantities, qualities, attendance, accident record, and housekeeping. They are observable facts and, as such, tend to be free of bias.

Performance Appraisal.   A yardstick used to measure how well an individual fits the job and fills the appropriate role in the organization.

Subjective Factors.   Those characteristics in an employee's approach to the job that cannot easily be converted to quantitative measures, but which must also be accounted for in the performance rating of an employee. They include such factors as dependability, initiative, adaptability, attitude, and personality.

Reading Comprehension

1. Distinguish between employee performance appraisal and job evaluation.

2. How important is it, when rating an employee's performance, that you use the same yardstick you use with other employees?

3. Distinguish between rating for performance and rating for pay increases.

4. Under what circumstances will an employee accept criticism in an appraisal interview?

5. Should performance ratings be treated confidentially, or is it all right to show one person's rating to another? Why?

6. What can a supervisor do during normal operations to help make subjective judgments more reliable when the time comes for performance appraisals?

7. Contrast the sandwich technique with the halo effect.

8. Would it be better to go easy during an interview rather than risk hurting feelings in such a way that the employee can't save face? Why?

9. What are some possible causes of poor employee performance, other than carelessness or lack of effort?

10. When the semiannual appraisal interview is over, why can't the supervisor forget about it for six months?

Supervision in Action
The Case of the Spoiled Lettuce. A Case Study in Human Relations Involving Appraisal of Employee Performance, with Questions for You to Answer.

At the close of the shift on Thursday, Andy Baker, a handler in the central division warehouse of the Waterman Wholesaling Company, made the biggest mistake of his career. He loaded 250 cases of perishable lettuce on a truck heading for St. Louis. It should have gone on the truck standing in the next bay, scheduled to make its run that night to Cleveland. The St. Louis truck was well on its way before the error was caught. Rico Lopez, Andy's supervisor on the loading dock, tried to catch the St. Louis driver at truck stops along the way, but after a couple of hours of frantic telephoning, he gave up. "There's $1,000 of the company's money you threw down the drain!" he shouted at Andy. "By the time that lettuce gets back here from St. Louis, it will be garbage."

"I checked the bill of lading, "said Andy, "and I checked my case count carefully. But I didn't understand that the shipping code we use for perishables is different from what we use for canned goods. Besides, the driver should have caught it."

"The driver thought the cartons contained celery, not lettuce. He'll be in trouble, too. But you are the guy who made the trouble for Waterman Wholesaling."

The following day Rico received a note from the personnel department through interoffice mail, advising him that his semiannual performance rating for Andy Baker was due next week. Rico seized this opportunity to straighten Andy out. On Monday afternoon he called Andy into the shipping office. "Sit down, Andy. The time has come for you and me to have a serious talk."

"About what?" asked Andy.

"About your performance rating. It is six months since we had our little talk, and your work has gotten worse rather than better."

"I thought my work had been getting better," said Andy.

"Better? After last week's foul-up! You are just lucky you weren't fired for sending those 250 cartons of lettuce off to St. Louis."

"But that was just a bad day for me." said Andy. "Most of the time my work has been good. You said so yourself a couple of weeks ago."

"I said that your attendance was finally on target, not that you work on the whole had improved," said Rico.

"What else have I done wrong?" asked Andy.

"Well, your attitude hasn't been all that it should be. Last month when the weather was so cold, every time I looked for you, you were inside standing under the space heater."

"What was I supposed to do? Stand out in the snow waiting for the next shipment?"

"You should have been showing some initiative. There is always a lot of stock that needs shifting around. If you have nothing to do, just come ask me and I'll keep you plenty busy," said Rico.

"I work as hard as the next guy on the dock," said Andy. "You never said anything about my shifting stock on my own before."

"If you took an interest in this job," said Rico, "you wouldn't make the kind of boo-boo you made last Thursday. That tops them all."

"Tops them all!" said Andy. "That's the first mistake I've made so far this year. You keep a logbook on the dock. You show me where I goofed up any other time."

Rico got out the logbook. After scanning it for a minute or two, he pointed out an entry to Andy. "See, you messed up a shipment of melons like this a couple of months ago."

"I forgot that," said Andy, "but I told you at the time that the coding system at Waterman is confusing. If you look at the other entries, you can see that I'm not the only person making that mistake."

"That's not the point," said Rico. "Your work has simply got to improve. I'm filling out this performance form on you today, and it won't be good."

"That's not fair," said Andy. "I'm doing my best. I'm sure that I do as well as the other handlers."

"I'm rating you now, not the other handlers," said Rico. "They will get theirs when the time comes."

1. How objective is Rico's appraisal of Andy's performance?
2. How valid was the critical incident of the mistaken shipment to St. Louis in judging Andy's overall performance?
3. What did you think of the way in which Rico conducted the appraisal interview?
4. Do you think that Andy's performance will improve? Why or why not?
5. If you were in Rico's place, how would you have handled the appraisal and the interview so as to get better results from Andy?

14

TRAINING AND DEVELOPMENT OF EMPLOYEES

Will employees learn without being trained?

Yes. That's the danger. Whether employees are trained systematically or not, they will learn. What they learn may be good, or, more likely, it will be only partially correct. In some instances, what is learned may be downright wrong. A good illustration is the case of an assembler of tiny parts in an electronics plant. Her work was regularly judged to be of poor quality. Her supervisor wanted to get her off the job. The assembler insisted that she was doing her work exactly like the others on the production line. On close investigation it was found that the assembler, who did her work with the aid of a binocular microscope, was looking through the microscope with only one eye at a time. No one had ever told her that to get the right depth of vision she had to use both eyes. As soon as she was instructed in this technique, which took only about three minutes, her work was as good as that of her colleagues.

The point is that there are four ways to provide training: hit-or-miss, sink-or-swim, trial-and-error, and structured and systematic. The only dependable way is the last one: structured and systematic. It is based on a careful study of what the job entails in terms of knowledge and skills and an orderly period of instruction provided by an individual (or individuals) who is well versed in training techniques and aware of the possible pitfalls in the learning process.

Why should a supervisor have to do the training? Isn't this job better done by a training specialist?

Make up your mind that training is your concern and one of the most important ones. It needs to be done day in and day out, for training is the only surefire way to build a work force that returns full value for every dollar invested in labor cost. As a supervisor, you no longer work with your hands. You are judged by your ability to get the people who work for you to produce accurately and well and to turn out more goods at lower costs. Employee training is your biggest tool in accomplishing that end.

When can you tell that training is needed?

Training needs are often the underlying cause of other problems. Be on the alert whenever you observe any of these conditions: too much scrap or rework, subpar production rates, operating costs that are out of line, a high accident rate, excessive overtime, and even a general state of poor morale. Any of these symptoms may respond better to a training program than to, for example, a crackdown on discipline.

What are the special rewards for a supervisor who does a good job of training workers?

In addition to making a better showing for your department in terms of better quality and quantity of output, training puts you in a favorable light in other ways. Effective employee instruction:

- Helps you handle intradepartment transfers better.
- Allows you more time for planning and scheduling your work.
- Provides a reserve of trained personnel in your department for emergencies.
- Wins the confidence and the cooperation of your workers.

Perhaps most important of all for a supervisor who wants to get ahead, training your employees makes you "available" for advancement.

When does good training begin?

When a new employee is hired. New workers who get off on the right foot are like a baseball team that gets off to a ten-run lead in the first inning. There's a good chance of eventual success.

Training recently hired workers, called *induction training* or *orientation training,* is a little like introducing friends at a club meeting where they are strangers. You'd want to introduce them around and try to make them feel at home. You'd show them where to hang their hats and coats, where the rest rooms are. If you wanted to have them think well of your club, you might tell them something about its history and the good people who belong to it. If you had to leave them for a time to attend to some duty or other, you would come back occasionally to see how they were getting along. It's the same way with new employees who report to you. Treat them as persons whom you'd like to think well of you and to feel at home in your department.

What should you tell brand-new employees about their jobs?

An induction talk should cover the following subjects, where they apply:

- Pay rates, pay periods, how employees are paid—by cash or by check—the day first pay is received, and the pay deductions
- Hours of work, reporting and quitting time, lunch periods, washup time
- Overtime and overtime pay
- Shift premium pay
- Time cards, where they are located, how to punch in and out
- How to report out sick

- What do do when late
- Location of lockers and washrooms
- Location of first-aid facilities and how to report accidents
- Basic safety rules, employee's as well as company's responsibilities under the Occupational Safety and Health Administration (OSHA)
- Explanation of employee's options under the company's benefit plans, such as group life and health insurance

Induction activities should include:

- Tour of department or company
- Introduction to co-workers
- Assignment to work station

Just this basic information is a lot for new employees to swallow at once. So don't be afraid to repeat what you tell them several times. Better still, give them some of the more detailed information in small doses. Some today, a little more tomorrow, and as much as they can take a week from now.

Note that in many companies a new employee receives an induction talk from a central service, such as the personnel or training department. As valuable as this talk may be, it won't help the new employee half as much as an informal, one-on-one chat with you.

How do you get down to the real business of training employees to do a job the way you want them to?

Training can be either the simplest—or the most difficult—job in the world. If you can grasp just four fundamentals, you can be a superior trainer. If you don't buy this approach, you'll spend the rest of your life complaining that employees are stupid, willful, or not like workers used to be in the good old days.

The foundation of systematic, structured job training (commonly called JIT, or Job Instruction Training) has four cornerstones:

Step 1. Get the Workers Ready to Learn. People who want to learn are the easiest to teach. So let trainees know why their job is important, why it must be done right. Find out something about the employees as individuals. Not only does this make them have more confidence in you, but it reveals to you how much they know already about the job, the amount and quality of their experience, and what their attitude toward learning is. This familiarization period helps the trainees to get the feel of the job you want them to do.

Step 2. Demonstrate How the Job Should Be Done. Don't just tell the trainees how to go about it or say, "Watch how I do it." Do both—tell *and* show them the correct procedure. Do this a little at a time, step by step. There's no point in going on to something new until the trainee has grasped the preceding step.

Step 3. Try the Workers Out by Letting Them Do the Job. Let the employees try the job—under your guidance. Stay with the trainees to encourage them when they are doing right and to correct them when wrong. The mistakes they make while you're watching are invaluable, since they show you where they have not learned.

Step 4. Put the Trainees on Their Own *Gradually*. Persons doing a new job have to fly alone sooner or later. So after they have shown you that they can do the work reasonably well while you're standing by, turn them loose for a while. Don't abandon them completely, though. Make a point of checking on their progress and workmanship regularly: perhaps three or four times the first day they are on their own, then once or twice a day for a week or two. But never think they are completely trained. There's always something the employee can learn to do, or learn to do better.

Training the four-step way is costly, isn't it?

All training, structured or catch-as-catch-can, is costly. It is the results that count. You may obtain inexpensive training by simply having a new employee work along with an experienced one. That way the costs won't show up immediately on the books. Or you can spend a little out-of-pocket money on a systematic plan such as the four-step method.

At one Johns-Manville Corporation plant in 1975, supervisors tried it both ways while breaking in new operators of extruding machines that convert raw materials into plastic pipe. The unstructured way put new employees on their own at about $60 per trainee. The structured plan cost almost $440 per person for the first trainee. When the total cost of the program was spread out over ten new employees, however, the cost per trainee averaged closer to $80. But what about the results? There was a big difference. The actual time for a new employee to reach a job-competence standard was 16.3 hours for the unstructured way, compared with 4.6 hours for the systematic way. And that was not the only saving. The structured employees operated their equipment almost two-thirds faster during training and turned out only 5.3 pounds of scrap per individual compared with 22 pounds for the unstructured.

How much should you teach at one time?

This depends on (1) the speed with which a trainee can learn and (2) how difficult the job is. Each learner is different. Some catch on quickly. Others are slow. It's better, therefore, to gauge your speed to the slow person. Try to find out why the person has trouble learning. With new employees it may simply be that they are nervous and trying so hard that they don't concentrate. So be patient. Give them a chance to relax. And when they complete even a small part of the task successfully, be sure to praise them.

What's the difference between acquiring "knowledge" and learning a "skill"?

Knowledge is information that can be learned from reading, from listening to an expert, or from keen observation. Skills are ordinarily learned only by doing them. For example, in operating a manually shifted automobile, you may be told that it is vitally important to reach certain minimum speeds before shifting from one gear to another. To apply this information, the operator will need to acquire a very special skill, a "motor" skill. Smooth shifting of gears will only take place after hours of practice learning the "feel" of pushing in the clutch and coordinating that with a sense of how fast the auto is moving. And all of this must tie in with a special movement of the gear stick by hand. Almost all jobs that require an individual to place his or her hands, or feet, or eyes on the material or equipment at the workplace require a unique combination of information and motor skills. In simple terms, the trainee on a job must learn a theory (acquire knowledge) and also learn a skill (application, learned through practice, of a combination of physical and perceptual abilities).

What can you do to make the job easier to learn and to teach?

Jobs that seem simple to you because you're familiar with them may appear very hard to a person who has never performed them before. Experience has shown that the trick to making jobs easier to learn is to break them down into simple steps. That way, an employee needs to learn only one step at a time and then add steps, rather than try to grasp the whole job in a single piece.

JOB BREAKDOWN SHEET FOR TRAINING

Part: Shaft

Operation: In-feed grind on centerless grinder

IMPORTANT STEPS IN THE OPERATION Step: A logical segment of the operation when something happens to advance the work	KEY POINTS Key point: Anything in a step that might: Make or break the job Injure the worker Make the work easier to do, i.e., knack, trick, special timing, bit of special information
1. Place piece on plate against regulating wheel.	Knack—don't catch on wheel
2. Lower lever-feed.	Hold at end of stroke (count 1-2-3-4) Slow feed—where might taper Watch—no oval grinding
3. Raise lever-release.	
4. Gauge pieces periodically.	More often as approach tolerance
5. Readjust regulating wheel as required.	Watch—no backlash
6. Repeat above until finished.	
7. Check.	

Figure 14-1. Sample job instruction breakdown. This illustrates steps in an operation that advance the work, together with the appropriate key points.

Breaking a job down for training purposes involves two elements: First, you must observe the job as it is done and break it into its logical steps. For instance, if the job is to in-feed grind on a centerless grinder, the first step would be to place the piece on the plate against the regulating wheel. The second step would be to lower the lever-feed and grind. The third step would be to raise the lever-release. And so on until the job is finished.

Second, for each step in a job breakdown, you must now consider the second element—called the *key point*. A key point is anything at a particular step that might make or break a job or injure the worker. Essentially, it's the knack or know-how of experienced workers that makes the job go easier for them. The key point for the first step in the centerless grinding job in the previous paragraph would be to know the knack of not catching the workpiece on the wheel. For the second step it would be the knowledge of how to avoid tapering or oval surfaces.

Figure 14-1 shows how this centerless grinder job might be broken down into seven steps with their appropriate key points for training purposes. Table 14-1 lists a number of factors that typically become key points for training purposes.

TABLE 14-1 KEY-POINT CHECKLIST

Key points are those things that should happen, or could happen, at each step of a job which make it either go right or go wrong. Key points include any of the following:

1. *Feel.* Is there a special smoothness or roughness? Absence of vibration?
2. *Alignment.* Should the part be up or down? Which face forward? Label in which position?
3. *Fit.* Should it be loose or tight? How loose? How tight? Can you show the trainee? When can you tell that a part is jammed?
4. *Safety.* What can happen to injure a worker? How are the safety guards operated? What special glasses, gloves, switches, shoes are needed?
5. *Speed.* How fast must the operation proceed? Is speed critical? How can you tell if it's going too fast or too slow?
6. *Timing.* What must be synchronized with something else? How long must an operation remain idle—as with waiting for an adhesive to set?
7. *Smell.* Is there a right or wrong smell about anything—the material, the cooking or curing during the process, the overheating of a machine?
8. *Temperature.* Is temperature critical? How can you tell whether it is too hot or too cold? What can you do to change the temperature, if necessary?
9. *Sequence.* Is the specified order critical? Must one operation be performed before another, or doesn't it make any difference? How can the worker tell if he or she has gotten something out of order?
10. *Appearance.* Should surfaces be glossy or dull? Should the part be straight or bent? How can you correct an unsatisfactory condition?
11. *Heft.* Is weight important? Can you demonstrate how heavy or light a part or package should be?
12. *Noise.* Are certain noises expected (purring of a motor)? Unacceptable (grinding of gears)?
13. *Materials.* What is critical about their condition? How can the worker recognize that? When should the material be rejected? What should be done with rejected material?
14. *Tools.* What is critical about their condition? Sharpness? Absence of nicks or burrs? Positioning? Handling?
15. *Machinery.* What is critical about its operation? How is it shut down in emergencies? What will damage it? How can this be avoided?
16. *Trouble.* What should be done in the case of injury to persons or damage to materials, parts, products, tools, or machinery? How can damage be recognized?

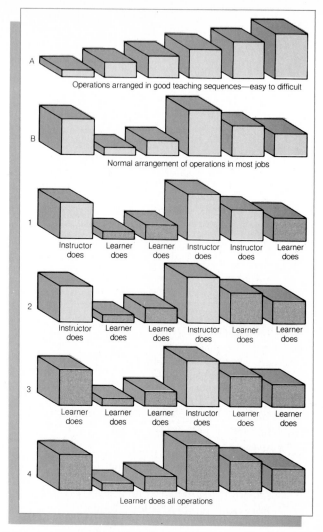

A — Operations arranged in good teaching sequences—easy to difficult

B — Normal arrangement of operations in most jobs

1 — Instructor does / Learner does / Learner does / Instructor does / Instructor does / Learner does

2 — Instructor does / Learner does / Learner does / Instructor does / Learner does / Learner does

3 — Learner does / Learner does / Learner does / Instructor does / Learner does / Learner does

4 — Learner does all operations

Figure 14-2. Arranging a preferable learning sequence. The blocks on Line A are arranged by size to illustrate the preferable sequence for learning a job made up of six operating segments of increasing difficulty. Realistically, however, the segments of a complex job are more likely to be arranged in a sequence like that shown on Line B: the difficult segments are mixed up with the easier ones. Nevertheless, each segment of the job must be performed in the prescribed order and, therefore, should be learned in that order. What can the supervisor-instructor do under these circumstances? Lines 1 through 4 show how effective learning can be arranged by repeating the entire job over and over with the instructor performing the most difficult segments first and the trainee the easiest. With each repetition, the trainee performs in the proper sequence an increasingly more difficult segment or segments until, as shown on Line 4, the trainee performs the entire job alone.

Where will the key points for a job be found?

They may be found in a number of places: in an operating or maintenance manual prepared by the manufacturer of equipment; in a record of "bugs" or peculiarities that has been gathered on a particular operation, procedure, or piece of equipment; or in the mind and/or know-how of an experienced operator. One of the reasons that training results are often poor when an experienced employee has been asked to break in a new one is that the older employee may "conveniently" forget or, more likely, not be aware of key points that she or he has come to take for granted through years of experience. Since experienced employees have "internalized" these key points, they may no longer be conscious of what they are doing. Their descriptions of the job may be either incomplete (missing key points such as "speed up the engine if you feel that the auto is about to stall while shifting gears") or altogether wrong (such as "depress the clutch pedal after you have moved the gear shift.")

As you (or a trained observer) break down a job for training purposes, you'll want to check all three sources of key points. Table 14-1 also lists a number of factors that help to identify key points for training purposes.

In what sequence must a job be taught?

The best way to teach a job is to start with the easiest part and proceed to the most difficult. This isn't always possible, of course. But if you can arrange your employee training in this sequence, learning will go more smoothly and teaching will be easier. Figure 14-2 shows how you can arrange your training sequence so that the learner works up to the difficult parts gradually.

How soon should you expect an employee to acquire job skill?

This, too, depends on the employee and on the job being learned. But, regardless, it's smart to set a timetable for learning. This can be a very simple one like Figure 14-3, or it can be as detailed as you like. The important thing is to use it to (1) record how much each worker knows already; (2) indicate what each worker doesn't need to know; (3) plan ahead for what each worker has to learn; and (4) set definite dates for completing training in each phase of the job.

An analysis such as that illustrated in Figure 14-3 is sometimes called a skills inventory. It tells you what skills each worker has acquired as well as the total skills capability of your department.

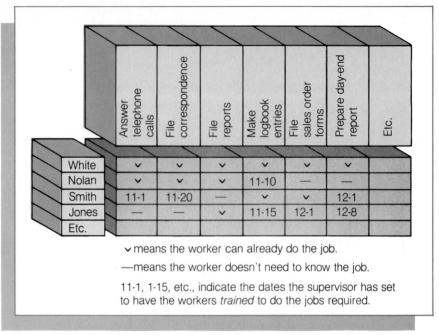

	Answer telephone calls	File correspondence	File reports	Make logbook entries	File sales order forms	Prepare day-end report	Etc.
White	✓	✓	✓	✓	✓	✓	
Nolan	✓	✓	✓	11-10	—	—	
Smith	11-1	11-20	—	✓	✓	12-1	
Jones	—	—	✓	11-15	12-1	12-8	
Etc.							

✓ means the worker can already do the job.

— means the worker doesn't need to know the job.

11-1, 1-15, etc., indicate the dates the supervisor has set to have the workers *trained* to do the jobs required.

Figure 14-3. Sample job instruction timetable or skills inventory. This illustrates (a) jobs in which the employee has already been trained, (b) jobs in which the skills or knowledge is not necessary, and (c) dates for training of various individuals in specific jobs or skills.

How expert should you expect a trainee to become?

It used to be that a supervisor would expect an employee to learn every facet of the job. A pipefitter could measure, cut, thread, and join galvanized, lead, and copper pipe and make every kind of joint. Today, in most industrial situations, the supervisor will expect a pipefitter to know about and do only so much pipefitting as is encountered on the particular job in a specific plant. The same would apply to a telephone operator, who would be expected only to be able to manage the particular kind of equipment one company had, not all the kinds of hookups available. For this and other reasons, the concept of progressive levels of skills (or competencies) is helpful for training purposes. A supervisor can decide (1) what knowledge and skill is absolutely basic to the job at a minimum level of competency, (2) what knowledge and skill will bring the trainee up to an intermediate stage of competency (which may take a month or more, according to the job), and (3) what knowledge and skill will be needed to bring the employee up to a mastery level (and this may take months or years of broadening experience.

Must supervisors do all the training themselves?

No. Instruction is a job that can be delegated—provided the employee who is to conduct the training is a qualified trainer and provided a job breakdown sheet with key points has been prepared. Just as you must know the ins and outs of teaching a job, any employees you appoint as instructors must also know how to train others. This means that they should have completed a course in Job Instruction Training (JIT) or have been thoroughly indoctrinated by you or by the company's training director in how to train. Few things are worse than bringing a new employee over to an older employee and just turning that person loose. If the older worker doesn't know how to train, chances are 1,000 to 1 that the new employee will never learn the job correctly. And the training process itself will be slow and costly. So don't depend on an older employee to show a new one the ropes.

Caution: Even if you have a qualified job instructor in your department, you can never completely delegate your training responsibility. It's up to you to show a personal interest in every trainee's progress and to supervise the training just as you supervise any other of your responsibilities.

Can you depend on an employee to learn a job by reading an equipment manufacturer's instruction manual?

Absolutely not. It's a very exceptional person who can learn how to operate equipment solely on the basis of an instruction manual. Instruction manuals are valuable training aids, however, and they will help you draw up job breakdown sheets. But they are no substitute for personal instruction.

How much training can be accomplished through outside reading and by correspondence instruction?

If employees are ambitious to learn and to improve themselves —and if they are the rare persons who can absorb knowledge and skills through reading and self-help—they can learn much through reading or through correspondence courses. But make no mistake about it, this is the hard way! Few employees are up to it. And despite the claims of many advocates of correspondence courses, the percentage of workers who have learned their jobs this way is very small.

This is not to say, however, that outside reading combined with personalized instruction by the supervisor is not effective. It is, but the two must go hand in hand.

How good is group training?

Personalized training seems to be best for job skills, but it is expensive and time-consuming. Training employees in groups is obviously less expensive. And for many purposes it is just as effective as individualized training. Sometimes, as when explaining the theory behind an operation, it's even better. If you are working with disadvantaged employees such as those under the Comprehensive Employment and Training Act (CETA) of 1973, the U.S. Department of Labor offers this advice:

> Group instruction generally doesn't work; use the individualized approach. Find out exactly what the individual doesn't know and concentrate on teaching that rather than a rounded course of instruction. Use a frequent method of testing to provide feedback on learning progress. Instruction must be set for each individual at his or her own pace without peer group pressures or public disclosure of ignorance.

How good are the various automatic, self-teaching systems?

There are a number of devices and systems that, in many instances, have proven to be very effective for employee training. *Programmed learning,* for example, exposes a trainee to a small block of information and then tests the trainee immediately to see if the material has been grasped. If the trainee answers the question(s) correctly, he or she moves ahead in the lesson. If the trainee cannot reply correctly, he or she either repeats the block or is exposed to the same information in a different form and then takes the test again. The trainee keeps trying at each level of information until he or she passes the knowledge or skill test. Information and skills, learned in small bits like this, make learning simple—and often quicker and more effective than with traditional methods.

When the programmed materials are presented and tested by means of mechanical and visual devices (such as a television screen), the system is called a **teaching machine.** Today, many of these programs and devices are linked to a computer. When learning is acquired this way, it is called **computer-assisted instruction** (CAI).

How quickly do people forget what they have learned?

According to the Research Institute of America, the startling figures in Table 14-2 indicate how fast our learning disappears unless we keep at it.

So for employees to become expert at the job you're teaching, they must practice constantly. And you must keep repeating the important things that these figures show they are likely to forget. This is one reason why follow-up (Step 4) in training is so vital.

What's the purpose of visual aids?

The classic Chinese proverb still tells the story best: One picture is worth 1,000 words. Any device that helps trainees visualize what you're telling them speeds up the learning process. After all, most of us use our eyes to pick up 80 percent of what we know. So it's only natural for training that utilizes the visual sense to be more effective.

Visual aids may include a variety of devices, such as transparencies, slides and filmstrips, and motion pictures. Visual aids may also be simple and obvious, such as writing on a blackboard or demonstrating a point on a machine. Practically nothing beats making the demonstration right on the equipment a worker will use.

In the last few years, audiovisual instruction has increasingly invaded the training field. Tape cassettes linked to programmed texts, audio-TV cassettes with capsulated instructions, and closed-circuit television demonstrations and lectures—live or on tape—have demonstrated their ability to ensure consistent instruction. In the main, however, such methods are prohibitively expensive and are used only selectively where their cost can be justified.

TABLE 14-2 LEARNING RETENTION RATES

Time Interval Since Learning	Percentage Forgotten	Percentage Retained
$\frac{1}{3}$ hour	42	58
1 hour	56	44
$8\frac{3}{4}$ hours	64	36
1 day	66	34
2 days	72	28
6 days	75	25

How good is apprentice training?

Traditionally, the top-notch, all-around skilled artisans have been schooled through apprenticeship. This is a long, thorough, and costly practice. It may take anywhere from 12 months to 4 years. A man or woman who has learned a trade through an approved apprenticeship program will be able to handle with skill almost any kind of job that occurs within that skill class. But jobs have tended to become more and more specialized, and much of what the person who has completed apprenticeship knows never gets used. For this reason the percentage of employees trained through apprentice programs becomes lower and lower. Most employees today are trained for only one specific job at a time. Emphasis is placed on acquiring just enough competency to perform a single job. As a result the training is more to the point, is done faster, and costs less.

What's vestibule training?

When employees are trained by the company on the kind of work they are hired to perform before they begin to work on in-production materials, the training is called vestibule training. It gets its name from the fact that such training is often done outside the area—as if it were performed in the vestibule of the company before actual entry into the working area.

Can you teach old dogs new tricks?

Yes. Older workers can and do learn new methods and new jobs. And although they may learn at a slower rate than younger workers, this is mainly because older workers frequently have to unlearn what was taught them in the past. Older workers often don't have the same incentive to learn that younger ones do. They tend to feel more secure in their jobs and have less interest in advancement. For these reasons, Step 1—getting the worker ready to learn—is of prime importance when teaching older workers.

How do you get employees to want to learn?

Employees must see how training will pay off for them before they pitch into training with a will. So show the younger employees how training has helped others to get ahead, how it has built job security for them and increased their incomes. For older workers, stress the prestige that skill gives them with other workers. Show them how learning new jobs or better methods makes the work more interesting.

Telling workers why a job is done a certain way is often the key to securing their interest. To see the necessity for training, an employee needs to know not only *what* to do and *how* to do it, but *why* it needs to be done.

How smoothly should the training process proceed?

The learning process doesn't go smoothly for most people. We all have our ups and downs. Expect trainees to learn quickly for a while, then taper off to a plateau temporarily. They may even backslide a little. That's the time to reassure them that their halt in progress is normal. Don't let them become discouraged. If necessary, go through the demonstration again so that they can get a fresh start. And pile on the encouragement.

If supervisors are responsible for training, what's the purpose of a company's training department?

The function of a company training department varies from organization to organization. But almost all training directors agree that unless supervisors are sold on training as their responsibility, the efforts of the training department won't be very effective.

Generally, the training department people are experts in teaching methods. They won't lay claim to technical skill about the job (except in cases where technical specialists are employed for certain types of instruction, such as blueprint reading). The training department serves best as an aid and a guide to supervisors in improving the skills of their workers.

For example, training directors can be of real help in determining specific training needs. They can help you recognize and interpret the training symptoms mentioned previously. You'll want their help, too, in learning how to be a good instructor and in training some of your key employees to be trainers. And the training department is invaluable in getting you started in making job breakdowns and training timetables.

Certain employee training is best done by a central training group. Such general subjects as company history and products, economics, and human relations are naturals for them. Other classroom-type instruction (for instance, in arithmetic and work simplification) lends itself to centralized training, too. But when the training department does these jobs for you, you must still assume the responsibility for requesting this training for your employees and for making sure they apply what they learn to their work.

Key Concepts

1. In the absence of a sound training effort, employees learn haphazardly and often inaccurately. Only by careful planning, systematic instruction, and responsible follow-up can a supervisor be certain that employees will learn how to perform their work accurately and in the most effective manner.

2. Learning rarely can begin until trainees are properly prepared to learn. They must first be made aware of the value of the information they are expected to absorb, aware in such a way as to arouse their interest—to motivate them to provide their own initiative in making the training process productive.

3. The process of instruction should utilize many techniques and appeal to many senses. Demonstration of a skill should (a) feature exercise and repetition, (b) involve showing as well as telling how a job is correctly performed; and (c) make an impact on the eyes, the ears, and the senses of smell and touch.

4. Trainees can absorb only a little at a time, and this information ideally should be arranged in a sequence which advances the learning from the familiar to the unfamiliar, from the easy to the difficult, from the simple to the complex.

5. Learning is accelerated to the degree that training provides the learner with insights—intellectual, sensory, and procedural—into the essentials that make the performance of a task successful or not.

Supervisory Word Power

Job Breakdown Analysis. Segmentation of a particular job into those important elements, or steps, during which the employee must perform, induce, or supervise an action that advances the work toward its completion.

Job Instruction Training. A systematic four-step approach to training employees in a basic job skill: (1) prepare the workers to learn, (2) demonstrate how the job is done, (3) try them out by letting them do the job, and (4) gradually put them on their own.

Key Point. The unique insight, knack, trick, timing, or special information that enables a worker to advance the work or task through a particular step in skillful and accident-free fashion. Literally, the make or break of the job.

Programmed Instruction. A self-administered teaching technique (using a specially prepared text or electromechanical device) which presents information in very small, readily absorbed bits. These bits are followed immediately by related questions that test the trainee's comprehension and that must be answered correctly before the trainee proceeds with the lesson.

Reading Comprehension

1. In what ways can a training specialist supplement the efforts made by supervisors to train their employees?
2. How does apprentice training differ from Job Instruction Training?
3. Contrast vestibule training with induction training.
4. Explain why a high accident rate in a machine shop might be related to the absence of, or an inadequate program for, employee training.
5. How does the acquisition of knowledge differ from the learning of a skill? In what way are the two related?
6. Compare the preparing-to-learn phase of training with the identification of a key point.
7. Why is individual rather than group training usually preferred for disadvantaged people (such as those trained under CETA) and for specific job skills training generally?
8. Would it be a good idea to let an employee learn all about the operation of a new machine by reading the manufacturer's instruction manual.
9. Why isn't it a good idea to always teach a job in exactly the same sequence as that in which it is performed?
10. In what way should the training of an older worker differ from that of a younger one?

Supervision in Action
The Case of the Perplexed Reservations Clerk. A Case Study in Human Relations Involving Proper Orientation and Training, with Questions for You to Answer.

When Malcolm finished his preassignment training as a reservation clerk at Border to Border Airlines, his supervisor rushed him immediately into action. That was on Monday morning. On the following Thursday morning, Malcolm was having a difficult day. For one thing, the computer had been down for two hours, and the backlog of requests was enormous. In addition to this, three of the requests he had been asked to field had turned out to be disasters. A customer called from Kansas City wanting a flight to Dallas at 10 a.m. Malcolm made and confirmed the reservation. A few minutes later, Malcolm handled a similar request. As he made his call to the computer, he discovered that he had failed to observe a coded notation on the screen. When he checked with Sandy at the next terminal—the clerk who had been assigned to break Malcolm in—Malcolm discovered to his dismay that this meant that the flight was no longer scheduled daily. It flew only on Tuesdays and Fridays. When Malcolm tried to call the customer back, he was informed that she had left for the airport.

"That's tough," said Sandy. "You'll hear from the airport about this one."

"Nobody told me about what the notation meant," said Malcolm.

"It's all in the instruction manual," said Sandy.

Later that morning, a customer called asking about a complicated routing for a special-discount, midweek flight to San Francisco with stopovers in Denver and Salt Lake City. Malcolm became completely confused and, after several false starts, told the customer that he would have to call back when the terminals weren't so busy. The customer hung up vowing to try another airline.

To cap it off, Malcolm's supervisor, whom Malcolm hadn't seen since Monday, showed up with a complaint.

"Malcolm," he said, "the auditor who monitors your calls tells me that you've been averaging only about 10 per hour. Even for a new clerk, that's a pretty dismal record. You ought to be handling at least 15. The experienced clerks are in trouble if they don't average 20."

"I've been very careful with each call, and the time seems to get away from me," said Malcolm. "In fact, one call tied me up for ten minutes and then the customer got angry when I told him I was too busy to spend more time with him right then."

"You did what?!" said the supervisor.

"I was very busy after the computer had been down, and the information he wanted was something special that wasn't covered in my preassignment training. So I did my best and then said he'd have to call back later."

"Never do that again," said the supervisor. "You should have known that if a request is beyond your knowledge at this time, you should signal for me and I'll switch the customer to a specialist."

"I didn't know that," said Malcolm.

"Sandy should have told you," said the supervisor. "Nevertheless, you're going to have to work on getting your call-handling rate improved. From what I hear, you're spending too much time on each call talking about meaningless things."

"But at the preassignment school we were told to be pleasant with each customer," said Malcolm.

"You seem to overdo it," said the supervisor. "Be courteous when you greet a customer, but don't pass the time of day. Stick to business. And when the reservation is confirmed, close the conversation promptly."

"That's easy to say," said Malcolm, "but it's hard to do without being discourteous."

"You'll learn how to do it if you just keep my advice in mind," said the supervisor as he walked away.

1. What is another name for the preassignment training that Malcolm received? What are some of the things that he may not have learned there?
2. How effective was the "breaking-in" training that Malcolm received from Sandy? Why?
3. In regard to the customer who wanted information on the trip to San Francisco, what key point had not been provided to Malcolm?
4. Identify some of the things that the supervisor failed to do, or did wrong, in training Malcolm for his job.

Model 4

Assessing Employee Performance

Experience shows that supervisors who follow this sequence of steps are likely to get better results when assessing and trying to improve employee performance than supervisors who don't.

Step 1. Ask for the employee's evaluation of his or her performance and then give your evaluation.

Step 2. Identify what you think needs to be done to maintain or improve that performance.

Step 3. Ask the employee to suggest how the desired improvement can be achieved.

Step 4. Agree on an improvement plan.

Step 5. Get commitment to the plan and set up a review.

The Situation

Marion, the supervisor of an airlines reservation section, is about to appraise the performance of Sally, a telephone reservations clerk. In Marion's opinion, Sally's performance is pretty good, with the exception of the above-average length of time she spends on each transaction.

Dialogue

1. Marion: Hi, Sally, pull up a chair. I won't keep you very long. I just wanted to have a chat with you about how things are going. We haven't had a chance to talk for a while except for a few words now and then on line. How're you doin'?

2. Sally: Fine, Marion. No complaints. Everything seems to be going well.

3. Marion: Good. I'm glad to hear that. In general I agree, but let's try to be more specific. How do you rate your performance as an agent?

4. Sally: Well, I think I'm pretty good. I think I handle customers well. I know my codes. I keep up with fare and route changes. I get along with most people. Yes, I'd say I'm doing well.

5. Marion: And I'd say the same thing. You *are* doing well. I agree—you do know your codes and you do keep up with changes. You get along well with everybody, as far as I know. I also agree that you handle customers well—with some exceptions.

6. Sally: Oh, what do you mean?

7. Marion: Well, the data shows that your transactions tend to be longer than the length of the average call. The department average is 2 minutes and 50 seconds. Your average is $3\frac{1}{2}$ minutes.

8. Sally: Maybe I get more complicated transactions than most others.

9. Marion: I don't think that's the case. We know that calls vary in length mainly because of what the customer wants and how the customer asks for the information. But we also know that complicated transactions and simple transactions average out in the long run. When an agent consistently has transactions that are longer than average, it's usually because he or she is *letting* the customer talk too much. In sampling your transactions, it's become clear to me that you are not handling some of your customers as efficiently as you could.

10. Sally: Since I don't get to monitor other agents' calls, I have no way to compare, so I'll just take your word for it.

11. Marion: There is no question about it in my mind. Since all your other skills are excellent, I thought we should talk about what we could do to improve your skills in how to manage complicated transactions or long-winded customers. What do you think we could do that would help?

12. Sally: I don't know, Marion. Maybe I could monitor an agent who's especially good at that and learn the way.

13. Marion: That's a good idea. Or maybe you could sit with me and together we could monitor a few agents. That way I could point out some of the techniques they are using. How does that sound?

14. Sally: Sounds find.

15. Marion: Do you remember the training program you had on this technique two years ago?

16. Sally: Yes. I learned a lot from that but I guess I've forgotten some of it.

17. Marion: Do you think it would be helpful to review the manual and the audio cassettes for that program?

18. Sally: Yes, that might help. And that shouldn't take long.

19. Marion: Okay. I'll get one of those from the training center tomorrow and I'll drop it off at your station.

20. Sally: Fine.

21. Marion: How long do you think it will take you to review that material?

22. Sally: Give me until the end of the week for that.

23. Marion: All right. Then why don't we plan to do the monitoring together first thing Monday morning?

24. Sally: That sounds good.

25. Marion: Let's go over what we've decided. Tomorrow I'm going to get you the training manual and cassettes for the training program on techniques for handling difficult customer calls. You'll review that material by the end of the week. Then on Monday morning, we'll both monitor several agents together—say for two hours.

26. Sally: Okay. I'm willing to give it a try.

27. Marion: Look, don't misunderstand. You're a good agent. You just need to sharpen *one* of many skills you have. I think this plan plus several weeks of practice using what you learn will bring your average down to where it should be. Let's meet one month from today to review the results.

28. Sally: You mean September 8?

29. Marion: Yes, first thing September 8. Okay, good. See you Monday.

Model Analysis

A. Identify by line numbers in the dialogue where Marion has applied Step 1 by asking for Sally's own evaluation of her performance and then by giving Sally hers.

B. Identify by line numbers in the dialogue where Marion has applied Step 2 by identifying what she thinks Sally should do to maintain or improve her performance.

C. Identify by line numbers in the dialogue where Marion has applied

Step 3 by asking Sally to suggest ways to achieve the desired level of performance.

D. Identify by line numbers in the dialogue where Marion has applied Step 4 by obtaining an agreement from Sally about a plan to improve her performance.

E. Identify by line numbers in the dialogue where Marion has applied Step 5 by (1) getting a commitment to the plan from Sally and (2) setting up a date for a review.

F. Recall, and describe briefly, a situation involving the appraisal of an employee whose performance needed improvement. Try role playing the supervisor, with someone else in the group taking the part of the subordinate. Get feedback from the group and from the instructor to (1) sharpen your sense of when to apply each of the model's steps and (2) sharpen the skill with which you handle each of the steps.

Model 5

Coaching to Improve Performance

Experience shows that supervisors who follow this sequence of steps are likely to get better results when coaching employees to improve their performance than supervisors who don't.

Step 1. Observe and analyze the employee's performance beforehand.

Step 2. Identify for the employee the area that needs improvement.

Step 3. Demonstrate how the task should be performed and ask the employee for questions about your demonstration or instructions.

Step 4. Have the employee demonstrate the task to you and then give the employee feedback on that performance.

Step 5. Set up a date to review subsequent performance.

The Situation

Caroline is the supervisor of the transportation department for a major manufacturing company. Cindy is a transportation clerk who gets a great many of her requests by telephone. Caroline has already applied Step 1 of the model, and by observing Cindy's performance and analyzing where it needs improvement, Caroline has observed that Cindy has a disturbing habit of having callers hold on an open line without knowing what's going on. Another thing that Caroline believes needs improvement is Cindy's telephone style, which comes across to callers as bored and indifferent. Caroline would like to hear Cindy's voice project a little more animation and interest, especially when she first answers a call.

Dialogue

1. Caroline: Oh, Cindy, there you are. Right on time. Please sit down. How was your vacation?

2. Cindy: It was great, Caroline. I loved every minute of it.

3. Caroline: From your description, it sounded like a great place to relax.

4. Cindy: It was.

5. Caroline: Cindy, you've done an excellent job in your first year here. I want to tell you again how pleased I am with your work.

6. Cindy: Thanks, Caroline.

7. Caroline: There are two things you could do that would improve your effectiveness. I've had comments about them from several people in the company and I've observed you on the phone, and I think I can pinpoint what needs to be done. One of these is procedural. When you get an inquiry on the phone, you proceed to get the information requested without telling the person on the line what you're doing. That leaves them wondering if you are still on the line. The other thing is a matter of style. It concerns how you answer the phone. A minor change there could make a big difference.

8. Cindy: I didn't realize there were any complaints about me. I haven't had any trouble with anyone on the phone since I started working here.

9. Caroline: I know you haven't, and no one is saying that you don't do an excellent job. I'm talking about two ways in which you could improve your performance. Two simple ways.

10. Cindy: All right. What are they?

11. Caroline: First, whenever you get a question on the phone that requires your finding some information somewhere, say, "I'll get that information for you. Would you like to hold or may I call you back?"

12. Cindy: But sometimes I can get the information in less than a minute.

13. Caroline: Then ask them to hold. Remember, 60 seconds seems like a long time when you're waiting on the phone.

14. Cindy: All right. That's easy enough.

15. Caroline: Good. Now, the other thing you need to think about changing is how you answer the phone. You're probably not aware of how you come across to others.

16. Cindy: I just say, "Transportation Department."

17. Caroline: Well, that's *what* you say, but that's not *how* you *say* it. Now, I can't imitate you exactly, but what you say is something like, "Transportation Department." [sing-song]

18. Cindy: [upset] I don't sound like that at all.

19. Caroline: Cindy, I said *something* like that. I'm not poking fun at you. I'm trying to pinpoint what you're doing. If you were to say it the way you did the first time—"Transportation Department"—and then add your name—"Cindy Davis"—you'd avoid negative reactions by the callers.

20. Cindy: But that sounds so cold and matter-of-fact. I'd rather sound friendly, because I am. Don't you think that's a better way to deal with the people who call?

21. Caroline: I do, and I'm not suggesting that you stop being friendly. But maybe if you were matter-of-fact when you first answered, that would help.

22. Cindy: Well, if you think that would help, I'm willing to try it.

23. Caroline: Good. I'm glad you are. Let's try it now to see how it sounds.

24. Cindy: You mean here?

25. Caroline: Yes, I'll give you a telephone ring and you make believe you're answering the phone.

---

26. Cindy: Okay.

27. Caroline: Ring.

28. Cindy: Transportation Department.

29. Caroline: "Transportation Department, Cindy Davis," okay? Ring.

30. Cindy: Transportation Department, Cindy Davis.

31. Caroline: Again. Ring.

32. Cindy: Transportation Department, Cindy Davis.

33. Caroline: Good. Now let's try it again, but this time I'll ask for some information. Ring.

34. Cindy: Transportation Department, Cindy Davis.

35. Caroline: Good morning. This is Caroline Collins. I'd like to know if a stop in Dallas on my way to Los Angeles would cost anything extra and at what times in the afternoon on September 15 flights leave for Dallas.

36. Cindy: I'll get that information for you. Would you like to hold or may I call you back?

37. Caroline: Perfect. Now, if you'll practice those two things a little, they'll come naturally after a while. Will you do that?

38. Cindy: Sure.

39. Caroline: [rises, so does Cindy] Remember, these are minor things, but they'll help keep our clients happier. Try them. I think you'll feel comfortable doing them in no time at all.

40. Cindy: All right, Caroline. I'll work on them.

41. Caroline: Come in again next Friday first thing in the morning and we'll see how it's working out.

42. Cindy: Fine. I'll see you then.

Model Analysis

A. In carrying out Step 1, what areas of Cindy's performance did Caroline feel needed improvement?

B. Identify by line numbers in the dialogue where Caroline applied Step 2 by telling Cindy what aspects of her performance needed improvement.

C. Identify by line numbers in the dialogue where Caroline applied Step 3 by showing how the task should be performed and asking for questions.

D. Identify by line numbers in the dialogue where Caroline applied Step 4 by having Cindy demonstrate the task and by giving her feedback on her demonstration.

E. Identify by line numbers in the dialogue where Caroline applied Step 5 by setting up a date for reviewing Cindy's subsequent performance.

F. Recall, and describe briefly, a situation where a supervisor's coaching might have helped improve the performance of an employee. Try role playing the supervisor, with someone else in the group taking the part of the employee. Get feedback from the group and instructor to (1) sharpen your sense of when to apply the model's steps and (2) improve the skill with which you handle each step.

The activating (sometimes called the directing) phase of the management process encompasses the pivotal functions of the management process. When plans and controls are in line and the departmental organization is in place, success depends on how well the supervisor is able to get his or her work force moving toward the established goals. Supervisors, more than other managers, must devote the major portion of their time and effort to the directing activity. This vital activity encompasses three skills in particular, which will be presented in this part.

1. Leadership, so clearly related to motivation, requires the development of personal skills for influencing staff members in the pursuit of departmental goals.
2. Communications, the mainstream of interpersonal relations, requires the capability for exchanging useful information in such a way as to ensure effective employee action.
3. Orders and instructions, the most direct form of implementing supervisory authority, require a working knowledge of all aspects of the communications process.

How the leadership/communications picture looks to supervisors

Although 68 percent of all supervisors say they have great confidence in their ability to motivate employees, supervisors don't speak so much of leadership as of how they feel about its outcomes. For instance, here are some leadership-related comments about *what supervisors find most rewarding about their work:*

"Working with understanding employees."
"Improving the enthusiasm of my employees."
"The respect received from employees."
"Seeing individual employees work together as a department."

Statistically, supervisors seem confident about their oral communicating ability but not so confident about their ability to communicate in writing. Here's what the survey figures showed:

How confident are you of your ability to:	Percentage expressing a great deal of confidence
Talk to employees on a one-on-one basis?	88
Write clear memos, letters, and reports?	68

Interestingly, on the subject of communications coming downward from above, the majority of supervisors (82 percent) say they get information about changes in company plans and policies from their bosses or through company newsletters or formal channels. This compares with only 18 percent who say they depend mainly on the grapevine. Related comments show how the absence of good communications—in any direction—can cause some supervisors to identify this as the *most frustrating aspect of their work:*

"Lack of communications."
"Not getting needed information."
"Not being informed about what's going on."
"Depending on grapevine communications."

15

THE ARTS OF LEADERSHIP

What is leadership?

Everyone will give you a different answer to this one. My definition is this: *Leadership is the knack of getting other people to follow you and to do willingly the things that you want them to do.* It should go without saying that these things should be legitimate. They should represent actions that will advance your department toward its goals of higher productivity, improved quality of product or service, and conservation of its resources.

What personal skills does leadership require?

Here again, answers will differ. Most people will agree, however, that good leaders have mastered the following skills:

Persuasion.   Some would call this sales ability. It is the ability to assemble and present to others a good case for what you think should be done. Persuasive talent alone will not make you a leader.

Influence.   This is the ability to exert power over others. Many people possess or are given power, but few learn how to use it. Supervisors, for example, have the power and authority of their position. They have the power of greater knowledge of departmental and company operations than is possessed by their employees. They also have the power that comes from the prestige that is commonly associated with their work. None of this, however, will make you a leader until you learn to use this power to move others.

Rapport.   In this sense, rapport is the art of creating among others a willingness to cooperate. It has a great deal to do with what behavioral scientists call "interpersonal skills." It requires a deep understanding of motivation and the ability to perceive the needs of others. Leaders first establish rapport, then use their powers of influence and persuasion to activate individuals and groups in the pursuit of worthwhile goals.

Are good leaders born or made?

A very few are born that way. Most leaders learn their skills. They do so mainly through hard work and careful study of their employees and the situations in which they do their jobs.

Are leaders always popular with the people they supervise?

The best leaders seem to combine the knack of leading and the knack of winning friends. But most leaders must be satisfied with respect and followers. Why? Because many of the decisions you must make as a leader will not always favor everybody. Sometimes they will please nobody. Chances are you won't win any popularity contests among employees.

Why should you want to become a leader?

The job of a leader is an unbelievably tough one. But the rewards are high. You'll find them in increased prestige and status among the people with whom you work, among your friends, and in your community. And to many leaders the heady exhilaration of making decisions that prove to be correct is reward enough. To others it's mainly a sense of mission. To still others it's the satisfaction that power brings. In industry or in public service, you can have all these in varying degrees. You may even have more money—since leadership is a quality that business traditionally pays a high price for.

How are motivation and leadership related?

Motivation is a power that arises within an individual to satisfy a need. As you've seen earlier in discussions about Maslow and McClelland's views of motivation, these needs cover a broad span, from the need for survival and safety to the need for self-esteem and fulfillment, and from the need for achievement to the need for affiliation and power. Leaders, as shown in Figure 15-1, act to provide satisfaction—or by offering a means of satisfaction—for the needs of others. Leaders don't really motivate. A leader succeeds by first understanding the needs of others and then by applying persuasion and influence to show others that they will get the most satisfaction from following the leader's views.

A person can have motivation without another person's leadership. Leadership, however, cannot succeed without motivation on the follower's part. Take Mary, for example. She has a powerful need to show that she can perform a higher-level job. This may be strong-

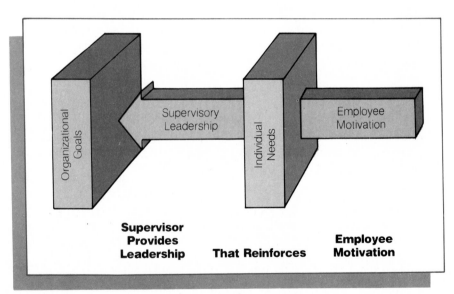

Figure 15-1. How leadership and motivation are related.

enough motivation for her to attend night courses so as to acquire the necessary knowledge and skills. She will do this with or without the encouragement of her supervisor. On the other hand, there is Peter. He has the same aptitudes as Mary. With additional training, he, too, could perform a higher-level job. Peter's supervisor sees this aptitude and offers Peter all sorts of encouragement and assistance in acquiring the necessary skills. Peter, however, is content to stay where he is. His social needs are very strong. He wants to enjoy working with the people he's become friendly with. Enrolled in a night course at the supervisor's suggestion, he soon drops out. The leadership failed, despite the supervisor's influence and persuasion, because the supervisor was not properly tuned to Peter's motivational needs.

Turn Peter's situation around a little bit and look at it again. Suppose Peter is such a fun-lover that his work suffers. His boss tells him that if his performance doesn't improve, he'll lose his job. Peter's reaction is: "So what! I can get another job." At this point the supervisor uses the knowledge of Peter's social needs to persuade him that he'll enjoy working with his friends at his current job more than he might enjoy working with strangers at some other job. Peter accepts this advice and gets his act together so that he can hold his present job. The leadership provided by Peter's supervisor has succeeded. The supervisor established rapport and was tuned to Peter's motivational needs. She used the power of her position to influence Peter's judgment about the consequences of his performance. And then she persuaded Peter that it was in his best interests to improve the quality of his work.

What are some of the personal qualities we like to see in our leaders?

Although our leaders don't always measure up to our expectations, there are a number of characteristics that most of us respond to. The following qualities are not only desirable, they also tend to provide the foundation for leadership effectiveness:

Sense of Mission.   This is a belief in your own ability to lead, a love for the work of leadership itself, and a devotion to the people and the organization you serve.

Self-Denial.   This essential of leadership is too often played down. It means a willingness to forgo self-indulgences (such as blowing your stack) and the ability to bear the headaches the job entails.

High Character.   Few persons become successful leaders who aren't honest with themselves and with others, who can't face hard facts and unpleasant situations with courage, who fear criticism or their own mistakes, or who are insincere or undependable.

Job Competence.   There's been too much talk about the insignificance of technical job skill for the supervisor. A person who knows the job that is being supervised has one of the best foundations for building good leadership.

Good Judgment.   Common sense, the ability to separate the important from the unimportant, tact, and the wisdom to look into the future and plan for it are all ingredients that tend to make the best leaders.

Energy.   Leadership at any level means rising early and working late. It leaves little time for relaxation or escape from problems. Good health, good nerves, and boundless energy make this tough job easier.

Here is a word of caution, however. The "trait" approach to leadership can be misleading. Some natural leaders display only a few of these desirable characteristics. You have only to consider Hitler and Mussolini to find some of these traits missing.

Is there one best way to lead people?

No. Here's where a lot of us have been fooled. Take this situation. Bob Smith supervises three material handlers. Each has become an absentee problem. Listen to how Bob deals with each person:

To Alice: "It's time you get on the ball. I want to see you in here five days a week every week from now on. Otherwise, I'll put you up for discharge."

To Sid: "Your absences are getting to be a headache for me and the rest of us here. You'll have to see that your attendance improves. Let's you and I work out a way to overcome this problem."

To Terry: "Take a look at your absence record. Not good, is it? I'll leave it up to you to figure out some way to straighten it out."

Which method do you suppose works best? The answer is that all get good results. Alice, Sid, and Terry are no longer attendance problems. The reason? There are at least three basic kinds of leadership because there are at least three basic kinds of people. To be a successful leader, you need, for starters, to be able to master all three techniques.

What are the three traditional, and most basic, kinds of leadership?

Autocratic, or Directive, Leadership (the kind used with Alice in the last section). Many people think this technique is old-fashioned, but it often works. The leader makes the decisions and demands obedience from the people supervised. The trouble is that the supervisor had better be right.

Democratic, or Consultative, Leadership (used with Sid). This is very popular today. The leader discusses, consults, draws ideas from the people supervised, lets them help set policy. It makes for involvement and strong teamwork. Some critics call this "compromise leadership."

Free-Rein, or Participative, Leadership (used with Terry). This kind is the most difficult to use. The leader acts as an information center and exercises minimum control, depending on the employee's sense of responsibility and good judgment to get things done. Advocates of this approach also call it participative or integrative leadership.

Are the traditional approaches the only way to lead?

Not at all. Two somewhat related approaches have become popular in recent years.

Results-centered leadership is akin to the "work itself" approach to motivation or to what you have read about Management by Objectives on pages 131, 132, and 239. Using this technique, the supervisor tries to focus on the job to be done and to minimize the personalities involved. In effect, the supervisor says to the employee, "This is the goal the organization expects you to reach each day. Now let's work together to see how your job can be set up so that you can make your quota."

Contingency, or situational, leadership maintains that leaders will be successful in a particular situation only if three factors are in balance. This approach, advanced by Professor Fred Fiedler and documented in many studies, asks the leader to examine (1) the extent of rapport or good feelings between the supervisor and those supervised; (2) the nature of the job to be done, in terms of how carefully procedures and specifications must be followed; and (3) the amount of real power invested in the supervisor by his or her superiors.

Where does the contingency approach work best?

As the term "contingency" implies, the approach that works best depends upon the situation. (See Figure 15-2.) Surprisingly, the authoritative approach, which uses forceful directing and controlling, is most effective in either very favorable or very unfavorable circumstances. That is, it works best when relationships are either very good or very poor, job methods are precisely defined, and the leader's true authority is either very strong or very weak. In the fuzzier, or

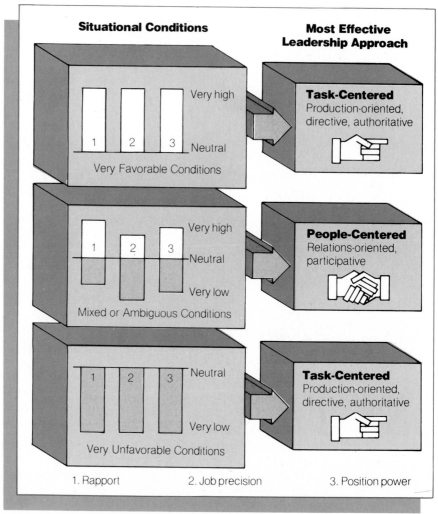

Figure 15-2. Choosing leadership style according to the situation.

middle, situations, the participative approach is likely to be more successful.

In other words, the *authoritative approach* works out best (1) in situations where the supervisor has lots of real power, the process requires strong control, and rapport with employees is good; and (2) in situations where just the opposite conditions prevail.

The *participative approach* is best where the supervisor's authority hasn't been clearly spelled out by top management or acknowledged by the employees, where the process and procedures are somewhat flexible, and where the rapport between supervisor and employees is only middling good.

The contingency approach tends to explain why dictatorial supervisors can be effective in some situations and not in others. Similarly, it helps to show where participative leadership may work best and to suggest where it might fail. An authoritative approach looks good for assembly-line workers or for labor crews cleaning up the area. A participative approach seems favorable on jobs for which exact procedures are hard to set or for jobs that require creativity or initiative. These conclusions are contingent on the authoritative leader's having either high or low position power and high or low rapport, and on the participative leader's having moderate rapport and only so-so authority.

The terminology is getting a little confusing. Where do task-centered and people-centered leadership fit in?

Followers of the contingency theory are more likely to use the term *task-centered* for authoritative leadership and the term *people-centered* for anything from democratic to participative. Later on in this chapter, you'll find that a couple of famous researchers characterize the task-centered type as having a "concern for production" and the other as having a "concern for people." The terms aren't as important as grasping the idea that the two approaches differ in the focus of their attention. Some leaders are overly preoccupied with the job to be done. Others may worry only about the people who perform the work. In a page or two, you'll see that the experts believe that good leaders balance their attention between both factors.

Which kind of leadership is best?

Many successful managers will tell you that democratic leadership is the best method to use. The fact is that whereas the democratic way may involve the least risk, you'll hamper your leadership role if you stick only to that method. You can play a round of golf with a driver, but you'll get a much better score if you use a wedge in a sand trap and a putter on the greens.

Suppose you have a problem of cutting down on scrap in your department. You may find it better to consult in a group meeting with all your workers to let them decide how they'll approach the problem (democratic leadership). Then the inspector, when informed of your plan, can adjust inspection techniques accordingly (free-rein). Merely tell the scrap collector how you want the waste sorted (autocratic). You see, you'd be using all three kinds of leadership to deal with the same problem.

Figure 15-3 illustrates what one noted authority calls the continuum of leadership styles. At one extreme the supervisor relies on absolute authority; at the other, subordinates are allowed a great deal of freedom.

How much does a supervisor's personality have to do with leadership?

A good personality helps. Employees may react more easily to a supervisor who has a ready smile and who is warm and outgoing. But personality must be more than skin-deep to be effective. Much more important is your real desire to understand and sympathize with the people who work for you. Fair play, interest in others, good decisions, and character will help make you a stronger leader than if you rely solely on personality.

Likewise, one kind of leadership may fit your personality better than the other two do. And you may rely more on this kind of leadership than on the others. But work hard to keep from depending on just one approach.

What do employee personalities have to do with the kind of leadership you exercise?

Noted author Auren Uris advises that you'll find the following connections between leadership methods and types of personality:

● Aggressive, hostile persons do better under autocratic leaders. Their latent hostility must be firmly channeled to confine their work to constructive ends.

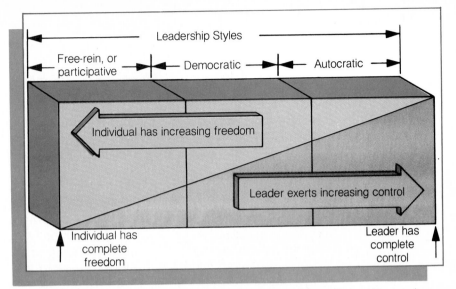

Figure 15-3. Continuum of leadership styles. Adapted from Robert Tannenbaum and Warren H. Schmidt, "How to Choose a Leadership Pattern," *Harvard Business Review,* March–April, 1958, pp. 95-101.

● Aggressive, cooperative persons work better under democratic or free-rein leadership. Their self-assertiveness takes constructive paths, and they will head in the right direction when on their own.
● Insecure persons, who tend to depend on their superiors, do better under the firmer hand of the autocratic leader.
● Individualists, or solo players, are usually most productive under free-rein leadership—if they know the job well.

Uris calls this point of view "followership." It is based on a well-established fact that certain kinds of persons naturally follow certain kinds of leaders better than others. The trick is to match them when you can.

What kind of leadership works best in an emergency?

Autocratic leadership is fast. When an emergency arises—say a live-steam hose breaks loose and whips about, endangering lives—you wouldn't want to pussyfoot around consulting employees as to what to do. You'd probably shout, "Hey, Smitty, cut the steam valve! Carl, watch the safety!"

Should your leadership approach be varied according to an employee's age?

One school of thought believes it should—provided that you are talking about a person's emotional maturity, not a chronological age. The **life-cycle theory of leadership** presumes that individuals—and newly formed groups of employees—move through progressive stages of emotional maturity. These stages can be likened to chronological ages. For example, children usually need firm, autocratic leadership. As children mature and start to "grow up" emotionally, they generally respond most favorably to democratic leadership. A mature person, however, is most likely to appreciate the opportunities for achievement that participative leadership offers. So it is with employee groups. A newly formed department will probably require tight, autocratic leadership. As time passes and people in the group get to know each other's capabilities and quirks, as well as the boss's, a democratic, consultative form of leadership will probably get the best results. A fully mature group, one that really knows its strengths and weaknesses, can be trusted to respond most effectively to participative leadership. You should be warned, of course, that many children are old beyond their years, and that many adults never do grow up. The same is true of employee groups. Individual or group, what counts here is emotional maturity.

What kind of supervision generally gets the best results?

At first it may seem hard to believe that supervisors who place less emphasis on production goals actually get higher production from the employees they supervise. This is only one aspect of the picture of the successful supervisor drawn as a result of a landmark study made in 1948 at the University of Michigan. Supervisors in high-production groups were characterized in the following ways:

● Their own bosses gave them a freer hand than was given to supervisors in low-production groups.
● They were more employee-centered and spent more time in supervising and less time on mechanical and paperwork details.
● They encouraged employees to contribute their ideas on how best to get things done.

Note how close these findings come to describing free-rein, or participative, leadership. Rensis Likert, who had much to do with pursuing the Michigan studies, came to believe that participative leadership, which he called "System 4," is the only form of leadership truly in tune with twentieth-century life. You may not be able to use it in every situation, but where you can, it brings the best results.

Must a people-centered leader always get participation?

No. If you plan your big targets by first asking for and considering the opinions of your employees, they'll understand that there isn't time to handle every decision that way. Participation is a long-range affair. If you show that you want and respect employees' opinions —and that your decisions are affected by these opinions—you'll have achieved the goal of making employees feel they are part of a team. An occasional oversight or an infrequent decision made without their counsel won't destroy the feeling that generates cooperation.

By sowing the seeds of participation generously, you'll also find that you won't have to take over many of the minor decisions that occupy your attention otherwise. Employees who know from experience that their opinions are desired know in advance how the team (their team and yours) would act if it had a chance to go into a huddle. They'll act accordingly.

Theory X, Theory Y. What's this all about?

To get along with people effectively, you must make a couple of fundamental decisions. First you must recognize your responsibility for managing human affairs at work. But you must always weigh this concern of yours against the practical urgencies of technical and administrative matters.

Douglas McGregor, late professor of industrial management at the Massachusetts Institute of Technology, had much to offer supervisors in his thoughtful work *The Human Side of Enterprise*. Most of today's management thinking was forged to meet the needs of a feudal society, reasoned McGregor. The world has changed, and new thinking is needed for top efficiency today. That's the core of this unique philosophy of pitting Theory X against Theory Y.

Theory X, the traditional framework for management thinking, is based on the following set of assumptions about human nature and human behavior:

1. The average human being has an inherent dislike of work and will avoid it if possible.
2. Because of this human characteristic of dislike of work, most people must be coerced, controlled, directed, or threatened with punish-

ment to get them to put forth adequate effort toward the achievement of organizational objectives.

3. The average human being prefers to be directed, wishes to avoid responsibility, has relatively little ambition, and wants security above all.

Do these assumptions make up a straw person for purposes of scientific demolition? Unfortunately, they do not. Although they are rarely stated so directly, the principles that constitute the bulk of current management action could have been derived only from assumptions such as those of Theory X.

Theory Y finds its roots in recently accumulated knowledge about human behavior. It is based on the following set of assumptions:

1. The expenditure of physical and mental effort in work is as natural as play or rest.

2. External control and the threat of punishment are not the only means for bringing about effort toward organizational objectives. Individuals will exercise self-control in the service of objectives to which they are committed.

3. Commitment to objectives depends on the rewards associated with their achievement. The most important rewards are those that satisfy needs for self-respect and personal improvement.

4. The average human being learns, under proper conditions, not only to accept but also to seek responsibility.

5. The capacity to exercise a relatively high degree of imagination, ingenuity, and creativity in the solution of organizational problems is widely, not narrowly, distributed in the population among both men and women.

6. Under the conditions of modern industrial life, the intellectual potentialities of the average human being are only partially realized.

What makes Theory Y so applicable today?

Under the assumptions of Theory Y, the work of the supervisor is to integrate the needs of employees with the needs of the department. Hard-nosed control rarely works out today. Here are McGregor's words:

The industrial manager is dealing with adults who are only partially dependent. They can—and will—exercise remarkable ingenuity in defeating the purpose of external controls which they resent. However, they can—and do—learn to exercise self-direction and self-control under appropriate conditions. His task is to help them discover objectives consistent both with organizational requirements and with their own personal goals. And to do so in ways that will encourage genuine commitment to these objectives. Beyond this, his task is to help them achieve these objectives: to act as teacher, consultant, colleague, and only rarely as authoritative boss.

Where does the Managerial Grid fit in?

The Managerial Grid helps supervisors to assess their leadership approach. The grid, devised by industrial psychologists Robert R. Blake and Jane S. Mouton, makes two measurements of a leader's approach: concern for production and concern for people. As shown in Figure 15-4, these two factors are typically plotted on a grid chart. The least concern for each factor is rated 1, the highest 9. To judge your own approach, first rate yourself according to your concern for people; say you think it is fairly high—a 6 score. Next rate your emphasis on production or job results; say you rate that as medium—a score of 5. You then find your place on the Managerial Grid by putting a mark on the chart 6 squares up and 5 squares across.

Blake, Mouton, and others have given nicknames to various places on the grid. The lower left-hand corner (1,1) could be called the cream puff, a supervisor who doesn't push for anything. The upper left-hand corner (1 for production, 9 for people) can be called the do-gooder, a person who watches out for people at the cost of overlooking production needs entirely. The lower right-hand corner (9 for production, 1 for people) is the hard-nose, a supervisor for whom production is all that counts. The supervisor near the middle of the chart (5 for both production and people) is the middle-of-the-roader, a person who makes a reasonable push for both concerns. In the eyes of many, all supervisors should strive to make their leadership performance score 9,9 (highest for both production and people) so that they might be called professionals.

The grid implies the need for leadership that is fully balanced between all-out concerns for both people and production. This is somewhat at odds with the contingency approach, which suggests that certain situations respond best to a task- (or production-) centered leader and other situations to a people-centered leader.

Are there any other tips for leaders?

Advice for leaders is free and plentiful. And most of it makes sense for the person who can put it into practice.

Be Predictable. People want to know where they stand with the boss—tomorrow as well as today. You might borrow a page from the books on child psychology. The experts have studied the maladjustments and the frustrations of kids. They suggest one good rule for handling them: Be consistent. If a child is praised for an act today and bawled out for the same act tomorrow—bingo, tears. If the child

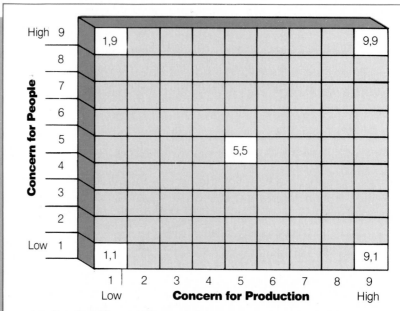

1,9 Comfortable and Pleasant. Attempts are made to promote harmony and goodwill. Issues which may cause disruption are smoothed over with the hope that things will continue to go well in the work situation.

9,9 Quality Achievement. People work together to get high quality results and are willing to measure their accomplishments against the highest possible standard. All involved support and hold one another accountable for actions influencing the result.

5,5 Accommodation and Compromise. With this go-along-to-get-along, "don't-rock-the-boat" approach progress may be made but only within the company's rules and regulations.

1,1 Do-Nothing Neutrality. An apporach associated with low concern, "passing the buck," and skillfully camouflaged, "doing little or nothing."

9,1 Produce or Perish. Results may be achieved for a short time. Used over the long term, it motivates people to "beat the system" or, at the very least, decreases their willingness to contribute.

Figure 15-4. The supervisory grid. From Robert R. Blake and Jane S. Monton, *The Grid for Supervisory Effectiveness,* Scientific Methods, Inc., Austin, Texas, 1975, p. 5. With permission of the copyright holders.

tries to help with the dishes, breaks one, and gets a scolding —watch out for tantrums. If you embarrass the child in front of others, look out—the cat may be painted green just to make it look ridiculous, too. It's the same thing for adults.

Put Yourself in the Employee's Place.   Maybe you recall the last time you were at a ball game. Did you find yourself leaning with every pitch—trying to put body English on foul balls? Do the same thing with people. This mental shift can become a regular and desirable habit. It will help you understand, predict, and direct the responses of people.

Show Your Enthusiasm.   If you sincerely like an idea, the way an employee did a job, or your next assignment, show this feeling to others in words and manner. It is a mistake for a supervisor to "play it cool" in relationships with employees. The personal atmosphere you create determines if people will have the welcome mat out for you.

Be Interested in Employees' Welfare.   People want a supervisor or manager "whom they can trust in time of need, to whom they can go when they need advice about personal affairs," according to Brehon Somervell, past president of the Koppers Company, Inc. "It is a good outfit, indeed," when employees can "ask the boss."

Treat Employees Equally.   Men and women insist on a leader's having a sense of fair play. They want to believe they are being given assignments on their merits and that the boss won't play favorites. Favoritism a sign of weak character and can wreck an organization.

Key Concepts

1. Leadership requires the ability to develop rapport with others and to apply appropriate persuasion and influence so as to obtain their willing cooperation in pursuing legitimate organizational goals.

2. Approaches to leadership range along a broad spectrum from those that are purely autocratic to those that are highly participative.

3. The techniques of leadership can be learned, provided the individual has the strength of character and the energy this responsibility demands.

4. The supervisor should strive to match his or her leadership style and approach to the specific situation and to the personalities of subordinates.

5. The success of leadership depends less on technique than on the creation of enthusiastic attachment and deep-seated trust between supervisor and subordinate. This relationship can be fostered by modern views of human nature (such as Theory Y) and by balancing concerns for production with concerns for people.

Supervisory Word Power

Contingency Model of Leadership. The belief that the leadership style that will be most effective in a given situation can be predicted by examining the intensity of three interacting factors: (1) the rapport between the leader and subordinates, (2) the precision with which the prescribed job methods must be followed, and (3) the amount of real power the organization has invested in the leader.

Continuum of Leadership. A range of leadership approaches that progresses, with no clear-cut distinctions, from the extremes of autocratic control by the supervisor to complete freedom for subordinates.

Managerial Grid. A method of evaluating a supervisor's approach to leadership by comparing the extent of his or her (1) concern for production and (2) concern for people.

Theory X. An essentially negative approach to human relations whereby a supervisor presumes that most people don't like to work and, accordingly, must be pushed, threatened, and disciplined; that they wish to avoid responsibility and prefer job security above all. Employees must therefore be pushed constantly and threatened with loss of security and other punishments when they don't produce.

Theory Y. An essentially positive approach to human relations in which a supervisor presumes that, given meaningful work, most people will try hard to achieve, especially when there is an opportunity to improve their regard for themselves. Given these opportunities, most people will provide their own initiative and objectives and exert self-control to attain them.

Reading Comprehension

1. Describe three skills that successful leaders must develop.
2. Compare *autocratic* leadership with *democratic* leadership.
3. Which kind of leadership is best in an emergency? Why?
4. Give an example of how an individual's motivational needs offer an opportunity for effective leadership action on the part of a supervisor.
5. If an employee tends to be aggressive but cooperative, which style of leadership might be most suitable? Why?
6. Provide examples of the use of a leadership style at three different points along the continuum of leadership styles.
7. Which kind of maturity is most important in applying the life-cycle theory of leadership? Why?
8. If you had to choose between a supervisor who was predictable and consistent and one whose enthusiasm was contagious, which one would you rather work for? Why?
9. What might a supervisor do to move his or her placement on the Managerial Grid from 3,7 to 7,7? In what way is the Managerial Grid related to Theory X and Theory Y?
10. According to Fiedler's contingency model of leadership, what is likely to be the best approach in a situation where the supervisor has been newly appointed, relationships with the new group are stand-offish, and the task to be performed requires great accuracy? Why?

Supervision in Action
The Case of the New Sales Supervisor. A Case Study in Human Relations Involving Leadership, with Questions for You to Answer.

Ada Force had just been appointed supervisor in a suburban department store. Before her promotion to the management level, she had been a salesperson for five years. Her work on that job had consistently been of superior caliber.

When Ada assumed her new position, her boss, the store manager, reviewed with her the scope of her responsibilities. He made a strong point about the goals of improved customer service and an increase in the amount of sales per customer. To attain these goals in her department, said the store manager, Ada would have to tighten up on a number of employee practices that had become lax. In particular, he didn't want customers to be left unattended, especially during the lunch hour and just before the store's closing. Ada agreed to do her best to attain these goals and to get her staff back in line whereever there was a problem. Then she headed out to the floor for her new assignment.

Except for a little good-natured roasting, Ada's former co-workers wished her well on her new job. And for the first week or two most of them were cooperative—even helpful—while Ada was adjusting to her supervisory role. When Ada spoke briefly to her staff one day (at a morning meeting just before the store opened) about the department's objectives and the need for tighter observance of store rules, no one voiced an objection.

Late Friday afternoon during Ada's third week as a supervisor, however, a disturbing incident took place. Having just made the rounds of her department, Ada stopped in the washroom. There she saw two of her old associates, Mae and Fran, washing up.

"Say, guys. You shouldn't be cleaning up this soon. It's at least another 15 minutes until quitting time. There are still customers on the floor," said Ada. "Get back on the floor, and I'll forget I saw you in here."

"Come off it, Ada," said Mae. "You used to slip up here early yourself on Fridays. Just because you've got a little rank now, don't think you can come down on us." To this Ada replied, "Things are different now. Both of you get back on the job or I'll make trouble." Mae and Fran said nothing more, and they both returned to the floor.

From that time on Ada began to have problems as a supervisor. Mae and Fran gave her the silent treatment. The rest of the sales force seemed to forget how to do the simplest things. Sales checks were prepared improperly. Customer complaints increased. Merchandise was spoiled. By the end of the month Ada's department had the poorest performance record.

1. How should Ada have handled the washroom incident? Why?
2. What shortcomings do you find in Ada's leadership?
3. What do you think Ada should do about the silent treatment she got from Mae and Fran?
4. If you were Ada, what would you do to furnish the kind of leadership that would get your department's performance back on track?

16

EFFECTIVE ORAL AND WRITTEN COMMUNICATIONS

What is the significance of the term communications when used in connection with supervision?

The term *communications* is defined as the process in human relations of passing information and understanding from one person to another. As a supervisory responsibility, the process is frequently called employee communications, although the communicating process is equally important between supervisor and supervisor and between supervisor and boss.

The term was, of course, originally applied to mechanical and electronic means for transmitting and receiving information, such as newspapers, bulletin board announcements, computer printouts, radio, telephone, and video screens. Employee communications have many of the qualities—and limitations—of mechanical means, but they are infinitely more subtle and complex. So try to treat communications carefully.

How do communications activate the organization?

By providing the linking pin between plans and action. You may have put together the best set of plans ever and staffed your department with the best people available. But until something begins to happen, you will have accomplished nothing. Communications with your employees are what starts and keeps the whole plan in motion.

Good supervisors can't know too much about employee communications. Their leadership is affected by what information they can pass on to others through communications. Unless employees know how you feel and what you want, the best management ideas in the world go astray. This is especially true where group effort is essential.

Group attitudes will depend on how well you can interpret your company's interests and intentions to workers. And you'll need all the communicating skill you can muster to secure the cooperation so necessary from your work team.

What is meant by the communication process?

When psychologists and sociologists use this term they mean the entire process, or system, that enables an idea in one person's mind to be transmitted, understood, and acted on by another person. This process is illustrated in greater detail in Figure 17-1. It's enough to say at this point that the communications process involves the most basic of human relationships. As with leadership, it requires rapport along with a sensitivity to how others perceive ideas and information. It also requires better-than-average skill in using the spoken word, the written word, and the nonverbal signals that your face and body send out to others. Last, but far from least, it demands of supervisors that they be good at receiving communications from others. That is, they must be good listeners, too.

Is any one method of communications better than another?

Each situation has its own best method or combination of methods. To show some employees how much you appreciate their cooperation, all you may need to do is give them an occasional pat on the shoulder. But others may need frequent vocal assurance. Still others will believe only what you put down on paper. So it seems that the most successful communicating is done by supervisors who know many ways of getting their ideas, instructions, and attitudes across.

What are the two basic ways to set up an employee communications system in your department?

By using either a wheel (or satellite) or a web (or system network). In a wheel system, communications tend to be restricted. The supervisor stands at the center, or hub, as shown in Figure 16-1. Information is passed out to, and received from, employees via the spokes. Employees are not encouraged to exchange ideas between one another. In web networks, communications tend to be more open. The supervisor still stands at the center of the system, but employees are encouraged to exchange information freely in any channel they can find open.

In the wheel network the supervisor controls the flow of information. This helps to avoid inconsistencies in interpreting what was said. The wheel approach seems best with simple, repetitive tasks. It protects privacy and allows the supervisor to be very personal in talks with employees. But it tends to be slow and ponderous when new or complex problems are being dealt with.

In the web network the supervisor acts more as facilitator and verifier than as communicator. The system distributes ideas quickly and helps to get agreement for them and application of them on a broad front. The system does have drawbacks. Rumors often get out of control. Progress toward goals and changes in methods may not be fed back to the supervisor until too late. But advantages tend to outweigh disadvantages. Too, open communications invite employee participation in solving problems and helps build team spirit.

Should a supervisor use the company grapevine as a means of communication?

Listen to it. It's one way of getting an inkling of what's going on. But don't depend on it for receiving accurate information. And never use it to disseminate information.

The grapevine gets its most active usage in the absence of good communications. If you don't tell employees about changes that will affect them, they'll make their own speculations—via the grapevine. As a result, the grapevine carries rumors and outright lies more often than it does the truth. Surveys show that whereas employees may receive a lot of their information from the rumor mill, they'd much rather get it from a responsible party—the boss. You build good will by spiking rumors. So show employees you welcome the chance to tell the truth.

Some authorities, however, believe that if you talk to enough employees and prove yourself to be a reliable source of company information, the grapevine will work for you. This is probably true. But leaking information to the work group deliberately through the grapevine isn't the same—and may tend to isolate you in the end.

Some people talk about three-dimensional communications. What are they referring to?

Communication should not be a one-way street. For a complex, modern organization to function smoothly, communications must move in

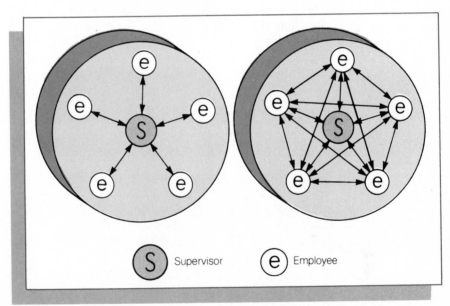

Figure 16-1. Examples of restricted and open communication systems. "Wheel" or "Satellite" System: Supervisor maintains control. There are no exchanges between employees. System is relatively restricted. "Web" System: Supervisor serves as stimulator and validator. There are few or no controls. There is free and open exchange among employees and between employees and supervisor.

three ways. Not only must you furnish information downward to employees, but employees must communicate their ideas and feelings upward to you. And since staff and interdepartmental cooperation is so important, there must be horizontal, or sideways, flow of information, too. This up, down, and across process is called three-dimensional communications.

Supervisors can't have the answer to everything that is happening in the company, can they?

No. But it is your responsibility to keep informed on matters of importance. If you don't know what's going on, you can't tell others. This applies to many areas that are of concern to employees—such as social security, pension plans, the way an incentive is applied, and leave of absence policy. When an employee asks you something you don't know about, you'll lose face if you have to say that you'll find out from someone else every time. Soon employees will figure you're not knowledgeable and will go to someone else—such as their shop steward—for information.

When you are caught unprepared, however, don't bluff. And don't say something like: "How should I know? Nobody tells me anything." Instead, strive to be in a position of confidence with higher management so that you can say: "I don't know the answer to that one. But I'll certainly try to find out and let you know as soon as I can."

Do employees believe what you tell them?

Not all the time, any more than you believe everything you hear. But if you shoot as straight as you can in all your conversations with them, they'll look to you as a reliable source of information. It is just as important that employees have confidence in the purpose of your communications. They should never wonder, "Why did the supervisor say that?"

If the reason you complimented an employee yesterday was so that you could stick that person with a hard job today, there will be suspicion the next time you offer praise. If you would build confidence, avoid trickery and don't blind yourself to the inferences an employee may draw from what you say. Better to be brutally frank about your purpose—"I'm having this heart-to-heart talk with you now because we're going to crack down on low producers"—than to "smokescreen" your intentions—"I want to get your ideas as to what you can do to improve your output."

Is there danger in overcommunicating with employees?

Yes, although this isn't the most common hazard. Supervisors who run off at the mouth continually, who are indiscreet, or who violate confidences do overcommunicate or communicate wrongly. It's much better to speak only about what you are certain than to get a reputation for being a blabbermouth.

Some supervisors, too, in their eagerness to keep employees fully informed, try too hard. They find themselves spending too much time communicating information that employees don't need or have no interest in.

How can you decide what to talk to employees about?

Talk about those things employees want to know—those things that directly affect them or their work. Talk about work methods, company rules, pay practices, the values in employee benefits, opportunities for advancement, your appraisal of how well the employee is doing the job.

Talk also about department and company matters that are news—while they are news. Your influence as a communicator will be watered down if what workers hear from you is only a stale confirmation of something they have learned from another worker or from their union representative. Your employees should depend on you for information.

Are there things you shouldn't talk about?

Yes. Politics and religion are dangerous subjects, as are other intensely personal matters. Steer clear of these issues—even if an employee brings up the subject.

On the subject of business economics—which should be discussed with employees if they are to get a good perspective of their work environment—be careful to let employees form their own judgments and express their own opinions.

Whatever you say, don't make comments, even in fun, that have sexual overtones. These can easily be misinterpreted by a member of the opposite sex as a form of sexual harassment.

How much communication should you have upward with your boss?

Just as your success as a leader depends on how freely employees will talk to you and tell you what's bothering them, your superior, too, needs similar information from you. Make a point of keeping your boss informed on:

Matters for Which the Boss Is Held Accountable by His or Her Superior. This would include performance standards, such as deliveries, output, quality. If you see that you're not going to be able to meet a schedule commitment, don't yield to the temptation of trying to conceal it. Instead, build confidence with your boss by saying: "I want to warn you that Job No. 1257 won't be finished on time. We ran into off-grade material and had to rework some of the units. I can guarantee that delivery will be made by next Tuesday, however."

Matters That May Cause Controversy. If you've had to take action that may be criticized by another department, your boss should know about it to be able to talk intelligently about it if interdepartment disagreements are brought up. Suppose the quality-control section has advised you to shut down a line because production is off-standard, but you've thought that you must keep it running in order to make a delivery date. Better get to your superior fast—with the facts.

Attitudes and Morale. Middle and top managers are continually frustrated because of their isolation from the work group. They need your advice and consultation as to how people in the company feel, generally or about a specific issue. Make a point of speaking to your boss on this subject regularly. Tell your boss about good reactions as well as bad. But never play the role of informer or go to your superior with information gained in confidence.

Which kinds of communications are likely to speak louder than words?

Your actions. Talking and writing are the communications media most frequently used, of course. But regardless of what you say, employees will be most affected by what you communicate to them by your actions. What you do—how you treat them—is the proof of your real intentions. When you go to bat for an employee who is in trouble, that's concrete communication of how well you value that person's contributions to your production team.

Even on simple matters, such as training an employee to do a new job, the act of showing how to do it (demonstration) is eloquent even when no words are spoken.

The best kinds of communications are generally those that combine the spoken or written words with action. "Show and tell" is a good formula for you to remember.

Body language. What's that?

The way your body or facial expressions tip off to others what is really on your mind. These nonverbal signals are revealed by a frown, a nervous touching of the nose, the way you shrug your shoulders, or a gesture with your hands. Rightly or wrongly, these can be misinterpreted. For example:

● Head-nodding forward can mean agreement; shaking the head from side to side, disagreement.
● Finger-drumming or foot-tapping may mean: "Hurry up. Get to the point."
● Puffing out the cheeks may signal doubt or reluctance.
● Eye-rolling often expresses disbelief.
● Turning down the corners of the mouth may indicate criticism, discontent, or even disgust.

Don't be overly concerned with your own body movements. They probably come naturally to you. But do be observant about those of others; these can often provide better clues to what is on a person's mind than what he or she may be saying.

How can you avoid having an employee take offense at what you say?

Each of us has a great big ego—and some of us are more sensitive than others. The tone of your voice, your choice of words, your tactlessness may make an employee feel menaced or hurt. Whenever you put something in such a way that an individual may infer a threat to pay or status, personal feelings will get in the way of rational thinking.

Take this example of a statement to an employee: "You remember I told you they wouldn't approve that transfer you asked for. Well, they won't."

Compare the tone of that statement with this way of saying the same thing: "I'm sorry, but the super won't approve that transfer right now. You recall, we thought it might have to be held up as long as we're short-handed here and they're full in the keypunch department. But you speak to me about it again in the spring, and we'll try it when we're slack in this department."

Watch out, too, when you start a conversation. Sometimes you can be more aggressive than you intend to be, especially when speaking to a superior, or when you're afraid you won't get your point across. That's because it sometimes takes courage. You have to push yourself, and some of that push gets into your voice.

Don't start an appeal this way, for example: "Now listen, I know you won't agree with me. But you've got to listen." This makes the tone of your message aggressive. It puts you on the defensive and may defeat your purpose.

How can you be sure that people understand what you mean?

To begin with, don't be afraid to repeat what you've said. That's the advice of Don Kirkpatrick, former president of the American Society for Training and Development and an expert communicator. But, Don advises, don't overdo it. Hearing what you have said and grasping its meaning can be two different things. For this reason, an attempt to get feedback from the employee ought to be a basic part of your communications routine.

A simple feedback device is to ask an employee to repeat back to you what you have said. If the person can't do this, it's the signal for you to tell your story over again.

Another way is to get the employee to ask questions. What is asked will tip you off to areas of weak understanding. And once a conversation is established on a give-and-take basis, communications are always improved.

Always keep in mind, however, that a common reason for poor understanding is that words can mean one thing in one relationship and something very different in other situations. Everyone has ideas, for instance, of what is meant by faster, slower, harder, up a little, and bear down. To make the meaning clearer, be more specific. Say, "Go a little slower—down to 2,100 rpm." Or, "I want you to bear down a little harder on quality this month. Last month we had complaints about poor finishes on six of the cabinets you turned out. Will you be especially careful about the application of the 00 emery cloth in the future?" Said with this explanation, "bear down" takes on explicit meaning.

Should you keep personalities out of the picture?

Don't be impersonal or cold-blooded in your approach to people. In fact, you should tailor your presentation to best fit the person you're talking to. Some employees like rough language. Others feel it is a sign of disrespect. Some employees respond well to an informal request, such as "When you've got time, will you sweep up the loading dock?" Others want you to be more formal, as with "Please get a broom and sweep the shipping platform. Start now and be sure it's done by three o'clock."

On the other hand, it's a good policy to deemphasize personalities in your communications. Think of communications as a process essential to the firm's organization. Try to avoid interference from personal factors that don't belong in the picture. Watch your tone so that it is objective and keeps emotional opinions out. There are helpful ways of rising above personalities. For instance:

"Now let's look at this from the point of view of company policy."

"This isn't between me and you. This is a question of whether office discipline will be maintained or not."

"Let's get back to the facts of the case."

"This is really a question of interpretation of the union contract. Let's see what they say in personnel."

It should go without saying, of course, that bias and prejudice should be held in check. You will arouse anger and resistance if you let your prejudices about sex, color, religion, handicaps, age, or national origin creep into your communications.

What will encourage employees to communicate with you?

Good faith, mutual confidence, welcoming their ideas, and a friendly attitude are the foundations on which employees will learn to talk to you. But a more specific way is for you to develop the fine art of listening.

Real communication is two-way. In the long run people won't listen to you if you won't listen to them. But listening must be more than just a mechanical process. Many employees (in fact, most people) are poor communicators. This means that you have to be an extraordinary receiver to find out what workers may be trying to say.

Here are four basic suggestions that may improve your listening power:

Don't Assume Anything. Don't anticipate. Don't let an employee think that you know what is going to be said.

Don't Interrupt. Let the individual have a full say. The employee who is stopped may feel there will never be an opportunity to unload the problem. If you don't have the time to hear an employee through just then, ask that the discussion stay within a time limit. Better still, make an appointment (for the same day, if at all possible) for a time when you can get the whole story.

Try to Understand the Need.   Look for the real reason the employee wants your attention. Often this may be quite different from what appears to be the immediate purpose. For instance, the real reason for a request for a half-day off may be that an employee is testing his or her standing with you as compared to another worker who has recently gotten a half-day off.

Don't React Too Quickly.   We all tend to jump to conclusions. The employee may use a word that makes you see red, or may express the situation badly. Be patient in trying to make sure that you are both talking about the same thing. Above all, try to understand—not necessarily agree with—the other's viewpoint.

You may also want to check yourself in relation to some other irritating listening habits shown in Table 16-1.

Can listening be overdone?

Listening should make up at least a third of your communications. But it shouldn't take the place of definite actions and answers on your part.

When an employee begins to ramble too far afield in discussions, return to the point with astute questioning.

If an employee is wrong on a point of fact, make that clear, even if it means contradicting the individual. But watch your tone!

When conferences or group discussions tend to turn into purposeless rap sessions, it's time for you to set talk aside and take action.

Finally, when an employee comes to you with a problem and its solution is clear to you, give a straightforward reply. It does help, if you have the time, to permit the individual to develop the solution. But when the employee has come to you by virtue of your knowledge and experience, chances are a direct answer is wanted, not a session of hand holding.

Which kind of communications is best for a supervisor's job?

For a supervisor, nothing can beat face-to-face communications. This way the common situation is shared with whomever you're talking to. And right at the time, you get a chance to see where your timing, tone, or choice of words has misfired. The biggest drawback to

TABLE 16-1 SELF-CHECK FOR LISTENING LAPSES

Are you guilty of any of the following?
Place a check mark in the appropriate column.

	A Never	B Once in a while	C More often than I like to think about
1. Not setting aside what you're doing (or providing a convenient time) to give an employee your full attention when he or she seeks it.			
2. Monopolizing the conversation, failing to let the employee fully state an idea or respond fully to your queries.			
3. Fidgeting with a pencil or some document on your desk, and often trying to study the document, while the employee is speaking.			
4. Not being able to resist looking at your watch or the clock while the conversation is going on.			
5. Asking—or implying—that the interview be speeded up since you have something important to attend to.			
6. Failing to look at the employee while he or she is talking.			
7. Jumping ahead to force a conclusion before the employee has made whatever point it is that he or she intends to make.			
8. Finding yourself asking a question that has already been answered but overlooked by your inattention.			
9. Rejecting an employee's suggestion or request not so much because it might not be worthwhile as because you may have to expend additional effort to explore its value.			
10. Using a conversation initiated by an employee on one subject as an opportunity to switch the conversation to a subject that is more to your interests.			

Instructions: Score 5 points for each mark in column A, 3 for each in column B, and 1 for each in column C. Fewer than 25 points indicates that you are a very irritating, and perhaps poor, listener; 25 to 35 points means that your listening habits could be improved; and more than 35 points means that you're too good a listener to be true.

face-to-face communication is that it can be very time-consuming. You may feel at the end of some days that you've done nothing but talk. This can interfere with other work.

Because person-to-person communication, talking to one person at a time, is so time-consuming, you will want to consider some of the other effective ways for communicating to employees. There are many forms of communications and an almost infinite combination of them. Combinations are usually more effective than any particular technique used by itself. To aid in your choice of technique, think of employee communications in two ways—either person-to-person or with groups of employees.

How can person-to-person communications be conducted effectively?

A maximum of "custom tailoring" for the individual is not only feasible but definitely in order. This becomes increasingly important as the relationship accumulates a common background. That's because an individual who is addressed singly but in the same way as everyone else is usually resentful in proportion to the degree of previously assumed familiarity.

Spoken. In spoken communication the immediate solution is shared, and the person addressed is aware of the conditions under which the message takes place. Therefore, haste, tone, mood, gestures, and facial expression may seriously affect the way the individual reacts.

1. **Informal Talks.** Still the most fundamental form of communication. They are suitable for day-to-day liaison, direction, exchange of information, conferences, review, discipline, checking up, and maintenance of effective personal relations. Even if brief, be sure they provide the opportunity for a two-way exchange.

Face-to-face communication should always be used (in preference to the telephone) when the subject is of personal importance to either party.

2. **Planned Appointments.** Appropriate for regular appraisal review, recurring joint work sessions, and so forth. The parties should be adequately prepared to make such meetings complete and effective by being up to date, by providing adequate data and information, and by limiting interruptions to the fewest possible.

Many supervisors have regular planned appointments with each major subordinate—daily (brief), weekly (longer), and monthly (extensive).

3. **Telephone Calls.** For quick checkup, or for imparting or receiving information, instruction, or data. They play a part in the personal relationship of the individuals concerned, which is sometimes overlooked. Your telephone personality sometimes contradicts your

real self. An occasional personal note can alleviate the sometimes resented impersonality of routine calls, which may sound indifferent.

Written.   All messages intended to be formal, official, or long-term or that affect several persons in a related way should be written. Be sure that you use only a written communication to amend any previous written communication. Oral changes will be forgotten or recalled inaccurately.

4. Interoffice Memos.   For recording informal inquiries or replies. They can be of value, too, if several people are to receive a message that is extensive, or when data are numerous or complex. A memo can be a simple way of keeping your boss informed without taking up his or her time. Memos should not be overused, or they will be ignored.

5. Letters.   More individualized in effect than a memo and usually more formal. They are useful for official notices, formally recorded statements, and lengthy communications, even when the addressee is physically accessible. Letters are often valuable for communicating involved thoughts and ideas for future discussion and development, or as part of a continuing consideration of problems.

6. Reports.   More impersonal than a letter and usually more formal. Reports are used to convey information associated with evaluation, analysis, or recommendations to supervisors or colleagues. They are most effective when based on conferences, visits, inspections, surveys, research, or study. Reports should carefully distinguish objectively determined facts from estimates, guesses, opinions, impressions, and generalizations.

How can you communicate most effectively with groups of employees?

Plant or office groups that are uniform in status, age, sex, compensation level, occupation, and length of service provide a valid basis for highly pointed messages. This approach helps avoid the gradually numbing stream of form letters, memos, and announcements that really have meaning for only a few of the recipients. Establishment of such groups on a continuing basis helps to build a sense of unity and group coherence that fosters favorable group reaction and group response, especially where there is routine personal contact among the members.

Spoken.   Effective spoken communication with groups calls for special skills. Those that are effective in a committee of equals may be inadequate in a mass meeting. Ability to conduct a conference of your own staff doesn't mean you will have equal ability to participate effectively as a staff member in a conference called by your superior. Conflicts of interest need more tactful handling than does a discussion of factual topics.

1. Informal Staff Meeting.   This provides an opportunity for development of strong group cohesiveness and response. Properly supplemented with individual face-to-face contacts, it is an outstanding means of coordinating activities and building mutual understanding. Hold brief, informal staff meetings daily (if your schedule permits)—early in the morning, at the end of the day, or at lunch.

2. Planned Conferences.   Relatively formal affairs. The most common error is for the person calling the conference to set up the agenda without previous consultation with those who will attend. It is usually desirable to check with most of the prospective participants in advance; to provide time for the preparation and the assembling of needed data, information, reports, and recommendations; and to allow an opportunity to make suggestions on the agenda and conduct of the meeting.

Properly conducted, a planned conference can be extremely useful. If improperly managed, participation will be limited or misdirected. As a result, it can be not only wasteful of time but even harmful in effect.

3. Mass Meetings.   Meetings of large numbers of employees or managers. They can be a valuable means of celebrating occasions, building morale, changing attitudes, meeting emergencies, introducing new policies or key personnel, or making special announcements. Mass meetings can also be used to clarify confused situations, resolve misunderstandings, and identify dissident elements. But such procedures require of the presiding individual great skill and a forceful personality. And there is always the danger of interference or interruption.

Written.   The effect of a single, isolated written communication to a group of employees is generally unpredictable. But a carefully planned program of written communications can develop a desirable cumulative effect.

4. Bulletin Board Notices.   For lengthy or formal announcements. These notices can be used for a series of illustrated messages and are most effective when readership is constantly attracted by changes and by careful control of content, including prompt removal of out-of-date material. Most bulletin board announcements should be supplemented by other forms.

5. Posters.   Small or large, situated at suitable locations, used in series, and changed frequently, posters can do much to supplement your other communications media. The usual and most effective subjects are safety, quality, and good housekeeping.

6. Exhibits and Displays. Can serve a useful purpose when appropriate space is available, and when they can be properly prepared. Such preparation is often expensive. The most common subjects are company products, advertising, promoting quality production, increasing safety, cutting waste and costs, and stimulating suggestions.

7. Audio and Visual Aids. Films, filmstrips, easel presentations, video and audio cassettes, and other special audio and visual materials have great potential value but are only as good as the way they are used. Few are self-administering. A good film will be far more effective, for instance, if presented with a soundly planned introduction and follow-up. Much material that could be of considerable value will be relatively worthless if not presented appropriately. Careful, competent preparation and planning should be applied to the use of all audio and visual materials.

Key Concepts

1. Effectiveness of employee communications depends on the extent to which supervision and management strive to maintain an open, honest, and comprehensive network. The resultant effectiveness of the communications effort will become a major factor in strengthening or weakening organizational performance.

2. The supervisors who are most successful in discharging their total responsibility are those who place themselves at the focal point of the communications network in their organization.

3. An effective exchange of information depends on the sending and receiving of messages, a process that is greatly improved by use of listening skills, feedback techniques, and reinforcing actions by both parties.

4. Whereas information exchange is greatly influenced by nonverbal factors—such as anxieties and apprehensions, attitudes and emotions, personality, tone of voice, and gestures—a great deal of business information must inevitably take its shape through the tyranny of words, written or spoken.

5. Communication techniques are most effective (a) when used in combination with one another rather than singly and (b) when appropriately attuned to the situation and individuals involved.

Supervisory Word Power

Communications Medium. The method, manner, form, or technique by which information is communicated, such as attitude, performance, appearance, speech, demonstration, or deed; conversation, discussion, dialogue, interview, conference, or lecture; writing, memorandum, letter, report, or book; telephone, recording, radio, public address system, or television.

Communications Process. The giving and receiving of information as a result of thinking, doing, observing, talking, listening, writing, and reading. In supervision, the exchange (especially of accurate meaning) between supervisor and employee, leading to a desired action or attitude.

Feedback. Information provided by those engaged in the communication process that serves to clarify and/or verify understanding and to indicate either agreement or dissent.

Information. The knowledge (such as basic background data about a particular job), skills (such as a specific work procedure), and feelings (such as a display of confidence in an employee's ability to respond favorably) that are exchanged in the communications process through the various media.

Listening. The conscious, active process of securing information of all kinds (including feelings and emotions) by paying acute attention to what people say and how they say it—for the purpose of improving the communications process and, consequently, the quality of understanding and performance that depend on it.

Reading Comprehension

1. Why is communication needed in an organization in the first place?

2. What kinds of information are usually handled by a management information system (MIS)? Can an organization do without an MIS?

3. Of the wheel and the web communication networks, which is more restricted and which more open? What are some advantages and disadvantages of each?

4. Discuss the shortcomings of the grapevine.

5. How can the credibility gap between a supervisor and the employees be narrowed?

6. If a supervisor finds that the department cannot deliver an important order on schedule, should the boss be told about it immediately, or should the supervisor wait until the order is finally shipped? Why?

7. Is it ever possible for a supervisor to overcommunicate? If so, it is harmful? How?

8. What techniques will help supervisors to listen more effectively?

9. How does feedback improve the communications process?

10. Discuss the pros and cons of a supervisor's holding a mass meeting with everybody in the department.

Supervision in Action

The Case of the Tangled Grapevine. A Case Study in Human Relations Involving Communications, with Questions for You to Answer.

Mary Lou was appointed head teller of the Arlington branch of SNB bank six months ago. The branch, which employs eight tellers, is located in a rapidly growing suburban community. Unlike the bank's main office and other branches that work some nights and weekends, the Arlington branch works only from 9 a.m. to 5 p.m. Monday through Friday. The SNB bank is an old one. It places great emphasis on proper relationships and formal channels of communication. Whenever changes in procedures are made, the main bank first issues a bulletin to all supervisors. Only after the supervisors have had a chance to get this information are general announcements made to rank-and-file employees.

Last week one of the drive-up tellers was asked by a depositor when the branch would be open Saturday mornings, as the main bank was. The teller said that it wasn't likely, since most of the tellers had taken their jobs with the assumption that there would be no Saturday work. "That's interesting," said the depositor. "My sister, who works at your head office, implied that a change in banking hours was imminent." On a coffee break the drive-up teller mentioned this to two of the employees who were in the lounge at the time. Bill, one of the more talkative clerks in the bank, ventured the opinion that "where there's smoke, there's likely to be fire. I'll bet that plans are already under way to open this branch on Saturdays. And, as usual, we'll be the last ones to know."

Two days later Jill, a savings teller, asked Mary Lou whether there was any truth to the rumor that the branch would soon be open Saturdays.

"I can't believe that this could happen in the near future," said Mary Lou. "Other branches like ours did not begin to open Saturday mornings until after their weekly deposits exceeded $500,000. We are nowhere near that level now. Anyway, nobody has said anything to me about it. As you know, if any changes are planned, we supervisors are informed before anyone else."

"If the Arlington branch wants me to work on Saturdays," observed Jill, "I'll have to quit. I want to spend time with my family on the weekends. I can always find another five-day, 9-to-5 job elsewhere."

"Don't worry about it," said Mary Lou. "It's just a rumor. I don't know how stories like this get started. It's probably someone like Bill. He sees ghosts around every corner. Anyway, I'll let you know right away if anything develops along that line."

At the end of the week Jill again asked Mary Lou about the rumored change in the bank's operating times. She was especially concerned now because she had a chance to take another job whose hours would suit her better. She had to make up her mind right away. Mary Lou again assured her that there was nothing in the works for additional openings. On the strength of this, Jill turned down the job opportunity.

Two weeks after this incident, the SNB *Bulletin to Supervisors* had the following announcement:

Beginning the first Friday of next month, all branches, regardless of size or deposits, will be open for business from 9 a.m. to 9 p.m. It is expected that all full-time employees will share this extended schedule equally.

Mary Lou immediately gathered her tellers together at quitting time and relayed the announcement to them. The news was not received enthusiastically.

"There goes my weekend," said one employee.

"Next move will be for Saturdays," said Bill.

"It won't be all that bad," said Mary Lou. "By rotating schedules, each of you will only have to work every fourth Friday."

"That's not good enough for me," said Jill. "I'm not about to work on Friday nights. That's league night for my bowling team."

"I'm sorry about that," said Mary Lou.

"You should be," said Jill, "especially after telling me to pass up a job where it was guaranteed that I wouldn't work anything but straight 9 to 5, five days a week."

"I didn't guarantee anything," said Mary Lou.

"Well, you sure weren't clued into what the bank was going to do," said Jill. "You really didn't have any more information about this change in hours than we did. You said it was all a rumor, and it turned out to be true. Next time I'll listen to the grapevine."

1. Did it make any difference that the details of the rumor were inaccurate?
2. Could Mary Lou have avoided this situation? How?
3. What should Mary Lou do, if anything, to make the next shift less difficult for Jill?
4. What should Mary Lou say about Bill's comment that Saturday work will be next?

CHAPTER

17

GIVING ORDERS AND INSTRUCTIONS

In what ways are orders and instructions linked to the communications process?

Orders and instructions are the most direct, authority-based kinds of communications. The supervisor should make absolutely sure that an employee has understood what must be done. Other kinds of communications tend to stress not only understanding, but acceptance of the message. Figure 17-1 illustrates what must take place during an effective communications exchange. With orders and instructions, the supervisor is the person to initiate the message. In most instances, the supervisor wants the employee to engage in a specific, often precise, form of action. As a consequence, employees are usually the receivers in order/instruction situations. It would be

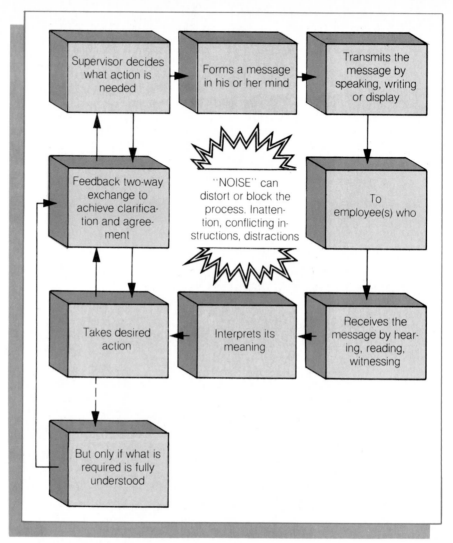

Figure 17-1. The communications process.

good if they fully agreed with the wisdom of what you were asking them to do, but in a majority of cases they have little choice. Overall company policies, procedures, and departmental schedules and process constraints narrow down their freedom of actions. As their supervisor, your first responsibility is to make sure that employees know what to do. Your second is to make sure that they do it and do it properly. If you really understand the communications process, you will, of course, be better able to meet both these responsibilities.

How can you get better results from the instructions and orders you issue?

By being sure your order is the right one for the particular situation at hand and by being specific about what the employee is to do and what kind of results you expect.

Your orders are even more effective when you use care in selecting the person most likely to carry them out well. And you add power to your orders by being confident (not cocky) and calm as you deliver them. Finally, your orders will stand the best chance of accomplishing what you intend if you make a practice of checking to be sure they are carried out at the time and in the manner you prescribe.

Should you repeat an order?

Yes, by all means. Repeat your instructions to be certain the employee understands them clearly. All of us are expert at misunderstanding. So give a worker an opportunity to ask questions if there seems to be doubt about what you want. In fact, it's a good practice to ask the employee to repeat your instructions back to you. That way you can readily find out where the stumbling blocks might be.

When should you *ask* an employee to do something?

As often as possible. It used to be thought that order giving was a one-way street, that all a supervisor had to say was, "I tell you. You do it." Such an attitude gets you nowhere. Today's workers want and deserve more consideration. And many of them have labor unions to back this desire. In addition, we now know lots more about employees' attitudes. For instance, psychologists who study employee behavior tell us that most workers will rate a boss high and will cooperate more willingly as a result if the boss gives orders pleasantly. We know, too, that employees like to feel they are offered some say in decisions that affect them and will work harder when they have had a chance to participate.

So there's nothing wrong and there's much good in saying, "Will you try to get that machine cleaned up before quitting time?" Or, "Won't you please make an effort to get to work on time Monday?"

Generally speaking, a request carries the same weight as a direct order. But it does impart a feeling that workers have some freedom of action, that they can question any part that bothers them. And it's especially useful with thin-skinned employees who tend to see every boss as a dictator.

When should you command an employee to do something?

Commands are dangerous. But they may be necessary in emergencies. In case of accident or fire, for instance, your instructions should be direct, clear, and unequivocal to avoid conflicting actions.

Orders should be specific and firm, too, in operating situations that demand active leadership. It's desirable to be especially decisive, for instance, in directing a crew that requires rapid coordination on an unfamiliar job—as in supervising a crew that is lowering a 100-ton machine onto its foundations, or starting up a new and complex machine.

But, in general, commands cause resentment. It's best to avoid them until you need them. If you use commands only occasionally, your employees will know that you're not being bossy just for the sake of showing your authority. They will recognize that your change in approach is necessary and will snap to accordingly.

So try to look at your orders as solutions to action-demanding situations that both you and your employees must see in the same light if orders are to be carried out willingly and well.

What should you do when an employee willfully refuses to do what you ask?

The first piece of advice and the toughest to follow is: Don't fly off the handle. Count to 100 if insubordination makes you want to blow your top. Then ask yourself whether the order or assignment was a fair one and whether you've chosen the proper person to follow it. Have you made yourself understood?

If you think you've done your part, next try to find out what the employee objects to. Ask for specifics: "What is it that you object to? Why do you think it's unreasonable?" Chances are an employee who is willfully disobedient is looking for an excuse to blow off steam. It may be that if you listen for a couple of minutes, the resentment will pass. For that reason it's wise not to talk about your authority or threaten with discipline. Not then, anyway.

But if an employee is stubborn and can't or won't be cooled off or have a change of mind about doing what you say, you're faced with a disciplinary problem. You still have alternative choices of what to do, so don't be quick about firing, penalizing or suspending. You may find it prudent not to insist—at that moment—that the order be carried out. Or you may want to modify the order so that it will be accepted. If you choose to do either of the latter, however, don't let the matter drop there.

Find an early opportunity to talk calmly, constructively, and in private. Don't permit the employee to think that you were soft. Let it be known that you will take disciplinary steps if the employee doesn't straighten up and fly right.

Your other choice is to take whatever disciplinary action your plant permits—that same day, while the incident is fresh in everyone's mind. But this is a choice supervisors should avoid if possible. Punishment is a last resort only. That's why it's unwise to force a showdown situation—especially if there are other employees watching or listening or if you'd like to change your mind later.

When should you put an order in writing?

Whenever you change an order that was previously in writing, put the new order in writing, too. Or if you give an order that must be carried over into another shift, it's wise to jot it down in writing—on the bulletin board, in the department logbook, or as a note to be passed on to the employees concerned. This is more reliable than word of mouth.

When instructions are complex and contain variations from normal in amounts and sequence, it's wise to write them down, too. On the other hand, don't depend too much on written orders. Not everyone follows written instructions easily. In fact, if you do write instructions down, look for an opportunity to review them orally with employees to see if they understand them. That way the written orders serve the employees as a reference.

Is it wise to let employees use their own judgment in following your instructions?

Sometimes it's a good idea just to suggest what you want and then let the employees use their own discretion in carrying it out. This leaves it up to them whether or not anything will be done and how it will be done. For instance, "I wonder if there's anything you can do to get this job finished by quitting time." Or, "It looks as if our scrap record will be off this month. Is there something you can do to get it back on the beam?"

Such an implied order stimulates initiative and cooperation —among more responsible workers. It's a form of delegation, and it helps develop your employees' judgment.

The suggestion approach is risky to try with inexperienced or unreliable people. And you shouldn't use it when you have decided in advance exactly what you want done and how. After all, you can't expect your workers to be mind readers.

Should you let anyone else give instructions to your employees?

Unless you have expressly asked someone else to pass along orders to people who work directly under you (and this should be done only infrequently), it's best to see that you're the only one who gives orders to your employees. Otherwise, your employees will find themselves working for two bosses. And your status and effectiveness will be weakened.

You were hired to direct your employees. That's your responsibility. If someone else tries to take over this part of your job, it's up to you to politely, but firmly, hold on to your rights. If your boss makes a habit of bypassing you in issuing instructions to your employees, you should speak to your boss at once about it. Be tactful, of course, but be convincing that this works against department morale and efficiency; otherwise, you're in for trouble.

Should you give an order when you're angry?

If you can avoid it, don't give orders when you're uptight. There's always the possibility that you'll make a threat that you can't, or won't want to, carry out.

You probably know of a case similar to this one: Ralph, machine-shop supervisor, has just been chewed out by his boss for the number of damaged hand tools charged to his department. So as soon as the boss leaves, Ralph turns his anger on his employees. "Next one who turns in a damaged tool, no matter what the reason, you'll pay for it out of your own pocket." So what happens? That afternoon Sylvia, who has been with the company 15 years and who is as conscientious as can be, accidentally ruins a micrometer. Who does that put on the spot? Nobody but Ralph!

How is your tone of voice important?

Remember the story of the cowboy who said, "When you call me that, smile." Employees are the same way. They'll read your voice like a book to hear whether you're trying to throw your weight around, whether you mean what you say or are just blowing smoke. So when you give an order that's going to be hard to carry out, smile to show that you know what you ask isn't easy. But let the tone of your voice show that you expect it to be done regardless.

Should you ask an employee to do anything you wouldn't do?

You don't have to do everything you ask others to do. But, in principle, you should show that you'd be willing to do it if you had to.

Giving orders is a test of your leadership mettle. General Patton used to say that an army was like a piece of cooked spaghetti. You can't push it, you can only pull it. You might not have to lead an army, but you should always imply your willingness to stand up where the shots are being received.

If there's a dirty or unpleasant job, be sure you expose yourself to the same conditions your workers do. If they must work in the rain or cold, get out there with them. If they have to get in the muck under a machine, show that you're not above getting your hands dirty, either.

But shouldn't each person be handled differently?

Yes, if you can find time. Some people like their bosses to be specific about what they want done. Others need only a suggestion. Still other people work best when given a free hand. To assign orders accordingly, you'll want to improve your ability to size up people. Then you will improve your supervision by tailoring each order to fit the individual.

Should you approach groups differently than individuals?

Yes, mainly because you will be dealing with many chances of misinterpretation rather than one. As seen in Chapter 4, work group relationships are highly complex. A participatory approach usually works best with them. Not only will group members want to talk among themselves about the implications of your orders, they will also be able to anticipate "interfacing" difficulties in carrying them out. For example, if the new procedure calls for rerouting of sales orders, Grace may know that this will cause problems with the way she exchanges data with George. Knowing this in advance will enable you to alter the procedures for a smoother exchange.

Admittedly, the participatory approach is time-consuming and invites hair-splitting and irrelevant objections. But, as the Japanese managers have learned, the time invested at the initial stages of change (such as when new orders or procedures are introduced) pays off with faster, trouble-free implementation once everyone understands what must be done.

One rule to follow in group instructions is that you should pin down exactly who is to do what. If you don't, you're likely to discover that each person is waiting for someone else to carry the ball. And, especially with groups, it's a good idea to follow up your oral instructions with written ones.

How can active listening help gain acceptance for your orders?

When supervisors actively listen to an employee's negative reaction to an order, for example, they may hear the reason for that resistance. Most of the time, however, we tend to put our minds into neutral when others resist us. We engage in passive listening, hardly hearing what the other person says, and we're ready to attack again. Compare these two examples:

Passive Listening

Employee: What does the scheduling office think I am, Rick—a miracle worker? There is no way this job can be finished today!

Supervisor: That's the order, whether you like it or not. Just make sure you've finished it by 5 p.m.

Employee: I'm already behind schedule because of the computer breakdown this week. Doesn't anybody understand what kind of pressure that puts on me?

Supervisor: Look, I don't make up the schedules here. It's my job to see that they get carried out. We're all under pressure this week. So, like it or not, you've got to get hopping right away so that we meet the deadline.

Employee: I'll do it, but this is the last time you're going to treat me like dirt.

Active Listening

Employee: What does the scheduling office think I am, Rick—a miracle worker? There is no way this job can be finished today!

Supervisor: Sounds like you're really angry about it, Joe.

Employee: You're darned right I am. I've been working all week to catch up after the computer went off line. Now that I'm about on schedule, this lousy order comes in.

Supervisor: As if you didn't have enough to do already. Seems as if you're shoveling sand against the tide.

Employee: Yeah. It's all uphill around here. I can hardly catch a breath.

Supervisor: You feel like it's unfair to unload a rush job on you when you've been trying so hard to get back on schedule.

Employee: That's right. I'm willing to pull my share of the load, Rick, but it's discouraging to feel that you're being dumped on all the time.

Supervisor: You feel that we have been asking more than you can handle?

Employee: Not more than I can handle. I can get this lousy job out today. But it sure puts me near my breaking point.

Supervisor: I understand how you feel. Actually, Joe, we haven't been picking on you. The whole shop is in a bind this week. But I appreciate your taking on what seems like an unjustified overload.

The difference between the two examples is that the supervisor is actively listening in the second one. Joe is, in effect, saying that he is being misused. Rick is listening and responding to make it clear to Joe that he appreciates the feeling Joe is expressing. Active listening won't solve all order-giving problems, but it does provide a good base for acceptance. It helps to show that the supervisor is not just mechanically passing on instructions and that the supervisor views the employee as a human being with very personal feelings and problems.

What can supervisors do to detect hidden resistance to an order?

By trying to put themselves in the employees' shoes. When you are giving an order, it is only natural for you to see the need only from the top down. If you turn yourself around mentally, you may begin to see what the need is from the bottom up. One good way to get this turned-about feeling is to answer an employee's challenge with a response that reflects what the employee has said. For example:

Employee's challenge: Just who is responsible for those filing cabinets, anyway?

Supervisor's response: Do you feel that someone is trying to take over your authority for them?

Employee's challenge: Isn't it about time that younger, more able people get a shot at a promotion before the older guys do?

Supervisor's response: It seems to you that younger people should get a chance now.

Employee's challenge: How does the company think I'm going to turn out clean letters on this obsolete console?

Supervisor's response: You really are fed up with this machine, aren't you?

Employee's challenge: Don't you think my work has gotten better over the last few months?

Supervisor's response: Sounds as if you feel that your work has picked up since we last talked about it.

Responses like this are not sweet talk. Their purpose is to keep open the flow of communication from the employee. Kept talking to a sympathetic ear, the employee may expose the real source of irritation. If so, the supervisor may be better able to shape the order or instruction to the employee's preference. Or at the very least, the supervisor may be able to take the sting out of the assignment.

Technically speaking, this approach provides empathy (understanding of, not necessarily sympathy for, another's feelings). This, in turn, helps to establish rapport (harmony, closeness, and confidence) between supervisor and employee.

What can be done to avoid ambiguity in instructions?

Many words and phrases have a double, or at least an unclear, meaning. Here is a list of troublemakers. Avoid words or terms like these when handing out assignments. Instead, try to add clarifying details to make them more specific.

- *Quality factors,* such words as *good, smooth, well-done,* or *clean.* Try instead: *fewer than three rejects per day, so smooth that a dust cloth won't catch on the surface, a steak without a trace of red in it, completely free of the grease that protected it when shipped.*
- *Quantity factors,* such words as *large, small, heavy,* or *tight.* Try instead: *over ten inches, smaller than a ten-cent piece, over two ounces, as tight as a 20-psi wrench can make it.*
- *Time factors,* such terms as *quickly, as soon as possible, in a few days.* Try instead: *25 per minute, within 24 hours, by Thursday at 2 p.m.*

Which guidelines in particular may keep a supervisor out of trouble when directing, ordering, assigning, or instructing?

There are no assurances that employees won't get hung up about a particular assignment, but here are 11 guidelines that should minimize trouble:

1. Don't Make It a Struggle for Power. If you approach too many order-giving situations in an I'll show-you-who's-boss frame of mind, you'll soon be fighting the whole department. Try to focus your attention—and the worker's—on the goal that must be met. The idea to project is that it is the situation that demands the order, not a whim of the supervisor.

2. Avoid an Offhand Manner. If you want employees to take instructions seriously, then deliver them that way. It's all right to have fun, but be firm about those matters that are important.

3. Watch Out for Your Words. As you have seen, words can be unreliable messengers of your thoughts. Watch the tone of your voice, too. Few people like to feel that they are being taken for granted or pushed around. Most employees accept the fact that it is the supervisor's job to hand out orders and instructions. Their quarrel is more likely to be with the way these are made.

4. Don't Assume That the Worker Understands. Give the employee a chance to ask questions and to raise objections. Have the employee confirm an understanding by repeating what you've said.

5. Be Sure to Get Feedback Right Away. Give the employee who wishes to complain about the assignment a chance to do so at the time. It's better to iron out resistance and misunderstanding before the job begins than afterward.

6. Don't Give Too Many Orders. This is an area where a communications overload will be self-defeating. Be selective in issuing instructions. Keep them brief and to the point. Wait until an employee has finished one job before asking that another be started.

7. Provide Just Enough Detail. More complex jobs require more information than less complex ones do. Some workers need more detailed instruction than others do. Think about the information needs of the person you're speaking to. For an old hand there's nothing more tiresome than having to listen to familiar details.

8. Watch Out for Conflicting Instructions. Check to make sure that you're not telling your employees one thing while supervisors in adjoining departments are telling their people another.

9. Don't Choose Only the Willing Worker. Some people are naturally cooperative. Others make it difficult for you to ask them to do anything. Be sure that you don't overwork the willing person. Make sure the hard-to-handle people get their share of the rough jobs, as well.

10. Try Not to Pick on Anyone. It is a temptation to punish a person by handing out an unpleasant assignment. Resist this temptation if you can. Employees have the right to expect the work to be distributed fairly. So if you have a grudge against an employee, don't use a dirty job assignment to get even.

11. Above All, Don't Play the Big Shot. New supervisors are sometimes guilty of flaunting their authority. Older supervisors feel more confident. They know that you don't have to crack the whip to gain employees' cooperation and respect.

Key Concepts

1. Supervision implies the need to exercise authority—the need to direct and control the activities of subordinate employees. To discharge this responsibility, supervisors must regularly issue orders, instructions, directions—and, occasionally, commands.

2. In a free society, an employee's reaction to the exercise of authority tends to be highly individualistic. Whereas one person may respond readily to a peremptory order, another may cooperate only when a direction implies the prerogative to accept it or not. Accordingly, it is essential that successful supervisors understand and anticipate the response pattern of each employee who works for them.

3. Issuing orders is an act of communication. As such, orders are susceptible to the shortcomings and misfires that obscure, distort, or otherwise interfere with the exchange of information. Therefore, clarity, consistency, restatement, and rapport are essential to the order-giving process.

4. Manner and tone, sensitivity and empathy provide a footing for the understanding and acceptance of a supervisor's orders and instruction—even the most arbitrary commands. When employees can be helped to grasp the reason for, and the rationality of, the directions they are expected to follow, they are likely to accept directions more readily and to carry them out with greater alacrity and enthusism.

5. Effective order-giving is based on effective communication; techniques such as active listening can improve communication and thus help identify and overcome resistances and encourage cooperation. Following proved guidelines can improve a supervisor's chances of success in getting employees to understand and accept orders and instructions.

Supervisory Word Power

Active Listening. Giving the speaker full attention, listening intently and being alert to any clues of unspoken meaning or resistance, and actively seeking to keep the conversation open and satisfying to the speaker.

Command. To exercise authority forcefully with the expectation of obedience.

Instruct. To furnish knowledge or information in a disciplined, systematic way with the expectation of compliance.

Noise. Any kind of distraction or impedence, physical or emotional, within an individual or as a part of the environment that distorts or obstructs the transmission of a message (such as an order or instruction) from one individual to another.

Passive Listening. An attitude of general indifference to the speaker's need to communicate, placing the entire burden of the exchange on him or her.

Request. To ask courteously, to make known your wishes without the implied assurance that they will be fulfilled.

Reading Comprehension

1. When should a supervisor be expected to repeat an order?
2. Under what circumstances might a supervisor command an employee to carry out an order?
3. Contrast a request that something be done with a suggestion that it might be done.
4. When you give orders, why is it important to try to get the employee to understand the situation in the same way you do?
5. In an instance of an employee's apparent willful disobedience, what recourses are open to the supervisor?
6. What are some disadvantages of passing orders through other people?
7. Under what circumstances should a supervisor try to refrain from issuing orders?
8. Why might a supervisor approach order giving with groups of employees differently than with single employee?
9. Why should supervisors try to develop the ability to listen actively when giving orders?
10. Give some examples of how objective terms and specific numbers can be used in orders to improve their clarity.

Supervision in Action
The Case of the Snarled Parking Lot. A Case Study in Human Relations Involving the Knack of Giving Orders and Instructions, with Questions for You to Answer.

Dr. McClinans, the director of administrative affairs for a Midwestern technical training institute, had been concerned for some time about the way in which staff personnel regularly ignored or disobeyed the school's parking regulations. His policy had been to assign parking spaces in order of seniority, with the most convenient spaces going to the senior staff members. Employees with the least seniority were placed in remote parking lots. On rainy days, however, these junior employees regularly cruised the senior parking lots looking for spaces that might be open. This was a distinct possibility, since staff hours varied according to the day of the week or whether employees were on daytime or evening schedules. It was a great source of irritation to older staff people to arrive at the institute for work only to find that their assigned spaces were occupied. Often, by the time the license plate of the interloper was identified, the car had been moved.

To counter this problem, Dr. McClinans regularly had the parking lots patrolled by security officers who were instructed to ticket the cars of parking violators. This practice was aided to some extent by the way in which parking lots were color-coded. Each staff person who applied for parking privileges was issued a color-coded decal that designated the particular lot in which that person's car could park—red, yellow, green, and so forth. When a security officer saw a "red" car in a "yellow" parking lot, it was simple to place a ticket on it and to report the decal number to the administrator's office. Violators who were caught were made to pay fines: $2 for the first offense, $5 for the second, and $25 for the third. Nevertheless, the parking lot interlopers were an ingenious group. They often knew the security patrol schedule and would be in and out of the prohibited lot before they were identified. Some drove unregistered cars to work so there could be no identification by the color-coded decal system.

Dr. McClinans finally reviewed the whole system and decided to revise the policy. His decision was to assign parking lots to a group of individuals rather than individuals to specific parking spaces. This would provide greater flexibility, he thought. Furthermore, he decided that he could overassign parking spaces by 10 percent, since there were always about that many no-shows on any given day or at any given time.

To carry out this new policy, Dr. McClinans had his administrative assistant revise assignments so that, for example, 55 of the most senior staff members were assigned to the red parking lot, which had 50 available spaces; 88 of the next most senior to the yellow parking lot, which had 80 spaces; 110 to the green lot, with 100 spaces, and so on. Next, Dr. McClinans issued a general announcement to describe the new procedure. Tech Institute General Order No. 276, dated December 10, read:

Beginning January 1, no one will be issued a specific parking space at the institute. All assignments will be on the basis of a particular lot only. Each employee will, before January 1, be issued a new color-coded decal designating his or her lot. All employees will be expected to respect the new assignments. However, should you arrive at your parking lot and find that there is no space for you, you may seek an open space in the next most senior lot. As in the past, employees who willfully ignore this new assignment policy will be fined.

W. X. McClinans, Director of Administration

January 1 was a holiday, but when the institute opened on January 2, chaos broke out. One senior staff member, finding his old parking space occupied by someone else's car, parked his car in the turning lane so as to block access and egress. A yellow car driver purposely rammed the fender of a red car driver who was trying to take the last open spot in the yellow lot. The red driver insisted that the new policy gave her first claim.

Many less senior employees headed directly for the best parking lots and cruised around till they found a space. Those that couldn't find spaces added to the traffic congestion in already closed lots. Three people assigned to the green lot reported to the director that more than seven spaces were occupied by drivers from red and yellow lots. When the security patrol tried to prevent drivers from entering unfilled, more convenient lots, they were reported by the drivers to the director as not cooperating in the new assignment plan. Drivers of those cars that were ticketed by the security patrol refused to pay fines on the grounds that they had tried to respect the new assignments as best they could or that they had not willfully ignored the regulations.

On January 3, Dr. McClinans and his assistant locked the door to the administration office and turned off the phones. "What shall we do now?" asked Dr. McClinans.

1. If you were Dr. McClinans, what would you do now? Would you try to make the new system work, or would you rescind General Order No. 276 and try a fresh approach? Why?

2. What are three main failings in the way in which instructions for the new systems were given to the staff?

3. What could Dr. McClinans have done to make the instructions regarding the new system clearer?

Delegating Effectively

Experience shows that supervisors who follow this sequence of steps are likely to get better results when delegating tasks and assignments than those supervisors who do not.

Step 1. Explain the need for delegation to the subordinate.
Step 2. Use the delegation of the task to motivate the employee.
Step 3. Explain the task and ask the employee's view of the assignment.
Step 4. Specify the responsibility and authority involved.
Step 5. Confirm the employee's understanding of the delegated task or responsibility and its authority, and to set up a review.

The Situation

Andy is supervisor of an engineering and design department. He has just received approval from his boss to purchase a copying machine for the department. He is too busy right now to examine the pros and cons of the various machines on the market himself. Therefore, he wishes to delegate this task to Mary, one of his subordinates.

Dialogue

1. Andy: Thanks for coming in, Mary. Have a seat. Listen; Ms. Stein has given approval for a new copy machine. But before we can make a decision on which one to buy, we need some information and she's asked me to get it. There is a kind of a rush on this, and I can't get to it right away, so I'd like you to take over this job for me.

2. Mary: Well I'm no expert on copy machines.

3. Andy: You don't have to be. We need someone who is well organized to collect information on what we need from people in the department, and someone I can rely on to get the job done in a week. You're very well organized and exceptionally reliable. I don't think anyone could handle this better than you could.

4. Mary: Well, I appreciate your confidence, but tell me what's involved.

5. Andy: Well, I want you to go to the library and do some research on the different features of all the leading copy machines. Prepare a list of those features; then talk to everyone in our department that uses the copy machine. Find out from each of them which features are important to them, and how many photocopies they make in a month. Total the responses for each feature and total the numbers per month, and get me that information one week from today. How does that sound to you?

6. Mary: I'm not sure I know what you mean by features.

7. Andy: Oh . . . you know, things like copies per minute, enlargements, copying on both sides, collating. Understand?

8. Mary: Oh, I see.

9. Andy: And when you tally the responses for me I'd like to have your recommendation on which one you think would satisfy the largest number of users.

10. Mary: Okay—I'm just wondering, are the users going to be willing to talk to me about this or are they going to want to talk to you directly?

11. Andy: I'm sure you'll have no difficulty. I will notify them that you have this authority and how important it is.

12. Mary: I think that would help.

13. Andy: Well, do you have any questions?

14. Mary: How much time should I take and when should I do it?

15. Andy: Start this morning and take as much time as you need to get this job done by next week. Don't worry about your regular work piling up—I'll take care of that. Any other questions?

16. Mary: . . . I don't have any questions right now. However, if I do have some later, can I come in to talk to you about them?

17. Andy: Oh, sure—not only can you see me any time, but if you run into any difficulties, I want to know about them immediately. Anything else?

18. Mary: No . . . I guess that's it.

19. Andy: Good! Now, before you go, let's make sure I've been clear in explaining what I want done. Why don't you summarize what I've asked you to do?

20. Mary: You want me to make a list of features of the most popular copy machines. Then survey everyone in the office who uses the copy machine and keep a tally of features most needed. You also want me to find out how many copies per month each user makes—then total that. Then you want my recommendation on what copier would best fit our needs.

21. Andy: That's a good summary and you're confirming my judgment that you can do the job.

22. Mary: Well, I hope so! And I thank you for giving me a chance at this.

23. Andy: Well, you'd better get started, and I'll expect a report from you by next week sometime.

24. Mary: Okay. I'm on my way.

Model Analysis

A. Identify by line numbers in the dialogue where Andy applied Step 1 by explaining to Mary the need for the delegation.

B. Identify by line numbers in the dialogue where Andy applied Step 2 by using the delegation of the task to provide motivation for Mary.

C. Identify by line numbers in the dialogue where Andy applied Step 3 by explaining the delegated task to Mary and asking her view of the assignment.

D. Identify by line numbers in the dialogue where Andy applied Step 4 by specifying the amount of responsibility and authority involved.

E. Identify by line numbers in the dialogue where Andy applied Step 5 by (1) confirming Mary's understanding of the delegated responsibility and authority and (2) setting up a review.

F. Recall, and describe briefly, a situation where a supervisor may wish to delegate a task to a subordinate. Try role playing the supervisor, with someone else in the group taking the part of the employee. Get feedback from the group and the instructor to (1) sharpen your sense of when to apply each of the model's steps and (2) improve the skill with which you handle each step.

Model 7

Giving Orders and Instructions

Experience has shown that supervisors who follow this sequence of steps are likely to get better results when giving orders or instructions than those supervisors who do not.

Step 1. Explain the problem to be handled or the task to be assigned. (In effect, give the order or instruction in the form of an explanation.)

Step 2. Ask the employee's view of the assignment—in order to be certain that it is clearly understood and also to obtain any suggestions the employee may have on how to carry the task out properly.

Step 3. Summarize the agreed-on understanding of the assignment and its method of implementation.

Step 4. Confirm the employee's understanding of the final agreement and set up a time or date for review.

The Situation

Frank is the supervisor of the collections department for a warehouse distributor of industrial parts and supplies. Fred is a departmental employee who specializes in making collections (called "receivables" for "accounts receivable") by telephone from the firm's customers, mostly small machine shops and manufacturing plants in the area. It is typical for some customers to be late in their payments, and Frank wants to initiate a new system for speeding up these payments.

Dialogue

1. Frank: Good morning, Fred. How are you today?
2. Fred: Fine, Frank.
3. Frank: Sit down. How about some coffee? How are things going in collections this week?
4. Fred: They're going fairly well so far. The biggest problem's Universal. They're over 60 days now, so I told them yesterday that if we don't get a substantial payment before the end of next week, we'll have to put them on a cash-with-order basis.
5. Frank: Good. You know, you've done an outstanding job in keeping our receivables in line. I've told you this before, but I want you to know how much I appreciate what you're doing.
6. Fred: Thanks, Frank. It's always good to know that your boss thinks you're doing a good job.
7. Frank: Not good—outstanding! But even though you've been keeping our receivables in line, we're hurting. With interest rates where they are, the cost of carrying receivables is eating into our profit margin. That's why we've decided to add a monthly interest charge to all accounts that aren't current. So we have to notify the customers, and since this is your bailiwick, I thought you should be involved in deciding how we go about doing this. What do you think we should do?
8. Fred: Well, let's see. Today's the 20th. If we send out a letter to all accounts today telling them this charge starts on the first of next month, they should all get it by the first.
9. Frank: Yes, they would, but maybe we should give them some advance notice.
10. Fred: How much advance notice?
11. Frank: What do you think—30 days?
12. Fred: Okay.
13. Frank: Anything else?
14. Fred: Well, I talk to a lot of customers every day. I could tell them all about it on the phone.
15. Frank: Yes, that's a good idea. You're talking to everyone who's behind in their payments, so that would reinforce the message for the people who need it most.
16. Fred: I guess we ought to reprint our invoices so that there is a statement about this new interest charge. A lot of companies do that.
17. Frank: Yes, we should add a statement to the invoices. But instead of reprinting our invoices now, let's use a rubber stamp at least until we've used up our present supply of invoices.
18. Fred: Okay. I suppose we probably have enough invoices to last us another four or five months, so that gives us time to think about printing the statement on the next batch we order.
19. Frank: Well, anything else?
20. Fred: I guess we have to notify the billing clerks to add this charge every month to all accounts that aren't current.
21. Frank: Well, I'll take care of that. Why don't you write a statement for the stamp and draft a letter to the customers? Now, the tone of the letter is

important. We want them to understand that we regret having to add this charge, but that our costs require it.

22. Fred: Sure, I understand.

23. Frank: Okay. Now let's go over what needs to be done. You're going to draft a letter today to the customers and a statement for the invoices. You'll also start telling all the customers you talk to on the phone about the new policy. I'll set up the procedures for the billing clerks.

24. Fred: Right.

25. Frank: Any questions?

26. Fred: No.

27. Frank: Okay. You tell me what you're going to do.

28. Fred: I'm going to write a letter to the customers explaining our new policy on overdue accounts which will go into effect on the first day of the month after next. I'll write it carefully so nobody gets their nose out of joint. I'll also write a statement which will be put on our invoices by rubber stamp, and I'll also start telling everyone I talk to about our new policy. And you'll take care of dealing with the billing clerks.

29. Frank: Right! Now, I want to go over both the letter and the invoice statement before you go ahead with them. What time do you think you'll have them ready by?

30. Fred: I should have them in about an hour.

31. Frank: Fine. Let's meet here at 11:30.

32. Fred: Fine, Frank. I'll see you then.

Model Analysis

A. Identify by line numbers in the dialogue where Frank applied Step 1 by explaining the task to be assigned.

B. Identify by line numbers in the dialogue where Frank applied Step 2 by asking Fred for his view of the task and instructions and how he might carry them out.

C. Identify by line numbers in the dialogue where Frank applied Step 3 by summarizing his and Fred's agreement about the instructions and the method of implementation.

D. Identify by line numbers in the dialogue where Frank applied Step 4 by (1) confirming Fred's understanding of the agreement and (2) setting up a time for review.

E. Recall, and describe briefly, a situation where a supervisor has issued an order or instruction to an employee. Try role playing the supervisor, with someone else in the group taking the part of the employee. Get feedback from the group and instructor to (1) sharpen your sense of when to apply each of the model's steps and (2) improve the skill with which you handle each step.

5

COPING WITH PROBLEM PERFORMERS

Happily, the great majority of employees perform effectively under routinely considerate supervision. When situations become stressful—at home or at work—most employees seem to be able to adapt without special treatment. There are, however, a significant number of employees who do not. These are the problem performers who appear with disturbing frequency even in well-run departments. They require special attention from their supervisors. Accordingly, the objectives of this part are to:

● Help you to become aware of, and to counsel effectively, employees whose performance is weakened by personal problems such as emotional stress, mental illness, and drug and alcohol abuse.
● Help you to develop a sensitivity to employees' complaints and grievances and to handle them fairly and positively.
● Help you to be able to administer firmly both positive and negative discipline as the need arises.

What supervisors think about the problem of problem performers

Supervisors are not preoccupied with deeply disturbed problem performers, but people who break rules or who are absent or late do show up as significant problems. For example:

To what extent do the following conditions cause problems in your department?	Regularly (%)	Sometimes (%)
Employees with deep personal or emotional problems	4	29
Enforcing rules and regulations	7	40
Employee absences or lateness	11	40

Counseling, however, is a skill that many supervisors feel they lack. For example, compared with 17 other skills, supervisors express the lowest degree of confidence in their ability to counsel an employee who abuses alcohol or drugs. Whereas many emotional problems are not as severe as those manifested in "substance abuse," the required counseling techniques remain much the same.

Grievance and disciplinary problems seem to be taken in stride by most supervisors. These problems occur frequently, but supervisors imply that because of good support from top management and their own skills in handling grievances, the time spent on them is kept to a minimum. Obviously, they'd like to keep it that way. Here's what the survey figures show:

How much time and attention do you spend on the following activities?	Above average (%)	About average (%)
Involved in employee grievances and/or disciplinary matters	9	28

This activity ranked lowest in a list of 16 activities, with "dealing with supervisors and staff people in other departments" highest, at 21 percent above average and 57 percent about average.

There seem to be two reasons why supervisors minimize their concern about complaints and grievances, which are surely the most difficult problems to handle when they arise. First, supervisors say that their companies back them up when needed; second, they themselves have acquired confidence in exercising the required skills.

18

COUNSELING TROUBLED EMPLOYEES

Who are these troubled employees?

They appear on your work rolls in many forms. They are the chronic absentee, the rule breaker, the boss hater, the psychosomatic, the person who's lost self-confidence, the alcoholic, the pill popper, the troublemaker, and, yes, even the work-obsessed. These are the people whose performance or behavior on the job is unsatisfactory. Many of them have good potential, but they function far below their capabilities. Their performance represents a problem to themselves and to their supervisors. Ultimately, many of these troubled employees become the subject of grievances and discipline. In this chapter, we'll be talking mainly about those employees who are troubled by emotional problems rather than about willful malcontents, although there's good reason to believe that the latter, too, are driven to their extremes by emotional problems.

Why worry so much about them?

Simply because there are so many of them. Authoritative estimates place the number of potentially mentally disturbed employees at one out of every four or five American workers.

There are many sociological and humanitarian reasons for being concerned about problem workers. One big reason is that a problem employee is also probably a problem husband, son, daughter, or wife. But industry's concern, admittedly, is primarily an economic one. Problem employees are expensive to have on the payroll. They are characterized by excessive tardiness and absences. They are difficult to supervise. And they have a tendency to upset the morale of the work group. Consequently, a supervisor should worry about (1) hiring problem employees in the first place, (2) handling them on the job so that they reach an acceptable level of productivity with the least disruption of the company's overall performance, and (3) determining whether troubled employees have become so seriously maladjusted that they need professional attention.

How can you recognize an employee with an emotional problem?

Be careful here. There are a vast number of employees whose problems are minor or temporary. With a little help and patience, they are able to get themselves back on the track. Among this group, there are a few whose emotional problems are very deeply rooted. Their disturbances are very serious and are beyond the kind of relief a supervisor can be expected to offer. Unfortunately, it is very difficult, even for a trained observer, to tell when an employee has crossed over the line into the more serious category. Generally speaking, the symptoms of employees with emotional problems are similar. These people tend to run away from reality. They do this by going on sick leave or by making too-frequent visits to the dispensary; they may believe that their supervisors are against them, or blame their failures on other people and other things rather than accepting any blame themselves.

Many problem employees fall into these categories: They are perpetually dissatisfied, are given to baseless worries, tire easily, are suspicious, are sure that superiors withhold promotions, believe their associates gossip maliciously about them. Some are characterized by drinking sprees, are given to drug abuse, are insubordinate, or have ungovernable tempers.

Among themselves, problem employees differ widely, just as more normal people do. But within the framework of their symptoms, they are surprisingly alike in their reactions.

Are emotionally disturbed employees insane?

Most emotionally disturbed employees definitely are not "crazy." In fact, a psychological consultant for Eastman Kodak Company, Ralph Collins, says, "One out of four workers is subject to emotional upsets that visibly disturb his or her work." Such employees' behavior under certain kinds of stress is not normal. When goaded by fear (such as the threat of a bill collector) or by anger (because of being refused a day off), they may act in a way that you would describe as "crazy." But they are not (except for a very few) insane or even abnormal.

What about psychotic and neurotic employees?

Both terms sound pretty ominous. But only the employee with a psychosis is seriously ill. The most common type of psychosis is schizophrenia, or split personality. Schizophrenics live partly in a world of imagination. Especially when the world seems threatening to them, they withdraw. They may be able to adjust to life, even have a successful career. But when they lose their grip, their problem is beyond the scope of a lay person.

On the other hand, most people are neurotic to a degree. People who have exaggerated fears, who feel the need to prove themselves, or who are irritable, hostile, opinionated, timid, or aggressive (which somewhere along the line describes most of us) have the seeds of neurosis in them. It's when this condition becomes exaggerated that a neurotic employee becomes a problem to associates and to the supervisor.

Here are a just a few examples of neurotic employees: the lift-truck operator who boasts about drinking and sexual prowess; the supervisor who gets pleasure from reprimanding an employee in front of others; the mechanic who visits the nurse every other day with some minor ailment; the records clerk who meticulously arranges the workplace in the same manner every day, who can't begin the job unless everything is exactly right.

What makes problem people problems?

The key lies in the word *adjustment.* Most problems that bother neurotic employees are trivial. And they often can adjust to them readily. They may for months, years, keep their disturbed feelings hidden—even from themselves—then be stricken by a fear that is so great they can't control it. And then they may do something that they can't explain even to themselves. They may have lost, perhaps temporarily, the ability to adjust.

What sort of management action can put pressure on employees with emotional problems?

All human problems are the result of cause and effect. A supervisor does something and an employee can't adjust—the result, a human explosion. Typical of some managers who unthinkingly put stressful pressure on workers are:

● The supervisor who thinks it's smart psychology to set production and quality goals just a little higher than an employee can reach. What could be more frustrating?
● The supervisor who thinks it's poor psychology to praise an employee for doing a good job. Is there anything so damaging to a person's morale than to do something well and have it taken for granted?
● The supervisor and management personnel who think that employee relations are better whenever the threat of a layoff hangs over employees' heads.

What are the signs of a worried worker—the employee who is about to become a problem?

Until now we've been discussing the general symptoms of problem employees. But you'll be more interested in pinning down the specific kinds of behavior that make employees a problem in your company. That way, you'll be better able to know what to do to aid them.

Some specific signs of a worried worker are:

Sudden Change of Behavior. Pete used to whistle on the job. He hasn't lately. Wonder what's wrong?

Preoccupation. Judy doesn't hear you when you speak to her. She seems off in a fog. When you do get her attention, she says she must have been daydreaming. Is something serious bothering her?

Irritability. Albert is as cross as a bear these days. Even his old buddies are steering clear of him. He wasn't that way before.

Increased Accidents. Bob knocked his knuckles on the job again today. This is unusual. Up until a couple of months ago, he hadn't had even a scratch in five years.

More Absences. Sara is getting to be a headache. She wasn't in this morning again. She never was extra dependable, but now you'll have to do something to get her back on the ball.

Increased Fatigue. Mary seems to live a clean life and keep good hours. But she complains about being tired all the time. Is it something physical or is she worried about something?

Too Much Drinking. Ralph was so jittery at his machine this afternoon, you felt sorry for him. And he had a breath that would knock you over. You know he used to like going out on the town, but this is different.

What can you do about your troubled workers?

Let's make this clear. We are not talking here about psychotic persons or the ones with serious neurotic disorders. We'll talk about them later on.

You can help troubled employees toward better adjustment only after you have reassured them that you are trying to help them keep their jobs—not looking for an excuse to get rid of them. No approach does more harm with persons who have emotional problems than the better-get-yourself-straightened-out-or-you-will-lose-your-job attitude. You have to believe, and make them believe, that your intentions are good, that you want to help. Then, you must give them every opportunity to help themselves. This approach is called *counseling.*

How do you counsel employees?

The researchers in this field suggest that a supervisor can best counsel employees if these five rules are followed for each interview:

1. Listen patiently to what the employee has to say before making any comment of your own.

2. Refrain from criticizing or offering hasty advice on the employee's problem.

3. Never argue with an employee while you are counseling.

4. Give your undivided attention to the employee who is talking.

5. Look beyond the mere words of what the employee says—listen to see if the person is trying to tell you something deeper than what appears on the surface.

What results should you expect from counseling?

Recognize what you are counseling an employee for, and don't look for immediate results. Never mix the counseling interview with some other action you may want to take—such as discipline.

Suppose Ruth has been late for the fourth time this month. The company rules say she must be suspended for three days. When talking to Ruth about the disciplinary penalty, try to keep the conversation impersonal. Your purpose at this point is to show her the connection between what she's done and what is happening to her.

Now in the long run you may wish to rehabilitate Ruth because she's potentially a good worker. This calls for a counseling interview. And it's better to hold the interview with Ruth at a separate time. (Of course, it would have been better to hold the interview before she had to be disciplined.)

A counseling interview is aimed at helping employees to unburden themselves—to get worries off their chest. Whether or not the conversation is related to the problem they create for you at work is not important. The payoff comes as they get confidence in you—and consequently don't vent their hostility and frustrations on the job. Experience seems to show that this will happen if you are patient. It won't work with every troubled employee, of course, but it will with most of them.

How do you start a counseling session?

Find a reasonably quiet place where you're sure you won't be interrupted and won't be overheard. Try to put the employee at ease. Don't jump into a cross-examination. Saying absolutely nothing is better than that. If Ralph has become a problem because of spotty work, you can lead into the discussion by saying something like this: "Ralph, have you noticed the increase in the orders we're getting on the new model? This is going to mean a lot of work for the company for a long while ahead. I guess it has meant some changes, too. How is it affecting the operation of your machine? What sort of problems has it created?"

In this case, you are trying to give Ralph an opportunity to talk about something specific and mechanical. If you listen to his ideas, he may begin to loosen up and talk about his emotional problems or his worries.

How effective is active listening at this stage?

In many ways, counseling *is* a refined form of active listening. Look back on pages 314–316, where active listening is described in detail and compared with passive listening. Troubled employees feel much more valued when your listening is active and are more likely to talk freely about what is bothering them. This helps to bring about a desirable relief in emotionally caused tensions.

How many counseling interviews should you have with a problem employee? How long should a counseling interview last?

These are hard questions for clear-cut answers. For a less serious case, one interview might clear the air for a long time. With employees whose emotional problems are more serious, it may take five or ten 15- to 30-minute conversations just to gain confidence. And with still others, the counseling will have to become a regular part of your supervisory chores with them.

You can readily see that counseling can be time-consuming. That's why it's so important to spot worried workers early and take corrective action while you can help them with the minimum drag on your time.

As to how long an interview should last—you can't accomplish much in 15 minutes, but if that's all you can spare, it's a lot better than nothing. At the very least, it shows the employee you're interested in the problem. Ideally, an interview should last between three-quarters of an hour and an hour.

How can you recognize when an employee needs emotional first aid?

Dr. Harry Levinson, a nationally recognized authority and founder of the Levinson Institute, advises that the basic steps (Figure 18-1) for you to take in administering emotional first aid are to:

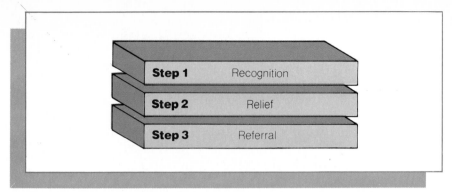

Figure 18-1. Levinson's three-phase guideline for supervisors to take in counseling troubled employees.

1. Recognize the emotional disturbance.
2. Relieve acute distress by listening (counseling).
3. Refer cases beyond your limits to professional help.

To recognize the employee who needs counseling help, says Dr. Levinson, look for three major signs:

Extremes. The ordinarily shy person goes even deeper into a shell. The hail-fellow-well-met steps up social activities to a fever pitch.

Anxiety. If withdrawal or activity brings no relief, the employee may become panicky or jittery, show extreme tension, flush in the face, or perspire heavily.

Breakdown. If still unable to cope with the anxiety, the problem employee may break down altogether and be unable to control thoughts, feelings, or actions. Thinking becomes irrational. The person doesn't make sense to others. Emotions may become irrational. For instance, the tidy person may become slovenly, the quiet person noisy.

How can you provide relief for the emotionally troubled employee?

Dr. Levinson suggests you may be helpful simply by letting the emotionally disturbed employee know how much the current distress is affecting the job—and how much of this the company will tolerate. Above all, a person under stress may add to it materially with fears of what the company might do if and when it discovers the condition. If you can offer some rule of thumb ("We appreciate the fact that you have something bothering you. And we're willing to go along with your present performance for a couple of weeks or so. But if it doesn't improve after that, we'll have to find a solution.") even if it's not entirely sympathetic, you at least provide something concrete to guide the employee's actions.

If the employee voluntarily brings the problem to you, you can help most by listening, advises Dr. Levinson. This is more difficult than it appears, he cautions. Listening must mean truly *nonevaluative* listening—no interruptions, advice, prescriptions, solutions, pontifications, or preaching.

When should you call for professional help?

Dr. Levinson offers this rule of thumb: *If after two listening sessions you seem to be making little headway in establishing confidence, you should report the case (in confidence, of course) to the company nurse or the company physician.*

Dr. Levinson also advises that your approach in referral should be that of opening another door for additional help. Don't ever suggest by action or word that the employee is "crazy," hopeless, or unworthy of attention.

Is an accident-prone employee likely to be emotionally disturbed?

Dr. Gerald Gordon, of the Du Pont company, which has one of the best safety records of any company in the world, had this to say:

Our studies have revealed a small group of individuals around whom occupational injuries seem to cluster in disproportionate numbers. Obviously there is something more than hard luck plaguing a man whose career shows a long series of injuries. What's back of his trouble? The answer is that *the accident maker is suffering from a form of mental illness so widespread that it may be found to some degree in most of us*. . . . It is the failure of the employee as a whole person that is the core of his problem. He tends to evade the rules, both of working and of living. . . . In most cases the potential accident victim has a long service record and is well trained for his job. But all too often he's a victim of his own bottled-up emotions, which he turns against himself.

What can a supervisor do about an accident-prone employee?

Du Pont's Dr. Gordon advises that so-called accident-prone employees can be helped fairly easily if they are discovered early enough and something is done to help them:

> In my opinion, the fact that a worker violates a safety rule is more important than *why* he violates it. Pampering the emotionally disturbed individual only serves to increase his demands and, at the same time, aggravates the severity of his illness.
>
> If a supervisor openly and honestly exercises his authority to obtain good performance, he is helping both the employee and the company for which they both work.

Absentees are a special kind of problem people. How lenient should you be with them?

It depends on the reasons for absence. Professor P. J. Taylor of London University, who was formerly medical director of Shell (UK) Ltd., observes that 60 percent of all absences are due to serious or chronic illness and 20 percent to acute, short-term illnesses such as the flu; 10 percent feel unwell because of a minor illness such as a cold and they do or don't report to work according to their attitude about their jobs; and the final 10 percent are completely well but feign illness to enjoy a day off.

It is the group of absentees who make up the bottom 20 percent who are suspect. Industrial psychologists call their virus "voluntary absence." In many, this is deeply rooted. The Puritan ethic of work does not apply to them. There is an inevitable conflict between the desire for more leisure and more work. This tug is especially evident among younger workers.

Many authorities, however, still contend that employees who are chronically absent from work are mentally ill. They reason that the reality of work must be so unbearable to these emotionally disturbed employees that they literally escape from reality be staying away from work. Regardless of the reason, you can help reduce absenteeism by:

● Firming up your rules about it.
● Being consistent in applying penalties.
● Trying to get at the reasons why an employee is frequently absent.

The last method requires the counseling technique. It is important that each individual case be followed up promptly. In your discussion of the problem with employees, be sure to permit them to explain their reactions to the job itself, the people they work with, the working conditions, their tools and equipment, the kind of training they receive. You thus avoid their feeling that you are placing all the blame on them. And if they are specific in their reactions, you then have specific complaints, rather than vague dissatisfactions to deal with.

Don't overlook, however, the power of job satisfaction in luring absence-prone workers back to the job. Surprisingly, however, physical working conditions seem to have little effect. In company after company, attendance figures show little variation between the dirty, unpleasant areas and those that are clean and well lighted. Even most incentive schemes aimed at reducing absences are relatively ineffective. Closeness of the work team, its homogeneity, and the state of its morale seem to have the greatest effect.

How effective is counseling in reducing absenteeism?

Success depends on the root cause of individual absences. See how the patterns and the motivations differ:

Chronic Absentees.   The people who have little capacity for pressure, either on the job or off, may be prime candidates for counseling. But first they must be made fully aware of the consequences of poor attendance. Theirs is a habit, usually of long standing, and correction requires pressure to attend as well as hand holding.

Vacationing Absentees.   The people who work only so long as they need the cash and who then treat themselves to a day or two off are difficult cases. These employees are often extremely capable on the job, but they feel no deep responsibility for it. Vacationers make a conscious choice to be absent and are rarely helped by counseling.

Directionless Absentees.   The younger employees who have as yet found no real purpose in work may simply follow the lead of the vacationer, who appears to lead a footloose, exciting life. A Dutch-uncle talk with the directionless absentee may be more effective than counseling.

Aggressive Absentees.   The persons who willfully stay away from work in the hope that their absence will cause an inconvenience for you are probably emotionally disturbed. This kind of behavior, however, requires professional counseling to correct it, not the kind of ordinary supervisor can provide.

Moonlighters. The persons who hold more than one job are often either too tired to come to work or faced with conflicting schedules. Straight talk, rather than counseling, is prescribed. When attendance is affected, the moonlighter must be forced to make a choice between jobs.

Occasional Absentees. The persons who seem to have slightly more absences than the rest of your staff are probably prime candidates for counseling. Their absences are legitimate. Their illnesses are real. Their problems are often temporarily insurmountable. These people deserve a mixture of sympathy, understanding, and sometimes outright advice.

In summary, you can probably help people who are absent for the following reasons:

1. Getting to work is a problem, real or imagined.
2. Off-job pressures are so strong that they weaken the employee's resolve to get to work.
3. The employee is imitative, easily led or misled.
4. The work appears boring, disagreeable, or unattractive.
5. Working relationships are unpleasant.
6. There are in fact off-job problems—child care, serious illness, court appearances—that need immediate attention.
7. Absence or lateness has become a habit.

You will have difficulty helping people who are absent because of these reasons:

1. The work or the pay associated with it holds no strong attraction.
2. Off-job pleasures have a greater appeal than work.
3. The employee is willfully absent in order to disrupt or inconvenience the organization.

What can you do for alcoholic employees?

Whatever you attempt, proceed slowly and cautiously. Not all heavy drinkers are alcoholics. And the more they drink, the less likely they are to admit to anyone (even themselves) that their ability to handle liquor has got out of their control.

An alcoholic employee is really just another kind of problem employee—only the case is an aggravated one and may need the help of a professional (discussed later). Nevertheless, many alcoholic workers have rescued themselves with the aid of Alcoholics Anonymous, an association of exalcoholics who, because they don't preach and because they emphasize the individual's need to face weaknesses, have perfected the art of listening without being either sympathetic or critical.

Your best bet, however, is to recognize an alcoholic in the early stages. Then you can apply the same techniques to gain the person's confidence that you would with any other problem employee. Your objective is to provide security at work and to help with talking out problems. If these employees can be helped to recognize that excessive drinking is a problem they aren't handling, then you can refer them to the company doctor or nurse, who in turn may be able to persuade them to look into Alcoholics Anonymous or to visit a psychiatrist or a special clinic for alcoholics.

How can you tell whether or not you've got an alcoholic employee on your hands?

To guide you in recognizing alcoholic employees, Professor Harrison M. Trice of Cornell University advises that you look first to the employee's absence record. A sharp rise in overall rate of absences almost always accompanies the development of drinking problems, he says. In a study of 200 cases of alcoholism in industry, Professor Trice also noted three differences from the normal conception of absences among problem drinkers:

Absences are spread out through the week. Neither Monday nor Friday absences predominate (probably because the alcoholic is trying to be careful not to draw attention to the condition).

Partial absenteeism is frequent. A worker often reports in the morning but leaves before the day is over.

Tardiness is not a marked feature of alcoholism in industry. The widespread notion that a problem drinker comes late to work was not substantiated by Professor Trice's study.

How should you approach counseling an employee you believe to be an alcoholic?

Alcoholism requires a special form of counseling, say those who have coped most effectively with it. For example, the U.S. Department of Health, Education and Welfare in its *Supervisors' Guide on Alcohol Abuse* offers these hints to supervisors who are faced with this problem among their employees:

1. Don't apologize for confronting the troubled employee about the situation. Your responsibility is to maintain acceptable performance for all your employees.

2. Do encourage this employee to explain why work performance, behavior, or attendance is deteriorating. This can provide an opportunity to question the use of alcohol.

3. Don't discuss a person's right to drink. It is best not to make a moral issue of it; HEW views alcoholism as a progressive and debilitating illness, which, if untreated, can eventually lead to insanity, custodial care, or death.

4. Don't suggest that the employee use moderation or change his or her drinking habits. A person who is an alcoholic cannot, at the start, voluntarily control drinking habits.

5. Don't be distracted by the individual's excuses for drinking—a difficult spouse, problem children, financial troubles. The problem as far as you are concerned is the employee's drinking and how it affects work, behavior, and attendance on the job.

6. Don't be put off by the drinker's assertion that a physician or a psychologist is already being seen. The employee may claim that the physician or the psychologist doesn't consider the drinking a problem, or that they think the use of alcohol will subside once the "problems" are worked out. Therapists probably wouldn't say that if they knew the employee's job was in jeopardy because of alcohol abuse; they would attach a new importance to the drinking habits.

7. Do remember that the alcoholic, like any other sick person, should be given the opportunity for treatment and rehabilitation.

8. Do emphasize that your major concern as a supervisor is the employee's poor work performance or behavior. You can firmly state that if there is no improvement, administrative action—such as suspension or discharge—will be taken.

9. Do state that the decision to accept rehabilitative assistance is the employee's responsibility.

10. Ann St. Louis, personnel counselor for Canada's Department of National Revenue, whose program maintains a 90 percent recovery rate among alcoholic government workers, adds this thought:

An employer—far better than wife, mother, minister or social agency—can lead an alcoholic to treatment by "constructive coercion." Give an employee every chance to take treatment, but make it clear that he must cooperate or lose his job. This has proven to be more effective than loss of friends or family.

How widespread is drug addiction among employees?

It is not so pervasive as you might think. Because regular drug use is incompatible with regular attendance, drug users tend not to select most regular or demanding kinds of employment. Attempts on a company's part to screen out hard drug users before employment have not been particularly successful. Dismissal afterward can be difficult because drug users are good at hiding the tools of their habit even if they cannot conceal its symptoms.

Symptoms of drug use are well known. At work they manifest themselves objectively in terms of poor or erratic performance, tardiness, absenteeism, requests to leave early, forgetfulness, indifference to deadlines and safety, and in many instances theft of company property.

Treatment and rehabilitation for drug users are as difficult and complicated as for alcoholics, and the treatments are somewhat similar. Policies of companies against drug addiction, however, tend to be firmer than against drinking and alcoholism. For one thing, the addict is different from the alcoholic because many addicts try to involve other people in drugs. The danger of an alcoholic's inducing another employee to begin alcoholism is slight. Then, too, drug use is illegal; in most instances, use of alcohol is not.

Here again, a supervisor's responsibility should be limited to the detection of drug addiction, prevention of its use or sale on company property, and counseling and referral—if indicated—of drug users to the appropriate company authority.

What makes some people overwork to the point of sickness?

A great many people suffer from work addiction. To mask deep emotional problems, and sometimes very real difficulties in their economic or home lives, they burrow into their work. It is a form of retreat from reality. It helps them forget what seem like insurmountable problems. The difficulty from a supervisor's point of view is that the work of work addicts tends to be nonproductive. Paradoxically, as these work-obsessed individuals intensify their diligence, it impedes their output. Furthermore, they often stir up such waves in the office or plant that they cut down the output of their associates.

It is difficult for a supervisor to do much other than to recognize the work addict. These compulsive individuals are usually highly moral, ambitious, intelligent, honest, and intensely loyal to their employer. At higher levels, they are the persons who stuff the briefcase for what is often needless work in the evening or weekends. They suffer from anxieties and depressions and generally will not respond to advice to take it easy. They need professional therapy that aims at improving self-understanding, flexibility, and creativity.

What do the professionals do for problem employees that the supervisors can't do?

Two kinds of industrial professionals usually work with mentally disturbed employees who are beyond the supervisor's limits to help adjust:

● The psychiatrist is a fully qualified physician who has practiced medicine before qualifying for this specialty. An industrial psychiatrist, because of specialized training and experience, can diagnose more closely what an individual's trouble is and prescribe the proper kind of treatment. No supervisor should try to do either.

● The counselor, or industrial psychologist, works with the great majority of emotionally disturbed employees who do not need full-scale psychiatric treatment. Because of specialized training, the counselor's biggest asset is the ability to listen understandingly to an employee's account of problems. The professional counselor has an advantage over the line supervisor, since the counselor doesn't have the authority to discipline, promote, or fire the employee and therefore has a greater chance of winning the employee's confidence.

Key Concepts

1. Troubled employees are those people who, for one reason or another, have not found a way to adjust satisfactorily to the hardships of life or work. Their failure to cope causes them to behave unproductively or erratically on the job and to interrupt regularly the harmony of the shop.

2. Problem employees can be recognized by such disharmonious conduct as sudden changes in behavior, preoccupation, irritability, increased accidents or absences, unusual fatigue, irrational anger or hostility, heavy drinking, or symptoms of drug abuse.

3. Constructive counseling by a supervisor can help a great many problem employees to improve or control their behavior, provided that the degree of their maladjustment is slight and the underlying causes are not intense.

4. Counseling requires that supervisors themselves be well adjusted; that they be willing to listen, even to hostility directed toward them; that they permit the employee to dominate the interview; and that they refrain from offering judgments.

5. It is critical, morally as well as medically, that a supervisor recognize the limits of his or her ability to counsel and the inability of many problem employees to accept nonprofessional counseling. In these instances (and they are frequent), the supervisor should confine his or her efforts either to suggesting professional counsel or to referral to the company personnel office.

Supervisory Word Power

Adjustment. The process whereby healthy as well as disturbed individuals find a way to fit themselves to difficult situations by yielding to a degree and by modifying their feelings and their behavior to accommodate the stresses of life and work.

Hostility. A feeling of enmity or antagonism; an aggressive expression of anger displayed by problem employees as an unconscious, unwitting relief from fears about their security or other feelings of inadequacy.

Neurosis. An emotional disorder, relatively mild in nature, in which employees have feelings of anxiety, fear, or anger that drive them unknowingly or unwillingly to say and do things they would not normally choose to say and do and which often act against their own interests.

Psychosis. A severe mental disorder or disease in which employee feelings of hostility or persecution are gravely magnified and actions are irrational and unmanageable to the extreme.

Withdrawal. A passive way for emotionally disturbed employees to cope with their anxieties, in which they retreat from confrontations, appear unduly preoccupied, discourage social overtures, and keep very much to themselves.

Reading Comprehension

1. Why is it a good idea for supervisors to identify and attempt to help the troubled employees in their work force?

2. List at least five symptoms of an employee with an emotional problem.

3. Differentiate between a neurotic employee and a psychotic employee.

4. Which kinds of problem employees are supervisors likely to be able to help, and which kinds had they best refer to a more highly qualified counselor?

5. Describe the essentials of a counseling interview.

6. What symptoms characterize an extremely disturbed employee who ought to receive professional help without delay?

7. In what ways are the accident-prone employee, the alcoholic, and the drug-addicted worker similar?

8. Discuss the difference between valid absences resulting from a bona fide illness and those absences that psychologists describe as voluntary absences. What is the supervisor's role in minimizing the latter?

9. What should a supervisor stress when counseling an employee who has shown signs of being an alcoholic?

10. Why are professionals such as psychiatrists and industrial psychologists better able to handle seriously disturbed employees than a supervisor is?

Supervision in Action

The Case of the Document Clerk's Sicknesses. A Case Study in Human Relations Involving Absenteeism, with Questions for You to Answer.

Aretha Ford, deputy assistant director of the Water Control Unit of a western state environmental protection agency, pondered her unit's absentee record. There were a couple of real losers on the list. She had tried very hard to get them back into line, with little success, and she had just about made up her mind to speak to the director about starting administrative procedures to separate them. But what caught her eye was the record of Beno Axelsone. His absence record had been steadily climbing above the unit's average for the past three years.

Beno was a medium-grade documents clerk with nearly 12 years of service in various state agencies. He had come to the Water Control Unit about 4 years ago. His overall performance was just about satisfactory. He was relatively quiet and showed little initiative. Nevertheless, he managed to do his work satisfactorily so long as he was there. The problem was that he regularly used up his sick leave with a variety of short absences. Each of these absences, taken one by one, seemed legitimate. Because he was a documents clerk, it was a nuisance when he was not there. It meant that someone had to search his files for critical records if these were needed in a hurry, as they often were when a call came from the state capitol or from Washington for information.

Aretha decided to speak to Beno about his increasing number of absences. She asked her secretary to call Beno into her office. Here is what transpired.

"Beno, can we talk a little this morning?" said Aretha.

"Yes, Ms. Ford," answered Beno.

"How have you been feeling?" asked Aretha.

"Fine, fine," said Beno.

"No problems at home?" asked Aretha.

"Everyone's got problems, Ms. Ford," replied Beno.

"What kind of problems do you have?" asked Aretha.

"I got no problems," said Beno.

"I thought maybe you did," said Aretha.

"Why?"

"Because I notice that your sick leave days have been steadily increasing in the last year."

"I'm entitled to them, aren't I? I have 12 years' service with the state now."

"You are entitled to them if you are sick. But you seem to be sick so often."

"I can't help it if I'm sick."

"Well, you cause us a problem when you are out so often."

"I do my work all right, don't I?"

"When you're here you do. But you have missed 24 days so far this year."

"I'm entitled to them. I've earned them."

"You are entitled to them only if you are sick."

"I am sick when I'm absent. I can't help it."

"Are you sure there isn't something at home that causes you to be sick so often?"

"I don't know what you mean, Ms. Ford. I get sick because I'm not as healthy as some other people, I guess."

"The records show that you are among the few in the department who are sick so often they use up their entire sick leave."

"Isn't that what the sick leave is for, Ms. Ford? To let me stay home without losing pay when I'm sick?"

"Yes, but you and a couple of others in the unit are the only ones who are sick so often."

"That's what I mean. Others get sick, too. And when they get sick, they stay home. I don't stay home unless I'm sick. I've worked for the state 12 years and my record is good."

"Well, your absence record isn't that good, and I'd like to see you improve it."

"I can't help it if I'm sick, Ms. Ford. My work record is good with the state. You can't get rid of me because I get sick a little more than others who are lucky to be healthy."

"I didn't say we were going to fire you. I only want your absence record to improve."

"Why are you putting this pressure on me because I get sick? I do my best. I can't help it if I'm not well."

"Beno, I'm not trying to get you fired. All I want is for you to improve your attendance. All right?"

"I'll try, Ms. Ford, but I'm doing my best anyway."

Beno left the office. Ms. Ford looked again at the records and shook her head. Why, she asked herself, is it so hard to get employees to admit that their absences cause a problem?

1. What is your estimate of the rapport Aretha established between herself and Beno? Who is at fault?
2. What is your reaction to Beno's reason for being absent so often?
3. How might Aretha have probed further into Beno's problem?
4. What did Aretha fail to do in discussing this problem with Beno?

19

HANDLING COMPLAINTS AND AVOIDING GRIEVANCES

How much attention should supervisors pay to employee complaints?

Just as much as is necessary to remove the employee complaints as obstacles to their doing a willing, productive job. That's the main reason supervisors should act as soon as they even sense a complaint or grievance. A gripe, imagined or real, spoken or held in, blocks an employee's will to cooperate. Until you've examined the grievance and its underlying causes, an employee isn't likely to put out very much for you. And if the complaint has merit, the only way for you to get the employee back on your team 100 percent is to correct the situation.

Can you settle every grievance to an employee's satisfaction?

No. It's natural for people sometimes to want more than they deserve. When an employee complains about a condition and the facts don't back him or her up, the best you can do is to demonstrate that the settlement is a just one—even if it isn't exactly what the employee would like.

Jake may want the company to provide him with work clothing on a job he considers dirty. Suppose you are able to show Jake that the working conditions are normal for the kind of work being done, that other workers in the company doing the same kind of work provide their own coveralls, and that this practice is common in the industry. Jake should be satisfied with this answer. He's getting equal treatment. But there's nothing to prevent Jake from still feeling dissatisfied with the settlement of his complaint. He may still feel the company should provide work clothing.

Look at it this way, though. You didn't give Jake the brushoff. You listened to his argument attentively. You didn't give him a snap answer. You checked with other supervisors and with the manager to see what the company practice was. You found out that the company practice conforms with that of the industry. All this adds up to something of value in you that Jake can see. He can take his troubles to you and get a straight answer. That's good leadership!

Is there danger in trying to talk an employee out of a complaint?

Talk if you will. But don't try to outsmart an employee—even if that's what the employee may be trying to do to you. Grievances are caused by facts—or what an employee believes to be facts. Clever use of words and sharp debating tactics won't change these facts or dissolve the grievance.

Patience and sincerity are the two biggest keys to settling a grievance. In many cases, just listening patiently to an explanation will result in the employee's forgetting the grievance.

What is meant by an imagined grievance? If it's a figment of a worker's imagination, why give it serious attention?

Marie, an unskilled machine operator, files a grievance saying that you've been picking on her, accusing her of doing substandard work. As far as you're concerned, Marie is off her rocker. In fact, you've hardly paid any attention to what she's been doing. Where'd she ever get a notion like that?

Well, where did she? Let's see. Your department has been pretty rushed lately—that's why you haven't seen much of Marie. You've been spending a good deal of your time with two new apprentices that have just been turned over to you for assignment. *You* knew that their presence had nothing to do with Marie or her job. But did Marie?

Here's how Marie looked at the situation: "I've been here four years busting a gut for Joe. So what does he do when they send up a couple of bright young apprentices? He puts me on the blacklist. He thinks he's going to freeze me out of my job by not speaking to me for two weeks. Then when he does, he tells me that the last batch of fasteners I turned out have to be reworked. And first thing this morning he jumps me for breaking a drill. Next thing I know he'll have one of those apprentices showing me how to do a job I've done for four years. Or taking my job on some phony pretext and bumping me back to the foundry. I'll squawk now before it's too late."

Marie has imagined this grievance, hasn't she? She's got the situation all wrong, too. But if Joe doesn't take time out right now to get to the bottom of this complaint, he'll have a real problem on his hands. Joe will make a good beginning by saying, "Marie, if I've been picking on you, it certainly wasn't personal. In fact, if I thought you had any complaint, it was that I hadn't been giving you enough attention. For the last couple of weeks, I've let you pretty much alone because you're an older hand here. I feel I can trust you to go ahead without my standing over your shoulder. But somewhere maybe I've gotten off the track. Can you tell me what you mean by picking on you? I certainly want to get this matter straightened out."

What's the most important thing you can do when handling grievances?

It can't be said too often: Above all, be objective, be fair. Get the employees' point of view clear in your mind. If they have an opportunity

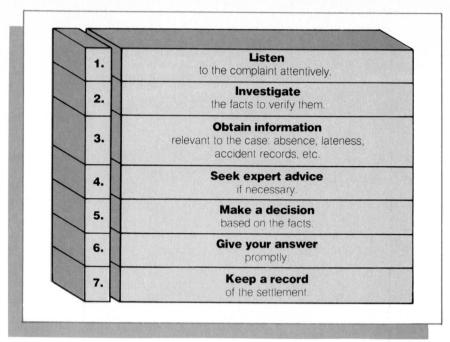

1.	**Listen**	to the complaint attentively.
2.	**Investigate**	the facts to verify them.
3.	**Obtain information**	relevant to the case: absence, lateness, accident records, etc.
4.	**Seek expert advice**	if necessary.
5.	**Make a decision**	based on the facts.
6.	**Give your answer**	promptly.
7.	**Keep a record**	of the settlement.

Figure 19-1. Grievance handling process.

to make themselves understood, their grievances may turn out to be something different from what appears on the surface.

To be really fair, you must be prepared to accept the logical conclusion that flows from the facts you uncover. (See Figure 19-1.) This may mean making concessions. But if the facts warrant it, you often have to change your mind or your way of doing things if you are to gain a reputation for fair dealing.

If you find you've made a mistake, admit it. A supervisor isn't expected to be right all the time. But your employees expect you to be honest in every instance—even if it means your eating crow on occasion.

Should a supervisor bargain on grievances?

No. Be like a good baseball umpire: Call each one as you see it. An umpire who blows a decision is really in for trouble if he tries to make up for it on the next call. It should be the same way with grievances. An employee either has a case or hasn't a case. Consider each case on its merits. And don't let the grievances become political issues.

Should supervisors change their story if they find the facts won't support their original conclusions?

Supervisors have no other choice if on investigation they find their actions or decisions have been wrong. But they should avoid this embarrassing situation in the first place. Just be sure to get the facts—all the facts. Get them straight to begin with—before you give the employee or a shop steward your decision. It costs you nothing to say, "Give me a couple of hours (or a couple of days) to look into this matter thoroughly. Just as soon as I know all the facts, I'll be able to discuss this grievance so that we come up with the fairest solution."

In trying to round up the facts of a case, explore further than just the obvious places. For example, if the grievance involves a dispute over pay, look beyond just the time-card and payroll data. Ask yourself: Has the worker been upset about the jobs assigned? Has the worker had a fair share of easier jobs? Have we had occasion to turn the worker down on a bid for a better job? Does the worker know how to fill in a time card properly? Does the worker know the procedure for getting credit for machine breakdown time? Have the worker's materials and tools been up to standard?

All these factors could affect a person's pay and should be examined before you commit yourself.

Records are especially useful in assembling the facts and in backing you when you present your decision to the employee or the union. If your complaint is that output has been below par, you'll need the worker's records and the records of others to prove it.

Isn't there a danger that if you make a big thing of a grievance, you'll encourage the employee and the union to think it's more legitimate than it really is?

There's that chance. But you've got to risk it. In the long run, treating each grievance with care and consideration pays off. That's different, of course, from giving in on a grievance. That might lead employees to believe you're soft and that you'll make concessions just to avoid arguments.

On the whole it is best to follow this rule for handling grievances: Be businesslike in your discussions. Talk with an employee someplace where you'll be free from distractions and interruptions. You should by all means treat the grievance as a private matter; discuss it away from other employees. Once the employee refers the grievance to the union for handling, don't attempt to settle it except in the presence of the union representative.

When you have made your own investigation and are ready to discuss how the grievance should be settled, advise the union steward. Ask the steward to invite the employee to be present. After all, your reply is to the employee as well as to the union. Even though the employee has gone to the union for representation, you still want to maintain your personal relationship. And the employee can observe that you maintained the initiative, that the steward didn't have to tell you off.

As in any business situation, handle all your discussions in a civil tone. Avoid discussing personalities. Keep the steward's focus, as well as your own, on the grievance situation. Show the steward you, too, wish to settle it fairly. Keep control of your temper, even if the employee or steward doesn't. Resist the temptation to blow your top. It's all too easy to permit a grievance to fall to the level of a personal squabble among you, the employee, and the steward. Avoid this at all costs.

When you give your decision on a grievance, how specific should you be? Should you leave yourself a loophole?

A supervisor is paid to make decisions. When the grievance has been fully investigated and you've talked it over with the parties involved, make your decision as promptly as possible. Be definite in your answer. State your decision so that there's no mistake about what you mean. If it involves a warning rather than a more serious penalty—for breaking a safety rule, for instance—don't give this kind of reply: "I'll withhold the warning this time, but next time it happens it won't be so easy for you."

Instead, use this clear-cut approach: "There appears to be a good reason to believe that you misunderstood what I expected of you. So I'll tear up the warning and throw it away. Next time, you'll get a written warning. And if it happens a second time, it will cost you a week off without pay."

It is also a good idea to make sure that the worker understands the reasons for your decisions. For instance, in the safety warning case above, the supervisor might have said: "Ordinarily, ignorance of the rule is no excuse. The rule is in the employee handbook and has been posted conspicuously in the department. Your case seems to be different because you asked me about this rule last week, and you misunderstood what I told you about it. I told you that you were to report any injury, no matter how minor, to me before going to the nurse. You seem to have thought that you didn't have to report the injury so long as you didn't go to the nurse—which you didn't. I've explained it now that I want to know about every injury—and I'll decide whether we treat it here or send you to the dispensary."

Must you give your decision right away?

No. But don't sit on it forever. Nothing breaks down the grievance procedure like procrastination. If you can't make up your mind on the spot, or need to check even further than you did originally, tell the employee and the steward that you'll give a definite answer this afternoon or tomorrow. Stick to this promise. If you run into an unexpected delay, let them know about it. For instance: "Sorry I can't let you know this afternoon as I'd hoped, because the paymaster has been tied up all morning. I won't be able to check the time sheets until late this afternoon. But I will let you know first thing in the morning."

Suppose your boss or your boss's superior asks you to hand down a grievance decision that you don't agree with. Should you accept responsibility for it?

This is that old supervisor-in-the-middle situation. It's bound to come up from time to time. Sometimes you'll find that company practice is easier on the employee than you think it should be. Sometimes just the reverse is true—company policy is tougher than what you'd do if you had no one but yourself to answer to. In either case, don't pass the buck. If you as a supervisor say that you agree with the employee but the company manager can't see it your way, you destroy the whole management teamwork. If you don't agree with company policy, try to adjust your own thinking. In any event, and hard as it may be to swallow, you should pass the decision along as your own.

Should a supervisor help employees save face if they have had a grievance go against them?

It seems as if it's asking too much for a supervisor to be noble about winning a grievance—especially when the employee or union has been nasty or aggressive in pursuing it. But here again, it's a bad practice in the long run to make the employee eat humble pie. If you help employees save face, they may be considerate to you when the tables are turned. If you rub in the decision, you may irk them so much that they'll be on the lookout for a gripe they can't lose.

This shouldn't be interpreted to mean that you must be so downright nice as to appear as if you were sorry you were right. Try saying something like this: "I've checked your complaint from every angle, but it still looks like no to me. You made two comparisons when you stated that I was playing favorites. In each case the facts show that both employees you referred to outranked you in both output and quality of production. On my scorecard they deserve the better assignments. I'm far from glad that I had to say no to you. But I am glad that you brought your position out into the open. Perhaps now that I know how you feel, I can give you some help to improve your performance so you can do some of the jobs requiring greater skill."

What's the best way to wind up a grievance settlement?

Carry out your part of the bargain and see that the employee does, too. Once an agreement has been made, follow through on corrective action promptly. You may lose all the good will you've built in settling the grievance if you delay in taking action.

How important is the grievance procedure as such? Wouldn't it be simpler if employee grievances were all handled informally?

Where a union is involved, the grievance procedure becomes a very important matter. The procedure may vary from company to company (see Chapter 28), but in any case your guide should be: Know the authorized grievance procedure in your organization and stick to it. It's up to you, too, to see that the steward also observes the provisions of the grievance clause.

Take special notice of what may appear to be tiny technicalities, and be sure you observe them. For instance, some contracts call for the supervisor to give an answer within 24 hours after the complaint has been presented in writing. Be sure you do, so that you can't be accused of stalling or even lose the grievance entirely on such a technicality.

Of course, it would be desirable if grievances could all be settled in a casual, informal manner. But where a union is concerned, experience shows that it's best to be businesslike and to stick to the letter of the contract procedure. On the other hand, don't get so engrossed with the process itself that you overlook the original purpose of the grievance procedure—to settle grievances fairly and promptly.

What happens to grievances that go unsettled?

They continue to fester. Frequently a supervisor feels that he or she has taken care of a complaint just by soft-soaping the aggrieved employee. This is a mistake. The grievance will continue to simmer in the employee's mind, even if nothing more is said about it to the supervisor. And dissatisfaction is contagious.

An unsettled grievance is like one rotten apple in a basket. It spoils the good ones—the good ones don't make a good apple of the rotten one. An offended or angry employee tends to make other employees lose confidence in the supervisor. The co-workers may encourage the dissatisfied employee to pursue the matter if it appears that you have been evasive.

When does a grievance go to arbitration?

Most union-management contract agreements call for a grievance to go to arbitration if the grievance cannot be settled at any of the steps of the authorized procedure. Once the complaint has been turned over to an impartial arbitrator, the arbitrator acts somewhat like a judge, listens to the facts as presented by both parties, then makes a decision. The arbitrator does not mediate, that is, try to reopen the discussions between the company and the union. Both parties agree to abide by the decision.

Where are grievances most likely to occur?

It's hard to pinpoint just what situations are most likely to breed grievances. But there are some indicators for you to follow:

● First of all, don't lose sight of the fact that grievances are symptoms of something wrong with employees, or with working conditions, or with immediate supervision.

● Second, employees are most likely to be worried about situations that threaten their security: such things as promotions, transfers, work assignments, layoffs, the supervisor's evaluation of their performance, and mechanization or elimination of their jobs.

TABLE 19-1 COMMON GRIEVANCES AND THEIR CAUSES

Grievances (listed in order of their frequency)	Typical Causes (as an employee sees it)
Wages and Salary	
1. Demand for individual wage adjustment	I'm not getting what I'm worth. I get less than other people doing work that requires no more skill.
2. Complaints about job classifications	My job is worth more than it pays and it should be reclassified.
3. Complaints about incentive systems	The method used to figure my pay is so complicated that I don't really know what the rate is. My piece rate is too low. You cut my rate when my production went up.
4. Miscellaneous wage complaints	You made a mistake in figuring my pay. The wages here are too low for what you ask me to do.
Supervision	
1. Complaints about discipline	My supervisor doesn't like me and has it in for me. Any mistakes that I made were because my boss didn't instruct me properly. My supervisor plays favorites.
2. Objections to general methods of supervision	There are too many rules and regulations. The rules are not posted clearly.

For an indication of situations that stir up grievances, together with some ideas of how employees are likely to feel about them, take a look at Table 19-1. It is based on (and updated from) studies made by the U.S. Bureau of Labor Statistics.

TABLE 19-1 COMMON GRIEVANCES AND THEIR CAUSES (continued)

Grievances (listed in order of their frequency)	Typical Causes (as an employee sees it)
Seniority and Related Matters	
1. Loss of seniority	I was unfairly deprived of seniority when the department was reorganized.
2. Calculation of seniority	I didn't get all the seniority due to me.
3. Interpretation of seniority	You didn't apply my seniority the way it should have been when assigning overtime.
4. Layoffs	I was laid off out of sequence. You didn't recall me in sequence.
5. Promotions	There is no chance to get ahead in this job. You promoted the other person ahead of my seniority.
6. Disciplinary discharge	The company has been unfair. What I did didn't warrant this severe a penalty. You were just looking for an excuse to get rid of me.
7. Transfers	I've had more than my share of dirty work. I don't want to work in the mixing department. Will you get me off the midnight shift?
General Working Conditions	
1. Safety and health	The lockers are too crowded. This place is unsafe because it is too damp and too noisy and there are dangerous fumes.
2. Discrimination	You're giving all the choice work to the white people in the crew. If I were a man, I would have been recommended for the promotion.
3. Sexual harassment	You embarrassed me by making those remarks.

I t's easy to see that it would be better to prevent grievances in the first place. What can you do to keep from having to wait until one occurs?

The trick lies in detecting situations that breed grievances and then correcting these situations. Don't make the mistake of planting seeds of trouble where trouble doesn't exist, though. A perfectly happy worker may be able to find something to complain about if you ask directly, "What is there about your job that you don't like?" Better leave that type of open-ended prospecting to company-directed attitude surveys.

As a rule of thumb, however, you can reduce the number of grievances by applying common sense to your relationships with your staff. For example:

1. Give employees prompt and regular feedback about how well they are doing their jobs. Uncertainty in this area is a major source of employee dissatisfaction.

2. Remove, or try to ease, minor irritations as they arise. The presence of unnecessary aggravations tends to magnify the more serious complaints when they occur.

3. Listen to and encourage constructive suggestions. Take action whenever it is reasonable and nondisruptive.

4. Make certain of your authority before making a commitment to an employee. Then be sure to keep your promises.

5. Render your decisions as soon as possible when responding to employee requests. A prompt no is often more welcome than a long-delayed yes.

6. If you must take disciplinary action, do not make a public display of it. Keep it a private matter between you and the employee.

Key Concepts

1. A vigilance toward those conditions which induce employee grievances, combined with (a) an attitude that invites rather than turns them away and (b) a cheerful readiness to deal with them justly and harmoniously, has inestimable value in creating and maintaining good morale.

2. A grievance, even when trivial, unjustified, or fancied, can be very real to the employee who raises it; consequently, it deserves serious and empathetic consideration by the supervisor.

3. Unless objectivity, consistency, and absolute fairness characterize a supervisor's handling of grievances, his or her rulings are unlikely to gain the acceptance from employees that is needed to maintain harmony and discipline.

4. A careful and thorough examination of all the specific facts, events, and attitudes that make up the circumstances of a grievance is a fundamental step that must be taken in its eventual resolution.

5. Grievance discussions should be conducted by the supervisor in a businesslike manner; the settlement concluded without undue delay; and corrective action discharged promptly without future prejudice toward the complainant.

6. Complaints and grievances can be held to a minimum by maintaining constant surveillance of conditions that foster them and by developing an open and sensitive communications network along with fair standards of performance and objective treatment of those who fail to meet them.

Supervisory Word Power

Arbitration. The process of bringing an unsettled grievance before an impartial third party to evaluate the arguments of both parties (usually management and union) and to decide which party's case has the most merit. Typically, the decision of the arbitrator is final and binding on all concerned.

Grievance. A job-oriented complaint stemming from an injury or injustice, real or imaginary, suffered by an employee, of which redress or relief from management is sought.

Reading Comprehension

1. Contrast a real grievance with an imagined one.

2. Why should every complaint be treated as if it were important?

3. For supervisors to be fair in settling a grievance, they must expect that occasionally they will lose one. Why should they resist the temptation to give in on one grievance so that they can win on another?

4. In searching for facts that contribute to a grievance, what are some of the places where a supervisor should look?

5. How specific and conclusive should a supervisor's settlement of a grievance be?

6. Is it wise for a supervisor to refer an employee's complaint to a staff department rather than to try to deal with it first? Why?

7. To what extent are grievances handled differently when there is a formal grievance procedure prescribed by the labor contract?

8. Name several administrative procedures and situations from which grievances are likely to arise.

9. Is it a good idea to ignore or belittle minor irritations and complaints? Why or why not?

10. What are some ways that effective communication will help to minimize the number and severity of employee complaints?

Supervision in Action

The Case of the Delayed Reply. A Case Study in Human Relations Involving Grievances, with Questions for You to Answer.

When Lew first brought his complaint to the attention of his shop supervisor, Belle Baker, he felt fairly satisfied. "Belle listened to what I had to say about why I should have gotten the overtime rather than the man from the second shift," Lew told his benchmate. "I can't see how Belle can handle it any other way than to give me what's coming to me." This conversation took place the day after Lew had spoken to his supervisor.

Three days later when Lew saw that his paycheck didn't reflect any additional money, he spoke to Belle again. "What happened to that overtime pay I spoke to you about? I figured that so long as I didn't hear from you, the company had approved my request. How long do I have to wait for my money?"

"Well, now," said Belle. "I didn't promise you that you'd get the money. All I said was that I'd look into it. But I've been so busy lately that it clean slipped my mind. Tell you what. I'll go up to payroll this afternoon for sure and find out what can be done."

That afternoon Belle checked the matter with the personnel manager and with her boss. They both listened to the facts. Then they showed Belle that a similar case had been settled at a third-step grievance with the union—with no overtime pay for the employee concerned.

Belle didn't look forward to telling Lew that he wouldn't get the overtime, so for a couple of days she avoided going into Lew's part of the shop. The following payday, however, Lew went up to Belle's desk: "I still didn't get the overtime pay. Are you going to do something about it or aren't you?'

Belle then told Lew that he wasn't entitled to the overtime pay. Lew replied, "We'll see about that. My shop steward told me to file a written grievance and said that's the only way to get any action around here. And I can already see that the steward is right!"

1. Do you think the written grievance could have been avoided? How?

2. If Lew really had no case, will it make any difference in the long run whether he files a grievance or not? Why?

3. How could Belle have improved her handling of this complaint?

4. If you were Lew, what would you think of Belle as a supervisor?

CHAPTER

20

HOW AND WHEN TO DISCIPLINE

What is the real purpose of discipline?

The real purpose of discipline is quite simple. It is to encourage employees to meet established standards of job performance and to behave sensibly and safely at work. Supervisors should think of discipline as a form of training. Those employees who observe the rules and standards are rewarded by praise, by security, and often by advancement. Those who cannot stay in line or measure up to performance standards are penalized in such a way that they can clearly learn what acceptable performance and behavior are. Most employees recognize this system as a legitimate way to preserve order and safety and to keep everyone working toward the same organizational goals and standards. For most employees, self-discipline is the best discipline. As often as not, the need to impose penalties is a fault of management as well as of the individual worker. For that reason alone a supervisor should resort to disciplinary action only after all else fails. Discipline should never be used as a show of authority or power on the supervisor's part.

Why do employees resent discipline?

Employees don't object to the idea of rules and regulations, but they frequently object to the way a supervisor metes out discipline. In civil life, if a person breaks the law, the police officer only makes the arrest. The person is tried before a jury of peers who are guided by the rulings of an impartial judge, who in turn determines the punishment.

Now compare the civil procedure for handling lawbreakers with what happens in the company. As supervisor, you're often called on not only to put the finger on the wrongdoer, but also to hear the case and decide the penalty. To many employees this seems unfair because you've acted as police officer, judge, and jury.

So don't take your job as disciplinarian lightly. It's a great responsibility and requires impartiality, good judgment, and courage on your part.

Incidentally, when rules are thought by the work group to be reasonable, the group itself will impose a discipline to keep its members in line.

Why do employees break rules?

As in most personnel problems, only a small percentage of workers cause disciplinary problems. People who break rules do so for a number of reasons—most of them because they are not well adjusted. Contributing personal characteristics include carelessness, lack of cooperation, laziness, dishonesty, lack of initiative, chronic lateness, and lack of effort. The supervisor's job, as a result, is to help employees to be better adjusted.

People break rules less often when the supervisor is a good leader, when a sincere interest is shown in employees, when employees get more enjoyment from their work. After all, if an employee finds the work uninteresting and the boss unpleasant, is it surprising that the employee will find reasons for being late or for staying away from work altogether?

If the supervisor gives the employees little or no chance to show initiative on the job or to discuss ways the work should be done, there should be no surprise if the employees talk back, shirk their responsibilities, or create a lot of scrap. That's what some people do who can't express themselves any other way.

Sometimes the real reason an employee breaks rules or seems lazy on the job has nothing at all to do with working conditions. The employee may be having worries at home—money problems or a nagging spouse—or may be physically sick. You might ask, "What concern is that of the supervisor?" It isn't—unless the supervisor wants that employee to be more cooperative and productive at work. If you're smart enough to see the connection, then you can do much to improve this worker's performance. Don't snoop in personal affairs, but do offer a willing and uncritical ear. Let the employee get to know that you're an understanding person, that the boss is someone to talk to without getting a short answer or a lot of phony advice.

So when an employee breaks a rule, make discipline your last resort. Instead, search hard for the reason the employee acts that way. Then try to see what you can do to remove the reason.

What kind of handling do employees expect from a supervisor in the way of discipline?

Justice and equal treatment. Being soft, overlooking nonstandard performance, and giving chance after chance to wrongdoers does not win popularity among most employees. In fact, it works the other way to destroy morale. That's because the majority of people who work hard and stay in line are frustrated and disappointed when they see others get away with things. Of course, no one likes to be punished. But everyone likes to be assured that the punishment received is in line with the error. ("Let the punishment fit the crime" is the advice given in Gilbert and Sullivan's *Mikado*). No one likes to be treated better or worse than anyone else for the same fault.

Some people talk about negative discipline and say positive discipline is better. What does this mean?

When you have to penalize someone, that's negative. If you can get an employee to do what you wish through constructive criticism or discussion, that's positive.

Supervisors, more than employees, understand that disciplining is an unpleasant task. All a supervisor wants is to run the department in peace and harmony, to see that things get done right, and that no one gets hurt. The supervisor who can establish discipline through good leadership won't have to exercise negative discipline through scoldings, suspensions, or discharges.

What is meant by progressive discipline?

The penalties for substandard performance or broken rules get increasingly harsh as the condition continues or the infraction is repeated. (See Figure 20-1.) Typically, a first offense may be excused, or the worker may be given an oral warning. A second offense elicits a written warning. A third infraction may bring a temporary layoff or a suspension. The final step occurs when an employee is discharged for the fourth (or a very serious) infraction.

What is the "hot-stove" rule of discipline?

It is used to illustrate four essentials of a good disciplinary policy. (See Figure 20-2.) If the stove is red-hot, you ought to be able to see it and to know that if you touch it, you will be burned; that is the principle of *advance warning.* If you touch the hot stove, you get burned (penalized) right away; that is the principle of *immediacy.* Every time you touch a hot stove, you will get burned; that is the principle

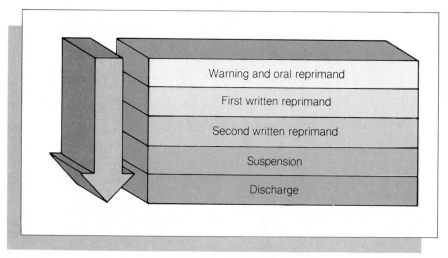

Figure 20-1. Example of progressive discipline.

of *consistency.* Everyone who touches a hot stove will get burned because it plays no favorites; that is the principle of *impartiality.*

How far can a supervisor go in handling discipline?

That depends on your company's management policy—and on the labor agreement, if your company has a union.

Legally, a supervisor can hire and fire. But firing is a costly action. To break in a new employee can cost anywhere from $500 to several thousand dollars for a skilled mechanic. So most companies have tried to approach discipline from a positive direction. And since discipline puts a supervisor in such a responsible position, many companies have carefully spelled out just how far a supervisor can go before having to check with the boss.

Labor unions, in their desire to provide the maximum protection from injustice or unfair treatment, maintain that discipline shouldn't be handled by management alone. Unions contend that they, too,

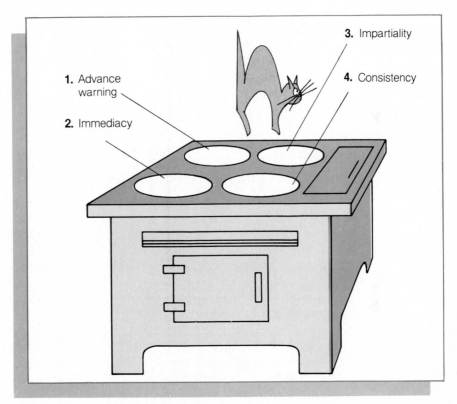

1. Advance warning

2. Immediacy

3. Impartiality

4. Consistency

Figure 20-2. "Hot-stove" rule for discipline.

should help decide on an employee's punishment. How much say a particular union will have depends on how successful the union has been in writing this privilege into the contract or in establishing precedents for its participation.

So tread carefully in disciplinary matters. Find out from your company's policy-level management (your immediate superior or the personnel manager) just how far the company wants you to go—and how much involvement you must allow the union.

How should you proceed when you're angry?

It's a very unusual person who can think and act sensibly when angry. For that reason it's a good idea for a supervisor not to take any disciplinary action while boiling over. How can this be accomplished? Try one of these:

Count to 100. An oldie, but it works.

Take a Walk. Ask the employee to walk with you over to the window or to your office—anything that takes time. This is especially good, since it gets the person away from other employees and from familiar surroundings where you may be resisted.

See the Employee Later. Simply tell the employee you'll speak about the matter in a couple of hours. This gives you a chance to cool off, to think the matter through, and to check with your boss, if necessary.

What determines the action you should take?

Facts rather than feelings. No one can make a decision without all the facts, or at least all that can be reasonably gathered. If a situation arises that looks as if you've got to take disciplinary action, look hard before you leap. Take time to investigate. Let the employee tell the full story—without interruptions. Check with witnesses for their observations. Look in the company records to see what other supervisors have done in the past. Speak to your boss or the personnel manager to get their advice.

For instance, someone tips you off that Will Jones is going to take home a baby Stillson wrench in his lunch box tonight. You stop Will at the time clock. Sure enough. There's the wrench tucked underneath a wad of sandwich wrappers. Your first reaction is to fire Will on the spot for stealing. But should you?

Suppose, on checking, you found any of these circumstances:

- Will had asked the toolroom supervisor for the wrench and received permission to borrow it overnight for a home-repair job.
- Two of Will's co-workers tell you Will had said he was just borrowing the wrench overnight and planned to return it in the morning.
- Will could prove that the wrench was one he actually had bought himself to use on his job.
- When checking with the personnel department, you found that the company had agreed with the union not to fire any ten-year employee for petty thefts, that the most Will's penalty could be for a first offense would be one day off without pay.

Wouldn't any of these facts change your decision?

How effective are warnings?

Warnings can do a lot of good—if you make them more than idle threats. Your warnings put employees on notice that their performance isn't up to standard. It gives you a chance to explain a rule that they may have taken only lightly before—and to make the penalty clear to them. When you warn employees, that's the perfect time for you to be constructive, to offer help, to practice positive discipline.

To make a warning a valuable piece of evidence in a union grievance, you should always make a written record of it. You'd be surprised how much weight arbitrators and union officials give to notations that you have written in your pocket notebook or the department logbook, or have inserted in the employee's personnel file.

Some companies make this written notation a formal practice by requiring supervisors to fill out a form to be filed by the personnel department. These notations are called written reprimands, and copies of the reprimand are sent to the employee and the union.

Under what circumstances can you fire an employee?

As you mentioned previously, the supervisor's authority is limited by the company's policy and by its agreements with the labor union, if one exists.

Speaking generally, however, some employee offenses are worse than others. Drinking or sleeping on the job, smoking in restricted areas, willfully destroying property, and falsifying time cards are often charges that result in discharge. It is easier to generalize about offenses such as fighting on company property and gross insubordination. All these wrongdoings have one thing in common—they are single incidents rather than an accumulation of minor offenses, and many of these single acts require immediate action by the supervisor.

To handle any of these serious offenses and still leave yourself free from reversal later on, there's an effective action you can take. It's short of discharge, but it certainly gets the culprit out of the company quickly and legally. This action is called *suspension.* It follows the advice arbitrators give employees: "Obey first—argue later."

To suspend an employee, you merely say something like this: "You've come to work with a load on. I think you're under the influence of liquor right now and are unfit to do your job. You could be subject for dismissal for being in this shape. I haven't made up my mind yet whether that's what I'll do. But in the meantime, you're suspended. Punch out your time card and don't come back to work until I call you. I'll try to let you know definitely tomorrow."

By suspending, you have demonstrated your willingness to enforce your authority when needed. And yet you have protected both yourself and the company from looking weak, foolish, or indecisive. If tomorrow, in the opinion of your boss, the personnel manager, or the company's lawyer, you can't make the discharge stick, you and the company are still in an effective position. It's when you cast the die—fire a employee and then have to take him or her back—that you have to eat crow.

When can't you make disciplinary action stick?

Here are some famous last words: What's difficult about discharging a third-rate employee? Get rid of the person whose work is poor, who talks back, or breaks a rule.

Many supervisors with that attitude have ended up behind the eight ball. And the company has been involved in an arbitration case, had to fork over back pay to a discharged worker, and even faced a charge of an unfair labor practice. Why? Because the situation that requires the most delicate handling is the provision for discipline and discharge. Dead beyond recall are the days when a supervisor could act and talk tough, when an employee had no recourse but to curse.

As difficult as the discipline problem is, many discharges or other penalties could be made to stick if the following mistakes weren't made:

No Clear-Cut Breach of Rule.   In one company a supervisor fired an employee for sleeping, only to see the decision reversed by the arbitrator. The union brought out the fact that the supervisor had made the observation from 60 feet away. The arbitrator ruled that at this distance the supervisor was "likely to see what he wanted to see."

Inadequate Warning. Arbitrators frequently feel that workers are entitled to sufficient warning that their conduct won't be tolerated —even though the rules and penalties are in an employee manual. Typical is the case where an employee has had a record of poor attendance for months without having been disciplined. Suddenly the supervisor cracks down without warning and fires the employee.

Absence of Positive Evidence. Take this case of loafing—always a difficult charge to make stick: The company went along with the supervisor and fired a worker caught loafing. The arbitrator reversed the company because (1) the supervisor had not been in the department continually but had popped in and out during one afternoon and (2) the person's job entailed occasional waits for material. Furthermore, the company could produce no time sheets that showed reduced output in black and white. The arbitrator ruled that the supervisor might have come into the department at the times the employee had been legitimately waiting for materials.

Acting on Prejudices. Real or imagined discrimination or favoritism weakens a disciplinary ruling. If a supervisor has shown that she has it in for a worker and just waited for an opportunity to enforce a penalty, an arbitration case may bring this out. If the supervisor has let others get away unpunished with the same offense for which she punishes another, she'll have a hard time justifying such unequal treatment.

Inadequate Records. The value of written records of warnings and reprimands can't be overemphasized. It's especially valuable for documenting action taken to correct an accumulation of minor offenses. You may not want to discharge a person who's been late the first time—or even the fifth. But when it gets to be a frequent and costly habit, you'll want to take action. Unless you've build up a record of warnings and kept a file of them that can be shown to the union and an arbitrator if necessary, your case will be hard to prove.

Too-Severe Punishment. Many arbitrators recommend "progressive punishment" and look unfavorably on too-severe discipline—especially for first offenses. For instance, a supervisor in a can company noticed a worker away from his work station ten minutes before the end of the shift. A look at the employee's time card showed that he had punched out a half minute early. The man was fired because not long before that he had received a written reprimand for doing the same thing. He had been warned that the next time he'd be fired. An arbitrator ruled that a penalty was called for—but not such a severe one. Do it progressively, the arbitrator said—just a little tougher each time. A lighter penalty would keep an old (seven years' service) and valuable employee on the payroll.

How can you make sure that your records will support a disciplinary action?

By taking care to make the proper records at each step of a progressive disciplinary action. Follow carefully your company's policies and procedures in this matter. The legal concept of "due process" is gradually taking hold in all areas of employment, especially those involving job security. This means that an employee, regardless of union representation, is entitled to a fair and just hearing under adequate legal protection. Under such circumstances, a supervisor's opinions and recollections will not carry much weight. They will have to be supported by specific documentation. Records that help to provide this documentation include:

● *Regularly kept records,* such as time cards showing absences and latenesses, visits to the dispensary, production and quality control tallies, and the like.
● *Written complaints* from customers or other contacts that can be identified without qualification with the individual who is to be disciplined.
● *Examples of unsatisfactory or careless work,* including mistyped letters, incorrect tabulations on reports, damaged goods—all tagged or marked in such a way as to identify the culpable individual.
● *Written summaries of appraisal and/or disciplinary conferences.* These should contain specific rather than general statements, including dates, figures, and clearly described incidents. The hard part here is that the law seems to say that copies of these reports (which are retained in personnel records) must be given to the individual at the time they are written.

What consideration should be given to an employee's good work record?

There's danger in carrying the rule book too far. Treating each offender equally does not mean that you should not weigh personal factors, too. For instance, what was the worker's attitude when the rule was broken? Was it done deliberately or accidentally? Was the worker emotionally upset by a circumstance beyond control (such as worrying about a sick child at home)? How long has the person worked for the company? What kind of work record has there been? Remember, it costs money to fire a good employee. Even civil courts put on probation a guilty person who has been considered a good citizen in the past.

In many instances, it is also good to wipe an employee's slate clean now and then. For example, if an employee who had a poor absence record two years ago has been near perfect since then, the employee should not have the past record brought up if at a later date there is another absence problem.

Key Concepts

1. Only a relatively small percentage of any work force ever becomes involved in disciplinary problems to any great extent. These tend to be the more poorly adjusted individuals, who find it difficult to accept the regulations and conformity imposed on them by an organized activity.

2. The great majority in the work force usually exert the necessary self-control to keep themselves out of trouble. The state of their morale, however, is significantly influenced by the way in which their supervisor maintains discipline with others.

3. To be effective for all members of the work force, discipline must be essentially a positive effort. It should be exercised as much to encourage and reward desirable employee behavior as to penalize and discourage undesirable conduct.

4. There are two hallmarks of effective employee discipline: (a) punishment should be suitable to the importance of the offense and should become progressively severe only as offenses are repeated and (b) discipline should follow the "hot-stove" rule; that is, it should be given only if there has been adequate warning, and it should be immediate, consistent, and impartial.

5. The supervisor's role in maintaining discipline requires unusual objectivity and integrity. Not only must the supervisor identify and apprehend transgressors, he or she must also determine the nature and extent of guilt and impose the penalties. Even then, the supervisor can never be sure that his or her decisions will not be modified or reversed by an appeal to higher authority.

Supervisory Word Power

Discipline. The imposition of a penalty by management on an employee for the infraction of a company rule or regulation in such a manner as to encourage more constructive behavior and to discourage a similar infraction in the future.

Due Process. An employee's legal entitlement to a fair hearing, usually before an impartial party and with appropriate representation, before discipline can be meted out.

Penalty. A punishment or forfeiture imposed by management on an employee in order to impose discipline. Typically, such penalties include suspensions, loss of time and/or pay, demotion, or loss of job—that is, discharge.

Reprimand. A severe expression of disapproval or censure by management of an employee, usually written as well as oral, and retained in an employee's personal file.

Suspension. The temporary removal by management of a privilege (particularly the right to report to work and receive pay for it) from an employee until the proper penalty for a rule infraction has been determined and imposed.

Warning. A reprimand so worded as to give formal notice to an employee that repetition of a particular form of unacceptable behavior, such as infraction of a rule, will draw a penalty.

Reading Comprehension

1. Discuss the similarities between rules and regulations at work and laws in civil life.

2. In what way does the enforcement of discipline in business differ from that in civil life?

3. What kind of people are most likely to break work rules regularly?

4. Distinguish between negative and positive discipline.

5. What kinds of restraints are placed on a supervisor's authority to handle discipline independently?

6. When Carlos saw Jane sneaking out early again, he fired her on the spot, even though he hadn't given her any prior warning. What should he have done to make discipline progressive?

7. The "hot-stove" rule is meant to help supervisors remember four important points about discipline. Briefly describe the four.

8. Explain the difference between suspension and firing or discharge of an employee.

9. Explain the importance of making written notations of discussions held with employees regarding disciplinary matters.

10. Describe at least three reasons why a supervisor's decision to discharge an employee might not be upheld.

Supervision in Action

The Case of the Missed Stitches. A Case Study in Human Relations Involving Employee Discipline, with Questions for You to Answer.

Business was booming at Ottobine Overall Outfitters, a manufacturer of heavy-duty work clothing. In the shirt department Phil Yasensky, section supervisor, had 35 sewing machine operators turning out nearly 2,000 denim work shirts a day. The quality-control inspector, however, had cautioned Phil several times about the stitching of seams. "Your operators frequently miss stitches and are often off the mark by a sixteenth to an eighth of an inch. And they are failing to catch and close the thread at the ends of the seams. We are going to get in big trouble with the buyers if you don't tighten up on your operation."

"Sorry," said Phil. "We are doing the best we can. The sales manager has made promises all over the lot. We are just about hitting our shipping dates as it is. And I've had to scrape the barrel to find 35 sewing machine operators."

"Don't blame me, then," said the inspector, "if you get hit with a truckload of returns from one of the big department stores. The little guys will take anything. But the big stores have an inspection routine that makes ours look like child's play."

As a matter of fact, no shirts were returned to Ottobine during this peak period. But when the sales staff made their next seasonal round of calls on customers, they received criticism for the poor quality of seam stitching on the work shirts. The word got back to Phil from higher management to correct this situation before the next season began.

Immediately, Phil carefully examined the work of his operators. There were only 20 regulars employed now, and it was easier to keep track of what was going on. Phil found that even among his regulars, however, the quality of seam work was not up to Ottobine's reputation for first-class work. Beginning on the following Monday, Phil advised the quality-control inspector to tighten up on her inspections. She was not to pass anything that was below specifications. At the end of the day, the report came to Phil's desk: Of the 1,000 shirts made, 95 had been rejected. These were returned to the operators, who had to rip out the seams and redo the sewing. Even then, many of the shirts had to be marked "seconds." Since the operators were on piecework (a wage-incentive system that enabled them to make about 20 to 30 percent over their basic hourly wage), the time spent on rework cut into their earnings. As a result, there was a constant battle between the operators and the inspector as to what work was acceptable and what was not.

"You'll have to straighten your operators out," the inspector advised Phil. "I am not going to spend all my time arguing with them. When their work isn't up to standard, I am going to reject it. You have been letting them run away with the shop. We will all be in trouble if you don't crack down."

The next morning, after having studied the reject tally for the previous day, Phil identified the operator with the poorest record—Annie Clark. He went out to her machine and picked up the shirt she was working on. "These seams won't do, Annie," said Phil. "If you don't get them 100 percent right by Friday, I'm going to have to let you go."

"What's wrong with that seam?" asked Annie. "It looks okay."

Phil got out the marker, a pattern that showed exactly where the seams should be. He demonstrated to Annie that her seam was a sixteenth of an inch off the mark.

"Look at this, Annie. Your seams are way out of line."

"They look pretty close to me," said Annie. "Besides, since when is a sixteenth of an inch off standard? Last month we were shipping stuff that was as much as an eighth of an inch off."

"We had a lot of temporary help then who didn't know any better. And we were under pressure from the sales department to ship. You are one of our regular operators. You've got to do better. There's no reason for your seams not to be on the mark."

Phil left Annie's machine and stopped to warn three other operators that their work was off standard, too.

On Friday morning Phil examined the inspector's quality-control record again. He found to his annoyance that Annie's rejects had dropped off a little, but she was far from perfect. The other three operators he had talked to had not improved as much as he had asked for, but their work was better than Annie's.

Phil called Annie into his office. "I'm sorry, Annie, but your seam work is still below what we can accept. I'm going to speak to the personnel department. You will be laid off. Don't come in Monday. We may call you when the plant gets busy. But for now, you are suspended because your performance is unsatisfactory."

"Why me?" asked Annie. "I'm not the only person around here who is having rejects. Anyway, the markers are too tight for the kinds of shirts we do for the department stores."

"Your work is not satisfactory," replied Phil. "I warned you at the beginning of the week that it had to improve. It's practically as bad today as it was then."

"It's not fair," said Annie. "You were happy enough to get my work when you were busy. And my quality was lots better than your temporary help then. Now all of a sudden, my work isn't good enough. If you're going to lay someone off, it ought to be all of us who are having rejects, not just me."

"Yours is the worst," said Phil. "And I am going to make sure that you are suspended until you can show me that you can measure up to Ottobine's standards."

1. What circumstances have contributed to this problem?

2. What do you think is wrong (or right) about Phil's approach to this problem? Why?

3. If you were the personnel manager for Ottobine, what would you do now? What would you suggest Phil do to make his discipline more effective?

Dealing with Employee Complaints

Experience shows that supervisors who follow this sequence of steps are likely to get better results when handling employee complaints than those supervisors who do not.

Step 1. Ask the employee to explain the complaint in detail.

Step 2. Reach an agreement with the employee as to the substance of the complaint—exactly what it is as opposed to a vague generalization.

Step 3. Ask the employee to suggest a solution to the complaint.

Step 4. Schedule a time for your investigating the complaint further and/or agree on an action plan to resolve the complaint.

Step 5. Set a date for a follow-up meeting.

The Situation

Bill is the supervisor of a stenographic, secretarial, and word processing pool in a large government agency. Susan is an experienced pool employee with good stenographic-secretarial skills. Susan is not satisfied with the assignments she has been receiving.

Dialogue

1. Bill: Sorry I couldn't see you yesterday, but the boss had me tied up all afternoon.

2. Susan: That's all right, Bill. I know how busy you are.

3. Bill: Well, talking to you is one of the more important things I have to do. Now, what can I do for you?

4. Susan: I wanted to talk to you about the assignments I consistently get in the steno pool. Somehow, I always get the worst assignments and I just don't think it's fair.

5. Bill: I'm sorry, Susan. What do you mean by the worst assignments? Tell me specifically what these are.

6. Susan: Now, Bill, you know very well that some people are more difficult to work with than others. For example, Mrs. Simpson dictates at an incredibly fast rate and does so for long stretches of time. Taking dictation from her is absolutely exhausting. Everyone in the pool dreads getting assigned to her, but in the last two months, I've been the only person in the pool assigned to her.

7. Bill: Is that the problem, the Simpson assignments?

8. Susan: No, that's just part of it. I also seem to be the only one who draws Mrs. Houston. She's another difficult person to work for. She doesn't dictate well. She dictates a lot of ungrammatical and clumsy sentences and she doesn't like suggestions for changes or even questions from stenographers, but after her dictation is transcribed, she has a horrendous number of changes and corrections, and blames the stenographer for them.

9. Bill: I can see why that would be difficult for you.

10. Susan: Then there is Mr. Lee. He is totally disorganized. He smokes those foul-smelling cigars and he keeps sending me for coffee even though I object and have told him so. I seem to be the only one assigned to him.

11. Bill: So the problem is that Mrs. Simpson, Mrs. Houston, and Mr. Lee are all especially difficult to work for and you believe you're the only person in the pool who draws them as assignments.

12. Susan: I know I'm the only one.

13. Bill: Well, it's a fact that Mrs. Simpson and Mrs. Houston specifically request you. They probably do that because they think you're the most competent person in the pool, but I don't know why you should be the only person to get Mr. Lee. Let's see . . . yes, you're right. He hasn't been assigned to anyone else in the last two months, but he hasn't specifically asked for you, so that's just been a matter of chance.

14. Susan: You mean it's just been my bad luck.

15. Bill: What I mean is, it hasn't been deliberate. Well, what do you suggest we do about all this?

16. Susan: I think assignments to these three people should be shared equally by everyone in the pool.

17. Bill: Even though Simpson and Houston specifically want to work with you?

18. Susan: I don't think I should be penalized because I'm competent.

19. Bill: How about Mr. Carter? He specifically requests you. Do you object to that?

20. Susan: No, he's a pleasure to work with.

21. Bill: Well, in general we operate on a first-come, first-served basis. I've made exception to this where some people have asked for specific stenographers. Until now, that hasn't caused any problems. Maybe I should stop making exceptions and just stick to first-come, first-served?

22. Susan: I don't know what the best way is, Bill. All I know is I don't want to be the only one to get stuck with those three.

23. Bill: Let me talk with some of the other stenographers this week. If some of them have similar problems, I'll put everything on a strict first-come, first-served basis. If you're the only one with this kind of problem, I'll see to it that assignments for those three people are shared equally with other stenographers.

24. Susan: That sounds fair enough. But how about the coffee bit? Can't you put a stop to that?

25. Bill: I think I can. I'll talk to Bob Lee about it today.

26. Susan: Thanks.

27. Bill: So, starting next week you should begin to see a change in these assignments. Why don't you come in again on the 28th so we can take a look at how it's going.

28. Susan: Fine, Bill, and thanks. I appreciate this very much.

Model Analysis

A. Identify by line numbers in the dialogue where Bill applied Step 1 by asking Susan to explain her complaint in detail.

B. Identify by line numbers in the dialogue where Bill applied Step 2 by getting an agreement from Susan about the substance of the complaint.

C. Identify by line numbers in the dialogue where Bill applied Step 3 by asking Susan to suggest a solution to her complaint.

D. Identify by line numbers in the dialogue where Bill applied Step 4 by getting an agreement from Susan on a plan of action to resolve the complaint.

E. Identify by line numbers in the dialogue where Bill applied Step 5 by setting up a date for reviewing the outcome of the plan.

F. Recall, and describe briefly, a situation where an employee has brought a complaint to a supervisor for resolution. Try role playing the supervisor, with someone else in the group taking the part of the employee. Get feedback from the group and the instructor to (1) sharpen your sense of when to apply each of the model's steps and (2) improve the skill with which you handle each step.

Model 9

Using Positive Discipline

Experience has shown that supervisors who follow this sequence of steps are likely to get more positive results when disciplining employees than are those supervisors who do not.

Step 1. State the performance problem.

Step 2. Ask the employee's view of the problem.

Step 3. Ask the employee for a solution to the problem.

Step 4. Agree on a plan to resolve the problem.

Step 5. Give the employee an oral or written warning and set up a date for review.

The Situation

Helen is the supervisor of the machining and polishing operations in a shop that fabricates metal trim for office furniture. She is dissatisfied with one aspect of the performance of Tony, a machining operator. She feels that it is time to correct that performance by using discipline in a positive manner. Accordingly, she has asked Tony to come to her desk to talk about it.

Dialogue

1. Helen: Ah, Tony, you're here. Good. Come and sit down. How are you doing?

2. Tony: Fine.

3. Helen: How is the course you're taking at the community college?

4. Tony: It's good. I like it. I think I'm getting a lot out of it.

5. Helen: Good. I'm glad to hear that. I think that kind of thinking is going to help you get ahead.

6. Tony: I hope so!

7. Helen: You know, Tony, you're a good machine operator. You rarely make errors, you're fast, and you're especially good at straightening out problem orders. You do good work.

8. Tony: Thanks, Helen. I appreciate that.

9. Helen: But there is one problem I want to talk to you about today. Now, you know that your job description calls for you to operate your machine as long as there are shop orders in your in-basket. It also calls for you to help out in polishing when you have finished all the work in your in-basket. The problem is that you have not been helping out in polishing. In the past month you have not logged in once in the polishing operation. Tell me, Tony, why is that?

10. Tony: I didn't know they really needed help in polishing.

11. Helen: I thought you understood that the polishers can't handle all the polishing there is and that we count on all the machine operators to spend a portion of their time polishing. That gives us flexibility to handle peak periods of machine operations and doesn't leave us with machine operators who are twiddling their thumbs when there are fewer shop orders.

12. Tony: I keep pretty busy, Helen.

13. Helen: I'm sure you do while there are shop orders in your in-basket, but I've noticed that you are often away from your workplace when your basket is empty.

14. Tony: I don't think I'm away that much.

15. Helen: Yesterday, you were away from your machine for almost an hour in the afternoon.

16. Tony: I just hate polishing. I did that for two years and when I was promoted to machine operator, I thought I was through with polishing.

17. Helen: You hate polishing.

18. Tony: Yeah, going back to polishing is like being demoted.

19. Helen: I see. Well, Tony, your job requires that you help out in polishing when you have the time, but you hate to polish because you feel it's like taking a step back. Is that a fair statement of the problem?

20. Tony: Yeah, it is.

21. Helen: How do you think we could solve this problem?

22. Tony: Let me do something other than polishing. There must be lots of other things I could do.

23. Helen: But we need your help in polishing.

24. Tony: Let me handle more machine orders.

25. Helen: That would mean the other machine operators would absorb your polishing time.

26. Tony: I guess it would.

27. Helen: Do you think the others would consider that fair?

28. Tony: I don't know. It might not bother them.

29. Helen: I think it would. In fact, I think some of them are bothered by the fact that you're not doing any polishing, and if this situation were to continue, some of them might begin doing the same thing you're doing. You can understand why I'd be concerned about that.

30. Tony: Yeah, I guess so.

31. Helen: It seems to me there's only one way to resolve this problem.

32. Tony: Yeah, I know.

33. Helen: Then you agree from now on, whenever you have finished handling all of the shop orders in your in-basket, you will log in and help in the polishing section?

34. Tony: Yes.

35. Helen: I have your assurance on that?

36. Tony: Yes.

37. Helen: Since this isn't the first time we've discussed this problem, I want you to consider this an oral warning. An oral warning is the first step in this company's discipline procedure.

38. Tony: Discipline? Does that mean it goes on my record?

39. Helen: No. An oral warning doesn't go into your file, but if I have to talk to you about this again, then you'll get a written warning and that will go into your file. Is that clear?

40. Tony: Yeah, that's clear.

41. Helen: As I said, Tony, you're an excellent machine operator. I have a lot of confidence in your ability to do the job properly, including the polishing. Let's plan to meet again on the 21st to see how you're doing. Let's make it at 4 o'clock.

42. Tony: At 4 o'clock on the 21st. Okay, Helen, I'll do as you ask. When I come back on the 21st, you'll see that everything is fine.

43. Helen: Now that's what I like to hear.

Model Analysis

A. Identify by line numbers in the dialogue where Helen applied Step 1 by stating the performance problem.

B. Identify by line numbers in the dialogue where Helen applied Step 2 by asking Tony's view of the problem.

C. Identify by line numbers in the dialogue where Helen applied Step 3 by asking Tony for a solution to the problem.

D. Identify by line numbers in the dialogue where Helen applied Step 4 by getting agreement from Tony on a plan to resolve the problem.

E. Identify by line numbers in the dialogue where Helen applied Step 5 by (1) giving Tony an oral warning and (2) setting up a date for review.

F. Recall, and describe briefly, a situation where a supervisor might wish to apply positive discipline to an employee whose performance is not acceptable. Try role playing the supervisor, with someone else in the group taking the part of the employee. Get feedback from the group and the instructor to (1) sharpen your sense of when to apply each of the model's steps and (2) improve the skill with which you handle each step.

Supervisors are judged by their ability to get employees to perform the organization's work. Productivity and quality considerations must be optimized. Accordingly, this part sets for the reader a number of task-oriented objectives:

● To become proficient at work design so as to be able to make job content and environment more attractive and job incumbents more effective.
● To be able to convert overall company plans into specific job assignments and departmental work schedules.
● To observe and measure work processes so as to develop job methods that simplify work flow and improve productivity while maintaining control over departmental costs.
● To gain an understanding of factors that contribute to poor quality and to be able to motivate employees to higher standards of workmanship.

How supervisors feel about productivity, costs, and quality

Problems and activities associated with the task-oriented "bottom line" of the supervisory job tend to dominate supervisor's time and attention. Here are some representative indicators from the survey:

Job Assignments and Scheduling	
Time and attention spent on each of the following	Ranking among 16 activities
Planning departmental production schedules	4
Making daily job assignments	9
Solving production-schedule problems	11

Productivity, Costs, and Quality	
Time and attention on each of the following	Ranking among 16 activities
Devising improved methods and procedures	2
Solving cost- or expense-related problems	8
Pressure from the boss for results on each of the following	Ranking among 10 results
Quality or accuracy of work	1
Keeping operating expenses in line	2
Output or volume of work	3

When asked about the sources of quality problems, supervisors acknowledged a great many but still seemed to place greatest blame, perhaps unfairly, on their employees. Here's the data:

When you encounter defects in workmanship, off-grade products, or inaccuracies, to what extent are any of the following sources responsible?	Greatly responsible (%)	Somewhat responsible (%)
Employee's carelessness	32	49
Company pressures for greater or faster output	22	43
Wrong or incomplete specifications or blueprints	18	42
Ineffective inspection or quality controls	17	43
Conflicting or imprecise operating procedures	15	49
Off-grade materials	15	37
Faulty or inadequate tools and equipment	14	36
Design deficiencies	13	44

21

JOB DESIGN AND ENRICHMENT

What is a job?

It is the task, duty, or chore assigned to one individual. It is the smallest unit of work performed by one employee in a particular unit, section, or department. Within a unit there may be many similar, almost identical jobs—such as the job of a filing clerk, keypunch operator, welder, pipe fitter second class, journeyman machinist, bench assembly hand, textile spinner, salesperson, bus driver, checkout counter clerk, and bank teller.

A job may be called a position or an occupation. The fourth edition of the *Dictionary of Occupational Titles,* published in 1977 by the

Employment and Training Administration of the U.S. Department of Labor, lists 20,000 different occupations. To illustrate how narrowly a job may be defined, this volume uses a nine-digit code for each occupation. Thus, a "boot and shoe side laster" who cements the last is designated 690.685.358; the laster who staples the last is 690.685.632!

Who decides how big or small a job should be?

This is a management decision, but it usually is carried out as a joint process. One or more specialists help the manager or supervisor make the decision. In a manufacturing plant, for example, an industrial engineer may provide the initial job design. In an office, a systems and procedures specialist may prescribe the job dimensions. Or the professional advice may be furnished by someone from the personnel department, such as a job analyst. Usually, however, a job just evolves as a company or an organization grows. As a particular job gets too big for one person to handle, it is divided into smaller, more specialized jobs. Later on these jobs may be fine-tuned—slightly reduced, enlarged, or modified in some way to best fit the organization's needs. A supervisor can make the most effective contribution to the design of a job in this fine-tuning stage.

What is meant by job design?

Job design is simply the process of dividing work into units that one person will be asked to carry out. Often called *work design,* it is the process of defining what a job should be. When existing jobs are reshaped in any way, the process may be more accurately called work or job *redesign.*

On what basis are jobs designed?

Two ways: to fit the process and to fit the people who must perform the jobs. Back in the days of scientific management, the aim was to design jobs that most perfectly supported the movement of the product or service as it was shaped by the manufacturing or administrative process. The ultimate idea was to have a machine do the work. When this couldn't be done, the job and the person were made to function as much like a machine as possible. This method of job design—the process-centered approach—was effective for a number of years. It wasn't particularly good for people, but it was good for efficiency.

Gradually, job design has acquired a greater and greater people-orientation. People aren't machines. They can never do what a machine can do as well as the machine can do it. But people can do an incredible number of things that machines can't do. People can think better. They can make changes more easily and faster. They are more flexible. They don't have to be programmed. People can solve problems more creatively, and they can make decisions based on information that only human beings can sense and consider. This is called the people-centered approach of job design.

Which approach to job design is better: the process-centered approach or the people-centered approach?

Neither—although the people approach was given so little attention for so many years, it still needs a lot of catching up.

Jobs are the means for getting work done, for helping an organization meet its goals. If a brass foundry, for example, has to make 6-inch gears, someone performing a job or jobs must make the pattern, put the pattern in the mold, fill the mold with sand, remove the pattern, lock up the mold, pour the molten brass into the mold, and shake out the mold after the metal has set. The design of each of these jobs must conform to the needs of the process.

On the other hand, thought must also be given to the person or persons who will perform these jobs. Is the job more challenging and more interesting if a single person performs the entire job cycle? Or would it be too fatiguing a job for one person? Or would the skill needed to make patterns be wasted on shaking out molds? The job designers—supervisors and specialists—must seek the best balance between process and people.

What limits the degree of people considerations in job design when the process or technical approach is used?

Limitations depend upon the extent to which:

1. The job is performed entirely by hand and at whatever pace is comfortable or attainable by the operator. Example: An assembler in a toy factory who puts together prefabricated parts to make a dollhouse.

2. The job is performed with the assistance of a machine, which dictates some of the conditions the employee must accept or maintain. Example: A stenographer who transcribes from a pedal-controlled dictating machine. The stenographer, who depends on the machine for voice inputs and cannot control the speed while the machine is running, can control the process by starting and stopping the machine.

3. The job is largely machine-controlled, machine-paced, or both, and leaves very little room for people considerations. Example: A packer at the output end of an automatic box-making machine who catches the boxes as they come off the line and places them into cartons. The operator must keep up with the machine and can shut it down only in an emergency.

When the process approach is used, what process or technical factors must be satisfied by the job design?

Several process factors must be satisfied by the job, whether or not it is accomplished entirely by hand or by automatic equipment.

Product Specifications. The finished product must be a certain size, shape, weight, and appearance. A customer who buys a refill for a ballpoint pen, for example, expects the refill to fit.

Process Flow Sequence. Whenever anything is produced or serviced, certain steps must be performed before other steps are performed. Roofers at a home construction site, for example, must wait until the frame and the rafters have been erected. An accounting clerk in the sales order department of a shoe company cannot prepare the customer invoice until after the order has been recorded and priced.

Time Constraints. The way in which a job is done almost always depends on two factors: (1) how long it takes to do the job (even in an automated bakery it will still take from 30 to 40 minutes to bake a loaf of bread) and (2) how soon the customer or client wants the product or service. If a company has a policy of shipping everything within 48 hours, the job may be designed one way; if the company makes few commitments about delivery dates, the job can be designed another way.

Costs and Profits. If cost is no object (for a product that has a high profit margin, for example), the job may be designed for maximum craftsmanship and quality. If the product has a low profit margin (so often the case with highly competitive items), the job may be designed to cut corners, to have a large machine input, and to put pressure on employees to get output at the sacrifice of quality.

What determines how efficiently the job will be designed under the process approach?

Three things: (1) the methods used to perform the job; (2) the tools, machinery, and computers used to assist human effort on the job; and (3) the arrangement of equipment and people.

The workplace layout (3) is especially critical, whether the job is hand-paced or machine-controlled. For jobs that are largely hand-controlled, the workplace design must go far not only in easing work flow but also in accommodating the physical aspects of human movements. Figure 21-1 illustrates a popular bench arrangement designed with the human body in mind. This approach typifies scientific management and the concept that the human body can be engineered somewhat like a machine. The engineering is soundly based on studies of human movement and body limitations. The studies were made in the early 1900s by Frank B. Gilbreth. In what he called motion study, each motion was broken down into its smallest element, a *therblig.* This technique, brought completely up to date, is called human factors engineering or *biomechanics.* Most contemporary equipment, ranging from automobile instrument panels to computer keyboard consoles, is designed with this in mind.

In today's office environment, with increased automation, *ergonomics*—the study of how workers react to their work environment—is a major consideration. In order to protect the health of workers and to ensure optimal efficiency, work surfaces (as illustrated in Table 21-1) must accommodate not only equipment but also the physiological and psychological needs of the workers.

How does the people-centered approach to job design differ from the process-centered approach?

It strives for maximum employee involvement in the design of each individual's job. It does not ignore process considerations. Instead, it encourages employees to view demands and restrictions as problems they are invited to help solve. The way in which this involvement takes place has led to its having many names: job en-

PART 6 • MANAGING WORK PRODUCTIVELY

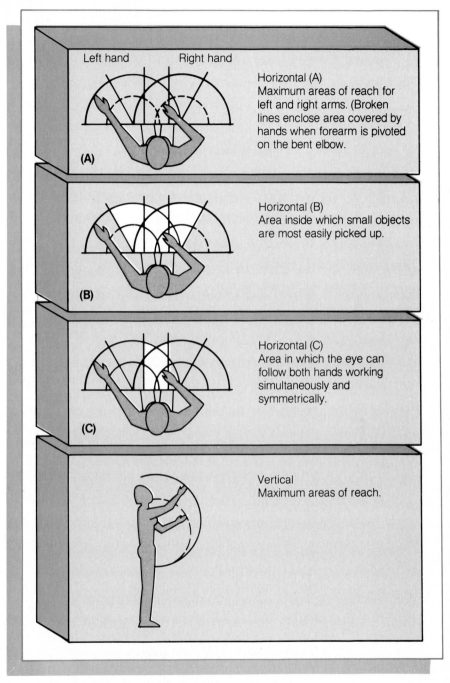

Figure 21-1. Workplace design for easiest reach.

TABLE 21-1 PROBLEMS EXPERIENCED BY SECRETARIES IN USING CATHODE RAY TUBE (CRT) DISPLAYS

Problems reported while using CRT displays	Age (%)			All Ages (%)
	Under 30	30–44	45+	
Eye strain	58	53	47	52
Back or neck problems	56	46	41	46
Down time	37	46	39	42
Loss of information because of equipment failure	38	34	28	33
Inadequate training	21	31	40	33
Headaches	39	31	23	30
Learning to operate the system	21	23	32	26
Other stress	17	24	26	23
Loss of information because of operator error	22	23	21	22
Static electricity problems	15	18	11	15
Confidentiality of stored information	6	6	6	7

Totals exceed 100% because of multiple responses.
Source: "The Evolving Role of the Secretary in the Information Age," survey done in cooperation with Professional Secretaries International Research and Education Foundation and conducted by C. A. Pesko Associates, Inc., 1983; sponsored by Minolta Corporation's Business Equipment Division.

largement, job enrichment, and work design or, sometimes, work redesign. The big difference is that the people-centered approach stresses genuine participation by employees, singly or in groups, in making their work effective and their jobs more attractive.

The boon to supervisors in the people approach is that it focuses everyone's attention on the "work itself" (another term sometimes used, defined in a later section). Supervisors aren't expected to be part-time psychologists or extraordinary leaders in seeking cooperation from their employees. It is the work that is examined, criticized, and restructured rather than human beings. The responsibility for these changes is no longer the sole burden of the supervisor, it is shared by all those employees who are able to, and wish to, get involved.

Certain elements of the people-centered approach are similar to those described for Quality Circles in Chapter 24. The latter is a joint management-employee effort, too, but it is more often a group-oriented approach than the one-on-one technique described here. Both approaches, however, have as a goal the improvement of the quality of work for the employee. All job designs that enable individuals to apply a greater degree of their natural skills and acquired talents, and by so doing optimize their productivity as well as their sense of genuine contribution, are said to have high "quality" and to improve the *quality of work.*

So that you may make a clearer distinction between the process-centered and the people-centered approaches and see where they overlap, comparisons have been provided in Table 21-2.

When the people approach is used, what organizational restrictions must be recognized?

As in the process approach, there are basic realities to which the job designers must give thought. For example:

1. The extent to which changes in job content and methods will affect only the individual employee. Example: A stock clerk in a supermarket finds it more efficient to stamp prices on items while they are in the stockroom rather than at the shelves. This decision affects no other workers and attains the results wanted: price-marked items on the appropriate shelves.

2. The extent to which job changes will be confined to a single department, section, or unit. Example: Employees in the purchasing department agree to rearrange their work so that order and posting clerks share some of the buying responsibilities. This work redesign fulfills the department's goals without interfering with, or affecting adversely, the quality and timing of its services.

3. The extent to which job changes will affect the entire company, organization, or system. Example: Machine shop employees and their supervisors wish to restructure their work in a way that will improve their operations but will require changes in plant scheduling procedures and a major revision in assembly and finishing operations.

Supervisors can usually encourage and assist job design in the first and second instances. Someone else (or a special committee with plantwide knowledge and authority) is needed to coordinate projects of the third kind.

What factors of job design are most likely to increase the motivational aspects of work?

Two authorities from AT&T (where more than 30,000 employees have been involved in work design), H. Weston Clarke Jr. and Richard O. Peterson, advise that there are six critical factors. When added to the job, these factors—or dimensions—help to meet organizational

TABLE 21-2 JOB—AND WORK—DESIGN CONSIDERATIONS

Process-centered Approach Degrees of process control:		People-centered Approach Degrees of organizational restrictions	
Low	Manual work	Low	Involves work of only one employee
Moderate	Machine-assisted work	Moderate	Involves work of group of employees within a department, section, or unit
High	Machine-paced work	High	Involves interfaces between departments or affects work of entire company, organization, or system

Process requirements that must be met:	Organizational requirements that must be met:

Product specifications
Process flow sequence
Time constraints:
    Process cycle time
    Promised delivery dates
Costs and profits
	Output, quality, and cost goals
	Job evaluation and wage schedules
	Motivational factors to be satisfied:
	    Functional completeness
	    Relationships with clients
	    Skills and task variety
	    Autonomy
	    Direct feedback from work itself
	    Opportunity for self-development

Areas affected by supervisor- and employee-initiated changes in job design structures which influence both approaches:

Work methods
Work tools and equipment
Support facilities
Workplace space and arrangements
Work schedules
Interpersonal relationships

needs and thus to promote productive performance in support of departmental or organizational goals. These dimensions include:

A Whole Job From Beginning to End. This functional completeness enables an employee to start his or her part of the work from scratch and see a definable product or service when the job is completed. Obviously, a worker in an auto factory cannot build a whole car. But it would be better if a wheel, for example, could be followed from the time it is uncrated until it is mounted on the car's hub.

Regular Contact with Users or Clients. The provision for an employee to have direct, consistent relationships with the person (department, regional office, or customer) who uses what is made or processed greatly enhances the individual's sense of being a person rather than an unknown cog in the machinery. Example: The person recording a sales order can call the salesperson for clarification if need be.

Use of a Variety of Tasks and Skills. The need to employ more than one skill and accomplish more than one task in getting the job done helps to relieve the sense of confinement and monotony. Example: An assembly worker uses a soldering iron as well as a wrench to join parts and to adjust critical mechanical tensions.

Freedom for Self-Direction. This is the reality as well as the feeling of autonomy—that the employee can run the show as far as the job is concerned. In particular, it provides the opportunity to make choices about how the work will be done. Example: At the General Foods plant in Topeka, Kansas, autonomous work groups of from 7 to 14 members decide for themselves how to divide the work, screen and select new members, and counsel members who do not meet team standards.

Direct Feedback From the Work Itself. The employee can tell immediately by looking at the finished product or service whether it has been done rightly or wrongly. The worker does not have to wait for the supervisor, an inspector, or an accounting report to get this information. Example: In one AT&T department, keypunch operators decided to schedule their own work, verify their own output, and keep track of their own errors. In work that had previously been judged dead-end and boring, turnover was cut 27 percent, and 24 clerks found they could do what 46 had previously done.

A Chance for Self-Development. Work that requires employees to stretch their minds and sharpen their skills makes these employees more valuable to themselves as well as to the company. It demonstrates that the benefits from work need not be one-sided, that both an employee's goals and a company's goals can be satisfied.

Should distinctions be made among the various kinds of people-centered job design?

Not necessarily, but it helps to add perspective to the ways that job design can be accomplished.

Job enlargement, for example, extends the boundaries of the job. First tried at IBM, the concept is to let manufacturing employees be responsible for the production step just before and just after the one they currently are doing. Thus, punch press operators might fill their own tote boxes and carry the punched parts to the next operation. It provides an opportunity to get away from a fixed place all day, a chance to converse for a minute or two with adjoining operators and to feel that the job isn't limited to the second or two it takes to load the press and wait for the die to stamp out a part.

Job enrichment is an outgrowth of the job enlargement concept. It allows participating employees to perform job-related activities that are usually done by specialists. For example, the punch press operators might set up their presses with the die required for each new job, inspect their own work with gauges typically used by roving inspectors, and maintain their own output tallies.

Work simplification, as you'll see in the next chapter, stresses employee participation in what is essentially a process-centered approach to work design. Using this technique, employees are trained to examine their jobs much as industrial engineers or methods and systems people might.

Goal-oriented management is the approach developed by M. Scott Myers while at Texas Instruments Company in Dallas. It is like "work itself," it emphasizes the need for supervisors to shift their thinking from "I am the boss who must think of everything" to "These are the goals we must reach together." Under the Myers system the supervisor leads (by "facilitating") and controls when necessary; employees are responsible for planning tasks and accomplishing them. Conversely, authority-oriented supervisors typically plan, lead, and control the doers, who have little say in planning how their work is to be accomplished. (See Figure 21-2.)

The *autonomous work group* is a group-centered concept originally developed at the Tavistock Institute of Human Relations in London, England, in work with coal miners. Its basic premise is that the social or human system and the technical or machine system are, in fact, one interlocked system. The goal is to build relatively independent work groups that can exert control over the technology (or process) involved in their work. This is the approach used at the General Foods plant in Topeka, Kansas, and at the Volvo auto assembly plant in Sweden.

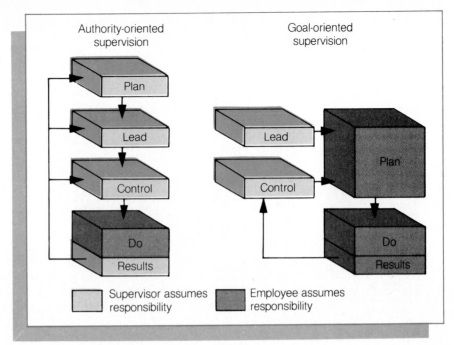

Figure 21-2. Job design differences using authority-oriented and goal-oriented supervision. Adapted from a concept developed by M. Scott Myers, *Every Employee a Manager*, McGraw-Hill Book Company, New York, 1970, p. 99.

Work itself was the term initially used by AT&T for the program it now labels *work design.* It typifies the people-centered job design approach featured in this chapter because it looks for a balance among process demands, organizational goals and restrictions, and employee abilities and interests.

Where does the biggest payoff come from in job design?

For the company or organization it comes in greater output per employee; improved quality of product or service; and—often most important—fewer absences, lower turnover rates, and greater cooperation from employees.

For employees there can be little doubt that job design adds a number of attractive ingredients to their work. Experts say that it improves the **quality of work** itself. It offers greater freedom and flexibility and at the same time makes the work more challenging. Job design utilizes more of an employee's skills and does this more effectively than traditionally frozen methods.

Must job design always be tied into a company-wide program?

Not at all, although it is helpful to know the steps that are typically followed:

1. A feasibility study is made to see if the program has the potential to pay off in a particular organization.
2. Supervisors and employees are trained in job design methods.
3. Together, they develop and pool ideas for departmental and company-wide improvements.
4. Changes that affect a single employee or that are limited to a department are put into place right away; those that are company-wide may take many months or even longer to implement.
5. Results are measured to make sure that the changes were really worthwhile.

There is no reason, however, that a supervisor cannot introduce informally many job design improvement factors—both process- and people-oriented. (See Table 21-3.) The principles are there to be applied. Organizational support and guidance give a great boost, but supervisory initiative can go a long way toward improving job design at the departmental level.

How can supervisors get started in people-centered job design on their own?

Simply approach directly the employees you think might respond. Try this uncomplicated method.

With an Individual Employee

1. You ask: If you could remake your present job so that you still got the same amount and quality of work performed, what would you do?
2. The Employee Suggests: New methods, different tools, restructured workplace layout, rescheduled stop and start time, fewer or additional things to do, changed relationships with other employees, revised paperwork, innovative ways of doing anything related to the job.

TABLE 21-3 IDEAS FOR IMPROVING JOB DESIGNS AND THE QUALITY OF WORK

Job change	How it improves job quality from an employee's point of view
1. Make the individual more accountable for some phase of his or her work.	Adds a feeling of personal responsibility for one's work.
2. Remove some of the minor checks and controls from the job.	Recognizes the individual's ability to proceed without close supervision.
3. Extend the job so that the individual performs all elements of it—a complete unit.	Enhances the sense of contribution, makes the work more meaningful.
4. Require that feedback reports go directly to the individual rather than being channeled through the supervisor.	Adds to the feeling of self-reliance and self-control.
5. Encourage the individual to rearrange his or her workplace to suit his or her idea of how best to improve effectiveness.	Demonstrates respect for the employee's ideas.
6. Add new and/or more difficult tasks that require skills not previously used.	Provides for growth and development on the job.

3. Together You and the Employee Check the Employee's Ideas Against

		OK	Not OK
a. Process constraints			
(1) Product specifications	_____	____	____
(2) Process flow sequence	_____	____	____
(3) Time constraints	_____	____	____
(4) Costs	_____	____	____
b. Organization requirements			
(1) Output and other goals	_____	____	____
(2) Relationships with other jobs	_____	____	____

4. Your Boss Approves, Suggests Modifications, or Disapproves.

5. Together, You and the Employee Implement the Job Design Plan. Example of job redesign for an individual: A chemical plant pumper now makes simple hookups to valves and piping, then operates on and off switches on pump motors. The operator asks to be allowed to replace leaking pipe fittings and pump packing as required, and to begin the shift an hour earlier on days when the work load is heavy. The company says it is okay to handle pump packing, but replacing pipe fittings would interfere with the job of pipe fitters in maintenance crews. Flexibility in starting time is approved.

With a Small Group of Employees

Follow steps 1 through 5 as above, except that allowances must be made for considerable interactions and adjustments among employees at steps 2 and 5. They will need to find ways to make each person's ideal job structure fit those of other employees. Example of job redesign for a group: Five office employees now have separate jobs. A sorts and delivers mail and serves as receptionist, B files all day, C transcribes dictation from a machine, D types records and form letters, E types letters and reports. Their redesign plan calls for all employees to share the mail job and the reception duties on a daily rotation basis. Otherwise, they suggest a rotation plan in which an employee works a full week each on filing, transcribing, form typing, and letter typing. The rotation cycle for these four segments repeats every four weeks. The company says okay so long as the work is done on time with no increase in errors.

Caution. Job restructuring may affect wage rates. The possibility of a change in wage and salary structure should be checked out with your boss, the personnel department, or both, at step 4 and before implementing step 5.

Is everything about job design all good?

Far from it. Like almost every other managerial technique, job design has its good points and its drawbacks as shown below.

Advantages	Disadvantages
Higher output per employee	Time taken in planning meetings
Better product or service quality	Cost of new tooling, machinery,
Less waste of materials	and other facilities
Fewer standby personnel	Longer training for new employees
Less absenteeism	Greater work space requirements
Lower total costs	Less efficient use of production
Flexibility in meeting changes	equipment because of its duplica-
Better use of employee talents	tion at some work stations
Greater employee initiative	High degree of managerial and
Shorter communication	supervisory commitment required
	Resistance from unions

Key Concepts

1. The "quality" of an employee's job—the work itself—probably has as much to do with the way that employee performs as does the nature of the supervision received.

2. The most favorable structure of jobs and work reflects a balance between (a) restraints imposed by the process and the organization and (b) those factors that provide the maximum degree of motivation for the employees who perform the work.

3. The nature of the production or administrative process dictates to a large degree how the work must be performed, but, except in extreme instances of machine-pacing, there is always room for adjustment to human needs.

4. Organizational considerations also exert great influence on the structuring of jobs by setting goals that must be met and by prescribing relationships that must be preserved.

5. Given the desire, managers and supervisors almost always have the opportunity to improve the quality of work within the established constraints by designing motivational factors into the job structure.

Supervisory Word Power

Job. The task, duty, chore, position, occupation, or work unit assigned by an organization to one individual to be performed routinely or repetitively on an hourly, weekly, monthly, or annual basis in return for wages.

Job Design. Known as job redesign or work design; the process of dividing work to be done by an organization into carefully structured and defined individual jobs so as to foster productivity and appeal to the employees who carry them out.

Quality of Work. The extent to which the work itself provides motivation and satisfaction because of the existence in the job design of functional completeness, contact with users, varied tasks and skills, autonomy, direct feedback from the work, and chance for personal growth.

Work Itself. The concept that the nature and the design of the job that employees hold will influence employee performance and satisfaction as much as or more than the interpersonal motivation provided by supervisors and management.

Workplace Design. The layout and arrangement of tools, equipment, and support facilities of the space assigned to an employee so as to make the job easier and less fatiguing.

Reading Comprehension

1. Why wouldn't a job stay the same forever? What sorts of things might cause it to change or might make an employee want to see it designed differently?

2. What is the basic difference between process-oriented and people-oriented job design?

3. At a furniture manufacturing plant, wood frames must be assembled and the glue allowed to set for four hours before the facing can be fitted. What two constraints on process redesign do these requirements represent?

4. Give two reasons why supervisors are often enthusiastic about the "work itself" approach to job redesign.

5. Although Margaret is a firm believer in people-oriented job redesign, she turned down Janice's suggestion because of "organizational restrictions." What most likely caused her to refuse the suggested change?

6. Name at least five factors that, if built into jobs, usually help to motivate employees.

7. After some changes had been made in the job, an employee complained to the supervisor: "This is job enlargement, all right, but it sure isn't job enrichment." What did the employee mean?

8. Which main functions does the supervisor carry out under authority-oriented supervision? Which under goal-oriented supervision?

9. Why would a company bother with job enrichment or redesign in the first place?

10. The head of production for an insulation manufacturer turned down a job design program because "it had too many disadvantages." What are four that might have been mentioned?

Supervision in Action
The Case of the Farm Equipment Repair Shop. A Case Study in Human Relations Involving Job Design, with Questions for You to Answer.

For years it was considered your good fortune if you could get a job at J. O. Shepley & Sons Farm Equipment Sales Company. The work was steady, the pay was adequate, and the management was considerate. As the firm grew larger, however, the work did not seem quite so attractive to many of Shepley's employees. Especially in the service and repair shop, there was a disturbing amount of turnover. Part of this was attributed to the entry into the area of larger factories that were able to offer higher wages to the kind of all-around service mechanics that work at Shepley's developed. But among those who stayed at Shepley's, there was a certain amount of dissatisfaction that was hard to pinpoint.

The service shop was not unlike a very large garage. It was equipped with overhead cranes and hoists large enough to lift an engine out of a tractor for repair. There were several small lathes, welding rigs, and other machines available for making or repairing small parts. During the summer the shop doors were kept open. In the winter they were closed to keep out the cold, for heating was provided only by a few space heaters mounted on the shop walls.

Six mechanics worked in the shop under the supervision of Mrs. Clem, a daughter-in-law in the Shepley family. Mrs. Clem was about 50 years old and had been working in the service shop since she was a teenage stock clerk. Her big advantage was her knowledge of spare parts lists and the location of manufacturer's replacement parts, which were kept in the company's rather extensive stockrooms.

Originally, the six mechanics had pitched in and worked together in groups of twos or threes on whatever job or equipment happened to be in the shop. With the growing variety of specialized farm equipment, however, Mrs. Clem thought that this approach was no longer efficient. Beginning a year ago, she had changed over the shop itself so that each corner was devoted to work on one type of equipment. The northeast corner was for tractors, the northwest corner for baling equipment, the southeast corner for mowers, rakes, and plows, and the southwest corner for planting equipment. In the center of the shop, Mrs. Clem placed the shop's machinery.

In addition, the shop doors were kept closed now and a modern air-conditioning and heating system was installed. Customers—farmers—who used to wander in and out of the shop while their equipment was being worked on now were asked to wait in a lounge in the showroom, where coffee was served and they could look at the new equipment for sale.

Under the new setup, one mechanic was assigned to each of the four specialty shops, the fifth mechanic was assigned to operate the lathes and similar machines, and the sixth mechanic did all the welding. The specialty shop mechanics would perform all the work in their areas, but when lathe work or welding was required, they would bring the part to the center of the shop or have the welder roll the rig to their area, where the work would be performed.

The lathe operator and the welder seemed to like the new arrangement. The main trouble was with the specialty shop mechanics. "I can't understand it," said Mrs. Clem. "I've put all these people in business for themselves. And air-conditioned the place to boot. They ought to love it this way. Besides, it is the only way to keep up to date on what's been put into all this new-fangled farm equipment. It was too much to expect everyone to know all about every tractor, plow, rake, windrower, and manure spreader we have to work on now. Furthermore, the old way was too slow, and our costs were too high."

1. What do you think might be bothering the dissatisfied mechanics?
2. What is good and bad about the new shop layout?
3. How do you react to Mrs. Clem's comment that since all the mechanics are in business for themselves, they ought to love the work?
4. Given the problem of the variety and complexity of the new farm equipment that must be repaired, how would you approach this problem to find a solution?

22

JOB ASSIGNMENTS AND WORK SCHEDULES

If a person has a job to do, why must supervisors get involved in making assignments?

To be certain that each employee's efforts are directed to the most important or the most pressing work to be done. A job simply defines the scope of an individual's work. In most instances supervisors must also provide specific direction in the form of job assignments. If six employees hold checkout-counter jobs in a supermarket, for example, the supervisor must assign each employee to a particular register, by time of day or by day of week. Making assignments, then, becomes a process of matching jobholders and the work that needs to be done.

Job assignments, or job matches, tend to fall into the three categories listed below:

1. **Repetitive, Routine Assignments.** An employee who has received an assignment reports to the same machine and performs essentially the same work over and over again for weeks or months until the assignment is changed. Repetitive assignments are typical of work in mass production operations or large organizations.

2. **Variable Routine Assignments.** As the department work load rises and falls or shifts from one order or product to another, the jobholders may also be shifted from one workplace, machine, or assignment to another. The duration of the assignment may range from an hour or two to a day or a week at most. Variable assignments are by far the most common, especially in job shops and smaller organizations.

3. **Special Projects Assignments.** An employee or a group of employees is given highly specific, usually nonrepetitive assignments that require extended time to complete (from a week to a year or two), with firm beginning and ending dates. Such assignments are most common with knowledge or professional workers and with technicians who are working in research and developmental operations.

How restrictive will a job definition be in determining the assignments an employee will accept or can handle?

This will vary. The point of designing, defining, and evaluating an employee's job is to provide some kind of specialized divisions in the work force. Obviously, you want to put an employee with the appropriate job skills on each task to be done. You wouldn't expect a lathe hand, for example, to do the work of a toolmaker. On the other hand, you wouldn't want to waste too much of an administrative assistant's talent on routine filing. People rightfully expect to work within reasonable limits of their job design, although they may accept extraordinary assignments temporarily or in emergencies. If these out-of-job-scope assignments are prolonged, however, you will run into trouble. The overqualified person will protest; the underqualified person may want a wage increase.

Which comes first, job assignments or the department's overall production schedule?

The production schedule comes first. It should guide the supervisor in making assignments. Said another way, each job assignment should be part of the supervisor's plan for meeting the overall schedule. Every assignment that steers an employee in another direction (a special cleanup job, an unanticipated request for a search of the files, or a nice-but-not-necessary embellishment) takes away from the overall schedule. These distractions may cause you to miss the schedule—or to add extra employees or overtime to meet the schedule.

Supervisors' major responsibility is to get out the work. Why should they be burdened with planning and scheduling?

Regardless of how much planning help supervisors may get from a company's centralized scheduling department, they just won't be able to turn out the work without detailed planning of their own.

Turning out the work requires skillful planning right at the department level. Planning transforms master plans into day-to-day operations. Otherwise the supervisor will waste (1) time—because of avoidable delays; (2) materials—because of haste, spoilage, or unnecessary inventories; (3) machines—because they are not operating at their best capacity; (4) space—because of overcrowding and poor coordination of incoming supplies and outgoing production; (5) personnel—because employees are not fully occupied.

How far ahead should supervisors plan their work?

Long-range planning should be handled largely by those in higher levels of management. Your target is necessarily much closer at hand. American Management Association studies show that supervisors spend 38 percent of their thinking time on problems that come up the same day, 40 percent on those one week ahead, 15 percent on those one month ahead, 5 percent on those three to six months ahead, and 2 percent on those one year ahead.

Check your own habits. If you feel you're too busy to worry about

anything but today, chances are you spend most of your time fighting fires that can be avoided by planning a week to a month ahead of
time.

Typically, a supervisor is responsible for short-range (or tactical)
plans and higher executives for long-range (or strategic) plans. In
military language, tactical plans are those concerned with a particular engagement or skirmish or battle; strategic plans are those on
which the major battle or entire war is based.

In what ways does good scheduling affect morale?

Employees have confidence in a supervisor who is willing and able
to plan their work well for them. One of the worst destroyers of morale
is the constant recurrence of emergency situations. Nothing breaks
down security like continual crises. Employees don't like change.
They fear it and would prefer that the company were run smoothly all
the time. Poor planning adds to that fear and often hits them where it
really hurts—in the pocketbook.

Good planning makes it possible for employees to go home at
night fairly certain of the job they are going to work on tomorrow. It
builds their respect for you. Employees want the feeling that they
know what they're doing at the company. If you've shown them that
you can schedule work smoothly, employees will be more willing to
pitch in when the occasional emergency arises.

Should you schedule your department to operate at 100 percent capacity?

No. This is a poor practice because it leaves no cushion for
emergencies. It's best to call on your past experience and plan only
for short periods at 100 percent. No department can run for very long
without some unforeseen emergency arising. These emergencies
may be only unexpected absences or special rush orders. But you
must leave room for them.

What happens if you underschedule your staff?

Exactly what you would expect: Employees find a way to stretch the
job to fill the time. One way to minimize this is to have a backlog of

second-priority jobs on tap for assignment. If regular orders are slow coming in, you can catch up with some of the work that often needs to be done but is not allowed for in the master schedule. These assignments might include cleaning out files in an office, sorting and discarding obsolete inventory in the stockroom, or any kind of general cleanup.

It should go without saying that if this condition persists, some employees must be transferred or laid off.

Can you expect as much from employees when they work overtime, or should you make an allowance for it in the schedule?

You should probably expect a 5 to 10 percent drop in productivity. Authorities differ on this one, probably because there has been very little definitive research on the subject. Stress and fatigue inevitably take their toll. The more extended the overtime, the greater the drop in output—and probably in the quality of work produced. My own impression is that a 10 percent figure is reliable for scheduling purposes.

What kind of special problems should you anticipate when scheduling shift work?

Shift work is becoming more, rather than less, common today—both in manufacturing and in office work. White-collar workers who never conceived of anything but a nine-to-five day now find themselves scheduled from 4 p.m. to 12 midnight. This is because their output is needed to keep a very expensive computer busy.

As you know, more than one shift usually creates a special set of problems for supervisors to contend with. For example:

Employee Attitudes.   Nightworkers feel left out. They need more attention from both day and night supervisors to make them feel they're really part of the team.

Employee Training.   More often than not, seniority prevails in staffing for the second shift. This means that the night gang is made up of beginners or relatively inexperienced personnel. So your training effort for nightworkers must be more patient and thorough than that for dayworkers.

Safety. Fatigue and poor lighting make nightworkers more susceptible to accidents than dayworkers are. Consequently, greater precautions must be taken, and education must be more detailed.

Communications. Projects carried from the day shift to the second shift frequently bog down or get off course because of faulty communications. Supervision ought to overlap—at least a half hour between shifts, preferably more. And logbook instructions should be written out in painful detail. What appears clear to the employee who's been working with a process all day may seem cryptic to the person who takes over at 4 p.m.

Cooperation. A little competition between shifts is a good thing. But if this competition grows into antagonism, you've got trouble. Typically, employees from the first shift leave the unattractive jobs—such as cleaning up spills—for the second shift. Or second-shift employees "forget" to prepare the equipment for a quick start-up by the day shift. Here's where it will pay off if you can devise ways to bring personnel from both shifts together occasionally—for production conferences and for recreation. If they get to know one another more intimately, mutual sympathy—and respect—are more likely to develop.

Shift work will always require special coordination and an extra effort on the supervisor's part to make certain that critical connections are not overlooked.

What about flexitime?

You may see more of this phenomenon. It is especially prevalent in government and in office work in smaller firms. Flexitime (flexible working hours) permits employees to choose their own working hours to some extent, provided they work the normal number of hours. Flexitime schedules (see Figure 22-1) generally include several (often six) hours of core time during which all employees must be on the job. An employee may choose to come to work an hour late and make up the hour after normal closing time, or an hour early and leave an hour before normal closing time. This kind of scheduling has advantages where transportation is a problem, and it appeals to many workers. It isn't so good where there is a need for continuous interaction between employees—for example, on an assembly line. It also requires a degree of cooperation between employees. For every person who may wish a variation, there may be a need for another employee to choose the opposite alternate to cover the job of the person who is early or late.

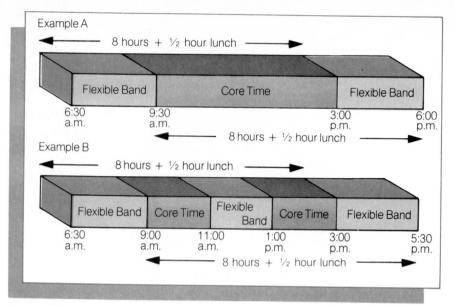

Figure 22-1. Two ways of designing flexitime schedules. From Barbara L. Fiss, *Flexitime—A Guide,* U.S. Civil Service Commission, May 15, 1974.

How do companywide plans dictate department-level schedules?

Through the preparation of a *master production schedule.* This sets the overall schedule for end items (or final products) that the company must make—in terms of number of units and their delivery dates.

Every final product consists of a number of different parts. Thus, to make an end item, a list of parts called a *bill of materials* must be prepared.

If a part is to be made in the plant, a *route sheet* must be prepared. This shows the operations that must be performed to make the part, their sequence, and the machines on which the work will be performed. The route sheet (sometimes called the order-of-work sheet) may also provide an estimate of the time needed to perform each operation.

It is usually the supervisor's task to assign each of the operations listed on the route sheet to a qualified worker in the supervisor's department.

What should supervisors do when they are pressured for faster deliveries or tighter deadlines?

Resist the desire to promise what you can't deliver. Hopes and expectations have no place in planning. Your schedules and promises must be based on fact. Only facts—available equipment and its condition, people and their reliability, material supply and its delivery—can be used as a successful base for planning.

A firm, dependable promise will satisfy most superiors. But don't yield to the temptation to be overcautious. Don't allow for more time than you think the situation actually warrants.

Don't say, for instance, "We can't possibly deliver these parts before the 16th," and then finish the job on the 11th. Others in your plant depend on the accuracy of your forecasts. If everyone allowed too much leeway, that would eat up time and money just as overscheduling might.

Give the best sure date you can figure on. Otherwise you'll lose friends and respect among your associates and your superiors.

When a supervisor draws up work schedules, what personnel time factors should be considered?

Planning a work schedule involves many employee variables—all of which must be accounted for in your final plans. Here are some of the most recurrent:

Holidays	Absences
Vacations	Shift rotation
Rest periods	Meal reliefs
Leaves of absence	Quits and discharges
Training time	Time off to vote (where applicable)

A study made by the department of economics of the University of Michigan in 1977 turned up some valuable information for scheduling purposes. This study found that the average employee spends 27 minutes a day on unscheduled breaks in addition to whatever is allowed in the schedule. This means that when estimating labor hours required, you should figure in another 10 percent to make up for the facts of working life.

If your company has no planning department, what can you do to schedule production smoothly and efficiently?

Don't try to improvise. Work up some sort of schedule and use it as a guide for assigning work and checking completions. As each order reaches you, make a rough estimate (based on experience or time study) of how long it will take—the number of worker-hours or machine-hours per operation. Then build up machine loads. At all times, know how many hours of work are ahead of each operator and each machine.

Check regularly with supervisors in the departments before yours and after yours. This way you keep track of when to expect goods to work on and when the next department expects goods from you. If your timing gets off, you're likely to have employees standing around waiting for work or you will hear the same complaint from the department that's waiting for goods from you.

Keep an eye constantly on supplies. On a regular basis, check to see that you have enough operating supplies on hand, such as raw materials, packaging materials, and any other items that you add to the product in your department.

Each afternoon start checking to see that there will be enough materials and work in process on hand to keep your employees busy the next morning. If you anticipate delays, try to maintain a backlog of low-priority jobs that can be set up and torn down quickly.

What is a Gantt chart? How does a supervisor use it?

During World War I Henry Laurence Gantt, an industrial engineer, developed the first production control chart. Its form seems obvious today, since most organizations now use one or another version of it to plan and chart output performance. Its essentials are displayed in Figure 22-2.

To understand the unique value of the Gantt chart, put yourself in the place of a supervisor who has just been handed five production orders, stamped serially from 101 to 105. These orders indicate what machines the work must be processed on, the sequence that must be followed, and the estimated number of hours it will take each machine to complete its work.

These orders contain essentially the same kind of information found on a route sheet. The route sheet, however, often includes operations performed in different departments. Thus, it is not unusual for the supervisor to collect this information from several route sheets, or the production-control department may issue a number of separate orders to each departmental supervisor.

If the supervisor were to load the machines (they could be benches, work stations, desks, and so on) with the assumption that each order must be finished before another one is begun (straight-line or point-to-point scheduling), the schedule would be something like Chart A in Figure 22-2. The flow of work would be orderly, but the equipment would be extremely underutilized. Worse still, many orders would be delayed. To correct these deficiencies, Gantt overlapped orders and disregarded the sequence in which they were accepted, while still rigidly adhering to the operation sequence each order specifies. Chart B in Figure 22-2 shows how the supervisor can juggle orders, starting number 105 on machine B and number 102 on machine C and at the same time beginning number 101 on machine A. By rearranging and overlapping the jobs, all five orders can be finished by Friday afternoon. Furthermore, the supervisor has greatly increased the overall machine utilization. Machine A is now scheduled to be in operation 18 of the first 24 hours of the week (through Wednesday). It works 4 hours on 101, 4 hours on 104, is idle for 2 hours, then works 4 hours on 102, 6 hours on 105, and is idle again until the close of the shift on Wednesday. Machine B utilizes 22 hours during the same period: 4 hours on 105, 8 hours on 101, idle for 2 hours, 6 hours on 102, and 4 hours on 103. Machine C utilizes all 24 hours: 10 hours on 102, 2 hours on 105, 2 hours on 101, and 10 hours on 104. This predicts utilization rates of 75 percent, 92 percent, and 100 percent. Whereas the supervisor might not be able to juggle the work so efficiently all week long, it indicates what judicial overlapping of jobs can accomplish.

Is the Gantt chart useful only for production scheduling?

Far from it. If you look closely at the Gantt chart, you will see that it is essentially a bar chart which shows commitments and/or progress against time. It has many variations and is used widely in almost every imaginable situation to plan and control projects. It need not be limited to hourly or daily controls. Many offices use it to help chart progress over a period of weeks and months.

What is a milestone chart?

It is very much like a Gantt chart, except that its focus is on the completion of a significant phase of an activity or program, rather

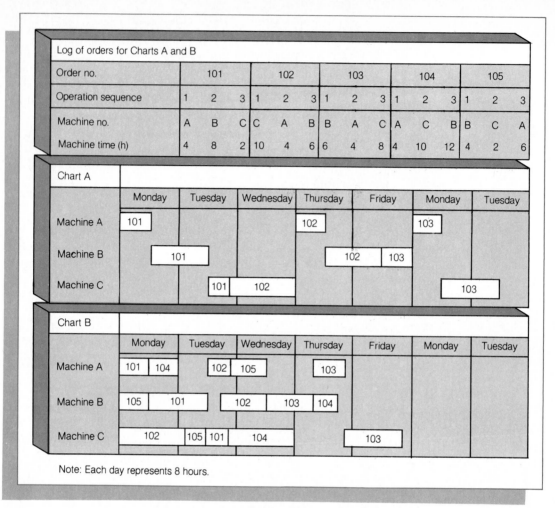

Figure 22-2. Development of a Gantt chart from a series of production orders. Chart A shows jobs lined up in sequence as they were received. Chart B shows jobs rearranged (overlapped) for maximum machine loading, with prescribed sequence of operations for each job maintained.

than on the starting date or the time needed to do the job. Using a milestone chart makes it possible to specifically relate actual progress to planned accomplishment. Figure 22-3 shows how a milestone chart can be used in order to plan a newspaper advertisement.

How does the PERT chart relate to the Gantt and milestone charts?

It combines the best aspects of both and adds some valuable elements of its own. Specifically, it borrows the ideas of juggling a number of different but related tasks of varying time requirements from the Gantt chart. PERT ties these to the critical events of the milestone chart and demonstrates graphically how these are all tied together. Finally, PERT enables the planners to identify the bottlenecks in a complex schedule, plan, or program.

What do the initials P-E-R-T stand for? Where is PERT used?

They stand for "program evaluation and review technique." In plainer English, PERT is a technique for planning any project that involves a number of different tasks that must be coordinated. It is a graphic technique that enables the planner to see the progressive

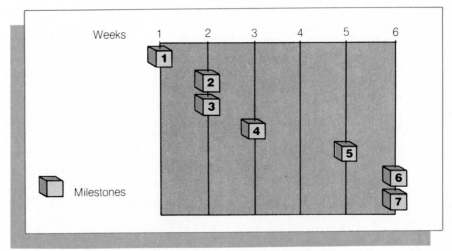

Figure 22-3. Milestone chart for planning a newspaper ad.

1. Complete data gathering from client.
2. Approve placement plans and schedule.
3. Present sample copy and art.
4. Approve final copy and art content.
5. Prepare finished art and complete typesetting.
6. Give final approval.
7. Deliver to scheduled newspaper media.

relationships among many jobs; PERT is also known as the critical-path method (CPM), arrow diagraming, and many other variations.

The technique dramatizes the value of conceiving of doing two or more things simultaneously. It may take 12 minutes to get a haircut, 5 minutes for a shoeshine, and 10 minutes to browse through the newspaper. You could take 27 minutes to do all three—in sequence, one after the other—or you could do all three in 12 minutes by doing them simultaneously or (as planners say) in parallel.

The PERT method is most useful for scheduling one-of-a-kind projects. It is used to plan and schedule construction projects such as roads, bridges, and dams. It is used to plan the building of very large engines, airplanes, and ships; PERT is helpful, too, in scheduling a number of jobs that must be done in a short period of time. For example, a plant closes for two weeks in the summer and tries to get everything cleaned and repaired during that period. It is also useful for starting a new program in a government agency or for introducing a new product to the market.

What makes PERT so different from ordinary scheduling methods?

The program evaluation and review technique helps a scheduler to plan ahead, to look for critical jobs that will tie up a whole program unless they are begun and completed before they create bottlenecks. For example, it may be logical to wait until a machine foundation pit has been dug and the concrete has been poured before constructing the supporting ironwork for the machine. (See Figure 22-4.) But if steel is in short supply and the ironwork job will take four weeks to fabricate, then perhaps it's wiser to begin this part of the job before digging the pit. And if there are several other jobs that can't be begun until the ironwork is in place, you can see how critical it is to anticipate the ironwork job and assure its completion in time; PERT charting helps you to identify these critical jobs ahead of time.

What is the basis for scheduling and assigning office and clerical work?

Office scheduling should be based on the same considerations given to production scheduling: (1) the number of tasks to be done, (2) the time it will take to do each task, (3) the number and qualifications of employees available to do the work, and (4) the capacity and availability of proper machines and equipment, when machinery plays a part. A good way to put this all together is to use a work distribution chart, which provides a rule-of-thumb guide to indicate how much work the department can handle with its present staff.

Figure 22-5 shows how repetitive, routine work in an office might be balanced among eight employees by means of a work distribution chart. (Machine capacity and availability are not considered to be factors in this example.) Note that this supervisor has tried to group together activities of roughly the same skills level into the job assignments for each person. For example, Apgar handles all the mail and part of the copying—fairly simple work. Bond and Crisi handle filing and the balance of the copying—slightly more difficult work. Dalt and Eigo have secretarial jobs, whereas Finch's job is mainly stenography. Grey is a keypunch operator who also handles the check-writing machine, and Hruska is a posting clerk.

What's meant by short-interval scheduling?

This is an industrial engineering technique for improving output by means of issuing many specific work assignments of relatively short duration. Called by various proprietary names by a number of man-

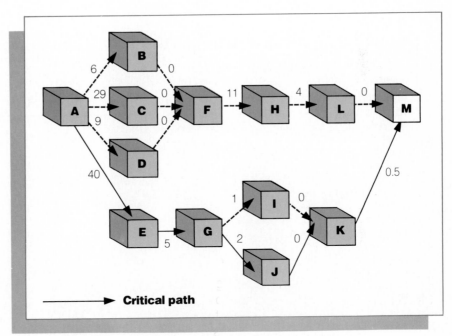

Figure 22-4. PERT chart for the installation of a large machine.

agement consulting firms, short-interval scheduling has met with growing popularity in office applications because of its unusual suitability to clerical work and some in service work, such as maintenance and repair jobs.

In essence, the short-interval scheduling technique calls on the supervisor to block out only a small portion of work at a time for each employee, rather than lining up a whole day's or week's work at once. For example, you give a filing clerk a sheaf of correspondence and say that it should be filed within the next half hour. Or you hand a dozen invoices to a clerk and ask for their preparation within the hour. When each of these particular blocks of work has been completed, you assign another chunk of work (that again covers only a short interval in the workday) to each employee.

A key advantage of the short-interval approach is that in a very short time you will know whether an employee is keeping up or falling behind in output. This system also forces you to estimate and enforce output standards, and it calls your attention to typical wishful thinking on management's part. For example, in the past you may have assumed that a clerk could handle 70 documents in a day. When you break this assignment up into 10 documents per hour, you might be surprised to discover that unexpected peculiarities in your kind of work make it impossible for the clerk to average more than 7 documents per hour—and consequently only 50 or 60 per day.

WORK DISTRIBUTION CHART FOR OFFICE PLANNING AND SCHEDULING

Tasks or activities to be done each week	Total time (in hours) for each task each week	Weekly time distribution in hours per employee							
		Apgar	Bond	Crisi	Dalt	Eigo	Finch	Grey	Hruska
Mail in	15	15							
Mail out	15	15							
Dictation	20				10	10			
Transcription	30				10	10	10		
Typing	80			10	20	20	30		
Copying	30	10	10	10					
Filing in	25		20	5					
Filing out	15		10	5					
Keypunching	30							30	
Check writing	10							10	
Posting	50			10					40
Total hours	320	40	40	40	40	40	40	40	40

Figure 22-5.

Short-interval scheduling functions well because many clerical people are not capable of, or particularly interested in, establishing or following for themselves a work schedule of a duration of much more than an hour. Consequently, they tend to welcome your taking the responsibility for the planning and scheduling part of their job.

Short-interval scheduling may be difficult because it depends on (1) the accuracy with which you can estimate reasonable work loads; (2) the extent to which you can find time to make these estimates and assignments; (3) the degree to which you observe and control performance and make the necessary adjustments in your expectations; (4) the effectiveness with which employees can be motivated to accept a work pace that is higher than that to which they have been accustomed; and (5) the ability and time available to train people to work with greater skills, concentration, and persistence.

Whether your office installs a formal short-interval scheduling system or not, however, the principle is a sound one for you to follow. You'll find that you can apply the general idea informally, even sporadically, and still get unusually good results.

How can you get the most from your staff's job assignments without asking for what's unreasonable?

Much of this has to do with how you plan your own day. Not only will you be able to maintain tighter supervision of your work force, you'll also be setting an example of self-management for them. For example, here's a brief list of things to do that will give you a head start each day on your job assignments:

Before the Day Begins:
1. Check the production schedule and/or work order for the day.
2. Check to make sure the equipment to be used is ready for operating.
3. Check the supply of material, stock, forms, etc., that will be needed to complete the work.
4. Line up a firm work schedule for the day and plan your job assignments accordingly.

At the Beginning of the Shift:
5. Check attendance and assign employees to work stations or specific orders or projects.
6. If necessary because of absences, balance the work force by rearranging assignments or by securing additional help from other departments, if available, for temporary assignment.

7. For all new, special, or temporary projects or assignments, make it clear when the work should be completed.

During the Day:

8. Stay on the floor immediately before and after rest and lunch breaks and for a full 15 minutes before quitting time.

9. Check periodically to make sure that employees are at their work stations and not roaming aimlessly.

10. Check periodically to make sure that employees are not idly waiting for materials, instructions, or assignments.

11. Make a list of unsolved problems that have come up that day. Think about ways to solve or minimize them the next day.

12. Think ahead about what must be done the next workday: (a) check the production schedule and/or work orders coming up, (b) check equipment and materials that will be needed, and (c) have clear in your mind the job assignments for the next day.

Key Concepts

1. An optimum matchup between (a) a job and its requirements and (b) an individual's capabilities and interests adds greatly to departmental productivity and employee satisfaction.

2. Departmental schedules descend from an organization's overall or master schedule. Failure of one department to meet its schedule contributes to delays in other departments and often prevents the organization from meetings its goals and commitments.

3. Job assignments must be made within the constraints of departmental schedules; thus short-term assignments may fall below the optimum, but long-term planning should seek the best possible matchups.

4. Few shops can meet schedules calling for 100 percent of capacity; allowances should be made for unanticipated delays caused by machine breakdown, materials shortages, and employee absences. On the other hand, prolonged underscheduling of the work force leads to overstaffing and lowered productivity.

5. Supervisors should master a variety of planning and scheduling techniques for handling a number of different scheduling problems: the Gantt chart for both long and short production runs; PERT or CPM for one-of-a-kind projects; the work distribution chart for standing assignments; short-interval scheduling for jobs that vary greatly in the time needed to perform them; and flexitime for staggering employee arrivals and departures.

6. Effective job assignments and scheduling will not automatically take care of themselves; they require constant surveillance and selective decisions on the part of the department supervisor throughout the day.

Supervisory Word Power

Gantt Chart. A chart that enables a planner to schedule jobs in the most productive sequence while also providing a visual means for observing and controlling work progress.

Milestone Chart. A variation of the Gantt chart which focuses the planner's and controller's attention on the schedule of events necessary to bring a project to successful completion.

PERT Chart. A graphic technique for planning a project in which a great number of tasks must be coordinated; this chart (1) shows the relationship between the tasks and (2) identifies the critical bottlenecks that may delay progress toward the project's completion.

Short-Interval Scheduling. A scheduling technique that calls for the issuance to employees of work assignments of relatively short duration, usually less than two hours. This enables supervisors to be in almost constant touch with employee productivity throughout the day.

Work Distribution Chart. A device for visualizing how the tasks or activities of a department—and the times needed to perform those tasks—are distributed among its workers in order that equitable workloads may be planned.

Reading Comprehension

1. Describe two simple ways to record plans without becoming overly burdened with paperwork.

2. Why would it not be wise to plan for as much production on the night shift as on the day shift?

3. An electric motor manufacturer is considering flexitime on its assembly line. Is that a good idea? Could flexitime have any advantages if used in the office instead?

4. If a supervisor's company provides a master production schedule, why does the supervisor have to schedule at all? What is the supervisor's role in carrying out the master plan?

5. What are some of the things a supervisor should do to make the work of a central planning and scheduling department more effective?

6. In what ways is a Gantt chart like a calendar? Different from a calendar?

7. In what ways is a PERT chart similar to a Gantt chart? What is its principal difference?

8. What is the critical path? Why is it called "critical?"

9. Peggy was moved from supervising manufacturing workers to a new job involving supervising office workers. How much of what she learned about scheduling in her old job can she use in her new job? What will be different in her new job?

Under what circumstances is short-interval scheduling particularly effective?

Supervision in Action
The Case of the Muddled Job Priorities. A Case Study in Human Relations Involving Job Assignments in a Shipping Department, with Questions for You to Answer.

Tom Varga, supervisor of the shipping department, was being hassled by his boss about the low productivity and poor delivery performance of his crew.

"Tom," said his boss, "you've been on this job six months and I don't know what we're going to do with you. There's hardly a week goes by that we don't have the sales division on our backs about late deliveries or about mispacked items. And, as if that weren't bad enough, the accounting department tells me that you're running over budget in labor hours per pounds of items shipped and that you bill more overtime than can possibly be justified."

Tom had no answer to these complaints. About all he could manage to say was, "I'm sorry about all this. I'm doing my best, but I'll go back and try my darnedest to correct these problems."

"You'd better," said Tom's boss, "I'm beginning to lose my patience. I've about run out of excuses to protect you from the heat that's coming down from upstairs."

Tom returned to the shipping department determined to find out what was going wrong there. His first thought was to speak to Dierdre, the shipping clerk, about the flow of orders. Her desk was piled with shipping orders, but Dierdre was nowhere to be seen. Tom thought she might be out supervising a truck loading, but she wasn't there. Nor was she in the stock-picking aisles. "I'll check with her later," Tom thought to himself, and went to find the lift truck operation.

Charlie, one of the drivers, was sitting on his rig when Tom found him. "What job are you working on now?" asked Tom.

"Nothing at the moment," said Charlie. "I finished the Zepco order ten minutes ago and I've been waiting for you to tell me what to do next."

"You ought to know without my telling you," said Tom.

"Well," said Charlie, "the last time I started to work on an order on my own, you jumped all over me and told me not to proceed without getting an OK from you or Dierdre."

"That was when we were having all that trouble with mixed-up shipments," said Tom. "That's all been straightened out now. Just go to the shipping desk and pick up the next job on the list."

"Okay," said Charlie as he drove off, "will do."

Next, Tom roamed the storage aisles observing the men and women who were picking orders. Things were moving very well in the areas where small items were stacked. In fact, the pickers looked overworked there. One of them told Tom that the crew was falling behind in a truckloading at that moment. In areas where the large units were stored, however, handling was moving at a snail's pace.

"What's holding things up here?" Tom asked of two idle stockpickers.

"We're waiting for the lift truck to pick the heavy cases out of the racks and put them on our hand pallets, but the drivers are busy loading trucks right now. Anyway, things have been slow in this area all morning," one of the stockpickers replied.

"Why don't you go over to the small-carton area and give them a hand there? They are busy right now and need help."

"Nothing doing," said the stockpicker. "My job is in this area, not working with the small cartons. If we ran over there every time they fell behind, we'd never get our own work done and you'd be all over us."

"I do expect you to use your judgment once in a while," said Tom. "Get over to the small-carton area right away and give them a hand."

"Okay," said the stockpicker, "but you better tell them to pitch in over here when we need help."

Tom shook his head and went back to the shipping clerk's desk. Dierdre was bending over the desk examining an order, along with Mona, one of the stockpickers.

"Where have you been, Dierdre?" asked Tom.

"Oh, I was up at the sales order section checking out one of the shipping orders that didn't seem quite right," said Dierdre.

"Why did you go over there? What do you think the telephone is for?" asked Tom.

"It seems easier to handle these things in person rather than by telephone," said Dierdre.

"And what is Mona doing out here at the desk when there's a jam-up back in the small-carton section?"

"There was a problem about one of the orders, and I came out to look it up on the master sheet," said Mona. "When Dierdre came back, I waited to see if we could both straighten it out."

"That's not your job," said Tom. "Dierdre and I will get it taken care of and let you know what it's all about. Meanwhile, get back to your area."

"Okay," said Mona.

Tom and Dierdre then began to examine the master shipping sheets.

1. What are some of the things that seem to be wrong with the way jobs are assigned and carried out in Tom's department?
2. If you were Tom, what would you do to improve job assignments in the stockpicking areas?
3. What might Tom do to straighten out job assignments among the lift-truck operators?
4. What will Tom have to do to get his department under control and properly productive?

23

IMPROVING PRODUCTIVITY AND CONTROLLING COSTS

What is productivity?

There are many definitions and most of them are complex. Yet productivity is a very simple and vital concept. Dr. C. Jackson Grayson, chair of the American Productivity Center, says it best of all: "Productivity is the process of getting more out of what you put in. It's doing better with what you have."

How is it measured?

Technically, *productivity* is a measure of how efficient a person or an operation is by comparing (1) the value of the output result with (2) the cost of the input resource. It is usually expressed as a ratio (or rate). For example, productivity of a hand assembly department in a furniture factory might be stated as five chairs per labor hour. The number of chairs is the output; the labor expended is the input. If the furniture factory wished, it could convert both figures to dollars. If so, the value added to the chair by the assembly operation might be estimated at $3 each, or a total of $15. If an assembler is paid $5 per hour, then the productivity of the assembly operation would be $15 divided by $5, or 3:1.

Ratios can also be converted to percentages, and some companies state productivity that way. For instance, the 3:1 ratio is 300 percent and the 2:1 ratio is 200 percent. Very often you will hear productivity compared to what it was previously. This is usually expressed as a percentage increase or decrease. For example, if your department's productivity ratio was 2:1 last year and improved to 2.2:1 this year, it would be correct to say that your productivity had improved by 10 percent:

$$(2.2 - 2.0) \div 2.0 = 0.10 = 10\%$$

How is productivity related to methods improvement and cost control?

Productivity measures not only tell supervisors how much they are getting from the available resources, they also indicate how effective the process methods employed are and how well costs are controlled.

How can supervisors tell how good their departmental productivity is?

Few people can say for sure what is good or bad. But you can easily tell whether your productivity is improving or falling off. There are four basic possibilities, as shown in Figure 23-1:

- If output remains the same but costs go up, productivity is *falling.*
- If output remains the same but costs go down, productivity is *rising.*

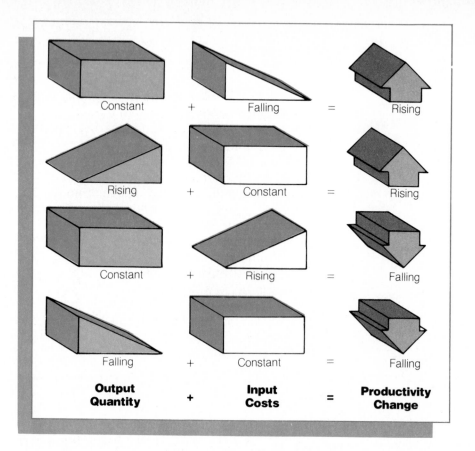

Output Quantity	+	Input Costs	=	Productivity Change
Constant	+	Falling	=	Rising
Rising	+	Constant	=	Rising
Constant	+	Rising	=	Falling
Falling	+	Constant	=	Falling

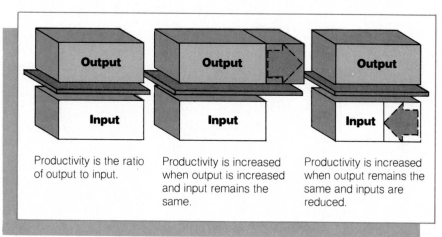

Productivity is the ratio of output to input.

Productivity is increased when output is increased and input remains the same.

Productivity is increased when output remains the same and inputs are reduced.

Figure 23-1. (a) How relative changes in output quantities and input costs affect productivity. (b) Two basic ways to increase productivity.

- If output goes up and costs remain the same, productivity is *rising*.
- If output goes down and costs remain the same, productivity is *falling*.

If output and productivity both change, you will have to use this formula: Productivity equals output value divided by input costs.

Are productivity considerations limited to manufacturing operations?

No. The same principle applies everywhere. In many clerical and service operations, productivity measures are made exactly as in manufacturing. A typist's productivity, for example, would be the number of letters or lines typed per hour worked. A supermarket checkout counter clerk's output would be the number of items checked (or dollars taken in) per day. A bank teller's productivity would be the number of transactions handled per hour, day, week, or month.

The only limit to the application of productivity is the need to obtain a reliable measurement of output. It is difficult, for example, to measure the value of a nurse's output, although many hospitals talk about the number of patients tended by one nurse per shift as a measure of productivity.

Another factor to watch is the impact that quality demands have on productivity. If quality requirements are raised, output may drop accordingly. Or, if product specifications are loosened, output may rise solely because of this change and not represent a real improvement in productivity.

What factors can contribute to productivity improvement?

There are two basic ingredients that supervisors can work on to improve productivity.

Technological Factors. These include:

- Product or service design. Some things are easier to make or deliver than others.
- Plant and equipment. Up-to-date and well-maintained facilities and equipment make a big difference in productivity.

● Process layout and methods. Congestion and backtracking hinder productivity; order and unimpeded flow accelerate it.
● Condition of materials. Presorted and stacked parts speed machine loading. Carbonless forms with preprinted routing instructions improve typing efficiency.
● Extent of power used. Electricity, steam, compressed air, fuel—these all apply leverage to human effort.

Human Factors. The obvious ones are ability, knowledge, and motivation. What is not so clear is the extent to which dozens of other people-oriented factors are important. Among those that deserve attention are individual education, experience, levels of aspiration, work schedules, training, organizational groupings, personnel policies, leadership, and—very important—pay practices.

What may not be so important as was once thought is the physical environment, but it cannot be ignored.

See Figure 23-2 for an indication of the relative input of human factors in operations with varying degrees of technology.

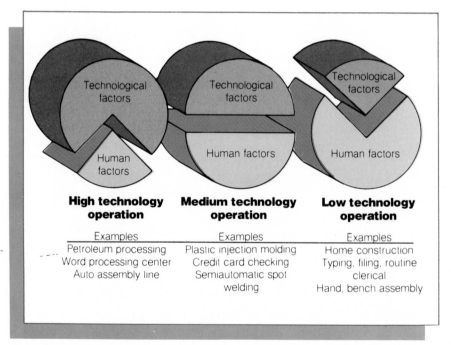

Figure 23-2. Relative impact of human factor as compared with factors on productivity.

What role does employee job satisfaction play in improving productivity and controlling costs?

It is the most important factor not yet fully exploited. In high-technology industries—such as petroleum refining—job satisfaction may be a smaller, though still vital, factor than technology. In most work, however, there is an increasing need to place major emphasis on the role of job satisfaction. In the long run, people control the work pace. They can be devilishly clever in thwarting machines.

Supervisors must try to match jobs with each person's own kind of job satisfaction. Productivity gets its strongest boost from the human side when supervisors support employees in their individual search for job satisfaction. The trick, of course, is to balance employees' needs for satisfaction with the organization's need for productivity and cost control.

In what ways is the Quality Circle movement related to the human element in productivity improvement?

It is at the heart of it. As you'll see in the detailed discussion of Quality Circles that appears in Chapter 24, that movement, which began as a way to improve quality by involving concerned employees, quickly showed that its benefits spilled over into productivity improvements as well. In fact, in many organizations, Quality Circles are aimed as much at productivity as they are at quality.

What has work measurement got to do with all this?

It provides the foundation stone. Work—human effort—is the basic input into most operations. Unless you have a good idea of how much work is entailed, it's almost impossible to know where to look for productivity improvements or to tell whether or not you've accomplished anything when you're through. *Work measurement* is the term generally applied to any method for finding out how long it takes to do a job. Work measurement usually refers to the time it would take an individual to accomplish a specific task. However, when a worker is assisted by, or paced by, a machine, this may also be considered. Since human accomplishment is affected by how much physical effort and skill go into the job, work measurement usually takes those into account, too.

What are the main ways in which work is measured?

Making *time studies* of the actual job as it is performed (using some sort of stopwatch) is by far the most common way. Other methods range from rough-and-ready measures to ultrasophisticated techniques.

The crudest measures involve simply looking at historical records that show how much an employee has produced in a day, week, or month.

The most elaborate approach uses tiny building blocks of time units based on *motion studies.* Experts add the time for every motion required on a job (lifting, pulling, straightening, and so forth) to find the total time needed. The measuring units are called *predetermined elemental time standards.* These are referred to with a variety of proprietary names, such as MTM, Work Factor, and ZIP Standard Data.

Still another very useful method for work measurement is work sampling, which will be described on pages 427–430. This method is especially suitable for supervisory use, although many work improvement analysts rely on it almost exclusively.

Whatever the work measurement technique—precise or rough-and-ready—the times that are found become time standards, or simply *standards.* These standards for various jobs are accumulated in a company's record files or are often available (for jobs commonly performed in commerce and industry) for purchase from consulting firms.

How is work measurement data used?

Time data is widely used for a number of practical purposes. It enables managers and supervisors to:

1. Estimate accurately how long future jobs will take.
2. Establish reliable work schedules.
3. Provide employees with specific work standards in terms of either (a) time allowed to get a job done or (b) number of output units that must be produced in a certain time period.
4. Estimate the labor costs for products to be made or services to be performed.
5. Provide a basis for employee wages, especially those that include extra pay (wage incentives) for work that exceeds the time standard.
6. Provide fundamental measures for productivity.

What causes standards to become loose and unreliable measures of productivity?

A time or cost standard is *loose* when an average employee putting forth normal effort is able consistently to undershoot the standard by a very large margin. Most fair standards, however, are set with the expectancy that good workers will be able to undershoot them by as much as 25 percent. Performance in excess of that should be investigated, for the standards may be loose.

Several factors determine the time allowed in the standard: methods and materials used on the job when studied, the way the job was set up, the way materials were supplied and taken away, the quality specifications, and the method of timekeeping. Changing any of these factors will loosen (or tighten, if the change causes the job to take longer) the standard.

You, as the supervisor, are responsible for observing when any of the original standard conditions are changed. If you slacken your standard of acceptance in order to rush a job through, you help loosen the standard. If you fail to observe and report a change in method or tool used, you help build slack in the standard.

Most supervisors are pretty alert to major changes in the way a job is done and quick to report them. But frequently standards become loose not because of any one big change but as a result of the accumulation of many minor changes. This is all the more reason you should keep on your toes, watch for the first signs of a loosening rate, and then take action accordingly.

Regardless of the cause of a standard's looseness, it should be obvious that a loose standard can give a false impression of high productivity. Loose standards should be reported and revised. Otherwise, employees as well as management will find their efforts increasingly uncompetitive with those of domestic and foreign challengers.

What is work sampling? How good is it?

Work sampling is a rough-and-ready approach to work measurement. It is relatively easy to do. It has some shortcomings, but it is especially suitable for supervisors who wish to get a quick idea of the productivity of their departments.

Work sampling (also called *ratio delay*) is accomplished by making random observations of various activities in the work area. It enables a supervisor to find the proportion of delays and interruptions that occur as related to the total time to do a job. For instance, if you wanted to find out how much of the time a lift truck was actually out of operation, you'd visit the truck a predetermined number of times a day, say, ten. These visits would not be at regular intervals; they would be at random. If in ten days you made 100 observations, and if during 23 of them the truck was idle, it would be statistically safe to conclude that the truck was idle 23 percent of the time. You could make the same sort of study on any number of items—so long as you make enough observations and the observations are made at random. If one were to make observations every hour on the hour, this would introduce a pattern that might bias the results.

How is a work sampling study conducted?

The observer records what each employee is doing at the instant the employee is observed. The record is made by checking a box under each of a set of previously determined categories. Different categories are used by different companies, but a fairly typical list might be:

Working. This means actually performing work—running a machine, using a tool, entering records, and so forth.

Preparing to Work. Under this heading would come such things as observing a job to determine how to proceed, listening to instructions, and asking questions relative to the job.

Travel. This would include getting tools or supplies and walking or riding to the job in the case of, say, a maintenance worker who is sent out from a central location or a clerk going to and from a copying machine.

Delay. This category is usually for delays for which the employee is not responsible—waiting for materials or waiting for some other worker to finish part of the job.

Idle. This is time for which the worker is responsible—time spent talking (not about the job), "roaming," or simply looking off into space.

Figure 23-3 illustrates a fairly detailed work sampling study of typical clerical operations.

Do employees object to work sampling?

Not usually, if it is properly explained to them beforehand. They should be told that the purpose is not to check up on individual employees but to determine what management can do to make it possi-

WORK SAMPLING STUDY OF CLERICAL EMPLOYEES

Observation Sheet

Name	Random Observation Times								
	9:09	9:57	11:18	1:15	2:43	3:11	3:52	4:21	4:39
Chavez	7	8	1	1	3	5	6	3	1
Yost	2	1	6	4	1	3	7	6	2
Albers	7	4	5	1	8	1	1	3	8
Dowdy	7	8	7	4	1	1	2	1	8
Calabrese	4	1	2	5	7	5	1	4	1

Activity Category Code Numbers
1. Typing
2. Taking dictation
3. Transcribing from machine
4. Clerical activity at desk

5. Away from desk, but in office
6. Talking, telephoning
7. Personal
8. Not in office

Date: 7/21   Supervisor (Observer): F. Diehl

Summary of 990 Observations

Category	Number of observations	Percentage of observations
1. Typing	487	49.2
2. Taking dictation	23	2.3
3. Transcribing from machine	86	8.7
4. Clerical activity at desk	71	7.2
5. Away from desk, but in office	36	3.6
6. Talking, telephoning	68	6.9
7. Personal	113	11.4
8. Not in office	106	10.7

Figure 23-3.

ble for them to work more steadily and effectively. Excessive travel, for example, may show the need for more convenient location of tools and supplies; waiting for other employees may indicate a need for better scheduling. Even if there is excessive idle time because employees are loafing on the job, the supervisor will realize that control must be tightened. Generally, however, sampling shows that the delays for which the employee is not responsible account for the greatest amount of wasted time.

What does methods improvement mean?

Methods improvement is any change in the way things are being done today that will show up in lower cost or better quality in the finished product or service tomorrow. The process of methods improvement is simply the organized use of common sense to find better ways of doing work. You need no stopwatch, no calculator, no motion-picture camera—only pencil, paper, good judgment, patience, and ingenuity.

More specifically, in methods improvement you put an operation, or a given way of doing a job, under close inspection and analysis. You give it this microscope treatment to eliminate every unnecessary step and to find the quickest and best method of performing each of the necessary steps.

For trained analysts, the basis of methods improvement is work measurement or work sampling data.

Is methods improvement known by any other name?

Methods improvement has many names, and it takes many forms. Sometimes it's called work simplification, time-and-motion study, operations analysis, methods engineering, systems engineering, methods and systems (especially in offices), waste reduction, or motion economy. Some people even believe that mechanization and automation are just advanced forms of methods improvement.

Methods improvement is usually effected by observing each minute detail of a job, then analyzing the details for ways to do the job better. That's the kind of methods improvement we'll talk about in this chapter. There are many other approaches (such as using motion pictures to observe and record, time studying, and so forth) that can be, and are, used effectively by methods engineers.

Where do work improvements come from?

Any employee can have a good idea. When a company has a formal suggestion system, one of its main purposes is to provide a channel for handling employees' ideas. If your company does not have a suggestion system, you are the most likely one for an employee to bring suggestions to. Either way, a department whose employees initiate lots of ideas for work improvement makes a supervisor look good.

The best ideas for work improvement, however, are likely to come from first-line management. One authority has estimated that one work-improvement idea from a supervisor is worth ten from another employee. That's because the supervisor has a better overview of the job than a worker does. An astute supervisor can see the forest as well as the trees.

In many companies a methods department is staffed by methods engineers whose job is to simplify and improve work procedures. They help supervisors do a better job of lowering costs. They need your cooperation in spotting cost-cutting targets and in making the improved methods work after they are installed. You should form a habit of working hand in hand with the method department. You can do a lot for them, and they can do much for you.

Are methods improvements limited to manufacturing or production jobs?

By no means. They have been applied by expert and novice alike to such diverse fields as construction, supermarkets, and endless paperwork systems in offices. Lillian Gilbreth, a noted pioneer in work simplification, made great improvements in hospital care by rearranging nurses' stations and by rescheduling food service, housekeeping, and patient care activities.

How do supervisors go about improving their cost and productivity controls?

There are six good ways to chop away at costs and improve productivity. Each approach provides you with a different wedge for getting at the roots of each problem. If one technique won't work, try another—or a combination of two or three.

Reduce Waste. Where can you find waste in raw materials and operating supplies? How about people? Are you wasting their efforts? Are you getting the most from utilities, or are you wasting water, steam, electricity?

Save Time. Can you speed up or double up your equipment? Will time studies show you where time itself can be saved? Are you doing everything you can to get full use of your employees' time?

Increase Output. You can cut cost rates—and improve productivity—by stepping up the amount of work put through your department. Sometimes there's a rhythm that goes with high production that's lost with lower production. Sometimes when you cut back, you need the part-time services of several different people, whereas if you increased output, these same people would be working 100 percent of the time. With the higher output base, cost rates would actually be lower.

Spend Wisely. Cutting costs rarely means that you stop spending. In fact, it's a popular and true expression that you have to spend money to make money. Often top management is more alerted to the need for spending to save during a cost-cutting campaign than at other times. So look for ways to spend money on mechanization or replacement of machines with slow feeds and speeds with newer ones.

Use Space More Intelligently. Space—for storage, manufacturing, and shipping—costs money. This cost goes on whether output is high or low. If you can figure out how to get more use of the same space, you cut costs. Double or triple stacking of pallet loads, for instance, cuts storage charges for space by a half or two-thirds.

Watch Your Inventories. It may make supervisors feel comfortable to know that they have a big backlog of materials and supplies to use or items to be shipped, but this is a very costly feeling. Generally speaking, it's a good idea to stock as little as you can safely get away with, especially if supplies can be purchased and delivered quickly. When using up materials in storage, it's also a good idea to use up the oldest stock first, before it gets soiled, damaged, or obsolete.

What kinds of questions can lead you to find opportunities to improve productivity or cut costs?

Ask challenging questions—questions that probe into every detail. You are probably familiar with Rudyard Kipling's famous poem:

I keep six honest serving men
They taught me all I knew;
Their names are What and Why and When
And How and Where and Who.

This often-quoted poem is your personal key to work simplification. Use it to remind yourself to ask:

● Why is the job done in the first place? Perhaps the job can be cut out altogether. Why is each of the details necessary? Give the third degree to each step. Is it really a must, or is it done "because we've always done it that way"?
● What is done? Have you recorded each detail so that you actually know? When operators pick up a part, for instance, they may not only be picking it up, they may be aligning it for insertion into the machine, or feeling the surface for burrs.
● Where is the detail done? Why is it done at that place? Where could it be done better, faster, more cheaply, more easily?
● When is it done? Why is it done then? When should it be done to do it better, faster, more cheaply, more easily?
● Who does it? Why does this person do it? Who might be better equipped, better trained, have more available time to do it more cheaply?
● How is it done? Why do we do it this way? How could the method be improved by doing two or more operations at once, by mechanizing it, by using a fixture?

Another list of helpful, leading questions follows:

● Has the trend in your department's usage of a particular input been upward over the past months or year? If so, can it be justified by a parallel increase in output? If not, why?
● Are you accepting as "normal" a bottleneck or delay that might be reduced or eliminated if other factors were changed?
● Have you been using and reusing the same work or production schedules for a long period of time? If so, they may be "standardizing" assignments that are no longer appropriate or efficient.
● Do you accept or require the same standards of performance from equipment and/or employees today that you did a year ago? If so, you should check to see if these standards are still operative, or whether or not changes in equipment speeds and capacities, for example, or in specified output requirements for the operation have been decreased or withdrawn.

● Is the *yield*—the extent of usage you get from a given material or supply—the same or greater than it was a year ago? For example, does a gallon of detergent cover the same square footage of wall or floor space that it did previously? If not, is this the result of a less-effective substitute product or of waste in its application?

● Have you observed equipment that is unusually idle recently? Are you accepting too high a degree of unused machine capacity or space anywhere? If so, this represents an input resource that might be used more effectively somewhere else.

● Are you satisfied with how busy your employees presently are? If there are not enough assignments to keep a particular employee fully occupied, are there other places or assignments this human resource can be used more effectively?

● Are there instances where the process flow of work from one desk to another, for instance, backtracks instead of moving smoothly from station to station? Retracing of steps and movements is wasteful.

● Are there instances where the same work is done twice (such as having a verification take place at two different work stations) without good reason? Duplication of effort is a major source of work improvement projects.

● Has there been an increase in errors, mistakes, or service complaints in any of your operating areas? To what can this be attributed? Does it represent a condition that requires a work improvement effort?

● How much time and effort does it take to set up a new job in your department (such as changing over from processing one kind of form to processing another) compared with the length of time that job will be worked on? If it takes half a day to get ready to run a one-day job, that suggests that something could be improved. Slow start-ups or setups, even on routine assignments, are good targets for improvement.

● How much time and effort does it take to put away materials and shut down equipment at the end of a shift or run, compared with the time spent productively on that particular assignment? Overly long shut-down, wash-up, and put-away periods are susceptible to work improvement.

In what phase of a job does the greatest room for improvement lie?

In the operations that actually do something to the product—shape it, change it, add to it in any way that makes it worth more. These operations are called the value-added operations because they add to the value of the product. Look at each job as if it were divided into three steps:

Makeready.   This includes the effort and the time that go into setting up the equipment or the machine or placing the parts in the machine. A painter makes ready to paint a house by mixing the paint, raising the ladder, spreading the drop cloths, and so forth.

Do.   This is the actual work that adds value to the product. A painter adds value to the house by putting a coat of paint on it. A worker adds value to a piece of $\frac{1}{8}$-inch iron rod by cutting it into 2-inch lengths for bolts. Value is added by heading it. And value is added again when threads are cut on the other end.

Put-Away.   This phase covers anything that's done after the "do" is finished. It includes unloading, disposing, storage, transfer, cleanup. The painter puts away by taking down the ladder, removing the drop cloth, cleaning up any spots on the floor, washing the brushes, and storing the materials and equipment.

The reason you're advised to concentrate on a "do" operation is that if you eliminate it, you automatically eliminate the makeready and the put-away associated with it.

How can you develop new and better methods?

Uncovering delays and finding out what's wrong are valuable accomplishments, and their worth shouldn't be minimized. But this effort doesn't pay off until you've devised a better way to do the job. There are many approaches from which to choose:

Eliminate.   First look for the chance of dropping out the detail or the entire operation. There's no point in wasting time improving methods if the job doesn't have to be done at all.

Combine.   Doing two or more things at once saves time. Often it saves additional time by eliminating transportations, storages, and inspections that previously took place between operations.

Change Sequence.   Frequently you can do things more easily or cheaply by changing the order in which they are done. For example, it is best to finish a part only after the shaping operations have been completed.

Simplify.   After you've searched the first three approaches in this list, look for ways of doing the job in a simpler manner. Here's where you try to cut down on waste motions, replace hand operations with mechanical ones, and provide fixtures for positioning and chutes for feeding. But remember, don't try to simplify until you've first tried to eliminate, combine, or change sequence.

In what ways does motion economy help improve productivity?

Motion economy is the use of the human body to produce results with the least physical and mental effort. Figure 21-1 showed its value in designing workplaces. It's been given long study by methods engineers and physiologists. Here are some of the principles of motion economy that are generally agreed on as aids to getting a job done with the least labor.

Motions Should Be Productive.   Every motion a person makes should be concentrated on "do" operations that bring the job closer to a finish. Hands, for instance, should not be wasted in holding the work; they should be released for more value-added operations.

Motions Should Be Simple.   The fewer parts of the body used, the better. Use a finger and a thumb rather than the whole hand. Grasp an object by reaching with the forearm rather than with the whole arm. Motions should be along curved paths rather than straight lines, because most of the body members swing from a joint in a circular motion.

Motions Should Be Rhythmic.   Arrange the work so that it's easy to work with smooth motions. It's easier, too, for hands to move in opposite directions and in similar motion paths.

Make Workers Comfortable.   The workbench, the tool, the chair should all be arranged so that the operator feels comfortable whether the work requires sitting or standing or walking.

Combine Two or More Tools.   Picking up and laying down tools takes time. It's quicker to reverse a tool with a working edge on either end than to pick up and lay down two separate tools.

Pre-Position Tools and Materials.   Having things arranged so that they are already aligned before the operator picks them up speeds the job. If a part needs to be turned over or around, the job needs positioning.

Limit Activity.   A person works comfortably within the swing of the arms forward and up and down. If the person has to reach or stretch beyond that normal work area, turn around, bend, or stoop, it takes time and is fatiguing.

Use Gravity When Possible.   Materials can be fed by gravity through bins and chutes. The part then comes out the bottom of the chute right at the worker's hand each time.

Who takes care of automation?

The highly engineered and/or large-scale approaches to improving productivity are usually the responsibility of engineering specialists and computer systems people. *Automation*—once thought of as simply a form of stepped-up mechanization with a degree of self-control in the process—has exploded in some industries. In fact, hundreds of thousands of fully automatic devices called *robotics* are already in place in hundreds of manufacturing plants. But it is the computer that has made the big difference. It has enabled engineers to look at an entire process—department-sized or even plant-sized—and to tie the scheduling and operation of dozens of separate machines and subprocesses into a whole. When this happens, the term applied is "computer-assisted manufacturing," or "computer-integrated manufacturing," or, sometimes, "data-integrated manufacturing." Productivity gains of better than 50 percent are commonplace as a result of using such automated systems.

Supervisors may or may not have an opportunity to make significant inputs into automation decisions. One thing is sure, however: supervisors are the ones who will be charged with making automation work. As a consequence, supervisors will be expected to ease the problems associated with shop-floor changes, to counsel employees about relocations and displacements, and to train them to handle the new system.

Where does value analysis fit into this picture?

To my way of thinking, value analysis (also called value engineering) is simply methods improvement focused on a product rather than on a process. However, Lawrence D. Miles, who conceived of value analysis while at the General Electric Company in 1947, defined it this way: "Value analysis is an arrangement of techniques which makes clear the functions the user wants; establishes the appropriate costs for each; then causes the required knowledge, creativity, initiative to be used to provide each function at that cost."

Miles's "functions" are of two classes: use and esteem. The use function provides the action that customers want from the product or service. An esteem function pleases them and causes them to buy it. Take an automobile. Use function: transportation. Esteem function: chromium trim.

The objective of value analysis is to keep the use and the esteem functions that customers want—but at a lower cost. Value people do not directly lower cost. They only provide criteria for decision makers (including supervisors) whose actions will lower cost. A value analysis study usually consists of five phases:

1. Gathering information to identify functions.
2. Creating ideas to serve functions at less cost.
3. Evaluating ideas for practicality.
4. Investigating sources of supply and improvement.
5. Reporting findings to decision makers.

Where should you begin your cost-cutting efforts?

Pick the likeliest spots—those that your records show to be out of line with past performance. Be especially critical of operations that show a trend upward. Some costs will naturally be up one month, down the next. These variations may have little substance (although it's worth looking into them to find the causes). Costs that creep steadily out of line might not appear spectacular, but in the long run they hurt most.

One supervisor, in checking cost accounts, noticed that charges for supplies had risen steadily for seven months—up $12.50 one month, up $9 another, up $17 the next, and so forth. Month by month the increases were nothing to get excited about. But in seven months this item had shown a net gain of $98.25 per month! Even if this expense were now to stay constant at the new level, in a year's time the additional expense would total $1,179! What was the cause? Seven months ago the purchasing department had changed the supplier of protective aprons all workers were required to wear because of the danger from acid splashes. The supervisor had heard the employees complaining about the inferior quality of the new aprons but had shrugged it off as just another gripe. Actually, the new aprons were wearing out just a little bit faster than the more expensive kind—but this little bit more inched up until it meant $1,179 per year. How was the situation corrected? The supervisor got together with the purchasing agent and the supplier to find an apron that better suited the conditions in the shop—and as a result brought the operating supplies expenses back into line.

What are some chief criticisms employees have toward cost-cutting or productivity improvement campaigns?

Employees often think that management itself throws away money through poor planning and downright misjudgment as to what's really important—and that applies to supervisors, too.

Here are some typical worker opinions:

"One employee saved the company about $2,000 one day and the next day almost got laid off for turning in 20 minutes overtime."

"We put in a new machine, then ripped it apart and sent it away. It probably cost the company $500 to do it. They waste lots of money by not planning the big things."

"They changed construction of this particular item four or five times, got just short of production, and then the whole thing was called off. What that cost I couldn't even guess!"

Sitting as you do on the management side of the fence, you can understand the reason behind many moves that look wasteful to employees. But the tip-off for you is that the employees frequently don't see the situation the way you do because no one has taken time to make it clear.

Your cue to selling cost reduction is to give employees the facts and help them see that cost cutting (or profit improvement) helps them; it does not work to their disadvantage.

In the face of prevailing employee attitudes, how do you get the need for productivity improvement over to workers?

Remember, the biggest fear of both employees and unions is immediate loss of jobs. If the big picture means only that jobs will be shuffled, not entirely eliminated, emphasize this point. If there must be layoffs, handle the layoff procedure as well as you can. Show all employees who work for you that you'll do your best to protect their job rights (as well as you can in line with the improved methods). Take the lead in talking with employees about to be laid off to be sure they understand how to handle their insurance and hospitalization and how to apply for unemployment. Can you help them with suggestions about where to get another job? Be sure to tell them about their chances of being recalled to work.

What is the best way to get through employee resistance?

Try these five approaches:

1. Talk to employees about cost reduction in terms that are meaningful to them. Get their point of view, or they'll never be able to get yours. In face-to-face conversations, show them how the company's interest in profits is exactly the same as a worker's interest in higher wages and more security. Show that one can't be achieved without the other.

2. Get the cost picture down to earth. Don't talk in global terms of standard costs, of productivity ratios, or even about hard times. If company sales have fallen off, talk in terms of the reduction of specific parts being made in your department: "Where we made 250,000 the first quarter, our schedule calls for only half as much production this quarter." If rising material charges are a factor, pick up a product your employees make and tell them: "Last year, steel for this item cost 55 cents, now it costs 62 cents—a rise of 12 percent."

3. Set specific goals. Don't just say: "We've got to cut costs to the bone." Have a specific program in mind. "Our records show that machine costs have got to be lowered. We'll have to figure a way to use new tools or change our methods to do this." Or, "Scrap cost us $12,000 last month. This month let's get it down below $10,000."

4. Invite participation. Let employees know that you need their help and that help means more than just cooperation. Let them know you'd welcome their ideas on how to go about it.

5. Explain why and how. Reasons for a specific change should be spelled out. Employees need your help, too, in deciding how to accomplish the cost-cutting objectives you set.

How helpful are cost-reduction committees?

Many companies have achieved great results by using cost-reduction committees to spark a cost-reduction campaign. Committees provide lots of chances for participation and tap a big reservoir of people for ideas. If you know others are doing the same thing, it's a boost to your morale.

How good are employee suggestion plans for getting ideas from your employees?

It depends on the company, the way the plan is carried out, and the manner in which the supervisor supports the plan. Some companies have had phenomenal success with plans. Others have been unsuccessful. The National Association of Suggestion Systems reports that on the average you can expect 238 suggestions per year for every 1,000 eligible employees; of these suggestions, about 25 percent will be worth accepting.

To make your company's plan a success, get interested in it. If you adopt a negative attitude, employees will be cool toward the plan, too. Find out what part you play in the plan's administration, and recognize that the degree to which your employees participate will be a measure of how well you stimulate cooperation.

Key Concepts

1. Productivity is akin to efficiency. It compares (a) the value of the product or service produced with (b) the cost of all the resources (labor, materials, equipment) that are used to make the product or provide the service. Productivity and cost controls form the "bottom line" for supervisory performance evaluation.

2. Productivity improvement and cost control are dependent on two inputs: technological factors and human factors. Responsibility for the former is shared by all members of management, whereas the latter is primarily the concern of the first-line supervisors.

3. Supervisors can contribute to the reduction of technological costs by reducing waste of raw materials, supplies, utilities, and floor space and by keeping machinery that is well maintained and operating at its scheduled capacity.

4. Work measurements of the times needed to perform tasks or jobs are typically converted into time or work standards. In turn, these standards form the basis for work schedules, job assignments, wage incentives, budgets, product or service costs, and ultimately a company's pricing structure.

5. The time needed to perform a task is directly related to the way in which the job is performed. The time needed can almost always be reduced through the application of methods-improvement and motion-economy techniques that simplify work procedures and utilize work-assistance devices, tools, and machinery.

Supervisory Word Power

Motion Economy. The selection and use of the human movements that are the quickest, most comfortable, and least fatiguing in performing a particular task.

Productivity. The measure of efficiency that compares the value of outputs from an operation with the cost of the resources used.

Standard Costs. The normal or expected cost of an operation, process, or product (usually including labor, material, and overhead charges), computed on the basis of past performance, estimates, or work measurement.

Work Improvement. Any of many systematic methods of work analysis (especially methods improvement) aimed at finding simpler, faster, less physically demanding ways of accomplishing a given task while at the same time increasing productivity and reducing costs.

Work Measurement. The determination, by systematic and (ideally) precise methods, of the time dimension of a particular task. How much work is there to be done? How long will it take a particular machine or a trained person to do it properly?

Work Sampling. A technique for finding out what proportion of employees' time is used productively on job assignments, compared with the proportion that is not.

Reading Comprehension

1. What two factors determine the productivity measurements of an operation? Why is high productivity better than low productivity?

2. A bank estimated that each transaction handled by a teller contributed 9 cents to the total value of the bank's services. The average teller receives $4.50 per hour and can handle 75 transactions per hour when fully occupied. What is the productivity of the average teller expressed as a ratio? As a percentage?

3. Why is work measurement sometimes called the foundation stone for productivity improvement?

4. How does a predetermined time standard differ from a time study? How are they similar?

5. Why should a supervisor become concerned with a loose time or cost standard?

6. What factors that detract from productivity are likely to be uncovered by a work sampling study?

7. Identify at least four major ways that a supervisor can go about cutting costs and improving productivity. Give examples for each.

8. Why do changeovers from one product or process to another tend to interfere with productivity?

9. Why are employees often suspicious of, or even outrightly hostile toward, productivity improvement and cost reduction programs? What can a supervisor do to minimize these suspicions and hostilities?

10. Compare, for the sake of value analysis, the use function and the esteem function.

Supervision in Action
The Case of Nora Nelson's Cost Overrun. A Case Study in Human Relations Involving Cost Control, with Questions for You to Answer.

Nora Nelson had been a collections supervisor at the Flexible Furnace Company for five years. Nora knew the department's operations from A to Z. When an employee ran into a problem, chances were that Nora would pitch right in. Working alongside the employee, Nora would get him or her out of trouble in no time.

Nora was also known to top management in her company as a person who was willing to cooperate—especially in trying anything new. When the systems people developed a different kind of recording format, they used to say, "If Nora can't make it work, nobody can."

Since the collections department had been looked on as a routine operation, the company had never examined the department closely for costs. But when a new comptroller was hired, every operation—including collections—was put under a magnifying glass. The conclusion was that Nora had gotten sloppy about overtime, use of operating supplies, and misuse of the telephone and copying machine. Consequently, Nora was issued a budget for these items at the beginning of the next month.

At the end of the month, Nora's boss called her into the office. "Nora," the boss said, "in checking over the figures for the collections department this past month, I find you're about 15 percent over budget. Will you see if you can't bring this back into line as soon as you can?"

The following day Nora called her work crew together. "People," she said, "we've got a real problem on our hands. We have an order from the front office to cut costs in our department 15 percent. It means there will be practically no overtime for a while. We'll have to watch how often we renew ribbons, cartridges, and the like. And I want you to keep your use of the telephone and the copying machine to a minimum." Without a dissenting voice, her staff vowed they'd pull together with Nora to make the necessary reductions.

At the end of the next month Nora was again called into her boss's office. "Nora, I hate to keep making an issue about this cost matter. I know that I rarely have to speak to you twice about any problem in the shop. Your collections continue to be good, but the fact remains that your department made no headway whatsoever against costs last month. I'm going to rely on you to make some progress by the end of next month."

Nora again went out to her work group. "Look," she said, "you're putting me in a bad light with the front office. We've got to get these costs under control. So I'm depending on you to give me cooperation."

At the end of that month Nora's department had cut costs approximately 3 percent. But by the end of the following month costs were back to where they were when Nora was first issued a budget. Nora wasn't surprised when she was called on the carpet again. When asked why she had been unsuccessful, her reply was, "I can't understand it. I expected my employees to give me a break. But now I don't know what to do except to get tough."

1. What do you think of Nora's approach to cost cutting?
2. What do you think of Nora's relationship with her employees? Why?
3. If you were Nora, what would you do to get costs back into line?

24

TOWARD A HIGHER QUALITY OF WORKMANSHIP

How much does poor quality cost?

It costs industry billions of dollars each year. It is most obvious in the form of product liability suits (a million claims for a total of $50 billion in damages in a year is not unusual) and manufacturers' recalls to repair defective goods. Billions of dollars are lost to poor quality, however, in two other ways.

Corrective Costs.   This is money down the drain for any of the following: (1) damaged parts and materials that must be scrapped or, at best, reworked; (2) the time and effort of doing poor work over; (3) the cost of warranties that presume errors will be made that must be corrected later; and (4) the cost of handling customer complaints. Corrective quality is by far the most costly—from 2 to 10 percent of sales revenue.

Preventive Costs. These are the costs of trying to prevent poor workmanship or defective goods in the first place. They include routine (1) inspection, (2) testing, and (3) quality-control procedures, including education and motivation programs. It is a rare organization where the costs of preventive quality, however, exceed 3 percent of total sales revenue.

Are quality problems limited to manufacturing plants?

Far from it. Poor workmanship causes costly quality problems in just about every line of work, including clerical. For example, a close watch should be kept on any of the following that applies to your organization:

● **Accounting.** Billing errors, payroll errors, accounts payable deductions missed, percentage of late reports, incorrect computer inputs, and errors in special reports as audited.
● **Data Processing.** Keypunch cards thrown out for error, deductions missed, computer downtime due to error, rerun time.
● **Engineering.** Change orders due to error, drafting errors found by checkers, late releases.
● **Hotel Operation.** Guests taken to unmade or occupied rooms, reservations not honored, inaccurate or missed billing.
● **Marketing and Sales.** Orders or prices written up incorrectly, errors in contract specifications, wrong copy or prices in advertisements and catalogs.
● **Maintenance.** Callbacks on repairs, wrong parts installed, downtime due to faulty maintenance.
● **Retailing.** Wrong product on shelves, incorrect pricing, merchandise damage in handling, storage, or shipping.

Philip B. Crosby, who conceived of Zero Defects, without which the United States would not have put men on the moon, states flatly: "There is no basic difference between manufacturing and service quality management except that one has tangibles as its product and the other does not. *Both require people to perform.*"

Who should have final responsibility for product quality – line supervisor or inspector?

Here's a question that gets plenty of batting around in many companies and has started many feuds between an otherwise successful supervisor and the inspection department. In the long run, responsibility must be fixed by your company's policy and its interpretation by your boss. But there's a long-standing rule of thumb that holds the best answer: Quality must be built into the product. No one can inspect it in.

Actually, few supervisors deny that they are responsible for product quality. The jurisdictional disputes arise over who's the best judge of quality—and who has the authority to stop production when quality falls below specifications. This is something you should try to have your boss make crystal clear for you. Otherwise, chaos will prevail.

Three plant operating executives I know were asked this same question. Here is the gist of each person's answer:

Supervisor's Primary Responsibility. One chief engineer says:

> The quality of a product depends on the coordinated efforts of the people who design and the people who produce. The inspector acts as the last hurdle the product must leap on its way to the customer. Many supervisors still take refuge in the old saw that "our job is to make, it is the inspector's job to inspect." This type of thinking must be rooted out if an organization is to thrive and grow. It is the primary responsibility of the supervisor to turn out work of acceptable quality.

Supervisor's Special Duty. A director of quality control says:

> The supervisor's responsibility for the quality of the department's products is not different from top management's responsibility for the profits of the company.
>
> The inspector's function is in many ways analogous to that of a treasurer. The inspector, like the treasurer, must compare present results against an agreed-to standard and, when the operation is not adhering to specifications, report these facts to the proper parties. This means that the inspector should forward this information to the department supervisor, who must make the decision of accepting or rejecting the questionable product.
>
> The key to quality of product is pride of workmanship, and quality is sharply reduced when the supervisor's duties are transferred to the inspection or quality control personnel.

Sometimes Automatically Controlled. A factory superintendent says:

> In those industries where mechanization and automation have been gone into in a big way, the immediate responsibility for the quality of goods lies primarily with the manager of quality control and the designer of the machinery, because the quality safeguards are (or should be) built into the machine or process. For example, weaving machines or printing presses will stop automatically if a thread is broken or if the paper is not properly lined up. In other plants . . . it is the responsibility of the departmental supervisors to train their operators so as to obtain the desired quality. Following this, the quality of the finished product becomes the responsibility of the supervisor, with the inspection department functioning primarily as the eyes of top management and the ultimate consumer.

What should you do if there is no inspection or quality-control department at your location?

If you make a product, the chances are that there will be an official inspection department somewhere in your organization—even if it doesn't carry on its activity in your department. If such is the case, you might first ask the central inspection department for advice in setting up your own quality checks. If you must go it alone or if yours is a service operation, however, try this analysis of your quality problem:

● What is my inspection problem? What do I have to do to maintain quality?
● Shall I assign the inspection to someone as a part-time or a full-time job?
● Shall I do the inspecting myself? If so, how much time can I devote to it?
● Should I try to inspect all the work produced or only a sample of it? Or should I confine myself to the first piece on a new setup only?

Once you have considered these questions and decided on your approach, you can proceed to the next question.

How can you make your own checks of quality?

Keep in mind these ten points:

1. Set up some specific quality standards, such as dimensions and appearance. Keeping examples of acceptable and nonacceptable work on exhibit helps.

2. Put specifications in writing. See that your employees get a copy to guide them.

3. Allocate some of your own time for inspection. The total amount isn't so important as doing a certain amount each day.

4. Pick the spots where quality can best be made or lost. There is no point in spending your time checking operations where nothing much can go wrong.

5. Make inspection rounds from time to time. Change the order of your trips frequently.

6. Select at random 5 or 10 percent of the pieces produced (for example, letters typed) at a particular station. Inspect each one carefully.

7. Correct operating conditions immediately where your inspection shows material to be off grade or equipment to be faulty.

8. Consult with employees to determine the reason for poor workmanship or unacceptable products. Seek their cooperation in correcting conditions and improving quality.

9. Check the first piece on a new setup or a new assignment. Don't permit production until you are satisfied with the quality.

10. Post quality records, scrap percentages, and so forth, keep employees informed of the department's performance.

How can you get employees more interested in quality?

It's been popular to complain about the I-don't-care attitude of some employees. Your viewpoint should be that if employees don't care about quality, it's because you have failed to sell them on its importance.

To get a worker to become quality-conscious, start right from the first day by stressing quality as well as output. Emphasize that the two must go hand in hand in your department. Whenever you show an employee how to do a job—especially a new one—be specific as to what kind of work is acceptable and what kind will not meet specifications. Explain the reason behind product quality limitations, and try to give your employees the little tricks of the trade that help to make quality easy to attain.

Why do employees make errors?

Generally speaking, there are six reasons why employees make mistakes—and most of them begin with management inadequacies rather than with employee shortcomings. Experience of companies who have improved their quality shows these potential causes of errors:

- Lack of training
- Poor communications
- Inadequate tools and equipment
- Insufficient planning
- Incomplete specifications and procedures
- Lack of attention

Poor communications, for example, can be overcome by taking the extra time to make sure each person fully understands the instructions. In written orders, don't leave loopholes that can lead to misinterpretation. One small company with a large staff of Spanish-speaking people had the workers repeat the orders that were given to them. It took a few minutes, but it actually saved time. Rejects and rework tumbled to a fraction of 1 percent.

Lack of attention, however, is completely different from the other potential causes of error and is perhaps the most serious. This is very personal and stems from employees' attitudes. You must reaffirm that management is interested in employees and will help them do their jobs to perfection. You, as a supervisor, must re-create the old-fashioned pride in one's craft. You must motivate employees so that they have a personal attachment to their jobs and will be proud of them.

It isn't all the employees' fault, of course. Quality experts, for example, observe that auto defects occur five major ways:

- A flaw in design that doesn't show up in testing
- A flaw in purchased or manufactured materials or parts
- A flaw in the manufacturing process itself
- A flaw in the tools and gauges provided
- A flaw introduced by sloppy workmanship or instructions that are not fully understood

What can you do to help employees understand that the customer is the real quality boss?

Try to provide employees with a customer's-eye view of your product. Workers who handle the same product every day tend to lose their objectivity. They begin to take minor defects for granted. To help them see the product as the customer does, get samples of customer complaints (about specific defects) and circulate them in your department. Explain how the customer uses your product—how it will be compared with a competitor's unit and how quality will affect its use. At an Ohio plant, supervisors and workers are selected to attend training sessions held for distributor salespeople. Employees hear at first hand the reasons for some of the things they do. "Our sales story really opened my eyes. I didn't realize what it takes to sell a pump," said one shop steward after attending the sales course. The net effect was a greater interest in high quality and lower costs.

At the plant of a manufacturer of small airplanes, where damage to aircraft bodies during production is a hazard, this approach is used to stimulate care among operators: "You wouldn't buy an $800 refrigerator with a patch on the door. Would you expect one of our customers to take a $1 million plane with a 2-inch patch on it?"

Probably nothing is more dramatic in a painful and costly fashion than when a company issues a recall to the owners of its products so that a defect can be corrected. Whereas the auto manufacturers get the full impact of the publicity (26 million autos were recalled in the first six years after the United States government cracked down on auto safety), many other firms in other industries have faced the same problem. For example, *The New York Times* cited on one day the following recalls:

● The electrical manufacturer who called back pacemaker heart machines with mechanical defects
● The major candy maker who recalled 4,000 fruitcakes with moth eggs in them
● The 20,000 tins of crab meat that went out with the wrong labels
● The thousands of cases of a soft drink that were ordered back because of contaminated lids
● The callback of the thousands of bottles of pharmaceuticals that went out with faulty caps

The granddaddy of all recalls occurred in October 1978, when Firestone Tire and Rubber Company announced its recall of 10 million steel-belted radial tires at a cost to the company of $230 million.

When things go wrong with quality or workmanship in your department, what steps do you take?

Supervisors at an Industrial Management Institute of the University of Wisconsin agreed on these 12 checkpoints for action:

1. Do you explain to each worker exactly what quality is expected on the job?
2. When work is rejected, do you make sure that the workers con-

cerned know what is wrong and exactly what is expected of them?

3. Have you a plan of close cooperation (for the purpose of improving quality) with the supervisor of the department from which your work comes and the supervisor of the department to which your work goes?

4. Do you get, or make, a list of all the defective work in your department each week or month so you can take definite steps to prevent similar defective work during the next period?

5. Do you set aside a definite amount of your own time for actual inspection of the work in your department?

6. Do you have a system for getting suggestions from your workers on how to improve quality?

7. Do you hold regular talks with each of your workers regarding the quality of the work that person is doing?

8. Are you making full and effective use of departmental bulletin boards for posting facts about quality and defective work and for exhibiting examples of good or bad work?

9. Do you keep your workers informed on the cost of defective work in your department?

10. Do you have any method for arousing pride of workmanship in your employees?

11. Have you systematically acquainted each worker with the relation between quality workmanship and job security?

12. Do your employees understand the value placed on quality performance when they are considered for raises or promotions?

If you can answer yes to most of these questions, you'll find that quality troubles will stay away from your door.

What is meant by statistical quality control?

Statistical quality control simply means that numbers—statistics —are used as a part of the overall approach for controlling quality. Statistics are tools and in no way relieve supervisor or employee from a concern with quality. Used properly, however, they can be of considerable aid.

In many industries, only the techniques of statistical quality control would make rigid specifications economically attainable. For example, J. C. Penney Co., Inc., orders millions of knitted garments each year. It uses various inspection and statistical methods to screen the thousands of samples submitted to the company for purchase. As a consequence, the company rejects 30 percent of the submissions, thus preventing subsequent disasters at the sales counters.

What are some of the tools of statistical quality control, and how do they affect the supervisor's job?

Greatly increased demands for precision parts have stepped up the need for better methods to measure and record the accuracy with which manufacturing people meet product specifications. Statistical methods speed up this measuring process, and more and more companies use them in some form or other. Don't let any fear you may have of mathematics prevent your using statistical methods.

Three statistical quality-control tools are encountered most commonly:

1. Frequency-Distribution Charts. Hold on. It isn't as bad as it sounds. Probably you'll recognize it by its more popular name—a tally card. If you were asked to place an *X* in the appropriate space for every shaft diameter you gauged in a given lot, chances are that you'd come up with a tally that looks something like Figure 24-1.

In this case the nominal shaft diameter was 0.730 inch with a tolerance of ±0.002. This tally gives you a picture of just what and where the shaft variations are instead of merely recording whether a shaft is good or bad. This frequency-distribution chart (or histogram) helps tell you the causes of the variation. The wide distribution in this case indicates tool wobble. A picture that showed parts bunched around

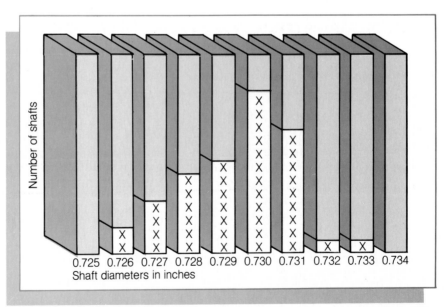

Figure 24-1. Simple frequency-distribution chart (or histogram) used in statistical quality control.

a point below or above the nominal 0.730 inch (say, at 0.728) might mean that the setup must be adjusted.

2. Quality-Control Chart. This is an hour-by-hour, day-by-day graphic comparison of actual product quality characteristics. On the chart are limits that reflect the person's or the machine's ability to produce, as shown by past experience. Statisticians make use of the knowledge of shop tolerances and analysis of previous frequency distribution tallies to establish these limits. Whenever the inspections plotted on the control chart show that the product is getting outside the predicted control limits, that's a signal for the supervisor or the operator to correct what is being done so that the product comes back into specification.

In Figure 24-2, the part being made is supposed to measure 0.730 inch. The tolerance specs are ±0.002, or from 0.728 to 0.732 inch. The quality-control statistician has predicted in advance from a frequency-distribution diagram that most production will vary within these control limits—the 0.7285 and 0.7315 lines. When quality stays within these limits, it is said to be on the highway. It is to be expected that a few products will fall outside the limits into the

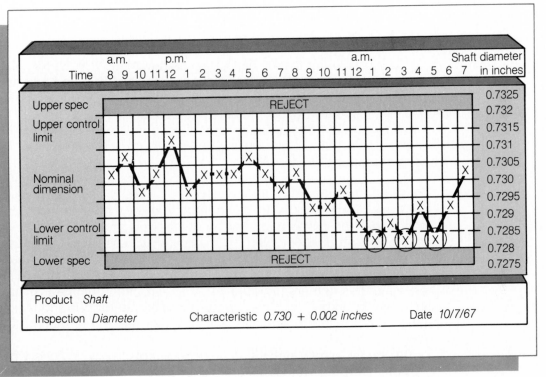

Figure 24-2. Quality-control chart.

shoulder. But when the trend of measurements indicates that product quality is drifting progressively into the shoulder area, it's time to check the process. Any product that goes beyond the upper or lower specification limits (goes into the ditch) is rejected.

The value of the chart lies in its telling the supervisor and the operator whether they are within bounds or whether they are losing control of the process, before the process goes completely haywire.

3. Sampling Tables. The trend today has been away from 100 percent inspection, which is costly and often misleading. (In a 100 percent check of a load of oranges, does this mean that each orange has been inspected for color, ripeness, thickness of skin, appearance? Or does it mean that each orange was inspected for appearance only?) The first solution to less than 100 percent checking was spot-checking, but this proved unreliable. Today most sampling is done according to the size of the lot of goods produced and according to tables designed by statisticians for this purpose. These sampling tables guide the quality-control manager in the determination of how large a sample to take and how often to take it.

Is there a connection between reliability and statistical quality control?

Yes, indirectly, and it often has a direct relationship to product liability claims. Reliability is defined as the probability of a product's performing a specific function, under given conditions, for a specified time, without failure. It must measure up specifically, therefore, to (1) what it's supposed to do (for example, for a bolt to hold 500 pounds of direct pull); (2) the circumstances under which it will be used (as at temperatures up to 185°C in an acid atmosphere); and (3) the length of time it should perform before it breaks or stops working (as for 25,000 fastenings or 39 months). Reliability can be determined either by direct test (using it until it fails) or by statistical computation (based on assumptions about the design and work characteristic of the product). Reliability is usually expressed as the (mean) time expected between failures—as, say, 1/0.002 or 500 hours. Because the assumptions made vary in the degree of confidence the estimator has in them, reliability figures are often qualified as having, say, 85 percent confidence (or being 85 percent sure to last as long as predicted but having a 15 percent risk of not lasting that long).

Reliability enters statistical quality-control considerations when you are deciding on the limits of variation, on how far from standard the product can be without being rejected. Obviously, the tighter the variable limits, the greater the reliability of the product. However, this does not mean that a perfect part will be reliable forever. It will be reliable only as long as it was designed to be under the specified operating conditions.

How important is nondestructive testing?

Increasingly so. The more valuable the product, the more important it is to test that product without destroying it. The farmer who candles eggs to be sure they are fresh is practicing nondestructive testing. Similarly, the company that x-rays a casting to see that it has no flaws is employing nondestructive testing. The principle of nondestructive testing is to make sure that your product is free of flaws without tearing it apart to find out.

The most common of all nondestructive tests is radiography, or, more simply, the use of X rays. Also widely used are sound waves, temperature flow patterns, magnetic fields, liquid penetrating dyes that show flaws under ultraviolet light, and eddy currents induced by high-frequency alternating currents.

What is Zero Defects?

It's the approach to quality that put an American on the moon. It was conceived by Philip Crosby at about the time that everything that could go wrong with the United States space program did go wrong. What Crosby did was to remove the emphasis on statistical quality control and expert quality monitors and place the responsibility for quality in the hands of the employees. Zero Defects (ZD) stresses personal motivation. It attempts to instill in each individual a pride in his and her work. It was the first quality program to put quality on a personal basis. ZD techniques are aimed at stimulating everyone involved to care about accuracy and completeness, to pay attention to detail, to improve work habits. In this manner we work toward reducing our own errors to zero.

Most other quality programs at that time attempted control by rejecting work that didn't measure up to minimum standards. Zero Defects reversed this philosophy. It aims for consistently high-quality products by eliminating all errors made by all the people designing, producing, selling, and servicing the item.

ZD programs anticipated what lawyers have learned from product liability suits: Defective goods can arise from errors and poor workmanship anywhere along the line.

What made ZD work so well?

ZD got results for a variety of reasons. The main ones, in my opinion, were as follows:

1. A Strict and Specific Management Standard. Management, including the supervisory staff, did not use vague phrases to explain what it wanted. It made the quality standard very clear: Do it the right way from the start. As Philip Crosby says, "What standard would you set on how many babies nurses are allowed to drop?"

2. Complete Commitment by Everyone. Interestingly, Crosby denies that ZD was a motivational program, but ZD did work because everyone got deeply into the act. From sweeper to clerk, everyone was encouraged to spot problems, detect errors, and prescribe ways and means for their removal. This commitment is best illustrated by the ZD pledge: "I freely pledge myself to make a constant, conscious effort to do my job right the first time, recognizing that my individual contribution is a vital part of the overall effort."

3. Removal of Actions and Conditions That Cause Errors. Philip Crosby claims that at ITT, where he was vice president for quality, 90 percent of all error causes can be acted on and fully removed by first-level supervision. In other words, top management must do its part to improve conditions, but supervisors and employees can handle most problems right in the department.

If ZD was so good, what's all the excitement now about Quality Circles?

If you agree with the participative aspect of ZD, then you'll probably agree that the Quality Circles movement is the next logical step forward. Both kinds of programs are based on the belief that quality cannot be produced or controlled by a single individual or department. Both programs conceive of quality as the result of dozens, perhaps hundreds, of interactions. These take place between the designer and the manufacturing department, between manufacturing and purchasing, between sales and production, between the keypunch operator and the computer programmer, and so on and on. In technical terms, quality is the end result of a complex system. With Quality Circles, quality is accepted as a starting point (as with ZD) and *then* concludes that only by bringing together the people who are directly involved in the system will the obstacles that block good quality and error-free performance be removed.

Quality Circles were conceived of by an American statistician, W.

Edwards Deming (abetted by Joseph M. Juran, a noted quality consultant) and introduced in Japan in the 1950s. Gradually, firms in the United States, such as General Motors and Westinghouse Electric Corp., got wind of the idea. These companies formed small groups of 10 to 15 employees to meet regularly to examine and suggest solutions to common problems of quality. By 1980, the number of U.S. firms using these circles grew to more than 200. Circles are found just about anywhere, in small companies as well as large, in hospitals as well as banks, in government agencies, and in offices as well as factories.

How does a Quality Circle operate?

Since the Quality Circle (QC) concept is based on maximum—and voluntary—involvement of employees from top to bottom of an organization, the QC programs are almost always initiated at the executive level. If the program doesn't get all-out support at that level, it probably won't work at any level. Next, the QC idea is fanned out into the total organization. It is typically spear-headed by a "facilitator" or "coordinator." That person helps to organize the departmental and interdepartmental circles. He or she also provides the necessary training in problem and opportunity identification and in methods improvement and problem solving.

Each circle is made up exclusively of volunteers, who meet on company time. They place personnel and labor relations problems off limits. Also prohibited are discussions about the performance or lack of performance of specific individuals. Ralph J. Barra, manager of the Westinghouse QC program, says that "a new circle will focus on simple workplace problems. Early achievements build confidence and experience." Later on, the circle will tackle more ambitious problems, ones that extend beyond its own control and involve other departments and other circles. As its expertise grows, the circle will shift gears from problem-solving to problem-preventing.

Is quality the only focus of QC?

It started that way, but most circles have found that quality is inevitably tangled up with every imaginable kind of operating problem. As a consequence, most circles will turn their attention to any troublesome problem. And most organizations with a QC program cite example after example of productivity improvement.

You may have observed by now that all quality improvement

approaches have much in common with productivity and cost improvement programs. There is a great deal of overlap. Many of the techniques of quality improvement have been borrowed from work simplification, for example. The reason for these similarities is that at the heart of all improvement programs are problem solving and decision making, as discussed in Chapter 9. The QC movement makes special use of all the approaches associated with problem solving, as shown in Figure 24-3. It does more, however. QCs utilize what appear to be the common truths of motivation, group dynamics, Theory Y, System 4, and participation that can lead an employee or group of employees to try harder. Employees try harder in a QC because the work itself is more challenging and fulfilling. QCs not only improve quality and productivity, they also improve the quality of employees' work life.

In what way is good housekeeping related to the quality of workmanship?

It is very hard to do good work in a sloppy shop. This applies to any kind of work, from assembling precision instruments to pouring white-hot iron in a foundry, from preparing purchase orders in a warehouse to sorting canceled checks in a bank. The insistence on neatness and cleanliness at the workplace also tells employees that the supervisor expects neatness and orderliness in their work.

At one Westinghouse plant, for instance, the QC program produced the side-effects of an end to washroom vandalism and graffiti and generally better housekeeping throughout.

Why are so many employees untidy in their work habits?

Neatness and cleanliness do not come naturally to most of us. Employees often feel that if they are working hard, the mess they create while doing so is justified. Supervisors sometimes feel the same way. This is a mistake. Supervisors need to be sold on the value of good housekeeping before they can sell it to their employees, and then they must persuade employees that good housekeeping is a basic part of their jobs.

Won't employees resent having to do their own cleanup?

Some will. They will protest that housekeeping is menial work, that they are depriving the sweepers of their rightful jobs, or that they aren't paid to clean. Each of these objections must be met with the

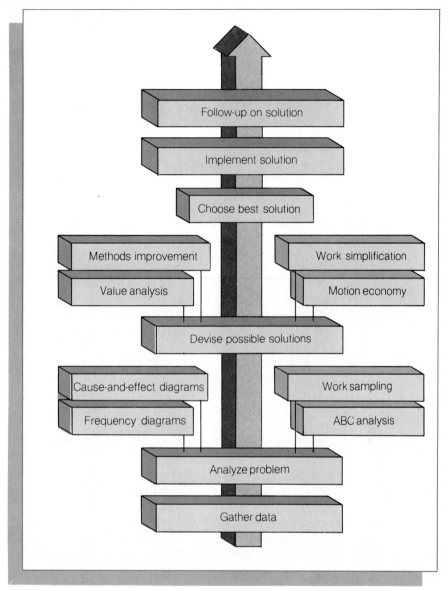

Figure 24-3. Problem solving in quality circles.

facts. Housekeeping need not be menial. Good care of the work-place has always been associated with craftmanship. It is a founda-tion stone in apprentice training.

Improved personal housekeeping has deprived few custodial em-ployees of a job. Usually it has enabled the custodial workers to become more effective and to show better results from their efforts.

As to housekeeping being part of the worker's job, formal job descriptions usually include "care of the workplace."

Many workers have pack-rat tendencies, too. They accumulate an unbelievable collection of junk at their workplace, if permitted. A certain amount of this should be left to the worker's own discretion—if it is kept neatly. But you should discourage collection of candy or food wrappers and old newspapers and magazines.

Poor housekeeping in the company is the result of poor work habits that have been tolerated by management—primarily the supervisor. The supervisor is the primary person in the drive to change these habits.

How can you sell a housekeeping program?

Housekeeping has many personal payoffs for those who practice it. When you are talking about better housekeeping to employees, don't present it in terms of just something the boss wants—"We'll be hassled if it isn't improved." Instead, show workers how good housekeeping improves the safety record and makes the department a safer place for employees to work. Emphasize that housekeeping actually makes production easier, quicker, and more accurate and that clean and neat surroundings take much of the drudgery out of work—and keep clothing cleaner, too.

Nothing is so convincing to employees as a demonstration of what good housekeeping is—and what it can do for them. Many people are puzzled when told to clean up. Each person has his or her own standards of what "clean" is, and these standards differ widely. So take a section of your department and see that it is arranged and cleaned to a minimum of what you judge can be maintained by your regular work force. Don't overlook anything—from wiping out the inside of lamp fixtures to stacking boxes squarely. Then gather your employees together so they can see what you consider good housekeeping. Let them see if you've missed anything, make suggestions, or protest standards they think are unattainable. Then hold them to the accepted standard.

Key Concepts

1. The cost of correcting defects and errors is high compared with the cost of preventing poor quality in the first place. Concerns for quality extend far beyond manufactured products into every kind of service provided.

2. Whereas quality must represent a total effort of all functions combined—design, materials purchasing, manufacturing or operations, and inspection—it is the first-line supervisor who is in the key spot to see that quality is built into the product or service as it is being produced.

3. Employees will work at higher levels of craftsmanship if they are properly trained; are equipped with the right tools, specifications, and instructions; and are highly motivated.

4. The concepts of Zero Defects and Quality Circles have been especially effective, since they illustrate that most errors of workmanship can be eliminated if each individual is properly motivated and supported throughout the entire organization.

5. Good housekeeping should be an essential part of every job. It is a contributing factor to good quality of workmanship. It, too, is dependent on proper employee education, well-defined and well-enforced standards, and motivation.

Supervisory Word Power

Acceptable Quality Levels.   AQL is a more general form of specification that tells a supervisor the kind of tolerance (in terms of percentage of rejects, extent of rework, number of defects, number of customer complaints, frequency of stockouts, extent of delays in service) limiting what will be judged as acceptable performance.

Defect.   Any variation (in the product or service) from specifications that falls outside the prescribed tolerances and thus causes (1) the product to be rejected, discarded, or reworked or (2) a service to be interrupted, declined, or delayed.

Rework.   To remanufacture, do over, adjust, modify, or otherwise repair a product or a service that has been rejected because of a defect.

Specification.   The definitions (preferably written) of expected performance of a product (or quality of a service), usually stated in finite measurements of size, shape, finish, durability, and so forth.

Tolerance.   Essentially a statement of precision that establishes limits within which the product or the service must meet the specification; for example, a machined part specified to be 1 inch in diameter with a tolerance of ±0.005 inch.

Reading Comprehension

1. Compare a line supervisor's responsibility for quality with that of an inspector.

2. The quality of the product is just as important—and just as variable—for nonmanufacturing workers such as keypunch operators, supermarket checkout clerks, bricklayers, bank tellers, waitresses, and file clerks as it is in the factory. What kinds of errors or defects might be detected in each of these jobs?

3. In the absence of an inspection department, how should a supervisor proceed to ensure the quality of the products the department produces?

4. How does statistical quality control differ from inspection?

5. In what way does statistical quality control depend on a reliability determination?

6. How good an idea is it for supervisors to conduct some of the inspections and tests themselves?

7. Besides poor workmanship, what are some of the things that can contribute to defects and errors?

8. In what way are Zero Defects programs and Quality Circle programs alike?

9. What is it about the Quality Circle approach that enables employees to contribute to the quality of their own work life?

10. Compare the housekeeping typists might be expected to do at their workplace with that of custodial workers who come to the office each evening.

Supervision in Action
The Case of the No-Fault Quality Problem. A Case Study in Human Relations Involving Quality Control, with Questions for You to Answer.

Jane Ryan, plant manager for Izod Precision Instruments Company, was puzzled. The plant had a sophisticated statistical quality-control program. Its suppliers of parts and materials were subjected to rigorous receiving inspections. Izod's employees were well paid and well trained and appeared to be well motivated. Despite all this, however, the plant's defects record had slowly deteriorated. The number of units that did not pass final inspection had steadily risen. Worse still, Izod had received a number of complaints from aircraft companies that used the plant's products in their instrument panels. In fact, Izod was facing a lawsuit. A leading commercial airlines was suing Izod for $5 million, charging that a malfunction in one of this plant's instruments had been a contributing factor in a landing crash that had killed three passengers and injured seven others.

Jane called her key supervisors into her office to review the situation with them and to get their suggestions. After outlining the problem, several supervisors volunteered opinions.

"All I can say, Jane," said Will Smith, supervisor of the machine shop, "is that the problem isn't in my shop. We have complete control. Our stuff meets inspection 100 percent."

Marie LaRoque, supervisor of the plating department, said, "I don't think the people in my department can be blamed. As you know, everything we get to plate has been okayed by the receiving inspectors. And everything we do is run through the automatic testing machine before it goes to the assembly operation."

Jack Gruber quickly spoke up. "Well, it's not in assembly. We double- and triple-check everything before it goes to final test."

Jane thought for a moment and then said, "If the fault doesn't lie in the producing departments, it must have something to do with our inspection procedures."

Al Brown, the chief inspector, looked up. "Hey, wait a minute, gang. Our job in inspection is to tell it like it is. We can't inspect quality into the product. We check everything against product specs. Incoming material seems to be all right. Inspections at each major point in the process are coming out okay. But at final test, it falls apart. The problem must lie in the design and inspection specs."

Everyone at the meeting turned to the engineering manager, Charles Ruiz. "You are getting the runaround, Jane," Charles said. "Those specs have been proved out thousands of times. Every machine, fixture, tool, and inspection device is capable of turning out 99.9 percent acceptable product—if, and it is a big if, employees in each department follow them carefully. The in-process inspections can't catch everything that could go wrong with a part. It's after everything has been assembled and the completed instrument put on the test block that we're finding the problems. My guess is that each of you supervisors is really only working toward passing the 'set' inspections. You and your employees cut corners on everything else. That's not error-free production. That's simply going through the motions."

Every supervisor tried to speak at once.

"I'm the most quality-minded guy in the plant," said Will Smith.

"The plating operation is almost completely machine-controlled," said Marie LaRoque.

"We put the stuff we get together right. We can't rework what's been done wrong elsewhere," said Jack Gruber.

"Inspection and test just does its job. The rest of you will have to straighten this out," said Al Brown.

"It's a proved fact that the design and inspection specs are all right," said Charles Ruiz.

Jane Ryan said nothing. She was now more puzzled than ever.

1. What do you think might be the real cause of the quality problem? Why?
2. Which supervisor or manager seems most at fault? Why? Which seems least at fault? Why?
3. What suggestions can you make to Jane to help her solve the quality problem at Izod?

PART

7

LEGAL CONCERNS OF SUPERVISION

T he law of the United States clearly separates supervisors from the people they supervise. In all areas of direct contact with employees, supervisors are declared to be, unequivocally, in the managerial chain of command. In three vital areas in particular, however, supervisors are not only the implementers and guardians of the law, they are also uniquely placed to see that the spirit of the law contributes to the opportunity, well-being, and harmony of employees entrusted to their supervision. The purpose of chapters in this part, then, is to enable supervisors:

● To grasp the intentions and the ramifications of legislation that guarantees equal employment opportunities so as to be able to implement these laws properly.
● To acquire the knowledge and skills needed to educate the work force in accident-free practices and to enforce standards of safe conduct.
● To comprehend the basic labor management laws so as to safeguard management prerogatives and maintain harmonious union relationships.

Highlights of supervisors' reactions to areas of legal concern

Supervisors seem to take the legal aspects of their jobs in stride. They appear relatively free from bias against minorities or labor unions. All in all, they do not devote an inordinate amount of their time and attention to legal concerns, or even as much as one might wish in safety matters.

Attitudes Toward Treatment of Minorities

With only a few exceptions, survey figures indicate a rather progressive attitude toward all classes of minorities. Here is how supervisors responded to this key question: For each kind of minority employee listed below, how would you describe your company's treatment of that group? Check the phrase that best describes that treatment.

	Treated More Harshly Than Others (%)	Treated Same as Others (%)	Given Special Treatment (%)	Not Applicable (%)
Older workers	3	83	11	2
Younger workers	4	91	4	2
Black workers	3	74	14	9
Female workers	4	82	10	3
Hispanic workers	1	71	8	20

Only the opinions of engineering-oriented and government supervisors differ much from these averages. Percentages for these two groups expressing "special treatment" bias were 21 and 25 for women, 29 and 33 for blacks, and 17 and 26 for Hispanics.

The Safety Issue

Observers might infer that safety is only a minor problem. When asked to rank the time and attention spent on safety-related matters, supervisors ranked it near the bottom of their priorities, 14th out of 16. Paradoxically, however, supervisors ranked their confidence in enforcing OSHA regulations 15th in a list of 18 skills. The low rankings in each case may be attributed somewhat to the views of white-collar supervisors, 16 percent of whom said that safety "didn't apply" to them!

Labor Relations

About 42 percent of all blue-collar supervisors surveyed, and only 14 percent of white-collar ones, said they supervised employees represented by a labor union. On average, 77 percent of those whose employees were unionized said that relationships with the shop steward were "good." Some 20 percent reported them as "fair," and only 3 percent said they were "poor." It is hoped that supervisors have learned to live amicably with the union without sacrificing their management rights.

CHAPTER

25

EQUAL EMPLOYMENT OPPORTUNITIES FOR ALL

I n the eyes of the law, who is a minority employee?

Just about anyone who is not a middle-aged white male of European heritage and the beneficiary of a fairly adequate primary education. Minorities include blacks, Mexican Americans, Spanish-speaking Americans, American Indians, women (white as well as black), disadvantaged young persons, handicapped workers, and persons over 40 years of age. The basic equal employment opportunity laws say that an employer cannot discriminate against a person because of race, religion, sex, national origin, or age. In trying to make these laws work, various agencies of the United States government have interpreted them to apply to all victims of prejudice and discrimination, especially those who are undereducated and have grown up in extreme poverty such as occurs in many ghettos and rural areas.

What has caused this concern for minorities today? Hasn't America always been a land of struggle as well as opportunity for the latest wave of immigrants?

Great social forces at work in the past 30 years have altered the values of many people. Family lifestyles and marriage patterns have radically changed. A great many people enjoy relatively affluent living. This makes for harsh comparisons with those who do not have jobs or are relegated to second-class work and often second-class pay. The power of television and instant communications intensifies the awareness of these differences. People—especially those who believe that their second-class status is the result of discrimination—are impatient for improvement. The newer laws are a direct expression of the public's general dissatisfaction with these conditions and its wish to provide equal employment opportunities.

What is the legal basis for equal employment opportunity programs?

There's no reason for you to be bogged down with the details, but for reference purposes here are the major laws with a brief description of their main points.

The *Equal Pay Act* (June 1963) amended the long-standing Fair Labor Standards Act of 1938 to require the same pay for men and women doing the same work.

Title VII of the Civil Right Act (1964) is the biggie. It prohibits employers, unions, and employment agencies from discrimination (race, sex, or national origin) in hiring; in wages, terms, conditions, and privileges of employment; in classifying, assigning or promoting, and extending or assigning use of facilities; and in training, retraining, and apprenticeship.

Executive Orders 11246 and 11375 prohibit discrimination in employment for organizations having contracts of $10,000 or more with the federal government. They require that these organizations institute affirmative action programs. Specifically, these contractors—and there are hundreds of thousands of them, including almost all large organizations—cannot:

- Make any distinctions based on race, sex, or national origin in any conditions of employment, including fringe benefits and pension plans.
- Distinguish between married and single people of one sex and not the other.
- Deny employment to women with young children unless the same policies apply to men with young children.
- Penalize women because they require time away from work for childbearing.
- Maintain seniority lists based solely on sex or race.
- Deny a woman the right to a job for which she is qualified even though the state may have "feminine protective legislation."

In 1971 the United States Supreme Court ruled in the *Griggs* vs. *Duke Power* case that if any employment practices or tests had an adverse (or differential) effect on minorities, the employers were guilty until they proved themselves innocent. In other words, if a test or a requirement (no matter how well intended it is, such as the requirement of a high school diploma) actually screened out minorities, it had to be shown indisputably that it was related to successful performance on the job. A company that requires a high school diploma for a floor sweeper's job, for example, would probably be in trouble. Based on this decree, the government said that exceptions could be made only if the company could prove that discriminatory selection practices were truly related to the job, that is, bona fide occupational qualifications (BFOQ). These are discussed in Chapter 11 and later in this chapter.

Revised Order IV (1971) strengthened equal employment opportunity guidelines to require that contractors (1) analyze their work force to determine whether women are underemployed and (2) set numerical goals and timetables by job classification and organizational unit to correct any deficiencies. This order was tested by the landmark AT&T consent decree of 1973, in which the nation's largest employer agreed to make fundamental changes in personnel policies and to promote women as well as men into jobs from which they were traditionally excluded.

The *Age Discrimination in Employment Act* (1967) forbids discrimination against workers 40 to 64 years old in hiring, firing, promoting, classifying, paying, assigning, advertising, or eligibility for union membership.

The *Rehabilitation Act* (1973), especially Section 503, requires employers with a federal contract of $2,500 or more to take affirmative action to hire and promote handicapped persons.

The *Vietnam Era Veteran's Readjustment Assistance Act* (1974) requires certain affirmative action in the employment of veterans.

How about the handicapped?

The *Rehabilitation Act of 1983* is designed to improve employment opportunities for disabled people. The Act requires employers with more than $2,500 in federal contracts or subcontracts to take "affirmative action" in hiring and promotion of those considered handicapped. The law further requires employers receiving grants and other federal financial assistance to be "nondiscriminatory" in considering disabled people for employment. The law defines disabled people as individuals who (1) have a physical or mental impairment (the term "impaired" is preferred by many) which substantially limits one or more major life activities, (2) have a record of such impairment, or (3) are regarded as having such impairment. So you can see that the definition is almost all-encompassing.

What is meant by affirmative action?

In enforcing the provisions of equal employment opportunity laws, the Equal Employment Opportunity Commission (EEOC) has encouraged firms to engage in *affirmative action programs.* When these firms are handling federal contracts, the EEOC insists that they engage in such programs. Affirmative action programs consist of positive action taken to ensure nondiscriminatory treatment of all groups that are protected by legislation that forbids discrimination in employment because of race, religion, sex, age, or national origin. These programs emphasize that results count, not good intentions. If company statistics on pay or promotion, for example, show that the current status of minority groups is inferior to that of most other employees in that company or geographic area, the company may be directed to set up an affirmative action program. Companies with federal contracts over $50,000 and with more than 50 employees have no choice. They must have a written program in good operation.

Obviously, equal employment opportunity legislation was designed to protect minority groups of all definitions from discrimination and specifically to encourage more rapid utilization of blacks and women in the work force. Note that the law is not a labor-management law: It is directed at employers, and they must comply without obstruction by a labor union, if one is present.

Do the new laws make it illegal for your company to refuse to hire members of a minority group?

Yes, if you do not hire them because of the color of their skin or because of their religion. The equal opportunity law (Title VII of the Civil Rights Act of 1964) actually goes further than that. It prohibits employers in interstate commerce from discriminating against job applicants because of race, color, sex, religion, or national origin, except where religion, sex, or national origin is a bona fide occupational qualification (BFOQ) reasonably necessary to the normal operation of the business. For example, religion may be a bona fide occupational qualification for an educational institution supported by a religious denomination. Or there may be a legitimate pay differential because of sex if the job content for a man and a woman is truly different in physical requirements.

Other restrictions prohibit separate lines of progression for men and women or separate seniority lists. Advertisements must indicate that the jobs are open to both men and women. Furthermore, the need to provide separate facilities is not considered an excuse for not employing women unless it would be unreasonably expensive. And the law considers that discrimination against married women is no longer acceptable.

In trying to comply with the law, you cannot shift the responsibility to the preferences of your customers or others who come in contact with your employees. For example, you can't say, "Our customers prefer to deal with men" or "Our customers don't like blacks."

The equal opportunity law is a federal law. It supersedes conflicting laws of some states and supplements or reinforces existing laws (such as those preventing discrimination on the basis of age) in other states. The law was initially legislated to apply to larger firms, but by 1968 it applied to all employers with more than 25 employees.

What is meant by reverse discrimination?

This is what many persons believe happens to men and also to members of the white race when preference in employment is shown to women, minorities, or both. In the *Bakke* case of 1978, the Supreme Court said in effect that it was wrong to use quotas designed to accommodate women and blacks in such a manner as to withhold employment from eligible men and whites. At the same time, however, the Supreme Court upheld the principle of affirmative action programs.

As you can infer, supervisors must tread a very unbiased line in this matter. They must be sure to support the principle of equal employment opportunity and affirmative action; yet they must also be careful not to use these guidelines unfairly to discriminate against nonminorities.

You hear of unemployed persons and of the hard-core unemployed: What's the difference?

The majority of unemployed persons are people who move in and out of the work force temporarily as they lose or quit one job and seek another. There are millions of other unemployed persons, however, who are out of work more of the time than they are employed. These are the especially disadvantaged. Typically, they have these characteristics that make them a challenge to their supervisors when they finally find what they hope to be a good job:

● They are school dropouts, usually with only a sixth- or seventh-grade education. Many do not speak or write English. As many as 30 percent have less than fifth-grade reading and arithmetic skills.
● They are unemployed heads of households, men and women with large family responsibilities that tend to overwhelm them with problems.
● They have poor work histories. Few have worked at anything but day labor or in casual service as dishwashers or porters, for example. They have not been prepared for work by their families, their communities, or their schools.
● They are plagued by personal problems. They have little experience in managing a regular income and may need help in handling credit, balancing a diet, or even learning how to cash a paycheck.

Recently employed hard-core or disadvantaged persons are troubled by job and business conditions that others accept as routine. They often have difficulty in getting along with the boss or with their co-workers. For example, one 24-year-old ghetto youth said that he reacted at first to orders from his supervisor the way he'd react to being pushed around by a street-gang leader: "I had to learn not to take orders personally. When someone told me to get this or do that, I'd get mad. Finally, I learned that the boss was reacting to the pressure of his job and had nothing against me." In like fashion, many of the disadvantaged view rules and regulations as something devised to harass them, not as reasonable guidelines for organized behavior that everyone has to follow.

Is it true that many disadvantaged people get "tested" out of jobs?

It was true to a great extent until 1971, when the United States Supreme Court (*Griggs* vs. *Duke Power*) handed down a decision barring "discriminatory" job testing. Few tests, however, are intentionally discriminatory; it is just that most tests have been built around cultural models of white, middle-class people. As you can see by definition, privileged people are not typical of the hard-core unemployed, and tests—when used indiscriminately—screened out the latter. Nevertheless, as a result of the Supreme Court decision, testing for selection, placement, or training in industry has been modified to identify aptitudes and skills of disadvantaged persons rather than unwittingly to separate out from the labor force people with untapped potential.

Federal guidelines for employment testing require that tests be validated (if adverse impact is present) so that the test really measures what it says it measures and does not exclude minorities or women in a discriminatory fashion. Tests must be validated on two counts.

Content Validity.   This means that the test content is truly related to the job requirements. It would be unfair to give a complex typing test requiring 100 words per minute when the job requires only the simplest sort of typing at 60 words per minute.

Construct Validity.   This means that the test is put together in such a way that it does not screen out applicants who could pass the content part if only they could understand the test questions themselves. For example, applicants might be able to demonstrate mechanical aptitude if they could read the questions. Perhaps the test should be administered orally rather than in writing.

What works and what doesn't work in training hard-core employees?

Training fundamentals do not vary from situation to situation or from person to person. It is more a matter of intensifying the fundamental techniques. Companies like Chrysler, Western Electric, Lockheed, and the Equitable Life Assurance Society have found that the following guidelines need special emphasis:

1. Make the Training Specific.   Avoid generalizations and abstractions. Talk about concrete things such as pounds, inches, steel, and paper. Show how each new subject relates to a job or to a product.

2. Rely on Demonstrations. Actions and illustrations, plus live demonstrations, communicate far more effectively than do words alone with an audience for whom speaking, reading, and other verbal skills are underdeveloped. Repeat and repeat the demonstration until you are sure the trainee has understood what you are doing.

3. Overtrain Rather Than Undertrain. Err on the side of providing more information and more skills than are needed for the work to be done. That way, trainees will be less likely to underperform on the job, and they'll have more confidence in their ability to do it well.

4. Offer Personal Aid. It may not seem germane to a training effort for a supervisor to help a trainee get a ride to work, have a garnishment reduced, or even provide jail bail, but it helps to keep the trainee's mind on what is being learned and, of course, it builds confidence in the boss.

5. Provide Lots of Follow-Up. In some cases, the most meaningful training takes place when a supervisor shows a trainee again on the job what may have already been shown in training. That's because it is on the job that learning becomes most relevant and least academic.

6. Reassure and Recognize Frequently. It may seem like pampering to assure a person repeatedly that progress is good, or to tell that person (and others) constantly how well the work is going; but with people who have been on the receiving end of put-downs most of their lives, it takes an overabundance of encouragement to reinforce their confidence in themselves.

7. Use the Buddy System. Appoint a co-worker, preferably a disadvantaged person, from whom the trainee can get private counseling. The first days on a new job are often full of hazing and mistakes. At one St. Louis plant, for instance, a trainee inadvertently was doused with oil on his first day in the shop. He would not have returned to the job after lunch, he said, if his buddy hadn't shown him that it was an accident and that it wouldn't happen again.

Why do so many women work outside the home?

Many women simply have no choice. Others work outside the home as so many men do, for the sheer exhilaration and satisfaction they get from their jobs.

Whereas many women may work to earn extra money, nearly half of those in the labor force have to work because they are single, widowed, divorced, or separated (and thus self-supporting), or because they are married to husbands who have low incomes. All these women must earn in order to subsist.

It is instructive to look at the turnaround in the nature of women earning money since the beginning of this century. United States Department of Labor figures reported that in 1900 only one out of twenty married women was at work while two out of every three women in the labor force were single. By 1971, four out of every ten married women were at work, and only one out of every four women in the work force was single. In 1971, 55 percent of the women in the work force were married (the rest were single, widowed, or divorced). Regardless of marital status, the increase in the number of women working has been nothing less than spectacular, as illustrated in Figure 25-1.

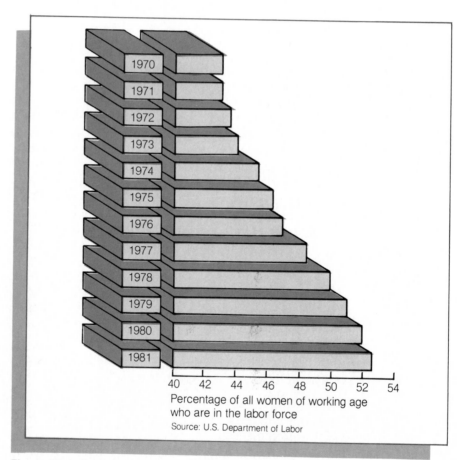

Percentage of all women of working age who are in the labor force

Source: U.S. Department of Labor

Figure 25-1. Growth in the percent of women who work.

In what ways might a woman's basic reason for seeking employment affect her job performance?

A glib reply would be to say that her performance will be affected in exactly the same way as a man's. It can be presumed, for example, that a single man may not be so highly motivated by wage rates and job security as a man with a family. Similarly, it can be presumed that a 19-year-old woman engaged to be married may not be so career-oriented as a 35-year-old unmarried woman. If these presumptions are correct, it would imply that a young man might respond less favorably to boring work than a married man would. And a young woman might be less interested in long-term advancement opportunities than a middle-aged one would be. Following this line of reasoning (and based on my own experience and that of dozens of other managers with whom I've discussed this problem), I think it is reasonable to anticipate a woman worker's attitude and resultant response to motivations on the basis of her reasons for working and the extent to which she expects her job to contribute to her life goals.

For example:

A relatively young woman, newly entered in the work force, may have only short-term work goals. Good pay, an attractive workplace, a chance to socialize, holidays and vacations, and a friendly boss probably rank highest on her list of requirements. Another young woman, especially one with advanced education and a liberal view of the woman's role in society as well as in marriage, might rate most attractive only those jobs that offer intellectual challenge and a chance to prove her true worth as an individual. Either young woman may be difficult to manage: the former, because her mind is not on the bigger picture; the latter, because she wishes to approach her work not as a subordinate who routinely follows orders, but as an intellectual equal whose opinion and judgment are sought and accepted. Obviously, there will be a little of each view in each woman because these examples represent the extremes of a spectrum; most young women are somewhere in between.

A working wife (or mother) may be so dominated by family responsibilities that her job can mean little else to her than a source of needed income. If so, pay may be her biggest motivator, with the hope that the workday will not drain her energies, emotional as well as physical, to the detriment of her home life. At the other end of this spectrum is the wife or mother for whom work is her most rewarding effort. Such a person is far more likely to expect mental stimulation at work and to exert pressure for equitable treatment. In between, of course, are the women who find both family and work rewarding and for whom work may or may not be necessary. These women will be neither docile nor excessively aggressive. They are more likely to fit the concept of an average, well-balanced employee and will respond most predictably to normal, unselfconscious, good supervisory techniques.

An older woman, married or widowed, who returns to the work force at middle age represents another challenge to sensitive supervision. If she has worked at a specialty before "retiring" to raise children or to manage her home, her skills are likely to be rusty, and she may need to adjust to the sustained pressures (and often impersonal nature) of the workplace. But she is typically steadier, more patient, and less demanding than many people in the work force, men as well as women. Since this group of potential employees seems to keep growing in the United States economy, the returned-to-work woman represents a particularly attractive employee to seek out and encourage.

Somewhere in this mix is a large group of women who view work in exactly the same manner as men traditionally do. These career women look to work not only for income and occupation, but as the principal avenue for fulfilling their life-career goals. Typically, they are competent, dedicated individuals. Treat them that way, regardless of whether they work for you or with you as associates or serve you in a staff capacity, or whether you work for one of them. These women seek no unusual quarter. All they ask is to be provided with the opportunity to perform at the level of their competence without favor or prejudice because of their sex. This is all that men with similar ambitions should ask for, too.

For most women, what appears to be the main ingredient missing in the labor market in general and in their jobs in particular?

An opportunity equal to that of men for securing intellectually challenging employment and a chance for advancement in proportion to their performance and capabilities. Too often in the past, the traditional or stereotypical attitude of management and supervision was essentially protective. The question asked was "Is the work fitting for a woman?" not, "What is she capable of?" Accordingly, women generally found themselves restricted to secretarial and clerical routines in the office and to bench work or nonthink jobs in the plant. Even today, one-third of all women working are found in only seven occupations: secretaries, sales workers, private household service workers, elementary school teachers, bookkeepers, waitresses, and professional nurses.

According to the U.S. Department of Labor, in 1980, of all managerial and administrative jobs, women held only 24.6 percent. Of clerical jobs, however, women held 80.3 percent of the total. Of professional and technical jobs, women held 41.7 percent, but this was because women dominated almost completely the nursing and elementary school teacher areas. Women hold only 5.7 percent of the relatively skilled craft positions in the United States and 40 percent of factory work, mainly at the less-skilled levels. It is little wonder that women complain they have been channeled into the less attractive and often lower-paying jobs and industries.

In the eyes of many, worse still has been the tendency for a supervisor to grow dependent on the know-how and can-do of a particular woman worker while at the same time concealing the true extent of her capabilities from others in management; thus her advancement and development are stymied, to say nothing of limitations that are put on her income. And of course there are endless instances where the capability of an individual is freely acknowledged in an organization, so long as it is confined to activities considered suitable for women. The figures cited in the previous paragraph are a direct reflection of this pervasive attitude.

The time has come—in fact, is long overdue—for supervisors and managers to open, rather than to block, the way outward (in terms of job scope) and upward (in terms of training, status, and financial opportunity) for the women who work for them. The returns to the supervisor who is progressive and liberated in the management of women will find *all* the employees more highly motivated and with a greater loyalty and devotion to the company objectives.

How differently from men should you treat women at work?

There should be no basic difference in how you supervise women. The principles of sound, equitable, and considerate management should apply fully as well to the supervision of women as to the supervision of men. It probably can't be repeated often enough that a person is a person is a person. Regardless of sex—and color and national origin and religious preference—the starting point in good human relations is recognition of each person's unique individuality and the conviction that he or she will respond most favorably when treated with respect and thoughtfulness.

But women are different from men, aren't they?

There are some distinct and indisputable biological and physiological differences between the sexes, but they are not nearly so many nor so pronounced as we once thought they were. And there is the question, often unanswered by the researchers, of how these differences affect behavior—if, in fact, they do affect it at all.

Practitioners of human engineering, for example, in designing gear for the work-station environment, take into account such factors as a woman's (on an average) thinner skin and less hirsute body (and her consequently greater sensitivity to colder temperatures). A woman's more acute color perception enables her to handle color-related assignments (again, on the average) better than her male counterpart does. Her shorter stature and smaller fingers make her a better bet for jobs that might physically cramp the average man's bulk. A woman's elbows are slightly curved inward and more supple at the joints than are the more muscular male's, giving her an edge in jobs where flexibility of arm rotation is desirable. Most men are stronger than most women, too. This has led, in many states, to legislation limiting the weight of the load a woman might carry on her job; in many occupations and industries it has also provided an excuse for reserving some jobs exclusively for men.

Observations such as these about men and women have led to the widespread practice (now generally prohibited by federal legislation) of classifying jobs as either men's or women's. The Equal Employment Opportunity Commission, on January 24, 1969, set down guidelines making it unlawful to place help-wanted ads segregated in this manner unless a bona fide occupational qualification (BFOQ) dependent on some of the delimiting factors listed above truly exists.

It should be obvious that, in principle if not always in practical fact (because of the limits of the available labor market), for any job there is a woman or a man who can perform it satisfactorily. To prejudge suitability or capability on the basis of sex alone (except as noted above) is patently unfair and illegal.

But what about absences and turnover?

The most serious disagreement, when a person is being judged for job suitability, revolves around a woman's menstrual cycle and her child-bearing capability—and the effect these have, if any, on her attendance and her job stability. It is a foregone conclusion of many employers that a woman worker will be absent one or more days a month during her menstrual period. The statistical facts do not bear this out. Study after study over the years purports to prove one view or the other, but a study made in 1970 by the U.S. Department of Labor showed that women lose only 5.2 days a year because of illness or injury; men lose slightly fewer, 5.1. The surprise in this study was that single women were absent from their jobs 3.9 days a year compared with 4.3 for single men. In any event, for working wives and mothers, there is always a time conflict when a child or a husband becomes sick; often the woman will remain home to provide the necessary care.

What about the charge of excessive job turnover that so many managers imply is related to women who drop out from the labor market to marry and have children? The evidence seems to show that, give or take a little (and excepting the 25 to 55 years for turn-over), absenteeism and turnover for women are not significantly different from what they are for men. Much more seems to depend on the individual, the family situation, the company worked for, the nature of the job itself, and the supervisor.

Can a woman do every job a man can do?

For every job a man now does, there is a woman, somewhere, who can do it as well or better. But, in general, there is no good reason to demand that women do every job that men do. In a great number of jobs requiring heavy physical effort, women—compared with men—have limited capabilities.

In spite of such limiting factors, to say nothing of stereotyped thinking in making job assignments, the latest United States Census reported one or more women in every one of the 479 occupational classifications. In fact, there were thousands working as welders, drafters, and painters and at maintenance crafts. Certainly, the employment of so many women in nontraditional jobs is an object lesson on the speciousness of withholding from any woman the opportunity to perform the kind of work for which she may be qualified.

Must women receive the same pay as men?

Absolutely! Ever since the passage of antisex discrimination legislation, the law is unrelenting in its insistence that women receive pay equal to that of men for equal work, and rightfully so. Separate seniority lists, positions so constructed as to artificially support a pay differential between men and women, and other wage biases based on sex are severely penalized.

If women are equal to men, what's the point of offering women assertiveness training?

First of all, assertiveness training, like almost everything else to do with the sexes, should be based solely on individual needs. Many men who are timid about speaking up could use the same kind of training. Assertiveness training is essentially an awareness and communications program. Women, far more often than men, are cast into situations where their role is expected to be supportive or compliant. They may be expected to accept orders and instructions that are demeaning without questioning them. Others in a work group may take for granted that the women members will follow docilely whatever plans the others adopt. Or a woman may be passed over for a promotion or a choice assignment without complaining about the injustice of the decision. Psychologists and sociologists reason that this apparent timidity is the result of the ways girls and women are treated by their parents and by society. Regardless of the reason, a lack of assertiveness (speaking up for oneself) tends to penalize the organization as well as the individual.

Assertiveness training stresses effective ways to handle sexist putdowns, conflicts with co-workers and superiors, situations where your ideas should be given serious consideration, and situations where your interests won't be protected or advanced unless you do it yourself. It does not advocate aggressive behavior, whereby an individual ignores the rights of others. It does, however, stress the right to be taken seriously, to be listened to, and to get a fair shake in assignments, promotions, and careers. Participants in assertiveness training seminars are advised against being "pushy," "hard to manage," or nitpicking about job responsibilities. Instead, the emphasis is on direct, open, honest, rational communications. It assumes that those who overlook the rights of nonassertive individuals do so without thinking and will give due consideration if properly informed. The informing, however, is up to the abused individual.

But what about charges of sexual harassment?

The statistics cited are shameful. Apparently, there are a great many men who purposely or inadvertently mix sexually-oriented behavior or overtures with their work. Supervisors are the persons most notably (if not justifiably) charged with such harassment. Obviously, they are also the ones who must guard against any actions that give substance to the charge.

In a study of federal office workers, for example, a majority of women listed these types of occurrences that they found sexually oriented and particularly distasteful:

1. Confrontation with letters, phone calls, or materials of a sexual nature.
2. Pressure for sexual favors in return for preferred job assignments or job security.
3. Touching, leaning over, cornering, or pinching—regardless of how non-sexually-oriented the intentions might be.
4. Pressure for dates off the job, for whatever reason.
5. Sexually suggestive looks or gestures.
6. Teasing, joking, remarks, or questions that have sexual overtones.

The message seems clear. Men, and women, who want to play games or seek favors with sexual implications must not do so at work. Supervisors have the responsibility for maintaining the proper levels of sexual decorum, even to the point of appearing stuffy and straight as a consequence.

What characterizes the younger work force?

First of all, it is within this group that the highest levels of unemployment occur, especially among black teenagers. As a consequence, the typical younger worker under 25 enters the labor force with a jaundiced eye toward business—toward what is called the establishment. The disadvantaged younger worker, especially, enters the labor market keenly distrustful of the establishment's intent.

Younger workers may come from backgrounds that are rich or poor. Their education may be complete or they may be dropouts from the school—or straight—scene. They may have ambition in the traditional sense—to achieve—or they may wish only to collect enough paychecks to underwrite their next adventures. They may be white Caucasians or black, Puerto Rican, or Chicano. Their politics may be radically left; they may be head-knocking, hard-hat right; or they may have no social concerns at all. Their distinguishing characteristics are (1) a deep preoccupation with themselves as individuals with unique prerogatives and (2) an almost universal suspicion of everything traditional.

The disadvantaged younger workers begin the battle for survival, let alone work, with several handicaps—most of which are neither of their own choosing nor of their own making. They suffer from all the usual wounds of the poor—poor background at home, poor education, poor diet, poor health, poor legal protection. They may be white, but the chances are that their skin is brown, yellow, or black. The probability is that they have never worked at a decent job with fair pay or in an enlightened environment. They may never have enjoyed any of the social comforts that the vast majority experience. Their politics may be militant, but they are more likely to be nonexistent. Their distinguishing characteristics are (1) an outlook that recognizes no values beyond those of today, (2) a disbelief in the possibility that business will ever provide an honest opportunity to succeed, and (3) a hopeless feeling that the cards are stacked against them.

Deep down, the typical younger worker asks, "What's in it for me now?"

Deep down, the disadvantaged younger worker asks, "What's the use of trying?"

How serious does this make the generation gap in business?

It is at its most critical in the realm of what any older person will accept without complaint and what a younger person will refuse to do, regardless of pay. Whereas an old-timer will brag about the scars from welding sparks, a 22-year-old packs up and quits. A veteran grimly clenches his nostrils as he seals up a coke-oven door in a steel mill; the recent high school graduate balks at that and asks his union steward to get him off that job. A woman who has worked for years as a blotter clerk in a stock broker's cage swallows her boredom; a young woman says that life is too short for that.

What is the root of this difference? The answers vary. Some say it is the permissiveness and the relative affluence in which most young people have grown up. Others say it is simply the difference between a compelling reason to earn a full-scale livelihood (as most older, married persons must) and the wish only to make enough cash for walking around. Regardless, younger persons are not docile. Either the job must be made more tolerable for them—or they will walk away from it.

What are the main complaints you hear from younger workers?

Complaints differ in number and intensity according to the industry and the geography, but these three seem to shout the loudest for attention:

1. "I Want the Same Rights As My Boss." Despite demurals by many about the value of an education, better-educated young people, especially, equate their advantage with authority. They want to be able to challenge their bosses on just about anything that has to do with the job. For example, in one large auto assembly plant, the company typically retains the right to maintain order and efficiency, to hire and lay off, to assign and to transfer, to determine starting and quitting times. Said a grizzled union officer at that plant, "To the young person, this means the company has all the rights. When the employee, who seems to be just part of the machinery, challenges a supervisor, there may be discipline, and this raises another cry of injustice."

2. "I Won't Work Where My Health or Safety May Be Endangered." Young people do not want to prove their ruggedness. They think that to do so is foolish. Just as the appeal to go off to war to prove oneself has been seen by many as an older person's trick on the young, so thousands of young people find it difficult to accept the fact that all work cannot be made clean, cool, and accident-free. Sometimes, of course, this complaint is exaggerated to include any job that might not be particularly pleasant.

3. "I Expect Improvements to Be Made Fast." Young workers simply do not want to wait. They certainly will not accept promises, even when made in good faith. Change, for them, must come as soon as a condition warrants it. Nor do they want to be burdened with a responsibility for making this change or with a comprehension of its difficulties. With a specific complaint, for example, they protest that the grievance machinery is too slow. Says one worker, "If a situation is unfair, I don't want to wait a year while it goes through channels. I want the benefits of the change right now." Underneath this impatience, of course, is a mistrust of management's intention—a belief that time is being used as a way to delay action and possibly to avoid it altogether.

What can a supervisor do to better motivate and manage young workers?

Supervisors should take their cues from younger workers' complaints. Specifically, a supervisor must:

1. Exert Authority Only From Reason. Dependence on power invites rebellion. A supervisor's authority ought to make sense in terms of its conservation of effort and resources, its recognition of the humanness of employees, its understanding of the value in change as well as in conformance.

2. Learn to Move Faster in Making Changes. This century moves ever faster in its development of knowledge and technology. Tradition has lost much of its value and meaning. It should be tested constantly against current needs. Letting go of the old must be achieved with dispatch. Neither progress nor capable young workers will wait very long for you to embrace the new.

3. Convey the Meaning of Each Assignment. There is nothing unique about the younger worker's cry for relevance. Men and women have wished to gain this from their work since time began. In order to apply oneself, one needs to know why a job must be done a certain way, why it must be done at all, and how it relates to what is going on around one.

4. Make Sure the Younger Workers Know What Results Are Expected of Them. Vague admonitions rather than specific goals and targets will weaken a younger person's resolve. Make certain, too, that the wage system is clearly understood—exactly how pay will be related to accomplishment.

5. Provide Support and Assistance. Especially in job training, a supervisor's desire to help employees become proficient is welcomed as an expression of respect and confidence.

6. Praise Freely When It Is Deserved. Younger people are less confident of their performance and need constant feedback as to its quality. Conversely, when you criticize, it is important to be tactful. Similarly, discipline must appear to be reasonable rather than arbitrary.

7. Enrich the Nature of the Work. Monotony stems from repetition that allows no room for improvisation and ingenuity. By stretching the limits of each job and by incorporating into it elements of depth, employees will have the freedom, should they choose it, to provide their own variety while they are still committed to a specific, demanding goal.

When does a worker become considered as older?

The Age Discrimination Employment Act categorizes people between 40 and 65 as older. Most authorities, however, observe that by age 45, employees have become older. They are mature, settled, experienced, and usually well trained. But they already have family responsibilities, often heavy ones; and signs of both physical aging and emotional wear are becoming evident.

What is important to keep in mind is that age affects each person differently. Its effect depends on a large number of factors: heredity, durability, physical condition, exposure to weather, extreme living or working conditions, climate, indulgence in food or drink, drug abuse, and emotional and psychological strains. Nevertheless, it is a good rule of thumb for a supervisor to look for signs of change due to age in any employee over 50 years old. Changes may be physical or mental, slight or marked. Changes may affect the older worker's performance for better or for worse. But change there is.

How do older workers compare with younger workers in their desire and ability to hold their jobs?

On the all-important matters of job turnover, older workers stand head and shoulders over younger workers. In an important study made by the U.S. Department of Labor, workers over 45 were found to be twice as likely to stick with one employer as those under 25. These findings were generally the same for older women as for older men, if not better.

What are the chief assets of older workers?

They have many. According to Dr. William A. Sawyer, formerly medical director of the Eastman Kodak Company and later medical consultant to the International Association of Machinists, AFL, these are the assets older workers take to work.

Safety. They have far fewer accidents.

Attendance. They have a better absence record. They are sick less often, although their illnesses tend to last longer than those of younger people.

Judgment. The variety of their work and social experiences tends to improve older workers' judgment and to familiarize them with a variety of work situations.

Loyalty. Broad experience has helped older workers to recognize good supervision when they get it—and to reward that supervision with the loyalty it deserves.

Skill. Once acquired, job skills rarely start to fade before a person reaches 60, often not until much later.

What are the chief drawbacks of older workers?

Older workers have many liabilities. But their experience and skills often permit them to compensate for the liabilities. On the whole, older workers tend to be:

Slower.   Age slows athletes and workers. But whereas older people work more slowly, they may make fewer mistakes.

Weaker.   Their strength fades, too, although by now they may have learned to work more intelligently, not harder.

Less Resilient.   Older workers haven't the endurance they once had. Fatigue—mental and physical—sets in faster. And illnesses and accidents keep them off the job longer than they would a younger person. But remember, they are less likely to have either happen.

Suffering from Poor Eyesight.   Near vision may suffer—they may need bifocals to correct it. But if vision also includes the ability to understand what we see, then older workers aren't much worse off than their sharp-eyed children.

Is it true that older workers learn less readily than younger ones?

This is a tricky question because the learning process is so complicated. It's best answered by saying that older persons with their greater experience, could learn just as quickly as younger persons—if the older persons were as well motivated. Younger people learn faster because they want to learn, because they see learning as a key to their futures. Older persons may see no benefit from learning. They have done their bit, they may think. So why try to learn something new?

Under what conditions do older workers learn best?

Knowledge of how well they are doing is especially important to older persons. This is a form of motivation that experience has taught them to recognize. The value the older workers place on their pride is so high that in a learning situation, an error is less acceptable to them than to younger persons.

Take this example. Pete is 56 years old and has been on the same welding machine for ten years. Now his plant buys a gas arc welder and assigns Pete to learn how to run it. Pete's boss, Jane, first shows Pete the many ways in which the gas arc technique is similar to what he's been doing. Then she points out where the welding method differs from the old—and demonstrates what happens if Pete should make a mistake. After Pete has tried out the new machine under Jane's supervision for an hour or so, Jane lets him handle it by himself for the rest of the day. First thing in the morning, however, Jane gets together with Pete and inspects the work he's turned out. They agree as to what's acceptable and what's below par. While Jane stands by, Pete reruns the off-quality material until he gets the hang of how to do the job right. Once Pete has the quality problem licked, Jane gives him a pretty specific idea of how fast he's supposed to work. That way Pete can judge for himself if he's running out enough work.

Day by day Jane lets Pete know how well he's doing as to quality and quantity of work until both Jane and Pete are sure that Pete can handle the job by himself. In other words, Jane hasn't made a nuisance of herself by explaining to Pete the things Pete already knows about his new job. But Jane does emphasize the job's newfangled aspects and is very definite in letting Pete know how well he's doing.

Under what conditions do older workers have the most difficulty in learning a new job?

Older adults have the most trouble learning a new skill when that skill conflicts with one they have already learned. Experience grows strong roots. When learning a new skill means cutting off those roots, the older workers may not be psychologically ready to learn something new.

To make a difficult learning task easier, it's wise to demonstrate to older workers the similarities between what they have been doing and what you're asking them to do now. For instance, in the case of the older typist, the supervisor could show that the processes for handling word processing equipment are basically the same, that the differences are mainly a matter of degree. It's always easier for anybody to learn if the move is gradual from the familiar to the unfamiliar.

At what sort of work will older persons find it hardest to become skilled?

At machine-paced work. Most older workers do much better at jobs they can pace themselves. An older person's loss of speed is often combined with a loss of responsiveness to what a situation demands. For instance, a very old person who is crossing a street may cautiously look up and down the road to see if there are any oncoming cars. But by the time the person evaluates the situation and decides it's safe to cross, he or she may step into the path of an oncoming vehicle. The person simply can't see and analyze a situation fast enough for decisions to be reliable. The same is true to a lesser degree for almost any older worker.

Similarly, many persons over 50 have proved to make poor retail sales workers simply because they found it difficult, if not impossible, to pace themselves to the fast-changing sales situation.

For this reason, as a worker's age increases, it's best to assign jobs requiring caution and accuracy rather than those requiring the worker to react quickly or to keep pace with a machine or a group of faster workers.

How can you motivate older workers?

By understanding them and helping them to understand themselves. As all of us grow older, the gap widens between what we are and what we'd like to be. It's only natural for us to adopt an I-am-what-I-am attitude—especially when someone asks us to improve or to change our ways. In fact, the very stability that makes older workers an asset also makes it harder for them to learn, since this stability is based on their having found contentment with their present lot. So the problem of getting them to want to change, or to do better, resolves itself in your ability to get them to try.

To get older persons to try, you must help them to be less critical and less self-conscious. Show them what other older workers are doing—in your company, if possible. Urge them to talk to others who have changed.

A word of caution: Keep performance standards high—for both output and quality—for older workers. There should be no rewards for age in terms of relaxed requirements. It is precisely these qualities that make older workers valuable to the organization.

What about the right to privacy—for any employee—in the work place?

The law regarding the crucial right to privacy at work is not as clear as it might be. It varies from state to state, too. In general, however, the law works two ways: (1) employees are entitled to know what information is on file about them and (2) supervisors are restricted in their efforts to find out confidential information about their employees or to pass on to others outside the company information that has been gathered about an employee. Here are some examples of practices that are illegal or generally thought to be an invasion of employee privacy:

- Monitoring or recording telephone conversations without the employee's knowledge and consent.
- Using extraordinary means—such as calling a neighbor—to check on an employee's absences or off-job behavior.
- Random searches or "fishing expeditions" through an employee's locker or personal space at work. A search is acceptable only when a person in authority needs specific information for operations.
- Releasing information about an employee's performance to others outside the organization without the employee's permission.

Key Concepts

1. A large body of equal employment opportunity legislation places a great responsibility on supervisors to make sure that these laws are effective in the workplace.

2. Minority and disadvantaged workers represent a special kind of supervision problem in that they often enter the work force poorly prepared in terms of education, environmental conditioning, and job skills.

3. Sweeping generalizations as to why women work are misleading: A woman may work for a variety of reasons—as the primary source of her livelihood, to supplement the income of her family, and/or to fulfill her own need for achievement.

4. Prejudice and preconceived notions rather than documented statistics distort the reputation of women as to the dependability of their attendance and their job stability. Women are just as reliable as men are on both counts, and the comparison improves as women grow older.

5. Young workers represent a special kind of supervision problem in that they bring to work very high expectations but very little self-discipline.

6. The more obvious limitations of aging people—a deterioration in pace, strength, eyesight, and resilience—are more than counterbalanced by their experience, skills retention, superior attendance, steadiness, safe working habits, and loyalties to their company and management.

Supervisory Word Power

Aging. The process in which persons grow older and during which they suffer to one degree or another from obsolescence, physical or mental wear and tear, and a general wasting away of knowledge or skill because of insufficient use or challenge.

Disadvantaged Worker. An employee or candidate for employment who, because of shortcomings in education and environment, enters the established and more stable world of business and opportunity with penalizing handicaps.

Discrimination. A distinction that is made in favor of, or against, a person (typically, but not necessarily, a member of a minority group) in employment, placement, training, advancement, pay, or working conditions.

Minority Worker. An employee or candidate for employment who, because of color, national or geographic origin, religion, impairment, education, sex, or age represents a relatively small segment of workers in a particular employment situation.

Young Worker. Generally any employee or candidate for employment between the ages of 18 and 25, although increasingly anyone, regardless of age, who embraces the views of youth toward work—that it should be meaningful and its decisions participative.

Reading Comprehension

1. If a minority-group employee doesn't measure up to the job, should the employee be the only one to blame? Why?

2. What is meant by affirmative action?

3. Which technique do you think would motivate the company's hard-core van driver most—an offer of membership in the company's recreational club or allowing the driver to take the keys to the van home at night? Why?

4. Why do you suppose so many married women participate in the work force now compared with the number doing so at the turn of the century?

5. Compare a possible difference in attitude toward her work on the part of a young single woman and of a married woman of 30.

6. Discuss the charge that women are more prone to be absent and to change jobs than men are.

7. What's wrong with classifying a job as either a man's or a woman's?

8. When a younger employee is dissatisfied and blames his or her unrest on the meaninglessness of the work, what is the possibility of this charge being justified? What should the supervisor do about it?

9. Why do you suppose older workers have fewer accidents than younger ones do?

10. Would it be a good idea for a supervisor to assign newly hired older persons to a fast-paced team of employees in the hope that they would learn the ropes more quickly in that kind of atmosphere? Why?

Supervision in Action

The Case of the Unexpected Resignation. A Case Study in Human Relations Involving Supervision of the New Labor Force, with Questions for You to Answer.

Paul Garcia had been hired by Inter Ridge Company as part of its contribution to an urban coalition employment program. Paul was typically underdeveloped in reading and arithmetic skills, but he was bright, quick, and personable. He responded well to the remedial programs and to the specific job training that Inter Ridge Company offered. As a starting position, however, the only job the company could place Paul on was that of a mail deliverer. Paul appeared to like the job, nevertheless. In particular, he enjoyed going about from office to office. It gave him a chance to chat with people and to make new friends. Unfortunately, it also gave him a chance to carry on a little business on the side—that of running the balota numbers in the building. In the course of the day, Paul would pick up about 25 numbers slips along with about $25 in cash. His deal with the numbers man was that Paul kept $5 of this daily take, and if someone hit the numbers, Paul would get 10 percent of the winning sum.

Paul began his mail job in May, and the first Tuesday in July a clerk in the shipping department hit the numbers for $1,500. Paul was elated. The next day, however, Paul saw his supervisor, Mr. Kent, and told him that his aunt, who had helped to send Paul to the city, was very sick and he'd need a week off to go home to visit her. Mr. Kent told Paul that this would be impossible. Paul should postpone his trip to the weekend and try to see his aunt then. Paul said nothing, but the next day Paul's sister called the office and told them that Paul had an upset stomach and couldn't report for work that day. Mr. Kent heard nothing from Paul for the rest of the week or during the next week either. On the Monday following the second week of absence, Paul's sister came to the Inter Ridge Company personnel office and asked for Paul's paycheck. He had decided to resign and had a job elsewhere, she said.

1. Do you think that Paul's resignation could have been avoided? Why?
2. How do you explain Paul's running the numbers when he had a steady job?
3. Was it a good idea for Mr. Kent not to have given Paul the time off when he wanted it?
4. What do you think could be done at this point to reinstate Paul in his job with Inter Ridge Company?

26

EMPLOYEE SAFETY AND HEALTH AND OSHA

What causes accidents?

People do, mostly. And for a variety of reasons. Sometimes employees are careless. Sometimes the boss hasn't given proper instructions. Sometimes employee attitudes are to blame. Sometimes the supervisor hasn't helped employees to understand the dangers involved in their work. Sometimes equipment fails. Sometimes machines are not properly guarded. But there is *always* a person who could have prevented the accident by taking proper protective or control action.

Consider the case of one of the worst industrial disasters. It took place in 1976 in the North Sea when an oil well plug blew out on a drilling rig, killing dozens of workers and ruining a multimillion-dollar enterprise. The accident investigation by the Norwegian Royal Commission turned up the following human errors:

● The work itself was not properly laid out. There was no plan for the job. If there had been, a blow-out preventer would have been on hand and ready to insert before the crews removed the valve housings. As it was, the preventer was not even fully assembled, and its parts were on two different decks of the rig.
● The essential parts of the plug were not clearly marked and had become mixed up at the key point of installation. Many of the parts looked alike, and the errors were hard to recognize before the well could no longer be capped.
● Operator and supervisory training was weak. The supervisors were long on experience, but they did not fully understand the principle of the capping (or plugging) operation or the assembly of the preventer. Furthermore, the supervisors had made little or no effort to pass on to their employees the skills they did have.
● Everybody, supervisors and operators alike, assumed too much. They assumed, for example, that a major safety valve was locked in place simply because it should have been; they did not check it out.
● Finally, many members of the crew had been working overtime shifts beyond their limits of endurance. The operator who forgot or was too tired to check the valve had been on the job for over 30 hours.

What role does the federal government play in the prevention of accidents?

Since 1971, a major one. Until that time the safety of an employee at work was largely the result of efforts on behalf of state governments, insurance companies, independent safety organizations such as the National Safety Council, and the employer. Passage of the Williams-Steiger Occupational Safety and Health Act of 1970 (effective April 1971) and the creation of the Occupational Safety and Health Administration (OSHA) have put the federal government and the Department of Health, Education and Welfare (HEW) squarely into the safety act in every significant plant and office in the United States. The purpose of OSHA is to establish safety and health standards with which every employer and every employee must comply. And to make sure that there is compliance, OSHA makes more than 100,000 inspections annually.

How much leeway for variances does OSHA permit?

Very little. The act minces no words. For example, the General Duty Clause states that each employer:

1. Shall furnish to each employee employment and a place of employment that are free from recognized hazards causing or likely to cause death or serious harm to employees.

2. Shall comply with occupational safety and health standards promulgated by the act.

The poster that OSHA requires each employer to display in the area adds this:

> The act further requires that employers comply with specific safety and health standards issued by the Department of Labor.

The standards (called National Consensus Standards) are derived from the American National Standards Institute (ANSI) and the National Fire Protection Association (NFPA) and are supplemented by the Established Federal Standards, which were derived from previous acts. Set down in a tightly packed, 250-page volume called "Occupational Safety and Health Standards; National Consensus Standards and Established Federal Standards," published by the *Federal Register* (Vol. 36, No. 105, Part II), May 29, 1971, the standards specify just about everything imaginable. They include specifications for guarding walks and walking surfaces, means of egress, powered platforms, environmental controls, noise, radiation, hazardous materials, sanitation, first-aid services, fire protection, compressed gases, material handling, machine guards, portable tools, welding, electrical installations, and particular attention to paper, textiles, laundry, sawmill, and bakery operations.

There was justified criticism of OSHA in its early years. The enforcement agency came on too strong, in the eyes of many, and some of its standards were either vague or unreasonable. The regulation about toilet seats, for example, ran on to more than 1,000 words, leaving no room for common sense. Much of this kind of bureaucratic arrogance and inflexibility has been dissipated, however. The general opinion now is that OSHA is a good law and that its implementation helps to make the work environment safer and healthier.

What happens to a company when it doesn't meet the OSHA standards?

It is given a citation. A severe penalty follows if the problem is not corrected. More specifically, the citation is issued to the manager in charge of the facility. It may even be issued, for example, to a supervisor who refused to make certain that a prescribed machine guard was in place. A company and an individual may seek a temporary variance from the standard, but in most instances the only recourse is to take corrective action as soon as possible. In many cases, heavy fines and even jail sentences have been imposed on companies and managers who failed to comply promptly with the citation.

Some accident hazards are more serious than others, aren't they?

Yes, and OSHA tries to separate them out. For example, it recognizes five categories of violations or potential hazards:

● *Imminent danger.* Any conditions or practices that could be expected to cause death or serious physical harm immediately, before the danger could be eliminated. In this case, a company can be shut down quickly by a court order.
● *Serious.* Conditions where there is a substantial probability that death or serious physical harm could result from the alleged violation, whether the employer knew of or, with reasonable diligence, should have known of the hazard. Guidelines have been set up in the OSHA Compliance Operations Manual to help evaluate such terms as "substantial probability."
● *Willful and repeated.* Violations are willful when the employer either intentionally or knowingly violates the act or, although not consciously violating it, is aware of hazardous conditions without making an effort to eliminate them. Repeated violations are those for which a second citation has been issued.
● *Nonserious.* Violations that are not serious but have a direct or immediate relationship to occupational safety and health.
● *De minimus.* A violation that has no immediate or direct relationship to the safety and health of the employees. No citation is issued.

How far beyond safety does OSHA extend?

The Occupational Safety and Health Administration looks deep into the areas of employee health that may be affected by substances in, or conditions of, the process or working environment and into *general sanitation* on the premises. These sanitation standards are spelled out under the section General Environmental Controls. An important area is housekeeping. For example, containers for waste disposal must be available and should be the kinds that don't leak and can be sanitized. Extermination programs must be in effect for vermin control. Food and beverage consumption on the premises is regulated.

Washrooms, toilet facilities, and water supplies are considered. Provision must be made for clearly labeling potable and nonpotable water. Toilet facilities are specified according to the number and sex of employees. Showers, change rooms, and clothes-drying facilities must be provided under certain circumstances.

To what extent does OSHA specify accident recordkeeping?

It insists that every company or separate establishment maintain a log of illnesses and accidents as they occur. Beyond that, the forms already used by your organization to monitor these matters and to investigate accidents are probably satisfactory.

The OSHA log (Form 200) is used to record each occupational injury or illness and identify whether it has caused a fatality, a lost workday, a permanent transfer to another job, or a termination of employment. In the area of *illness identification* OSHA has expanded typical coverage; OSHA requires a report on occupational skin diseases or disorders, dust diseases of the lungs (pneumoconioses), respiratory conditions and poisoning due to workplace exposure to toxic materials, disorders due to other physical agents, and traumas (emotional shocks).

In addition, OSHA standards require that additional specialized records be maintained on such items as scaffolding, platforms, man lifts, fire extinguishers, cranes, derricks, and power presses. These records should include maintenance and inspection dates. Still other records are required for radiation exposure, flammable and combustible liquids inventories, and monitoring logs of toxic and hazardous substances.

Whereas your company will probably specify what records must be kept and who will maintain them, the supervisor—as in so many other areas—is a pivotal person in collecting the data.

How has OSHA affected safety training?

It has made it mandatory. Supervisors are expected to make certain that safe procedures are taught not only to new employees but also as an ongoing program.

General safety training applies to the proper observance of safety regulations, routing for emergency egress in case of fire or other common danger, accident and injury treatment and reporting, and fire and explosion emergency activities.

Specific employee training required by OSHA applies to occupational health and environmental controls, hazardous materials, personal protective equipment, medical and first aid, fire protection, materials handling and storage, machine guarding, and—for welding—cutting and brazing.

Where do employees fit into the OSHA picture?

The law insists that they, too, act safely within established standards—provided that employers live up to their responsibilities. In other words, an employee who refused to wear the safety glasses provided by the employer in prescribed areas could be cited. A bearded employee might be required to shave to make his respirator fit. Specifically, OSHA states:

> The Williams-Steiger Act also requires that each employee comply with safety and health standards, rules, and orders issued under the Act and applicable to his conduct.

Employees have several important rights under OSHA, however. For example, they may:

1. Request an inspection if they believe an imminent danger exists or that a violation of a standard exists that threatens physical harm.
2. Have a representative (such as a union steward) accompany an OSHA compliance officer during the inspection of a workplace.
3. Advise an OSHA compliance officer of any violation of the act that they believe exists in the workplace, and question, and be questioned privately by, the compliance officer.
4. Have regulations posted to inform them of protection afforded by the act.
5. Have locations monitored in order to measure exposure to toxic or radiation materials, have access to the records of such monitoring or measuring, and have a record of their own personal exposure.

6. Have medical examinations or other tests to determine whether their health is being affected by an exposure and have the results of such tests furnished to their physicians.

7. Have posted on the premises any citations made to the employer by OSHA.

Where do most industrial accidents happen?

Accidents can happen anywhere. But the most common places for industrial accidents to happen are:

● Around hand lift trucks, wheelbarrows, warehouses, cranes, and shipping departments. More industrial accidents (nearly one-third) are caused by handling and lifting materials than by any other activity.

● Near metal- and woodworking machines, saws, lathes, and transmission machinery such as gears, pulleys, couplings, belts, and flywheels.

● On stairs, ladders, walkways, and scaffolds. That's because falls are the third most common source of industrial injury.

● Anywhere hand tools are used. Chisels, screwdrivers, hammers, and the like account for 7 percent of industrial disability.

● Everywhere electricity is used, especially near extension cords, portable hand tools, electric droplights, wiring, switchboards, and welding apparatus.

Where are most office accidents likely to occur?

Offices may be safer than factories or construction sites, but 1 out of every 27 office workers is injured each year. These accidents tend to happen in the normal work areas or in stockrooms, where makeshift ladders or stools are often used to enable an employee to reach overhead storage space. In the offices themselves, the culprits are the most innocent of booby traps: a small plastic wastebasket left in an open aisle, desk or file drawers left open, and electrical extension cords. These are easy to trip over or walk into. Then there are swivel chairs that tip over, spilled coffee on a polished floor, letter openers that accidently stab, unanchored filing cabinets that tip, loaded file boxes that strain the backs of those who carry them, and even paper edges that cut the fingers and gummed envelops that cut the tongue.

How can you prevent accidents from happening?

For years the National Safety Council has said that accident prevention depends on the three E's—engineering, education, and enforcement:

● To *engineer* a job for safety is to design the equipment, lay out the work, plan the job, and protect the individual—all with accident prevention as a first ingredient. Safety guards on machines are one example of engineering. Arranging the job so that employees work in another room instead of one where toxic fumes are generated by the process is another example. Still another is the wearing of protective eye shields, gloves, or safety shoes.

● To *educate* for safety is to show employees where, why, and how accidents can happen and to develop in them safe work habits and the desire to avoid injury. Helping workers to analyze the danger spots in their jobs and training them to build a defense against each is an example of education for safety.

● To *enforce* safety is to make an actuality of the slogan "Safety first." Employees work most safely when they want to be safe, but they need guidance in the form of regulations and discipline to protect safe workers from those who would cause accidents through unsafe acts.

Isn't accident prevention the safety specialist's job?

Safety engineers do an excellent job of carrying out the three E's of safety. But they would be the first to admit that without the supervisor's help, safety programs would flop. The supervisor is the key safety person, especially in education and enforcement.

Doesn't insurance or workers' compensation take care of accident costs?

Not by a long shot. A company's liability insurance usually pays only the cost of a worker's compensation for an injury received at work. The cost of liability insurance to a company depends on how good a safety record the company has. The difference between a good and a bad record isn't peanuts. It means real money in insurance rates. "Workers' compensation" is a term applied to the procedure of most state governments for determining how much money an employee should get to compensate for the injury—assuming that it leaves the employee temporarily or permanently disabled to some degree.

It's been estimated that for an accident that comes to $1,000 for compensation, a company pays another $5,000 for related expenses. Examples of related expenses are cost of time lost by employees who stop to watch or assist; time lost by supervisors helping and investigating the accident, making changes in production schedules, and assigning and breaking in new workers; cost of medical care; loss of material, damage to equipment, productive time lost on machines, and—not to be overlooked—cost of the insurance that pays for the compensation.

With whom does accident prevention begin?

Good supervision is the starting place for an effective accident-prevention program. No amount of machine guards or safety rules will stop accidents from happening if supervisors aren't absolutely sold on the fact that it can be done—and that it's their responsibility.

Take the slogan "Safety first." What does it mean to you? Does it mean "Safety measures come ahead of everything else in my department," or is it just another slogan? Keep asking yourself that question every time you urge a worker toward higher production or better quality. Be sure that you don't ever give quantity or quality priority over safety. If you do, you'll find that your accident record suffers—and someone may get hurt.

One of the best examples I know of in setting the highest possible priority for safety takes place at a Du Pont plant in Germany. Each morning at the Du Pont (Deutschland) GmbH polyester and nylon plant, the director and assistants meet at 8:45 to review the past 24 hours. The first matter they discuss is not production, but safety. Only after they have examined reports of accidents and near misses and satisfied themselves that corrective action has been taken do they move on to look at output, quality, and cost matters.

Shouldn't the individual employee have a responsibility for safety?

Yes! People cause accidents. Supervisors can't be everywhere at once. They shouldn't want to be. So in the long run it will be your employees who cause—or prevent—accidents in your company. But they won't prevent accidents unless you've gone all the way down the line to show them how.

First of all, you've got to instill in employees the belief that *they* are the most influential source of accident prevention. Do this—with the aid of your safety engineer, if you have one—by discussing the accidents that have happened in your organization. Seize every opportunity to let employees see cause and effect for themselves.

Preaching is not much help. Instead, when an accident happens, talk it over with one—or many—of your employees. Get their ideas on how it could have been prevented. Ask them if similar situations could arise in their jobs. Continually bring the conversation around to the human element.

Second, help your employees to develop safe working habits. People have to be trained to work safely just as they must be trained to work accurately. Few persons are just naturally cautious—or know instinctively where danger lies. The first day on the job in a foundry, a worker may be worried most about burns from the hot metal and hardly realize that eye injury, dermatitis, and crushed toes are just as likely to happen. The supervisor can start the worker out right, however, by explaining all these things, by showing how such accidents can happen, and by showing how to do the job so that they don't happen.

The third step in helping employees to be safe lies in the supervisor's ability to enforce job instructions for safety. Too many employees think of safety as "Don't do this or that"—as just so many rules and regulations. To get acceptance of job methods—as well as rules—you've got to show why they are necessary. And let employees know of the danger to themselves and your dissatisfaction when they don't follow the guides you've established for them. If you catch yourself saying, "Workers in my department just won't wear their safety goggles," its no one else's fault but your own. It's up to you to see that they do. Reason and encourage first. But penalize if you don't get conformity.

What is an accident-prone employee?

Examination of safety records often shows that just a few employees account for the bulk of the accidents—that the great majority of employees rarely have accidents. Those people who get injured frequently are spoken of as *accident-prone.* This means that for one reason or another they have an innate tendency to have accidents and hence are prone to injury. Psychologists have shown, however, that only a small percentage of so-called accident-prone employees are truly accident-prone. Most of these habitual sufferers can actually be made accident-free by proper job placement, training, and encouragement. So if one of your workers appears accident-prone, don't give up. Encourage the development of work habits that will protect the worker as well as the co-workers. (See Chapter 18, "Counseling Troubled Employees.")

How effective are safety posters?

This is a debatable subject. Most authorities feel that "scare" posters on highways have done little to reduce accidents. Posters in the company can be more effective when they are keyed to your area's condition and your own safety program. For instance, if your emphasis is on safety goggles this month, posters that reinforce or repeat this emphasis will help. The mistake is to expect a series of posters to do your safety job for you. They'll help a little. But the big job is up to you.

Posters, like other forms of communication, need to be changed frequently in order to attract fresh attention. It's better to have none then to have a dust-covered one that's been on a bulletin board for two or three months.

Should a supervisor give an injured employee first aid?

That depends on the practice in your company and on your own qualifications. There should be no question, however, about your responsibility to see that an injured employee gets first aid—quickly and properly. Permit only trained people (such as graduates of the Red Cross first-aid course) to attend the patient. Know who these people are ahead of time and how to summon them without delay.

If your plant has a nurse or a physician who has been called, stay until you are sure that the injured employee is under medical care.

What can you do about employees who you think are malingering?

Check with the company medical department, if you have one. Avoid charging employees with faking illness or injury unless your medical department can support you. Otherwise, you may have a hard time supporting your viewpoint. If workers feign sickness, ask yourself what there is about the job or about the employees that makes them want to get away from work so badly that they'll put on an act. In the long run, the answer to malingering lies in better understanding and in improving the employee's attitude.

How do you prevent lifting and material-handling accidents?

Heavy loads are only one reason for lifting accidents. Most lifting accidents happen because an employee doesn't have the knack of lifting with the legs, rather than the back. If you try to pick something up by bending over it and pulling backward and upward with your arms, it tends to strain the muscles and ligaments in the back. Instead, get as close to the object as possible. Crouch down beside it; if it's a case or carton, get the inside of your thighs as close to it as possible. Get a firm grip with your hands and arms. Keep your back straight as you pull the object toward you. Then simply stand up.

Try this knee-lift method yourself until you get the feel of it. Whenever a new employee enters your department, show how it's done. Let the person practice the lift a few times while you watch.

Of course, it goes without saying that when loads get too heavy—over, say, 50 to 100 pounds—you should instruct employees to get help. This may be another pair of hands or a lift truck, jack, crowbar, block and tackle, crane, or any handling device that suits the purpose.

Accidents often happen when a worker trips when carrying materials. That's one reason clean floors and aisles are so important.

Accidents that happen while using mechanical lifting devices are frequently the result of overloading or improper usage. Make it a point to check load ratings on slings, cables, and cranes. Don't permit an inexperienced employee to operate any mechanical equipment without first showing the person the right way.

How do you prevent accidents on machinery, machine tools, and power-transmission equipment?

Not only is machinery the number two cause of accidents in manufacturing and construction, it also causes the most severe injuries. Since the turn of the century, both employers and machine builders have done much to protect machine operators through the judicious use of safety guards and devices. But don't take this action for granted. Whenever a new machine is installed in your department, inspect it before it goes into action. Try to be certain in your own mind that a worker would be adequately protected.

Many machine tools cannot be fully protected. So it's a good practice to caution employees about wearing loose clothing, long-sleeved shirts, string neckties, and so forth, around moving machinery. Stay with new and old employees alike until you're sure that each is aware of the danger a machine holds and how to steer clear of trouble. Of particular importance is knowledge of how to shut machinery down in a hurry. You should drill machine operators until they know enough about "off" and "on" control locations so that they can turn their machines off blindfolded.

How do you prevent falls?

In theory, falls can be prevented 100 percent. In practice, it's not quite that easy. One big obstacle to perfection is that employees tend to take falls for granted. It's the mark of a timid person, workers often say, to worry much about them.

To minimize falling injuries in your department, keep an eye out for these causes:

Unsafe Floors and Work Surfaces.   See that employees keep floors and workplaces swept clean. Don't permit spillages to remain unguarded or uncleaned for even a minute. Your keen interest in this matter helps dramatize its importance.

Unsafe Ladders, Stairways, and Scaffolds.   Ladders should never be used if there is any doubt about their condition or suitable length. Stairways should have railings and be well lit. Scaffolding should be checked by a qualified mechanic or an engineer.

Improper Footwear.   There's a lot of stress on use of safety shoes to protect the feet. But sensible, low-heeled shoes, with soles in good shape and uppers laced to support the foot, are an excellent guard against falls, too.

Unsafe Practice.   Employees may think you're nagging if you insist they hold on to a railing when going up or down stairs. But if you insist on safe practices when walking and climbing, or especially when working overhead, they will respect you for your interest in their welfare. That's the point to stress—how safe practices protect them and not just the shop's accident record.

How do you prevent hand-tool accidents?

Squashed thumbs and scraped knuckles by the hundreds of thousands bear painful tribute to the misuse of hand tools. Tools in bad shape, such as a chisel whose head looks like a mushroom, should be taken out of service and repaired or thrown away. Proper tools for the job should be available, and employees should be instructed as to the danger in using the wrong tool for a job—as in using a knife as a screwdriver or a file as a driftpin to remove a drill from a chuck.

Some employees, especially those who have not come up through the apprentice ranks, won't know how to handle tools properly unless you show them how. In securing employee cooperation in this, appeal to their sense of professional skill. No one likes to look like an amateur. So see that a file is used with a handle and never hit with a hammer (it might shatter), thumbs are out of the way of handsaws, and open jaws of monkey wrenches are facing you when you pull on the handle.

Portable hand tools all have their own peculiarities, too. Check with the manufacturer's instruction manual to be certain you know, and your employees follow, the maker's guide for safe use.

H ow do you prevent low-voltage electric shocks?

The term *low voltage* covers anything under 600 volts. Since deaths due to contact with 110 volts (ordinary house-lighting circuits) are common, it's absolutely foolhardy to take any chances with electrical hazards. Injuries from electrical sources happen from touching live parts, short circuits, accidental grounds, overloads on the system, and broken connections.

Advise your employees to report to you any evidence of hot wires, tingling shocks from machines or equipment, abnormal sparking, frayed insulations, loose connections, or any other electrical fault. Don't investigate the cause yourself. Get the plant electrician—and quickly.

Portable electric power tools should always be grounded before being connected to an electric outlet. This is done by connecting a separate wire between the frame of the tool and a good ground —such as a pipeline or I beam. Today many companies have grounded, three-prong outlets to accept three-prong plugs, but the existence of a three-prong plug doesn't guarantee that the circuit is grounded. Check with the building electrician on this.

Electricity's safety valves are fuses, fused switches, and circuit breakers. These protect equipment and circuits from overloads. Disconnect switches are dangerous. Do not permit production operators to touch them. That's the job for an electrician.

If one of your employees is knocked out by an electric shock, see that he or she is removed from the electrical source first (be careful, or others may also be shocked) and then given artificial respiration.

Frequency and severity — what's the difference?

Both are measures of how good your plant or department's safety record is. *Frequency* tells how often accidents have occurred. *Severity* tells for how long injured persons are disabled. The key to each measure is the *lost-time accident.* If an employee is injured and loses no time from work, the accident is not computed in the records. If the employee does lose time, it is.

Take this example: Supervisor Anne has 50 employees averaging 40 hours work a week each. In 12 months one worker is injured. Total time lost is 37 days.

Injury frequency rate =

$$\frac{1 \text{ injury} \times 1,000,000}{50 \text{ workers} \times 40 \text{ per week} \times 50 \text{ weeks per year}}$$

= 10 lost-time accidents per million hours worked

Injury severity rate =

$$\frac{37 \text{ days lost} \times 1,000,000}{50 \text{ workers} \times 40 \text{ hours per week} \times 50 \text{ weeks per year}}$$

= 370 days lost per million hours worked

Note that OSHA insists on using its own special formula, which is based on the assumption that 100 employees will work fifty 40-hour weeks for a total of 200,000 hours annually. Thus, the OSHA formulas are:

Frequency = number of incidents $\times$ 200,000 $\div$ total hours worked

Severity = number of lost days $\times$ 200,000 $\div$ total hours worked

National Safety Council figures (compiled the traditional way) show that frequency rates range from a low of 1.2 accidents per 1 million hours worked in the communications industry, to an average of 6.5 for all industry, to 28.4 for construction, and to a high of 36.7 in underground coal mining. Severity rates are lowest in wholesale and retail trades (71 days lost per 1 million hours worked); they average 695 days for industry in general, amount to 2,642 for construction, and reach a high of 7,542 in coal mining.

What's key-point safety?

Key-point safety is a form of job analysis in which the supervisor lists the safety hazards on the job and the preventive measure an employee should take for each.

TABLE 26-1   KEY-POINT SAFETY PLANNING

Job Planning	Hazard	Safe Practice
Get material on job	Acid stored in tank	Wear full eye protection and acid-resistant gloves
Dig out sewer	Hand tools	Keep tool handles dry
Repair sewer	Acid splash	Shut off tank outlet valve; proper use of chisels
Backfill	Hand tools	Keep tool handles dry
Clean up	Acid on surface	Use water freely on hands or any place acid splashes; spread lime on ground to neutralize acid

Suppose you were a maintenance supervisor in a chemical plant. You're about to assign a work crew to repair an acid sewer. You'd first fill out a key-point safety-planning card. It might look like Table 26-1.

The next step is to discuss the key points with the operator who has to follow them. Have the operator repeat the instructions—and follow up to see that safety is being practiced on the job.

If you supervise a job that is done about the same way each day, and consequently has the same hazards most of the time, you'll want to make up a permanent key-point safety card for each job. Post it at the machine or the workplace. Quiz workers regularly about it. (See the section on key points in Chapter 14.)

How do you investigate an accident?

If an accident should happen in your department or to an employee under your supervision, one of the best ways to prevent its happening again is to investigate the accident to find out exactly why it happened. Once you have determined this, you can establish safeguards to protect individuals from any unnecessary dangers. This is an important point to understand, since there is a little risk in everything we do—even staying at home in bed. But many of the chances employees take are unnecessary. Accident investigation will uncover these and enable you to do something about minimizing them. When checking on accidents, your object is to find causes, not to fix the blame. Look for answers to such questions as these:

● *What happened?* Who got hurt? How badly? What material was spoiled? Was any equipment damaged? Does it need repair before being put into operation again? Who, besides the injured individual, was involved?

● *Why did it happen?* Was it solely human error? If so, was it due to a lack of skill? Of knowledge about key points? Was it mainly carelessness? What part did the process play? Was it functioning properly or erratically at the time? How about the equipment involved? Was it in good working order? Did the individuals involved know how to operate it properly?

● *What needs to be done to prevent this from happening again?* Does it require special training? A specific new rule or regulation? A change in process procedure? Different kinds of equipment? Additional safeguards on the equipment?

● *What steps have you taken to prevent recurrence?* How much of the above have you put into practice with improved training and instruction? Have you worked out a prevention plan with process engineers, systems designers, or housekeeping and maintenance staffs?

● *What still needs to be done?* Do you need further assistance from your boss or from the appropriate staff departments? Should you enlist the help of the safety committee? Have you set up a follow-up procedure that won't be dropped until the entire prevention plan is implemented?

How much good is safety clothing if employees won't wear it?

It's generally been proved that employees will wear safety goggles and other protective clothing *if* they have been trained to do their work with it, *if* they understand how it protects them, and *if* everybody—co-workers as well as the supervisor—expects them to wear it.

To make safety clothing more acceptable to employees, there are many things you can do:

1. Let employees help decide which kind of protection suits the situation best. Discuss the hazardous situation with them first. If working near a degreaser requires wearing a respirator, talk over with them the various kinds of respirators available. Give them a chance to make suggestions as to what they think is best.

2. Offer a selection. If employees say that such and such a safety goggle makes them uncomfortable, it helps if you can offer a choice of three or four kinds. "Surely," you can say, "you ought to be able to find one that you like."

3. Set an example yourself. If the job calls for hard hats, wear the heaviest, brightest one yourself. Then you can say, "I know that the hard hat looks uncomfortable. But I hardly even know I'm wearing it anymore."

4. Get help from the informal leaders in the work group. If you can get an older, respected employee to set the style in safety gear, other workers are likely to follow suit.

5. Show you mean business. If employees can't be cajoled, encouraged, or led to wear their safety clothing, then take disciplinary action. If you're consistent and if the protective equipment is suitable, OSHA and even most unions will back you up strongly on this point.

What sort of fire prevention measures should you enforce?

Good housekeeping is one of the best. Where floors, benches, desks, corners, and machines are kept clean and neat, fire has a hard time getting a foothold. Watch out for material piled too close to overhead sprinklers, fire extinguishers, and hoses. Material too close to the sprinklers cuts down on their effectiveness. Blocked fire extinguishers may mean the difference between a fire that is put out in a few seconds and one that gets a toehold in a minute. And never permit a fire extinguisher or a fire bucket to be used for any purpose other than to fight fires. Also check regularly to see that they're full.

Check with your safety engineer, personnel manager, or superior to determine the best practices for handling flammable liquids, such as solvents of any kind. Some of the precautions will seem overdone, but in the long run no safety measure with flammable materials can be too extreme.

Don't be lenient with employees who smoke in unauthorized areas. It may seem like a little thing. But it's the carelessly flipped butt where people don't expect it that can cause the big trouble.

Set this rule for yourself and your employees: Regard every open light, every flame, every match and cigarette, every bit of oily waste or thimbleful of flammable liquid as potentially dangerous. Discipline taken to enforce safety measures is the least difficult to gain support for from labor unions. So sell each employee on the personal stake held in fire prevention in the plant or office.

How does the National Fire Protection Association (NFPA) differentiate between the kinds of fires?

The NFPA and the Underwriters' Laboratories, Inc., recognize four kinds of fires:

Class A. Ordinary combustible materials such as wood, which are put out by a quenching agent like water.

Class B. Flammable liquids or greases such as gasoline, which require a blanketing or smothering agent like foam.

Class C. Involving energized electrical equipment (including computers and copy machines), which requires a nonconductive extinguisher such as a dry chemical or CO_2.

Class D. Fires of combustible metals where the quenching agent must cling to surfaces, conduct heat away, and smother burning.

What's the significance of the four classifications?

Each kind of fire is fought with a different kind of agent. Most wood and paper fires (A type) are fought with the typical soda-acid extinguisher or a hose—both of which use water as a quenching agent to cool off and wet down the fire.

Oil, grease, and solvent fires (B type) are fought with foam-type, dry chemical, or carbon-dioxide gas extinguishers. These all act to blanket the fire by keeping the air away from it. Water on a fire like this would simply spread the fire around. Lighter oils would float on top of it.

An electrical fire (C type) *could* be put out with almost any kind of extinguisher, but the person holding the hose or extinguisher (if it's soda-acid) would get a severe, possibly killing, shock. That's why a bromotrifluoromethane, dry chemical, or CO_2 extinguisher must be used; none conducts electricity.

Burning metal fires (involving such substances as magnesium, uranium, sodium, and potassium, and now known as D-type fires) have been controlled for years by G-1, a graphite granule and phosphorus powder applied by scoop or shovel. But a new dry powder in fire extinguishers flows freely and provides a heat cake to cool metal. It has a sodium-chloride base and additives to assist flow and water repellence. Its ability to cling to vertical surfaces makes it quite suitable for magnesium casting fires, since it is not necessary to bury the casting.

The point is that you need the right kind of extinguisher for each fire. Usually you can depend on your safety engineer or insurance company to be certain that the most suitable extinguisher is handy to the kind of fire that might start. But you should make a habit of knowing what kind of fire-fighting equipment is in your department, how to use it, and on what kind of fire. Then see that your employees know, too.

Figure 26-1 shows NFPA's recommended markings to indicate which kind of extinguisher is good for what kind of fire.

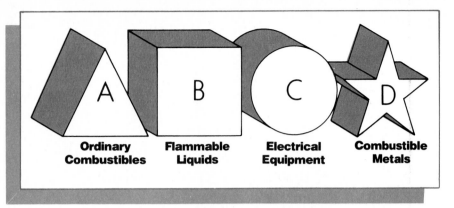

Figure 26-1. NFPA recommended markings for fire extinguisher use. Markings placed on extinguisher indicate suitable use for each class of fire. Extinguishers suitable for more than one class of fire may carry as many markings as appropriate. When symbols are colored, A is green, B is red, C is blue, and D is yellow.

In case of fire, what should you do?

Experts disagree as to which one of these things you should do first. But they all agree that these three things should be done immediately:

1. Report the fire by telephone, or see that the message is carried to the company or local fire department. Many building-wrecking fires have gotten away from persons who were sure they could put them out themselves.

2. See that employees are evacuated. Safety to persons comes before property. See that all employees in the department know about the fire and are evacuated from the building or out of the area—except those officially designated to fight the fire.

3. Fight the fire with hand extinguisher or hose. Speed is absolutely essential—thus the need for keeping fire extinguishers unblocked and knowing how to use them.

What conditions should a supervisor look for when making safety and sanitation inspections?

Conditions and OSHA requirements vary, but you'll find a good starting set in Table 26-2. For each item listed, it is a good idea to check with your superior to see what the specific OSHA standard is so that you can know exactly what to look for.

What can be done to make safety committees more useful?

If you or your company has organized departmental safety committees, see that the committee has a real job to do. Don't let meetings turn into coffee klatches. And don't use them solely as a sounding board for your inspirational appeals for safety. Treat the safety committee as a business organization:

Assign Specific Problems. If your medical department or first-aid room tells you there's been a rash of small cuts on hands and arms, get the committee to investigate this condition to find out what the facts are, where they occur, and to whom. Then ask for a specific recommendation on how to correct the situation.

Expect Results. Make it clear that being on a safety committee entails more than sitting in on a meeting. Assign area safety responsibilities to the members. Let them assist with inspections. Ask for a report of minor accidents in each area. Have the members tell what improvements have been made, what more can be done.

Have Members Participate on Investigations. Talking about safety isn't as effective as getting out on the floor to see what's being done about it. Use this opportunity to demonstrate the company's efforts and expenditures for safe working conditions. Emphasize that unsafe practices are just as important to watch out for.

Delegate Duties. If the committee plans a safety competition, let it handle the publicity, the method of making awards, and the establishment of rules. Committee members know their co-workers better than anyone else does—and can guess what will work best.

What's the best way to sell safety to your employees?

There are three keys here:

Believe in Your Product. "If you'll study your job with me so that you always do it the safe way, I'll guarantee you'll never get a cut or a bruise, let alone lose an eye—as someone might who doesn't work safely."

Know Your Product. "'Safety first' is more than a slogan here. There's a safe way and an unsafe way of doing every part of your work. Before you start up your machine, see that your safety goggles are on. Check the tool; is it firmly in the chuck? Now stand clear as you push the button to start the motor."

Show Benefits to Employees. "Safety practices are designed with one person in mind—and that's you. These practices not only

TABLE 26-2 SAFETY AND HOUSEKEEPING CHECKLIST

	Condition Okay	Needs Correction
Unsafe Practices:		
Employees operating without authority	_____	_____
Employees working at unsafe speeds	_____	_____
Employees making safety devices inoperative	_____	_____
Employees using unsafe equipment	_____	_____
Employees lifting improperly	_____	_____
Employees assuming unsafe positions	_____	_____
Bulletin Boards and Safety Signs:		
Clean	_____	_____
Readable	_____	_____
Material changed frequently	_____	_____
Material removed when obsolete		
Protective Equipment and Clothing:		
Equipment and clothing in good condition	_____	_____
Equipment and clothing used when needed	_____	_____
Additional equipment or clothing needed	_____	_____
Sufficient storage space for equipment	_____	_____
Floors:		
Loose material	_____	_____
Slippery, wet, or oily	_____	_____
Badly worn or rutted	_____	_____
Garbage, dirt, or debris	_____	_____
Stairways and Aisles:		
Passageways, aisles, stairs unblocked	_____	_____
Stairways well lighted	_____	_____
Aisles marked and markings visible	_____	_____
Lighting:		
Lamp reflectors clean	_____	_____
Bulbs missing	_____	_____
Any dark areas	_____	_____
Material Storage		
Neatly and safely piled	_____	_____
Passageways and work areas not blocked	_____	_____
Fire extinguishers and sprinklers clear	_____	_____
Machinery:		
Machines and equipment clean	_____	_____
Sufficient containers for waste materials	_____	_____
Guards on and operating	_____	_____
No drips or oil leaks	_____	_____
Cutoff switches accessible	_____	_____
Buildings:		
Windows clean and not broken	_____	_____
Painting and upkeep satisfactory	_____	_____
Door jambs clean	_____	_____
Fire doors unblocked	_____	_____

TABLE 26-2 SAFETY AND HOUSEKEEPING CHECKLIST (*continued*)

	Condi-tion Okay	Needs Correc-tion
Employee Facilities:		
Drinking fountains clean	_____	_____
Locker rooms and toilets clean	_____	_____
Soap and towel supply satisfactory	_____	_____
Tools:		
Right tools for the job	_____	_____
Tools used correctly	_____	_____
Tools stored properly	_____	_____
Tools in safe condition	_____	_____
Electrical hand tools grounded, used properly	_____	_____
Ladders in good condition, used properly	_____	_____
Electrical:		
Motors clean	_____	_____
No exposed wiring	_____	_____
Temporary wiring removed	_____	_____
Switch boxes closed	_____	_____
Proper fusing	_____	_____
Pressure:		
Gauges working properly	_____	_____
Cylinders secured from falling	_____	_____
Pressure vessels inspected regularly	_____	_____
Steam:		
Steam or water leaks	_____	_____
Insulation condition	_____	_____
Gases, Vapors, Dust, and Fumes:		
Ventilation all right	_____	_____
Masks and breathing apparatus available where needed	_____	_____
Dust-collection system satisfactory	_____	_____
Material-Handling Equipment:		
(Check for cleanliness, safe condition, and operation)		
Cranes, platforms, cabs, walkways	_____	_____
Chains, cables, ropes, block and tackle	_____	_____
Industrial trucks	_____	_____
Railroad equipment—rolling stock, tracks, signals, roadbed	_____	_____
Conveyors—drives, belt condition, guards	_____	_____
Elevators, hoists	_____	_____
Hand trucks and wheelbarrows	_____	_____
Fire Protection:		
Hoses and extinguishers well marked	_____	_____
Hoses and extinguishers not blocked	_____	_____
Extinguishers inspected regularly	_____	_____

make your job safer, they often make it easier. And we can show you the records to prove that the safety device won't cut down on your earnings. Safety here at work pays off for your family at home, too. They can relax knowing that you are working the safe way, that they needn't fear that someday you'll come home in an ambulance."

Key Concepts

1. An accident is evidence of something wrong in the workplace—with the employee, the machinery, the methods, the materials, or the supervision. Only responsible people can recognize these wrongs—and correct, guard against, and avoid them.

2. The Occupational Safety and Health Act of 1970 has placed a great deal of the responsibility for implementation on supervisors. Supervisors are involved in accident reporting, are required to see that equipment that monitors hazardous conditions is operating properly, and are responsible for informing employees about and training them in safety matters pertaining to their jobs.

3. Most accidents can be prevented by a combination of (a) proper job and equipment design; (b) effective employee communication and training; and (c) consistent adherence to, and enforcement of, the prescribed safe practices.

4. Assuming that a company has done its part in providing safe working conditions, employees themselves must accept responsibility for their own safety and must be motivated and trained to do so effectively.

5. Safety practice responds favorably to participative encouragement: the more deeply employees become involved in planning for and ensuring safety, the safer their own work habits become.

6. Fires are a significant cause of loss and injury in industry, careful inspections are necessary to locate hazards, and it is desirable to develop and enforce rules on how to prevent fires and on how to handle them if they do occur. Four classes of fires may occur, and you should know how to use a specific means of extinguishing each class that may be found at your work site.

Supervisory Word Power

Accident.   An unplanned or uncontrolled event in which the action or reaction of an object, material, or person results in personal injury.

Hazard.   A potentially dangerous object, condition, or practice that is present in the workplace, to which employees must be alert and from which they must be protected.

Lost-Time Accident. An accidental injury at work that causes an employee to lose time from the job and thus becomes recorded in official statistics.

Spontaneous Combustion. Ignition of a substance (such as oily cotton waste) with the heat generated by the rapid oxidation of its own constituents when exposed to air and with no other heat source applied.

Worker's Compensation. Financial reparations or awards granted by an employer (often in accord with rate tables prescribed by a state's legislature) to an employee who has suffered an injury at work that is judged to have permanently restricted the employee's earning capacity.

Reading Comprehension

1. Differentiate between the three E's of safety.

2. What is the purpose of OSHA? What are employees' rights under the act?

3. Why do so many serious fires start in out-of-the-way places?

4. What can a supervisor do to instill safety consciousness in employees?

5. What limits the effectiveness of safety posters, safety campaigns, and other appeals for safety?

6. What is the danger in trying to put out a fire yourself, without first calling the fire department?

7. Distinguish between injury frequency and injury severity rates.

8. When investigating an accident, what role should key-point safety play?

9. Would it be a good idea to make the wearing of safety clothing optional? Why?

If a company's safety committee turns up nothing but slogans, what might you suggest to make their suggestions more useful?

Supervision in Action

The Case of the Six-High Stack. A Case Study in Human Relations Involving Safety, with Questions for You to Answer.

Mike studied the OSHA poster on the wall of the Dairy/Drug chain store where he was employed as a stock clerk. Mike's job consisted of unloading cases from trucks, opening cartons in the stockroom, wheeling their contents out into the store proper, stamping prices on each item, and placing these items in their assigned shelf space. If Mike understood the OSHA poster correctly, it meant that he did not have to do anything that he thought was unsafe. And here he was piling these heavy cartons as they came off incoming trucks six high in the stockroom. Why, that was outright dangerous! They might topple down on someone's foot if the person weren't careful. To say nothing of the fact that he was going to strain his back for sure, lifting the fifth and sixth cases above chest level to stack them. Mike decided that he was going to do something about this right away. He went looking for Edna, the assistant store manager.

"Hey, Edna," Mike said, "from now on, I'm not stacking those incoming cases like you want. Not until you provide some sort of racks so that they are only stacked three or four high. The way it is, those cases are a safety hazard. Somebody's going to have a bad accident if they fall. And it may be me. We ought to have a powered lift truck out in that stockroom anyway. Or at least someone to help me stack cases when a truck comes in."

"Who do you think you are fooling?" asked Edna. "You're just looking for an excuse to get out of the heavy work here. We have been stacking cases six high for years, and I never saw one fall. And neither did you."

"We've been lucky," said Mike. "OSHA wants us to step in now and make sure no accident can happen because of an unsafe practice. And stacking cases six high is unsafe."

"We'll see what's unsafe around here," said Edna. "In the meantime, get that truck unloaded. And keep on stacking the cases six high. Otherwise, there won't be room in the stockroom to walk around or to sort out the case contents. *That's* what might really cause an accident."

"No way," said Mike. "I know my rights. Stacking six high is a threat to my safety. Dairy/Drug has got to remove any hazards that are likely to cause me or anyone else serious bodily harm."

"As a matter of fact," said Edna, "I'd like to see one of those cases fall on your head where it would do some good. But the heaviest case can't weigh more than ten pounds. And besides, those cases aren't going to fall. That's a safe way to stack them. You are just looking for trouble. Or for someone else to help you do your work."

"Since you put it that way," said Mike, "I am not going to stack those cases at all until the OSHA inspector comes in here and tells me whether it is safe or not. I'll keep on moving stock out into the store, but I won't unload trucks."

1. What do you think of Mike's argument?
2. How do you think Edna has handled this situation?
3. If you were Edna, would you insist that Mike unload trucks? Stack cases? How high?

27

THE SUPERVISOR'S ROLE IN LABOR RELATIONS

What role does the first-line supervisor play in labor matters?

In the eyes of the law, supervisors are the responsible agents of their companies. Your employers are held responsible for any action you take in dealing with employees or with labor unions, just as if they had taken the action themselves. For this reason, if for no other, it is essential that a supervisor be familiar with labor law on two particular points: (1) the way in which your actions affect labor unions in their attempts to gain or retain bargaining rights for employees, and (2) the labor contract that your company may have signed with a union and the impact this has on policies, practices, and procedures that make for amicable labor relations.

How does a labor union get the right to bargain for your employees in the first place?

Within certain limits, labor unions have the legal right to try to persuade a company's employees to allow the union to represent them in the employees' dealings with management. Management also has the right to try to persuade its employees that they might be better off without union representation. At some point in this process, the union is entitled to ask for a recognition election among the company's employees. This election is supervised by the National Labor Relations Board, an agency of the United States government. If the union wins the election, management must then bargain collectively with employees through the union. If the union does not win a majority in the election, the union has no further say in labor relations matters at that company. It may, however, petition for another election at a later date.

During a contest for recognition by a labor union, what should the company's supervisors do?

You've pretty much got to take your instructions from the company, even if your personal inclination is to remain neutral or even to support the union's membership drive. Under these circumstances, most companies will expect supervisors to support the company's position. In that case you may be asked to:

● Represent the company to your employees in a positive way. "This is the company's record for fair treatment. I don't think you really need a union to get a good deal here."
● Raise questions about employees' relationships under union representation. "Have you been told what your strike benefits will be? Is it clear to you what the union will ask for in the way of dues?"

On the other hand, there are a number of things that your company cannot ask you to do, nor should you do them on your own. For example:

● Don't promise rewards for not joining the union.
● Don't make threats about what will happen if the union wins, such as saying that the plant will be closed or the union will call a strike.

● Don't pressure employees to commit themselves to the company. You can't, for example, ask what employees' attitudes are toward the union, whether or not they have signed a representation card, or whether they went to a union rally.

● Don't try to spy on employees' union activities. Don't stand near the door at a union meeting to see who is attending or even to count noses.

● Don't invite employees into your office to discuss the union. This, like most of the points already mentioned, is considered by the law to be intimidating and to imply an ultimate discrimination against employees who show an interest in union membership. When in doubt about what to do or say, ask your boss before doing or saying anything. Labor law is both expansive and complex; it takes an expert to interpret it properly.

What does collective bargaining include?

Collective bargaining takes place only after a labor union has won a recognition election. When authorized representatives of the employer and authorized representatives of the employees bargain together to establish wages, hours, and working conditions, this process is called *collective bargaining.* Various labor laws have determined what are fit matters for collective bargaining and what are not. Generally speaking, however, the term *working conditions* is so broad that almost anything that affects employees at work or the manner in which they carry it out can be included.

The mere fact that a matter, such as the establishment of wage rates, is a fit subject for collective bargaining doesn't necessarily mean that the union can control the way it is handled. The union can bargain for its position, and management has to bargain in good faith over the issue. But the company does not have to accept the union's position. Several considerations will determine its final disposition: the reasonableness of the union demand; the desirability of the demand to employees, management, and stockholders; the ability of the company to pay for its cost; the judgment of management as to its worth; and, finally, the bargaining strength or weakness of the union or the company.

Does collective bargaining end with signing of the contract negotiations?

Collective bargaining usually starts with the negotiation of the union agreement and the signing of the labor contract. But it doesn't end there. Supervisors, managers, employees, and union stewards must live with the agreement for the next 365 days or longer. Applying the contract and interpreting its meanings from day to day are what make collective bargaining effective. The contract, like any other contract, is rarely changed during its life. But there are dozens, sometimes hundreds, of occurrences between supervisor and employee that require astute judgment on how the situation should be handled to best carry out the meaning of the contract. It is such interpretation and differences of opinion between management and unions that make labor relations a key supervisory headache and responsibility.

Wasn't everything much simpler before the Wagner Act?

There's no denying that supervisors had a much freer hand in dealing with employee matters before the Wagner Act. But there is also considerable evidence that, unions or not, supervision has actually become more intelligent and more effective since the right of employees to organize has been protected by law.

The Wagner Act (correctly called the National Labor Relations Act) describes the conditions under which workers can bargain collectively through their authorized representatives. The act did not create any new rights. It was intended to safeguard and enforce existing rights.

The Wagner Act does not set up any specific working conditions (as so many people erroneously believe) that employers must give to their employees. It does not concern itself with the terms of the union agreement. All it does is guarantee that employees may act in a group together—rather than as individuals—if they so desire, in bargaining for their wages, hours, and working conditions.

The supervisory job has been made tougher where unions exist, simply because whenever a supervisor deals with an individual employee's problem, he or she must always take into account the whole employee group's position as set forth in the labor contract.

Supervisors in the past have been charged with unfair labor practices of interference and discrimination. What's this all about?

Supervisors are most directly affected by the section of the Wagner Act that prohibits unfair labor practices. Actually, there are five unfair labor practices, but the following two most frequently involve supervisors.

Interference.   This would most likely take place during a union's organizing drive or a National Labor Relations Board (NLRB) representation election. Supervisors should be especially careful at that time to avoid (1) any actions that affect an employee's job or pay, (2) arguments that lead to a fight over a union question, (3) threatening a union member through a third party, or (4) dealing without advice from top management with any of the organizing union's officers.

Discrimination.   This term applies to any action (such as discharge of an employee, layoff, demotion, or assignment to more difficult or disagreeable work) taken by any member of management on account of the employee's union membership or activity. To be on safe ground, once a union has won recognition it's wise not to discuss union matters as such with employees, or to express an opinion for or against a union or unionism. This is good practice off duty as well as on.

The simplest way to avoid charges of discrimination is to disregard completely an employee's union membership when you make decisions regarding job assignments, discipline, and promotions. Before you act, make sure in your own mind that you have separated ability, performance, and attitude toward the job from the employee's stand on unionism or zeal in supporting it.

Why don't supervisors sit in with the management bargaining team at a union contract negotiation?

Bargaining is a delicate matter of strategy and power. It's a little like playing poker. If there are too many kibitzers, a good hand can be spoiled by unwanted expressions and remarks.

If your company does not invite you to sit in on negotiations, don't feel slighted. Not many companies have other than a handpicked bargaining team of the top plant management group.

How does the supervisor's day-to-day administration of the contract influence contract negotiations?

In many ways. If day by day a supervisor neglects or ignores grievances, assigns jobs unfairly, or neglects safety and other working conditions, collective bargaining will be made more difficult. Each time during the year you throw your weight around thoughtlessly or take advantage of letter-of-the-law loopholes in the contract, you add to the store of incidents that the union representatives will bring to bear in order to win their demands at contract time.

Take seniority as an example. Suppose you stand on your management right (and the absence of a specific contract clause to the contrary) to assign overtime only to the workers you favor, regardless of their seniority. Once or twice you defend your position by saying that the overtime required the special skills of the two class A operators you held over. But the union observes that several times you've held over class A operators just as a convenience: The bulk of the work could have been done by laborers. When contract time rolls around, you can bet that the union negotiators will be in there pitching for a definite clause to spell out exactly how overtime will be distributed.

It's far better to handle your decisions reasonably and equitably during the year so that at contract time the union will accept more general provisions. This leaves the details to be worked out during the year on a mutual basis as the occasion arises. Experience seems to show that the more general type of contract is easier for all members of management to administer.

How did the Taft-Hartley Act change the Wagner Act?

The labor law of the land is the National Labor Relations Act (the Wagner Act) as amended by the Taft-Hartley Act (Labor-Management Relations Act) in 1947. The Taft-Hartley Act clarified and added to the list of unfair practices that could be charged against management. But more significantly, the act imposed on unions certain controls over their organizing activities, their internal union organization, and their collective bargaining methods.

Under the law, unions and their agents are forbidden to:

● Attempt to force an employer to discharge or discriminate against former members of the union who have been expelled for reasons other than nonpayment of regular union dues or initiation fees.
● Attempt to force an employer to pay or deliver any money or other things of value for services that are not performed. This outlaws featherbedding and other make-work practices.
● Restrain or coerce other employees into joining or not joining a union.
● Require excessive or discriminatory fees of employees who wish to become union members.

In addition, individual employees are protected in their desire to bargain or not to bargain collectively:

● They may take up a grievance directly with management—provided that the settlement is in line with the union contract and a union representative is given an opportunity to be present.

- If they are professional employees, they have a right to vote with a company's other professional employees on whether they want a collective bargaining unit of their own.

Other significant changes enacted by the Taft-Hartley Act are:

The 60-Day Notice of Contract Termination.   If either the company or the union wants to end the contract, it must give the other party 60 days' notice—even though the contract has a definite termination date. During the 60-day period no employee can strike or slow down; management cannot alter, in a manner contrary to the contract requirements, the employment status or working conditions of any employee.

The 80-Day Injunction.   Should a labor dispute, in the opinion of the President of the United States, imperil the health and safety of the nation, procedures are set up so that after proper investigation the President may petition the federal district court for an injunction to stop the strike or lockout. During this 80-day cooling-off period, certain other procedures must be followed. Toward the end of the cooling-off period, if the dispute remains unsettled, the NLRB must take a secret ballot of employees to ascertain whether they wish to accept the terms of the employer's last offer. If still unsettled after 80 days, the strike or lockout may resume.

Right to Sue for Damages.   Both companies and unions may sue in federal court for damages caused by breach of contract. Employers may also sue for damages arising out of illegal strikes and boycotts.

Plant Guards' Units.   Plant guards are permitted to form their own bargaining group but may not bargain collectively through a union associated with other employees.

Freedom of Speech.   Employers and unions are given equal rights to speak their minds freely about each other—except when they actually utter a "threat of reprisal, or force, or promise of benefit." (Note that "promise of benefit" is not considered to restrict a union from describing the potential benefits to be derived from union membership.)

Union shop, closed shop, what's this all about?

The closed shop was outlawed by the Taft-Hartley Act. In a closed shop, a man or woman had to belong to the bargaining union before he or she could be hired. The union shop is somewhat similar. The difference lies in the fact that a person need not be a union member at the time of hiring. But an employee must (usually after a 30- or

60-day trial period) become a member of the union in order to stay on the payroll.

Under the Taft-Hartley Act, the only reason a union may force a company to fire a worker is that he or she does not pay union dues. This protects the individual from being discriminated against by the union. In the union shop agreement, it's common for a company also to sign a checkoff agreement with the union. This means that the company will collect employees' union initiation fees and dues and turn them over to the union. The employee must first sign an authorization card that gives the company permission to do so.

What is a right-to-work law?

When the Taft-Hartley Act outlawed the closed shop, it also permitted the individual states to pass laws making the union shop illegal. Such laws, enacted in 19 states (5 later rescinded them), are called right-to-work laws. In most of these states, membership in labor unions is discouraged, and either an open or an agency shop prevails where unions have gained recognition. In an agency shop, all employees must pay union dues (ostensibly for bargaining and other services), but they are not required to become union members. Thus, it is possible to have 51 percent of a company's employees union members and 49 percent nonmembers, even though 100 percent contribute to the union's administrative expenses.

Are there any other labor laws that a supervisor should know about?

Two important laws are the Walsh-Healey Public Contracts Act and the Fair Labor Standards Act. Generally, your company will watch for compliance, but since the laws influence decisions that affect you, here's a fast rundown:

Walsh-Healey sets the rules for any company that works on a government contract in excess of $10,000. The act forbids hiring boys under 16 and girls under 18. It limits the basic hours of work to 8 per day and 40 per week. The employer must pay time and one-half for overtime. The act sets up strict standards for safety, health, and working conditions and also may establish a minimum wage for a particular industry.

Fair Labor Standards (Wages and Hours Law) regulates methods of wage payment and hours of work for any industry engaged in commerce between two or more states. The law restricts the employment of children over 14 and under 16 to non-manufacturing and nonmining positions and will not permit the employment of children between 16 and 18 in hazardous jobs, including driving or helping a driver of a motor vehicle. The law sets the minimum wage ($3.35 an hour in 1981) and prescribes that time and one-half must be paid for all hours worked over 40 in a week. It also establishes what is "work" and what is not—such as waiting in line to receive paychecks, changing clothes, washing up or bathing, and checking in or out. (All this may be considered work in a union agreement if the parties so agree.)

The Fair Labor Standards Act also sets up guides for determining which supervisors must be paid overtime and which need not. In order to be classed as an exempt executive, a supervisor must:

● Have as a primary duty the management of a recognized department or subdivision.
● Customarily and regularly direct the work of two or more other employees, exercise discretionary powers, and have the power to hire or fire or make suggestions and recommendations which will be given particular weight in the hiring, firing, advancement, and promotion of subordinates.
● Not perform nonexempt (clerical, nonadministrative) work more than 20 percent of the time (40 percent in retail trade).
● Receive a salary of at least $155 per week.

If an employee's salary is over $250, there are fewer restrictions on what he or she can do and still be exempt from overtime.

Nonexempt employees include almost all wage-roll and clerical people; overtime provisions of the law apply to them. Professional employees who require advanced knowledge, customarily acquired through prolonged instruction and study of a specialized field, are usually considered exempt. However, apprenticeship, a college degree, and routine training will not necessarily qualify an employee as a professional.

What is the purpose of the Disclosure Act of 1959?

Officially designated as the Labor Management Reporting and Disclosure Act of 1959, Public Law 86-257 (also known as the Landrum-Griffith Act) compels employers to report:

● Payments to labor union officials, agents, or shop stewards (for purposes other than pay for work).
● Payments to employees (other than regular wage payments) or to

groups or committees of employees for purposes of persuading other employees regarding choice of a union or other union matters.
● Payments to a consultant on labor union matters.

Payments that must be reported also include reimbursed expenses. More important, the law also compels a labor union to make a more complete disclosure regarding the sources and disbursement of its funds.

The law is aimed primarily at (1) preventing unethical collusion between a company and a union or other interference with the due process of collective bargaining, (2) preventing the misuse of a union's funds by its leaders, and (3) otherwise minimizing the possibility of labor "racketeering."

Why do employees join labor unions?

Employees join labor unions for at least three reasons:

1. The union offers services and security in collective activity that many individuals cannot, or do not wish to, provide by acting alone. That's the underlying purpose of labor (or trade) unions: to promote, protect, and improve—through joint action—the job-related economic interests of their members.

2. Membership is often compulsory. In three-quarters of the labor agreements, an individual must join or at least pay dues if she or he wants to obtain or keep a job. The idea behind compulsory membership is that everyone should pay his or her fair share of the cost of the benefits derived from unionism and that no one should get a free ride.

3. Membership provides a sense of independence from management's power to hire, promote, or fire at will. No matter how fair-minded a management may try to be, many individuals feel "pushed about" or helpless in today's increasingly large and complex organizations. For many such individuals, union membership provides a feeling of strength that is otherwise lacking.

What is the outlook for growth in labor union membership?

Only one in four American workers belongs to a labor union. Changing values among workers and management's enlightenment would seem to forecast a decline in membership in the future. As mentioned earlier, many states have enacted right-to-work laws, which preserve the right of an individual to refuse to join a union even after the union has been certified as the legal bargaining agent. Many companies seek to start up new plants on a nonunion basis, too, not because of lower wages (many pay higher wages) but because they believe there is potential for higher productivity in nonunion operations.

Why does a supervisor's authority in labor relations vary according to the employing organization?

Your primary responsibility to your company in labor matters is to protect the interests and the rights of management. How far supervisors can exercise authority in carrying out this responsibility will depend on the extent to which the front office feels that supervisors can act without first checking to see if their decisions are in line with company policy.

In most companies supervisors have no authority to adjust wage rates directly; they are limited merely to reporting a wage-rate request and analyzing the job conditions. On the other hand, in most companies supervisors are expected to take direct and immediate action in the case of willful damage to equipment, unsafe actions, or refusal to follow a work assignment.

But regardless of administrative differences from company to company, the first-line supervisor is usually the first contact between employees and management and between union representatives and management. Since what you do and say in labor matters has such vital consequences to your company's overall relationship with employees and their representatives, you must be alert to your company's labor practices. Your actions are not confined only to yourself and a single employee. They could very well have companywide impact. Under certain circumstances, your actions could cause your employer to be charged by the union with breaking the contract, or even with breaking the law.

How far does a union shop steward's authority go?

A steward is to the union what you are to the company. It's a union steward's job to protect the rights of union members just as it's yours to protect the rights of management. But in protecting these rights, union shop stewards have no authority to run your department or to tell you or any employee what to do.

You may get the impression that a steward is telling you what to do. A new steward may even feel that it is his or her job to do so. All the steward has authority to do, however, is to advise you or an employee of how the steward understands the contract to limit your actions and decisions. It goes without saying that you are the department executive, and you are not obligated to share your responsibility with anyone.

It is good practice, however, to keep stewards informed of what you are doing—so that they can make their position known. It also shows that you are not trying to take unfair advantage of the stewards.

How friendly should a supervisor be with a shop steward?

Be as cordial as you can without giving up your right to run your department. You may personally resent a steward who is a continual thorn in your side. But remember, the steward is an elected representative of the group. Stewards speak not only as individuals but also for the employees they represent.

You can gain confidence, if not cooperation, from shop stewards if you let them know what's going on. They have status to protect, just as you do. If you try to keep them in the dark or treat them as if they are insignificant, they may react by showing you just how important they are. So don't keep a steward at arm's length. Get to know him or her as you would any other employee. You will have many mutual problems. There's nothing wrong with enlisting a steward's help in solving some of them.

Suppose you are planning to start up a second shift on one of the machines in your department. You intend to post a bidding sheet for a new operator. You lose nothing by telling the steward of the new job opportunity in advance. And it gives you a chance to enlist the steward's help when you say "We're going to be needing a good operator to run the number 6 machine on the second shift. We agree with the union that the job should go to the worker with the most seniority who is really qualified to do a good job. But let's see that we get some good people bidding."

Some stewards just won't cooperate. How do you handle them?

You can help aggressive stewards blow off steam if you maintain a constructive approach and show them you understand their problems. After all, their jobs can be thankless ones. Check yourself, too, to be sure that it's not your own aggressive actions that make a steward hard to get along with. Try to approach each problem not as a battle between the two of you, but as a problem that you are both trying to solve in accordance with the labor agreement. Don't say only, "Let's see what the contract says." Show that you, too, are interested in justice for your employees: "Let's see how we can do the most we can for this employee without making a decision that is out of line with the contract."

Always keep in mind, however, that it is cooperation you are seeking, not co-management.

What should be your attitude toward an existing union?

Don't be anti-union. Adopt the attitude that once your company has made an agreement with a union, your best bet is to work as hard as you can to get along with that union. Don't waste your energy trying to undermine the union. Instead, put your efforts into making your department a better place to work.

It would also be a big mistake, however, to turn over to the union your interests in, and your responsibilities to, your employees. It's more important than ever, when your company has a union, to show employees that you still consider them your department's greatest asset. If you abandon their interests, you're likely to find employees looking to their union representatives rather than to you for leadership.

Should you feel hurt when your employees display strong loyalties to their union?

No. An extensive study of employees' loyalties showed rather conclusively that it's natural for workers to have dual loyalty—to their supervisors and to their union leaders. Employees look to their boss for sound business judgments and for the satisfactions that come from doing a purposeful job under good working conditions. Employees look to their union for the social prestige of belonging to an influential group and as a protector of their economic interests and job security. An employee who works for a good company and a considerate boss and who also is represented by an honest, active union enjoys this relationship. Asking an employee to choose between the boss and the union would be a little like asking a child to choose between mother and father.

Why is there a grievance procedure? Wouldn't it be better to settle gripes informally without all the red tape?

Most union contracts establish a step-by-step grievance procedure. Experience has shown both management and labor that it's best to have a systematic method of handling complaints. Without a formalized procedure, management (in dealing with unionized employees) would find it difficult to coordinate labor and personnel practices from department to department.

The formal procedure provides an easy and open channel of communications for employees to bring complaints to the attention of supervision. And it guarantees that these complaints won't be side-tracked or allowed to ferment without corrective action being taken. Good supervisors and wise managements know that an unsettled grievance, real or imaginary, expressed or hidden, is always a potential source of trouble. The grievance machinery helps uncover the causes and get the grievance out into the open (See Chapter 19.)

Is there a standard grievance procedure set down by law?

No. The actual grievance procedure will vary from company to company. It will depend on what the company and the union have agreed on and have written into the labor contract.

A typical grievance procedure has from three to five steps:

● Step 1. Supervisor discusses complaint with employee and union steward.
● Step 2. Superintendent and industrial relations manager discuss complaint with union grievance committee.
● Step 3. Plant manager and industrial relations manager discuss complaint with union grievance committee.
● Step 4. General company management discusses complaint with national union representative and union grievance committee.
● Step 5. Dispute is referred to impartial umpire or arbitrator for decision.

It should be emphasized that a serious and a prolonged effort should be made by both parties to settle the grievance at each of the steps—including the first.

Why do supervisors sometimes get overruled?

If supervisors have made every effort beforehand to be sure their decisions and actions are in line with the company's interpretation of the contract, there can be only three reasons why they should be overruled. The supervisor may have acted on insufficient or incorrect facts. This is probably the most common reason. The supervisor may occasionally be made the sacrificial lamb when the company realizes at the third or fourth step of the procedure that its interpretation of the contract won't stand up to the union's position. Or both the supervisor and the company may be overruled by the arbitrator at the last step.

Why don't grievances go right to the arbitrator in the first place?

Unions and managements seem to agree on this point: They'd both rather settle their household quarrels between themselves than invite a stranger in to settle disputes. Both parties reason, and rightly, that they know more than anyone else about their affairs. In the long run, union and management must learn how to settle their differences themselves without continually depending on a third party. It's been said by both union and management that nobody wins an arbitration. But when it's needed, peaceful arbitration is far better than strikes or lockouts.

What's the purpose of the NLRB?

The National Labor Relations Board (NLRB) is made up of five members appointed by the President of the United States. Its duty is to:

● Administer the National Labor Relations Act and, in so doing, determine proper collective-bargaining units.
● Direct and supervise recognition elections.
● Prevent employers, employees, and unions from violating the act by carrying out unfair labor practices, as defined in the statutes.

The NLRB is not a federal court with power to settle disputes, but it makes the major decisions about how the NLRA should be interpreted. Since it is not a court, you may occasionally read of a company or a union petitioning a federal district court or the United States Supreme Court to set aside a ruling made by the NLRB. The federal court or the Supreme Court, in such a case, would have the final say—not the NLRB.

Key Concepts

1. In dealing with employees and labor unions, the laws of the land (the National Labor Relations Act as amended by the Labor-Management Rela-

tions Act) view supervisors as responsible agents of the companies they work for. In the eyes of labor laws, supervisors *are* the company.

2. The import of actions taken by supervisors in their conduct with their employees is not limited to their own departments; the actions can affect labor relations in the entire company.

3. Regardless of a supervisor's attitude toward organized labor, he or she is bound to behave in accordance with labor laws (which protect the right of employees to bargain collectively) and to abide by the agreements regarding wages, hours, and working conditions as set down in the company's labor contract.

4. Especially where labor unions and shop stewards are part of the daily routine in an organization, it is a prime objective of the supervisor (a) to maintain the supervisor's own interest in, and responsibility toward, the well-being of employees and, further, (b) to protect his or her rights as a manager to motivate, direct, and control this staff—modified only by the contractual limitations.

5. Employees' grievances are in the primary domain of the supervisor. It is in the supervisor's interest to listen to, understand, and resolve them at the first level of management rather than to have them move beyond his or her control into the formal channels of referral.

Supervisory Word Power

Arbitration. Settlement of a labor dispute or employee grievance by an impartial umpire selected by mutual agreement of the company and the union.

Collective Bargaining. The process of give and take between the management of a company and authorized representatives of its collective employees (a labor union) to reach a formal, written agreement about wages, hours, and working conditions.

Grievance Procedure. A formalized, systematic channel for employees to follow in bringing their complaints to the attention of management. Typically, it prescribes a progression of appeals from lowest to highest authority within the company and the employees' organization.

Labor Contract. The written agreement that binds a company's management and its employees' organization (labor union) for a stipulated period of time to certain conditions of pay, hours, and work, and any other matter the parties deem appropriate.

Unfair Labor Practices. Those practices engaged in by either management or labor unions that are judged by the federal labor law (National Labor Relations Act) to be improper, especially in that they (1) interfere with the rights of employees to organize or (2) discriminate against them for labor union activities.

Reading Comprehension

1. Distinguish between a recognition election and a collective bargaining session.
2. What three principal matters are always fit subjects for collective bargaining discussions?
3. Contrast negotiations for a collective bargaining agreement and the day-to-day administration of that contract.
4. What is the difference between unfair labor practices involving interference and those involving discrimination?
5. Compare the objectives of the Wagner Act with those of the Taft-Hartley Act.
6. How do the closed shop, union shop, and agency shops differ? Which is most closely associated with right-to-work laws?
7. Give three reasons why employees join labor unions.
8. Contrast a shop steward's responsibility under a labor contract with that of a supervisor.
9. Describe a typical grievance procedure. At what point does a supervisor usually bow out?
10. Contrast the role of an arbitrator and that of the NLRB in settling labor disputes.

Supervision in Action
The Case of the Suspended Dye Mixer. A Case Study in Human Relations Involving Labor Relations, with Questions for You to Answer.

"Eddie, this is the third time this year you've pumped the wrong mixture into a dipping tank," said Frank, the supervisor of a chemical plant, to a dye mixer. "I can't understand how you can make such a mistake. You mustn't be paying enough attention to what you're doing. So I'll give you something to help you remember. Punch out now, and don't come back to work until next Monday. And if the same thing happens again, you'll be fired."

Eddie punched out, but before doing so, he checked with his shop steward, Tammy. "We'll see what we can do for you," he was told by the union representative.

That afternoon Tammy spoke to the supervisor. "Don't you think that a suspension is a little steep for Eddie? You've never done this to anyone else."

"No," said the supervisor. "And nobody else has pumped the wrong mixture three times in a year. Our contract says we can take necessary disciplinary action to correct poor performance. Eddie has had enough chances. Now he needs to know we mean business. Besides, Eddie's attendance has been lousy lately. He's been late a couple of times this month and was absent at least once when he wasn't excused. And you should have heard the hassle he gave me last week, too. Eddie's head is getting too big for his hat, and he needs something to put him straight. The suspension will have to stick."

The shop steward's only reply was, "We'll see about that."

The union filed a written grievance. When the case came before the plant superintendent, here's what the steward said then: "Sure, it looks as if Eddie made a mistake. But when I checked up, it wasn't at all clear to me. Eddie says that Frank's directions were confusing, that he misunderstood. In fact, Eddie says that on one occasion recently he asked Frank to explain his orders over again and all he got from him was 'You understand what I mean.'"

"Besides, when I spoke to Frank about this case, Frank was more interested in telling me all the other things that were wrong with Eddie than about the pumping mistake. In fact, he went so far as to say that Eddie's head was getting too big for his hat and he was going to straighten him out. It's my opinion that Frank had it in for Eddie and gave him the business the first phony excuse he could find."

The plant superintendent turned to Frank. "Is this true, Frank? Let's hear your side of the story again."

1. If you were Frank, how would you explain your position?
2. What do you think of the shop steward's defense to protect Eddie?
3. What sort of mistakes do you think Frank made in handling this case? Why?
4. What do you think of Frank's relationship with Eddie? With Tammy?

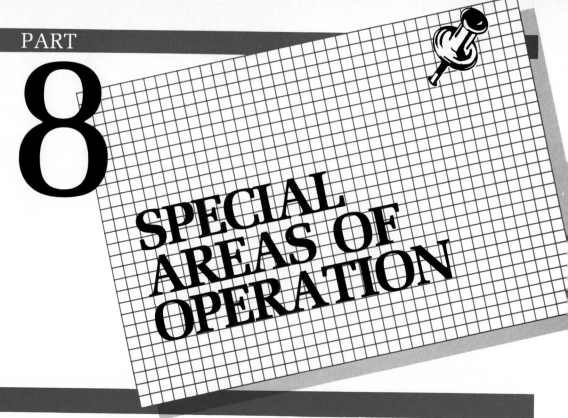

PART

8

SPECIAL AREAS OF OPERATION

Technology, especially that associated with computers, reaches far into the supervisors' world. It makes its deepest inroads, however, outside the factory floor in the remote areas of clerical support and knowledge work. As a consequence, the supervision of white-collar workers, engineers, and other professionals has increasingly taken on many of the features of blue-collar supervision. In particular, more emphasis than ever before is placed on paperwork productivity and high performance among clerical and knowledge workers. And, as the complexity of organizational processes grows, the pressure also intensifies to combine the planning and control aspects of blue-collar and white-collar operations. In many organizations this unity is accomplished through management information systems. Accordingly, this part will deal with these vital, special areas of supervisory concern in order to help the reader:

● To identify the aspects of clerical and office work that make such work unique so as to be able to manage office support staffs more effectively.
● To understand the idiosyncrasies of those engineers and other professional employees whose jobs require advanced knowledge and training so as to be able to create the most supportive and productive work environment.
● To comprehend the way in which a management information system (MIS) and computer technology operate, and to use both to strengthen planning, communications, and controls in your department.

How supervisors feel about problems with clerical support staffs, engineers, and professional employees

Generally speaking, supervisors of white-collar employees (including clerical support staffs, engineers, and professional employees) enjoy a freer relationship with their subordinates than do their blue-collar counterparts. Supervisors of white-collar employees and engineers spend less of their time in the nitty gritty of daily job assignments and are less plagued by employee absences and lateness. There is also less pressure from above to keep their employees satisfied. Much of this is reflected in the belief that the work of office staff support and professional employees offers greater opportunities for participative management techniques. Specifically, survey figures show the following:

---

1. How much attention do the following conditions get from your boss or other superiors?

Keeping employees satisfied	Less than moderate attention (%)
Blue-collar	19
White-collar	27
Engineers	34

2. To what extent do the work layout, process, or procedures in your department allow employees an opportunity for the following:

	Provides a good opportunity (%)
Perform a complete job from start to finish	Blue-collar 66
	White-collar 68
	Engineers 69
Use a variety of skills	Blue-collar 52
	White-collar 61
	Engineers 67
Make decisions affecting the work performed	Blue-collar 42
	White-collar 54
	Engineers 60

3. To what extent do you ask employees to help solve problems, set work goals, or establish work methods?

Half the time or more (%)	
Blue-collar	63
White-collar	78
Engineers	80

28

SUPERVISING THE OFFICE SUPPORT STAFF

H ow does office support work differ from typical blue-collar and factory work?

Office administrative support work typically deals with transactions rather than with tangible products that others use or consume. Administrative services also differ from professional or personal services such as those provided by a barber, a lawyer, a restaurant, a dry cleaner, and a hotel. Unlike almost any other kind of activity, the outputs of office support work are nearly inseparable from the processes, or transactions, that produce them. Furthermore, they tend to be provided only on demand by other departments in the same company or by clients and customers. In this way, too, office support output differs from products that can be manufactured for inventory or passed along to distributors and retailers to sell later on.

From a supervisor's point of view, this means that an employee's performance is also inseparable from the department's output. The department will be judged by others not solely on the merits of the piece of paperwork delivered, but also on the basis of the manner in which the service was rendered. Thus, timeliness, responsiveness to requests, and courtesy are of great importance in establishing a department's performance.

What has caused the tremendous growth in office support occupations?

Two things, in particular: (1) the general shift from a production-oriented economy to a service-oriented one, and (2) the application of computerization and automation to service processes. This second factor has caused such great improvements in productivity that, instead of putting clerical people out of work, it has triggered a demand for their services that has multiplied beyond anyone's expectations.

Employment figures here are revealing. In 1960, there were 24 million blue-collar workers and 28.5 million white-collar workers of all kinds. By 1982, the employment of blue-collar workers had risen by only 5.6 million, for a gain of 23 percent. The number of white-collar workers, however, grew by 25 million (or 88 percent) to 53.5 million. (See Figure 28-1.) In fact, about 60 percent of the 14 million jobs created in the U.S. economy during the 1970–1980 decade were in nonsales office support jobs. In 1982, the number of office support workers totaled about 18 million, or about 18 percent of all workers. Included were such workers as bank tellers, billing clerks, bookkeepers and cashiers, estimators, file clerks, office machine operators of all kinds, receptionists, secretaries, stenographers and typists and wordprocessors of all kinds, statistical clerks, shipping clerks, and stock clerks.

To what extent are office jobs in one company similar to those in other companies?

To a very great extent—in general. In their detailed particulars, however, office jobs may vary radically from company to company. For

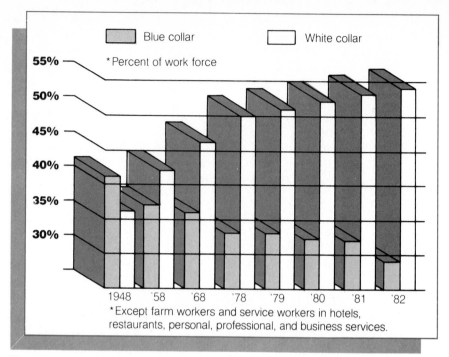

Figure 28-1. Shift toward white-collar work. Statistical abstract of the United States 1982. *Except farm workers and service workers in hotels, restaurants, personal, professional, and business services.

example, the Bureau of Labor Statistics lists dozens of classifications of clerical work by job titles such as those given earlier. With regard to details and amount of work performed, however, these carefully defined jobs frequently differ from one office to another.

Office support and administrative work, of course, covers a broad range of occupations, mainly clerical, which support specialized activities in manufacturing—such as sales order, purchasing, scheduling, accounting, inventory control, and data processing departments. In today's world, data processing is often the term used to cover any kind of work involving data and information recording, manipulation, retrieval, and transmission.

Are office support and related white-collar workers different from blue-collar workers?

From a supervisor's viewpoint, they are. Office workers may have the same number and variety of motives that blue-collar workers have, but they have them to a varying degree. For instance, job status is of great importance to most white-collar workers, whereas it is usually of secondary importance to blue-collar workers. The same is often true of working conditions. On the other hand, wages are of serious importance to both.

To supervise office, clerical, and other white-collar workers successfully, you'll have to study their idiosyncrasies and deal with them accordingly.

How important is pay to white-collar workers?

Very important. For years it was a mistaken impression that office workers enjoyed their working conditions and status so much that their wages were of little importance. This isn't true, as the survey figures show. White-collar workers tend to feel underpaid and overworked.

Do office employees take fringe benefits for granted?

Yes. On the whole, clerical workers don't turn handsprings just because you give them a 15-minute coffee break, for instance. If anything at all, they view fringe benefits negatively. In other words, they're more likely to complain about what you don't give them (and the ABC Company next door does) than to be much impressed —and grateful—for what you do for them.

Of what part of their jobs are office employees likely to be most critical?

Your attention to the human side of an office employee's job is likely to be the critical factor of your success or failure in supervising. Studies show that office employees place high importance on the social and human aspects of the organization.

One feature of office work that makes it particularly attractive is the opportunity for employees to talk together while they work. Although this can sometimes be disruptive, it is a powerful force in knitting a work group together, and it offers a form of real job satisfaction quite apart from pay and status.

There is a negative aspect, however, to the office employees' concern for the social side of the work. Office employees (compared with blue-collar workers) are often critical of others who have better or worse education, dress differently, or live in inferior or superior parts of town. The office work group strives for homogeneity. The pressure is strong for conformance. Any newcomer has a hard time breaking down the "keyboard curtain." Offbeat newcomers will find it almost impossible to gain acceptance unless you introduce them gradually—and stand by to give them assurance when needed.

So strive hard to put together people who have similar interests. Don't put too much emphasis on technical skills. A good disposition in a typist will go a long way toward offsetting slow fingers.

M ust white-collar workers be handled with velvet gloves?

It helps—so long as there is a firm hand inside them. Remember that white-collar workers choose that kind of work because it implies social distinction. Consequently, they expect their supervisor to act and speak courteously. They won't complain because you're a little stiff and unbending as long as you treat them with genuine respect.

W hat is it about office support work that makes it so difficult to schedule and supervise?

Transaction requests and sequences are at once unpredictable and inflexible. Office processes don't function like an auto assembly line, with all tasks focusing on the products to be made. Instead, there are always a number of tasks in progress, and these are usually waiting for—or overwhelmed by—requests for transactions to take place. For example:

1. Requests for service are triggered by a number of events, many of which are on different time schedules. Employees often have to wait for the mail to arrive with orders, claims, and requests; a customer to telephone or arrive in person (as with airlines and hotel reservations); or a job to be completed in another department.
2. Work may be delayed by overloaded equipment or employees. Few offices can "equip for" or "staff up" to a peak load. Instead, they plan on average workloads. Typically, there are many periods in the schedule when the work process is overloaded or underloaded.
3. A great deal of coordination between jobs and people cannot be programmed in advance by the system. Supervisors must perform a lot of the fitting. They must see, for example, that files needed by an authorized clerk to perform an eligibility check are retrieved by a file clerk when needed.

4. There is always a limit on the extent of employee specialization that can be afforded. Not all employees can be trained to perform all tasks. On the other hand, there will not always be enough specialized work to keep an employee exclusively on his or her specialty; that person may have to pitch in on other kinds of work.

Office jobs are routine, often boring. What can you do to relieve the monotony?

Be careful with this one. What may appear to be monotonous work to you may be just what the doctor ordered for your office workers. Unless you see real signs of boredom, don't upset the office applecart by well-meant, but resented, attempts to liven up the job.

When a worker indicates that the job is boring, one sensible move to make is to find ways of varying the daily routine. Can tasks usually done in the morning be shifted to the afternoon? Can the worker develop a different and more stimulating order of work without disturbing the routines of others?

Better still, look for ways to rotate work assignments. If sorting mail is a tiresome job, break it up into smaller pieces so that each of five people share it for only one day each week. Likewise, if the reception desk is a pleasant assignment in your office, don't give this choice plum to only one person. Make it an assignment that several employees can look forward to each week.

In the office, as in the shop, jobs often become boring simply because employees can't see the point in what they're doing. They think they're just another cog in a machine. To counteract this form of the blues, sharpen your listening technique. Ask employees for their opinions about office procedures. See if you can't adapt some of their ideas. Let them establish their own way of doing minor tasks. It's said over and over again: To get employees interested in their work, you've got to get interested in them.

Even programming, which seems so exciting and challenging, has its duller side. Routine program maintenance is considered tiresome by programmers. Most of them want an occasional crack at the rewarding work of creating new programs. As with so many office support tasks, rotation of assignments helps to relieve monotony.

How effective are participative and job enlargement techniques in motivating office workers?

Apparently there is an endless horizon for goal sharing and laissez-faire management in the office. In a notable job enrichment program at American Telephone and Telegraph Company, supervisors in the treasury department changed the jobs of 120 women employees so that these jobs would include appeals to learning, achievement, recognition, responsibility, and advancement. The supervisors in this "work itself" program decided that these employees should research, compose, and type their own letters without being checked. Results were dramatic. Turnover of employees dropped 27 percent, and 24 clerks did the work that 46 had previously done. In all, savings totaled $558,000 in 18 months. After that experiment, which took place in 1965, the program expanded. Keypunch operators were given full units of work, such as the payroll for an entire department, and were asked to schedule their own days as well as to maintain their own quantity and quality records. Telephone operators were encouraged to use their own words, rather than prescribed phrases, when speaking to customers. By 1980 over 30,000 AT&T employees had taken part in this program. Many other companies have had comparable success with such programs. The Prudential Insurance Company, for example, has a "job design" program in 100 of its divisions, and over 2,000 employees have benefited from the changes.

What about Quality Circles for office work?

QCs seem to be as effective in offices as they are in factories. The same principles prevail—a participative, systematic approach to solving operational problems. At Westinghouse, for example, where there are over 1,100 QCs, about one-fourth of them are directed toward office support problems. In fact, QCs have revolutionized the role of secretaries at Westinghouse by facilitating the installation of word processing centers. Now those people who used to be called secretaries are full-fledged administrative assistants. Instead of spending a major part of their time taking and transcribing dictation, they now take over tasks their bosses used to handle. They organize conferences, sit in on task forces, and prepare and present research data and the like. In one Westinghouse plant, the office QC realized that money was being wasted by preparing and mailing separate envelopes that were directed toward a central location. Now this correspondence is consolidated and is mailed in one large batch. In another office, the QC reviewed the storage files and threw out more than half of them that were deemed as unnecessary. The rest were consolidated in a central file that reduced the entire space occupied by that office by one-fifth.

How do you handle the career-oriented office worker?

More than 80 percent of all office and clerical employees are women. Many of them (in the beginning) do not view their work as a lifetime career. Handling these employees takes the greater part of your time and your skill. But there is a significant and increasing group of office employees who desire more from their work than just a place to occupy their time between high school and motherhood. These are career-oriented employees.

The career woman or man needs stimulating assignments, a chance to learn—even if there's small chance to get ahead. Be careful not to have this attitude: "What's the point of letting Amy learn how to strike trial balances? She won't stay here long enough to become a chief accountant." It's true that in the past there was little or no chance in many offices for promotion for women. But legislation and social awareness (see Chapter 25) have opened the door for advancement. Regardless of the sex of the individual, nothing dashes cold water into the face of an ambitious person so much as having the boss block chances for improvement at every turn.

Many people to whom work is a complete outlet will willingly accept broad assignments and won't confine themselves to narrow job descriptions. These willing workers get satisfaction from the importance derived from doing more and doing better. So give them a chance to flex their muscles.

Should you treat your secretary differently than other office employees?

The relationship between a boss and his or her secretary is a delicate one. Technically, supervising a secretary is just like supervising any other clerical employee. But anyone who's ever had a secretary will tell you that in practice it doesn't work out that way.

First of all, your secretary is doing work for you personally—in contrast with other kinds of workers who are more likely to see their work as being done for the company. A secretary often has access to confidential matters—both about business and about your own affairs. This makes it difficult to be reserved and impartial in your relationship. On the other hand, you should avoid being too intimate. A dignified distance between boss and secretary will wear better in the long run. Be friendly, but keep your friendliness on the formal side. In the office it looks better to the rest of the employees—and to outsiders—to be businesslike.

In many organizations, the position of secretary has been redefined and retitled as that of administrative assistant. This is more nearly appropriate to the responsibilities and status usually associated with the work. And along with these changes, in many instances, the time-honored—or demeaning—assignment of managing the coffee urn has been dispensed with. Or, in the best of relationships, it is a task that is shared good-naturedly.

What's the best way to hold on to your good office support workers?

Surprisingly for some people, it is not through long vacations or exotic fringe benefits. The two biggest reasons for job jumping are (1) lack of interesting work and (2) lack of prospects for additional responsibility. It is important to provide a favorable balance of job conditions in order to attract and hold the best office people. Accordingly, interesting work, attractive salaries, good location, adequate fringe benefits, the company's reputation, and the treatment received from supervision go into the mix.

Don't make the mistake of thinking that most younger clerical people do not take their work to be a serious occupation. For the most part, secretaries and other clerical candidates tend now to think in career terms rather than in terms of "just a job." They want to make a contribution to the company's activities and want this viewpoint recognized by their supervisors. Furthermore, the drive for women's equality on the job puts far greater stress than ever before on upward mobility from the typing pool and the file room.

In human resources staffing for an office, how much output can you expect from filing clerks, typists, and stenographers?

This is a little like shooting at a moving target. Under normal conditions a filing clerk can take good care of 60 file drawers. (Incidentally, you can ordinarily fit 4,000 sheets of paper into a single file drawer.) The Administrative Management Society once recommended the following standards of performance: typing, about 70 words per minute (although many firms accept 45); shorthand, 120 words per minute (although most firms accept 80); and transcription from notes, 45 words per minute (although here again, the standard for many firms is only 30).

In 1973 the U.S. General Services Administration's National Archives and Records Services prescribed these far more conservative rates:

- To type from copy a standard page of 30 to 40 lines: 3 pages per hour
- To transcribe one standard page: 25 minutes
- To address envelopes by typewriter: 140 envelopes per hour
- To type letters from steno notes: 2 letters per hour
- To type form letters: 20 letters per hour
- To type average straight copy: 42 words per minute
- To take shorthand: 24 words per minute
- To transcribe shorthand notes: 15 words per minute
- To transcribe machine dictation: 30 words per minute

You might conclude from these contradictory figures that staffing should be based on careful study of the unique nature and demand of the work performed in your particular office.

How error-free should you expect office support workers to be in performing their work?

According to many authorities, you can be satisfied if your people meet the following standards of performance:

Filing Cards. Only 1 misfile out of each 10,000 units.

Filing Correspondence. Only 3 misfiles out of 1,000 letters.

Keypunching. About one-half of 1 percent wrong, excluding errors corrected by the puncher.

Cutting Mail Stencils. About one-half of 1 percent of all items incorrect, or about 3 percent of all stencils with an error.

Preparing Checks. One oil company found that good clerks can still be expected to make errors on six-hundredths of 1 percent of all vouchers.

Preparing Invoices. One public utility found that four-tenths of 1 percent contained clerical errors, but that the best employee made errors on only about one-tenth of 1 percent of the work.

Should there be a limit to the number of paperwork forms used in a single office?

Form design and control is a science in itself. But it is usually a wise idea to make one person in your office a forms "commander"—with absolute authority to say yes or no on any new form. Your other people will then take the forms problem seriously. Duplication of information from form to form can be avoided; forms can be consolidated, and the proliferation of forms that demand time and attention can be minimized.

Such a control procedure ought to apply also to such insidious kinds of forms as (1) the unprinted kind that's run off casually on the copying machine and (2) the monthly letter that requests tabulated information. This informal type of form frequently sneaks by forms control; yet it is just as time-consuming as a printed form for the recipients to handle.

What are some rules of thumb for minimum levels of records retention and retrieval?

Despite the trend toward automated offices, records and correspondence files are still the heart—and bane—of most office systems. It makes sense to keep these files as slim as possible. In practice, however, it isn't all that easy. One expert suggests you weigh these eight factors before relegating anything to your filing cabinets:

1. How useful is this information for the operation of your department?
2. How often do you need this information?
3. Does it summarize other records (which can be discarded now if you hold on to just this one record)?
4. Can this information be duplicated easily from other sources if you need it (so that it need not be held in your files)?
5. Is the information essential for meeting government or company regulations? (The latter test is sticky because so much can be justified as conforming to company policy.)
6. Is it necessary to retain this document for legal purposes? Might it be needed later as evidence to avoid or to settle suits about unemployment, accidents, specifications, deliveries, contracts, and so forth?
7. How important is this material to persons other than those in your department? Is your file the main source for this information? Do others depend on you to maintain this record?
8. How long should you hold on to this information? Can it be marked with a green tab for removal after six months? A yellow tab for discard after a year? Should it be branded with a red flag if it must be held indefinitely?

How important is productivity in the supervision of office support work?

It is just as important as productivity in manufacturing, construction, mining, and other product-oriented activities. First of all, office support staffs in business and government simply couldn't handle the overwhelming demand for service if they were only as productive today as they were a decade ago. Second, office operations in business offer the unique opportunity to create what is often called the "third profit." Traditionally, business managers have recognized the "first profit," which is the profit from the production operations. They also acknowledge the "second profit," which results from the sales effort. Only in the last decade or so have they seen the potential in the "third profit." This is the profit to be gained from efficient operation of the administrative support activities of an enterprise. For example, suppose a company realizes a 5 percent profit on gross sales ($5,000 on sales of $100,000). It can estimate that a like reduction of $5,000 in administrative office costs will have the same effect on corporate profits as if there were an increase in sales of $100,000. In other words, a reduction in office costs of $5,000 can make the same contribution to profits as an increase of 20 times that amount in sales.

What factors contribute most to office productivity?

As with manufacturing and production operations, office efficiencies are attributable to two major sets of factors: (1) the human element and (2) the technical element. To be effective, office workers must be properly trained and motivated. This responsibility is placed squarely in the supervisor's bailiwick. It goes without saying, however, that even the best trained and most highly motivated people will not be effective unless their work is laid out in a systematic pattern and sequence and is aided by appropriate tools and equipment. In this regard for the efficiency of systems and mechanization, the supervisor will usually find guidance and support from staff specialists. For the moment, we will turn our attention to the human factor in office productivity and talk about the technical factors later on in this chapter.

Significantly, a major study of white-collar employees in 1978 turned up four opinions of note. When interviewed in a Louis Harris poll (*The Steelcase National Study of Office Environments: Do They*

Work?), office workers responded this way to four productivity-related questions:

1. I could *probably* do more work than I am doing now: 32 percent.
2. If conditions and circumstances were changed, I could *certainly* do more work: 77 percent.
3. I'm either sometimes or often unclear on just what the scope and responsibilities of my job are: ranked 4th among 12 problems.
4. The most serious problem preventing me from getting my job done well is not getting good enough instructions and information from my supervisor: 16 percent, but ranked first among 11 other problems.

What is the role of systems and procedures in office management?

This deals with the study and improvement of information, communications, and paperwork flow within an organization. It is usually conducted by trained specialists with the advice of various department supervisors. Typical areas investigated are forms and records, paperwork preparation and flow, work measurement and standardization, equipment usage, and computer adaptability. In principle, systems and procedures is not unlike work simplification.

What characterizes office support work from a systems point of view?

Martin F. Stankard, in his *Successful Management of Large Clerical Operations* (McGraw-Hill Book Company, New York, 1981) offers this simplified viewpoint. There are, he says, three factors in every clerical system:

Transactions. These are sequences of events with a definite beginning and end, each with a specified input and output. To receive reimbursement for a damaged automobile, a client must file her or his claim (the input), it must be processed internally by the insurance company, and she or he must receive a check reimbursing her or him (the output).

Processes. These are sequences of tasks that must be accomplished to complete a transaction or series of transactions, as illustrated in Figure 28-2. The claim must be received (where it awaits processing). It must proceed through a sequence of tasks,

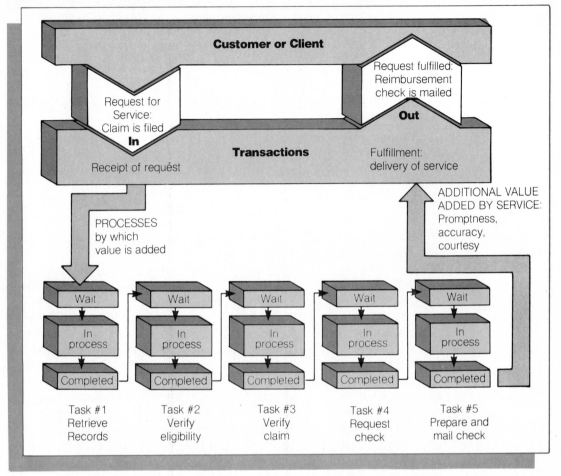

Figure 28-2. Example of what happens in a clerical processing system.

such as retrieval of the client's records, verification of eligibility, verification of client's claim, request for payment, issuance of the check, and mailing of the request to the client. At this stage, the processing is completed.

Value Added.   This is what makes a transaction worthwhile to the client, customer, or department being served. Typical values include not only the most visible output, as when a person receives a claims check, but also getting the check promptly, accuracy of the amount received, a sense of having reliable information during the exchange, and friendliness and courtesy in the client's dealings with the service organization.

In applying work simplification to office methods, where should you begin?

Work simplification is too often left up to the systems and procedures department. Actually, there are many simple improvements you can make or initiate on your own. As a starter, try any of these approaches:

● Look for single steps of a job that are performed by more than one person. These steps can often be combined or eliminated.
● Look for identical data being recorded on more than one form. A single, well-designed form can often replace two or more forms.
● Look for records that are seldom used. Question their value. These are the ones most susceptible to elimination.
● Look for records that duplicate other records. Those records can usually be consolidated.
● Look for people doing too little work. Chances are that half your people could do more work than they do now if work flow were smoother and assignments were better planned.
● Look for people doing too much work. About one-tenth of your people will take on too big a work load—and often not do it as quickly as it might be done if assignments were better balanced.
● Don't pass up small opportunities. Especially where many employees or transactions are involved, pennies saved can add up to hundreds of dollars. For example, your typist can save a separate operation in making file cards by slipping a card and a carbon inside each envelope while addressing it. Or for some correspondence purposes, the reply can be written on the back or bottom of an incoming letter—or a form designed for this use can be substituted for typed letters.

How will the trend toward word processing affect office support work?

Word processing is the production of written communications (letters, forms, reports, and so forth) through a systematic combination of automated equipment and human effort. It requires a major change in office staffing and procedures. In its simplest phase, word processing combines dictation equipment with automatic typewriters. In its most advanced stage, word processing uses (1) machines that store data for forms and letters and have features for correcting, revising, deleting, and aligning copy; (2) machines that set type from the output of the storage unit; (3) computers to link all this together;

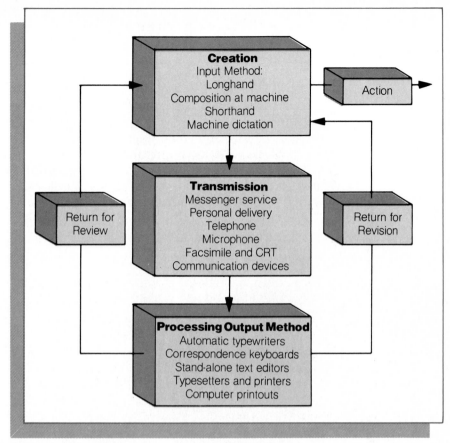

Figure 28-3. Basic word processing system.

and (4) telephones or satellites to transmit data in its raw or printed form between departments in one building or between plants and offices thousands of miles apart. Figure 28-3 illustrates a basic word processing system. Right now, about 25 percent takes place in an integrated system. The balance is more likely to be handled by electric and electronic typewriters using inputs from dictating and other semiautomatic equipment.

Experts say that even the simple word processing systems save between 15 and 40 percent of secretarial and typing costs. Obviously, word processing is changing the work of secretaries, typists, file clerks, and those in mail rooms, duplicating services, and telephone operations. It will also require the addition of personnel specialized in such skills as grammatical construction, correspondence procedures, and conceptualization and operation of electronic office equipment in systematic arrangement.

What is the trend in office automation?

Computer-assisted office operations are galloping ahead at an increasing rate. Estimates are that three out of four clerical jobs will be affected by 1990. Such automation will not necessarily do away with jobs, but it may change them radically. Some jobs will become more interesting and challenging; others will become more boring. Nevertheless, as this occurs, the productivity of the office will improve at a rate of about 20 percent per year.

What forms will office automation take?

It will appear in many different forms. Word processing, for example, is only one of five building blocks that constitute a completely auto-

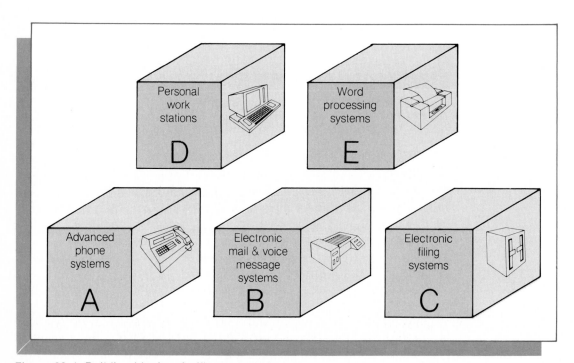

Figure 28-4. Building blocks of office automation.

matic office. (See Figure 28-4.) Other areas affected by automation include:

Advanced Telephone Systems. These systems can perform a variety of services, such as transferring or forwarding calls without operator assistance, placing calls in line at a busy extension, automatically seeking the least-cost routing for a call over a trunk line, and recording and listing all calls on an extension.

Electronic Mail and Message Systems. These involve interconnected terminals for transmitting and receiving letters and memos in text form and teleconferencing.

Automatic Work Stations. These equip technicians, professionals, managers, and others with a computer or a terminal connection to a computer and data base that enables the individual to perform a great deal of his or her own data retrieval and analysis.

Electronic Filing Systems. These go far beyond paper files, microfilm, and microfiche. Information can be placed in storage via keyboarding, transfer from a word processing unit, optical character reading, and, increasingly, laser-based optical scanners. The information is placed on various types of magnetic and laser optical discs and when retrieved is given in text form, on microfiche or microfilm, or displayed on CRT terminals.

When requisitioning office machines, how can you be sure these machines will pay off?

A fancy new machine frequently has great eye, or gimmick, appeal. Or if the office down the floor has one, there's a tendency for you to want one for your department, too. For these reasons it's a good idea to look hard before you make a strong plea to your boss for that new machine. First, you might check the answers to these four questions:

1. How much does the machine really cost? Not just what someone said it costs, but the price of the model your office will need. Then, too, what will be the installation charge? The cost of operating supplies? The cost of maintenance?

2. Will your employees use it effectively? Are they capable of using it without further training? Will they like to use it? If you can get only one, will there be a squabble over who has priority for its use?

3. What are the machine's payoff characteristics? Will it save labor? How much? Will it produce more copies? Better copies? Can one person perform a complexity of jobs on it? How soon will it pay for itself in saved labor or supplies?

4. Is this machine what your office needs now? Will it fit into your ex-

---

isting paperwork system? Is its speed something that's nice to have but not absolutely necessary at this time? Will it be outmoded quickly?

How can you minimize work peaks and overloads?

P. K. Eschbach, a perceptive office manager for the Blue Diamond Corporation in Nevada, has suggested this approach:

1. Prepare your staff for flexibility by rotating jobs and assignments among different employees. Almost every job can thus be handled by more than one person. This is especially valuable during vacation periods when doubling up or filling in is a necessity.

2. Put your job procedures into writing so that the person who has to fill in will have a reasonable idea of what's to be done and how to do it. Such written procedures need not be overly detailed or comprehensive.

3. Schedule work assignments far in advance. You'll be surprised how many peaks can be melted ahead of time simply by pushing anticipated routine work ahead on the schedule. Furthermore, when you know that Tom will be out on vacation at such and such a time, that Jack is planning to get married in June, and that Ella is expecting to give birth in October, you can plan fill-in assignments beforehand.

4. Build a backlog of substitute pinch hitters. Keep in touch with good employees who have left your employ to set up housekeeping or who have recently retired. Frequently you can call on them to step in at a moment's notice and with a minimum of instruction.

5. Set up an interdepartmental employee loan program to meet emergencies. Of course this can be done only if working relations between departments are good. But there's much to be said for swapping employees back and forth. It makes for a break in monotony for the employees, too—provided they aren't made to feel like so much chattel.

6. Clean up as much work as possible ahead of known peak periods. Don't go into a month-end closing, for example, with a backlog of unfinished routine work. Carefully plan ahead of time the specific work assignments for the peak period. That way, each employee starts with a clean slate and with full knowledge of what's expected when the pressure is on.

Of course, you can always resort (with your boss's approval) to the employment of professional temporary people or to the extension of work into overtime for regular employees. The latter course of action is a dangerous habit to get into, however. Employees tend to take the overtime for granted and may resist future solutions to peak-period staffing that do away with it.

What are the most likely accident hazards in offices?

More than half of all serious office accidents are caused by falls. The most common hazards are highly polished floors, a single unsuspected step just inside a door, unanchored rugs, wet or slippery stairs, poor lighting, extension cords, ladders, and wastebaskets.

Office people also have a penchant for cutting or bruising themselves on relatively simple equipment such as paper cutters, scissors, razor blades, moving parts of typewriters and comptometers, electric fans, mail carts and dollies, and glass-top desks.

Office fires also take their toll. Watch out for employees who carelessly throw matches or ashes in wastebaskets, who smoke when using flammable typewriter-cleaning fluid, or who use the floor for an ashtray.

What are reasonable office safety rules to enforce?

The American Management Association lists these as being especially applicable to office work:

1. Open doors slowly to avoid hitting anyone approaching from the other side.
2. Don't stand in front of closed doors.
3. Use the handrail when you go up or down stairs; don't carry materials so heavy or bulky that you have no hand free with which to grip the railing.
4. Don't tip back in swivel chairs.
5. Don't run or horseplay in the office. Don't play practical jokes.
6. Don't yank at file-cabinet drawers. If they're difficult to open, ask the maintenance department to repair them.
7. Never stand on the open drawer of a desk or file cabinet.
8. Never stand on chairs—especially swivel chairs—to reach something on a high shelf.
9. Don't leave drawers of a desk or file cabinet standing open.
10. To remove staples, use a staple remover only.
11. Keep razor blades and other sharp equipment in a closed container so that employees won't be cut while reaching into a drawer.

To what extent can you monitor personal telephone calls?

In today's society most people have come to take the telephone privilege for granted. They use the telephone indiscriminately in their own homes, so it's hard for them to feel that they're doing something wrong when they make free use of telephones in your office. This doesn't mean that you should make no attempt at all to control telephone use. When a dozen employees bang away daily on commercial telephones, the telephone bill will accelerate wildly. And of course, even with a WATS line, such use ties up the telephone for business purposes and can also be a costly employee time waster.

Probably the most effective approach to telephone control is to combine an appeal to fair play with a certain amount of hard-nosed checking. Try to set some acceptable standards for personal calls, such as (1) no charge for calls made within the area, (2) permission granted to call home when weather or business delays normal arrival, and (3) no criticism for incoming or outgoing personal calls that don't exceed five minutes each or for making no more than two calls per day. Admittedly, critics may ask why such calls should be permitted at all. The reason is that limited, reasonable usage seems better than unlimited, surreptitious usage. If you can arrive at a permissible standard, you also imply your prerogative to enforce this standard. You'll also feel freer to question anyone who is frequently on the telephone or who uses it for long periods of time. You can ask such users directly whether the call is personal or not. If the call is not a personal one, there's no reason why you can't press for details about it.

In summary, what are some sound approaches to use to stimulate interest and cooperation among office support staff personnel?

Office work tends to be increasingly routinized as it becomes more automated and controlled. It is often the price that workers pay for greater productivity. As a consequence, supervisors must try continually to inject a humanizing, motivating element into daily work life. For example, you might try to:

● Make sure that each person understands the value you place on his or her contributions. "It may seem to you, Paul, that you're only a keyboard caught in a web of computer chips. But to me and the company, you're indispensable. We depend on your good work to keep us going."

● Offer all the information needed for a person to do the job well. "As far as your job goes, Mary, there are no secrets in this department. This procedures manual and the operating files are for your use. And if you can't find what you need to know from these sources or from your associates, ask me and I'll try to dig it out for you."

● Assign each individual the authority to tap the resources related to his or her responsibilities. "You have my okay, Barbara, to use the telephone, the central terminal, the copy machine, and the materials in the stock rooms whenever you need them to proceed with your job. If you need additional help, you can ask Natalie to give you a hand."

● Give employees an opportunity to solve work-related problems and to assist you in decision-making. "You're closer to your work than I am, Rauel. I'll be expecting you to solve many of the day-to-day problems as they arise. And, from time to time, I'll be asking you to give me your views on the long-range problems that affect the whole department."

Key Concepts

1. Office administrative and support work is unique in many ways, but especially in that its transactions are valuable in and of themselves, must be performed on demand, and cannot be stored like a tangible product for later use or sale. Furthermore, the performance of office support employees is often inseparable from the service they render, either adding or detracting value from it.

2. Office employees, typically, are reluctant to commit themselves to a deep involvement with either the company they work for or its management; consequently, they tend to be either coolly aloof or cynical toward most efforts to arouse their enthusiasm.

3. Social and human aspects of the work situation seem to hold far greater importance for office workers than for their counterparts on the assembly line. Office workers' liking or dislike for the people with whom they work tends to dominate their attitudes and, as a result, their performance.

4. Office employees respond most favorably to (a) work that is varied, interesting, and truly challenging and (b) situations where supervision is effective and fair and opportunities to improve and/or advance are real.

5. The productivity of office support employees can be measurably improved by application of systematic analysis, work simplification, and various forms of office automation.

6. Periods of extreme peak work loads with slack periods between are a problem because they require keeping a large enough staff to handle the peaks or paying expensive overtime or temporary help wages. Planning ahead by doing routine work in advance, training the staff to be flexible in work assignments, and cooperating with other departments can help avoid the strain caused by the peaks.

Supervisory Word Power

Data Processing. Transmission and manipulation of data, paperwork, records, and other information essential to the production and distribution of goods and services. This may be accomplished manually, mechanically, or electronically or by some combination of these means.

Forms Control. An administrative control technique for standardizing, coordinating, and minimizing the number of forms needed to carry on properly the functions of the organization.

Office Automation. The application of electronic devices to any or all aspects of office support work, including telephone, mail, and message systems; word processing; records filing and retrieval; and personal work stations.

Office Support Staff Members. White-collar workers who perform work typically of a clerical nature in an office (as opposed to a manufacturing area) of an industrial or a commercial enterprise or an institution.

Records Retrieval. The methods and techniques used to locate and recover data, documents, and information from filing systems, libraries, data bases, and other records storage or retention areas.

Word Processing. A specialized aspect of data processing that involves a systematic approach to producing written communications (letters, forms, reports, and so forth) by integrating human skills with highly complex, automated equipment.

Reading Comprehension

1. In what important ways does office work differ from blue-collar employment?

2. How likely is it that a stenographer's duties in an office in Missouri would be similar in fundamentals to those of a stenographer in a plant in Massachusetts?

3. Which is more likely to be important to a white-collar employee: status or pay?

4. How might a supervisor minimize the monotony of some office jobs? When should the supervisor exercise caution in making changes?

5. Which is more important in improving white-collar productivity: the technical or the human factor?

6. What are the key ingredients of a job enrichment or "work itself" program?

7. Name the three factors that characterize a clerical system.

8. What is meant by the "additional value added" by clerical work?

9. What sort of problems do peak-work-load periods cause in an office? How can they be minimized?

10. What kind of accident accounts for most of the serious office injuries?

Supervision in Action

The Case of the Peak-Period Backlog. A Case Study in Human Relations Involving Office Support Work, with Questions for You to Answer.

In one Southwestern insurance company, new policy registrations typically peaked each year in May. This caused the office supervisor, Kendra Tarducci, to schedule overtime for both recording and registration clerks during that period. Sometimes the work piled up so badly that temporary help was employed. However, with the introduction of computers, a good part of the previously scheduled overtime became unnecessary. Nevertheless, the registration section still had to hand-post certain original documents. Accordingly, the office supervisor continued to schedule overtime for this group of 6 registration clerks during the month of May. The 15 recording clerks in the department continued to work their normal schedule.

By mid-May, Kendra noted that even though the work load for the recording group appeared no heavier than usual, a backlog in their section was steadily building up. On the 21st of the month, she received a request from the underwriter, who asked that the posting be brought up to date immediately. Kendra called her entire department together right away and urged that the work pace be generally speeded up in order to keep abreast of the policy registrations. Several of the senior recording clerks spoke up to cite examples of unusual problems caused by the computer recording system. These, they claimed, took an inordinate amount of time to handle. It would be impossible to catch up or stay abreast with recording without working overtime. Kendra, in turn, carefully and logically explained how each of the new problems could be handled without delay. She was certain, she said, that the recording group could get the work done without overtime. At the end of the week, however, the backlog was greater than ever.

Kendra then went to the chief underwriter, George Smith, and asked whether overtime could be authorized for the recording clerks to catch up. "No," said George. "One of the reasons we put in this new system was to cut down on overtime. There's no reason in the world why your department should have fallen behind. You'll have to get the recording section back on track without extra hours or extra help. It's bad enough that you have the registration clerks on overtime."

1. If you were the office supervisor, what would you do now?
2. What factors contributed to Kendra's problem?
3. Was the underwriter reasonable in his request? Why?
4. How could this situation have been avoided?

29

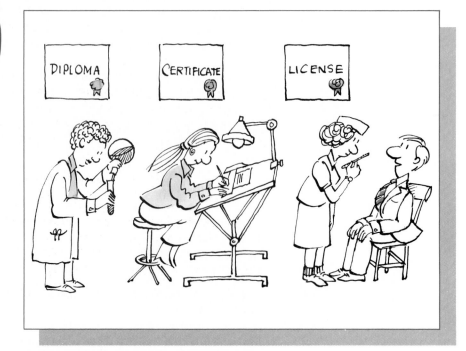

SUPERVISING ENGINEERS AND OTHER PROFESSIONAL EMPLOYEES

What distinguishes engineers and other professionals from the great majority of other workers?

They manipulate information and knowledge rather than machines, materials, assembly parts, or paperwork. For this reason, Peter

Drucker, the great management analyst, has called them "knowledge workers." Drucker makes this point:

> Fifteen to twenty years ago manual workers were the central productive factor in this society. Today, in our society, and increasingly in *all* developed societies, the central cost factor —which is not quite the same as the central productive factor— consists of knowledge workers. These people do not work with their hands, do not use brawn or manual skills. They use concepts and theories.

Drucker believes that business profits cannot improve without an intense application of this "knowledge talent." And he insists that it is "information," not "technology," that diffuses through our economy at the faster rate today. Consequently, the engineer and the scientist, together with the vast body of technicians and others who apply specialized knowledge, must be made more productive if our society is to grow and improve.

Who, besides engineers, can be included in this body of professional and knowledge workers?

There is a growing army of people who combine an advanced or specialized education with work requiring a high degree of mental effort such as analysis, reasoning, interpretation, and creativity. Their occupations cover a wide scope. Knowledge workers are engineers, scientists, researchers, planners, and technicians. They are librarians, editors, economists, market analysts, statisticians, data processing designers, programmers, and the like. They include, of course, doctors, lawyers, nurses, dentists, architects, and all other occupations generally regarded as professional. The real test of a knowledge job, however, is the degree to which it requires the incumbent to apply a specialized body of knowledge or information, usually acquired by extended study in colleges or universities and considerable experience in that particular field.

In what way will the progress toward greater automation and computer applications affect the growth in the number of knowledge workers?

It won't do away entirely with blue-collar or routine clerical work, but it will develop an intense demand for highly skilled artisans and

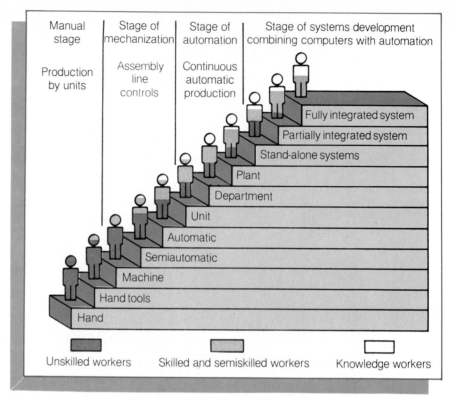

Manual stage	Stage of mechanization	Stage of automation	Stage of systems development combining computers with automation
Production by units	Assembly line controls	Continuous automatic production	

Fully integrated system
Partially integrated system
Stand-alone systems
Plant
Department
Unit
Automatic
Semiautomatic
Machine
Hand tools
Hand

Unskilled workers   Skilled and semiskilled workers   Knowledge workers

Figure 29-1. Gradual increase in percent of knowledge workers as industrial process progress from manual to automated and computerized systems.

knowledge workers with advanced, specialized training. Figure 29-1 (adapted from a figure prepared originally by the International Labour Organization in Geneva, Switzerland) illustrates the trend. Automation has already hit hard at repetitive, strong-back, no-think jobs. At the same time it shifted much of the blue-collar factory employment to white-collar or service industries. Computers, the whiz kids of automation, then descended on almost every conceivable office or clerical operation. But, initially at least, the net effect was to create more jobs. The trend today, however, is toward (1) a leveling off of routine clerical work and (2) a growth in specialized, conceptual jobs to support computer activities and to serve in fields opened by technology, automation, and computerization. There is little doubt that Peter Drucker is correct. We are entering the age of the knowledge worker.

To what extent does a higher level of education make a difference in the knowledge worker's expectations?

The higher the level of education beyond high school, the more the employee will put a premium on a job that offers (1) real challenge, (2) the chance to make a contribution to society, (3) the ability for self-expression, and (4) free time for outside interests. Furthermore, most people with college degrees do not believe that hard work, alone, will pay off. Many young people with advanced degrees find themselves at odds with what business offers them. For example:

- Most organizations place greater emphasis on job security than do these highly educated people.
- On the other hand, most organizations expect greater conformity in behavior and acceptance of corporate goals and values than graduates are ready to give.
- Furthermore, organizations believe the ability to work with groups is more important than people with advanced degrees think it is.

As a supervisor of college-trained knowledge workers, then, you face the difficult task of trying to bring together organizational and individual goals. Your best bet is to look for some sort of trade-off. For example, you may have to give a little in demands for conformity of dress and behavior in return for exceptional job results. Or, you may have to provide more flexible working hours in exchange for unstinting dedication to the work to be done. As to the need to work with groups, some highly creative people may do their best work alone—and their interests should be accommodated as much as possible. But for most organization members, the need for them to sacrifice some of their independence to the work group is so great that noncooperating individualists may be a luxury the organization cannot tolerate.

Between high and low performers among knowledge workers, are the expectations much different?

In some areas they are. According to one study of engineers and engineering managers employed in aerospace and technology-based companies, poor performers—just as much as high performers—expect salary increases, challenging work, and more job freedom. The big difference lies in expectations of promotion to a managerial position or of assuming positions of greater complexity. In actual fact, the high performers get their wishes fulfilled, whereas the poorer performers are disappointed.

These attitudes imply that supervisors are more likely to run into apathy and performance problems with their less effective employees. The danger would appear to be that supervisors will be called on to spend a disproportionate amount of their time counseling and motivating second-rate and third-rate employees. On the other hand, the high performers among knowledge workers tend to be self-starters and to be able to work effectively with minimum outside direction and stimulation.

How different are engineers, scientists, and other knowledge workers from other employees?

They are different from other employees in that they feel they are different. They believe that they are professionals and resent treatment that indicates they are thought of as ordinary workers. For example, the average engineer tends:

● To view the job as interesting and challenging and to be proud of the field. The average employee does not usually have this viewpoint.
● To rate challenge, advancement, and salary as key factors of the ideal job. There's not too much difference here, except that technically oriented people are more likely to expect to find these rewards at work—and to find another job if they don't.
● To feel that the degree of professionalism of the job is not understood by either the company or the general public.
● To be an avid reader of employment ads and to be readily open to pirating overtures by other companies.

In what ways do scientists differ from engineers?

Engineers apply scientific information. Scientists develop this information. They usually have more advanced education than engineers do. More important, their viewpoint is more academic or theoretical; the engineer's is more practical.

Scientists are even more concerned than engineers about operating in a freewheeling way. For example, one frustrated manager laments: "They like to take coffee breaks whenever they want to."

Other distinctions are more troublesome. Observes one person who must deal with scientific personnel: "Our research and development people simply won't defer to another person's priorities or backlog. Even though the job they want done may seem fairly trivial, they want it right away. For example, a scientist may wait three months for a machine to be delivered. If it comes in at 4 o'clock Tuesday afternoon, it has to be running by 9 a.m. Wednesday. They make it seem that the whole project will go down the drain otherwise." Still another observer complains: "The main problem in the design of laboratories is pinning the research people down to what they want and getting them to relinquish some of their more exotic ideas." You'd better be prepared to accept the fact that the more highly educated the employees are, and the more intellectual and creative their work, the more likely they are to be touchy to deal with.

But are engineers really professionals?

The weight of opinion is that engineers are not more than partly professional, despite the fact that many states license them as professional engineers. If they were truly professional, goes one opinion, they would have a rounded balance of specialized training and experience, professional legal responsibility, professional personal relationships, and professional ethical relationships (qualities generally attributed to a professional). Another viewpoint says: "It depends on the engineer's attitude about responsibility to society. Some research engineers are outstanding in applying science to meet some objective, but then show only the technician's limited interest in what their endeavors actually do to people." The point, however, is that most engineers—and technicians—do consider their work professional. Regardless of the harsh judgment of others, they think they are a cut above rank-and-file employees. They respect their superiors only if the superior encourages them to display a disciplined—or professional—attitude toward their assignments.

One big problem with engineers stems from their great need to be right. William D. McGuigan, who has managed thousands of engineers, puts it this way:

Criticism of an engineer's ideas tends to be translated into personal criticism—of his intelligence, competence, standing in the community, and even his ancestry. Thus, particular care must be taken to minimize criticism, particularly in the initial stages when ideas are still in an intuitive stage. The desire to avoid being wrong may make engineers poor decision makers. One role of the manager of such people is to assume this responsibility, making it his neck that is out rather than theirs. Furthermore, engineers also tend to be critics themselves. Thus the very tendencies which make an engineer—to be meticulous, detailed, analytical—are the factors least needed by a manager of engineers—particularly of creative ones.

What other kinds of employees might be thought of as professionals?

Webster defines a profession as "a calling requiring specialized knowledge and often long and intensive preparation." The so-called learned professions—theology, law, and medicine—all require intense, advanced, and specialized education, guided experience; and some form of licensing. However, many other occupations have acquired professional status: Teaching is one of the more obvious. Accounting is another. Many people in technical occupations (such as laboratory technicians, drafters, programmers, and surveyors) are often thought of as professionals—even though not every professional stipulation is met in every case or to a full degree. In addition, many clearly definable occupations—such as traffic manager, purchasing agent, systems analyst, and training director—have tended to develop professional standards of practice. When jobholders adhere to high standards of responsibility—and maintain a high level of self-discipline—in the execution of their jobs, they may think of themselves as professionals and expect to be treated accordingly.

In what ways can hospital personnel be considered professionals?

Registered nurses (RNs) are, without doubt, professionals. Licensed practical nurses (LPNs) consider themselves professionals, too, although technically this may not be so. Laboratory technicians, because of their long training and the precise quality of their work, are usually granted professional status, also. But there's something unique about hospital and related health care work that tends to make all hospital employees feel that their work is professional. First of all, they assist, in one way or another, the most respected professionals of all—medical doctors. Second, the ultimate impact of their efforts, no matter how humble, on the health—even the very life—of human beings demands a sterner self-discipline than is required in most jobs.

What characterizes work as professional?

These four unique characteristics differentiate professional chores from administrative and managerial work:

Professional Work Is Investigative in Nature. Professional assignments always involve conducting investigations for the purpose of drawing scientific conclusions or solving technical problems. Obtaining and recording data, making analyses and computations, and similar activities (although they may be performed by a professional) are not peculiar to professional work. Such activities are characterisitc of the work of nonprofessional technicians. Therefore, by definition, a person not directly concerned with drawing conclusions or solving problems based on technical investigations is not doing professional work.

Professional Work Requires Individual Contributions. A professional worker is primarily concerned with the execution of technical work and not primarily with planning, organizing, and directing work carried out by others. Even though he or she may be a leader of a team or group attempting to reach a common objective, the professional will, nonetheless, be making a substantial part of the contribution personally and directly. In such a case, the other team or group members, both professional and nonprofessional, act as extenders or multipliers of the leader. In other words, professional technical persons are employed to carry out technical assignments, and any team or group that they lead or coordinate is brought together primarily to assist. The professional knowledge worker therefore differs from a managerial employee, technical or otherwise, whose position exists for the prime reason of organizing, directing, and controlling the work of others.

Professional Work Is Not Routine or Repetitive. It does not follow a pattern or cycle, nor does it consist of specified duties and responsibilities, as does the work of most managerial or administrative positions. Professional work often consists of a series of assignments, each having a definite beginning and an end, and in most cases each is quite different from the others with respect to the steps taken in carrying it out and the end results achieved. Therefore, the professional position is neither defined nor limited by reporting relationships or responsibility for resources—human, physical, or financial. Rather, it is defined and limited by the technical complexity of assignments carried out.

Increases in the Importance and Difficulty of Professional Work Do Not Occur in Discrete Stages. Professional work covers a wide range of complexity. The range can be defined at one end by the type of assignment given a beginning, inexperienced engineer or scientist; and at the other end by the most complex kind of assignment given to a professional employee. Between these extremes, of course, assignments represent a progressive order of complexity in a more or less continuous spectrum.

In what ways can supervision modify their approach when dealing with individuals who have a high sense of their professionalism?

Try any of these actions to suit the unique needs of professional employees:

1. Realize that professional employees want to be recognized as members of a profession. The professional employees are often career-oriented rather than company-oriented. They are usually individualists who are constantly evaluating themselves. They dislike regimentation and compulsion.

2. Ensure credit and recognition from top management for outstanding work and unusual accomplishments. Generally, professional employees are jealous of their own ideas and accomplishments. They understandably resent the supervisor who takes credit for their work. They want their unusual contributions to reach the attention of top executives.

3. Give proper dignity to the title of each position held by a professional employee. Job titles are important and should be consistent with the stature of the responsibilities involved. The use of the term *engineer* in jobs that do not require formal technical training and professional status should be avoided. Similarly, such titles as Junior Engineer or Class B Planner have an adverse effect on the professional's morale.

4. Adopt liberal policies with respect to time off for personal reasons. Knowledge workers enjoy a work environment where clock-punching and other rigid controls are absent. They are frequently required to work extra hours to meet emergencies, or voluntarily spend a considerable portion of their own time coping with their employer's problems. This is considered part of the game. Accordingly, when personal matters require their absence, they expect to be allowed reasonable compensating time off.

5. Encourage knowledge workers to take part in the activities of their professional or technical societies. Since stature in the profession is important, professional interests should be promoted at every opportunity.

What is it that knowledge workers are most likely to complain about?

The typical knowledge worker resents being asked to do what he or she considers subprofessional work—routine work of a technician or clerk. The knowledge workers also feel that their salary is determined more by seniority than by merit, and they resent this. Furthermore, they dislike being regimented and believe they should be allowed to manage themselves—at least to a reasonable degree. Engineers, for example, claim they need more technical and nonprofessional help—ranging from drafters and technical writers to clerks and typists; they would like management to better define project and company goals; and many complain that communications are inadequate on scope, planning, and progress of their projects.

What do supervisors find most wanting about knowledge workers?

Typical criticisms are: "They lack experience, common sense, and maturity." "They lack practical knowledge of market needs and company problems." "They are technically strong but naive in the realm of business practicality." Supervisors may also say: "They don't keep abreast of their field" or, worse still, "They don't have the ability to determine when a job is complete." If you are aware of these tendencies, you can avoid being taken by a surprise when professional performance doesn't measure up to your expectations.

How can you keep researchers and engineers from carrying their projects past the point of no return?

Research in any field, social or technical, is largely unpredictable. Progress, furthermore, is made in small steps. And research personnel, by their very nature, are eternally hopeful and optimistic. Be prepared to listen to the plea for just $1,000 more or just one more week's work or just one more something to clear up the difficulties that seem to be bogging down progress. It will take not only good judgment but courage as well, on your part, to decide to abandon a project after considerable time and money have been spent on it. Therefore, be comforted by the generally accepted fact that between 50 and 90 percent of all research projects come to no useful end. It obviously makes a great deal of difference, however, whether the 50 or 90 percent is dropped after $1,000 has been spent or after $100,000 has been spent.

Engineering and other technical projects, whereas more definitive, often present the same sort of problem to the manager. The main danger here lies in the tendency of the engineer to broaden the scope of the project. Firm goals and specific budgets that are agreed on at the start seem the best ways to avoid undeserved prolongation of engineering projects.

How closely should research people be supervised?

Most experienced managers believe that supervision of research people should not be too close. One missile scientist, for example, defined what the supervisor should do as "just leave me alone." Scientific personnel seem to respond best to colleague authority. That is, they want their work approved by other scientists as well as by the supervisor. Despite this preference, many authorities still believe that close supervision is necessary to prevent scientists from straying too far afield. This approach, however, is most effective where scientists are engaged in development work rather than in exploration of new fields.

Happily, the true professional is basically self-regulating. A supervisor, therefore, need not necessarily know more than the subordinate scientists do—or bear down continually on them. The supervisor should function as a catalyst, a bridge to higher management, a coach, or even a critic. But if you function as a warden or a turnkey, the professional resents, rather than respects, both the concept of supervision and the person who supervises.

How much control of time and workmanship should you exert over employees who perform engineering or development work?

The hourly cost of engineering and creative work is typically very high. It is best controlled not by excessive personal supervision but by the maintenance of a few simple tabular records. For example, project cost control should compare hourly inputs with those in the original estimates. A continuing record should be kept of nonproductive time that accrues to individuals because of the failure to assign them to specific projects. Work sampling studies, which make random observations of what engineers, designers, and researchers actually do in the course of a week, often reveal that more than 25 percent of the knowledge worker's time is nonproductive for one reason or another. (See Chapter 23 for a discussion of work sampling.)

As to quality of work, it is just as important to establish quality standards for the knowledge worker as for manual, routine, or clerical work. Many engineering organizations maintain detailed checklists of design items that must be inspected and verified to prevent errors and omissions. Standards typically include dimensioning, lettering, preparing title blocks, and procedures for issuing drawing numbers.

What's the best way to keep younger knowledge workers interested in their work?

Impatience characterizes young knowledge workers. They want to make their mark fast. So it's important to get across to them in a challenging manner the idea that big achievements rarely come easily or quickly. Point out that the little successes are essential. Show that they in turn become the foundation on which reputations are built and from which more important tasks can be attacked.

A variety of job assignments, including job or project rotation, also keeps a job from becoming dull. Whereas it's natural for some individuals to want to move ahead immediately to more difficult assignments, under proper guidance they can continue to learn and to gain versatility by working on a number of jobs that are essentially of the same complexity. This way they gain breadth, if not depth.

Probably the greatest offense to guard against when dealing with younger specialists is to reject ideas out of hand. You must listen—and listen objectively—to their suggestions. Avoid being overcritical. You want to nurture an inquiring mind with a fresh approach. You'll discourage it quickly if you revert too often to "We've tried that before and it won't work here."

One sure way to disenchant young college graduates is to flagrantly misuse their talents. Expect them to do some routine work, of course. But don't make their daily work just one long series of errands. This includes such break-in assignments as performing routine calculations, digging up reference material, and operating reproduction equipment. One large manufacturing company recently interviewed a number of promising engineers who had left them. The company found that the overwhelming complaint was that the company not only did not provide work that was challenging but also expected far too little from them in the way of performance.

As a sidelight to this, it is important not to overselect engineers or other technical people for your department. If the nature of your work is such that you can't keep good personnel working near their capabilities, they are almost certain to get jaded. Overstaffing, too, can lead to the same kind of problem. Keeping good knowledge workers waiting around for assignments to materialize frequently results in boring, unproductive idleness. Most technically oriented departments would probably function better with too few employees than with too many.

What is the best communications pattern to encourage among knowledge workers?

It should be free and open and encouraged to take place at the lowest possible level. Knowledge workers should feel free to consult other workers across organizational lines. Informal groups develop from these contacts, and this fosters cross-fertilization of ideas and innovation. Often the best solutions to problems come from these informal communications channels.

What sort of relationships should you maintain with your knowledge workers?

It is a matter of being both firm and soft. On the one hand, you should let them know exactly what it is that you expect from them. Knowledge workers can be great hairsplitters and "sea lawyers." That is, they can debate endlessly, and sometimes expertly, about issues and conditions that have not been firmly established. As such, you must be fairly rigid in setting up explicit ground rules. Then allow them maximum creativity while working within these limitations.

On the other hand, it's a good idea to present your role to knowledge workers as that of a facilitator rather than a boss. It is better to be criticized by them for "not doing anything" than to draw their resistance by continually riding herd on them. You can be sure that most knowledge workers believe that they are doing the really important, brilliant work of the organization. If, in fact, they do perform well, give them all the credit you can. They tend to respond better, anyway, to suggestions than edicts. "We" is a better pronoun than "I" in discussing problems. As one perceptive manager put it, "Let them feel you are the tug to their cruise ship," even if the opposite is true.

In that regard, it is even a good idea to acknowledge your own vulnerability. Concede that you may be as likely to be wrong as they are. Don't make the mistake of trying to act out the role model of the tough, assertive boss. It's more effective to be hesitant in problem situations, allowing your employees to come to the fore with their solutions.

Finally, try to avoid direct confrontations. Don't say such things as "You're wrong." Instead, modify your approach by saying something like: "Perhaps I don't have all the facts that you do, because I can't see it the way you do. Will you explain your position again to me?" As with any kind of conflict, it helps to defuse anger by depersonalizing the issues. Disagreements should focus on facts and issues, not personalities.

Should you handle nonprofessional employees — such as those involved in hospital work — differently from the professionals where both groups are in close daily contact?

This problem occurs regularly, and it is difficult to handle. It requires a delicate touch on the part of the supervisor. The situation seems especially critical in hospital work. Some of the personnel are undeniably professionals; others merely think that their work is professional. The true professionals are typically granted certain status and privileges. When you withhold these conditions from the nonprofessional staff, you tend to demoralize them, or at least to lessen their dedication—a dedication that is so badly needed. On the other hand, things can get out of hand if housekeeping employees, for example, refuse direction on the basis of their "professionalism."

In the main, it would appear better to lean a little in favor of too much recognition of rank-and-file employees than to reveal an attitude that judges their work to be routine or, worse still, menial. For that reason the word *dedicated* occupies a special place in describing the work of hospital employees. It tends to place their efforts above those of people employed in other industrial or service occupations without, at the same time, leading these employees to demand or expect status and privileges equal to those of the recognized professionals on the staff.

Conversely, experience has shown that registered nurses and technicians sometimes want all the status associated with professionalism without wanting to assume their share of its self-discipline and responsibilities. For example, the practice of tipping nurses and presenting them with gifts has tended to detract from their professionalism. Pervasive as the practice is in hospitals today, it is not consistent with a policy of equal treatment of all patients regardless of income, reputation, or disposition. The rule of thumb for the true professionals might be to treat them will full respect for their status but at the same time to let them know you expect the ultimate from them in dedicated service.

What criteria should be used when appraising the performance of knowledge workers?

One guideline has been provided by the National Society of Professional Engineers. It cautions, however, that evaluations are essentially a matter of judgment and not a matter on which there can be hard-and-fast rules about how to rate. Nevertheless, the society suggests the criteria and possible weightings shown in Table 29-1. Most appraisal systems seem to be informal rather than formal. Typically, a manager observes the knowledge worker and discusses the work with him or her, judging output by projects completed successfully, process and product improvements, patents, and published articles. Some companies feel that productivity and performance should be measured over a period of years (perhaps three years) because so many projects take a long time. Shorter-interval rating could be misleading, they say.

TABLE 29-1 APPRAISAL STANDARDS FOR ENGINEERS

Criterion	Point Value
Job and technical knowledge	15
Application and productivity	10
Originality and initiative	20
Quality of work	15
Judgment, planning, and organization	10
Cooperation	3
Effective communication	8
Leadership	6
Attitude	4
Dependability and responsibility	10
Capacity for learning	9
	110 maximum

Those companies that use appraisal forms most often include the following factors: attitude and cooperation, reliability, productivity, job and technical knowledge, judgment, planning and administrative skills, contribution of workable ideas, accuracy, adaptability, personality, quality of work, capacity for development, leadership ability shown, relations with other workers, drive, and ability to communicate.

What can you do to retain good professional people on your staff?

You have to work hard at it, because professionals and other knowledge workers are highly mobile. This means that unemployment among them is usually low, and they can often pick and choose their jobs. Private companies must compete for these professionals not only with other companies but also with federal agencies.

The best approach is to offer (1) as much freedom of job direction as possible and (2) truly worthwhile and challenging assignments. Assuming that pay scales are equitable, this kind of employee will stick to an employer under even miserable working conditions if the task is interesting enough and the supervisor is understanding enough. The employee may appear to be discontented; knowledge workers are very able and vocal complainers. But they also can get so wrapped up in their work that you couldn't persuade them to leave even if you wanted to.

What about advancing people who are good at their specialty, but have poor management potential, into the managerial ranks?

Some companies handle the problem by rewarding outstanding researchers and other specialized knowledge workers with a two-track promotion plan. One track is for those who want, and have the potential, to advance by the management route; the other is for those who want to stick to research. The idea is that persons who want to devote their talents to research can still achieve the same pay and status as the persons who go into supervision and management. Even if your company does not follow this plan, it is probably better in the long run to keep good researchers researching than to advance them into management echelons if their personalities and inclinations are not suitable.

Task force or project assignments: How do these affect supervisors of knowledge workers?

It puts great demands on the supervisors to coordinate one set of specialized skills or knowledge with several others. In medical research, for example, a parasitologist may have to work effectively with a tissue specialist. On a mechanical design project, a metallurgist may have to work with structural, aeronautical, and chemical engineers. On an urban development project, economists, sociologists, and behavioral scientists may have to work together with land-usage engineers, planning specialists, and architects.

Leadership of such interdisciplinary teams requires a unique balance. On the one hand, the leader will extract the greatest contributions and cooperation from the participatory approach. On the other hand, the leader must also exert firm progress and cost control to keep team members focusing on the project's objectives and scheduled completion date.

The situation is complicated further because members of task forces often are assigned only temporarily to a particular project. They owe their more permanent allegiance to managers of the specialized departments from which they have been detached. Thus, knowledge workers find themselves torn between two bosses and two sets of standards. There is no easy solution here. The project supervisor must recognize this possibility and maintain a flexible approach to minimize its effect.

Where does the so-called matrix organization fit in?

The matrix organization is closely associated with special projects, task forces, and committee work. It presumes that each group of specialists is organized in a separate, but typical, line organization. You can picture this part of the matrix as a series of vertical organizational chains hanging from a clothesline. (See Figure 10-6.) The other part of the matrix (the horizontal segment) occurs when one or more project managers are given authority to use the time of a number of different specialists. These project managers come in horizontally from the left side of the clothesline to pick out from each vertical organization the particular specialists needed. The matrix (or grid) has the net effect of putting each specialist into a square from which he or she looks (1) upward to the manager of the specialized organization and (2) sideways to the manager of the project to which he or she is assigned.

Matrix organizations are becoming increasingly popular, since so many modern problems need solutions that stem from many sources rather than a single one. Matrix organizations are most commonly found in engineering, research and development, planning, and investigational work.

The matrix organization, however, is by no means the only way to organize knowledge workers. Whatever the organizational form may be, its purpose should be to bring these informed people together to get jobs done, not to classify jobs and establish barriers between zones of authority and responsibility. The most effective organizational groups for these people are often the informal ones set up by the knowledge workers themselves.

Key Concepts

1. Engineers, scientists, and other knowledge workers tend to have a high regard for their field of work and for themselves. They feel that their professionalism puts them a cut above rank-and-file employees, and as such they expect more freedom and the right to conduct their work with less outside direction and control.

2. True professionalism stems both from the nature of the work and from the way in which it is carried out. The work is investigative, individualistic, creative, and nonrepetitive. Its conduct requires high standards of performance, self-discipline, and ethics.

3. Professional conduct is encouraged by (a) assignment of professional levels of work; (b) recognition of the self-motivating, self-evaluating, and self-controlling capabilities of the individual; (c) provision of dignified surroundings and status; and (d) intelligent knowledgeable supervision.

4. Because of the comparatively high levels of education and social acceptance that most knowledge workers have attained, they tend to have a naïve confidence in their own abilities and judgments which often makes them hold out against strong direction, criticism, and control, regardless of their justification.

5. There are a growing number of subprofessional and paraprofessional occupations whose work borders on that of the professional; the contributions of this segment of the labor force can be improved and maximized by extending to it professional status and treatment.

Supervisory Word Power

Engineer. A person who applies scientific information to the design, construction, or use of machinery and equipment.

Interdisciplinary Team. A group of employees with different specialized skills who are assigned, usually temporarily, to a project or to a task force.

Knowledge Worker. A person who applies specialized knowledge or information, usually acquired by extended study and considerable experience, to an occupation that requires a high degree of mental effort such as analysis, reasoning, interpretation, and creativity.

Paraprofessional. A specially trained individual who works along with professionals but in a subsidiary and support relationship.

Professional. A person whose occupation requires highly specialized training and experience, legal responsibility—such as a license to practice the occupation—and prescribed standards of performance and ethics.

Scientist. A person whose occupation is concerned with the development of information based on a study of the facts, truths, and laws that define the arrangement of the physical and material world.

Technician. A person skilled in the application of a particular art or trade or of one of the engineering or scientific disciplines.

Reading Comprehension

1. In what ways do engineers and other knowledge workers think they are different from ordinary workers?

2. If knowledge workers are so jealous of their professional status, does that mean that managers can exert no control over their performance? Explain.

3. What is it that distinguishes professional work from nonprofessional work?

4. If a choice had to be made, would a professional tend to defend the profession or the employer most vigorously? Why?

5. Compare a knowledge worker's attitude toward the length and regularity of the hours of work with that of, say, a clerk in a large office.

6. If a knowledge worker balked at being asked to perform regularly subprofessional work, such as filing correspondence, would it be a good idea to insist on the assignment? Why?

7. Why should a supervisor want to bring to a conclusion a knowledge worker's research project just when the individual wants to continue it until it is certain the best solution has been reached in the research?

8. Contrast the supervision considered ideal for a knowledge worker with that considered necessary for an assembly line worker.

9. To what extent does it make sense to consider noncertified occupations professional because of the professional demands of the work? Give some examples.

10. In an electronics research firm organized in a matrix structure, engineers, scientists, and technicians representing a number of disciplines are being assigned temporarily as needed to project managers. What are two difficulties the project managers might encounter?

Supervision in Action
The Case of the Missed Deadlines. A Case Study in Human Relations Involving Knowledge Workers, with Questions for You to Answer.

Joan, a project leader, supervises a group of three mechanical engineers. Their mission is to redesign a gear track for a motion-picture projector in which Teflon gears are to be substituted for bronze ones. When Joan was first handed the assignment from the chief engineer, she called her group together. She explained that the new design would have to conform to a new set of parameters. For example, the new gear train had to be totally enclosed and dust-free and operate at speeds of more than twice the speed of the bronze ones, and the gear box would have to be interchangeable with previous models. Furthermore, this called for a crash program—the project was to be completed within three months. After the preliminary discussion, Joan proceeded to make specific job assignments. She asked Sabra to draw up a table indicating the range of Teflon gears available in stock sizes. She asked Tom to develop a gear-box design that would be readily interchangeable with existing and projected models. She asked the veteran in her group, George, to develop sketches for the new gear-train design.

At the end of the next week, Joan met with each of the engineers to check their progress. She found that Sabra had gathered all her information within a day or two and then had turned her efforts toward another project. Tom, on the other hand, had no designs to show and had spent only a few hours during the week talking to members of the production department about assembly specifications. The rest of the time he had spent on another urgent project. George had made a few preliminary calculations and then set the project aside in the belief that it would be next to impossible to develop a design to meet the new operating specifications using a synthetic material.

In speaking to each of the engineers at this time, Joan listened carefully and discussed the progress or lack of progress without criticism. In her own mind, however, she decided that the group would never meet the project deadline if she didn't set more rigorous timetables for each intermediate target. That Friday afternoon Joan laid out a schedule pinpointing what sort of progress would be expected from Sabra, Tom, and George by the following Friday. Joan's secretary typed the schedule and distributed it to all three. The following Friday, when Joan met with each of the engineers to discuss progress, she discovered that none of them had made any significant progress during the week.

1. If you were Joan, what tack would you try now?
2. What could be some of the reasons why Joan's original approach did not work?
3. Was there anything fundamentally wrong with her follow-up approach? Why?
4. Why didn't each engineer accomplish more during the first week of the project?
5. What could Joan have done to get the project moving faster in the first place?

30

THE COMPUTER AND MANAGEMENT INFORMATION SYSTEMS

What, really, is a management information system? Why is it so important?

At its root a management information system (MIS) is plain old accounting, but with a much broader base and an electronic twist. MIS is important because it can provide an informed basis for all management decisions. When the system is a good one, decisions are likely to be good. When the system is skimpy or overdone or misleading, decisions will suffer.

A modern management information system tries to keep track of everything that may help to make a manager's decisions effective. In a manufacturing company, for example, MIS collects and analyzes information about product development, production, marketing, and finance. In a service company such as a commercial airline, MIS may encompass other functions, such as aircraft operation, maintenance, scheduling, and customer sales and ticketing. (See Figure 30-1 for an example of a comprehensive management information system for a manufacturing company.)

The ultimate objective of a MIS is to tie together all of a company's past and present data into a great big library with instant electronic recall. Managers at all levels draw from this library (called a data bank) any kind of information that aids short-range or long-term decisions. Few organizations reach this ideal. Most management information systems operate in functional pockets with separate systems for each important activity. Production and inventory control may form one system, for example, and payroll accounting another. These functional systems are only loosely tied into the overall company MIS, with little cross-referencing between them. The goal, however, is gradually to link all separate MISs into a fully integrated system.

In what way does the computer help MIS?

The computer makes a modern MIS possible. A management information system needs a device to collect, store, analyze, and transmit an immense array of data. The computer performs this function in the form of integrated electronic data processing, or EDP, and it does it at fantastic speeds.

How does the computer work?

Supervisors need not know its inner workings. It helps, however, to think of a computer as made up of a number of black boxes that are its *hardware.*

Memory or Storage Unit.   This operates by changing numbers coded in decimal form to binary form—known as the base-2 number system—so that each number (or *bit*) can be turned either on or off. The vital memory unit is usually a fundamental part of the computer's

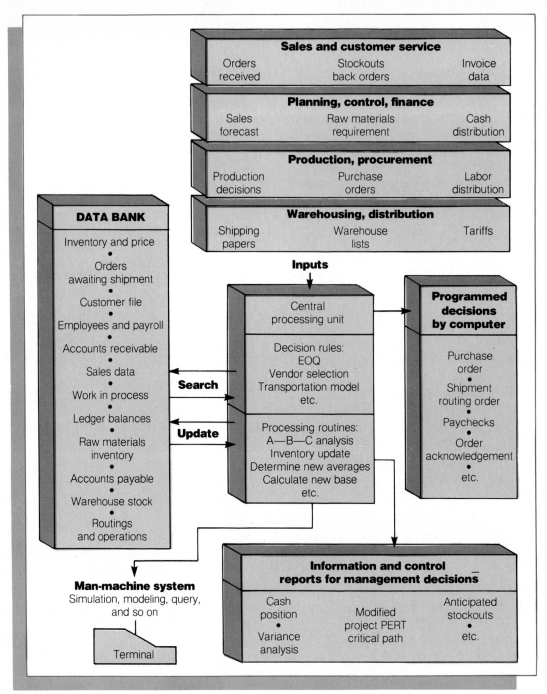

Figure 30-1. A management information system in a manufacturing company.
Joel E. Ross, *Modern Management and Information Systems,* Reston Publishing
Company, Inc., Reston, Va., 1976. Used by permission.

innards. The storage unit may actually be inside the computer or somewhere outside, attached by an electrical "umbilical" cord.

Arithmetic Unit.   This device manipulates the bits—especially to add, subtract, or multiply them—at incredible speeds.

Control Unit.   This handy device fetches instructions from the memory, decodes them, and then tells the other units of the computer what to do.

Input-Output Units.   These are what you chiefly see when you look at a computer. Input devices (see Figure 30-2) connect the heart of the computer to keyboard machines, punched-card machines, tape and disk drives, optical scanners (which "read" the magnetic

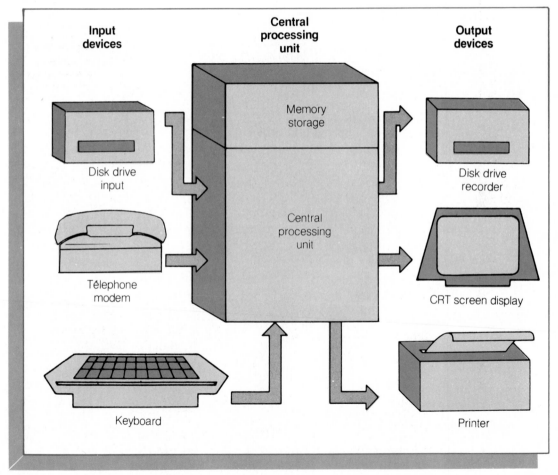

Figure 30-2. Hardware components of a small computer system.

numbers on checks, for instance, or the wand used at supermarket checkout counters to read grocery package labels), and telephone modems to pick up electronic voice inputs. Output devices are not unlike the input media except that the most visible devices are the video display tube (CRT, for cathode ray tube) and the printer (which looks like a typewriter but is driven automatically by the computer). When the computer output is in printed form (such as a typical "print-out" report) it is popularly known as "hard copy." If you will look back at Figure 30-1, you'll see the various outputs at the lower right, indicated by rectangles with curved bottoms.

What is the central processing unit?

This is the heart of the computer. Nicknamed the CPU, it includes the memory, arithmetic, and control units.

What do computers really look like?

They come in three sizes and forms. First, there is the giant "mainframe" computer that only large companies, government agencies, and other sizable institutions own. Smaller firms may obtain usage through computer service companies. Then there are the desk-sized "minicomputers" that thousands of smaller organizations use. These perform operations somewhat reduced in scope from those of the giant computers. Finally, there are the millions of "microcomputers," often called "personal computers." These look very much like the schematic drawing shown in Figure 30-2. Even if your firm has access to a mainframe computer, the chances are that what you will mainly see are the various input and output devices, unless you are directly involved with operation of the computer itself. The difference between the personal computer and the mainframe computer is only one of degree. The principles of their operation are essentially the same.

What converts operational data and information into a format the computer can process?

Data and information must be arranged beforehand in such a way that it will flow through the computer to do what management wants it to do. Highly skilled specialists, called programmers, translate the data into a computer language. Three computer languages commonly used by programmers are:

COBOL (COmmon Business Oriented Language) is designed especially for business. It employs English words and sentences almost exclusively.

FORTRAN (FORmula TRANslation) may be used for business, but its principal application today is for scientific work where mathematical equations are solved.

BASIC (Beginners' Algebraic Symbol Interpreter Compiler) is more complicated than either of the other two languages. It is especially adaptable for input and output users, however, which is making its application more common in business.

In addition, there are a number of programs that enable a person unfamiliar with computers to talk directly in conversational language with them.

Programmers, using computer language, produce instructions for a computer. These instructions are called programs. Programs are the *software* of the computer.

Other commonly used terms that apply to computer hardware and software appear in Table 30-1.

S hould a distinction be made between data and information?

It may seem like hairsplitting, but MIS designers insist there are good reasons to distinguish them.

Data can be described as merely facts and figures that, until processed, bear little relation to decision making.

Information is data that has been processed for specific use by managers and supervisors in decision making related to planning, organizing, directing, and controlling.

W here does the computer input unit get the information it processes in the first place?

The computer may get it from you or your department. It certainly gets it from someone or someplace in your organization. Here are some typical computer input sources: a sales order, an invoice from a vendor, a record of the invoice when it is paid, a talley of the day's production output, a charge against a credit card account, and the information on a quality-control chart. Whatever the input, it is often copied by a keyboard operator who transfers the data to punched

TABLE 30-1 SELECTED GLOSSARY OF COMPUTER TERMS

Bit. The smallest unit of information that the computer recognizes, a bit is represented by the presence or absence of an electronic pulse, 0 or 1.

Byte. A byte is to a bit what a word is to a letter. Usually, one byte is eight bits long.

Compatibility. A characteristic of some computers that allows a program developed for one system to run on another system.

Data base. A collection of interrelated data that is organized for ease of update and retrieval. For example, a personnel data base would include information such as employee names and Social Security numbers.

Disk. A revolving plate on which data and programs are stored.

Documentation. The printed material accompanying a program that describes what the program does and how to use it.

File. A collection of related records; an inventory file, for example.

Machine language. A program—consisting of a string of 1's and 0's—that the computer understands directly.

Memory. The section of the computer where instructions and data are stored.

Memory capacity. The maximum number of storage positions in a computer's memory. Typically, a microcomputer can have up to 128K (approximately 128,000) bytes of memory.

Menu. A list of alternative actions displayed on the video display screen for selection by the user; for example, ADD A CUSTOMER might be one option on a menu.

Microcomputer. A small computer in which the CPU is an integrated circuit deposited on a silicon chip.

Modem. A telephone hookup device that converts computer signals so that they can be sent over telephone lines; this allows microcomputers to communicate with larger systems, such as time-sharing networks.

Packaged software. Sometimes referred to as "off-the-shelf" software, this is usually used as is but can be modified to fit a business's particular needs.

Peripheral. A device—for example, a video display screen or a printer —used for storing data, or for entering it into or retrieving it from the computer system.

Prompt. A request for action that is presented to a user on a video display screen.

Terminal. A peripheral device through which information is entered into or extracted from the computer.

User-friendly (user-oriented). This describes software that is designed to be easily understood by the user.

cards, or more frequently now, to magnetic tapes or disks. A card-reader machine or disk drive then transfers the data into the heart of the computer. Increasingly, data is entered directly into the computer by the keyboarder or by such devices as the optical scanner.

What kinds of services do computers perform for MIS?

They can be classified under four main headings.

Recordkeeping. This is by far the most widely used service. It replaces or aids just about every imaginable kind of clerical activity that formerly was done by hand. Some experts say that 98 percent of all computer activity is recordkeeping. It can be done in batches, or it can be handled on-line as the transaction takes place. When a shipping clerk in a warehouse, for example, removes a case of goods from stock and keyboards this information at the same time into the computer, it is an on-line system.

Operations Control. This connects the computer to a process, such as petroleum processing, or to numerically controlled machine tools. The computer's control unit gets feedback information (measurements) from the process or tool. The computer compares this information with the standard measurement in its memory. If there is a deviation, the computer then instructs the necessary valves or motors in the process equipment to do whatever is necessary for the process to proceed correctly.

Planning and Simulation. This enables management to make forecasts and to try out a plan in advance. It does so by carrving out its procedures in a computer program modeled after its plan (a simulation).

Management Control. This is, of course, the management information system. It works in very much the same way as operations control, except that management action—rather than a physical process—is being helped. The computer rarely takes the action; it simply signals management that something should be done. A computer printout that places an asterisk next to items that are running over budget is a typical output of this system. A supervisor observes the asterisk and does whatever he or she thinks is necessary to correct the situation.

The computer end of MIS, then, is foolproof?

Yes—once the data gets inside the machine. Before data gets into the machine, however, there are innumerable chances for mistakes. Many errors in MIS occur at the very instant the original information is collected. This can take place anywhere along the line. The original sales order may have the wrong price on it, or the production figure written by the operator can be incorrect. Many errors are introduced, too, as the original data is prepared for input by keypunch and keyboard operators; and, of course, there is nothing to guarantee that the programmer has not made an error—or that the programmer was not misled by the manager who stipulated what the computer should do.

All these problems arise from human faults, not electronic ones. It is the reason close supervision is needed, together with an understanding of how the system works—especially outside the computer.

Where do supervisors fit into the MIS computer picture?

Supervisors become involved in computer operations in two basic ways:

1. You may simply be an *end-user* of computer output information. If so, make the most of this output. Understand what it means, what you are supposed to derive from it, and what kind of actions you are supposed to take on the basis of it. Is the computer printout you get a yard long, but only six items apply directly to you? Should you make a correction today? Or can you wait until the next report before you get moving?

2. You may be a *prime source* of inputs. If so, find out specifically what information your department is sending to the computer. Which records are selected for keyboarding? Exactly what form should they be in when they leave your department? Are the measures your employees are collecting exactly the same as those required for the computer? For example, are you tallying in inches when the computer needs metric figures? Or are you transmitting daily figures when the computer wants hourly data?

How can you get the most from your relationships with MIS designers and the EDP people?

Four things will help:

1. Ask For Only as Much Data or Information as You Need. It might be convenient to know what the reject rate is for every one of 578 parts in your department, for example, but this information would take far too many notches on a punched card. Instead, suggest that these parts can meaningfully be classified into only five types and that a reject rate according to these would be fine.

2. Be Ready to Compromise When Information Overlaps Occur. Say that you want an inventory report with items listed by part numbers and the supervisor in the next department wants them according to order numbers. Suggest that a single report that lists items by both part and order number might be feasible and an inexpensive compromise.

3. Let MIS and EDP People Know About Any Excess Information You Get That You Don't Need or Use. Let them know also if you receive duplicate sets of the same reports. You may be able to help them reduce the number of items gathered and reports issued.

4. Make Your Own Data Collections as Accurate as Possible. Then relay this data to EDP as promptly as is required and in the form specified.

Can supervisors design their own management information systems?

Yes. Even if their parent organizations have a MIS, supervisors can and should develop their own concept of how information needed for decisions is gathered and routed to them. Part A of Figure 30-3 shows a basic management information system. Part B shows how a

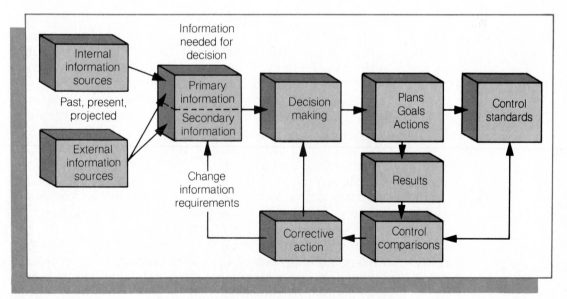

Figure 30-3A. Basic components of a management information system.

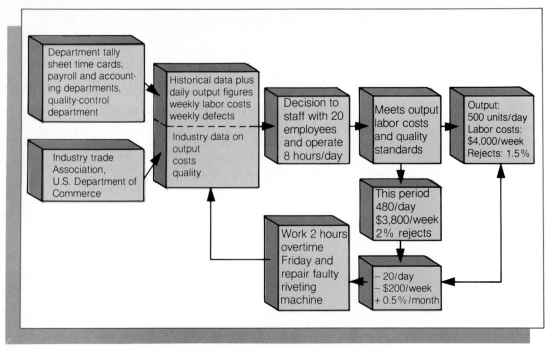

Figure 30-3B. Assembly supervisor's departmental information system.

supervisor can adopt the same principle to explain departmental information needs, sources, and uses. **Primary data** is information that is collected and analyzed for the specific purpose of running a particular operation. **Secondary data** is any useful information published by trade associations, business magazines, the United States government, or any other outside source.

Secondary data for your department may simply be the data you can gather from other departments in your own company, agency, or institution.

In part B of Figure 30-3 the supervisor set performance standards at 500 units per day, labor costs at $4,000 per week, and the average weekly reject rate at 1.5 percent. The supervisor based the decisions for these standards on past records for the department and on what could be learned about industry standards for similar operations.

To make the MIS work, the supervisor requested the following: daily output figures from the shop clerk; weekly labor costs gathered from the time cards, processed by the payroll section, and recorded by the accounting department, and the weekly defects rate from the quality-control department.

For this week the supervisor's daily output has been only 480, or

20 below standard. Labor costs were $3,800, or $200 less than budgeted. The weekly reject rate was up to 2 percent, or 0.5 percent over standard. On the basis of these control comparisons, the supervisor decides to take corrective action. The entire staff will work overtime for two hours on Friday to raise output. The supervisor will also place a maintenance request to fix a faulty riveting machine, to which the higher reject rate is attributed.

How is employee job content affected by computers?

It is likely to be radically affected if the work is clerical. Skilled typists, for example, have to change their complete approach when servicing a computer-assisted word processing center. Where typists formerly entered data in selected places on a standard form, they may now type these entries into a minicomputer, which then types the entire form on the basis of the entries provided by the typist. Check sorting, which is done by hand in many banks, will eventually be done by electronic scanning devices linked to a computer. The check sorters may still be needed, but their work will be directed toward gathering and presorting for computer reading. One check sorter will handle thousands instead of hundreds of checks per hour.

In many areas the traditional way of handling the job will simply disappear, if it hasn't already. As of 1980, for instance, the Library of Congress no longer prepares the familiar cards for library catalog files. Instead, the system has been shifted to keyboard operation. Most large libraries will follow suit, so that someone looking for a book will punch a keyboard and read the book's location from a cathode-ray tube.

Nothing, however, is likely to reduce the need for accuracy. Attempts to eliminate human error by computerization have generally been unsuccessful. Removal of one source of error, as when bank numbers are printed on checks with magnetic ink, simply highlights another source of error, such as placing checks upside down or backward in the optical scanner.

To what extent will computers replace people?

It is hard to say. During the first few decades of their use, computers created millions of new jobs. Unfortunately, some of these new jobs were created hundreds of miles away and in organizations different from those where jobs were eliminated. Some experts now believe the computer's impact on employment has topped out. It will neither create nor do away with jobs. Other experts foresee unimagined new uses that will again create millions of new jobs. Still other experts think that, if anything, the computer will now start to eat away at existing jobs. It is best to proceed on a case-by-case basis. Don't jump to conclusions about what computers will do to jobs in your organization. Wait until you gather all the facts.

What will be the impact of computers and centralized MIS on the supervisor's job?

There are two schools of thought here. The first says that computers will tend to squeeze out the need for middle managers, as illustrated in Figure 30-4. In this scenario, middle-level decisions will be programmed, leaving the first-line supervisor to make the nonprogrammed decisions that directly affect operations and employees. This would, of course, require supervisors to make more decisions and to make them more quickly. The second theory is that the numbers of managers at each level will not change much, but their jobs will. That is, all managers, including supervisors, will be expected to rely more on documented information than on hunch or intuition. In a way, this would place more value on a keenly analytical mind than on a supervisor's accumulated experience.

Either scenario puts more responsibility on the supervisor. The computer-programmed plans and schedules will always need ad-

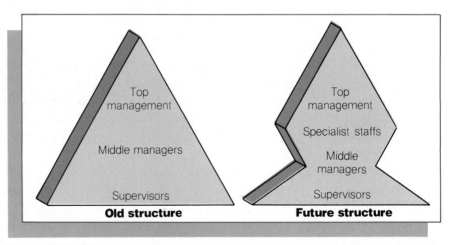

Figure 30-4. Structural changes in future organizations. Adapted from R. Trewatha and M. Newport, *Management: Functions and Behavior,* Business Publications, Dallas, 1976, p. 507. By permission.

justment on the shop or office floor. Supervisors must be alert to make these changes or to see that their employees make the necessary adjustments.

How does the systematization of information handling, especially with computers, affect people at work?

It has its good aspects and its unfavorable ones. Even these draw conflicting responses. For example:

1. Systematization reduces job tensions and conflicts by making things more orderly. There will always be conflict among people, jobs, and operations. The computer should lessen their intensity, however, because the interfaces will be fixed and predictable. Once an information issue is resolved between the production and the maintenance supervisor, it should be less bothersome, because it will arise in the same manner each time and can be anticipated.

2. Systematization creates job dissatisfaction because it requires individuals to fit their work into a rigidly prescribed format. Those employees who dislike close supervision and control will feel the same way about any system that makes similar demands. Supervisors must do a better job than in the past of placing people in work that best suits their concept of job satisfaction.

3. Systematization tends to make work monotonous because it reduces the opportunity to be creative. If the job is one that is fully dominated by the system, this will be true. People who prefer routine to initiative may like it, however. For many jobs the computer has just the opposite effect. It removes the routine and calls out for creative solutions to the problems it identifies.

4. Systematization depersonalizes work; people serve the machine more than the machine serves people. This is unfortunately true at lower levels of employment. At skilled and managerial levels, however, the system takes over much of the tiresome work and allows people to devote a greater portion of their efforts to work that matches their eduation, experience, and capabilities.

What can be done to make employees more adaptable to the MIS process, EDP, and computers in general?

Electronic data processing and other aspects of computer technology are with all of us to stay. Happily, employees coming out of high schools and colleges today are much more familiar with it than are those of previous generations. Nevertheless, there are several positive tacks that supervisors should take.

Try to Reduce Tension by Allowing Employees to Bring Their Irritations into the Open. Tempers are likely to flare highest when a new system is being debugged. Suppose Mike says, "Nothing matters anymore except getting the data to that electronic monster on time." Don't give Mike this reply: "That's too bad. If you can't keep up with it, maybe you better look for a job somewhere else." Instead, try saying something like this: "I agree that the computer now seems to be dominating our work in the department. Perhaps it won't be that way once we get used to it. After all, look how we adjust ourselves to the exact time for a TV show or a sports event. Let's stick with it and see if we can get the better of this situation."

Acknowledge That It's Only Normal to be Fearful of What the Computer May Do to Jobs and Job Security. Suppose that Selma says, "When they redesigned the last computer setup, six people in the payroll section were transferred to the sales order department, and not one of them likes it over there. What's going to happen when these MIS analysts finish up with us next month?" Don't dismiss Selma's fear as something silly. Instead, agree that computers and EDP have made changes in the company. And, yes, some of these changes have been hard to accept. But assure Selma that you will do whatever you can do to make certain that higher management is aware of her present contributions. You will also look around to see where and how her talents can best be used if there is a change in her job.

Focus Your Attention on Trying to Make Sure That People Are Assigned to the Work They Do Best and Like Best. Abe, Edna, and Malcolm like routine work so that they can socialize to the maximum; assign them to repetitive work that is undemanding mentally. Ella, Dixie, and Vortek have strong creative qualities; assign them to work that requires initiative. All six persons may have to work in a computer-oriented world, but usually enough different kinds of work are available to satisfy individual preferences. People and job matches won't be perfect, of course. But when supervisors show they are willing to make the effort, this act in itself helps to counteract anxieties about computers' depersonalizing the work.

Key Concepts

1. Management Information Systems (MIS) tie together all the relevant information needed to operate an organization and make this information available to managers and supervisors for problem solving and decision making.

2. Computer equipment (hardware) and instruction programs (software) enable management information systems to accomplish a wide variety of tasks in an incredibly short time.

3. Supervisors stand at both ends of the computer (or MIS) system. As end-users, they receive computer outputs that provide them with operational and cost data. As prime sources of input supervisors collect and transmit all sorts of sales, production, data, quality, and cost data to the system.

4. By applying MIS principles, supervisors can make up their own departmental MIS from time cards, scheduling, production tallies, quality specification, inspection, and other data related to departmental operations.

5. Computers and automation pose a real or imagined threat to many employees. Supervisors should face these problems openly and try to reduce tensions and dissatisfactions by making job assignments as attractive as possible.

Supervisory Word Power

Computer Language. A unique combination of symbols and instructions that readily converts to the binary arithmetic form understood by the computer. COBOL, FORTRAN, and BASIC are common languages for computer instructions.

Computer Program. A string of instructions written in computer language, which, when followed by the computer, carries out a given operation—such as preparing a payroll, computing merchandise prices, and maintaining perpetual inventory records.

Computer System. A unique combination of self-modifying (1) *equipment* (hardware) consisting of a central processing unit that stores, manipulates, and controls data provided to it by input devices and delivers information to users by means of output devices; and (2) *programs* (software) couched in special languages that instruct the computer what to do and how to adapt these instructions to the changing nature of new data (or feedback) it receives.

Information. Data—past or present facts, observations, or conclusions collected in numbers and words—that has been selected, arranged, and analyzed (processed) to make it useful for a specific human (managerial) activity.

Management Information System. A system made up of data processing devices, programs, and people, which collects, analyzes, exchanges, and delivers information to the organization in such a way as to help managers make the best possible decisions.

Reading Comprehension

1. Why is it that a management information system can be said to be an extension of an old-fashioned accounting system?
2. List and describe the functions of the four basic parts of a computer's hardware.
3. Distinguish between data and information.
4. What is the purpose of the computer program? What is its nickname?
5. What might be some sources of computer input data for a fast-food chain? For an auto insurance company? For a manufacturer of baby food?
6. Suppose the supervisor of the woodworking department of a furniture factory was asked to reduce the number of specific items requested on the weekly departmental record report. Would it be better to cut out data on the number of defects found, the average number of employees on the payroll, or the number of orders backlogged for next week? Why?
7. List some examples of primary and secondary data that might be used in a construction firm, a department store, and a manufacturing plant.
8. Discuss the extent to which computers might change the jobs of a bank teller, a machine tool operator, and a parts clerk in an auto parts store.
9. Systematization of information handling may have three undesirable effects. What are they?
10. Besides the obvious value of providing better information on which to make decisions, what particular advantage may a smoothly operating information system offer to employees? Why?

Supervision in Action

The Case of the Peak Poultry Season. A Case Study in Human Relations Involving Computers and Management Information Systems, with Questions for You to Answer.

"You'll have to stick with it for at least another month. I know that keyboarding is not your cup of tea. But that is a vital spot that must be covered for now." Valerie Banks, head of the sales order department of Pappy's Poultry Packing Plant was talking to Don Wardle, an employee of some five years. Pappy's is the largest chicken and turkey packer in the state. During the peak season, 120,000 birds per day go through the plant. They are dressed in various ways, frozen or packed in ice, and shipped off to dozens of supermarket warehouses in the Northeast.

During the fall and winter holiday season, the sales order department is a madhouse. Orders come in all day by telephone and teletype. Each customer presses for immediate delivery. But orders are far from standard. One customer may want a truckload made up of 1,000 whole turkeys in assorted weights, 500 cases of frozen parts, 200 cases of turkey loaf, and 300 cases of chicken breasts. Another may want a completely different order makeup.

Clerks in the sales order department perform three kinds of work. First, there is a variety of low-skill jobs such as typing forms, filing, and hand posting. Then there is the order entry keyboard operation that feeds input data to the computer. It requires a skilled employee who can work accurately at very high speeds. Finally, there is more complex work that involves liaison with the production and inventory control departments. It has been the practice to hire college students temporarily to perform the liaison work during the peak season. They learn quickly and seem to have the flexibility and the initiative needed to handle the sensitive relationships involved.

"Every time the peak season rolls around, Val, you pull me off the production and inventory control job and sit me down at this keyboard," complained Don. "I've got seniority around here and I ought to get my pick of the jobs."

"When the work load is lower, I am glad to let you handle the liaison job," said Val. "But at peak periods I've found that part-time college students catch on quickly to the hand calculations needed to convert our orders to data for production control. Most of them already know how to prepare the computer runs, and speed is not an important factor on the job. Keyboarding the sales orders requires top-flight speed, and you are certainly the fastest person on that job we've ever had."

"I want to put the keyboard work behind me," said Don. "I've served my apprenticeship and should be allowed to work full-time on the liaison job with production control."

"Our department isn't large enough for that kind of permanent specialization," said Valerie. "We all have to work where the need is the greatest."

"If you would hire one or two of those college temporaries a couple weeks before the work load began to peak, we could train them to be almost as good as I am on the keyboards," said Don.

"That wouldn't work," said Valerie. "The college kids catch on fast, I agree. But they get tired of the routine just as fast. And then they start to make errors. The mistakes we make inside the house between our department and production control can be patched up easily. The mistakes that affect our customers are nothing but trouble."

"Well, what about training Elda, the regular typist, to handle the keyboard work?" asked Don.

"Elda is simply too slow for that job. Besides, her accuracy isn't all that good," said Valerie.

"I don't care what you say," said Don. "It's not fair to marry me to the routine work when I have proved that I can use my knowhow and skill on a job that is more challenging. If you can't see it my way, I'm going to complain to the general manager. I'm sure that a more interesting job can be found for me, probably in the production-control department."

This conversation took place early in the morning. Don found a chance to talk to the general manager right before lunch. By the next morning, Don had been transferred to the sales order liaison job in the production and inventory control department.

1. What do you think of Valerie's decision to place Don on this job?
2. What alternatives might Valerie have tried? What are the strong points and drawbacks of each approach?
3. Assuming that Don had secured the transfer from the general manager, what would you do about it if you were Valerie?

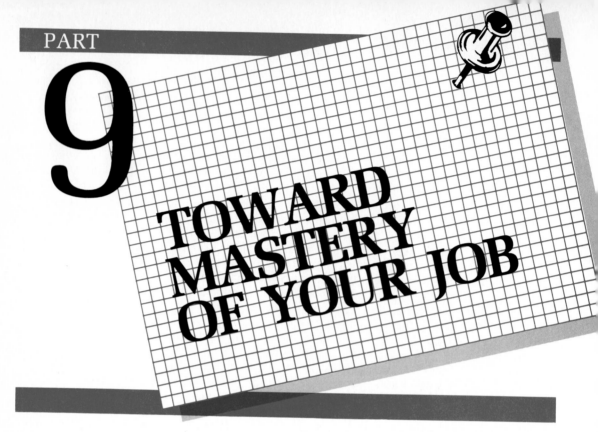

TOWARD MASTERY OF YOUR JOB

In the long run, most personal development is self-development. Supervisors who perform well in their work and who seek advancement do so mainly on their own initiative. They will be aided by their companies, of course, but much must be done on their own. The rewards, however, go much farther than salary increases and job advancement. Job competency at any level helps individuals to release their true potential and to attain an exhilarating degree of self-fulfillment. For those who would aspire to these levels, three chapters in this part set three related objectives:

● To analyze personal capabilities and shortcomings so as to construct a career plan with specific programs for developing key knowledge and skills.
● To become aware of the ways in which personal time is lost and job stress is generated, and to acquire methods and techniques for bringing about system and order in the normal workday.
● To acquire insights into the ways that are the most productive for gaining organizational support and for working harmoniously and profitably with your superiors.

How supervisors feel about their careers, their jobs, and their special competencies

The majority of supervisors seem more satisfied with their present positions than with thoughts about careers beyond these. A large portion of them are reasonably satisfied with their pay. They like their bosses, too, and say that their bosses are good listeners. In general, supervisors have an unusually high degree of confidence in their job skills. In particular, supervisors rate themselves as "very good" in managing their personal time and in handling stress. This is probably because so many supervisors realize how important these skills are and have made a special effort to master them.

It is significant, however, that there is a hard core of supervisors (one out of every five) who are not happy about their jobs, their bosses, or their performance. These supervisors, in particular, need to take a long, hard look at the careers they have chosen, and perhaps choose a new direction. All supervisors, however, should be prepared to regularly assess their knowledge and skills and to take responsibility for their improvement.

Here is a sampling of the relevant survey data:

---

1. How satisfied are you with your present job?

%	
27	Very satisfied
55	Satisfied
11	Neither satisfied nor dissatisfied
6	Dissatisfied
2	Very dissatisfied

2. How do you feel about the adequacy of your pay?

%	
38	About right
48	Not quite enough
13	Far too little
1	Too much

3. How would you rate your boss?

%	
63	One of the better things about my job
15	One of the poorer things about my job
22	Not an important factor in my job

31

TAKING CHARGE
OF YOUR CAREER

Are careers open only for professionally trained persons?

Far from it. Everyone's occupation offers an opportunity to create a path of continuous, purposeful progress. This is especially true of supervision, where progress can take place in two stages. You may, for example, develop an ever-expanding career in your present supervisory role. This can take place if you regularly set goals for your performance and acquire the knowledge and expertise needed to attain them. The great majority of supervisors choose this kind of career. They may never change jobs or employers, but their life's work grows more meaningful and satisfying every year.

Many other supervisors choose to make their present position a stepping stone toward a career that progresses ever upward in the organization. You may be one of these persons. If so, you must first demonstrate unusually good performance in your present job. At the same time, you must begin to acquire the skills needed to move you along your career path.

In either choice, your career, as well as your sense of personal accomplishment, will depend a great deal on how wisely and firmly you take the responsibility for your self-development.

What can self-development mean to you?

Just about everything. Not only can it mean the difference between your holding a mediocre job and your holding a good one, but it can also mean the difference between your enjoying life and not enjoying it.

Self-improvement should mean continual growth for you—not physical, of course, but mental. It should mean constantly assessing yourself—as a supervisor and as a person. It calls for setting your personal standards a little higher each year because as you grow older, experience should tell you more and more about what is worthwhile and what is not.

True self-development calls for a certain amount of self-dissatisfaction. It's when you become too satisfied with yourself—your performance as a supervisor or as an individual—that your growth stops and you lose your grip.

So be ambitious for yourself. Work holds high rewards for those who help themselves along. Mark it well: Over the long haul, your success will depend on your own efforts to improve.

How can you know how well you are doing on your job?

To map a plan for your self-improvement—the self-propelled road to a higher salary or a better job—the best place to begin is with a no-excuses permitted rating of yourself on your job. To do so, answer the questions on the Self-Rating Job Quiz in Figure 31-1.

To evaluate your score, add the scores for each of the questions. A total of 70 is par. A score of 100 is tops. Anything below 50 means there's something seriously wrong with your performance.

If your score is between 50 and 70 points, your whole approach to your job needs an overhaul. If your score is in the 70s, better set up a plan now for improvement. If your score is 80 or above, don't take your future for granted. Look again at your low spots and decide to take definite action to bring them up within the next three months.

SELF-RATING JOB QUIZ

1. Outline employee responsibilities:
   Do you as a matter of policy see that all employees know what
   you expect from them in terms of output, quality, attendance,
   and safety?
   a. In specific terms and on a regular basis.   10 points
   b. In specific terms but only when it applies to a new employee.   7 points
   c. Vaguely and only when a discipline problem arises.   3 points
   d. Can't remember when you last did this.   0 points

   Score: _____

2. Relationship with your employees:
   Do you discuss with your workers your appraisal of their performance and other factors affecting your relationship with
   them?
   a. Regularly.   20 points
   b. Not on a regular basis.   12 points
   c. Only occasionally.   8 points
   d. Hardly ever.   0 points

   Score: _____

3. Working conditions:
   Have you tried hard to see that working arrangements for you
   and your employees are conducive to good work?
   a. By active, regular steps (inspection, etc.) to ensure
      good housekeeping, safety, and job enrichment.   20 points
   b. By occasional but effective efforts to improve housekeeping,
      safety, and job enrichment.   14 points
   c. Only when forced to do so by your superior.   8 points
   d. Not in the last 12 months.   0 points

   Score: _____

4. Contacts with other departments:
   Do you try (whether or not aided by the company) to become
   better acquainted with supervisors in other departments and to
   learn more about their duties?
   a. By taking advantage of every opportunity and trying to
      establish more contacts.   10 points
   b. By attending company functions and following up all contacts.   7 points
   c. By seldom attending company functions and failing to follow
      up contacts.   4 points
   d. By never attending company functions and avoiding new
      contacts.   0 points

   Score: _____

Figure 31-1

5. Further education and training:
   Have you personally made it a policy to improve your own basic education so that it will best benefit you and your company?
   a. By taking night or correspondence courses and following a program of self-education.   **10 points**
   b. By conscientious efforts to train yourself when new problems arise on your job.   **8 points**
   c. By only rare attempts to improve your knowledge in the field of your work.   **4 points**
   d. In no way at all in the last 12 months.   **0 points**

   Score: _____

6. New assignments and ideas:
   Have you searched for ways to contribute new ideas and to accept assignments beyond the limits of your current job?
   a. By regularly submitting in writing carefully considered ideas, or looking for chances to carry out special assignments.   **10 points**
   b. By accepting additional assignments with enthusiasm and carrying them out with vigor.   **6 points**
   c. By occasionally informally suggesting ways for improving methods in your department.   **2 points**
   d. By doing just what your job demands and nothing else.   **0 points**

   Score: _____

7. Professional society activities:
   Do you belong to, and participate in the affairs of, professional or technical societies such as the National Management Association and the Industrial Management Clubs?
   a. More than one and attend most meetings.   **5 points**
   b. At least one and attend most meetings.   **4 points**
   c. At least one but attend only occasionally.   **2 points**
   d. No outside activity of this nature.   **0 points**

   Score: _____

8. Keeping posted on new technology:
   Do you make a point of keeping up with the latest developments that affect supervision and the technical side of your job by reading business magazines and technical journals?
   a. Regularly on company time and occasionally on your time.   **5 points**
   b. Regularly on company time.   **4 points**
   c. Rarely.   **2 points**
   d. Never.   **0 points**

   Score: _____

Figure 31-1 (continued)

9. Attitude toward company:
When not carrying out specific orders or under active supervision of your boss, how do you attempt to use your time?

a. Exactly as though you were running your own business.	10 points
b. Follow policies and instructions to the letter but no more.	7 points
c. Work effectively only under pressure for conformance.	3 points
d. Look for loopholes to avoid work.	0 points

Score: _____

Total: _____

Figure 31-1 (continued)

On what is a career development program based?

It has four components.

A Candid Self-Assessment.   You will have started if you have completed the self-rating charts in Figure 31-1 and Figure 31-2.

Firm and Realistic Goals.   These should be based on what you want to accomplish in your career specifically and in your life generally. They will be limited, of course, by the weaknesses that stand out in your job quiz (Figure 31-1) and personal inventory (Figure 31-2).

A Concrete Program for Development.   Every weakness points toward a corrective course of action. These actions should be spelled out in specific detail—a course to take, a book to read, a seminar to attend, an on-job practice to engage in. Action plans should also pin down the time to begin and complete each phase. A modest but concrete development program is far better than an ambitious but vague one.

Motivation and Commitment.   Career growth has its pluses and minuses. Upward movement usually means greater status and a more affluent lifestyle. It also means very hard work, sacrifice of leisure time, removal from the easy friendship with people in the department, and an occasional unpleasant decision to make. That is the trade-off. To go ahead, supervisors have to value the benefits above the new obligations. Without personal drive and commitment to the goals you have chosen, a self-development program becomes an exercise in self-deception.

PERSONAL EFFECTIVENESS INVENTORY

	Weak	Adequate	Strong	Needs improvement
1. **Oral Communication:** Effectiveness of expression in individual or group situations.	____	____	____	____
2. **Written Communication:** Ability to write clearly and correctly.	____	____	____	____
3. **Leadership:** Getting ideas accepted and guiding a group or an individual to do a task.	____	____	____	____
4. **Interpersonal Insight:** Perceiving and reacting to the needs of others, objectivity in perceiving impact of self on others.	____	____	____	____
5. **Planning and Organizing:** Ability to efficiently establish a course of action for self and others and get results.	____	____	____	____
6. **Problem Solution:** Identifying causes of problems, proposing solutions, and solving problems.	____	____	____	____
7. **Stress Tolerance:** Ability to perform under pressure and opposition.	____	____	____	____
8. **Creativity:** Ability to generate, recognize, and accept imaginative solutions and innovations.	____	____	____	____
9. **Decisiveness:** Ability to make sound decisions and take action.	____	____	____	____
10. **Flexibility:** Ability to adapt managerial approach to changing organizational needs and situations.	____	____	____	____
11. **Reasoning:** Ability to apply a sound reasoning and logical process to varying situations, problems, goals, and activities.	____	____	____	____

Adapted from *Guide for Preparing Individual Development Plans,* prepared by Richard F. Fraser and Chester C. Cotton for the Training and Career Development Branch of the U.S. Department of Agriculture's Agricultural Research Service at Hyattsville, Md., February 1977. By permission.

Figure 31-2

How are others likely to judge your potential for growth and improvement?

Your present employer will judge you most by what you accomplish on your job. If you have not mastered the art of meeting production schedules and quality standards and holding costs in line, you can probably forget about career growth. A good starting point in getting your boss's confirmation is to get agreement about exactly what it is he or she expects from you. Look back at Figure 10-7. It shows you how to make a supervisory responsibility survey. It lists 50 items that typically make up a supervisor's job and suggests that you and your boss get together to make sure that you both see eye to eye on all of them.

Assuming that you measure up to the basic responsibilities of your job, the other vital measures will be of your ability to plan, organize, direct, and control. To make a candid assessment of this functional potential, try rating yourself against the characteristics listed in Figure 31-2 (Personal Effectiveness Inventory). Better still, ask a good friend or your boss to do the rating. The list consists of criteria that many authorities believe are needed for success in supervisory and management positions. The purpose of the assessment is not only to affirm your strong points but, especially, to identify areas that need further development.

What is a career path? How is it found?

A career path maps out the most logical and practical roadway to a position, or series of positions, that an individual believes holds the most attractive occupational and personal rewards. As stated earlier, you may decide that your career lies in your present job. If so, you'll be mainly concerned with your improved performance, broader scope of responsibilities, larger salary, and heightened personal satisfaction.

If, however, your sights are on a career beyond your present position, you'll need to develop a more complex plan. Your target can be the next higher position in your organization, or it can be one at the same level but with a different range of responsibilities, or it can be a job much further up the management hierarchy. An example of a career path is illustrated in Figure 31-3. This individual—let's call her Patty—has picked a long-range target of becoming the general manager of a profit center. To get there, Patty has plotted a path that will move her from a staff-supervisory position in quality control (1)

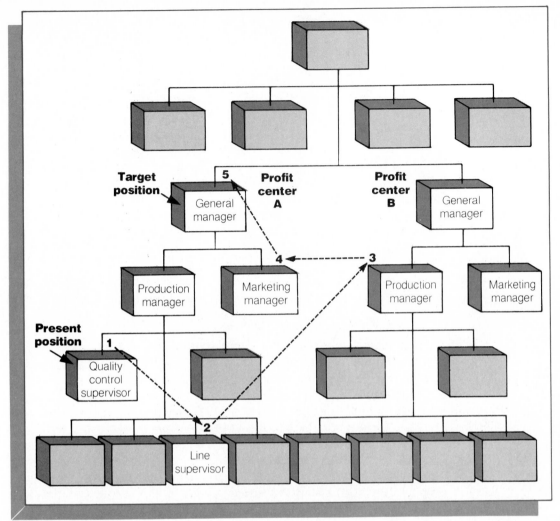

Figure 31-3. Example of a career path.

to being a production-line supervisor (2), then upward to production manager in a different division (3), across to an entirely different functional area as a marketing manager (4), and, it is hoped, after a number of years, to general manager of her original division (5).

To make her career path workable, Patty should include target dates for each move, say "in two or three years" or "in five years." And, most important, Patty's plan must identify (1) any personal weaknesses in her present performance and (2) the knowledge, skills, or experience needed to move her from one step to another along her career path. For example, Patty's performance on her present job may be marred by a poor employee safety record. She'll have to plan to do something to get that straightened out before she can realistically expect to get a crack at the line production job. Looking ahead to what it will take for her to move from the line job (2) to the divisional production manager's job (3), Patty may decide that she has to acquire a broader technical knowledge of the process. To do so, she may enroll in the appropriate technical course at a local university. The point is that each new job will have its own particular set of requirements. Patty will need to anticipate them and acquire the necessary credentials before she can seriously think about moving ahead to the next position in her career plan.

What happens to your career when you can't be spared from your present assignment?

Many ambitious supervisors have stumbled on this problem. It's mainly their own fault, not the organization's. If you have any idea of moving ahead, you must make a determined effort to select and train a replacement. Contrary to a popular notion, subordinates who perform well *do not* threaten their boss's job. If you have someone ready to step into your shoes, it shows your superiors that you are on top of your job. Better still, it makes you immediately available when a choice assignment crops up. And it prevents the possibility that your career will be stymied because "there is no one prepared to replace the key person in this department."

How can you make sure that your plan for self-improvement or for career advancement actually becomes reality?

Self-improvement is paved with good intentions. To avoid shortfalls in your plans, don't try to do too much too soon. Plan ahead for one step at a time. Do this planning in detail and do it realistically. Set targets that can be reached and place some kind of deadline for them, as shown in Figure 31-4. Put both your goals and your plans into writing. Tack them up in a place where they will constantly remind you of your commitment to them. Check your progress regularly.

SELF-DEVELOPMENT SCHEDULE

Supervisor: _Joe Smith_

Weak Spots	Plan for Corrective Action	When to Do It	Action Complete
Telling employees where they stand	Prepare calendar with a different worker to be talked to each week	At once	✓
Poor department safety record	Hold monthly meetings with work group	Begin June	✓
Keeping up with job technology	Subscribe to *American Machinist*	At once	✓
No activities outside of work	Join International Management Council	Next year	
Speaking in front of groups	Enroll in Dale Carnegie course in public speaking	Next winter	
Cost estimating	Take correspondence course in accounting	Not scheduled	

☐ This Year's Plan   ▨ Next Year's Plan   ▨ Future

Figure 31-4. Self-development schedule.

I t is easy to talk about self-motivation and commitment, but how does one develop it?

My guess is that you have a certain amount of it already or you wouldn't have come as far as you have. Nevertheless, the question has always bothered ambitious people. Here is one helpful way to think about this problem for yourself.

Try a Force-Field Analysis. This is done in five steps. (See Figure 31-5.)

1. Pick a goal you wish to reach or an action you plan to take as part of your development program. This action should help you reach your goal by changing (improving) your present behavior. This step is sometimes called the goal-action-change step. Your *goal* may be to prepare effective reports for higher management to read. The *action* may require your taking a night course at your community

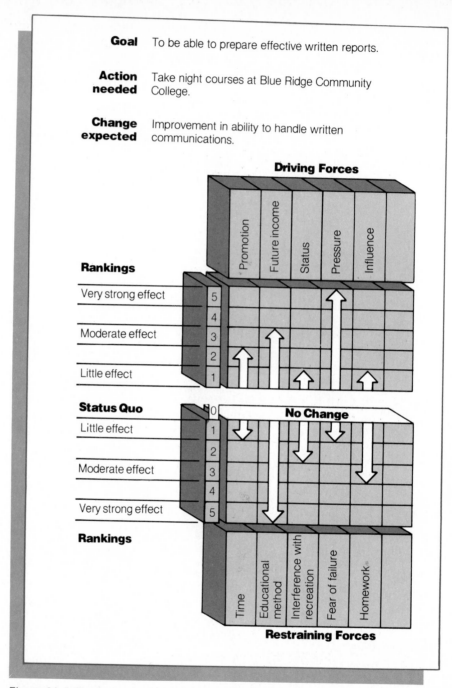

Goal To be able to prepare effective written reports.

Action needed Take night courses at Blue Ridge Community College.

Change expected Improvement in ability to handle written communications.

Figure 31-5. Example of a force-field analysis. Adapted from George A. Ford and Gordon L. Lippitt, *Planning Your Future*, rev. ed., University Associates, La Jolla, Calif., 1976, p. 49. By permission.

college in report writing. The *change* will be improvement in your written communications.

2. Make a list of at least five important forces that are *driving* you to make that change. For example, you want to get a promotion (key force is promotion); you hope to earn more money (key force is future income); your spouse would feel good about your improved status (key force is status); your boss is pressuring you for regular formal reports (key force is pressure); and you want the satisfaction of seeing your ideas influence higher management decisions (key force is influence).

3. Make a list of at least five important forces that are holding you back, or *restraining* you, from making this change. For example, you can't find the time (key force is time); you hate taking night courses (key force is educational method); the course is only given on your bowling night (key force is interference with recreation); you are afraid that you won't do well (key force is fear of failure); and you don't like the idea that you will have to do homework (key force is homework).

4. Now rank each force, driving as well as restraining, according to how strong it is. Use a ranking scale of 1 to 5, ranging from 1 as "little effect" to 5 as "very strong effect." This singles out what is really important in motivating you and what is truly powerful in holding you back. It also helps to expose low-ranking forces for what they are—excuses.

5. Try to match opposing forces. A strong driving force such as pressure may be all that is needed to motivate you to overcome a strong restraining force such as educational method. Hope for a larger future income may overcome your dislike of homework. The driving forces of promotion, status, and influence may not be so powerful as you thought they were when compared on the chart, but neither are the restraining forces of time, fear of failure, and interference with recreation.

What about networking and mentors?

You'll help your career along with either or both. *Networking* is what used to be called "connections." Today's differences are that networks are built by, or tapped by, an individual along lines of knowing what's going on and what's opening up in an organization rather than on formal lines of authority and status. Networks are very informal, and the individuals in them often have little or no direct influence. But, by working the network, you can do a better job of planning your career moves and in selecting the best preparation for them.

A *mentor,* on the other hand, is someone in a position of influence or authority who is interested in you and your career. A mentor is best utilized as an adviser. He or she will have a good idea of the best path to travel and what kind of training and skills you'll need to pursue it. It is not a good idea to expect a mentor to do much more than point the way. It is unfair to ask him or her to risk personal security and reputation on your behalf. If, however, a mentor goes out on a limb for you, don't let him or her down.

Behavior modification: what's that?

Personal growth and/or career advancement often requires that an individual break some long-standing habits. This is especially true in the area of interpersonal relationships. Many supervisors get hooked on a way of handling human problems that is ineffective. To improve their relationships, they must change—or modify—their approach. A proven way of accomplishing this is through behavioral modification, or **behavioral modeling,** sessions. In these sessions, supervisors are shown examples of a good way to handle a particular situation, such as imposing positive discipline on an employee. These examples are called "models." Supervisors practice these models at the behavioral modification session, then try to apply them to real situations on their jobs. They report their successes or failures back to the training group and try to practice their skills until perfect. There are several behavioral models in this book, placed at the ends of parts 1 through 5. Try them out to see if you can make the models work for you.

How can you attain the formal education needed for your career?

Face it, the person with the better education has an advantage over the person without it. But this doesn't mean you can't do anything about it. There's plenty you can do to improve your knowledge.

First, examine your own attitude toward further education. Is it strictly negative? If so, you'd better change in a hurry. Convince yourself that you, too, can learn new techniques and accept new ideas. If you want to learn, learning is made easier.

Next, pick out the soft spots in your educational armor. Is it reading and writing? Is it a weakness with figures? These can be improved quickly through correspondence and home-study courses or in an evening course at a local university. Adult education courses at your local high school also offer help in these areas.

If your weakness is in a technical line—say your company is processing chemicals or constructing complicated electronic equipment, or your job involves simple metallurgy—you can find courses at technical institutes and universities that will help you understand your processes better even if you don't become an expert.

Caution: You may not be able to take a course in physical chemistry, for instance, if you haven't had a previous course in basic chemistry. So your plan for improvement may often have to be a long-range one. Here's a suggestion. You may be able to enroll in an advanced course just as a listener. You can thus get a feel for the subject and its terminology, with only a little prior preparation.

In your programming, don't scatter your efforts indiscriminately. Pinpoint your educational efforts to strengthen your weak spots. Later on, if you like, you can add frills.

How can you take best advantage of your company's training and development program?

Show that you're interested. In most progressive companies today, the personnel manager or the training director is eager to help supervisors who want to help themselves. Don't be ashamed to ask for help, and don't think you'll be revealing a secret weakness. One of the necessary qualities of an executive is the ability for self-analysis and the determination to improve.

What is a management-development program?

Management development (it may also be called executive or supervisory development) is the term applied to the systematic inventory, appraisal, and training of management people. Programs vary according to an individual company's policies. Sometimes they include only top management people and often are not extended to the first-line supervisory level.

If there's a program in your company that applies to you, you'll probably hear about it from your boss. But don't expect your company to take care of your self-development program. It's really up to you.

Where can you go for outside help and guidance?

For educational guidance outside your company, try your local centers for adult education or vocational guidance, a nearby community college, or a university extension service. Or write either of the nationwide management clubs mentioned in Chapter 1. Another source to try is any nearby chapter of the American Society for Training and Development.

For information about specific correspondence or technical courses, write to:

American Society for Training and Development
600 Maryland Avenue, S.W.
Washington, D.C. 20024

American Society for Engineering Education
1 DuPont Circle, N.W.
Washington, D.C. 20036

National Home Study Council
1601 18th Street, N.W.
Washington, D.C. 20009

American Personnel and Guidance Association
1607 New Hampshire Avenue, N.W.
Washington, D.C. 20009

What will outside reading do for you?

Some people can learn a lot just be reading. Others find it difficult to get much from the printed page. But if you're one of the former, try to set up a planned reading program. Include in it at least one good newspaper (such as *USA Today* or *The Wall Street Journal*), one good news magazine (such as *Time* or *Newsweek*), one good management magazine (such as *Business Week* or *Industry Week*), and one good technical magazine or journal that serves your field (such as *American Machinist* or *Popular Computing*). Don't just subscribe to them or have your name put on the routing list. Read them—and try to apply what you find in them. In addition, you ought to set up a library of business books for yourself. The references at the end of Chapter 1 of this book make a good place to begin.

To what extent will career goals conflict with your other aspirations in life?

They can be compatible, but the higher one moves in a career, the more likely it is that other life values will suffer. This need not be, if you also build into the plans you make for your career a place for the other things you hold dear—family, friends, leisure, health, service, faith. You will be able to make such plans only if you have developed maturity, however. Maturity means the ability to stand outside yourself and make an honest judgment of your thoughts and behavior. It usually means—among other things—exercising a great deal of self-control, being able to hold your temper when others are losing theirs, accepting an occasional failure as well as success, and evaluating the talents and the intent of others fairly, regardless of your personal views.

If you have developed such a maturity, you may want to try two exercises that will help you understand much more about what is important to you.

Try a Life Inventory.   This requires that you go off alone for one hour and make up six separate lists about yourself.

● List 1.   These are the things I do well.
● List 2.   These are the things I do poorly.
● List 3.   These are the things I would like to be able to learn or to improve: skills, activities, attitudes, and feelings.
● List 4.   These are the things I would like to be able to stop: activities, habits, attitudes, and feelings.
● List 5.   These are the things I would like to have in life that I don't have now.
● List 6.   These are the things in life I value and would not like to lose.

Make each list as long as you like; each list ought to have at least five items, however. Don't worry about duplicates between lists. If you have compiled your lists thoughtfully and candidly, you ought to know more about yourself than before. Now, go back and look at your job quiz (Figure 31-1) and your personal inventory (Figure 31-2). Are there weak points on those lists that are explained by your life inventory? Are there items on your life inventory that would lead you to find new strengths on your job and in your personal assessment? Look at your goals and career plans. Do they conflict with your life inventory? In what way can your plans for self-development capitalize on what your life inventory shows?

Try Keeping a 24-Hour Diary.   Do it for one business day and for one weekend day. Get a big note pad and write down (1) every single thing you do, (2) whom you do it with, and (3) how long you spend doing it. You will find that many things you do, especially at work, are repeated over and over. For example, talking with one employee about quality for three minutes may be repeated five or ten times with other employees. You may also discover gaps of time in which you do nothing. Don't worry about that, either. The purpose of the diary is to tell you exactly what two days in your life are really like. If you keep this diary carefully and candidly, you will find many surprises—and some valuable insights into your job, yourself, and your life. It, too, will help you plan a better self-development program and generate a greater drive to fulfill it.

Key Concepts

1. Personal growth and improvement are the direct result of self-development. Other people may offer valuable advice and guidance, but each individual must furnish his or her own initiative, application, and persistence.

2. Plans for career development should be based on an objective assessment of present performance as compared with job demands and future opportunities for growth and advancement.

3. Self-development is a form of adult education directed at improving personal knowledge, skills, and attitudes. This education can be accomplished through formal instruction, guided experience, and relevant reading.

4. It is essential that plans for self-improvement be (a) practically related to both needs and opportunities, (b) specific in nature, and (c) firm in setting time and goals.

5. The objectives of self-development should extend beyond the confines of self-interest. Only by embracing socially responsible goals can personal achievement be truly fulfilling and individual maturity be attained.

CHAPTER

32

MANAGING TIME AND HANDLING STRESS

What's the connection between time management, stress, and your career?

One thing leads to another. Supervision is the kind of position where, by its nature, you are asked—or expected—to do more than most people can fit into a normal work day. If you can manage your time well, you have a fighting chance to accomplish the important aspects of your job and look good. If you are not very wise in choosing priorities for your time, you may work very hard indeed and still look bad in the eyes of your boss. Few things can be more frustrating.

Frustrations exert pressure on your mind and eventually on your nerves and body. Such pressure is popularly known as stress. The more important your job and career appear to you, the greater the possibility for stress. It follows, then, that if you manage your time well, stress will be minimized. And, if you are alert to the symptoms of stress, you can handle it—not by "toughing it out," but by sorting out your priorities so that your work load remains manageable.

The big time question: Are you really too busy?

That's the first question you should ask—and answer for—yourself. There's an old story about a farmer who told his wife he would plow the north field the next day. It goes like this:

In the morning he went out to oil the tractor, but he found that he was low on oil. So he went to the storage shed to get some. On the way he noticed the chickens weren't fed. He went to the corn crib to get them some corn, where he saw some sacks on the ground. That reminded him the potatoes needed sprouting, so he started for the potato pit to sprout the potatoes. As it happens, on the way he passed the woodpile and remembered he had to take some kindling to the house. He had picked up a few sticks when an ailing lamb passed by. He dropped the wood and reached for the lamb. Then . . . .

Guess we don't have to finish the story. It's important only if it means something to you. For instance, does it bear any resemblance to your own methods of operation? Do you, for example, start out to see the records clerk, run back to check a tote box of finished parts for quality, stop on the way to talk to a mechanic about a job to be done, then leave him or her to answer a phone, drop the phone to answer a question from an employee—and never get to see the person you started out to see?

All this may be exaggerated. But it points up a clue to why so many supervisors are too busy to do the job they ought to do. They lack system. So here's the cardinal rule of using your time better: The more systematic you are, the more effective you will be in the use of your time.

How much time can you call your own?

Only you can answer this properly. Nevertheless, you should approach the challenge of time management by trying to divide your time into two compartments: (1) the time that you *can* control and (2) the time that you *can't* control. When your boss wants you at a meeting, for example, that's time you can't control. So is the time you have to spend on an unexpected breakdown or when an emergency arises. In your own situation, there are probably a number of other demands placed on your time, not at your convenience but at that of someone else. It's a good idea to make a list of these potentially uncontrollable occurrences right now. This is important because you'll want to think about them in a different way than the time demands that you can control. As a consequence, your approach to time management can be guided by two general rules:

1. Systematize and prioritize the management of your controllable time. In this chapter, we'll suggest a number of proven techniques to help you do this.
2. Minimize the amount of your uncontrollable time. This has to be done in bits and pieces, and probably over a long period of time. And, since this time is often controlled by others, you'll have to work out ways to gain some concessions from them in the interests of your own flexibility while still accommodating their needs. We'll have some suggestions on this, too.

Where is your controllable time most likely to go?

A supervisor's time typically flies away from him or her in four different ways:

1. **Routine Work.** Checking time cards, filling out pay sheets, distributing pay envelopes, and answering mail, for instance. These are the little things in your job. But unless you keep an eye on them, they can take a big part of your time—as much as 20 or 30 percent.
2. **Regular Job Duties.** Such as supervising employees, assigning work, training new workers, checking performance, and counseling employees. This part of your job is the most important and should get the major part of your attention.
3. **Special Assignments.** Such as when your boss says, "Joe, will you find out how many hours it took to produce that Acme job last month?" or "Will you serve this month on the plant's cost-improvement committee?" These can be the little jobs that show how you save time for that extra effort.
4. **Creative Work.** Such as figuring out a new layout for your department or starting a training program to teach your employees new skills. Supervisors who really get ahead are often those who find time to use their imagination and creative ideas to improve work in their departments. You need to save time for this, too.

What can you do to save personal time?

First find out where your time really goes. For a week, keep a running record of what you do. Make it specific—for instance, "8:00, check time clocks; 8:15, call for raw materials; 8:25, supervising; 9:35, fill out computer sheets; 10:00, discuss absences with Charlie," and so on.

Next, analyze your time record according to the four categories listed in the previous question. Then add up how much time you spend for each kind of work.

Now ask yourself how much of the routine work you can delegate to a clerk or other subordinate. You should cut this time for routine work to the bone—say, less than 10 percent of your total time.

Look over your time allotment for regular job duties. Are you spending enough time on them? Are you doing everything you should? Are you doing some things that can be discontinued for more important efforts? You're the best judge, but you should devote something like 70 percent of your time to this phase of your job. Supervising, that is. Not stock chasing and running meaningless errands that less expensive help can do for you.

How about your special assignments? Are you accepting your share of the miscellaneous duties that crop up? Or are you getting the reputation as a shirker? On the other hand, avoid being so active on side-bar efforts that your regular duties don't get the proper attention. As a rule of thumb, hold your special assignment time to 10 or 15 percent unless your boss says otherwise.

Finally, does your time analysis show that you are just marking time on the job, or are you finding time to do something creative? Not only for the eager beaver (who finds that this is the path to promotion) but also for the old-timer, this devotion to trying to find new and better ways of doing things has a payoff: your job will become more interesting—and more rewarding.

To what extent can you budget your time at work?

This depends, of course, on how much of your time is under your control. Nevertheless, you can make good headway against both controllable and uncontrollable time limits by drawing up a time allotment plan (a kind of *time budget*) for yourself. A sample time budget is shown in Figure 32-1. Using the four categories of time usage already described, try roughing out a time budget of your own.

You'll want to account for 100 percent of your work time in this

	MONDAY	TUESDAY	WEDNESDAY	THURSDAY	FRIDAY
8	ROUTINE	ROUTINE	ROUTINE	ROUTINE	ROUTINE
9	Inspection and supervision of operations REGULAR	Individual work with staff REGULAR	Inspection and supervision of operations REGULAR	Individual work with staff REGULAR	SPECIAL WORK
10		Inspection and supervision of operations REGULAR		Control studies and reports REGULAR	Inspection and supervision of operations REGULAR
11			Division staff meeting REGULAR		Our staff meeting REGULAR
12 / 1	L	U	N	C	H
1	Interviews and contacts REGULAR	Interviews and contacts REGULAR	Interviews and contacts REGULAR	Interviews and contacts REGULAR	CREATIVE WORK
2	Planning and organizing REGULAR	Inspection and supervision of operations REGULAR	SPECIAL WORK	Inspection and supervision of operations REGULAR	
3 / 4					
5	ROUTINE	ROUTINE	ROUTINE	ROUTINE	ROUTINE

Figure 32-1. Plan your time this way—an example of a time budget.

budget, even though a portion of it cannot be controlled. The way to recognize the extent of uncontrollable time is to make an estimate of (1) the portion of your time that is uncontrollable and (2) the times of the day or week that are most likely to be absorbed by uncontrollable time. Then enlarge the budget for the category most likely to be affected. If, for example, you are likely to get the most time-eating distractions in the course of your regular activities on a Monday morning, make this part of your time budget larger than normal, as it is in Figure 32-1. If unexpected meetings are typically called on Wednesday afternoons, enlarge the special work budget (as in Figure 32-1) to anticipate the meetings.

The time budget has weaknesses, of course, but it provides a pattern for planning your time usage throughout the week. It will, for example, keep you from scheduling anything but routine work at the beginning and end of each day. It will remind you that control reports must be prepared on Thursday morning and that you'll be tied up with your own staff meeting Friday at 11. It will give you an incentive, too, for telling associates that you'll "be tied up on a special project Wednesday from 2 to 4 and Fridays from 10 to 11." Or, when an employee says that he or she would like to talk with you about an idea for improving work methods, you can make an appointment for Friday afternoon during your creative period.

How does a time budget differ from a daily schedule?

The time budget is an ideal, but practical, long-range plan. Your daily schedule focuses on what's supposed to happen today. It should include, first of all, those things you want to make sure actually happen today. These are your top priorities. In addition, you may want to add a number of things that you'd *like* to get done today, if you can find the time for them. These are less urgent than the other items and can be postponed until tomorrow, or later in the week, if you can't find the time today.

Your daily time schedule, or daily agenda, should always be written down. It is best to do this the night before, and it should certainly be done before your shift begins. Your daily time schedule needn't be fancy. Simply make a "laundry list" of items on your agenda for the day; then assign priority numbers to them. My guess is that it's a good day when you can get more than five other-than-routine items scratched off. Consequently, your "absolutely-must-do-today" list should be short. The "would-like-to-do-today" list may include a dozen or more items. You'll discover that a number of these items are repeatedly postponed; they never seem to move up to the top of your priorities. This is a signal, of course, to see if these can be delegated to others, or an indication that they don't belong on your personal time budget in the first place.

What can you do to manage your time better?

Here are five good tricks to remember:

1. Make Up Your Mind Fast.   This is not to advocate snap judgments, but it's a fact that 85 percent of the problems that face you aren't worth more than a few minutes of your time. So learn to say "yes" or "no," "we will" or "we won't." Employees and associates like working with decisive people—even when they aren't right all the time. And few things save time like a decisive answer—time saved for you and your employees.

2. Be Specific About Dates. You promise to get out an order "sometime next week." What happens? You're likely to find several deadlines coming due at the same time. If you're specific—Wednesday for Triangle and Thursday for Superior—you've started to systematize your thinking.

Or let's say Pete calls you on the phone. Can he drop by to see you? Any time, you say. So Pete drops by just when you're up to your ears in a line changeover. Pete doesn't get much attention, your changeover gets the "one-eye-only" treatment, and your time budget suffers.

3. Control the Telephone. It's a monster to supervisors in some shops. But it needn't be (if your boss will cooperate). If you can get someone else to answer it for you, do. Then call back when you have the time. Avoid using the telephone for routine messages that can be forwarded through the interoffice mails. And watch yourself so that you don't develop telephonitis and bother others with it unnecessarily.

4. Write Down Reminders. Don't trust yourself to remember things to do. Use a sure-fire reminder system, such as jotting down important jobs to be done on your desk calendar or in a pocket notebook. One supervisor we know jots down anything she feels she should remember or act upon on a little sheet of paper. Then she tosses it into a desk drawer. Each morning she shuffles the notes to see what she must do out of the ordinary for that day. When it's done, she simply tears up the slip.

5. Limit Chit-Chat. Conversation—with employees and fellow supervisors—is vitally important to your role as supervisor. But you've got to keep it under control or it will eat up all your spare time. So limit casual conversation to a few pleasantries, when you can. Nothing ruins your day quite so well as a couple of 20-minute conversations with your associates about the fish they didn't catch or the status of a do-it-yourself project.

H ow can you get your workday off to a better start?

The key to planning your time lies in your time budget (Figure 32-1). But since each day presents a set of new problems, you should try to take five minutes each morning to get yourself organized for the day ahead.

Start off by setting a time each day for reading your mail. The earlier you scan it, the sooner you can plan ahead. Every day, make a mental estimate of the time your paperwork will take up. Some days, routine replies and compliance will take less than half an hour. Other days, one request may take several hours to act on. So it's plain fool-ish to begin your work without first sizing up the job ahead.

In this regard, you can make good use of your desk calendar. Use it as a daily order of work. List the things you want to do that day, including the specific and nonroutine paper work to be handled.

Another good rule is to dispose of all mail and other paperwork before you go home each evening. That way you don't have to face a stack of unfinished work when you arrive the next morning.

If you delegate a big share of your work to your subordinates to save time, won't you be charged with passing the buck?

Not necessarily. Subordinates expect that they'll have to carry the ball along with you. After all, that's the name of the game. Further-more, most people want to feel important enough to the operation to be asked to do some of the boss's work. But even if this weren't so, it's imperative for other urgent reasons that you learn to delegate a good portion of your personal work load.

Delegation is an essential ingredient of good management. And, to be painfully frank, it's often the only way you'll be able to keep your head above water. The average managerial job is so fraught with responsibilities that you could worry yourself into an 80-hour, jam-packed week just checking up on every detail yourself. If you allow yourself to fall into that trap, you're on your way out as a super-visor.

Delegation means, of course, that you've got to trust others on your staff to do the job nearly as effectively as you'd do it yourself. And if you can steel yourself to leave them alone, they usually will. With a big difference, however. Others won't do the job exactly the way you'd do it yourself. They'll also regard some factors as more impor-tant than you think they are. Worse still, they'll overlook or ignore other factors that you think demand top priority. That's the way of del-egation. So learn to accept the fact of less-than-perfect results and to delegate just the same. Without delegation, you won't be able to make the grade as a supervisor and still maintain your cool.

In delegating to make better use of your time, there are two good rules of thumb to follow:

1. Try not to spend time working on tasks that are below your capabilities. (See Figure 10-8.) These are the things that you *can* do, of course, but that others should be doing for you.

2. Don't give your priorities to a series of trivial jobs while putting the big job on "hold." It's important that you take on the big job first. If the trivial jobs are urgent, then you should delegate them right away to the most qualified subordinates.

How can you use ABC analysis to control time?

ABC analysis is a concept that predicts that some 80 percent of your time will be spent on only 20 percent of your problems. (See pages 148–149 and Figure 9-4.) To make this idea pay off for you, the 20 percent of the problems that you work on should be rated as Class A—the vital ones. The president of a major appliance firm, for example, begins his day by labeling each task ahead as A, B, or C. Class B items aren't quite so important as A items. And Class C problems are very small fish, even though there are lots of them. The president goes after A items first, then tries to get to the B's. Invariably, says the president, a surprising thing happens. When he gets to the C's, he can "wipe out a lot of them in one sweep." These are the tasks, of course, that can be disposed of quickly with a telephone call, a jotted note, or a brief instruction to employees as you walk through the shop.

You say to concentrate your time on the "vital few" problems and let the "trivial many" await their turn. How do you recognize the vital few?

Experience will provide a good basis. You may waste a couple of hours the first time around on what turns out to be an inconsequential problem. The next time it comes up, however, you will either know how to dispose of it quickly—or you will know that you should put it far down on your priority list.

There are other ways, too, of judging a problem's importance. For example, ask yourself any of these questions:

Where Did It Come From? If the problem arises as a directive from your boss or a request from the sales department, it may need top priority. If it comes from a lesser source, perhaps you can delay it. In organizational matters, you must be realistic and hard-headed politically.

What Is Its Potential for Trouble? Some unsolved problems can cause other problems to pile up elsewhere. Suppose there is a machine that needs a minor repair. You put it off. But that machine is in the main line of flow in your operation. It is in a position to cause quality problems, and if it breaks down altogether it will hold up production. The repair problem is minor, but its potential for trouble is great. Get to it sooner rather than later.

Is It Aimed at Results Rather Than Activity?   Dr. George Odiorne, who popularized MBO, warns that supervisors and managers devote too much time going through motions that are essentially trivial. On paper, their efforts may look good; they write reports, keep their files up to date, and attend all the meetings. But they don't get results in terms of greater output, better quality, or lower costs. Odiorne says that these managers have wasted their time by falling into the "activity trap."

How Quickly Can It Be Disposed Of?   Watch your answer on this one. It is what R. Alec Mackenzie calls the "time trap." Many problems look as if they can be handled quickly. It is a temptation to jump into them without thinking. But what was supposed to be done with a three-minute phone call turns into several phone calls. What should have taken only a minute or two of discussion grows into a major hassle. Tasks that can truly be handled quickly should be grouped together and finished in one block of time. Problems that need a major effort should be budgeted for your undivided attention, with enough time allotted for their solution.

S o much for the time problem; what about the stress that so often is associated with it?

As stated at the beginning of this chapter, the pursuit of a career and the squeeze it puts on your time do not necessarily cause stress. As you have probably observed, some individuals thrive on pressure, whereas others seem to be crumpled by it. On the other hand, those people who learn to manage their time also reduce, if not eliminate, their stress. A good way to understand this relationship is to look at stress the way engineers do.

Suppose you were to suspend a steel beam on two cinder blocks—somewhat the way a bridge is supported—and to place a number of heavy weights on the beam. As you added the weights, these would place a *stress* on the beam and the beam would begin to flex a little under that stress. If you removed the weights, the beam would snap back into its original straight shape. If, however, you continued to add weights until the beam bent beyond its ability to flex and return to its original shape, the beam would be said to have suffered a *strain*. If you continued to add weights, the beam might not only be bent, it might break. Stress, then, so far as your work goes, is the weight or pressure that the situation places on you.

There is always a limit beyond which your mind and body will flex no longer. Gradually, you can begin to sense just how much pressure you can take before *you* get bent out of shape. As a consequence of this reasoning, you can "manage" stress by finding ways of relieving it, redistributing it, or removing it.

For example, you shift some stress to others by delegating. You remove some of it by obtaining additional resources (people, tools, information, and the like) to help out in your department. You can also make sure that stress doesn't all come at once by planning and controlling your personal time more effectively. The steel beam, for example, can carry a load of 100 tons in 24 hours, *provided* that no more than 5 tons are placed on it at a time. That's why so many bridges bear signs that read: "Maximum load is 10 tons." You can't go around wearing such a sign; employees and associates often have little sympathy for one's limits, anyway. Instead, you must learn exactly how much stress you can bear before you suffer a strain, and then develop a plan for managing stress so that it never exceeds that limit.

How can you tell when stress is beginning to get to you?

There are all sorts of danger signs. It may be that no one sign in particular is significant or conclusive. But when you can check off a number of symptoms, the chances are that stress is getting to you. It may do you serious damage, psychologically or physically, if you don't find a way to manage it. For example, you may be revealing signs of stress if you answer yes to any of the following:

● Are you becoming unusually irritable, a real bear for others to get along with? Are small things bothering you that didn't before? Are you dissatisfied with the way you're handling interpersonal relationships?

● Are you finding it increasingly hard to concentrate? Is the workday full of distractions? Are you having trouble finding time to get your head together to face difficult or complex problems?

● Are you becoming aware of an unusual spate of physical problems? Insomnia? Grinding your teeth while asleep? Diarrhea? Stomach cramping? Unusual premenstrual tension? Missed periods? Feelings of weakness or dizziness? Loss of appetite? Migraine headaches? Pains in the neck or lower back?

● Are you slipping into behavioral habits that you don't feel good about? Such as too much alcohol use? Too much smoking? Overeating? Dependence on sleeping pills, pain pills, or pep pills?

● Are things happening to you that you feel shouldn't happen? Such as minor cuts and bruises? Auto accidents? Slips and falls? Misplacing or losing personal objects such as keys, glasses, and notebooks?

Where is stress likely to come from?

Career counselors tell us that stress at work originates from three sources:

1. The Work Environment. This includes just about everything, from malfunctioning machinery, faulty materials, tight schedules, pinching budgets, and pressure-cooker deadlines to your hard-headed boss, your uncooperative associates, and your disinterested employees.

2. Your Inner Self. This is pretty deep stuff, but it includes such things as a loss of self-confidence, sensitivity to criticism about your performance, fear of failure, and doubts about your ability to cope with stress, wherever it originates.

3. Interpersonal Relationships. This combines the worst elements of the first two. Most work situations involve some sort of interpersonal transaction. For example, you may want a machine repaired in a hurry so that a critical order can be shipped. You've got to persuade the maintenance supervisor that this job should get his top priority. The degree of stress generated by this situation may depend entirely on your interpersonal skills. If you handle this transaction well, the machine will be back on line without delay. On the other hand, if you end up quarrelling with the other supervisor, the stress of the machine breakdown will be compounded by the stress of the quarrel.

Speaking only about stress coming from the supervisory job itself, which conditions are likely to need a fundamental improvement?

Harry Truman was partly right when he said, "If you can't stand the heat, stay out of the kitchen." The supervisory job is, by its nature, stressful. That's what makes it so invigorating and challenging. As another wise person once said, "If there were no stress, you might as well be dead." But there is a great difference between an invigorating amount of stress and too much stress. A basic goal in stress management, therefore, is to try to eliminate persistent but unnecessary stress. There's enough of the other kind already to make many of your days hectic. Among the basic sources of stress that should be corrected are the following:

● **Ambiguity About the Results for Which You Are Held Responsible.**   If your organization provides a job description for your position, make sure that it is specific about vital results such as output expected per shift, the acceptable percentage of rejects or errors, allowable expenses, and tolerance for employee absences, tardiness, and accidents. Be wary about performance expectations in these and any other areas that are described with such loose terms as "good," "better," "soon," and "improved." Ask, politely but firmly: "How good?" "How much better?" "How soon?" "How big an improvement?" These are reasonable questions, and they will do much to take the vagueness—and stress—out of the measurements by which you will be judged.

● **Inadequate Resources for the Job at Hand.**   Few things are more frustrating than when you are pressed to get results without having been given the resources to get the job done properly. You'll want to try to make certain that the performance demands that are made of you are matched from the start with adequate labor, equipment, materials, and supplies. Supervisors often make their biggest mistake by saying "yes" to a request before carefully sizing up the situation. This doesn't mean that you should say "no" all the time, either. It may mean that you'll need to say: "Yes, it can be done—*but only* by postponing Job No. 2"—or by allowing the staff to work overtime, or by subcontracting a part of the project, or by purchasing partially finished components, or by making any other necessary increase or adjustment in your resources, methods, and deadlines.

● **Conflicting Demands and Instructions.**   These often stem from having two bosses. This situation shouldn't happen, of course, but it does. And, as matrix organizations increase in number, it will happen more often. When faced with the stress of conflict in orders or instructions, don't let it pass by simply blowing off steam. Instead, make the results of such a conflict clear to both parties as soon as you can. Show them how it affects productivity, costs, or customer relations. Here, again, situations are most likely to be corrected for reasons that bring benefits to those who cause the situation.

There are sources of stress outside of work, aren't there?

Of course. Not only that, but the sources of stress outside of business are probably more powerful and less manageable. So far, we've talked about how to avoid or minimize stress at work, especially stress arising from time pressures. You should not overlook the very important matter of stress sources outside of work. These are often just as hard to avoid or reduce. The same principles prevail, however:

1. Alter or change the conditions of your personal environment to reduce stress, if you can.

2. Be realistic about your personal ambitions and capabilities, but don't undersell yourself to yourself.

3. Identify those necessary interpersonal transactions where your performance is unsatisfactory, and do something to improve your skills in those areas.

Admittedly, none of this is easy to do. Accordingly, if the strain you feel—from stress at work or elsewhere—is great, you'll need professional counseling. This might be obtained from a variety of professionals, including doctors, lawyers, and accountants; marriage counselors, psychologists, and clinical social workers; and religious or spiritual advisers.

Besides trying to control stress at the source, what else can you do personally to lessen its impact?

The three general approaches to management of stress, no matter what its origin, were outlined in the last section. In a more specific context, however, there are several other constructive things you can do to lessen the impact of stress on your system:

1. Understand Your Limitations and Live Within Them. Acknowledge such truisms as "Everybody can't be president" and "Rome wasn't built in a day." This calls for you to (a) be realistic about your true capabilities, (b) exploit them only as far as they'll carry you, (c) try not to move too far too fast, and (d) accept the fact that it's usually more satisfying to do well at a lesser job than to feel relentlessly pressured at one slightly above your capacity.

2. Get More Genuine Exercise. It's a fact that tensions are reduced when the blood circulation rises. Even if you're not athletically inclined, find a half hour each day to loosen up your body in some relaxing form of exercise. Such activity need not be too vigorous— walking, bike riding, bowling, or lawn mowing may do you as much good for relaxation purposes as jogging, tennis, or swimming.

3. Select and Pursue at Least One Diversion. Most important, this should be something you truly enjoy doing, not something that you feel is a matter of obligation. Let it be stamp collecting, woodworking or machine-shop work, local politics, gardening, gourmet cooking, card playing, or needlepoint. The test of a true diversion is that you will find yourself lost in it, that time flies and cares are forgotten during your involvement. The purpose of the diversion is to give your mind a rest from stress so that it can recharge its psychological energy cells.

4. Take Time to Look at the World Around You.   Most people who are troubled by stress tend to turn their vision inward. This is like trying to climb out of a pit by digging downward. The escape from pressure usually lies in the other direction, outside oneself. The world is a very big place and when you take 5 minutes to look at the morning or evening sky, it helps to place personal matters in perspective. Similarly, the act of getting concerned about other people's problems has a tension-relaxing effect. To test the degree to which you are inwardly turned, observe how well you can listen to others without interruption. Ask yourself how often you try to top another person's miseries with a story about one of your own. Does only the work that you do seem important? Many of us who would never think of ourselves as egotists are concerned only with ourselves. It's a malady brought on by stress. And one of the best proven cures for it is to immerse yourself in trying to come to the aid of others.

Key Concepts

1. An awareness of time, its incredible value, and its fleeting elusiveness, together with an ability to utilize and conserve it, is what distinguishes the outstanding supervisor from the ordinary one.

2. It takes self-discipline and conscious control to prevent personal time from being frittered away in nonessential, nonproductive activities. Inevitably, time waste leads to job stress.

3. Capable supervisors are tempted to consume too much of their own time by doing too much themselves, by retaining too many responsibilities, and by failing to delegate and distribute those time-absorbing activities that might better be carried forward by their subordinates.

4. Without system and order in one's personal life, combined with an organized approach in the analysis and discharge of one's personal work load, one squanders time resources rather than extending them.

5. Stress can be relieved, or managed, through routine delegation, by acquiring additional resources when needed, by more evenly distributing one's work load, and by planning and controlling personal time more effectively.

33

PUTTING YOUR BEST FOOT FORWARD IN THE ORGANIZATION

How can you put your best foot forward in an organization?

There are many ways to gain personal acceptance in an organization, but here are some that have been effective:

1. Demonstrate Your Job Competence. Few things gain respect like an individual's ability to do a job well. Your job is supervision. So show that you can run your operation like a clock, that companywide problems never have their origin with your department, and that you've got your employees well motivated and under control.

2. Become an Integral Part of the Information Network. Almost all organizations, public and private, derive a great deal of their power from the information they assemble and control. By becoming a part of the information network of an organization, you become an integral part of the organization. Accordingly, make an early effort to know (a) the extent of unique information the organization possesses, (b) how to gain access to it, (c) how to contribute to it, and (d) how to use it in your operation. This does not imply that you should try to tap secret documents. It does mean, however, that you should know how to obtain and exchange the data you need to improve productivity and smooth out operations in your department.

3. Go With the Flow of the Organization. That is, try to find a way to go along with the organization's standards and its general style of management. A maverick has a hard time proving his or her worth. It's better to give up a little of your independence in return for the support you'll eventually need if you are to be fully effective in any organization. After all, that's what an organization is—a cooperative effort. Loyalty, too, plays a part here. If you disagree with some of the things that are going on, don't stand aside and criticize; try constructively to improve them.

4. Build a Personal Support System. It can be awfully lonely in an organization without friends, especially without influential friends. Accordingly, it is wise to be somewhat selective about the people in the organization with whom you develop special rapport. Be cordial and courteous to everyone, of course. These qualities provide the lubrication that enables interpersonal contacts to revolve. But it is important that you go beyond that in making friends (business friends, not necessarily personal friends) with those people who are—or whose positions make them—influential in the organization. A first step is to develop a good relationship with the key person in the department that precedes or follows yours in the product or service flow. If you make things reasonably comfortable for them, they may be expected to come to your aid when you need help. A next step is to establish contacts in key staff departments (if you're a line supervisor; or in line departments if you're a staff supervisor). You'll want to be able to get confidential advice, and perhaps a little extra cooperation, from those in a position to do you good in payroll, accounting, sales order, field service, inventory, and production control, for example. In a great many instances, you will be able to develop this network only by first demonstrating that you will discharge your own responsibilities in a way that, at the very least, does not create problems for these key people. People for whom you do favors do you favors. People about whom you say good things speak well of you. That's politics, of course, but it's also the fact of organizational survival and success. Make no mistake: your personal support network depends on such tradeoffs.

What sort of attitudes and actions should you avoid?

Always keep in mind that an organization is a group of people working together toward common goals. Large organizations are made of many smaller, overlapping organizations. These are groups within groups. As a consequence, at any one time at work you'll be a member of many organizations. What you say and do to make you a hero in one organization may make you an outcast in another. If you're strong enough and right enough often enough, you can say and do just about anything you please and few people will take sides openly against you. Most of us, however, are not like the eight-foot bear who can "sleep anywhere he pleases." We've got to be more politic. This means that it's not too wise to take extreme positions. You needn't always be at the middle of the road, but you don't want to get too far away from the concensus that you can't make a compromise when good judgment dictates one.

● It's important, too, that you show others that you are willing to pull your weight in the total organization. There are always a number of dirty assignments; make sure that you take your share.
● You can't go far—or for long, either—with a win-lose attitude toward your peers. Resource allocations can spark battles between departments. Each wants the new clerk, the extra lift truck, first access to the computer terminal, and the like. If you insist on getting the most or the best every time, you'll inevitably make enemies. Organizations create mutual dependencies. You'll need to learn when to fight for a particular resource and when you will contribute more to the organization's goals if you let another department have the resource without a quarrel.
● It's also wise to avoid being characterized as a "negative," a person who resists every change. Try to check yourself before you think or say: "We've tried that before and it didn't work." "It isn't practical in the shop." "We're too busy with more important matters to be bothered right now."
● In another negative vein, many supervisors fall into the habit of criticizing everything the organization does. They think and talk interminably saying such things as: "The boss is lazy, the top executives don't know what they're doing, the company policies are stupid, they never spend money on what's important," and so on and on.

Don't fall into this trap. Admittedly, there are many things wrong in any organization. But, as a rule of thumb, think—and speak—positively about at least three out of four issues. If you can't convince yourself that this is true, you'll eventually place yourself outside the realm of influence in your organization. You'll be forever on the receiving—and carping—end rather than on the creating, changing, contributing end.

● Finally, don't hog all the credit. Most of your accomplishments depend on the contributions of others. When reporting progress, give others the credit they deserve, and then some. Go out of the way to tip your hat (in your reports to your superiors) to anyone who can reasonably be said to have been a party to a success. It costs very little to be generous and it goes a long way toward defusing any potential undercutting of your organizational ambitions. It should be obvious, of course, that a perfect way to make enemies is to place the blame for problems and failures on others in the organization. It's better to swallow the irritation than to develop a reputation as a buck passer or finger pointer.

How can you draw favorable attention to your capabilities without appearing offensive or objectionable?

The larger the organization, the more difficult it is for you to gain broad visibility. Doing a superb job in your own niche usually isn't enough. Your good works will go unrecognized elsewhere unless you make a conscious effort to display them. This does not mean that you make a nuisance of yourself in this regard. However, it should help you in both your present job and your career if you can do both of the following:

Find Ways to Exhibit Your Leadership and Initiative. It may be more comfortable for you to sit back and let others start a project rolling. After all, the old army saying, "Never volunteer!" has its merits; it keeps your extra burdens light. But if you really want to show your talents, this is one way of separating yourself from the pack. You'll want to pick your spots, of course. You don't want to become the company dray horse who can be counted on to carry all the heavy loads. Instead, try to be a part of the leading edge of those committees, projects, and operational changes that are being watched over or spurred from above. Sometimes all that is needed is for you to speak up in favor of a project that is stalled on dead center.

There are always opportunities, too, to institute a new method or procedure in your own department without waiting for a com-

---

panywide program. When you do so, be sure to go on record with a memorandum to your boss and to any of the staff departments to which it may have special interest. Suppose, for example, you institute a daily error-watch reporting system for your employees, and it makes an observable inroad into reducing errors. Send a copy of the form you use and the results obtained to your boss and to the quality control department.

Look for, or Accept, Challenging Responsibilities. This idea is an extension of gaining visibility for your leadership and initiative qualities. It will require an extra effort on your part, since these opportunities often will not come to you; you'll have to seek them out. They may be found, however, wherever a problem exists—within your own operations or anywhere in the total organization. You may many times accept a condition that you know to be unsatisfactory. You may assume that either nothing can be done about it or that it is the affair of someone else, usually one of the adjacent line or staff departments. Don't let the problem die there. Instead, try tackling a material shortages problem, or a duplication-of-effort problem, or a communications problem, for example. These often occur at the interface between departments. They give you a chance to work with others in positions of responsiblity outside of your department. It will usually be up to you to be the spearhead, but if you can bring about a solution or an improvement, you'll have something to show, not only upstairs but next door.

Of course, there are any number of ways that you can enlarge the scope of responsibilities within your own area of operations. I've rarely seen a boss who hasn't looked with favor on a subordinate who says, "What more can I do—within reason—to take some of the load off your shoulders?" or, "I've been getting my basic job under control; now I'm ready to tackle some of its aspects that you feel need extra attention."

How do you stay on the right side of your boss?

Nothing very complicated here. Know what your job responsibilities are. Do your own job well. Stay out of trouble with other departments—such as sales, accounting, and engineering—that the boss must deal with. Avoid petty bickering with the other supervisors. You may never get a medal pinned on your shirt for all this, but it will put you well up on the list of supervisors the boss knows can be depended on.

You might also try matching your views about your relationship with your boss with the checklist shown in Table 33-1.

TABLE 3-1   CHECKING RELATIONSHIPS WITH THE BOSS

Make sure you understand your boss's situation, including:
His or her goals and objectives.
Pressures on the boss.
His or her strengths, weaknesses, blind spots.
His or her preferred work style.

Assess yourself and your needs, including:
Your own strengths and weaknesses.
Your personal style.
Your dependence on authority figures.

Develop and maintain a relationship that:
Fits both your needs and your styles.
Is characterized by mutual expectations.
Keeps your boss informed.
Is based on dependability and honesty.
Selectively uses your boss's time and resources.

From John J. Gabarro and John P. Kotter, "Managing Your Boss," *McKinsey Quarterly,* Summer 1981, p. 30, with permission.

What things should you check first with your boss? What matters shouldn't you bother the boss with?

The usual answer is to bother the boss only with the big problems and to handle all the routine stuff yourself. But in practice, you'll want to be guided by the boss's own management style. Some bosses just can't seem to give up their control of an occasional trifle. If your boss worked himself up from the job you now hold, he may still want to do some part of it which he still enjoys, such as deciding whether a report form should be on pink paper or blue paper. Sure, it's foolish. But if he seems to be a bug on procedural details, better check with him first. It won't be the least bit surprising if he lets you make decisions a hundred times bigger without wanting to know anything about it except the results.

The principle here is that you've got to find out from your own experience just what your boss's delegation habits are. And then follow them.

If you're lucky enough to have a really approachable boss, try taking the Supervisory Responsibility Survey in Figure 10-7 with her or him. It may help both of you resolve the areas where you feel uncertain.

How much should you sweet-talk your boss?

In the eyes of most people, it's despicable to curry favor with your superior by substituting patronizing attention and "yes-manship" for the main responsibility of getting your job done. Such tactics may meet with short-term success, but in the long run the resentment you stir up among your associates will become a burden that is very difficult, if not impossible, for you to bear.

First be sure of what you mean by "sweet-talking" or by "apple polishing." Too often a supervisor whose performance is subpar, or whose skill in human relations is inadequate, accuses more successful associates of apple polishing. It's hard to get around the fact that supervisors who do their jobs well will be appreciated by their bosses. And if, in addition, their skill in dealing with people includes skill in getting along with their superiors, they will be in especially good graces with their bosses. To criticize such supervisors is "sour grapes." Better that you should reflect on your own approach and try to improve.

How successful are "yes men"?

The persons who say "yes" to all the boss's whims may be a comfort to the boss to have around. But such persons rarely achieve a true success. This doesn't mean you should say "no." The trick to making a hero out of yourself is to find ways that you can agree with the boss—to find ways that you can make his or her ideas and suggestions workable.

Consider this example: You're in a meeting with your boss. He or she suggests that the way to reduce costs is for each supervisor to cut his or her payroll 10 percent. You feel that this is an unreasonable proposition. Do you say, "Yes, it's a great idea"? Or do you say, "No, the idea stinks"?

Say neither. To say "yes" when you disagree is dishonest and only postpones facing up to the problem. To say "no" is tactless—it tends to get you a reputation of being a noncooperator, a grumbler, or a malcontent.

Try saying something like this: "I agree that we should make every attempt to cut our payrolls. And perhaps a 10 percent reduction will be possible, although we just can't afford to overlook the pressure we're getting from sales to speed up our deliveries. Suppose, in addition to taking a long look at our labor cost, we also see what we can do to spread out our production peaks. Perhaps, if we can just get the sales department to give a little bit, we can achieve a lasting reduction in work force."

This technique is called the "yes, but" method. It works because you are showing that you accept the principle of the boss's suggestion. And rather than contradict the boss, you are going along with him or her to explore ways of making his or her idea work out. If you use this approach, the boss will be more inclined to listen later on to suggestions that run counter to his or her own thinking at the moment.

What do you do if your boss asks you to betray the confidences of your employees?

Chances are slim that he or she ever will. But if the boss does, that's the kind of boss you better be careful with. Tell him or her you'll report disruptive activities that come to your attention, and let it go at that.

Don't confuse this issue with your very real responsibility to keep your boss informed of what's going on. Most top-level decisions that go wrong do so because they are based on inadequate information on what people are thinking and saying in the shop. It's up to you to channel your interpretation of feelings and attitudes to your boss so that she or he can make better decisions. As a matter of fact, much of what employees will tell you is told with the unconscious purpose of having you relay this information upstairs. Of course, you must only talk in generalities or about groups of employees, never about specific individuals.

Suppose, within a week's time, Maria Jones tells you that she's going to quit because she didn't get a raise, Pete Sandels lets you know he's working at another part-time job to make ends meet at home, and Ed Black says he is going to file a grievance because his wage rate doesn't include his doing the kind of work you're assigning him. What do you tell your boss? You don't tell the boss that Maria said this, Pete that, and Ed another thing. Instead, you say that in the last week you've heard three complaints that indicate that wage rates in the plant are getting out of line. That this is hurting morale. This is information the boss desperately needs from you. If the boss wants details, give only those which don't violate a request by employees that their conversation be treated confidentially.

What do you do about a boss who's too busy to take time with your problems?

This isn't all bad. It can mean that the boss has so much confidence in you that he or she trusts you to handle your problems without help. But the too-busy boss does point up the importance of timing when dealing with your superiors.

This can't be stressed too much: Find the right time and place for discussing problems with your boss. If she is irritable on Monday mornings, don't ask for favors then. If the boss is in a rush late in the afternoon, don't bring a long, involved problem to her attention at that time. Instead, rearrange your own schedule to get to the boss when experience shows she is the most relaxed and unlikely to be disturbed. One good method is to make an appointment. Call the boss on the phone. For instance: "Ms. Blake, I've got an inventory problem I'd like to have your guidance on. It will take about a half hour to go over it. Can we get together in your office sometime tomorrow morning—say, between 10 and 11 a.m.?" Your request, put this way, is pretty hard to turn down.

Another tip is to be certain that when you do talk with your boss, you're well prepared to present your problem. If you've left lots of loose ends, the boss will feel you're wasting time. And consequently will find reason to be busy the next time.

How can you tell how you rate with your boss?

There's hardly a supervisor alive who doesn't ask this question from time to time. You see the boss stop by Louis' office and chat with him for a half hour, whereas he passes you by with hardly a nod. "How come Louis is getting all the attention," you ask yourself, "while I can't get the time of day?" It's a pretty uneasy feeling. No wonder you found yourself unreasonable with the kids this morning.

You can watch some straws in the wind, however, that will tell you what the boss really thinks of your services.

● Do you get raises as frequently as your associates? If you feel that you do, chances are that your boss values your effort. Although the boss may not put appreciation into words, he or she may feel that the pay envelope will speak more loudly. So don't complain if that's the way the boss shows appreciation. Does the boss ask your opinion about matters that affect your department? Even if the boss doesn't make decisions in accordance with your suggestions, a boss who shows that she or he is interested in your reactions has shown you that you rate pretty high.

● Does the boss have a hands-off attitude toward your employees? Be thankful for the boss who lets you do all the direct dealing with employees—whether it's favorable or not.

● Does the boss criticize you when you've made a mistake? If so, she or he is letting you know where you stand. This way you have a chance to explain why—or to figure out a way to prevent it from happening again. It is much worse if your boss doesn't say anything to you but complains about your efforts to others.

● Does the boss back you up—even when you're on shaky ground? You can forgive bosses a lot of sins if they are loyal to you with superiors and associates.

● Does the boss know much about you and your family? Many bosses find it hard to get personal—even though they are interested in your welfare. So look for the little telltale indications that the boss knows what kind of house you live in, how old your children are, what model car you drive.

If you can answer "yes" to most of these questions, chances are that your boss rates you as an all-right supervisor. Sure, your boss probably feels there's plenty of room for improvement. But in the long run, he or she wouldn't trade you for any other supervisor.

The trouble with too many supervisors is that they expect the boss to be perfect in his or her relationship with them. Actually, it's often the other way around. Because you're in the official management family, your boss may feel that she or he doesn't have to square every corner with you, just as when you get home you drop your company manners—and show your family some of your grouchy side that you've been concealing all day.

What's the moral? Give your boss half a chance. Don't expect him or her to fall all over you just because you've done your job. Be satisfied if the good points outweigh the faults. And then see how much this realization will help you get along better with him or her.

How can you sell your ideas for improvement up the line in your organization?

When you go upstairs with an idea, the number of challenges increases. So try borrowing any of these 15 techniques used by successful salespeople to break down your "buyer's" resistance:

1. Go piggyback. Hitch your idea onto the current "hot" program in the shop. For instance, a waste-reduction drive is a good thing to relate to.

2. Make it easy to say "yes." Ask yourself whether you'd say "yes" if you were in the driver's seat.

3. Offer a trial run—like a salesperson's sample. If you want six machines, see whether you can buy one and then show how it pays off.

4. Buy now, pay later. If money isn't available, look into short-term leasing. All the company has to do then is risk one year's expense.

5. Knock down a straw man. If your boss has a pet peeve, show how existing equipment contributes to it and how your proposal will help.

6. Don't put all your eggs in one basket. For instance, if the problem is replacement of a battery of word processors, try selling replacement of part of the battery with known performers and the remainder of it with new equipment you haven't yet tested.

7. Prepare a rebuttal. Anticipate the soft spots in your proposal. Say, for example, you want a copy machine that requires an extra-firm foundation. If the committee asks whether this foundation won't boost costs, say you've selected a spot where the installation can be made without spending extra money.

8. Try the soft sell. Let the buyer see the advantages, then talk himself or herself into the proposal. If you mention to your boss that a conveyor would speed assembly, let the boss make the point that it would also cut costs.

9. Encapsulate your presentation. Even the busiest executives can spare 10 minutes (but seldom more) to listen to a profit-making idea.

10. Tie it into a package. If the company has a long-range program for developing new products, for instance, show how your proposed layout change fits these plans. Add other bits and pieces as you go.

11. Suggest a committee. If your proposal gets cool treatment, suggest that a committee review it. If the committee gives its blessing, this should carry weight when you resubmit the proposal.

12. Play the devil's advocate. You can take the wind out of an objector's sails by making all the critical arguments yourself—then answering them.

13. Horse trade. Suppose you suggest six projects and another department also submits several attractive projects. There isn't enough money to go around. Your move: Acknowledge the interest of the company as a whole and offer to postpone some of your projects if your top ones get quick approval.

14. Use the union. It has influence in many companies—especially on projects involving lighting, washrooms, cafeterias. Properly tipped off, it can push its interests when it talks to top management. (Caution: Use with discretion.)

15. Catch your prospect off guard. If your boss takes half a day to say "no" on a major project, try a smaller idea next. A switch from a small to a large request sometimes works, too.

When should you ask for a raise?

Watch your timing. Keep in mind four things: (1) organization policy, (2) the economic situation, (3) your boss's disposition, and (4) your own performance.

If your company has a fixed policy for reviewing and appraising your work and for issuing raises, don't buck the system. Find out when the review period is and what your salary range is (many companies will state that a supervisor, for instance, can make from, say, $1,250 to $1,600 per month—to go over the top figure, you've got to get the next-higher job). Then gauge your actions accordingly.

Of course, it's downright foolish to ask for a raise when your company is in an economic slump. If the slump is seasonal, wait until times pick up. Even then, don't make your pitch the day after the company loses a big order.

You needn't be told much about the good and bad times to approach your boss. Be smart about it. Wait a day or a month for the right time—if she or he tends to be temperamental.

And in every case, be sure that your job, and your work at it, deserves the increase. The days of giving you a raise (other than a general one that everybody may get to adjust to the cost of living) just because you've been a nice fellow and stayed with the company for 14 years are fast drawing to a close.

How do you go about asking your boss for a raise?

Assuming your timing is correct, you'll want to approach the raise problem in much the same manner you would if you were trying to sell your boss a new idea. Here are a few tactics to consider:

Come Right Out and Ask for It. The direct approach will force a "yes" or "no" answer, so be certain your performance warrants more money before you try it. To be on firm ground, have some facts on hand that can show how your job has grown bigger or how your efforts have become more effective: "I know the company expects to get a return on all the money it spends—including my salary. So I've made a list of new duties I've picked up since last year. And the shop records show that absences in my department are down 3 percent over last year, scrap is down 4 percent, and direct labor cost per unit has been reduced 7 cents."

Pick a Salary Goal. Instead of vaguely asking for "more money," it puts you in a better negotiating position if you can name the dollar figure you have in mind. Be certain that it is reasonable in light of (a) your performance and (b) what others are being paid in your organization. Don't set it too low, however. The chances are great that your boss will interpret your salary target as a top figure to consider and will work downward from there. The point of naming a salary goal is to establish the range of your request, with the thought that you may be willing to compromise between that and your current salary.

Start Your Campaign Early.   You will be at a disadvantage if you walk into your boss's office and suddenly ask for a raise. You should condition your boss for this request by periodically making him or her aware of your accomplishments. The purpose of this kind of communication is twofold. First, you want to be sure that the boss knows what you are doing that is especially commendable—and why. Second, you'll be establishing the fact that your accomplishments contribute to the boss's own performance and to the goals of the organization. Your boss will get your message. It may put the boss on the defensive, but he or she will begin to expect the day when you knock on the door and ask for that increase.

Stress the Value of Your Contribution.   People who get ahead are those who can—and do—point to their efforts to help the organization attain its goals. Specifically, find ways to document your productivity, dependability, management-mindedness, and initiative. Show how you do more than the minimum required without having to be pushed. Guard against making the plea that you need the money, however. It's a poor business argument. Your personal finances are your own affair. You weaken yourself in the boss's eyes by asking for a raise because you can't manage at home.

Wait and See.   In many companies, this is the only tack you can follow. But, generally speaking, it's wise for you to put a little pressure on from time to time. For instance, you might say, "I'm not asking for a raise at this particular moment, Ms. Jones, but I'd like to review my past six months' performance with you so that when raises are possible again, I'll be sure that my performance will warrant one."

What should you say when you do get a raise?

Be appreciative—but never, never treat it as a handout. Act as if it's something you've earned and consequently deserve. If the raise is smaller than you expected, ask the boss how you can do the kind of job that will deserve more money next time.

How about asking for a promotion?

Use essentially the same approach as in asking for a raise: (1) Cite the excellence of your performance on your present job, (2) demonstrate your readiness and qualifications for new responsibilities, and (3) emphasize how the new position will release untapped potential in you to contribute to the boss's and the organization's goals.

Key Concepts

1. Few people rise far in management without having found a way to harmonize their goals and actions with those of their superiors and the organization as a whole. To do so requires tact and a degree of compromise, but it does not necessarily mean that you must sacrifice your integrity.

2. Your acceptance and support by the organization will depend in large part on (a) how well you demonstrate competence in your job, (b) the readiness with which you accommodate group goals and consensus, (c) your contribution to, and use of, the information network, and (d) the power and influence of the personal support system you build.

3. "Yes-manship" achieves little in the long run; what most bosses do want, however, is a subordinate who "can do"—who can find a way to get things done, and preferably what the boss believes should be done. That is the boss's prerogative, and the successful supervisor must try to accommodate the boss's objectives.

4. Mutual confidence characterizes a good superior-subordinate relationship. Accordingly, you must apprise your boss of decisions and developments in your sphere of operations that affect his or her position and security. You must carry out this responsibility, however, without betraying the confidences that exist between you and your subordinates.

5. You do your superior a great service when you improve the quality of his or her performance and advance the status of his or her responsibilities. Generally speaking, the boss's successes become your successes, so it makes sense to bring to your boss ideas and methods for improving your department's operation and that of the entire organization.

INDEX

C